SUNDAYS

AND

SEASONS

1999

Augsburg Fortress

ABOUT THE ART

The most significant Christian symbol is the cross, reflecting the mystery of God's sacrificial love of creation given through Christ Jesus. The cover cross for *Sundays and Seasons* is meant to represent this mystery in a primal, direct, and rugged way. Exploding off the cover edges, this cross symbolizes the boundless and powerful life it gives while its metallic quality represents the sacred and precious nature of the Christian way.

The images in *Sundays and Seasons* symbolize the various and many beliefs and practices of the church. Some symbols are from of old, some newer. Some symbolize Christian truths, some Christian festivals, and still others Christian rituals. Primal and rugged in style, all the symbols form a family of imagery that, whatever their source or place, speaks anew of the power, beauty, and wonder of Christ Jesus and the church.

Nicholas T. Markell is a liturgical artist from Minneapolis, Minnesota. In 1984 he earned a Bachelor of Visual Arts degree at the University of Saint Thomas in Saint Paul, Minnesota, and in 1987 chose to respond more fully to his religious yearnings by studying for Christian ministry, earning a Master of Arts degree in theology and a Master of Divinity degree from the Washington Theological Union in Washington, D.C. Among his many studies was that of ancient Christian art and symbolism. Working in a variety of media and recognized for his artistic excellence, Nicholas's original art has won national awards and has been published, exhibited in shows, galleries, academic institutions, and installed in numerous churches across the country.

SUNDAYS AND SEASONS

Worship Planning Guide, Cycle A, 1999

ACKNOWLEDGMENTS

Scripture quotations, unless otherwise noted, are from the New Revised Standard Version Bible © 1989 Division of Christian Education of the National Council of the Churches of Christ in the United States of America. Used by permission.

The Prayers (printed in each Sunday/festival section) may be reproduced for one time, congregational use, provided copies are for local use only and the following copyright notice appears: From *Sundays & Seasons*, copyright © 1998 Augsburg Fortress. May be reproduced by permission for use only between November 29, 1998 and November 27, 1999.

Art: Markell Studios, Minneapolis, MN
Book Design: The Kantor Group, Inc., Minneapolis, MN

General Editor: Frank Stoldt
Editors: Dennis Bushkofsky, Eric Vollen

Manufactured in the U.S.A.   0-8066-3625-4   3-1203

99   98   1   2   3   4   5

CONTRIBUTORS

Annual Essays: Introduction, Frank Stoldt; A Pastoral Overview of Matthew, Mark Powell; The Old Testament in Worship, Robert Bornemann; Speaking and Singing about Jews, Franklin Sherman; Welcoming Adults to the Faith, Roger Prehn; Worship in Context, S. Anita Stauffer; What Makes Worship Lutheran? Robert Rimbo; Sundays and the Lesser Festivals, Paul Nelson; How to Plan Blended Worship, Scott Weidler; A Guide to Writing the Prayers, Walter Huffman; Hymn Mass, Gracia Grindal and Martin Seltz

Seasonal Materials: Images of the Season, Julie Ryan; Environment and Art for the Season, Augsburg Fortress Ecclesiastical Arts staff; Preaching with the Season, Mark Oldenburg, Ronald Roschke, Jann Fullenwieder; Alternate/Seasonal Liturgical Texts, Mark Bangert, Lauren Kirsh-Carr, Marty Hampton, Andrew Paul Fredel, Rodney Mruk, Kimmy Meinicke, Pam Werrel, Nancy Winder; Planning Ahead for the Season, Ordo for the Season, Dennis Bushkofsky; Assembly Song for the Season, Scott Weidler

Weekly Materials: introductions to the day, introductions to the readings, the prayers, calendar for lesser festivals and commemorations, Samuel Torvend, Craig Mueller; Images for Preaching, James Nieman, Ronald Roschke, Paul Jaster, Beth Gaede; Worship Matters, Kari Henkelman Keyl, Timothy Keyl, Randall Lee, D. Foy Christopherson; Let the Children Come, Vanessa Skaarvold; Service Music, Martin Seltz

Music Materials: mainstream hymnody, Timothy Guenther; popular song, Terri McLean; mainstream choral, Mark Bighley; popular choral, Jan Gilbertson, Bill Chouinard; children's music, Marilyn Comer; classic choral, Carlos Messerli; handbell, Cathy Moklebust

Contributing Editors: Norma Aamodt-Nelson, Carol Carver, Linda Parriott, Martin Seltz

COMPANION VOLUME

Worship Planning Calendar 1999 (AFP 23-2008; $20.00)

INTRODUCTION

ADVENT

CHRISTMAS

EPIPHANY

LENT

THE THREE DAYS

EASTER

SUMMER

AUTUMN

NOVEMBER

INTRODUCTION

Welcome to another year of grace! This newly prepared edition of *Sundays and Seasons* invites the reader to cross the familiar ground of the ecumenical lectionary and calendar, back to the very beginning of the church's three-year liturgical cycle. But this edition is more than simply starting over. It is, as the First Sunday in Advent suggests, a "wake-up call" to take what is worthy and move forward as children of light embracing the continual unfolding of God's gracious gifts. Employing a familiar structure, but in a greatly expanded and redesigned format, this volume is like "a householder who brings out of the treasury what is new and what is old" (Matt. 13:52).

FOUNDATIONS

Central is the understanding that "Sunday . . . is the primary day on which Christians gather to worship. Within this assembly, the Word is read and preached and the sacraments are celebrated" (*The Use of the Means of Grace* 6). This, then, is the foundation on which the resource is built: the *gathering* of God's people by the Holy Spirit, the reading and preaching of the *word* with song and prayer, the washing of the baptismal *bath*, the nourishment of the *meal*, and the *sending* out to participate in the mission of God for the world. Together with Reformed, Anglican, and Roman communities, Lutherans share this ecumenical pattern *(ordo)* of word and meal, bath and mission. Planners build upon this primal structure in ways that enliven the community's life, heal the brokenhearted, celebrate the joys and passages of God's people, and *announce the Word that sets us free* to love one another.

THE STRUCTURE OF THIS RESOURCE

At this volume's core are the lectionary readings, the church's calendar, and the *ordo* of Christian worship. A collection of gifted writers use these materials to provide a plethora of resources that weave the diverse ministries of Christian worship into a rich tapestry.

Annual essays introduce the Year of Matthew with its unique Jewish roots, call to mission, and model for contextualization. Hints about crafting prayers, planning blended worship, and choosing liturgical song are also offered, including a hymn mass set to familiar melodies that encourage even the smallest gathering to full, active, and conscious participation.

Seasonal materials focus on themes that inform the environment, preaching, music, and "accordion" of the ordo. New is an introduction to preaching the season— a reminder to preachers that the sweep of the lectionary and season shapes proclamation as much as the readings.

Weekly materials provide the "consumables"— introductions, readings, preaching images, songs and prayers, and hints that encourage the entire assembly to deepen its worship life. Greatly expanded are music suggestions for hymns, children, instruments, and choirs.

HOW TO USE THIS PLANNING GUIDE

At its best, worship is prepared by all of a congregation's liturgical ministers. Presiders, preachers, musicians, altar guilds, parish educators, and others are encouraged to gather on a regular basis to reflect on the readings and the season and to plan in advance. *Sundays and Seasons* cannot replace this "cross-functional" team nor does it prescribe liturgical praxis. Rather it serves as a tool for congregations to use the community's gifts in a manner that is congruent with the whole church.

A revised *Worship Planning Calendar 1999* (AFP 23-2008; $20.00) also has been prepared as a "workbook." Each two-page spread has room to note weekly planning decisions as well as daily appointments and devotions.

Finally, *Sundays and Seasons* is a work in progress. Much of its initial success can be credited to Samuel Torvend who, serving as editor for its first three years, created a volume that has achieved widespread use. His valuable insights along with many readers' careful suggestions shape the current resource. Please continue to offer your comments by calling (800) 426-0115, ext. 558 or sending an E-mail to: bushkofd@augsburgfortress.org.

Frank Stoldt, *General Editor*

A PASTORAL OVERVIEW of MATTHEW

Matthew's gospel comes first in the New Testament because in the early church it was considered the most important book in the Bible. It was called "the gospel of the church." In many ways, Matthew does in one volume what Luke does in two. He tells the saving story of Jesus while simultaneously providing an abundance of material intended to serve as instruction for those who continue the mission of Christ after Easter. True to its position in the canon, Matthew has exerted more obvious influence on the life and mission of the church than any other biblical document.

Not only has Matthew's effect been felt in the church, but also in society at large. A few years ago, *Reader's Digest* magazine conducted a survey to determine the three most-read chapters in the Bible. The winners were Matthew 5, Matthew 6, and Matthew 7—the Sermon on the Mount. Here we have the Beatitudes, the Lord's Prayer, and the golden rule. In the United States, this material is not just scripture, but part of the cultural heritage, as American as the Bill of Rights or Poor Richard's Almanac.

Every three years, the Cycle A lectionary draws on these and similar texts, presenting lessons that are, for the most part, very familiar to the active churchgoer and somewhat familiar to the average citizen. For preachers and worship planners, such familiarity can be both asset and obstacle.

We will consider three points as background to this year's experience of Matthew.

1) MATTHEW'S CONGREGATION(S)

The social setting for Matthew's gospel was a fairly prosperous, urban community marked by cultural diversity. It was, thus, a far cry from the social setting of Jesus himself—a more monolithic, rural, peasant environment.

Some think the first evangelist had pastoral responsibility for a number of congregations in such an area. Prominent among their needs were questions of social definition and legitimation. Matthew himself and the base membership of his church were certainly Jewish.

Indeed, most scholars now say it is better to regard them as "Christian Jews" than as "Jewish Christians."

But there was a difference. These Christian Jews were committed to making disciples of all nations (28:19), and a significant number of Gentiles were now being baptized. This fact alone, their enemies would say, offered proof positive that Christians were not "true Jews." Some of the Christians in Matthew's church are probably ready to agree and accept the break in a way that repudiates any connection to Judaism. Others want to solidify that connection and insist that the new converts observe the sacred traditions of the past.

The preceding description offers numerous contact points for ministry in our own society in 1998–99. The church remains committed to growing with regard to both size and diversity. In an increasingly secularized society, this commitment necessarily implies challenges to tradition, including sacred ones. Matthew, the evangelist and pastor of these congregations, does not "side" with either group, but he incorporates material that addresses the crisis throughout his gospel. Matthew's solution is not to play tradition and innovation against each other or to accept any "compromise" that dilutes the one (or both) at the expense of the other; rather, a paradoxical, uncompromising, absolute commitment to both tradition and innovation. A leader trained for the kingdom of heaven, Matthew says, is able to keep what is old and accept what is new (13:52).

2) JEWISH OR ANTI-JEWISH?

One issue of particular sensitivity in using Matthew's gospel today is the manner in which it represents the Jewish people, particularly their leaders. Time and again throughout this year, we will encounter cycle A texts that portray prominent Jewish figures in a bad light. Jesus calls the Jewish leaders a "brood of vipers" (12:34; 23:33) and views them as "evil" (9:4; 12:34; 16:4). In one chilling verse, Matthew presents "the (Jewish) people, as a whole" calling for Jesus' death and saying, "Let his blood be on us and on our children!" (27:25). Throughout the centuries, this verse has been quoted by anti-Semitic groups who wished to label Jewish people "Christ-killers" and portray them as accursed by God.

At the same time, many passages in Matthew's gospel display a strong Jewish orientation. Although the book ends with a commission to "make disciples of all nations" (28:19), Jesus' disciples are explicitly commanded during his earthly life to "Go nowhere among the gentiles (nations)" (10:5). Similarly, Jesus insists that he has been "sent only to the lost sheep of the house of Israel" (15:24). No other gospel emphasizes the Jewish matrix for Christianity or insists on its preservation as much as Matthew does.

Three points are helpful to remember when dealing with the difficult texts. First, they must be understood in light of the social setting already described. They betray the climate of inter-Jewish rivalry during a time of transition. It is important to recognize that the hostility against the Pharisees in Matthew is inter-Jewish not anti-Jewish. Within the historical context of Matthew's gospel, Jesus' harsh words are analogous to those of Israel's own prophets who would accuse the people of all sorts of sins and shortcomings.

Second, such critique, when offered from within, was always understood to assume God's fundamental acceptance of Israel. The whole reason Jesus comes is to save *his people* (that is, the Jewish people) from their sins (1:21). It is not likely that Matthew intends for us to think Jesus failed to accomplish this basic purpose. Ironically, the very text so popular with anti-Semites (27:25) is probably meant to affirm this acceptance and salvation. Jesus' blood does not bring condemnation but forgiveness (26:20). Unlike Pilate (27:24), Judas (27:3-5), and the chief priests (27:6-7)—who act in ways that will keep Jesus' blood from coming upon them—the Jewish people call for his blood to be upon them. Thus, they are forgiven and saved from their sins. It is likely that the line, "Let his blood be upon us and on our children" was part of the early Christian liturgy used in Matthew's church. By placing those words on the lips of the Jewish people, the first evangelist sought to remind his Christian Jewish community that Jesus died for other Jewish people too—even for those who, as rivals, come in for some pretty harsh prophetic critique elsewhere in the gospel.

Third, Matthew's gospel is radically opposed to any exercise of violence. Even if Jews were to be regarded as enemies (and it is questionable that they were), Matthew would counsel the members of his church to love their enemies, bless them not curse them, even—if necessary—turn the other cheek and suffer indignation rather than inflict any sort of misfortune on others (5:43-48). It is an incredible and tragic turn in history that the one book in the Bible that is most explicitly committed to nonviolence has been used to justify persecution of the very people who that same book says Jesus came to save.

3) GOD, JESUS, AND THE CHURCH

Matthew presents Jesus as Messiah, as Lord, and as Son of Man, but most important, he presents Jesus as the Son of God. For Matthew, this means that Jesus is the one in whom God is uniquely present and the one through whom God is made manifest in the world. Matthew tends to avoid attributing emotions to Jesus (compare Mark 10:14 to Matt. 19:14) or even presenting Jesus as asking questions (compare Mark 9:33-37 to Matt. 18:1-4).

What we might call Matthew's "Christology" is developed pastorally in response to the fundamental question, "Where is God to be found?" Matthew's gospel offers a threefold response to that question. First, Matthew wants to say that God is present in Jesus. Such an affirmation goes a subtle shade beyond an insistence that God *acts* through Jesus. When Jesus is born, Matthew can say, "God is with us" (1:27). Matthew believes, of course, that God has been present with the people of Israel in the past, before Jesus was born, but the presence of God manifested now in Jesus is unprecedented and superlative. On different occasions Matthew portrays people worshiping Jesus (2:11; 8:2; 9:18; 14:33; 15:25; 20:20; 28:9, 17; the Greek word used in all of these verses is *proskyne*). Jesus himself declares in Matthew 4:10 that people should worship *(proskyne)* no one except "the Lord God." Yet when people worship Jesus, they are not rebuked. As far as Matthew is concerned, God is present in Jesus to such an extent that worshiping him counts as worshiping the Lord God.

Second, Matthew affirms that Jesus is present in the church. The last verse of the gospel records Jesus saying, "I am with you always, to the end of the age"

(28:20). Matthew recognizes the literal or physical absence of Jesus (Matt. 9:15; 26:11) but reduces its significance by insisting that Jesus remains present with his followers nonetheless. Specifically, Jesus promises that he will always be with those who baptize people in the name of the Father, Son, and Holy Spirit, and who teach them to obey his commandments (28:19-20). Likewise, in Matthew 18:20, Jesus says that when two or three gather for prayer in his name he "will be among them."

Third, Matthew thinks the church is or must be present in the world. The church for Matthew is not a building or even a localized community, but a missionary movement. The church consists of believers who are going out into the world to be salt of the earth (5:13), to overcome the gates of Hades (16:18), and to make disciples of all nations (28:19). The mission of the church is to embody the presence of Christ (and therefore the presence of God) in the world. By making God present in the world, the church may be said to be "the light of the world" in Matthew (5:14) in the same way that Jesus is said to be the light of the world in other writings (John 8:12). The church *is* Jesus for Matthew—the living body of Christ making God present in our world just as Jesus did in his.

All three points are significant. Imagine someone asking today, "Where can I find God?" People would offer a variety of answers: in nature, in scripture, in other human beings, and so forth. Matthew would say, "In Jesus." Then, of course, the question becomes, "But where can I find Jesus?" Matthew would say, "In the church." But, and this is a significant *but*, Matthew would not think that our hypothetical seeker ought to find God by making his or her way to the church where God is to be discovered through Christ. Rather, Matthew assumes that it is God who does the seeking (Matt. 18:10-14). Matthew's answer to those who are looking for God in our world would be, "Don't worry. God—through Jesus, through the church—will find you."

FOR FURTHER READING

Hagner, Donald. *Word Biblical Commentary Series* (Dallas: Word Books, 1993, 1995).

Kingsbury, Jack Dean. *Matthew as Story*, 2d ed. (Philadelphia: Fortress Press, 1988).

Luz, Ulrich. *The Theology of the Gospel of Matthew* (Cambridge: Cambridge University Press, 1995).

Powell, Mark Allan. *God With Us: A Pastoral Theology of Matthew's Gospel* (Minneapolis: Fortress Press, 1995).

Senior, Donald. *What Are They Saying About Matthew?*, 2d ed. (New York: Paulist Press, 1996).

THE OLD TESTAMENT IN WORSHIP

Why do we use the Old Testament in worship? Or an even more basic question, Why do we use the Old Testament at all? Both questions are especially relevant as the lectionary brings us to the year of Matthew.

HOW JEWISH IS MATTHEW?

All four gospels make frequent use of the Old Testament in presenting the story of Jesus and the meaning of his life and ministry, but none so much as Matthew. More than sixty times—more than twice as many as in any other gospel—Matthew quotes the Old Testament.

Of these quotations some thirty are formally introduced by such phrases as, "as it is written" or "in order to fulfill," and are connected with specific events in Jesus' life. Some twenty more are quotations used in Jesus' teachings and discussions with others.

Little wonder that Matthew is seen as the most Jewish of the gospels! This Jewish character goes beyond Old Testament quotations. It can be seen in some of the stories and additions to common gospel materials, which are found only in Matthew and are strikingly similar to the kinds of stories and additions found in early Jewish commentaries, the *midrashim*. These midrashic additions are described by F. C. Grant as a "poetic and imaginative embellishment of the central narrative and message of the New Testament" (*The Interpreter's Dictionary of the Bible*, III, p. 304). Stories such as Herod's persecution, the wise men and the star in the east, the flight into Egypt, and Matthew's expansion of the passion and resurrection narratives—the dream of Pilate's wife, Pilate's washing his hands, the self-cursing of the Jews, the earthquakes, and the opening of the tombs—all reflect the style of ancient Jewish commentary.

It is not surprising, then, that traditionally the author of the first gospel has been seen as a Jewish Christian, maintaining the early ties that the followers of Jesus had with the synagogue. This explanation would be a natural one for the perceived "Jewish" tone and style of the gospel and its large use of the Old Testament.

More recently, however, a growing number of scholars have argued that, Matthew's extensive use of the Old Testament notwithstanding, the author is not a Jewish Christian but a gentile. These scholars see in Matthew a complete break with the synagogue and a rejection of the Jews too sharp to have been made by a Jewish Christian. In this regard they note passages that appear only in Matthew; for example, Matthew 21:43: "The kingdom of God will be taken away from you and given to a nation producing the fruits of it" (RSV), an addition not found in the Markan and Lukan parallels; and especially the self-cursing in Matthew 27:25, "Then the people as a whole answered, 'His blood be on us and on our children!'"—hardly the sentiments of one of Jewish heritage! Contrast Paul in Romans 9–11.

These scholars also see problems in Matthew's dealing with Jewish practices and beliefs. Even how he reads the Hebrew Scriptures may be questioned; for example, Matthew (unlike Mark and Luke) literalistically misinterprets the Hebrew parallelism of Zechariah 9:9 and so has Jesus riding two animals into Jerusalem. A Jewish Christian, they say, would know better. Strong influences of Greek rhetorical style are also seen in Matthew, especially in such passages as the Sermon on the Mount.

THE OLD TESTAMENT AS FULFILLMENT

If the author of Matthew is indeed a gentile and not a Jew, then his extensive use of the Old Testament only raises more acutely the question of why the Old Testament is important to the Christian. Matthew himself suggests an answer. In Matt. 26:47–56, at the outset of the passion narrative, Jesus is in Gethsemane and Judas and the crowd come to arrest him, and one of the disciples draws a sword and cuts off the ear of the high priest's slave. Jesus rebukes him: "Put your sword back.... Do you think that I cannot appeal to my Father, and he will at once send me more than twelve legions of angels? But how then would the scriptures be fulfilled, which say it must happen in this way?" (vv. 53–54). These verses with their reference to the fulfillment of the scriptures are found only in Matthew.

These scriptures—the Law and the Prophets and the Writings—are not just an historical setting for the gospel, but are an essential part of the confession of faith. They are part of the gospel proclamation of what God wills and purposes, how God acts in history. We call these writings the *Old* Testament, not to reject them, nor to supersede them, but to set them in a right perspective to the Christ event, God's self-revelation in Jesus Christ.

JESUS AND THE OLD TESTAMENT WITNESS

The Hebrew Bible with its great variety of witnesses and understandings is Israel's response to God's acting within their history, and as such is a witness to God's will and purpose revealed and fulfilled in Jesus of Nazareth. And when the followers of Jesus wanted to make clear the meaning of Jesus' life and person, they turned to their sacred writings, the rich heritage of the Hebrew Scriptures. So they spoke of Jesus as the fulfillment of all that is implied in the many figures and images and hopes found in the Hebrew Bible. Jesus is the high priest, the sacrifice of atonement, the Passover lamb; he is the true Israel, the servant, the righteous one, the sufferer; he is a prophet like Moses; and like David he is king, Son of God, messiah.

Readings from the Old Testament in connection with the gospel of the day provide an opportunity to explore these Old Testament images and figures and to reflect on what they mean in connection with Jesus. In John 10:11, for example, Jesus says, "I am the good shepherd," and the passage goes on in clear reflection of Ezekiel 34:11-16, where God is the good shepherd. Again, in John 15, when Jesus describes himself as the true vine and his followers as the branches, he is using the imagery of Israel as the vine God brought out of Egypt and planted (see Ps. 80:8 and Isa. 5:1-7). Jesus embodies in himself the true Israel and in him the church is the Israel of God.

The use of the Old Testament in the gospels always starts with Christ and looks back to the scriptures as it asks what is going on here, and what the meaning of these events is. One does not start with the scriptures searching for predictions, but with Christ as revealer and fulfiller of God's purpose which is witnessed in those scriptures.

In all four gospels Psalms 22 and 69 have a significant place in the story of Jesus' death: the cry from the cross—"My God, my God, why have you forsaken me?"—the dividing of the garments, the mockery, the thirst and bitter drink. They are used, however, not as predictions of the crucifixion and its details, but as expressions *par excellence* of suffering, and are applied to Jesus who has taken upon himself the suffering of humankind.

SOME THEOLOGICAL ASSUMPTIONS

The Old Testament is part of the Christian confession of faith and the proclamation of the gospel. It is used to interpret the meaning of God's revelation in Christ. The Old Testament also bears witness to some basic biblical understandings about God and humankind, which are not discussed in the New Testament, but simply assumed. Indeed, the Old Testament testimony to God's revelation in Israel provides the primary categories for understanding God's act in Christ. This notion should not surprise us, for Christianity began in the bosom of first-century Judaism.

Among these biblical understandings is that the revelation of God takes place in history, and so history has meaning. History is where God acts and reveals Godself. It is in history that God has called a people; it

is in history that God has revealed God's own will and purpose; and it is in history that God's rule will be achieved and proclaimed.

The Old Testament presents an unparalleled testimony to God, a personal God who addressed Israel, and through Israel all peoples. In brief, it testifies to the mighty God who acts, the holy God who comes, the righteous God who saves, the faithful God who forgives, the Lord of creation who makes known God's will and purpose.

At the same time that the Old Testament speaks about God it speaks about human beings and the human situation—the enjoyment of the world God created, the responsibility for it, the affirmation of life, the reality of mortality, the problem of sin and suffering, the source of hope and comfort, the vision of God's rule over all. The Psalms especially express all these moods and concerns. They are Israel's many-faceted responses to God's presence and activity in their lives, but in them we can also see ourselves and we join in their responses of petition and trust, of praise and thanksgiving. So it is that the Old Testament speaks about what it means to be the people of God—how even to be God's people depends upon the initiative and saving activity of God, how as God's people they are to live out that relationship, and how as a kingdom of priests they are made the instrument through which God's revelation shall come to all peoples.

Little wonder then that the Old Testament plays so essential and significant a part in Christian understanding and worship of the God who in Christ has acted in our history, who has come to save. And this is the answer to the question, Why do we use the Old Testament in Christian worship? It is because the Old Testament is not just a second book along with the New Testament, nor is it only a historical and cultural background for the New Testament. We use it because the Old Testament is the Word of God, bearing witness to the true living God, testifying to the situation of humankind and the world, and pointing to its fulfillment: the Word made flesh.

SPEAKING AND SINGING ABOUT JEWS

Matthew has often been called the most Jewish of the gospels. Its very first verse already strikes this note: "An account of the genealogy of Jesus the Messiah, the son of David, the son of Abraham." Luke takes his genealogy all the way back to Adam, but Matthew's main concern is to root Jesus in the history of his people.

Yet Matthew also depicts Jesus as constantly engaged in conflict with Jewish leaders, and his chapter 23 contains some of the most violent polemic in the gospels. "Woe to you, scribes and Pharisees, hypocrites!" says Jesus. He calls them "blind fools" and "blind guides," and exclaims: "You snakes, you brood of vipers!"

We are reminded by the fervor of these words that much of the New Testament, indeed most of it, was forged in the fires of controversy. In Matthew's case, it was the controversy between the new Christian movement and its parental faith, a conflict that centered on the question of who were the legitimate heirs of the ancestral covenant. It was no mere theoretical matter. It had a sociological expression involving direct competition, particularly in cities such as Antioch where this gospel may have originated, with church and synagogue on opposite street corners, so to speak. Matthew 10:16 and the following verses depict the conflict so intense as to include even physical violence.

The Gospel of Matthew, it is generally agreed, was written after the destruction of the Jerusalem temple in A.D. 70, and reflects the special bitterness of that time. Christians, who had been warned that "All who take the sword will perish by the sword" (Matt. 26:52), were charged with shirking their duty in defense of Jerusalem. They in turn could and did point to the city's desolation as demonstrating God's judgment on a faithless people. It was not a good moment in "interfaith relations"!

Jesus undoubtedly made a strenuous critique of the religious establishment of his day, as the prophets had before him. But in his words as reported in Matthew, we also have an overlay deriving from that later, post-A.D. 70 period. If we do not want these texts to contribute to interreligious hostility and stereotyping today, we need to find some way of distinguishing between these layers. It may mean not using certain passages at all, or accompanying their use with an historical explanation somewhat along the preceding lines.

Matthew has Jesus using the terms "Pharisees" and "hypocrites" practically as synonyms. It is quite possible, however, that Jesus meant to rebuke particular Pharisees whom he had diagnosed as insincere, or even the whole current generation of Pharisees, but not Pharisaism as such. Some scholars maintain that Jesus was closer to Pharisaism than to any other option within Judaism in his day. The Pharisees taught their followers to pray to God as Father, they believed in the resurrection, and they tried to be faithful in word and deed to what they understood to be God's will. After the destruction of Jerusalem it was clear that the Zealots had failed. The priests—without a temple—had lost their function, as had the Sadducean aristocracy. Meanwhile the Qumran community had been obliterated. Only the Pharisees—who were really a lay renewal movement—remained to rebuild Jewish life, and they are considered to be the direct ancestors of rabbinic Judaism, the form of Judaism practiced today. This connection is one reason to be sensitive in the use of the term.

Most Christians are ignorant of the history of postbiblical Judaism, and of the remarkable powers of self-renewal that it has shown, again and again. A study of a brief history of Judaism or of the writings of great Jewish thinkers, such as Martin Buber or Abraham Joshua Heschel, will prove illuminating. Perhaps the best antidote to anti-Jewish stereotypes is for Christians to meet Jews face to face in situations where personal sharing is possible. Living room dialogues such as the Interfaith Circles program (see For Further Reading) are one vehicle for this, as well as visits to synagogue services, especially if the rabbi or an informed layperson is asked to explain the service.

11

THE JEWS IN THE FOURTH GOSPEL

Cycle A is the year of Matthew, but as in the other cycles, it also uses readings from the Gospel of John, especially in the Lenten and Easter seasons. It is here that we face the problem that those who oppose the gospel are referred to not as "scribes and Pharisees" or other particular groups, but simply as "the Jews," as if Jesus and his disciples were not Jews themselves, and as if *all* Jews opposed them—a usage that has fostered the notion of universal Jewish guilt for Jesus' death.

The usual explanation for the vilification of Jews in the fourth gospel is that it was written at a time, late in the first century or even early in the second, when the separation between church and synagogue had become so complete that a "we–they" situation obtained, and all Jews whatsoever (except "those who believed in him") were lumped together as Jesus' opponents. Another intriguing possibility, suggested by many scholars, is that the phrase *hoi Ioudaioi* in the fourth gospel does not mean "the Jews" but "the Judeans"—that is, people from Judea. Evidence supports the presence of considerable antagonism in New Testament times between Judeans and Galileans, with the former regarding the latter as untutored provincials, lax in their observance of the law, and a source of dissident and rebellious movements. Conversely, the Galileans regarded the Judeans as part of the "power structure," willing to collaborate even with the hated Romans to maintain their privileges. The Jesus movement, as a Galilean movement, was almost destined to come into conflict with the Jerusalem authorities.

THE JEWS IN LITURGY AND HYMNODY

Since the decision was made following the Second Vatican Council to delete the phrase "the perfidious Jews" and to remove the infamous "reproaches" (described as "the reproofs addressed by the crucified Savior to his ungrateful people") from the Good Friday liturgy, the major causes of offense to Jews in the Roman liturgy have been eliminated, and *LBW* does not contain either of these elements. Eucharistic and other prayers do need to be monitored, however, as to what kind of image of the Jews and Judaism they present.

The same consideration applies to hymns, since they often play a powerful role in interpreting biblical texts. Hymns for Lent, and especially Good Friday, seem to fall into two groups, those that emphasize what

"they" did, and those that confess that "we" are responsible. Even a song such as Sydney Carter's "Lord of the Dance" has this problem, especially if we forget that the "they" in "they whipped and they stripped and they hung me high" refers to the Romans, not the Jews. At the opposite pole is a hymn such as "O sacred head now wounded," with its acknowledgement: "Mine, mine was the transgression." This may be called an existential interpretation of Jesus' death, rather than an historical explanation. The two are not contradictory. In fact they can be complementary, if we see that the motives of the actors in the original passion drama, including both perpetrators and bystanders, are similar to our own. The hymn "Ah, holy Jesus" gives this existential approach its classic expression (LBW 123).

On occasions when one wishes to stress the continuity between Judaism and Christianity, one can easily find many hymns that celebrate our common faith in the God of creation and of providential care. Every time we sing or say a psalm we are also celebrating that common faith. The song "Shalom" (WOV 724)—with words given in both English and Hebrew—is well known especially to Jewish young people, and could be used in an interfaith setting. Both the words and the tune, which can be sung as a round, are of Israeli origin. In Jewish usage, instead of repeating *Shalom chaverim*, the second part of the verse reads: *L'hitraot, l'hitraot, shalom, shalom*: "We'll see you again, we'll see you again, shalom, shalom."

FOR FURTHER READING

Cunningham, Philip A. *Proclaiming Shalom: Lectionary Introductions to Foster the Catholic and Jewish Relationship.* Collegeville, MN: Liturgical Press, 1995. Suggested introductory remarks that highlight the Jewish context of the readings and convey a positive image of Judaism. Usable also for most of the Revised Common Lectionary.

Interfaith Circles. A 24-unit discussion program designed for Christian-Jewish living room dialogue groups. For information write: Interfaith Resources, Inc., 1328 Oakwood Dr., Anoka, MN 55303, or phone (612) 421-1896.

Jergen, Carol, B.V. M. Frances and Rabbi Byron L. Sherwin. *Thank God: Prayers We Have in Common.* Chicago: Liturgy Training Publications, 1989. A collection of classic prayers from Jewish and Christian liturgies that can be used with integrity by persons of both faiths.

Neusner, Jacob. *The Fortress Introduction to American Judaism: What the Books Say, What the People Do.* Minneapolis: Augsburg Fortress, 1992.

ACTION RECOMMENDATIONS

1) Do background reading to enrich your understanding of Jesus' Jewishness and the Jewish background of early Christianity.

2) Learn more about the history of Judaism since New Testament times and about Judaism today. Invite a rabbi to speak at an adult forum or other event.

3) Recognize that Jesus' critique of religious hypocrisy applies to us, not just to others.

4) Interpret references to "the Jews" to mean "the Jewish authorities," "some Jewish leaders," "the Judaeans," "the people present," etc., according to the context.

5) Arrange for adults and/or youth to visit a synagogue service. Arrange with the rabbi to have an explanation of the service beforehand and a question period afterward.

6) Use the Interfaith Circles program (see For Further Reading) as the basis for a series of "living room dialogues" with six to eight persons from each faith.

7) Point out our indebtedness to the Jews for the psalms, other elements of the liturgy ("Alleluia," "Amen"), and the whole history of God's dealings with God's people.

8) Read contemporary Jewish thinkers such as Buber or Heschel and consider using one of their books as the basis for an adult study program.

9) During Lent and Holy Week, stress how "we" are responsible more than what "they" did. Use hymns that convey this message.

10) Be alert for expressions of anti-Semitism or other forms of bigotry in your community and speak out forcefully against them.

11) Consider not pronouncing the name "Yahweh," and avoiding biblical translations where it is used. Say "the Lord" instead (an equivalent to the Jewish custom of saying *adonai* in place of the name of God).

12) Use biblical translations that deal more kindly with Jewish people—particularly the Contemporary English Version (CEV), or the NRSV emended version of the Revised Common Lectionary by Gordon Lathrop and Gail Ramshaw, *Readings for the Assembly*, Minneapolis: Augsburg Fortress (Year A code: SC3-389).

WELCOMING ADULTS TO THE FAITH

Welcoming adults to the Christian faith is not the same as welcoming them to a church on a Sunday morning. Members of a congregation are often advised with "how to" techniques for helping people feel at home when they come to worship.

The focus is usually on a way for people to be more friendly and hospitable to strangers who walk in the door. Hospitality is important when strangers find their way into a church, but another more important task falls to the church, and that is the work of evangelism, or welcoming people to the faith of the Christian church.

When confronted with a person who is searching, the most common reaction is to set up a class or a series of classes using a textbook and perhaps lectures on church history, the sacraments, and the Bible. These classes, usually taught by the pastor, may be held over a period of two to six weeks, with the baptism celebrated either privately or on a Sunday when the congregation is present. Often, however, a sense follows—once the class is completed and the new members drift in and out of the church in varying degrees of activity—that something more or different could have occurred.

NEW POSSIBILITIES

The recovery of the catechumenate (meaning to "resound" or "echo in the ear") for the church has helped to bridge the gap between what ideally is hoped for and what realistically can be done. The catechumenate has a deep history in the church in the way that it serves to guide the seeker into faith and into a congregation. Although the temptation may be to move seekers as quickly as possible into the church, the catechumenate allows for the possibility of an intentional, open-ended process whereby each person who is exploring the Christian faith can do so in an unhurried manner. It allows individuals to go more deeply into prayer, corporate worship, scripture study, and works of compassion and justice.

The temptations for congregations are many: to short-circuit the process, to be concerned with setting up programs and activities merely to satisfy inquirers' direct requests, or to view inquirers as numbers, rather than disciples to be formed in the faith. What is happening with seekers is a life-changing event, with a new way of living being called for as people move into the Christian faith. The process of the catechumenate allows for an individual to be fully incorporated into the culture of the Christian faith.

FOUNDATIONS OF THE CATECHUMENAL PROCESS

The catechumenal process is built on several premises: that a formation in Christian discipleship is tied into information to learn; that the entire congregation is committed and involved in the process from beginning and beyond; that it is an open-ended process, with no time limits for "finishing the course"; that discipleship of individuals is more important than numbers; and that certain worship rites are essential and basic to the process. The catechumenal process is interdisciplinary in that it brings together liturgy, scripture study, prayer and personal devotions, and ministry in daily life. This process is adaptable for one inquirer or for several, and can be used in a variety of settings from the parish, to prisons, to college campuses.

The entire congregation is involved in a supportive, prayerful and evangelizing way, but the sponsor, the catechist, and the pastor are integral to the process. First, the sponsor can be someone chosen by the pastor and the catechist, in consultation with the inquirer, who will accompany the inquirer on this journey of faith to baptism and beyond into ministry. Potential sponsors to be considered are most effective if they are active members of the congregation, are willing to share their own faith stories, are caring and hospitable, and above all, willing to pray for the inquirer seeking a deeper relationship with Jesus Christ.

The catechist needs to be an active and committed Christian and a member of the congregation, skilled in leading people through scripture study and the teachings of the Christian church, and able to guide inquirers in prayer.

The pastor's role in the catechumenal process is to plan and preside at the liturgical rites, preach, serve as a resource person and study leader when requested by the catechist, pray for the unbaptized in the prayers of the church, and be willing to use the sacraments of baptism and communion in the fullest manner for which they were intended.

THE TIMES OF THE CATECHUMENAL PROCESS

The catechumenal process covers four "times": the *Time of Inquiry*, the *Time of the Catechumenate*, the *Time of Lent: Baptismal Preparation*, and the *Time of Easter: Baptismal Living*. Each of these times is open-ended and is not meant to be set in a rigid way that hampers the shaping of the person in the Christian life. An individual should be made to feel free to leave, or to postpone or lengthen any one of the times, without feeling pressured to continue just for the sake of hoping to complete the journey.

The time of inquiry is an opportunity for the inquirer to begin to explore the Christian faith, his or her own story of faith up to this point, and to study scripture, especially the Sunday readings. These gatherings are held weekly, and because of the deep nature of the conversation are considered to be confidential in nature. The keyword to the gatherings is flexibility. The group itself will need to decide the best time to meet. These meetings will allow catechist and sponsor to explore what brought the inquirer to the church. It will be a time to share something of the congregation's ministry (for example, committee chairpersons might share what they're doing), guide the inquirer through the worship service, conduct a tour of the church building, and model prayer and the devotional life.

When it is deemed appropriate, the inquirer will be welcomed into the catechumenate at a public worship service of the congregation called the "Welcome of Inquirers to the Catechumenate" (from *Welcome to Christ: Lutheran Rites for the Catechumenate*, Minneapolis: Augsburg Fortress, 1997, pp. 8–15). This welcome can happen at any time during the year.

After the inquirer is welcomed, the individual now enters the time of the catechumenate and may now be called a *catechumen*. This time is for the catechumen to explore in more depth the teachings of the church, the study of the Sunday scriptures, the developing prayer life, and involvement in following the way of the crucified and risen Christ in daily life. It is a time for the sponsor and catechumen to worship together and explore ways of ministry in the world.

When the catechumenate group believes it appropriate, the catechumen comes before the congregation for the "Enrollment of Candidates for Baptism" (*Welcome to Christ: Rites . . .*, pp. 18–21). This rite emphasizes the utter importance of baptism, and is the bridge for the catechumen from the time of the catechumenate into the time of baptismal preparation. It is most appropriately celebrated on or near the First Sunday in Lent.

The candidate, the sponsor, the catechist, the pastor, and the congregation now look ahead to the sacraments of baptism and communion. This time of baptismal preparation is more like a six-week long retreat than anything else. During this time the candidate considers the reality of evil in one's life, and the need for God's love realized for us in the death and resurrection of Jesus Christ. The candidate now deals with questions such as, Do I recognize the areas of my life that are wounded? Do I accept responsibility for failings? Do I desire to follow the way of Christ? Am I willing to live in the Christian community? Am I willing to leave behind all that is inauthentic and live life fully, whatever the cost? The questions aren't easy and they call the candidate to search deeply in order to root out all that might be in the way of life in Christ.

Prepared and ready for baptism, the candidate comes to the waters of life at the vigil of Easter to be washed, marked, and sealed in Christ. Because of the time the candidate has spent in coming to this event, the anticipation of the candidate, catechumenal team, and congregation can be seen and felt as the life-giving waters give birth again. All may feel the air of excitement as the first Holy Communion is offered to one whose life has undergone drastic changes, and who has come from the old practices and ways of life to the new life of Easter.

Now called *newly baptized*, the individual is ushered into the time of baptismal living, most likely the time from Easter to Pentecost if the baptism was celebrated at the Easter Vigil. This fifty-day period is spent in reflecting on baptism for daily living and on Holy Communion as food for the continuing journey. The newly baptized are helped to see that when one is baptized, its significance and importance do not end at the baptismal font, but that baptism is for life and for continued daily living.

During the times of preparation leading to baptism, the catechumens are confronted with ways of living in the world that are in keeping with Christian discipleship. Each individual is helped by the sponsor and the catechist to find ways of making the faith come alive in action. During this time of baptismal living, it might be well to ask each of the newly baptized to choose an area of ministry for the coming year. It might even be preferable to encourage each one not to do this ministry in the congregation, but rather to seek out places in the larger community for them to instill Christ's love.

On Pentecost, or a Sunday near its celebration, the newly baptized are again before the congregation for the "Affirmation of Vocation of the Baptized" (*Welcome to Christ: Rites . . .*, pp. 58–61). Together with sponsor and catechist, the newly baptized declare publicly their intention to pattern their life after Jesus Christ our Lord and to be sent out into the world in peace to serve and minister.

WHERE DOES A CONGREGATION BEGIN?

The catechumenal process may seem to end with the *Affirmation of Vocation*, however, living and serving for the sake of Jesus Christ never ends. The catechumenal process of worship, scripture study, prayer, and ministry in daily life is not just for the unbaptized, but it is the rhythm of life for all Christians.

Where, then, does a congregation begin if it chooses to be intentional about setting a catechumenal process in motion? A good starting point might be for the pastor and key leadership to begin praying for the unbaptized in the prayers of the congregation. Also, it might serve the congregation well to study the catechumenal resources of the Evangelical Lutheran Church in America, and the Evangelical Lutheran Church in Canada, namely *Welcome to Christ: Lutheran Rites for the Catechumenate; Welcome to Christ: A Lutheran Introduction to the Catechumenate;* and *Welcome to Christ: A*

Lutheran Catechetical Guide (Minneapolis: Augsburg Fortress, 1997).

God calls us to Jesus Christ and gives us a rebirth in the waters of baptism. Every congregation is summoned to grow in its own understanding as an "evangelizing congregation," which means that bringing seekers to the faith is not just the work of the pastor or evangelism committee, but rather, it is the task and mission of us all. The catechumenal process is an opportunity for everyone to participate in the mystery of death and life, the pattern of life for those who follow Christ Jesus.

WORSHIP in CONTEXT

Congregational worship always takes place in a context—a complex web of people in their various cultural and natural settings. It is the contexts in which we live that shape how we live and think; they shape our basic approach to life and relationships, faith and values. What we believe, and how we communicate, even how we dress and eat, how we arrange our furniture, and what art and music we like, are all shaped by cultural setting.

Congregational worship, being an activity of people assembled *together*, is of necessity contextual, and it reflects the people and their approach to life and faith. Worship thus relates to local culture, since our culture (basically defined) is simply our whole pattern of life and thought. However, the ways in which worship and culture relate are quite complex. For that reason, from 1992 to 1998 the Lutheran World Federation undertook an international study of worship and culture, looking at worship in the local contexts where it takes place Sunday after Sunday, season after season, on the various continents of the world. By 1996, the study team was able to summarize some conclusions in its "Nairobi Statement" (the complete text of which is included in *Christian Worship: Unity in Cultural Diversity*, pp. 23–28). What follows here are some excerpts from that statement, along with some commentary for congregations in North America.

This brief article can only mention a few issues; readers are encouraged to use the books listed at the conclusion.

> 1.3 Christian worship relates dynamically to culture in at least four ways. First, it is *transcultural*, the same substance for everyone everywhere, beyond culture. Second, it is *contextual*, varying according to the local situation (both nature and culture). Third, it is *counter-cultural*, challenging what is contrary to the Gospel in a given culture. Fourth, it is *cross-cultural*, making possible sharing between different local cultures. . . .

These four dynamics relate to all the components of Christian worship—not only to texts and music, but also to ritual actions and to the architecture and art, which together provide the visual environment of our worship (see the chapter on architecture in *Worship and Culture in Dialogue*).

Essentially, the four dynamics together point to the need for a balance between the local and the global, the particular and the universal. In worship, the local context is both affirmed and challenged, and the broader global character is recognized.

Because the one whom we worship is beyond us

and our own settings and concerns, the Nairobi Statement begins with attention to the crucial ways in which Christian worship is transcultural.

WORSHIP AS TRANSCULTURAL

Contemporary discussions of culture are usually about diversity and plurality—but in the church, it is vital to begin with what we have in common, that is, with what *unites* us. Our congregations may be culturally or ethnically diverse, but they are not polycentric. We who are baptized have but one center: the crucified and resurrected Christ.

> 2.1. The resurrected Christ whom we worship, and through whom by the power of the Holy Spirit we know the grace of the Triune God, transcends and indeed is beyond all cultures.

It is Christ alone whom we gather to worship, and it is because of Christ that our worship transcends all cultural and ethnic boundaries. The style of worship varies from congregation to congregation, but its content (Christ incarnate, crucified, and risen) and its essential shape or pattern (gathering, word, meal, sending) are the same around the globe.

WORSHIP AS CONTEXTUAL

Contextualization means building a bridge between worship and its local setting(s), so that worship is meaningful to people in their life situations, and that the gospel can take root more deeply in a given local place.

> 3.1. Jesus whom we worship was born into a specific culture of the world. In the mystery of his incarnation are the model and the mandate for the contextualization of Christian worship. God can be and is encountered in the local cultures of our world.

The proclamation of the word must always be contextualized. One obvious implication is that the readings be done from a translation with a linguistic style comprehensible to the congregation. Another essential implication is that in preaching, the connection must be made between the ancient Mediterranean contexts of the Bible and the context of today's congregation in *this* place, for there are enormous differences between the cultural contexts of the Bible and of North America today.

Hymns are an obvious area for contextualization. Indexes at the end of the *Hymnal Companion to Lutheran Book of Worship* provide the national and linguistic sources of all *LBW* hymns.

The commemorations in the *LBW* church year calendar can be occasions for reflecting a congregation's ethnic background, and helpful information is provided in *Festivals and Commemorations* (see especially the geographical index on p. 476). However, it is important to remember that these persons are remembered because of their witness to Christ; the commemorations are not times for ethnic glorification.

WORSHIP AS COUNTERCULTURAL

In Christian worship, local culture is critiqued when it is contrary to the gospel. In this way, worship can be said to be countercultural, and the call is for transformation. The very act of coming together—assembling for worship—is countercultural in a society where individualism reigns. In a nation where many stores are open seven days a week (and therefore in which there's no difference between the days), Christians mark Sunday as unique—not as a day of rest (that, in the biblical sense, is Saturday, the Sabbath) but as the day of resurrection—and hence as the day of corporate worship. In an era when family meals are becoming less and less common, we assemble as a parish family for the Lord's Supper.

> 4.1. Jesus Christ came to transform all people and all cultures, and calls us not to conform to the world, but to be transformed with it (Romans 12:2). In the mystery of his passage from death to eternal life is the model for transformation, and thus for the counter-cultural nature of Christian worship.

The church year, too, challenges us to transformation. Advent is a time of waiting and hoping in the midst of our society of instant gratification. In worship we delay singing Christmas carols until Christmas—not to follow some liturgical "rule," but to learn the value of waiting. And at Christmas we proclaim that God brings salvation to *all* people (Titus 2:11), in contrast to Santa Claus's distinction between those who are "naughty or nice."

Other, larger ways in which Christians worship contrast with North American culture. Ours is now largely an entertainment culture, yet Christians come to worship not to be entertained passively, but to participate actively in the liturgy and hymns.

WORSHIP AS CROSS-CULTURAL

The Christian church extends far beyond our local congregation; it is the communion of saints of every time and every place. To acknowledge the rich breadth of the whole church of God, from time to time we might incorporate into our worship elements from other places and cultures.

> 5.1. Jesus came to be the Savior of all people. He welcomes the treasures of earthly cultures into the city of God. By virtue of Baptism, there is one Church; and one means of living in faithful response to Baptism is to manifest ever more deeply the unity of the Church.

Both *LBW* and *WOV* include hymns from a wide variety of traditions. However, tokenism and eclecticism should be avoided, and elements from other cultures (whether musical, artistic, or ritual) should be understood and respected—because we worship the Christ who redeemed "saints from every tribe and language and people and nation" (Rev. 5:9c).

FOR FURTHER READING

Pilch, John J. *The Cultural World of Jesus: Sunday by Sunday, Cycle A.* Collegeville, MN: Liturgical Press, 1995. Insightful cultural background on the gospel readings for year A, and comparisons with contemporary western culture; helpful for preaching preparation.

Stauffer, S. Anita, ed. *Christian Worship: Unity in Cultural Diversity.* Geneva, Switzerland: Lutheran World Federation, 1996. An international exploration of the contemporary dynamics between the eucharist and the world's cultures, and contextualization methodologies; includes an extensive bibliography.

———. *Worship and Culture in Dialogue.* Geneva, Switzerland: Lutheran World Federation, 1994. An international examination of the historical and contemporary relationships between culture and Christian liturgy, church music, and church architecture/art. Detailed attention to Holy Baptism and eucharist in the cultural contexts of the New Testament, early church, and Lutheran Reformation.

WHAT MAKES WORSHIP LUTHERAN?

That particular question can stand for many others. What makes worship among Lutherans both evangelical and catholic? What sets our assemblies apart from those of our ecumenical sisters and brothers? What are those distinctive marks of Lutheran congregations gathered around word and sacraments? The first answer is "Not much." The second answer is "Quite a bit, actually."

AN ECUMENICAL CONSENSUS

Ecumenical consensus about worship—a common "core" of characteristics seen in recent worship books in a great variety of denominations—is growing. This consensus might be articulated as follows. This gathering of Christians uses gracious, life-giving signs and strong, clear words. Saying and doing the gospel of Jesus Christ in word and sacraments within a group of God's people is the central reality of much of Christian worship today. Since there is no empirical way to capture and express the essence of God, we construct worship using images, metaphors, and anthropomorphisms to express the gracious acts of God in their myriad forms. Our words, symbols, and gestures are profound and beautiful, and include many of those images the scriptures use to express the idea of God.

The people of God assembled in community in this place are of great importance, always to be respected and welcomed into the common prayer and praise, and never made to feel incompetent. The presiding minister acts as a guide, directing these people to the source of their life—word and sacraments—and encouraging these people to do their ministry in worship and in daily life. Musical leaders are dedicated to helping the people of God, not entertaining them. Assisting ministers carry out a representational as well as functional ministry as they act on behalf of all the people. The life of the assembly itself is a gift; in the breaking of the bread and the sharing of the cup people move beyond friendship to *koinonia,* the unity that is at the essence of the church.

Related to this *koinonia* is the desire of the assembly at worship to express its corporality, the fact that it is the body of Christ in spite and because of its great diversity, and that it is linked with the church throughout the world and throughout the ages. Thus the communion is both in and as the body of Christ.

Newly published worship books use amazingly similar terminology to identify the four-fold shape of worship in many churches: the gathering of the people of God, a central focus on the word of God read from scripture and proclaimed in sermon or homily, the importance of table fellowship with Christ and with his people in the meal, and a sending into the world for continued service. Within this basic shape can be found the differences between the churches, yet we see a consensus, marked by a simplicity that emphasizes the flow of the ordo while following this shape.

The liturgy offers a kind of order to the chaos of human life by providing a sense of stability for this assembly. The Sunday assembly raises the name of Christ in a society that is largely post-Christian and provides for community in a culture characterized by narcissism. Worship impacts the life of the world. The liturgy is not only about God; it is also about our lives and our world in light of God. Our worship judges our lack of justice, our abuse of creation, our neglect of service to others, and it provokes us to new considerations of what it means to be the body of Christ in the world.

In this worship, the offering can be seen as an important ritual act as we take the gifts of God and give them in praise to the giver, linking Sunday with the other days of the week, connecting this community with the whole creation, and coming to realize that music, drama, fine arts, skillful and sensitive choice of words, fabric creations, and so forth, are all gifts used by God's people in their offering of praise.

DISTINCTIVELY LUTHERAN MARKS

In her book *Worship,* Evelyn Underhill writes perceptively about Lutheran understandings of worship, beginning with Martin Luther's liturgical work. Luther did not seek to be an innovator, but rather worked to restore the balance of word and sacrament, moving from the medieval emphasis on the meal that led to the near exclusion of the word. Underhill rightly claims that for Lutherans the word is a sacrament, the sensible garment in which the presence of God is clothed. But in the generations after Luther, the eucharistic rhythm of divine initiative and human response was lost because of an overemphasis on the restoration of this balance which, in fact, moved to the opposite of the medieval extreme. Thus, Luther's desire, while coming closer to being a reality among us through changes in eucharistic piety over the past half-century, remains an unmet goal. The meal is yet secondary to the preaching of the word. When Lutherans greet their pastor on the way out of worship with "good job, pastor," they usually mean that the sermon was satisfactory. But the frequency of celebration of the Holy Communion *is* increasing in Lutheran congregations and appreciation for this sacrament continues to grow.

The distinctive marks identified by the Lutheran confessions themselves are becoming more common in our congregational practice. Article 7 of the Augsburg Confession defines the church as "the assembly of all believers among whom the Gospel is preached in its purity and the holy sacraments are administered according to the Gospel" (*The Book of Concord,* p. 32). Within Lutheran churches one notices signs that a new, vigorous, robust style of celebration is taking shape as theological and confessional awareness increase and ritual action becomes less threatening. Controversies of "high" versus "low" church are fading, largely due to a renewed appreciation for the abundance of ways to understand the Lord's Supper, especially as identified in the Lutheran confessions.

THE LORD'S SUPPER AS A MEANS OF GRACE

The Holy Communion is a "means" of grace. The forgiveness of sins is given through this means because, as

19

the *Smalcald Articles* (3:8:10) declare, "God will not deal with us except through his external word and sacrament" (*The Book of Concord*, p. 313). This gift is offered to the faithful "every Sunday and on other festivals" (24:1) according to the *Apology of the Augsburg Confession* (*The Book of Concord*, p. 249), and even more frequently to judge by the Large Catechism's (5:24) declaration that the Lord's Supper "is given as a daily food and sustenance so that our faith may refresh and strengthen itself" (*The Book of Concord*, p. 449).

THE LORD'S SUPPER AS BOTH SACRIFICE AND REMEMBRANCE

The confessions also identify the Lord's Supper in terms of sacrifice. Much controversy among Lutherans still surrounds the use of the word *sacrifice*, but the *Apology of the Augsburg Confession* (24:19) helps to clarify the legitimate, even necessary, use of that term:

> There are two, and only two, basic types of sacrifice. One is the propitiatory sacrifice; this is a work of satisfaction for guilt and punishment that reconciles God or placates his wrath or merits the forgiveness of sins for others. The other type is the eucharistic sacrifice; this does not merit the forgiveness of sins or reconciliation, but by it those who have been reconciled give thanks or show their gratitude for the forgiveness of sins and other blessings received. (*The Book of Concord*, p. 252)

Thus, the confessions reject the thought of the sacrament as a sacrifice of propitiation but clearly understand the eucharist as a sacrifice of praise.

The element of remembrance likewise is central to Lutheran thought about the Lord's Supper. This remembrance, however, understands Christ's sacrifice as a present event, here and now, with us still. This remembrance is articulated by doing what Jesus did: giving thanks. Though Luther removed eucharistic prayers in his liturgical reforms (thereby hoping to rid the church of the emphasis on propitiatory sacrifice) the situation is different today. The eucharistic prayer is itself a remembrance of God's mighty acts in salvation history, and especially in the paschal mystery of Christ crucified and risen. In congregations where the "consecration" is reduced to the narrative words of institution we risk losing the connection with Jesus' own act of institution—that is, blessing God. Without this form of prayer we miss an opportunity to remember the wonder of God's interaction with God's people throughout the ages, and we risk a return to a "magic moment" of consecration in which the words change the elements.

As already alluded to, preaching is of great importance among Lutherans. In fact the case can be made that Luther viewed the mission of the church as making the word of God come alive in oral and sacramental communication. While oratorical trickery, moralisms, a surfeit of anecdotes, and doctrinal lectures seem to have replaced proclamation in many congregations, Lutherans hold on to the promise of the real presence in the preached word just as in the eucharist. Lutheran preaching, both in the sermons of Luther himself and those of his spiritual descendants, are largely expository of the lectionary's scripture and thus are connected with the church's year, helping to achieve the balance of word and sacrament as Luther desired.

Congregational song is a vital ingredient of worship in Lutheran churches. For Lutherans, the eucharistic liturgy is musical; note the simple fact that *LBW* prints the text of the liturgy only in musical settings (as distinct from other traditions in which the liturgy appears in a text-only version). One may also note that *LBW* and its supplement, *WOV,* continue the standard Lutheran practice of providing a hymn collection with musical settings of the Holy Communion in a single book, thus indicating the importance of hymnody in the liturgy. From the beginning of the Lutheran reform movement, hymnody has been integral to the liturgy, not loosely attached to it.

What makes worship Lutheran is a combination of the catholic ecumenical consensus and the clear voice of the gospel proclaimed and sung. We continue to grow into that richness.

FOR FURTHER READING

The Book of Concord: The Confessions of the Evangelical Lutheran Church, Theodore G. Tappert, ed. (Philadelphia: Fortress Press, 1959).

The Use of the Means of Grace: A Statement on the Practice of Word and Sacrament. (Chicago: ELCA; Minneapolis: Augsburg Fortress, 1997).

Underhill, Evelyn. *Worship.* (London: Collins, 1936).

20

SUNDAYS AND THE LESSER FESTIVALS

Today many people live with several calendars, which they find themselves

juggling. Among these calendars are ones governing work and government

services. They have the home and family calendar

that keeps soccer practice and music lessons on

track. The schedule of bill paying is another calendar to observe. The annual round of birthdays and anniversaries for family and friends is yet one more. The Christian church also has several calendars.

The basic building block of time for Christians is Sunday. In the church, however, other calendars are at work as well. There is the yearly round of festivals like Christmas, Epiphany, Easter and Pentecost. The calendar of commemorations celebrates the lives of the saints. The secular calendar also makes an impact on Christian celebration; secular holidays such as Mother's Day and Father's Day, Memorial Day, and Labor Day have their particular impact on planning. The church and its people are not so much ruled by these calendars; rather, they use them to make an orderly witness to Christ in time.

One of the earliest distinguishing marks of Christians was their gathering together on the first day of each week to hear the story of Jesus and to celebrate the Holy Communion. We know from New Testament evidence they followed this practice even before Sunday, the first day of the week, was observed as a day free from work. It also made Christians noticeable to their unbelieving neighbors and to their Hebrew friends, family, and neighbors.

The earliest Christians, who were also Jews, likely continued to worship at the temple in Jerusalem (as long as it was possible) and also to attend synagogue and observe the Sabbath. Even while observing Sabbath—the seventh day of the week—they did not confuse it with the unique Christian celebration that took place on the first day of the week—Sunday: the Lord's Day, the eighth day. The earliest Christian church knew both Sabbath and Sunday and regarded Sunday as the unique Christian observance. It was focused not on rest from work (as Sabbath had been) nor on thanksgiving for creation (as Sabbath had been) but on the resurrection of

Jesus Christ from the dead (Luke 24) and his subsequent appearances to the apostles and others (see John 20:19 and John 20:26). It also focused on the new creation promised in Christ—hence the eighth day.

How do we know that Christians observed the Lord's Day—Sunday—with such noticeable devotion and commitment? Evidence for it includes Paul gathering with Christians "on the first day of the week" (Acts 20:7). The second-century testimony of Justin Martyr in his description of Christian worship to hostile unbelievers specifies that Christians worshiped on the first day of the week. Sunday was so important to Christian identity that the council of Nicea (A.D. 325) decided that the great annual feast of Christians—Easter—must always be observed on Sunday.

Virtually all congregations of the Evangelical Lutheran Church in America hold an assembly for word and sacrament on Sunday. They may hold several on that day. They may also hold additional assemblies on Saturday and other days of the week. Sunday continues to be an important part of Christian practice among us.

When *LBW* was published and approved by several church bodies in 1978 it described the Lord's Day, Sunday, in this way: "All Sundays of the year are festivals of our Lord Jesus Christ, for they are the weekly celebration of his resurrection" (*LBW, Ministers Edition*, p. 13). This principle was reaffirmed in 1997 by the Churchwide Assembly of the ELCA when it adopted *The Use of the Means of Grace* (Principle 6).

Since the publication of *LBW*, a new lectionary has been approved for use and is being used by more than 90 percent of ELCA congregations. The Revised Common Lectionary, produced by the ecumenical Consultation on Common Texts, is a Sunday lectionary. Providing three yearly cycles of readings (Old Testament—typological or semi-continuous; Psalm; New Testament; Gospel). It is not identical to the lectionary provided in *LBW* but does resemble it closely for Sundays.

SUNDAYS AND LESSER FESTIVALS

Since the ELCA authorized the Revised Common Lectionary for use in congregations, an old question has reemerged among some pastors, church musicians, and other worship planners. What is the relationship between the lesser festivals and Sundays? Should the integrity of Sunday and the careful use of the readings assigned to Sunday be the guiding factor in worship planning or should the recovery of the celebration of lesser festivals be encouraged by allowing them to "have precedence" over Sundays?

LBW worked out its own principle on this issue, which still guides practice in the ELCA:

> Lesser festivals have precedence only over Sundays for which the color is green and over the first and second Sundays after Christmas. Lesser festivals never have precedence over Days of Special Devotion [Ash Wednesday and the days of Holy Week].

Commemorations never have precedence over Sundays and Days of Special Devotion. In its calendar *LBW* designated the lesser festivals (*LBW, Ministers Edition*, p. 14). For our purposes here we will distinguish "precedence" as essentially meaning that when lesser festivals happen to fall on a Sunday assigned the color green in the calendar, the lesser festival will be observed with its proper elements—prayer of the day, lectionary readings, proper preface, and color—rather than the Sunday.

In conformity with these principles, approved in 1978 with *LBW*, the calendar we use now in the ELCA reflects the internal conflict between the absolute priority of Sunday and the precedence of lesser festivals.

The lesser festivals are in a real sense festivals of the Lord displayed in aspects of Christ's life and ministry and in the witness to Christ in the apostles, evangelists, and saints, as well as in the reformation of the church's life. They help to recover the sense of the communion of saints, which is so important to understanding the church. They have also contributed in many congregations to more frequent celebration of Holy Communion. Congregations often describe themselves as celebrating Holy Communion every second or third or fourth Sunday with the addition of festivals. Embracing the lesser festivals has allowed congregations moving toward a weekly celebration of Holy Communion to augment their usual practice with additional celebrations. It serves to enrich the sacramental life of the congregation and to place Christ in word and sacrament at the center of the assembly for worship.

Certain difficulties come with observing the lesser festivals in place of a Sunday. Most lesser festivals have only one set of readings rather than three, as the Sundays do. It means that days such as Reformation Day (when celebrated on Sunday) will proclaim the same readings each year. This limitation seems to turn back the reforms of the lectionary from a three-year cycle of reading of scripture to a one-year repetition. The careful planning in the RCL and the relationships among the Sunday readings will be disrupted when one set of them is replaced on a given Sunday by a lesser festival.

Until a careful and coordinated reform of the calendar and its principles is authorized and undertaken, the ELCA and its publishing house will uphold the *LBW* principles in the matter of Sundays and lesser festivals.

WHAT CAN WORSHIP PLANNERS DO?

Worship planners who decide to celebrate the lesser festivals will find help in *Sundays and Seasons* and in the resources supporting *LBW*. Worship planners committed to the Sunday observance will omit the lesser festivals that fall on green Sundays. Worship planners who wish to maintain the emphasis on Sunday and also employ the lesser festivals may want to consider some of the following possibilites:

- Announce the day by including the lesser festival in that announcement. "Today we celebrate the _____ Sunday after Pentecost. Today, (date), the church is also celebrating the festival of _____."
- Use the Sunday readings—for example, Proper 18.
- Commemorate the lesser festival by including a second prayer of the day from that festival after the prayer for that Sunday.
- Use the Sunday readings but connect to the lesser festival in the content of the intercessions.
- Make the relationship between the Sunday and lesser festival an occasion for preaching and teaching.

HOW to PLAN BLENDED WORSHIP

Worship is about unity. Through word and sacrament, prayer, song, sign, symbol, action, sound and silence we are united with God and with one another. Without denying our human individuality, we gather around the central images of our faith,

striving for Christian community. As the gathered people of God, we are called to leave behind our personal agendas as we encounter the living God in our lives—the same God encountered by all Christians throughout time and space, of all ages, genders, languages, and cultures. At the heart of preparing Christian worship is a vision that unites rather than divides.

This unity is not easy in North American culture during the latter years of this millennium. Individuality has become a normative characteristic for our culture. Yet, Christ's prayer that we may all be one stands as a vision for the not-yet-one church on earth. Worship can and should be a reflection of that vision.

Unfortunately, the vision often reflected in worship is not of one, but of many. To emulate our culture is often easier than being countercultural. Providing a variety of worship opportunities, each reflecting a particular style or taste, can be quite expected by the world's standards. But, if our vision—our ideal—is to reflect Christ's ideal, we should foster a worship life that brings people together, a much harder task than presenting a menu of offerings.

As Lutherans, we have a rich liturgical heritage on which to draw for resources. The vision for Lutheran worship has always centered around word and sacrament: gathering together and telling our stories, expressing concerns for and sharing joys with those present and with those who are absent, setting the table and eating a meal together, and finally being sent on our way home with the blessing and good wishes of the host. Whether we picnic outdoors with barbeque and paper plates, or enjoy a lavish holiday meal on the family's fine china, the pattern for community is the same.

Too often, we have approached worship in an all or nothing manner. Either we have used *LBW* by the book or we have abandoned it altogether for something more

contemporary or flexible and, therefore, relevant. The joy of committing oneself to the shape of the liturgy is that it enables worship planners to create a worship event that uses the best of a diversity of musical and leadership styles, while maintaining the integrity of our liturgical tradition, a tradition that connects us with other Christians throughout time and space and allows for full participation by all the people of God.

Music is often the scapegoat for our concerns about the relevance of worship in a contemporary context. For example, some opine that if we only change the style of music we use in worship, young people will be attracted to it. In reality, music of any style, if done with confidence and quality, can be appealing to almost anyone, regardless of age. Week after week we boldly proclaim that we believe in "one holy catholic and apostolic church." A church that is truly catholic embraces practice, language, and music of all God's people. A church that is truly catholic uses all that is worthwhile from the tradition, woven closely and carefully with that which is appropriate from the contemporary culture.

Music from various times and places, if it is the best choice for proclaiming the gospel message at any given point in any particular liturgy, needs to be embraced and sung heartily without apology. This embrace means that a Christian text set to music in a popular style can stand side by side with a German chorale, a jazz setting of a psalm, and a liturgical piece from the growing church in Africa. Such diversity, carefully planned over a lengthy period of time in the life of a congregation, will come to reflect the true diversity that is the church. Where this vision of music serving as a glimpse of the nature of the church is present, the reality is that in every liturgy, most worshipers will love some of the music and dislike other portions. But in our persistent and pastoral use of a variety of appropriate music, worshipers may gradually come to respect others who, although differing in musical tastes, are part of the same body of Christ.

23

A GUIDE to WRITING the PRAYERS

To intercede for others is at the heart of the definition of Christian prayer.

The genius of Christian prayer is our privilege and responsibility to pray to

God for others. When we pray for the hungry, the

poor, the dying, for nations at war, societies in

disarray, and nature contaminated by waste we stand in solidarity with everyone for whom Christ died. In such prayers we envision a world at peace, creation healed and cherished, and a community of faith living out the life of Christ. In such prayer we embrace the biblical picture of God's "kingdom come." With the whole creation, we long for final liberation from sin and death. Liturgical renewal in our day underscores the importance of restoring intercessory prayer in Christian lives by recovering its presence in the Sunday liturgy.

THE ROLE OF INTERCESSOR

Intercessory prayer is one of the basic baptismal rights and responsibilities of a Christian. In the early church, one of the first gifts conferred in baptism was inclusion in the community's prayers. Formerly excluded from the Prayer of the Faithful, the newly baptized were able to participate in this prayer, which served as segue into the eucharistic meal. (*LBW* simply uses the term *The Prayers* to designate the intercessory component of the liturgy. Other traditions refer to this same element as the *Prayer of the Faithful, Prayer of the Church, Prayers of the People, General Prayer, Universal Prayer, or The Intercessions.*) Just as the offering of bread, wine, and other gifts grow out of our everyday lives, so do the prayers. At the offertory we present signs of our lives accompanied by prayer asking God to take, redeem, and renew them in the eucharist.

Being faithful to the origins and meanings of this prayer, it should be led by a layperson. This leader must be a credible witness. In other words, voiced petitions must be supported by a sense of this person's own commitment to Christian life and ministry. The intercessor also must have recognized gifts of communication, as well as spiritual depth and commitment to the life and ministry of the congregation.

A standing program of study, prayer, and practical experience will be necessary if a congregation is to take this role seriously. Major portions of this material are based on a text for training congregational leaders in this ministry: Walter Huffman, *Prayer of the Faithful: Understanding and Creatively Leading Corporate Intercessory Prayer* (Minneapolis: Augsburg Fortress, 1992).

PREPARATION OF THE PRAYERS

Careful preparation of the prayers and Spirit-led presentation are complimentary themes in fulfilling the expectations of intercessory prayer in public worship. Those who deliver sermons or give musical offerings know the importance of preparation so that text *and* assembly may be honored. Deliberate preparation can free us to speak or sing from the heart.

One approach to gathering the prayers might look like this: the intercessor for the week or month establishes a network of people who supply the concerns to be included in the prayers. The pastor, other congregational leaders, and a team of intercessors help the prayer leader balance the "universal scope proper to Christian concern with the specific concerns of a given congregation." Such collaboration could take place in a weekly meeting or over the telephone. Some congregations have narthex books for individuals to note intercessory requests. Sometimes prayer requests come via pew cards or as part of the offering. If oral announcements take place during the offering, that might be a time to gather and announce prayer requests. While each congregation must find its own way of gathering petitions, a recognizable strategy is necessary if these are to be the "prayers of the people."

PRESENTATION OF THE PRAYERS

One of the contributions of the free-prayer tradition is the reminder that prayer is primarily an act rather than a composition to be read. Public prayer is an oral medium; it lives in the vocative mode.

Public prayer is in the praying and not just the reading of texts. As with all public communication, the style of presentation will be as important as the content. Body language, facial expression, tone of voice, and the environment impact one's delivery. So that the prayers may be heard and prayed by others, the leader must be practiced in communication skills that facilitate this liturgical ministry.

The following matters of presentation need to be addressed in terms of local appropriateness:

- More than one person may lead the prayers. Occasionally, they may be spoken by a variety of voices from the congregation.
- If the prayer leader uses notes or written pages, the material should be held in a special folder or the narthex book of intercessions, rather than held as loose-leaf pieces of paper.
- A basic requirement of the presentation is that the leader be heard and understood. That requirement will mean attention to matters of projecting one's voice or amplification. A deliberate pace is essential if the congregation is to accompany the intercessor in prayer. Spaces must be left for reflection, silent prayer, and, when appropriate, free prayer. Intercessors should seek out the advice of others as to their leadership style so they may become more effective in this ministry.

PROPERTIES OR SHAPE OF THE PRAYERS

INTRODUCTORY ADDRESS

Normally the assisting minister introduces the prayers with a formula such as: "Let us pray for the whole people of God in Christ Jesus, and for all people according to their needs" (*LBW*, p. 65). In place of this standard invitation, other variations reflecting the liturgical day or season may be used.

THE INTENTIONS

Historically the prayers have addressed five basic categories which serve as the norm for public intercessory prayer. Such intentions are strengthened with a balance of both universal and local dimensions. A list of traditional categories would include:

- The needs of the church

- The welfare of the nation and world
- Those with special needs
- The concerns of the local community
- The faithful departed

THE FORMAT

One of the most ancient forms of intercessory prayer—found in the bidding prayer for Good Friday—is an ideal one (*LBW, Ministers Edition*, pp. 139–141). Essentially it is the following:

- A bid or invitation to pray for a special need or intention
- Silence so the people may pray
- A brief collecting prayer
- Ending with a congregational response

A familiar formula used in many congregations consists of brief prayer paragraphs of several sentences followed by silence and congregational response. This is modeled in the Holy Communion Liturgy (*LBW*, p. 65). In addition to these forms, many other appropriate patterns exist for the prayers.

CONGREGATIONAL ASSENT

A hallmark of the prayers is the internal and external assent of the people who participate in them. A popular approach to such congregational involvement allows the people to respond to each petition in a shared, litanic fashion. While such responses normally remain the same throughout a given prayer, they may vary from Sunday to Sunday as a way to claim congregational attention to enrich the spirit of the prayer. A leader might end each intercession with "Lord, in your mercy," with the response being "Hear our prayer," or "Show us your saving power," or "Give your people joy and peace," etc.

CONCLUDING PRAYER

The assisting or presiding minister may conclude the prayers with a summary ending such as: "Into your hands, O Lord, we commend all for whom we pray, trusting in your mercy; through your Son, Jesus Christ our Lord" (*LBW*, p. 65). Like the introductory address, this conclusion could be varied ("Hear our prayers, eternal God, and cast the radiance of your mercy over the creation you have made in the image of Christ the Lord." The Epiphany of Our Lord).

HYMN MASS

KYRIE

Have mercy on us, Lord,
and hear our solemn prayer.
We come to hear your living Word;
it saves us from despair.

Have mercy on us, Christ,
and wash away our sin.
Pour out your grace and make us whole
that new life may begin.

Have mercy on us, Lord;
make sin and shame depart.
Renew us with your saving pow'r;
create in us new hearts!

SUGGESTED TUNES (S M)

LBW 89   Potsdam
LBW 309   Southwell

GLORIA

Glory be to God in heaven;
peace, goodwill, to all the earth.
Mighty God of all creation,
Father of surpassing worth:
we exalt you, we adore you,
we lift high our thanks and praise.
Saints and angels bow before you;
here on earth our songs we raise.

Glory be to Christ forever,
Lamb of God and Lord of love.
Son of God and gracious Savior,
you have come from heav'n above;
on the cross you died to save us;
now you reign at God's right hand.
Hear our prayer; restore, forgive us;
in your promise firm we stand.

Holy One we now acclaim you;
Lord alone, to you we call;
Holy One in faith we name you,
throned on high, yet near to all:
Jesus Christ, with God the Spirit,
in the Father's splendor bright.
For the peace that we inherit,
glory be to God on high!

SUGGESTED TUNES (8 7 8 7 D)

CON 168   Anxious Heart
LBW 358   Austria
LBW 405   Abbot Leigh
WOV 638   Joyous Light
LBW 408   Rustington
LBW 315   Hyfrydol

ALLELUIA

Alleluia! Lord and Savior;
open now your saving Word.
Let it burn like fire within us;
speak until our hearts are stirred!
Alleluia! Lord, we sing
for the good news that you bring.

SUGGESTED TUNES (8 7 8 7 7 7)

CON 316   Jesus, Lord and Precious Savior
LBW 250   Unser Herrscher
WOV 643   Irby
LBW 266   Gott des Himmels

LENTEN VERSE

We are turning, Lord, to hear you;
you are merciful and kind!
Slow to anger, rich in blessing,
and with love to us inclined.

SUGGESTED TUNES (8 7 8 7)

WOV 656   Kas Dziedaja
LBW 200   Omni die
LBW 494   Galilee

OFFERTORY

Oh, what shall I render in thanks to my Lord
for all the good gifts by which I am restored?
No treasure I tender could ever repay
God's mercy and faithfulness, new every day.

My hands take the cup of salvation you give;
I'll praise you, O God, for as long as I live.
My thanks will rise up as I call on your name,
with all of your people your goodness proclaim.

SUGGESTED TUNES (11 11 11 11)

WOV 644   CRADLE SONG

LBW 507   FOUNDATION

WOV 799   THE SINGER AND THE SONG

SANCTUS

Holy, holy, Lord most holy,
God of pow'r and God of might:
Heav'n and earth reveal your glory.
Hail, hosanna, Lord of light!
Blessed be the coming Savior.
Hail, hosanna, Lord of light!

SUGGESTED TUNES (8 7 8 7 8 7)

LBW 50   REGENT SQUARE

LBW 198   PICARDY

LBW 549   PRAISE, MY SOUL

WOV 747   WESTMINSTER ABBEY

AGNUS DEI

O Lamb of God, you bear the sin
of all the world away;
you suffered death our lives to save:
have mercy now, we pray.

O Lamb of God, you bear the sin
of all the world away;
you set us free from guilt and grave:
have mercy now, we pray.

O Lamb of God, you bear the sin
of all the world away;
eternal peace with God you made:
give us your peace, we pray.

SUGGESTED TUNES (C M)

WOV 675   DUNLAP'S CREEK

LBW 331   LAND OF REST

LBW 345   ST. PETER

NUNC DIMITTIS

Lord, in peace I leave this celebration
for mine eyes have seen your great salvation.
By your grace you prepared a light
that with brightness shines
through the darkest night
to all nations.

SUGGESTED TUNES (10 10 8 10 4)

CON 205   IN HIS KINGDOM

THANK THE LORD

Thank the Lord, your voices raise:
sing to God with highest praise!
Tell the wonders God has done:
freedom, life, the vict'ry won.
All who seek the Lord, rejoice;
proudly bear the name of Christ.
Go in joy where God will send.
Alleluia! Sing amen!
or, in Lent: God is faithful. Sing amen!

SUGGESTED TUNES (7 7 7 7 D)

LBW 407   ST. GEORGE'S WINDSOR

LBW 90   SALZBURG

LBW 130   ORIENTIS PARTIBUS

27

BIBLIOGRAPHY

COMPUTER RESOURCES

Lutheran Resources for Worship Computer Series. Lutheran Book of Worship Liturgies; With One Voice Liturgies; Words for Worship: 1998–1999, Cycle A; Graphics for Worship. Minneapolis: Augsburg Fortress, 1997 and ongoing. These CD-ROM resources enable worship planners to prepare weekly, seasonal, or occasional worship folders.

WORSHIP BOOKS

Libro de Liturgia y Cántico. Minneapolis: Augsburg Fortress, 1998. A complete Spanish-language worship resource including liturgies and hymns.

Lutheran Book of Worship. Minneapolis: Augsburg Publishing House; Philadelphia: Board of Publication, Lutheran Church in America, 1978.

Lutheran Book of Worship: Ministers Edition. Minneapolis: Augsburg Publishing House; Philadelphia: Board of Publication, Lutheran Church in America, 1978.

Occasional Services: A Companion to Lutheran Book of Worship. Minneapolis: Augsburg Publishing House; Philadelphia: Board of Publication, Lutheran Church in America, 1982.

With One Voice: A Lutheran Resource for Worship. Minneapolis: Augsburg Fortress, 1995. Pew, leader, and accompaniment editions; instrumental parts, organ accompaniment for the liturgy, and cassette.

THE LECTIONARY

Lectionary for Worship, Cycle A. Minneapolis: Augsburg Fortress, 1995. The Revised Common Lectionary. Includes first reading, psalm citation, second reading, and gospel for each Sunday and Lesser Festival. Each reading is "sense-lined" for clearer proclamation of the scriptural texts. New Revised Standard Version.

Lectionary for Worship, Ritual Edition. Minneapolis: Augsburg Fortress, 1996. This elegant, illustrated, hard-bound edition includes the complete three-year Revised Common Lectionary and lesser festival scriptural readings.

Readings and Prayers: The Revised Common Lectionary with LBW Prayers of the Day. Minneapolis: Augsburg Fortress, 1995.

Readings for the Assembly, Cycle A. Gordon Lathrop and Gail Ramshaw, eds. Minneapolis: Augsburg Fortress, 1995. The Revised Common Lectionary. Emended NRSV for inclusive language.

REFERENCE WORKS

Concordance to Hymn Texts: Lutheran Book of Worship. Robbin Hough, compiler. Minneapolis: Augsburg Publishing House, 1985.

Praying Together. English Language Liturgical Consultation. Nashville: Abingdon Press, 1988. Core ecumenical liturgical texts with annotation and commentary.

Indexes for Worship Planning: Revised Common Lectionary, Lutheran Book of Worship, With One Voice. Minneapolis: Augsburg Fortress, 1996. With many valuable indexes, this book indexes hymns and psalms for Sundays, principal and lesser festivals, and occasions. A brief summary of each biblical reading with prayer of the day, scriptural verse, and offertory make this a handy guide to the primary biblical, liturgical, and hymn texts for each Sunday.

The New Dictionary of Sacramental Worship. Peter Fink, ed. Collegeville: Michael Glazier/Liturgical Press, 1990.

The New Westminster Dictionary of Liturgy and Worship. J. G. Davies, ed. Philadelphia: Westminster, 1986.

Pfatteicher, Philip. *Festivals and Commemorations*. Minneapolis: Augsburg Publishing House, 1980.

———. *Commentary on the Occasional Services*. Philadelphia: Fortress Press, 1983.

———. *Commentary on the Lutheran Book of Worship*. Minneapolis: Augsburg Fortress, 1990.

Pfatteicher, Philip, and Carlos Messerli. *Manual on the Liturgy: Lutheran Book of Worship*. Minneapolis: Augsburg Publishing House, 1979.

Stulken, Marilyn Kay. *Hymnal Companion to the Lutheran Book of Worship*. Philadelphia: Fortress Press, 1981.

Van Loon, Ralph, and S. Anita Stauffer. *Worship Wordbook*. Minneapolis: Augsburg Fortress, 1995.

GATHERING FOR WORSHIP

Foley, Edward. *From Age to Age: How Christians Have Celebrated the Eucharist*. Chicago: Liturgy Training Publications, 1991. An excellent survey of Christian worship, music, environment, and theological concerns.

Open Questions in Worship. Gordon Lathrop, general ed. Minneapolis: Augsburg Fortress.

What are the essentials of Christian worship? vol. 1 (1994). The scriptural, historical, and ecumenical consensus on essential elements of Christian worship.

What is 'contemporary' worship? vol. 2 (1995). Contemporary church music, multiple services and diverse worship styles, and the meaning of the word "contemporary."

How does worship evangelize? vol. 3 (1995). Evangelism in American culture, liturgical leadership in evangelism, and the inclusive nature of the liturgy.

What is changing in baptismal practice? vol. 4 (1995). New developments in bringing adults to the faith, issues in infant baptism, and the relationship between baptism and life stages.

What is changing in eucharistic practice? vol. 5 (1995). Preaching, the eucharistic prayer, and admission to the eucharist.

What are the ethical implications of worship? vol. 6 (1996). Liturgy serving social justice, worship and the cosmos/environment, and liturgy in a secular world.

What does "multicultural" worship look like? vol. 7 (1996). Worship in North American culture, racial/ethnic-specific worship, and culturally diverse worship.

How does the liturgy speak of God? vol. 8 (1996). Images and names for God in worship, women and men preaching, and the trinitarian name invoked in the liturgy.

Ramshaw, Gail. *Every Day and Sunday, Too.* Minneapolis: Augsburg Fortress, 1996. An illustrated book for parents and children. Daily life is related to the central actions of the liturgy.

———. *1-2-3 Church.* Minneapolis: Augsburg Fortress, 1996. An illustrated rhyming primer and number book. For parents with young children, this book presents the fundamental actions of worship through numbered rhymes. A song for singing at home or in church school is included.

———. *Sunday Morning.* Chicago: Liturgy Training Publications, 1993. A book for children and adults on the primary words of Sunday worship.

Senn, Frank. *Christian Liturgy: Catholic and Evangelical.* Minneapolis: Fortress Press, 1997. A comprehensive historical introduction to the liturgy of the Western church with particular emphasis on the Lutheran traditions.

The Use of the Means of Grace: A Statement on the Practice of Word and Sacrament. Chicago: ELCA; Minneapolis: Augsburg Fortress, 1997.

LEADING WORSHIP

Adams, William Seth. *Shaped by Images: One Who Presides.* New York: Church Hymnal Corporation, 1995. An excellent review of the ministry of presiding at worship.

Hovda, Robert. *Strong, Loving and Wise: Presiding in Liturgy.* Collegeville: The Liturgical Press, 1981. Sound, practical advice for the worship leader from a beloved advocate of social justice and liturgical renewal.

Huck, Gabe. *Liturgy with Style and Grace,* rev. ed. Chicago: Liturgy Training Publications, 1984. The first three chapters offer a practical, well-written overview of the purpose of worship, the elements of worship, and liturgical leadership.

Huffman, Walter C. *Prayer of the Faithful: Understanding and Creatively Leading Corporate Intercessory Prayer,* rev. ed. Minneapolis: Augsburg Fortress, 1992. A helpful treatment of communal prayer, the Lord's Prayer, and the prayers of the people.

Singing the Liturgy: Building Confidence for Worship Leaders. Audiocassette. Chicago: Evangelical Lutheran Church in America, 1996. A demonstration recording of the chants assigned to leaders in *LBW* and *With One Voice.*

CELEBRATING THE SEASONS

Huck, Gabe. *The Three Days: Parish Prayer in the Paschal Triduum,* rev. ed. Chicago: Liturgy Training Publications, 1992. For worship committees, it is an excellent introduction to worship during the Three Days: Maundy Thursday, Good Friday, and Holy Saturday/Easter Sunday.

Hynes, Mary Ellen. *Companion to the Calendar.* Chicago: Liturgy Training Publications, 1993. An excellent overview of the seasons, festivals and lesser festivals, and many commemorations. Written from an ecumenical/Roman Catholic perspective, including commemorations unique to the Lutheran calendar.

The Promise of His Glory: Services and Prayers for the Season from All Saints to Candlemas. Collegeville: The Liturgical Press, 1991. And: Perham, Michael, et al., comps. *Enriching the Christian Year.* (Services and prayers from Lent through Pentecost). Collegeville: The Liturgical Press, 1993. New liturgical texts, prayers, litanies, and complete services for congregational use.

PROCLAIMING THE WORD

Brueggemann, Walter, et al. *Texts for Preaching: A Lectionary Commentary Based on the NRSV.* Cycles A, B, C. Louisville: Westminster John Knox Press, 1993–1995.

Craddock, Fred, et al. *Preaching through the Christian Year.* 3 vols. for Cycles A, B, C. Valley Forge, Pa.: Trinity Press International, 1992, 1993. In three volumes, various authors comment on the Sunday readings and psalms as well as various festival readings.

Days of the Lord: The Liturgical Year. 7 vols. Collegeville: The Liturgical Press, 1991–1994. Written by French biblical and liturgical experts, this series provides helpful commentary on the readings and seasons. Readily adapted to the Revised Common Lectionary.

Homily Service: An Ecumenical Resource for Sharing the Word. Silver Spring, Md.: The Liturgical Conference. A monthly publication with commentary on Sunday readings (exegesis, ideas and illustrations, healing aspects of the word, a preacher's reflection on the readings).

New Proclamation, Series A. 1998–99. Various authors. A sound and useful series of commentaries on Cycle A readings.

Reading the Lessons: A Lector's Guide to Pronounciation. Minneapolis: Augsburg Fortress, 1993.

PREPARING ENVIRONMENT AND ART

Huffman, Walter C., S. Anita Stauffer, and Ralph R. Van Loon. *Where We Worship*. Minneapolis: Augsburg Publishing House, 1987. Written by three Lutheran worship leaders, this volume sets forth the central principles in understanding and organizing space for worship. Study book and leader guide.

Mauck, Marchita. *Shaping a House for the Church*. Chicago: Liturgy Training Publications, 1990. The author presents basic design principles for worship space and the ways in which the worship space both forms and expresses the faith of the worshiping assembly.

Mazar, Peter. *To Crown the Year: Decorating the Church through the Seasons*. Chicago: Liturgy Training Publications, 1995. A contemporary guide for decorating the worship space throughout the seasons of the year.

Stauffer, S. Anita. *Altar Guild Handbook*. Philadelphia: Fortress Press, 1985. Guidelines for worship preparation.

HYMN AND SONG COLLECTIONS (see also p. 36)

Borning Cry: Worship for a New Generation. Compiled by John Ylvisaker. Waverly, Iowa: New Generation Publishers, 1992.

O Blessed Spring: Hymns of Susan Palo Cherwien. Minneapolis: Augsburg Fortress, 1997. AFP 11-10818. New hymn texts set to both new and familiar hymn tunes.

Dancing at the Harvest: Songs by Ray Makeever. Minneapolis: Augsburg Fortress, 1997. Songbook 11-10738. Acc ed. 11-10739.

Lead Me, Guide Me: A Hymnal for African American Parishes. Chicago: GIA Publications, Inc., 1987. A broad range of hymns, songs, and liturgical music often inspired by African American musical traditions. A Roman Catholic collection.

Lift Every Voice and Sing II: An African American Hymnal. New York: The Church Hymnal Corporation, 1993. An Episcopal collection.

Mil Voces para Celebrar: Himnario Metodista. Nashville: The United Methodist Publishing House, 1996.

Sound the Bamboo. Manila: Asian Institute for Liturgy and Music, 1990. Hymns from Asia.

Wonder, Love, and Praise. New York: Church Publishing, Inc., 1997. A Supplement to *The Hymnal 1982*.

PSALM COLLECTIONS

The Anglican Chant Psalter. Alec Wyton, ed. New York: Church Hymnal Corporation, 1987.

The Basilica Psalter. Jay Hunstiger. Collegeville: Liturgical Press.

The Grail Gelineau Psalter. Chicago: GIA Publications, Inc., 1972. 150 psalms and 18 canticles.

A New Metrical Psalter. Christopher Webber. New York: Church Hymnal Corporation, 1986. Metrical psalms, canticles, invitatories

with indexes for Sundays/festivals and suggested hymn tunes. Includes permission for local use.

The Plainsong Psalter. James Litton, ed. New York: Church Hymnal Corporation, 1988.

Psalm Songs. David Ogden and Alan Smith, eds. Minneapolis: Augsburg Fortress, 1998.

   Psalm Songs 1 for Advent-Christmas-Epiphany. AFP 11-10903.

   Psalm Songs 2 for Lent-Holy Week-Easter. AFP 11-10904.

   Psalm Songs 3 for Ordinary Time. AFP 11-10905.

Psalms for the Church Year. Various volumes by different composers. Chicago: GIA Publications, Inc., 1983–present.

The Psalter. International Commission on English in the Liturgy (ICEL). Chicago: Liturgy Training Publications, 1995. A faithful and inclusive rendering from the Hebrew into contemporary English poetry, intended primarily for communal song and recitation.

Psalter for Worship. (1996–8) Martin Seltz, ed. Minneapolis: Augsburg Fortress, 1995 and continuing. New settings of psalm antiphons by various composers with *LBW* and other psalm tones. Psalm texts included. Prepared for psalms appointed in the Revised Common Lectionary for Sundays and festivals.

   Psalter for Worship, Cycle A. AFP 3-556.

   Psalter for Worship, Cycle B. AFP 3-554.

   Psalter for Worship, Cycle C. AFP 3-555.

The Psalter: Psalms and Canticles for Singing. Louisville: Westminster/John Knox Press, 1993. Various composers.

Singing the Psalms. Various volumes with various composers represented. Portland: Oregon Catholic Press, 1995–present.

CHOIRBOOKS

The Augsburg Choirbook. (1998). Ed. Kenneth Jennings. AFP 11-10817. 67 anthems primarily from North American composers of the 20c.

European Sacred Music. (1997) Ed. John Rutter. OXF 0-19-343695-7. 50 choral masterworks primarily from continental European composers of the 16–19c .

Motettenbuch. (1959). Ed. Hans Holliger. BA 3451. 42 classic German motets from the 16–20c.

The New Church Anthem Book. (1992). Ed. Lionel Dakers. OXF 0-19-353109-0. 100 favorite anthems for mixed voices from the 16–20c.

The New Novello Anthem Book. (1996). Ed. Philip Brunelle. NOV 0-85360-705-2. 41 anthems primarily from English composers of the 19–20c.

100 Carols for Choirs (1987). Ed. David Willcocks and John Rutter. OXF 0-19-353227-1. 100 classic choral settings of traditional Christmas carols.

The Oxford Easy Anthem Book. (1957). OXF 0-19-353321-9. 50 anthems for a variety of voices primarily from English composers of the 16–20c.

DAILY PRAYER RESOURCES

Book of Common Worship: Daily Prayer. Louisville: Westminster/John Knox Press, 1993. Presbyterian.

For All the Saints. 4 vols. Frederick Schumacher, ed. Delhi, N.Y.: American Lutheran Publicity Bureau, 1994.

Haugen, Marty. *Holden Evening Prayer.* Chicago: GIA Publications, Inc., 1990.

Zimmerman, Joyce Ann. *Morning and Evening: A Parish Celebration.* Chicago: Liturgy Training Publications, 1996. An introduction to parish use of daily prayer. Associated volumes: Morning and Evening (texts and melody lines); Morning and Evening (presider, cantor, and accompanist edition).

PREPARING MUSIC FOR WORSHIP

Cherwien, David. *Let the People Sing!: A Keyboardist's Creative and Practical Guide to Engaging God's People in Meaningful Song.* St. Louis: Concordia Publishing House, 1997. A practical and pedagogical approach to leading congregational singing and improvising at the organ.

Cotter, Jeanne. *Keyboard Improvsiation for the Liturgical Musician.* Chicago: GIA Publications, Inc. Practical approach to keyboard improvisation.

Handbells in the Liturgy: A Practical Guide for the Use of Handbells in Liturgical Worship Traditions. St. Louis: Concordia Publishing House, 1996. Includes historical information on handbells in worship, ideas for structuring a bell program, and specific segments on the use of bells in the church year.

Haugen, Marty. *Instrumentation and the Liturgical Ensemble.* Chicago: GIA Publications, Inc., 1991. A resource for instrumental ensembles in liturgical settings.

Hopson, Hal H. *The Creative Use of Handbells in Hymn Singing.* Carol Stream: Hope Publishing Co. Resource contains specific handbell techniques to be used in accompanying congregational singing.

Leading the Church's Song. Mark Sedio, gen. ed. Minneapolis: Augsburg Fortress, 1998. Articles by various authors, with musical examples and CD recording, giving guidance on the interpretation and leadership of various genres of congregational song.

Rose, Richard. *Hymnal Companion for Woodwind, Brass and Percussion.* St. Louis: Concordia Publishing House, 1997.

Rotermund, Donald. *Intonations and Alternative Accompaniments for Psalm Tones.* St. Louis: Concordia Publishing House, 1997. (*LBW* and *LW* versions available separately.)

Weidler, Scott, and Dori Collins. *Sound Decisions.* Chicago: ELCA, 1997. Theological principles for the evaluation of contemporary worship music.

Westermeyer, Paul. *The Church Musician,* rev. ed. Minneapolis: Augsburg Fortress, 1997. Foundational introduction to the role and task of the church musician as the leader of the people's song in worship.

———. *Te Deum: The Church and Music.* Minneapolis: Fortress Press, 1998. An historical and theological introduction to the music of the church.

Wilson-Dickson, Andrew. *The Story of Christian Music.* Minneapolis: Fortress Press, 1996. An illustrated guide to the major traditions of music in worship.

Wold, Wayne. *Tune My Heart to Sing: Devotions for Choirs Based on the Three-Year Revised Common Lectionary.* Minneapolis: Augsburg Fortress, 1997.

PERIODICALS

Assembly. Notre Dame Center for Pastoral Liturgy. Chciago: Liturgy Training Publications. Published five times a year by . Each issues examines a particular aspect of worship practice. (800) 933-1800.

Catechumenate: A Journal of Christian Initiation. Chicago: Liturgy Training Publications. Published bimonthly with articles on congregational preparation of older children and adults for the celebration of baptism and eucharist. (800) 933-1800.

Cross Accent. Journal of the Association of Lutheran Church Musicians. Semi-annual publication for church musicians and worship leaders in North America. (800) 624-ALCM.

Faith & Form. Journal of the Interfaith Forum on Religion, Art and Architecture. Editorial office, (617) 965-3018.

Grace Notes. Newsletter of the Association of Lutheran Church Musicians. (708) 272-4116.

Liturgy. Quarterly journal of The Liturgical Conference, Washington, D.C. Each issue explores a worship-related issue from an ecumenical perspective. (800) 394-0885.

Plenty Good Room. Chicago: Liturgy Training Publications. Published bimonthly. A magazine devoted to African American worship within a Roman Catholic context. Helpful articles on the enculturation of worship. (800) 933-1800.

Worship. Collegeville: The Order of St. Benedict. Published through The Liturgical Press six times a year. Since the early decades of this century, the primary promoter of liturgical renewal among the churches. (800) 858-5450.

Worship '99. Published periodically by the Office of Worship of the Evangelical Lutheran Church in America. Articles and annotated bibliographies on a range of worship topics. (800) 638-3522.

SELECTED PUBLISHERS

AMSI
1599 Southeast Eighth Street
Minneapolis MN 55414
612/378-0027 General
612/729-4487 Fax

ABINGDON PRESS
201 8th Avenue South
PO Box 801
Nashville TN 37202
800/251-3320 Customer Service
800/836-7802 Fax

ALFRED PUBLISHING CO, INC
Box 10003
16380 Roscoe Boulevard
Van Nuys CA 91410-0003
800/292-6122 Customer Service
800/632-1928 Fax
818/891-5999 Direct

AMERICAN LUTHERAN PUBLICITY
BUREAU
PO Box 327
Delhi NY 13753-0327
607/746-7511 General

ARISTA MUSIC
PO Box 1596
Brooklyn NY 11201

AUGSBURG FORTRESS
PO Box 1209
Minneapolis MN 55440-1209
800/328-4648 Ordering
612/330-3300 General

BECKENHORST PRESS
PO Box 14273
Columbus OH 43214
614/451-6461 General
614/451-6627 Fax

BOOSEY & HAWKES INC
35 East Twenty-first Street
New York NY 10010
212/358-5300 General
212/358-5301 Fax

BOSTON MUSIC CO.
172 Tremont St.
Boston, MA 02111
617/426-5100 Retail
617/528-6199 Fax

BOURNE COMPANY
5 West 37th Street
New York NY 10018
212/391-4300 General
212/391-4306 Fax

BROUDE BROTHERS LTD
141 White Oaks Road
Williamstown MA 01267
413/458-8131

BROADMAN HOLMAN GENEVOX
Customer Accounts Center
127 Ninth Avenue North
Nashville TN 37234
800/251-3225 General
615/251/3870 Fax

C F PETERS CORPORATION
373 Park Avenue South
New York NY 10016
212/686-4147 General
212/689-9412 Fax

CHANGING CHURCH FORUM/
PRINCE OF PEACE PUBLISHING
200 E. Nicollet Blvd.
Burnsville, MN 55337
800/874-2044

CHESTER MUSIC
Music Sales Corporation
257 Park Ave. South
New York, NY 10003
212/254-2100

CHURCH HYMNAL CORPORATION
445 5th Avenue
New York NY 10016-0109
800/223-6602 General
800/242-1918 Customer Service
212/592-1800 General
212/779-3392 Fax

COLORSONG PUBLICATIONS
2533 7th Ave E
North St. Paul, MN 55109
612/773-5371
800/352-6567
612/773-4053 Fax

CONCORDIA PUBLISHING HOUSE
3558 South Jefferson Avenue
Saint Louis MO 63118
800/325-3391 Sales
800/325-3040 Customer Service
314/268-1329 Fax
314/268-1000 General

E C SCHIRMER MUSIC CO
138 Ipswich Street
Boston MA 02215
800/777-1919 Ordering
617/236-1935 General
617/236-0261 Fax
614/236-1935

EUROPEAN AMERICAN MUSIC DIST.
PO Box 850
Valley Forge, PA 19482
610/648-0506

CARL FISCHER, INC
62 Cooper Square
New York, NY 10003
212/777-0900

MARK FOSTER MUSIC CO
28 East Springfield Avenue
Champaign IL 61820
217/398-2760 General
217/398-2791 Fax
800/359-1386

GIA PUBLICATIONS, INC
7404 South Mason Avenue
Chicago IL 60638
800/442-1358 General
708/496-3800 General
708/496-3828 Fax

GALAXY COMMUNICATIONS
PO Box 101
Blaine WA 98230
800/333-7279 General
604/522-7955 General
604/522-7799 Fax

HINSHAW MUSIC CO, INC
PO Box 470
Chapel Hill NC 27514-0470
919/933-1691 General
919/967-3399 Fax

HAL LEONARD CORP
- PO Box 13819
7777 West Bluemound Road
Milwaukee WI 53213
414/774-3630 General
800/637-2852 Music Dispatch

HOPE PUBLISHING CO
380 South Main Place
Carol Stream IL 60188
800/323-1049 General
630/665-3200 General
630/665-2552 Fax

ICEL (INTERNATIONAL COMMISSION
ON ENGLISH IN THE LITURGY)
1275 K Street Northwest
Suite 1202
Washington DC 20005-4097
202/347-0800 General

IONIAN ARTS, INC
PO Box 259
Mercer Island WA 98040-0259
206/236-2210 General

THE LITURGICAL CONFERENCE
8750 Georgia Avenue
Suite 123
Silver Spring MD 20910-3621
800/394-0885Ordering
301/495-0885 General
901/495-5945 Fax

THE LITURGICAL PRESS
St. John's Abbey
PO Box 7500
Collegeville MN 56321-7500
800/858-5450 General
800/445-5899 Fax
320/363-2213 General
320/363-3299 Fax

LITURGY TRAINING PUBLICATIONS
1800 North Hermitage Avenue
Chicago IL 60622-1101
800/933-1800 Ordering
800/933-4779 Customer Service
800/933-7094 Fax

LIVE OAK HOUSE
3211 Plantation Rd.
Austin, TX 78745-7424
512/282-3397

THE LORENZ CORPORATION
PO Box 802
Dayton OH 45401-0802
800/444-1144 General

LUDWIG MUSIC PUBLISHING CO
557 East 140th Street
Cleveland OH 44110-1999
800/851-1150 General
216/851-1150 General
216/851-1958 Fax

MARANATHA!
30230 Rancho Viejo Rd
San Juan Capistrano, CA 92675
800/245-7664 Retail
800/251-4000 Wholesale

MASTERS MUSIC PUBLICATIONS, INC
PO Box 810157
Boco Raton FL 33481-0157
561/241-6169 General
561/241-6347 Fax

MORNINGSTAR MUSIC PUBLISHERS
2117 59th Street
Saint Louis MO 63110-2800
800/647-2117 General
314/647-2117 Ordering
314/647-2777 Fax

MUSICA RUSSICA
27 Willow Lane
Madison, CT 06443
800/326-3132

OREGON CATHOLIC PRESS
5536 Northeast Hassalo
Portland OR 97213
800/547-8992 General
800/462-7329 Fax

OXFORD UNIVERSITY PRESS
2001 Evans Road
Cary NC 27513
800/451-7556 General
919/677-1303 Fax

PARACLETE SOCIETY INTERNATIONAL
1132 Southwest 13th Avenue
Portland OR 97205

PLYMOUTH MUSIC CO
170 Northeast 33rd Street
Fort Lauderdale FL 33334
954/563-1844 General
954/563-9006 Fax

RANDALL M EGAN, PUBLISHERS
2024 Kenwood Parkway
Minneapolis MN 55405-2303
312/377-4450 General
*51 Fax

SUMMY-BIRCHARD INC.
Watner Bros
265 Secausus Rd.
Secausus, NJ 07096
201/348-0796

SHAWNEE PRESS
PO Box 690
49 Waring Drive
Delaware Water Gap PA 18327-1699
800/962-8584 General
717/476-0550 General
717/476-5247 Fax

THEODORE PRESSER CO
1 Presser Place
Bryn Mawr PA 19010
610/525-3636 Wholesale
610/527-4242 Retail
610/527-7841 Fax

WARNER BROTHERS PUBLICATIONS
15800 Northwest 48th Avenue
Miami FL 33014
800/327-7643 General
305/621-4869 Fax

WESTMINSTER/JOHN KNOX PRESS
100 Witherspoon Street
Louisville KY 40202-1396
800/227-2872 General
800/541-5113 Fax

WORD MUSIC CO
Thomas Nelson Company
P.O. Box 14100
Nashville, TN 37214
800/251-4000

WORLD LIBRARY PUBLICATIONS
3825 North Willow Road
Schiller Park IL 60176
800/621-5197 General
847/678-0621 General
847/671-5715 Fax

KEY TO MUSIC PUBLISHERS

ABI	Abingdon	FEN	Fentone	MERC	Mercury (Presser)
AFP	Augsburg Fortress	FLA	Flammer (Shawnee)	MFS	Mark Foster
AG	Agape (Hope)	GAL	Galaxy	MP	Music Press
ALF	Alfred	GEN	Gentry (Hal Leonard)	MSM	Morning Star Music
AMC	Arista	GIA	GIA Publications	MUR	Musica Russica
AMSI	AMSI	GS	GlorySound	MUS	Music 70 (Alfred)
AUR	Aurole	GSCH	G Schirmer	NGP	New Generation (ColorSong)
BBL	Broude Brothers	GVX	Genevox	NOV	Novello (Shawnee)
BEC	Beckenhorst	HAL	Hal Leonard: G Schirmer	OCP	Oregon Catholic Press
BEL	Belwin (Warner)	HIN	Hinshaw	OXF	Oxford University Press
BEN	Benson	HM	Hall and McCreary	PAR	Paraclete
BOH	Boosey & Hawkes	HOP	Hope	PEER	Peer Music
BNK	Banks (Intrada)	HTF	H T Fitzsimons (Hal Leonard)	PLY	Plymouth
BOR	Bornemann	HWG	H W Gray (Warner)	PRE	Presser
BRD	Broadman	INT	Integrity (Word)	PVN	Pavanne (Intrada)
BRE	Breitkopf	ION	Ionian Arts	RHP	Ron Harris Publications
BRN	Bourne	JEF	Jeffers	RIC	Ricordi
BST	Boston	JFB	J Fischer and Bro. (Warner)	RME	Randall M Egan
CAL	Calvary Press	KAL	Kalmus	SCH	Schott (European American)
CCF	Changing Church Forum	KIR	Kirkland House	SEL	Selah
CEL	Celebration Press	KJO	Kjos	SGM	Stained Glass Music
CFI	Carl Fischer	LAK	Lake State	SHM	Schmitt, Hall and McCreary
CFP	C F Peters	LAW	Lawson-Gould Publishing	SHW	Shawnee
CGA	Choristers Guild (Lorenz)	LB	Lutheran Brotherhood	SMB	Summy-Birchard
CHA	Chantry (Augsburg Fortress)	LED	Leduc	SMC	Southern Music Co
CHC	Church Hymnal Corporation	LEM	Lemoine (Presser)	SMP	Sacred Music Press (Lorenz)
CHE	Chester	LIL	Lillenas (Royal Marketing)	TRI	Triune Music
CLP	Warners: CCP/Belwin	LIN	Lindsborg Press	UNI	Unity Music
CPH	Concordia	LIV	Live Oak	VIV	Vivace
DOV	Dover	LOR	Lorenz	WAL	Walton
DOX	Doxology Music	LUD	Ludwig	WAR	Warner (Plymouth)
DUR	Durand (Presser)	MAR	Maranatha	WJK	Westminster/John Knox
ECS	E C Schirmer	MCF	McAfee Music Corp. (Warner)	WLP	World Library
EV	Elkan-Vogel	MEA	Meadowgreen	WRD	Word Music

MUSIC FOR WORSHIP KEY

acc	accompaniment	hc	handchimes	qrt	quartet	
bar	baritone	hp	harp	rec	recorder	
bng	bongos	hpd	harpsichord	sax	saxophone	
bsn	bassoon	hrn	horn	sop	soprano	
cant	cantor	inst	instrument	str	strings	
ch	chimes	kybd	keyboard	synth	synthesizer	
cl	clarinet	M	medium	tamb	tambourine	
cong	congregation	MH	medium high	tba	tuba	
cont	continuo	ML	medium low	tbn	trombone	
cym	cymbal	mxd	mixed	timp	timpani	
DB	double or string bass	narr	narrator	trbl	treble	
dbl	double	ob	oboe	tri	triangle	
desc	descant	oct	octave	tpt	trumpet	
div	divisi	opt	optional	U	unison	
drm	drum	orch	orchestra	vc	violoncello	
eng hrn	English horn	org	organ	vcs	voices	
fc	finger cymbals	perc	percussion	vla	viola	
fl	flute	picc	piccolo	vln	violin	
glock	glockenspiel	pno	piano	ww	woodwind	
gtr	guitar	pt	part	xyl	xylophone	
hb	handbells	qnt	quintet			

35

KEY TO HYMN AND PSALM COLLECTIONS

ASF   *A Singing Faith: The hymns of Jane Parker Huber*. Louisville: Westminster/John Knox Press, 1987.

AYG   *Another Year of Grace: The Collected Hymns of Carl. P. Daw, Jr*. Carol Stream, IL: Hope Publishing Co., 1990.

BH   *The Baptist Hymnal* (Southern Baptist Convention). Nashville: Convention Press, 1991.

CEL   *The Celebration Hymnal: Songs and Hymns for Worship*. Nashville: Word Music, 1997.

CHA   *Chalice Hymnal* (Disciples of Christ). St. Louis: Chalice Press, 1995.

CON   *The Concordia Hymnal*. Mpls: Augsburg, 1932.

CW   *Christian Worship: A Lutheran Hymnal* (Wisconsin Evangelical Lutheran Synod). Milwaukee: Northwestern Publishing House, 1993.

DATH   *Dancing at the Harvest: Songs of Ray Makeever*. Mpls: Augsburg Fortress, 1997.

G2   *Gather*. Second ed. Chicago: GIA, 1994.

GS2   *Global Songs 2: Bread for the Journey*. Mpls: Augsburg Fortress, 1997.

H82   *The Hymnal 1982* (Episcopal). New York: The Church Pension Fund, 1985.

ICEL   *The ICEL Resource Collection*. Chicago: GIA, 1981.

ISH   *In Search of Hope & Grace: The Hymns of Sylvia G. Dunstan*. Chicago: GIA, 1991.

LBW   *Lutheran Book of Worship*. Mpls: Augsburg; Philadelphia: Board of Publication, LCA, 1978.

LEV   *Lift Every Voice and Sing II*. New York: The Church Pension Fund, 1993.

LLC   *Libro de Liturgia y Cántico*. Mpls: Augsburg Fortress, 1998.

LW   *Lutheran Worship* (Lutheran Church–Missouri Synod). St. Louis: Concordia Publishing House, 1982.

MBW   *Moravian Book of Worship* (Moravian Church in America). Bethlehem, PA: Interprovincial Board of Publications and Communications, 1995.

NCH   *The New Century Hymnal* (United Church of Christ). Cleveland: The Pilgrim Press, 1995.

NSR   *New Songs of Rejoicing*. Kingston, NY: Selah Publishing Co., Inc., 1994.

OBS   *O Blessed Spring: Hymns of Susan Palo Cherwien*. Mpls: Augsburg Fortress, 1997.

PCY   *Psalms for the Church Year*. 8 vol. Chicago: GIA Publications.

PH   *The Presbyterian Hymnal* (PC-USA). Louisville: Westminster/John Knox Press, 1990.

PS1   *Psalm Songs 1*. Mpls: Augsburg Fortress, 1998.

PS2   *Psalm Songs 2*. Mpls: Augsburg Fortress, 1998.

PS3   *Psalm Songs 3*. Mpls: Augsburg Fortress, 1998.

PsH   *Psalter Hymnal* (Christian Reformed). Grand Rapids: CRC Publications, 1987.

PW   *Psalter for Worship*. 3 vol. (Cycles A, B, C.) Mpls: Augsburg Fortress.

REJ   *Rejoice in the Lord* (Reformed Church in America). Grand Rapids: William B. Eerdmans Publishing Co., 1985.

RS   *RitualSong: A Hymnal and Service Book for Roman Catholics*. Chicago: GIA, 1996.

SIC   *Singing in Celebration: Hymns for Special Occasions by Jane Parker Huber*. Louisville: Westminster/John Knox Press, 1996.

SPW   *Songs for Praise and Worship*. Nashville: Word Music, 1992.

STP   *Singing the Psalms*. 3 vol. Portland: OCP Publications.

TP   *The Psalter: Psalms and the Canticles for Singing*. Louisville: Westminster/John Knox Press.

TWC   *The Worshiping Church*. Carol Stream, IL: Hope Publishing Company, 1990.

UMH   *The United Methodist Hymnal*. Nashville: The United Methodist Publishing House, 1989.

W3   *Worship: A Hymnal and Service Book for Roman Catholics*. Third ed. Chicago: GIA 1986.

WAO   *We Are One in Christ: Hymns, Paraphrases, and Translations by Gracia Grindal*. Kingston: Selah Publishing Co., Inc., 1996.

WGF   *The Word Goes Forth: The Hymns of Herman Stuempfle*. Chicago: GIA, 1993.

WOV   *With One Voice*. Mpls: Ausgburg Fortress, 1995.

ADVENT

The guest is on the way

IMAGES OF THE SEASON

"Love, the guest, is on the way," we sing in Eleanor Farjeon's Advent carol, "People, look east" (WOV 626). Company's coming! Time to get ready! In times so long ago we can only imagine, those keeping watch over a town or village would be the first to spot movement along the road. The good news of the company's safe arrival would be shouted from the heights to those standing guard—or simply waiting—down below. The great bar pinning shut the castle or city gate would be shoved aside, the heavy door pulled open. At night, servants with blazing torches or lamps of oil would go running out to meet the approaching party and light the way. Exhilaration and joy would surround the travelers as they were ushered inside. The hosts would feel delightfully torn between pressing the visitors for all the latest news and leaving them alone for a while to refresh themselves and rest. Soon there would be time for feasting and mutually satisfying conversation.

Company's coming! But now in these last days, even as gated communities are beginning to reappear, retinues with oil lamps are not. And so, as our own guests are en route, we watch the weather channel, tune in to traffic reports, call the airline to monitor a given flight's progress. We fax and mail maps or information about ground connections; perhaps we ourselves drive to the terminal and idle in a passenger loading zone until we've just about memorized the messages repeated over the loudspeaker. Once our guests and their luggage have safely arrived, we feel delightfully torn between wanting to exchange all the latest news and allowing them to recover from jet lag.

Company's coming! Not some stranger or supervisor we have to impress, but friends or family whose love for us reaches across time and distance and makes us eager to get ready. Once our company gets here, we won't have to go out of our way to dazzle them with constant entertainment. Just being with them will be enough. Good shared memories will surface and surround us. A walk, or cup of coffee, or even a simple task undertaken together will become the substance of future memories. Because of the love and friendship that have drawn and kept us together, we trust that the visit will turn out to be one of the highlights of our year—and of theirs.

Company's coming! Our church year begins with this sense of joyful anticipation, of looking forward to welcoming one who loves us: Christ, the guest, who is already on the way.

Preparation for company entails not only making a way for them—giving directions, lighting the path, opening the door—but providing a comfortable place for them to stay once they get *in* the door. We may have to rearrange things and adjust our schedules to make room for the guests. We move the furniture to make room for a Christmas tree. We have to find space —create space—in order to prepare.

"Make your house fair as you are able," runs the carol (WOV 626, st. 1). "As you are able" are words of grace in a secular season fraught with stress. Christmas advertising and commercial decorating now begins before Halloween; the economy depends upon it. We can't escape from images promising the perfect Christmas if we just spend lots of money to get the desired effect. The authors of *Unplug the Christmas Machine* (Jo Robinson and Jean Coppock Staeheli. *Unplug the Christmas Machine: How to Have the Christmas You've Always Wanted.* New York: Quill, 1982) knowingly describe the pressures on women to be the Christmas magicians and upon men to act as the Christmas stagehands—all in frenetic service to fantasies that can never be fully realized. No way can most of us, balancing multiple responsibilities, produce a domestic tableau worthy of a magazine.

The season of Advent asks us to prepare *as we are able:* not in such a way that we end up too exhausted or preoccupied to receive our guests, but sufficient to help them feel at ease and warmly welcomed. Our preparations express to our company that their visit is a special occasion because they are specially treasured in our lives.

And precisely because of this strong sense of mutual love, the joyful momentum of anticipation can carry us along and override any lingering anxiety or compulsiveness. That momentum may just carry us into completing projects we've put off longer than we care to remember. "Company's coming" is a great pretext for accomplishing what only inertia seems to have kept us from doing.

Advent, the season of diminishing light and darkening skies, is a natural time to decorate. We want to brighten the gloom with vibrant colors and sparkling light. It may be the one time all year that the brass polish and paste wax come out to shine up the metal and the wood. Holiday linens and china emerge from cupboards and closets to adorn the table. Delicate ornaments from generations past are carefully unwrapped from their tissue paper and hung on the tree. Children's sturdier creations enjoy a place of honor. Boxes and paper are temporarily everywhere. Chaos accompanies the transformation.

And then there are the difficult years of bereavement or transition, when entertaining guests or decorating are all but unthinkable. "As you are able" might mean lighting a single candle and doing nothing more than trusting that there might be a future year when joy will once again feel possible.

Company's coming! It's time to get ready—open up—create room for them. We prepare *as we're able* so that the visit can proceed. Once our guest has arrived, we want the focus to be not upon all that we've done to prepare, but upon the visit itself.

During Advent we make ready at home. We rearrange things in church as well. Liturgical paraments and vestments in shades of blue mirror the deepening night. Candles flicker against the growing darkness. Away from the malls and traffic jams the liturgy helps us to create space where we can prepare ourselves and keep watch for Christ, the guest.

Our readings exhort us to be patient and walk in the light. They encourage us with visions of all creatures and all nations dwelling together in peace. They articulate our dreams: deserts blooming, exiles coming home,

and everyone able to see and hear and move about freely. The young woman will give birth. The righteous man will know an angel's visit. But then there are the nightmares: the Lord will come unexpectedly, like a thief in the night—and many will be left behind. The axe is at the root of the barren trees, and the winnowing fork is ready to clear away the chaff. Who can spare us from the wrath to come?

It is love, the guest, who is already on the way; whose power is stirred up for our sake. Christ is journeying toward us in the form of expected travelers and surprise ones. We see him in the faces of family members and friends of long standing, and in brothers and sisters with neither homes to decorate nor tables to spread. "Welcome one another," urges Paul, "as Christ has welcomed you." To our astonishment, the one whom we invite in is actually our host—whose dwelling, Isaiah promises, will be glorious. "Let ev'ry heart prepare him room; and heav'n and nature sing!" (LBW 39, "Joy to the world").

ENVIRONMENT AND ART FOR THE SEASON

At the beginning of the church year, the Advent season offers a good

opportunity to study the environmental impact of your church building's

physical presence in the community. Its physical

presence witnesses constantly. How and what does it convey about the gospel? Does it provide a clear message of God's abiding presence; a sense of invitation? Does its form and image convey that it is God's house? Does it convey a mission of faith that enlightens our lives upon entering? A good, well-designed and appointed liturgical environment does just that, in providing both shelter, spiritual refreshment, and transcendence.

In Advent the lectionary readings are rich in image and contrast. The themes of hope, the fulfillment of prophesy, the drama of salvation, and Jesus' presence in our lives provide remarkable opportunities to convey a tangible witness to the larger community. In Advent we reflect upon the past, live in the present, yet hope for Jesus coming again. As the church waits in expectation, there are practical avenues of application to follow in witnessing to this season.

EXTERIOR ENVIRONMENT

Exterior signage should welcome and provide information about the services of the Advent and Christmas seasons. Be selective in what you choose to place on exterior signage. Passing motorists cannot read small print or many words at a time.

Expect to receive visitors and lapsed members who may not be thoroughly familiar with everything about the building and its surroundings. Be ready with helpful and informative signs and symbols. Do entrances to the worship space have strong visual importance? Many churches have poor orientation on the site. Well-designed buildings have good creative art that focuses attention on the entrance. A liturgical designer can provide counsel in selecting creative symbolic art, sculpture, and landscaping that compliments and integrates the architectural design as a total statement.

In the Northern Hemisphere we have the shortest period of daylight during the Advent season, so it is especially appropriate at this time of year to evaluate exterior and entrance lighting. It is also a good time to clean and re-lamp all lighting.

Exterior blue Advent banners or simple blue garlands can visually distinguish this season. Develop a progression of subtle change to the decoration that reflects the period of expectation.

INTERIOR ENVIRONMENT

The narthex should be clean and uncluttered. Study the visual impact upon all persons entering the church, especially the visitor. First impressions are important! The entrance should fundamentally be viewed as a space of preparation and invitation for the worship that follows. Information about where to hang up coats and where to find a restroom or a nursery is important for the arriving worshiper. Posters about a variety of parish activities, or requests for donations blanketing one or more walls do not convey a sense of welcome and hospitality for worship. Good, well-defined seasonal artwork and photography can be especially effective in preparing people for worship that is to come.

The worship space itself should provide a key visual statement about the season of Advent. A blue processional banner may be an excellent resource for this purpose. It should be securely anchored, centrally visible, and immediately ready for use. Its design should be creatively developed, worthy of its use as a key visual messenger.

Decorating in the worship space should be restrained especially during this season, with special attention given to the design of central places of liturgical action. Take seriously the impact that textiles, simple blue paraments, and vestments have in keeping with the mood and theme of this season. Just as the music of the season expresses longing and expectation, so also should worship appointments convey these sensibilities.

If an Advent wreath is used, select one with good

proportion, scale, and style to offer warmth and visual beauty within the environment. Position it prominently and determine when it will be lit each week (perhaps with simplicity during the entrance rite, as the congregation prepares to hear the readings). Allow the wreath to be encircled with fresh greens that have scent and visual life. Never use dusty artificial greens.

Advent candles should be new each year and be of sufficient size to be seen throughout the worship space. Use four blue (purple) or white candles that comple-ment the parament color. Remember to instruct acolytes to light the candles in sequence to indicate a clear visible passage through time.

In the last half of this century, the early use of Christmas decorations during this season have clouded the intent of the Advent season. Powerful signs and symbols of the church—which communicate a sense of longing, and which call people to repentance, prayer, and preparation—are too frequently lost to sentimentality.

PREACHING WITH THE SEASON

"Every Advent," said a friend, "I feel like a character in a bad detective novel. I know what's going to happen, and yet I have to pretend to be stupid enough not to have figured it out. Good grief, everybody knows that Jesus is going to be born at the end of the story. After all, why else would the color for Advent be blue, than that we know the baby is a boy!"

We can understand and sympathize with this friend's frustration. Although we read Isaiah and sing "Oh, come, oh, come, Emmanuel," we are not looking forward to the appearance of God's chosen ruler/redeemer; we are looking back to it. We seem to spend these four weeks in a state of denial, pretending that we do not know about the nativity while we wait to celebrate Christmas.

But we do not spend Advent waiting and hoping for December 25. We do not even spend it waiting and hoping for Christmas. We spend it waiting for God to be true to promises. And the color of the season is blue not because "the baby is a boy," but because in our culture, the color of the sky is the color of hope.

The great word for Advent is a pun. Maranatha, the Aramaic cry of first-century Christians, means both "Our Lord has come" and "Come, O Lord." Advent is frustrating, among other reasons, because we have to balance both the affirmation and the prayer. On the one hand, Jesus has come. God has acted and we are living after the day of the Lord. Death and sin and every sort of oppression have been dealt their fatal blow. On the other hand, death and sin and every sort of oppression seem to be dealing fairly well with their fatality.

Advent reminds us that we are in the meantime, the time between the resurrection and the parousia, the time when mean things happen. We read Isaiah and sing "Oh, come, oh, come, Emmanuel," not because we're pretending not to know about the nativity, but because we can look around even on this side of the nativity and see that God's promises go unfulfilled. As Albert Bayly wrote,

Still your children wander homeless;
Still the hungry cry for bread;
Still the captives long for freedom;
Still in grief we mourn our dead.

Albert F. Bayly, 1901–1984

We do not have to pretend that we are ignorant of the birth of Christ in order to echo the prophets' prayer for God to act. In the meantime, we have every right to make our own the psalmists' urgent plea for God to carry out divine promises of liberation and justice and peace.

For these reasons, the lessons of Advent focus not only on Christ's coming in the past, but on Christ's promised return in the future. We proclaim a Christ

41

who is present in Advent, and our response to that presence is a longing for Christ's presence—or rather for Christ to be more widely, more clearly, more evidently present, not simply in our hearts, but in our world. We stand with the disciples on the mountain of the ascension, asking the risen Christ, "Lord, is this the time when you will restore the kingdom to Israel?" (Acts 1:6). If, with them, we accept with bad grace Jesus' command to wait in reverent agnosticism, it is not because we doubt his promise, but because we see a world in dire need of the restoration of the kingdom. The meaning of Advent is that Christ has already come, but has not yet come; that the reign of God has broken into our midst, but is still approaching. Things are not yet as God has promised they will be—but because God's promises are absolutely dependable, that promise will be fulfilled. The meaning of Advent is that in the presence of Christ, we are to wait and hope for the presence of Christ.

The preacher's task is formidable in this season, and not simply because many of the hearers will begin focusing on Christmas on the day after Thanksgiving (at the latest). Preachers need to paint a realistic picture of the state of this world without simply wallowing in countercultural despair. Preachers need to offer hope

based on the absolutely dependable promises of God without presenting that hope as "pie in the sky by and by." Preachers need to encourage people to wait for God to act without commending passivity. Preachers need to lead the cry of Maranatha! without letting either meaning drown out the other.

Thank heavens the readings offer help in all these efforts. And the readings do it by assuring that each Sunday the competing emphases are juxtaposed, that we will hear of Christ's coming in past, present, and future; that we will be assured of God's promise in a context that seems to deny God's trustworthiness; that we will be encouraged to wait for God's good time, yet to remain active in the meantime. The readings do this by providing several consistent streams running through the season. The first readings explore the notion of God's promise of worldwide peace, including not just the nations, but all of creation in shalom-talk about a chance to address ecological concerns. The second readings offer instruction about how Christians are to live in the meantime. Even if sermons have such a single, consistent focus throughout the season, the service itself would do well to reflect the variety, the scope, and indeed the perplexities of the season.

PLANNING AHEAD FOR THE SEASON

Waiting and anticipation are important focal points of the Advent season,

which is especially true in the midst of a culture that seems to introduce

Christmas earlier every year. While plenty of holi-

day merriment will take place from Thanksgiving

Day onward, it is useful for the church to celebrate Advent fully.

Waiting and anticipation are at odds with many cultural norms. Advent encourages us to carve out some margin in our lives. The spirit of retreat during Advent may encourage us to consider greater opportunities for silence within our corporate worship—silences already suggested within the Holy Communion liturgy, but that

might be more intentionally observed in this season: during the brief order for confession and forgiveness, before the prayer of the day, following the readings, following the sermon, before the post-communion blessing, prior to the benediction, and at other places. Considering the wall-to-wall sounds of commercial TV and radio, fifteen seconds of silence may seem like an eternity at times, thereby indicating why it may be so urgently needed in our lives. Advent asks us to value those silences.

42

The Advent season may in fact help us with those difficult silences in our lives when there seems to be nothing to say, whether in the face of prolonged pain or unsolved problems. The silences of Advent may teach us that there are times when we have reached the limits of our knowledge or our ability to control things and that we must simply keep silent.

This is not to say that the Advent season is without joy. Many hymns proper to this season announce a profound joy: "Wake, awake for night is flying" (LBW 31), "Prepare the royal highway" (LBW 26), "Rejoice, rejoice, believers" (LBW 25), and the Song of Mary. Some of these hymns are among the most exuberant of our tradition. There is a great story to proclaim in this season, even throughout our waiting and observance of intentional silences.

Among the activities to consider during this season would be having a "Jesse Tree" in the narthex or fellowship hall area. A "Jesse Tree" helps to focus part of our waiting time on those whom Jesus has called us to serve. A bare tree is decorated with paper ornaments, which serve as gift tags. The ornaments represent possible items to be given for needy people of various ages. If you have a congregational social ministry committee, it might be aware of the needs of individuals in the community, or the committee might have an ongoing relationship with local community organizations that work directly with homeless persons or those of more limited means. At any rate, you will need to acquire a list of possible gift items that could be used.

On the first two Sundays in Advent (adjust the timeframe as you need to locally) have worshipers select ornaments from the "Jesse Tree" which have gift suggestions written on them. Encourage children to be involved in the selection and purchase of the gift so that they are kept active in waiting and in serving others as well. Then on the Third Sunday in Advent have worshipers bring their wrapped gifts along with the gift tag itself securely attached to the outside, eventually to be distributed to those who are in need of the items. The congregation might be encouraged to bring the gifts forward in an offertory procession that day.

Consider an evening prayer service one weeknight each week throughout the Advent season. If your congregation has such a gathering during Lent, then establishing a similar pattern for Advent may be a possibility as well. All of the events might take place in a fellowship hall around tables (rather than in a more formal worship space), thereby lending a more relaxed and unhurried atmosphere to the whole evening. One simple agenda for Advent gatherings could be this:

- Light candles placed at tables as worshipers begin singing a hymn of light: "O Christ, you are the light and day" (LBW 273), "O Trinity, O blessed Light" (LBW 275), "Now all the woods are sleeping" (LBW 276), "Light one candle to watch for Messiah" (WOV 630), "O Light whose splendor thrills" (WOV 728), and "Christ, mighty Savior" (WOV 729), among others. Follow with a table prayer.
- Have a simple "potluck" meal, perhaps consisting only of soups, breads and salads.
- Make a handmade ornament or craft each week, focusing on a different spiritual dimension of either the Advent or Christmas seasons (stars, angels, etc.). The items actually made each week could be given to homebound persons, with additional materials and instructions given out for participants to re-create items at home for their own household celebrations.
- Close with a brief order of Evening Prayer
  A psalm (especially 16, 121, 126, 137 or others indicated for evening prayer on p. 178 of *LBW*)
  A short scripture reading
  The Song of Mary: "My soul now magnifies the Lord" (LBW 180) or "My soul proclaims your greatness" (WOV 730)
  Brief prayers of intercession
  The Lord's Prayer
  Dismissal (from Responsive Prayer 2, *LBW*, p. 167).

Keep the time focused on things that people of all ages can do together, so that families are brought together during this often hectic time of year.

43

ORDO FOR THE SEASON

Congregations do not have to do everything the same week in and week out, even if they still wish to have a basic shape for worship that is consistent throughout the year. Over the centuries, this basic shape of Christian worship has remained remarkably consistent regardless of the church's geography, politics, or religious traditions. The common pattern can be noted as such:

- Gathering
- Word
- [Bath]
- Meal
- Sending

Described in more detail in the "Shape of the Rite" in *WOV* as well as in the ELCA statement *The Use of the Means of Grace: A Statement on the Practice of Word and Sacrament* (1997), this common rite of the church can be celebrated in richly diverse ways that reflect the seasons of the church's year, the gifts of the local culture, and the skills and requirements of the parish community.

It is important for worship planners, and even worshipers themselves, to understand this basic shape, which underlies the Sunday eucharistic assembly no matter how simple or elaborate that gathering is. It is this basic shape or *ordo* that crosses the centuries and miles to provide unity among Christians of every time and place.

The way in which we gather might vary from week to week, and from congregation to congregation, but it still follows the same shape by and large. It still can be "the liturgy," even in congregations or denominations that do not consider themselves very *liturgical*. In fact the basic shape *is* the liturgy. Of course the way in which liturgy is dressed and molded in each Christian community is part of the excitement of the liturgy. Each region, each denomination, and each congregation may take this basic shape of the liturgy and make it

their own. With all of this discussion as a prologue to the shape of the liturgy for the year, let us look at some of the ways in which that shape can be molded particularly for the season of Advent.

ADVENT

Though it is not an essential part of the Holy Communion liturgy, an opportunity for public confession and forgiveness prior to the service during the season of Advent helps to underscore the preparatory characteristics of this season. The silences and waiting of this season work well with the silence often experienced as part of orders for confession. Advent calls us to watch for the signs of God's coming among us. Periods of public confession help us to watch also for the ways in which we thwart God's will in our lives.

The Kyrie, with its plaintive beseeching of God's mercy, seems to fit very well into Advent's yearning for God's coming. Exuberant hymns of praise, on the other hand, seem better suited to other more festive occasions.

Several congregations have made use of the seasonal eucharistic prayers, which are printed in the leaders edition of *With One Voice*. These fairly brief prayers would be a fine way for congregations to take up the practice of including a true prayer of thanksgiving as a part of the "great thanksgiving." Though the seasonal prayers are not long, they add a more complete reference to God's trinitarian work than is possible with the mere words of institution alone. The seasonal eucharistic prayer for Advent (Eucharistic Prayer A, p. 65 in *WOV*) confesses our complicity in bringing chaos and cruelty into the world. It also prays for justice to be born in our lives.

44

ASSEMBLY SONG FOR THE SEASON

During the season of Advent, our secular culture is loaded with more music than any other time of year. Most of it is Christmas music. And so the debate rages on in the church about whether to "allow" Christmas music into worship during Advent. The debate should never be about what is "allowed," but rather about what best accomplishes the purpose of Advent.

Yet Advent entices us into continual preparation for an encounter with the living God—here and now in our history. As we look back at the pivotal encounter with God (Jesus' life, death, and resurrection), we rely on the regular encounter with God through word and sacrament, anticipating the time when Christ will come again ushering in our eternal encounter with God in heaven. All these encounters between humanity and the divine are woven together in Advent. It is a time of excitement, frustration, and curiosity. The music that cradles the texts and actions of Advent worship needs to reflect these diverse sentiments. As you prepare Advent worship, read the texts carefully, being intentional about your vision for Advent, and choose music to accomplish this purpose.

Like a thief in the night, this season quietly slips into our lives, often overshadowed by the festivities of Thanksgiving. The themes of waiting and preparing for the end times have already been heard for nearly a month before Advent. Plans can either heighten or diminish this unique characteristic. If you wish to enhance the ambiguity with which we enter Advent, certain liturgical elements (such as a specific setting of the "Alleluia" as a gospel acclamation or offertory song) could be in place since All Saints Day. If a clear transition into the new church year is desired, the first Sunday in Advent may be an excellent time to introduce a new musical setting of the liturgy or other seasonal modifications.

The themes of Advent cry out for simplicity and ample use of silence. Just as rests in a musical score are an integral element in the rhythm, so is silence to our worship. However, in our current cultural context, we cannot assume that worshipers will know when and how to keep silence in a productive way. Perhaps before the prelude begins, a verse from scripture or a hymn stanza appropriate to the day can be noted. Worshipers can be invited to meditate on that text during the prelude.

Reserving the hymn of praise (Glory to God) until Christmas Eve, and singing only a setting of the Kyrie (Lord, have mercy) during the gathering is one of the church's traditional ways of keeping Advent. Many settings of the Kyrie make excellent processional music. Even the settings from *LBW* can work in this way, perhaps with an assisting minister singing in the procession.

This model makes a clear statement about the simplicity of Advent. It does, however, eliminate another opportunity to sing an Advent hymn. This simple opening could be contrasted nicely with a fuller and more festive gathering at Christmas.

In some congregations, the lighting of the Advent wreath can become a major production. In keeping with the simplicity of the season, it may be best to light the appropriate candles quietly before the service. If, however, lighting the wreath is something that worshipers treasure in keeping Advent, accompanying the lighting with an appropriate hymn stanza may be wise. "Light one candle to watch for Messiah" (WOV 630) is one example. Be certain to avoid songs that give made up names or themes to the candles. The candles of the Advent wreath simply help us to mark time, and to heighten our watching and waiting for the light of the world.

45

MUSIC FOR THE SEASON

VERSE AND OFFERTORY

Cherwien, David. "Verses for the Sundays in Advent." MSM 80-001.
U, org, opt hb.

Hillert, Richard. "Verses and Offertory Sentences, Part 1: Advent
through Christmas." CPH 97-5509. U, kybd.

Krentz, Michael. "Alleluia Verses for Advent." AFP 11-02564. SAB, org.

Wetzler, Robert. "Verses and Offertories: Advent 1–Baptism of Our
Lord." AFP 11-09541. SATB, kybd.

SERVICE MUSIC

Richard Proulx's *Missa Emmanuel* (GIA G-3489) is a contemplative
musical setting of the liturgy based on "Oh, come, oh, come
Emmanuel," and can be sung by a cantor or choir and congregation.

CHORAL MUSIC FOR THE SEASON

Berthier, Jacques. "Magnificat" in *Songs and Prayers from Taizé*.
GIA G-3719-P. Canon or chorale.

Brahms, Johannes/Hopson. "Let All the Gates Be Opened Wide."
CGA 736. U/2 pt, kybd.

Callahan, Charles. "The Lord Will Come." CPH 98-3090. 2 pt mxd, org.

Christiansen, F. Melius. "Wake, Awake." AFP 11-102. Also in *The Augsburg Choirbook*. 11-10817. SSAATTBB.

Ferguson, John. "Comfort, Comfort." AFP 11-02381. SATB, opt picc,
2 cl, tamb.

Hallock, Peter. "The 'O' Antiphons." ION CH-1030. SATB, org, hb.

Honoré, Jeffrey. "Rejoice, Rejoice, Believers." CGA 746. 2 pt mxd,
kybd, rec/fl, opt tamb.

Jean, Martin. "Advent Hymn." AFP 11-10801. SATB.

Jennings, Carolyn. "Climb to the Top of the Highest Mountain."
KJO C8118. SATB, opt children, org.

Jennings, Carolyn. "A New Magnificat." AFP 11-10479. Also in *The
Augsburg Choirbook*. 11-10817. SA/SATB, org, opt cong.

Johnson, Linda Lee, and Tom Fettke. "Be Strong in the Lord."
HOP GC827. SATB.

Niedmann, Peter. "Lift Up Your Heads, Ye Mighty Gates."
AFP 11-10774. SATB, org.

Ravenscroft, Thomas. "Remember Christians All." GIA G-4148. SATB.

Sirett, Mark. "Thou Shalt Know Him." AFP 11-10645. Also in *The
Augsburg Choirbook*. 11-10817. SATB.

Webster, Richard. "Adam Lay Ybounden." CHA 12-400002. SATB.

Weiland, Brent. "Christ Is Coming." AFP 11-10578. SATB, org, fl.

Zacharia, Cesare de/Larry Long. "Magnificat." AFP 11-10508. SATB.

CHILDREN'S CHORAL MUSIC FOR THE SEASON

Bostrom, Sandra. "Christ Is Coming." CGA 691. U/2 pt, kybd.

Clyde, Arthur. "Advent Candle Song." AFP 11-2408. U, opt cong,
kybd, fl.

Kosche, Kenneth. "Hosanna Now Through Advent." CGA 662.
U, kybd.

Mitchell, Tom. "People, Look East." CGA 505. SAB, kybd, fc.

Wold, Wayne. "Three Songs for Advent." AFP 11-9949. U, kybd.

INSTRUMENTAL MUSIC FOR THE SEASON

Hassell, Michael. *Jazz December: Piano Arrangements for the Season*.
AFP 11-10796. Pno.

Organ, Anne Krentz. *Advent Reflections for Piano and Solo Instrument*.
AFP 11-10864. Pno, B-flat/C inst.

Wold, Wayne. *Light One Candle: An Advent Organ Collection*.
AFP 11-10720. Org.

Young, Jeremy. *Gathering Music for Advent*. AFP 11-10798. 2 solo inst,
opt bass/vc, kybd.

HANDBELL MUSIC FOR THE SEASON

Hopson, Hal H. "Festival Collage and Variations." (PUER NOBIS)
AGEHR AG35031. 3 or 5 oct.

Moklebust, Cathy. "Come, Thou Long-Expected Jesus" in *Rise Up,
Shepherd, and Follow*. CGA. CGB184. 2-3 oct, perc.

Page, Anna Laura. "Hymn Descants for Ringers and Singers: vol. 1—
Advent, Christmas, and Epiphany." Full score ALF 11527.
Vcs/kybd 11529. 3 oct, kybd, desc.

Semmann, Barbara. "Advent Processional: Hark the Glad Sound" in
Processionals for the Time of Christmas. CPH 97-6252. 3 or 5 oct.

ALTERNATE WORSHIP TEXTS

CONFESSION AND FORGIVENESS

In the name of the Father, and of the ✛ Son, and of the Holy
 Spirit.
Amen

Christ is coming soon.
Let us prepare our hearts
as we confess our sins against God and one another.

Silence for reflection and self-examination

Most merciful God,
we confess our failure to watch for your coming
and to make ready your way.
We have sinned against you in thought, word, and deed;
we have not welcomed one another
as we have been welcomed.
Restore us, O God.
Open our hearts to receive you.
Clothe us in Christ
that we may live in the light of your day. Amen

The light of God's face shines upon us, and we are saved.
As a called and ordained minister
of the church of Christ, and by his authority,
I declare to you the entire forgiveness of all your sins,
in the name of the Father, and of the Son, and of the Holy Spirit.
Amen

GREETING

In days to come, God's holy mountain
shall be raised above the hills;
all nations shall stream to it.
Come, let us go up to the house of our God.
The grace of our Lord Jesus Christ, the love of God, and the communion of the Holy Spirit be with you all.
And also with you.

OFFERTORY PRAYER

God of mercy and grace,
the eyes of all wait upon you,
and you open your hand in blessing.
From all that you have given us,
receive these gifts,
signs of our thanksgiving and praise.
Fill us with good things at your table
that we may come to the help of all in need. Amen

INVITATION TO COMMUNION

Come to Zion with singing;
strengthen your hearts, for the Lord is near.

POST-COMMUNION PRAYER

Redeeming God, through these gifts
you gladden our hearts and refresh our spirits.
Grant us eagerness for your advent in our lives
as we watch for the coming of your Son,
Jesus Christ our Lord.
Amen

BENEDICTION

May the God of faithfulness
grant you to live in harmony with one another,
in accordance with Christ Jesus;
may the God of hope fill you
with all joy and peace in believing,
so that you may abound in hope
by the power of the Holy Spirit.
Amen

DISMISSAL

Go in peace. Walk in the light of the Lord.
Thanks be to God.

47

SEASONAL RITES

BLESSING OF THE ADVENT WREATH

The gathering rite for either the first week or all the weeks in Advent may take the form of lighting the Advent wreath. Following the entrance hymn and the greeting, one of the following prayers may be spoken. A candle on the Advent wreath may then be lit during the singing of an Advent hymn, such as "Light one candle to watch for Messiah" (WOV 630). The service then continues with the prayer of the day. On the second, third, and fourth Sundays in Advent, the number of candles lit prior to the service would be the total number lit the previous week. One new candle is then lit each week during the service.

Alternatively, candles of the Advent wreath may simply be lit before the service, without any special prayer of blessing. Candles may also be lit during the singing of an entrance hymn, the Kyrie, or the psalm for the day, without any special accompanying prayers or music.

1 ADVENT

We praise you, O God, for this evergreen crown
that marks our days of preparation for Christ's advent.
As we light the first candle on this wreath,
rouse us from sleep that we may be ready to greet our Lord
when he comes with all the saints and angels.
Enlighten us with your grace
and prepare our hearts to welcome him with joy.
Grant this through Christ our Lord
whose coming is certain and whose day draws near.
Amen

Light the first candle.

2 ADVENT

We praise you, O God, for this circle of light
that marks our days of preparation for Christ's advent.
As we light the candles on this wreath,
kindle within us the fire of your Spirit,
that we may be light shining in the darkness.
Enlighten us with your grace
that we may welcome others as you have welcomed us.
Grant this through Christ our Lord
whose coming is certain and whose day draws near.
Amen

Light the second candle.

3 ADVENT

We praise you, O God, for this victory wreath
that marks our days of preparation for Christ's advent.
As we light the candles on this wreath,
strengthen our hearts as we await the Lord's coming in glory.
Enlighten us with your grace,
that we may serve our neighbors in need.
Grant this through Christ our Lord
whose coming is certain and whose day draws near.
Amen

Light the third candle.

4 ADVENT

We praise you, O God, for this wheel of time
that marks our days of preparation for Christ's advent.
As we light the candles on this wreath,
open our eyes to see your presence in the lowly ones of this earth.
Enlighten us with your grace
that we may sing of your advent among us in the Word-made-flesh.
Grant this through Christ our Lord
whose coming is certain and whose day draws near.
Amen

Light the fourth candle.

48

LESSONS AND CAROLS

Stand

ENTRANCE HYMN

LBW 32   Fling wide the door
LBW 34   Oh, come, oh, come, Emmanuel
WOV 631   Lift up your heads, O gates

DIALOG

The Spirit and the Church cry out:
Come, Lord Jesus.
All those who wait his appearance pray:
Come, Lord Jesus.
The whole creation pleads:
Come, Lord Jesus.

OPENING PRAYER

The Lord be with you.
And also with you.
Let us pray.
Eternal God, at the beginning of creation you made the light that
scatters all darkness. May Christ, the true light, shine on your
people and free us from the power of sin and death. Fill us with
joy as we welcome your Son at his glorious coming; for he lives
and reigns with you and the Holy Spirit, one God, now and forever.
Amen

Sit

First Reading: Isaiah 40:1-11
CAROL
LBW 29   Comfort, comfort now my people
LBW 556   Herald, sound the note of judgment
WOV 629   All earth is hopeful (Toda la tierra)

Second Reading: Isaiah 35:1-10
CAROL
LBW 384   Your kingdom come, O Father
WOV 633   Awake, awake, and greet the new morn

Third Reading: Baruch 4:36—5:9
CAROL
WOV 626   People, look east

Fourth Reading: Isaiah 11:1-9
CAROL
LBW 87   Hail to the Lord's anointed
WOV 762   O day of peace

Fifth Reading: Isaiah 65:17-25
CAROL
LBW 33   The King shall come
WOV 744   Soon and very soon

Sixth Reading: 1 Thessalonians 5:1-11, 23-24
CAROL
LBW 31   Wake, awake, for night is flying
WOV 630   Light one candle to watch for Messiah
WOV 649   I want to walk as a child of the light

Seventh Reading: Luke 1:26-38
CAROL
LBW 28   Savior of the nations, come
WOV 632   The angel Gabriel from heaven came

Stand

RESPONSIVE PRAYER

Blessed is the One who comes in the name of the Lord.
Hosanna in the highest.
Show us your mercy, O Lord,
and grant us your salvation.
Give peace, O Lord, in all the world;
for only in you can we live in safety.
Let not the needy, O Lord, be forgotten,
nor the hope of the poor be taken away.
Shower, O heavens, from above,
and let the skies rain down righteousness.
Come, O Lord, at evening, with light,
**and in the morning, with your glory, to guide our feet
into the way of peace.**

THE LORD'S PRAYER

BLESSING AND DISMISSAL

Let us bless the Lord.
Thanks be to God.
May Christ, the Sun of Righteousness, shine upon you and scatter
the darkness from your path. Almighty God, Father, ☩ Son, and
Holy Spirit, bless you now and forever.
Amen

SENDING HYMN

LBW 26   Prepare the royal highway
LBW 27   Lo! He comes with clouds descending

49

NOVEMBER 29, 1998

FIRST SUNDAY IN ADVENT

INTRODUCTION

Of one thing we can be certain: our fragile, mortal lives will come to an end. We know neither the day nor the hour. Yet with our hearts enlightened by faith, we know that Christ—our life and our resurrection—is already with us in his word, his baptismal promise, his body and blood, his community of faith. We have been grasped and held for all time with Christ's steadfast love. In these gifts of grace, the people of God rejoice. Indeed, if there is any urgency, it concerns our mission in this fragile, broken world that yearns for light, life, and salvation.

PRAYER OF THE DAY

Stir up your power, O Lord, and come. Protect us by your strength and save us from the threatening dangers of our sins, for you live and reign with the Father and the Holy Spirit, one God, now and forever.

READINGS

Isaiah 2:1-5

The visionary message presented in this reading focuses on a future day when God establishes universal reign. At that time, the Lord will be recognized as God of all the earth. The prophet calls God's people to trust in the certainty of that reign even now.

Psalm 122

I was glad when they said to me, "Let us go to the house of the Lord." (Ps. 122:1)

Romans 13:11-14

Paul compares the advent of Christ to the coming of the dawn. We should anticipate his arrival and prepare for it as we would prepare to greet the new day.

Matthew 24:36-44

Jesus describes his second coming as a sudden unexpected event that will bring salvation or judgment upon people caught up in the usual affairs of daily life. Therefore, he urges people to be alert and expectant.

COLOR   Blue *or* Purple

THE PRAYERS

Calling to mind the hopes and longings of all people, let us pray for the church, the world, and all those in need.

A BRIEF SILENCE.

For the nations of the world, that turning from weapons of war they may walk in the way of peace, let us pray to the Lord.

Come, Lord Jesus.

For the church, that it may be alert to the signs of your coming, and proclaim your presence among us in word and sacrament, let us pray to the Lord.

Come, Lord Jesus.

For those living with depression, loneliness, or illness, and for all who wait for health and healing (especially . . .), that your light may be their hope, let us pray to the Lord.

Come, Lord Jesus.

For ourselves, that we may wake from sleep, and keep watchful for your advent, let us pray to the Lord.

Come, Lord Jesus.

HERE OTHER INTERCESSIONS MAY BE OFFERED.

We give you thanks for all the saints who dwell in the new and eternal Jerusalem. Make us glad for the gifts of this new year of grace, until we join all God's holy ones in light everlasting. Let us pray to the Lord.

Come, Lord Jesus.

Grant us steadfastness and patience, faithful God, as we wait in joyful hope for the fulfillment of your promises in Jesus Christ our Lord.

Amen

IMAGES FOR PREACHING

If knowledge is power, then Advent is about weakness. But its weakness derives from a peculiar *ignorance*. Four times over, the gospel reading for today declares that not knowing plays an important part in the divine design. Noah's cohorts did not know the nearness of the flood. The householder does not know the thief's itinerary. And likewise, disciples will not know the day of the Lord's coming. In the first two cases, however, the result of not knowing was destruction and plunder.

Is that what awaits us this season? Hardly blissful ignorance, it seems.

But our ignorance is not total. Although the faithful (let alone the angels or even the Son!) know not
when that day and hour will be, Jesus discloses that it
will surely happen. Paul's voice in Romans lends a note
of urgency. The end is not simply coming, but coming
soon, bearing its own distinctive quality. "For salvation
is nearer to us now than when we became believers. . . ." This insight is significant and comes with brac-
ing clarity. The endless, half-witted hours we waste on
the pettiness of life and our petty ways with others are
exposed for what they are. In place of that shadowy
existence, God's decisive end casts brilliant light on
every day that comes before it, including today, invest-
ing each moment with clear purpose and direction. If
the end really looks like salvation, then what will we do
in the meantime? We can live in readiness, wakefulness,
clothed presentably in the body of our Lord.

Advent ignorance is, therefore, most peculiar. With
all that we don't know in these darkening days, we do
know whose the end will be. The end belongs to our
Lord, whom Isaiah recognized as teacher and judge and
light for every nation. Our ignorance, our weakness this
season is of a blessed sort, for with it comes the power
to trust that the future rests in holy hands, so that our
hands may be set free for peace and praise.

WORSHIP MATTERS

Despite Advent's "keep awake" message, we may, at
times in our worship, catch someone "sleeping." The
organist plays only three stanzas when the congregation
is ready and waiting for the fourth. The acolyte lights
up the entire wreath. The choir misses its cue. The lector can't quite get out the words "licentiousness and
debauchery." Do we who keep watch over our worship's ebb and flow go ballistic when the unexpected
interrupts us? Or do we proceed with ease and good
humor, attending only to what really matters? By handling the unexpected with grace, we model for the
congregation the very posture Advent is coaxing us to
assume.

LET THE CHILDREN COME

Before the Advent wreath is blessed and lit, gather the
children around it. Engage their imaginations about

darkness and the comfort of light in dark times. Invite
them to join in the prayer of blessing (a prayer of this
type is in the alternate texts section for Advent). Model
a posture of prayer for them, such as the *orans* position
with hands outstretched, which they can duplicate.
They will be ministers of blessing. Teach them a simple
spoken or sung refrain that the whole assembly will
share sometime during the service. Make this a part of a
simplified gathering rite each Sunday during Advent.

MUSIC FOR WORSHIP
SERVICE MUSIC

LLC 184 (bilingual) provides a plaintive Kyrie in
f minor, well suited to the season of Advent.

GATHERING

LBW 25	Rejoice, rejoice, believers
WOV 631	Lift up your heads, O gates

PSALM 122

Farrell, Bernadette. "I Rejoiced" in PS1.

Joncas, Michael. "Let Us Go Rejoicing." GIA G-3437.

Proulx, Richard. "I Rejoiced When I Heard Them Say." GIA G-3780.
Choir, cong, kybd, fl, opt bass.

Walker, Christopher. "Ps. 122: I Rejoiced" in STP, vol. 2.

Witte, Marilyn. PW, Cycle A.

HYMN OF THE DAY

LBW 31	Wake, awake, for night is flying
	WACHET AUF

VOCAL RESOURCES

Bach, J. S./John Leavitt. "Zion Hears the Watchmen Singing."
GIA G3801. SATB, opt 2 vlns, vla, vc/bsn, bass.

Bach, J. S./John F. Wilson. "Wachet auf, ruft uns die Stimme."
HOP MW 1225. SATB.

Zipp, Friedrich. "Wake, Awake, for Night Is Flying." CPH 97-5389.
SATB, cong, brass, org.

INSTRUMENTAL RESOURCES

Bisbee, B. Wayne. "Wachet auf" in *From the Serene to the Whimsical*.
AFP 11-10561. Org.

Larson, Katherine Jordahl. "Wake, Awake, For Night Is Flying."
AFP 11-10634. Hb.

Oliver, Curt. "Wachet auf" in *Advent Keyboard Seasons*. AFP 11-10724.
Kybd.

Wold, Wayne. "Wake, Awake, for Night Is Flying" in *Light One Candle:
An Advent Organ Collection*. AFP 11-10720. Org.

51

ALTERNATE HYMN OF THE DAY

LBW 28   Savior of the nations, come
WOV 628   Each winter as the year grows older

COMMUNION

LBW 323   O Lord of light, who made the stars
WOV 703   Draw us in the Spirit's tether

OTHER SUGGESTIONS

OBS 79   Sweet coming for which we long

SENDING

LBW 33   The King shall come
WOV 744   Soon and very soon

ADDITIONAL HYMNS AND SONGS

WOV 627   My Lord, what a morning
DATH 50   Bright and Morning Star
GS2 18   Come to be our hope, O Jesus
SPW 75   Emmanuel

MUSIC FOR THE DAY

CHORAL

Boyce, William. "I Was Glad." NOV29 0454 0. SATB.

Cherwien, David M. "Hills of the North, Rejoice!" AFP 11-10731. SATB, org, opt brass/cong.

Erickson, Richard. "Light One Candle to Watch for Messiah." AFP 11-10887. SATB, org.

Hopson, Hal H. "O Day of Peace." AFP 11-10495. SAB, kybd, opt hb.

Hovhaness, Alan. "Watchman, Tell Us of the Night." CFP 6460. SATB, bar, org.

Howells, Herbert. "O, Pray for the Peace of Jerusalem." OXF 42.064. SATB, org.

Keesecker, Thomas. "Be Strong, Fear Not." CPH 98-3044. SATB, opt cong, gtr, kybd.

Larkin, Michael. "Rejoice, Ye People of Zion." AFP 11-10576. SAB, kybd.

Parry, C. H. H. "O Day of Peace." GIA G-2689. SATB, org, opt brass, timp.

Teschner, Melchior. "O Lord, How Shall I Meet You" in *Let All Together Praise.* CPH 97-565S. SATB, kybd.

Willan, Healey. "Rejoice, O Jerusalem. Behold Thy King Cometh" in *With High Delight.* CPH 97-504. SATB, org.

CHILDREN'S CHOIRS

Eltringham, Susan. "Let Us Go to the House of the Lord." KIR K120. U, kybd.

Lindh, Jody. "Advent Carol." CGA 648. U, kybd.

KEYBOARD/INSTRUMENTAL

Albright, William. "Nun komm, der Heiden Heiland" in *A New Liturgical Year,* ed. John Ferguson. AFP 11-10810. Org.

Bach, J. S. "Nun komm, der Heiden Heiland" in *Leipzig Chorales* and *Orgelbüchlein.* Various ed. Org.

Distler, Hugo. Organ Partita "Wachet auf, ruft uns die Stimme." Op. 8/2. BA 637. Org.

Wasson, Laura E. "Savior of the Nations, Come" in *A Christmas Season Tapestry.* AFP 11-10861. Kybd.

HANDBELL

Berry, Susan, and Janet Van Valey. "My Lord, What a Morning" in *E-Z Reader Spirituals.* LOR HB384. 2 oct.

McFadden, Jane. "Rejoice, Rejoice, Believers." AFP 11-10632. 2-3 oct.

Moklebust, Cathy. "Savior of the Nations, Come." CGA CGB173. 2-3 oct, perc.

Page, Anna Laura. "My Lord, What a Morning." LOR HB352. 3 oct.

PRAISE ENSEMBLE

Crouch, Andre/Schrader. "Soon and Very Soon." HOP. GC952. SATB/SAB.

Fragar, Russell. "Show Me Your Ways" in *Integrity's Hosanna! Music Songsheets: Shout to the Lord.* INT.

Hanson, Handt. "Once Again" in *Spirit Calls, Rejoice!* CCF.

Ylvisaker, John. "Wake Up Sleeper" in *Borning Cry.* NGP.

MONDAY, NOVEMBER 30
ST. ANDREW, APOSTLE

Andrew is known as a fisherman who left his net to follow Jesus, and fish for people. As a part of his calling, he brought others to Jesus, including his brother, and the boy with five loaves and two fish. Throughout the world, various countries celebrate Andrew whose missionary travels were legendary!

Your congregation can remember Andrew in devotions or meetings this week by connecting his missionary emphasis with the season of Advent. How are we called to invite others to the light of Christ that we celebrate during Advent and Christmas? How do you publicize your services during December, and how do you encourage your members to invite their unchurched friends and neighbors to join them for worship and other special events during this time of year?

THURSDAY, DECEMBER 3

FRANCIS XAVIER, MISSIONARY TO ASIA, 1552

Francis Xavier, considered a great missionary, helped form the religious order known as the Society of Jesus (also called the Jesuits). As he traveled throughout India, Southeast Asia, Japan, and the Philippines, Francis learned the native languages, wrote on the indigenous spiritual traditions, and drew connections between Christian and Asian religious practices.

As an Advent saint, Francis points to the light of Christ in the Far East and the Savior's advent in music, art, song, and ritual unique to the Asian world. To honor Francis consider singing "In a lowly manger born" (LBW 417, Japanese) or "Lord, your hands have formed" (WOV 727, Philippines). You may want to discuss how some people today are turning to Eastern spiritual practices such as the Buddhist concept of mindfulness to deepen their Christian experience of prayer.

DECEMBER 6, 1998

SECOND SUNDAY IN ADVENT

INTRODUCTION

In the scripture, prayers, and hymns of Advent, John the Baptist brings us to the Jordan River and the waters of baptism. He calls us to repent, for the reign of God is near. He calls us to the font of new birth, where we have been grafted into God's branch, the root of Jesse. He calls us to the holy supper, where we receive forgiveness in the life-giving fruit of Christ's body and blood. From the celebration of word and sacrament— from the center of our worship—we are called to go forth as a people whose mission is the proclamation of God's mercy for our suffering world.

PRAYER OF THE DAY

Stir up our hearts, O Lord, to prepare the way for your only Son. By his coming give us strength in our conflicts and shed light on our path through the darkness of this world; through your Son, Jesus Christ our Lord, who lives and reigns with you and the Holy Spirit, one God, now and forever.

READINGS

Isaiah 11:1-10

In the previous chapter Isaiah portrays God's judgment as the felling of a great forest. In today's reading the prophet describes the ideal ruler who will come in the future as a green shoot springing from the dead stump (David's royal line) of Jesse

(David's father). The reign of this monarch will be experienced as paradise regained.

Psalm 72:1-7, 18-19

In his time the righteous shall flourish. (Ps. 72:7)

Romans 15:4-13

Paul encourages Christians to welcome diversity and live in harmony with one another. In particular, the writings of the Hebrew Scriptures promise that Gentiles will be welcome among God's people.

Matthew 3:1-12

Just before Jesus began his public ministry, John the Baptist appeared, calling people to live in accordance with their words and speaking of the powerful one who was to come.

COLOR Blue *or* Purple

THE PRAYERS

Calling to mind the hopes and longings of all people, let us pray for the church, the world, and all those in need.
A BRIEF SILENCE.

Rouse our imagination to new visions of peace in the world, and send your Spirit of wisdom, knowledge, and justice to rest upon the leaders of nations. Let us pray to the Lord.

Come, Lord Jesus.

Stir the church to preach the message of John the Baptist, that we may bear the good fruit that comes from

53

repentance. Let us pray to the Lord.

Come, Lord Jesus.

Awaken us to care for those who are poor and forgotten, or the victims of violence and injustice, that they may know the good news that your kingdom has come near. Let us pray to the Lord.

Come, Lord Jesus.

Look with compassion on all who are hospitalized or ill (especially . . .), that they may abound in hope at your coming among us. Let us pray to the Lord.

Come, Lord Jesus.

Inspire this community of faith, that we may glorify God with one voice, and welcome others as you have welcomed us. Let us pray to the Lord.

Come, Lord Jesus.

HERE OTHER INTERCESSIONS MAY BE OFFERED.

We remember with thanksgiving John the Baptist, Nicholas, and all the saints who prepared the way of the Lord. Gather us, with them, into your great harvest of eternal life. Let us pray to the Lord.

Come, Lord Jesus.

Grant us steadfastness and patience, faithful God, as we wait in joyful hope for the fulfillment of your promises in Jesus Christ our Lord.

Amen

IMAGES FOR PREACHING

Why repent if all is well? Or put another way, Advent's call to repent itself presumes that something is terribly wrong. Behind this plea for repentance, then, is the recognition of deep division between the way things are and the way God would have them be. Probe the otherwise lovely images from Isaiah, test their assumptions, and this division snaps into crisp focus. Why would the poor need a righteous judge or the meek an impartial decision unless justice and fairness were just what they lacked? Why would coexisting animals—wolf and lamb, leopard and kid, and all the rest—be the prophet's vision of divine rule if they were not, in ordinary times, the very emblems of violent hostility straining the fabric of life? And why would Isaiah picture an earth flooded with knowledge of the Lord if not for the foolish idolatry that leaves it everywhere a desert?

Generations later, this same sort of division haunted Paul. If the welcome of Christ meant anything, he wrote to Rome, it would include within their church a welcome for circumcised and uncircumcised alike. But this he asserted precisely because reconciliation between gentile and Jewish Christians was as yet unknown. And the irony was that the divisions they preserved for the best of religious reasons were the very ones their Lord had in fact come to reconcile.

Every such division, whether malicious or well-intentioned, runs headlong into John the Baptist's cry for change, for turning and returning. For John's call recognized one final division: that between every earthly reality and the kingdom of heaven that was drawing ever near. With contrary signs of garments and food, in a contrary landscape unfit for human thriving, John spoke his contrary word. First, turn from all that fragments life into splinter groups and safe havens of religious self-satisfaction. And then, return to the one who is already returning, who approaches even now through the crucified to gather the harvest and purify it forever.

WORSHIP MATTERS

The image of chaff being pitched into unquenchable fire can leave us all a bit hot under the collar. The very word *repent* makes many squirm. Yet Advent without that cleansing fire of repentance simply isn't Advent. And squirming's not so bad if it helps us inch toward a fresh understanding of ourselves as would-be followers of Christ.

Repentance comes in many packages. It need not be limited to a brief gathering rite, hurriedly spoken and quickly forgotten. Repentance as a cleansing, refreshing change of heart can happen during well-planned silences: in the sermon, the prayers, the lighting of the wreath, the moment between "And also with you" and "Let us pray."

The confession and forgiveness itself may take on new meaning if occasionally placed within the liturgy of word and meal, rather than preceding it. An example is in the "Service of Word and Prayer" (*WOV*, p. 50), where repentance finds a fitting home as a response to hearing the preached Word.

LET THE CHILDREN COME

At this time of year, many parishes make food baskets, stock food shelves, and set up giving trees as a part of their outreach to local persons in need. Children can share in that outreach, and it can be rooted in the liturgical life of the church. Today is the commemoration of St. Nicholas, Bishop of Myra. He is the figure behind Santa Claus. Show them St. Nicholas and his care for those in need. He gave gold to a poor man with three daughters to prevent them from being sold into slavery. Here is an image for the life of the church: One who gives freely to any in need as we look for the coming of Christ.

MUSIC FOR WORSHIP
GATHERING

| LBW 26 | Prepare the royal highway |
| WOV 633 | Awake, awake, and greet the new morn |

PSALM 72

Hallock, Peter. "Psalm 72" in TP. WJK.

Haugen, Marty. "Every Nation on Earth Will Adore You" in PCY.

LBW 87   Hail to the Lord's anointed

Ogden, David. "In His Days" in PS1.

Schoenbachler, Tim. "Ps. 72: Justice Shall Flourish" in STP, vol. 3.

Witte, Marilyn. PW, Cycle A.

HYMN OF THE DAY

| LBW 36 | On Jordan's banks the Baptist's cry |
| | PUER NOBIS |

VOCAL RESOURCES

Busarow, Donald. "On Jordan's Banks the Baptist's Cry." CPH 98-2639. SAB, ob, org, cong.

Cherwien, David. "On Jordan's Banks." Full score AMSI 2020. Brass 2020B; hb 2020HB. SATB, org, opt brass, hb, timp, cong.

INSTRUMENTAL RESOURCES

Cherwien, David. "On Jordan's Banks the Baptist's Cry" in *Interpretations Book VII.* AMSI SP-104. Org.

Leavitt, John. "On Jordan's Banks the Baptist's Cry" in *A Little Nativity Suite.* AFP 11-10351. Org.

Zinsmeister, Karl. "Puer Nobis" in *Hymnworks for Handbells and Handchimes.* AMSI HB-24. 2-4 oct.

ALTERNATE HYMN OF THE DAY

| LBW 29 | Comfort, comfort now my people |
| WOV 762 | O day of peace |

COMMUNION

| LBW 25 | Rejoice, rejoice, believers |
| WOV 799 | When long before time |

SENDING

| LBW 332 | Battle Hymn of the Republic |
| WOV 626 | People, look east |

ADDITIONAL HYMNS AND SONGS

AYG 13	For the coming of the Savior
MBW 260	Rejoice, rejoice, the kingdom comes
NCH 114	Return, my people, Israel
PH 409	Wild and lone the prophet's voice

MUSIC FOR THE DAY
CHORAL

Bach, J. S. "Comfort, Comfort Ye My People." CPH 98-204. U, SATB, 2 vln, vla, cont.

Billings, William. "Rejoice, Ye Shining Worlds on High." CPH 98-328. SATB, kybd.

Buxtehude, Dietrich. "Prepare, O Children of the Lord." AFP 11-035. U, 2 vln, kybd, opt vc.

Distler, Hugo. "Lo! How a Rose E'er Blooming." CPH 98-1925. SATB.

Hunnicutt, Judy. "Make Straight in the Desert a Highway." GIA G-3981. SATB.

Kohrs, Jonathan. "What Is the Crying at Jordan." CPH 98-3299. SSAB, cong, brass, org.

Martinson, Joel. "Lo, How a Rose Is Growing." AFP 11-400003. SAB/SB, org.

Mitchell-Wallace, Sue. "The Advent Herald." GIA G-3393. Inst pts G-3393INST. SATB, org, ob/cl, cong.

Thompson, Randall. "Blessed Be the Lord God." PRE 392-03021. SATB.

CHILDREN'S CHOIRS

Pote, Allen. "Prepare!" CGA 705. 2 pt mxd, kybd.

Sleeth, Natalie. "O Come, O Come Immanuel." CGA 273. U, desc, kybd.

Sleeth, Natalie. "The Lion and the Lamb." CGA 296. U, kybd.

KEYBOARD/INSTRUMENTAL

Peeters, Flor. "Partita on 'Puer Nobis Nascitur.'" Peeters ed. 66746. Org.

Sedio, Mark. "Rejoice, Rejoice" in *Let Us Talents and Tongues Employ.* AFP 11-10718. Org.

Young, Jeremy. "On Jordan's Banks/O Come, Divine Messiah" in *Gathering Music for Advent.* AFP 11-10798. Inst, kybd.

HANDBELL

Kinyon, Barbara B. "What Star Is This That Beams So Bright" (PUER NOBIS.). CGA CGB111. 2 oct.

Moklebust, Cathy. "Rejoice, Rejoice!" in *The Bells of Christmas.* CGA. CGB146. 2 oct.

55

McFadden, Jane. "Pastorale on 'Lo, How a Rose E'er Blooming.'"
AFP 11-10522. 3-5 oct.

PRAISE ENSEMBLE

Carter, John. "Dancing into the Promise." Somerset/HOP. SAB.

Hanson, Handt, and Paul Murakami. "Give Us Your Vision" in *Spirit Calls, Rejoice!* CCF.

Robinson, Marc A. "Prepare Ye." KJO 8830. SATB, perc.

Yeager, Bill. "Wonderful Counselor" in *Praise Chorus Book*, 2d ed. MAR.

SUNDAY, DECEMBER 6
NICHOLAS, BISHOP OF MYRA, C. 342

Nicholas, fourth-century bishop in Asia Minor, is one of the most beloved saints, but we know little of his life apart from legend. According to tradition he devoted his life to good works, was generous to the poor, and died peacefully.

In some countries gifts are given on this day, perhaps with a visit from St. Nicholas himself. Families could observe this day by giving simple gifts, or inviting children to place their shoes outside their bedroom door. Traditional shoe-stuffers include chocolate coins, small tangerines, or gingerbread cookies. Since he is remembered for giving gifts in secret, St. Nicholas could make a visit to Sunday school children today (or in a children's message during worship). In addition to giving a small gift, he could talk about the practices of gift giving, doing acts of kindness in secret, and caring for the poor.

MONDAY, DECEMBER 7
AMBROSE, BISHOP OF MILAN, 397

While a catechumen, Ambrose was elected bishop and was baptized, ordained, and consecrated as a bishop on the same day! He was a respected and deeply loved bishop, and he was a famous preacher and defender of orthodoxy. With Jerome, Augustine, and Gregory the Great, Ambrose is considered one of the four doctors (teachers) of the Western church.

Ambrose was one of the first to write Latin metrical hymns; three of his texts are in *LBW*. The most famous of these is an Advent hymn, "Savior of the nations come" (LBW 28). Consider using this hymn sometime during this week. Note that like Luther centuries later, Ambrose wrote hymns as a means of strengthening faith during periods of hardship and distress.

FRIDAY, DECEMBER 11
LARS OLSEN SKREFSRUD, MISSIONARY TO INDIA, 1910

When Skrefsrud was in prison at age 19 he devoted his life to Christ while reading religious books and after talking with a visiting pastor. After attending a mission institute he went to India to minister to the Santals, a people of northern India who suffered terribly from social and political oppression. Skrefsrud's ministry among them included translating the gospels and the Small Catechism, and teaching agricultural and carpentry methods to raise their standard of living. He was a political activist and saw no separation between the spiritual and social aspects of Christian witness in the world.

Consider raising up the ways Skrefsrud is an Advent prophet in the same manner as Isaiah and John the Baptist. How are we called to point the way to Christ by working for justice and equality among all people?

SATURDAY, DECEMBER 12
DAY OF OUR LADY OF GUADALUPE

This feast is especially observed in Mexico where Our Lady of Guadalupe is their patron saint. In 1531, Juan Diego saw a vision of Mary and told the bishop that she wanted a church to be built on that spot where the cries of the poor and the oppressed would be heard. The hopes of the Aztec people were stirred by Mary appearing clothed like one of them.

In Mexico people rise early today to offer a morning serenade to Mary, followed by Mass and a festive breakfast. This day provides an opportunity to celebrate the importance of Mary in the church around the world, and especially in our Advent observance.

DECEMBER 13, 1998

THIRD SUNDAY IN ADVENT

INTRODUCTION

In today's gospel reading, Jesus points to signs of God's reign: the blind see, the lame walk, lepers are cleansed, the deaf hear. Those who thought themselves ignored by God now discover the merciful and healing presence of God's anointed servant. Echoing these words of Jesus, the prayer of the day asks God to open our eyes and ears so that we might see and hear God's strong and saving presence among us today: in word and holy supper, in the church and in our homes, in the silence of prayer and in the events of daily life. Strengthen your hearts, the Lord is near.

PRAYER OF THE DAY

Almighty God, you once called John the Baptist to give witness to the coming of your Son and to prepare his way. Grant us, your people, the wisdom to see your purpose today and the openness to hear your will, that we may witness to Christ's coming and so prepare his way; through Jesus Christ our Lord, who lives and reigns with you and the Holy Spirit, one God, now and forever.
or
Lord, hear our prayers and come to us, bringing light into the darkness of our hearts; for you live and reign with the Father and the Holy Spirit, one God, now and forever.

READINGS

Isaiah 35:1-10

In the previous chapter Isaiah described God's judgment on Edom as the turning of a garden into a wasteland. In contrast, the prophet now uses the image of the wasteland becoming a garden to describe the restoration of the exiled people of Judah to their homeland. Not only will the wasteland be renewed, but so also will God's people.

Psalm 146:4-9 (Psalm 146:5-10 [NRSV])

The Lord lifts up those who are bowed down. (Ps. 146:7)

or Luke 1:47-55

My spirit rejoices in God my Savior. (Luke 1:47)

James 5:7-10

The faith of Christians who are waiting for their Lord should

be marked by patience and by trust in God's compassion and mercy.

Matthew 11:2-11

In the early days of his ministry, John the Baptist proclaimed the advent of God's reign and bore witness to Jesus as the promised one of God. But even John had his doubts later, when Jesus demonstrated that God's reign was present in merciful deeds among the poor, rather than a terrifying day of judgment.

COLOR   Blue *or* Purple

THE PRAYERS

Calling to mind the hopes and longings of all people, let us pray for the church, the world, and all those in need.
A BRIEF SILENCE.
That our government may be a sign of the justice and dignity that belongs to all your children, let us pray to the Lord.
Come, Lord Jesus.
That bishops, pastors, diaconal ministers, associates in ministry, and all the baptized may be strong witnesses to the good news of your coming, let us pray to the Lord.
Come, Lord Jesus.
That you strengthen with your healing love all who are depressed, lonely, ill, or whose hearts are fearful (especially . . .), let us pray to the Lord.
Come, Lord Jesus.
That you bless the ministries of charitable organizations who serve the lives of those who are blind, deaf, lame, or speechless, let us pray to the Lord.
Come, Lord Jesus.
That during these busy days of preparation you calm our hearts with your gifts of patience, stillness, and hope, let us pray to the Lord.
Come, Lord Jesus.
HERE OTHER INTERCESSIONS MAY BE OFFERED.
We give you thanks for Lucy, and all the saints whose lives revealed your light. Bring us with them to the everlasting joy and gladness of your reign. Let us pray to the Lord.

57

Come, Lord Jesus.
Grant us steadfastness and patience, faithful God, as we wait in joyful hope for the fulfillment of your promises in Jesus Christ our Lord.
Amen

IMAGES FOR PREACHING

What can be said when hopes are crushed? What word is enough? A beloved companion suddenly dies. The longing for children goes repeatedly unmet. Ferocious disease reasserts its unstoppable course. What once was a bright future now chokes and confines. And though we may even know these experiences firsthand, still we puzzle at what to say. At best, our words can only gesture at such *barrenness* through verbal images and scenes. No wonder Israel remembered its days in exile using the language of wilderness. The rebellious nation, now a refugee, felt like a wasteland, parched and lifeless. But even these vivid terms had only the power of expression. They could never accomplish the restoration that was truly needed.

To the prophets, however, fell the remarkable vocation of uttering just such words. Powerful words that once visited judgment on an earlier generation now brought comfort and renewal. Isaiah's happy task was to speak fruitfulness: the desert in bloom and gushing with springs. Jesus, too, bore such powerful words, even becoming prophet to a prophet. John the Baptist, trapped in his cell and his uncertainty, heard the quenching news that healing had begun, ancient prophecies were complete, and the wait was over. In a surprising twist, the one to whom John had once testified now gave testimony to him, renaming the Baptist as chief among prophets, first among humanity, herald of the ever-nearing kingdom.

In the wasteland, our own words seem so empty and weak. Oddly, the same would have been true for the prophets but that they spoke the words of another. Beyond the limits of our cries, God speaks a lasting word to awaken life in the most desolate of places. And as the epistle for today remarks, those whose company is spent with such divine speech, even the prophets themselves, share the benefits of patience. To bear this lasting word on our lips this season grants us endurance before every sorrow, with strength to press on until fruitfulness returns.

WORSHIP MATTERS

As Isaiah says so well, we do see God's glory when weak hands and knees are given support, when those who fear are given reason for hope. When the blind, the deaf, and the lame come to our churches, can they, too, sense God's glory? Can those whom the world tends to dismiss as lost causes (those with mental illness, people living with AIDS/HIV, for example) find a welcoming community within our sanctuaries?

LET THE CHILDREN COME

One of the strong themes of Advent is hope for the coming of the Lord. The alternate prayer of the day sums up the hopes heard all through this season, "Lord, hear our prayer and come to us." Teach children the word Maranatha, "O Lord, come." Children are less hesitant than adults about picking up on new phrases. They may even join in a call and response, O Lord come! Maranatha! As Advent reaches its mid-point and the beginning of the great O Antiphons, the invitation for the Lord to come can be continued at home with the hymn, "Oh, come, oh, come, Emmanuel." It will serve as preparation for next week's gospel and the promise of the coming of Jesus, Emmanuel.

MUSIC FOR WORSHIP
GATHERING

LBW 35	Hark, the glad sound!
WOV 626	People, look east

PSALM 146

Haugen, Marty. "Bless the Lord, My Soul." GIA G-3339. SATB, cant, gtr, kybd, cong.

LBW 538   Oh, praise the Lord, my soul!

Martens, Mason. "Psalm 146" in TP. Cant, hb.

Porter, Thomas J. "Happy the Poor in Spirit." GIA G-3354. SATB, cong, kybd, gtr, C inst.

Wellicome, Paul. "Maranatha, Alleluia!" in PS1.

or

LUKE 1:47-55

LBW 180   My soul now magnifies the Lord

Schalk, Carl. "A Parish Magnificat." CPH 98-288. U, cong, org.

Smith, Alan. "Magnificat" in PS1.

Toolan, Suzanne. "My Soul Proclaims." OCP 10580. SATB, cant, cong, kybd, gtr, 2 solo insts, fl, ob, vc trio.

UMH 198   My soul gives glory to my God

W3 534   Tell out, my soul, the greatness of the Lord!

Witte, Marilyn. PW, Cycle A.

WOV 730   My soul proclaims your greatness

HYMN OF THE DAY

LBW 26   Prepare the royal highway
          BEREDEN VÄG FÖR HERRAN

VOCAL RESOURCES

Ferguson, John. "Advent Processional." AFP 11-10448. SATB.

Gieschen, Thomas. "Prepare the Royal Highway" in *Three Songs of Praise for Children*. CPH 98-2623. U/2 pt, kybd, hb.

Hemmerle, Bernhard. "Prepare the Royal Highway" in *For the Crowning of the Year: A Collection of Rounds and Canons for Advent and Christmas*. AFP 11-10509. U.

INSTRUMENTAL RESOURCES

Afdahl, Lee J. "Prepare the Royal Highway." AFP 11-10723. 3-5 oct.

Manz, Paul. "Prepare the Royal Highway" in *Six Advent Improvisations*. MSM 10-002. Org.

Ore, Charles W. "Prepare the Royal Highway" in *11 Compositions for Organ*, set V. CPH 97-6107. Org.

ALTERNATE HYMN OF THE DAY

LBW 556   Herald, sound the note of judgment
          (*alternate tune*: REGENT SQUARE, LBW 50)
WOV 629   All earth is hopeful

COMMUNION

LBW 14   Listen! You nations
WOV 635   Surely it is God who saves me

OTHER SUGGESTIONS

WOV 766   We come to the hungry feast

SENDING

LBW 553   Rejoice, O pilgrim throng
WOV 768   He comes to us as one unknown

ADDITIONAL HYMNS AND SONGS

ASF 18   O Promised One of Israel
CW 5   As angels joyed with one accord
H82 75   There's a voice in the wilderness crying
W3 355   When the King shall come again

MUSIC FOR THE DAY

CHORAL

Distler, Hugo. "Lo, How a Rose E'er Blooming." CPH 98-1925. SATB.

Fleming, Larry L. "Go and Tell John." AFP 11-10282. SATB.

Jennings, Arthur. "Springs in the Desert." HWG GCMR 580. SATB, T solo, org.

Jennings, Carolyn. "A New Magnificat." AFP 11-10479. SATB, opt cong, org.

Keesecker, Thomas. "All Earth Is Hopeful." AFP 11-10877. U/2 pt, kybd.

Laster, James H. "Prepare the Royal Highway." CPH 98-285. SATB, org.

Philips, Craig. "People, Look East!" SEL 405-103. U, kybd, opt desc.

Proulx, Richard. "His Name Is John." AFP 11-10777. 2 pt mxd, hb.

Willan, Healey. "Magnificat and Nunc Dimittis." CPH 98-144. SATB, org.

Wood, Charles. "O Thou, the Central Orb" in *The New Church Anthem Book*. OXF 0-19-353109-0.

CHILDREN'S CHOIRS

Leitz, Darwin. "The Magnificat." AFP EK12-467281. U, org/gtr, bass.

McRae, Shirley. "A Litany for Advent." CGA 570. U/2 pt, opt fl, glock, kybd.

Mitchell, Tom. "Song of Hope (Canto de Esperanza)." CGA 638. U, kybd, opt desc.

KEYBOARD/INSTRUMENTAL

Billingham, Richard. "My Lord, What a Morning" in *Seven Reflections on African American Hymns*. AFP 11-10762. Org.

Finzi, Gerald. "Carol" in *A Finzi Organ Album*. OXF 0193753685. Org.

Hassell, Michael. "My Lord, What a Morning" in *Jazz December*. AFP 11-10796.

HANDBELL

Hopson, Hal H. "Variations on 'Kingsfold.'" AFP 11-10703. 3 or 5 oct.

Matheny, Gary. "Puer Nobis." AMSI HB-3. 3 oct.

Moklebust, Cathy. "People, Look East." AFP 11-10805. 3-5 oct.

PRAISE ENSEMBLE

Alexander, Lowell/Steven V. Taylor. "Joy to the World." MEA 3100030168. SATB.

Nystrom, Martin, and Don Harris. "We Will Draw Near" in *Integrity's Hosanna! Music Songsheets: We Draw Near*. INT.

Sims, Randy. "You Are the Lord of Me" in *Spirit Calls, Rejoice!* CCF.

SUNDAY, DECEMBER 13

LUCY, MARTYR, 304

Lucy lived in Syracuse in Sicily, and at a young age died the death of a martyr under the persecution of the emperor Diocletian. The name Lucy derives from the Latin word for "light," and during Advent she is commemorated as one who bears witness to the coming light of Christ.

In Scandinavian countries St. Lucy's day is celebrated during the cold, dark days of winter with the ancient traditions of outdoor bonfires, roaring fires in fireplaces, and the lighting of Lucy candles. Many homes still keep the tradition of the eldest daughter rising early in the morning to serve the family coffee and sweet rolls. Your congregation could tell the legend of Santa Lucia at coffee hour today, and serve sweet breads in her honor. In addition to the traditional "Santa Lucia" hymn, consider singing "Rejoice, rejoice, believers" with its rich images of light and darkness.

MONDAY, DECEMBER 14

JOHN OF THE CROSS, RENEWER OF THE CHURCH, 1591
TERESA OF AVILA, RENEWER OF THE CHURCH, 1582

John and Teresa both were members of the Carmelite religious order during the sixteenth century. Teresa wrote of the states of prayer between meditation (quiet) and ecstasy (union). John's writings focus on his mystical thought and personal experience, rooted both in Scripture and in psychological insight. John and Teresa believed that authentic prayer leads to a greater love of neighbor and service to those in need.

The recent interest in spirituality has led many people to discover the depth of Teresa and John's spiritual writings. Because Advent is a time to emphasize

contemplation and prayer, consider using readings by them at an Advent prayer service, retreat, or other gathering. A discussion might focus on the connections between spirituality and service to others.

WEDNESDAY, DECEMBER 16

LAS POSADAS

For the next nine days many Mexican families observe the custom of *Las Posadas*, which means "lodgings." Groups of people wander through the neighborhood to mark the journey of Mary and Joseph to Bethlehem. They knock on doors, asking to come in, but a rude voice says there is no room. The visitors either respond that Mary is about to give birth to the king of heaven, or they sing an Advent carol foretelling his birth. Eventually the door is opened, and everyone is welcomed into a great party of traditional Mexican holiday food and singing.

Youth groups or other congregational gatherings could include this tradition as a part of a pre-Christmas party. Las Posadas can be a strong reminder of Christ's humble birth among the poor, and the importance of sharing hospitality.

DECEMBER 20, 1998

FOURTH SUNDAY IN ADVENT

INTRODUCTION

We do well to acknowledge that one of the reasons we celebrate the festivals and seasons of the year is our tendency to forget God's merciful presence. In word and sacrament we are not only reminded of God's promises, we also encounter the very presence of Jesus Christ. The liturgy of Advent names him Emmanuel, "God is with us." God comes to us in ordinary ways, offering extraordinary gifts: new life in baptism, gracious words to guide us on life's path, welcome food for the journey of faith. With Mary and Joseph and all the angels, we offer thanks to God for the one who was born to save us from the power of sin. Let us not forget: God is with us now.

PRAYER OF THE DAY

Stir up your power, O Lord, and come. Take away the hindrance of our sins and make us ready for the celebration of your birth, that we may receive you in joy and serve you always; for you live and reign with the Father and the Holy Spirit, now and forever.

READINGS

Isaiah 7:10-16

An Israelite and Aramean military coalition presents a serious threat to King Ahaz of Judah. In response, Ahaz decides to secure his throne and kingdom by asking mighty Assyria for help. In today's reading, Isaiah reminds him that human attempts to establish security will only fail. The prophet repeats the promise that God alone will make God's people secure.

Psalm 80:1-7, 16-18 (Psalm 80:1-7, 17-19 [NRSV])

Show the light of your countenance and we shall be saved. (Ps. 80:7)

Romans 1:1-7

Paul's letter to the Romans is devoted to presenting the gospel (or "good news") of God, which provides salvation for all who believe. This theme is introduced already in the opening words of the letter, where Paul expands upon the typical salutation to include a statement of faith.

Matthew 1:18-25

Matthew's story of Jesus' birth focuses on the role of Joseph, who adopts the divinely begotten child into the family of David and obediently gives him the name Jesus, which means, literally, "God saves."

COLOR Blue *or* Purple

THE PRAYERS

Calling to mind the hopes and longings of all people, let us pray for the church, the world, and all those in need.

A BRIEF SILENCE.

For the church throughout the world, that it faithfully announce that God is with us in word and at the table of the Lord, and in acts of kindness and love, let us pray to the Lord.

Come, Lord Jesus.

For the nations of the world, that you grant wisdom and compassion to all who govern and lead, let us pray to the Lord.

Come, Lord Jesus.

For those awaiting the birth of a child, and for all who watch and wait, that their hearts be filled with peace, and their fears turned to joy, let us pray to the Lord.

Come, Lord Jesus.

For all who live without hope, especially those who are hungry or homeless, depressed or lonely, sick or dying (especially . . .), that your merciful face shine on them, let us pray to the Lord.

Come, Lord Jesus.

For our families and congregations, that as we celebrate Christmas you draw us to the mystery of your love, and your gracious presence in our lives, let us pray to the Lord.

Come, Lord Jesus.

HERE OTHER INTERCESSIONS MAY BE OFFERED.

We remember with thanksgiving Mary and Joseph, and all who responded faithfully to your Word. May Emmanuel find welcome in our hearts until we join all your saints in the brightness of your glory. Let us pray to the Lord.

Come, Lord Jesus.

Grant us steadfastness and patience, faithful God, as we wait in joyful hope for the fulfillment of your promises in Jesus Christ our Lord.

Amen

IMAGES FOR PREACHING

Perhaps in concession to the larger culture, today's gospel reading sneaks in an early Christmas. But the birth in Matthew is a quiet and understated event, more of an afterthought whispered in the closing words of the final verse. Instead, the real energy is spent on *scandal*. No sooner is the happy couple introduced than the problem is presented, discreetly yet plainly: Mary is with child, but without Joseph! What's a faithful fiancé to do? Joseph reasons that discreetness is the better part of righteousness (if not personal pride), and resolves to act quietly.

Too bad Joseph needed to sleep on the matter, for it gave the angel of the Lord occasion to demand a more public path. What human faithfulness saw as scandal to be swept under the rug, God saw as opportunity to be dragged into the light. And it all raises the vexing question of where true righteousness rests in this familiar tale. Even the righteousness of Joseph (and he *is* praised for this in Matthew) falls short of God's unexpected righteousness with its roots sunk deep into scandal itself, emerging not so much despite human shame as through it.

If you think that claim overstated, then consider the seventeen verses *prior* to today's gospel, the cadence of "begats" with which Matthew's gospel begins. In the mind-numbing regularity of that genealogy, listen for the ruptures and wrinkles within that whole holy history. Just when we think Jesus came from pure stock, Matthew makes clear that his lineage included sinners and schemers. Astounding news: God chose a descendant of *them* to be savior of *us*. And even in Paul's briefer sketch of this pedigree, scandal leaps out. Jesus is the powerful, spirit-filled Son *not* because of his flesh or his forebears, but because he was raised *from the dead*. This one who knew the scandal of the tomb "will save

61

his people from their sins." It is the shocking sign of God with us still, the scandal from which true righteousness springs.

WORSHIP MATTERS

As the popular Christmas myth goes, Mary and Joseph are travelling from Nazareth to Bethlehem, supported only by the faithful old donkey (you know, the one the gospel writers forgot to mention). Whether Joseph and his betrothed actually were given support by their community remains a mystery. Equally mysterious is how faith communities today can be supportive of those engaged to be married.

Perhaps there are some ways to explore. We might include in our intercessions the names of those preparing for marriage. Engaged couples who participate in the community's worship life may wish to publicly announce their news to the congregation, and receive an appropriate blessing. Couples who are rarely seen at worship may gain from receiving a card signed by all at a fellowship gathering, wishing them well and promising prayer and support.

LET THE CHILDREN COME

Today's gospel gives three names and titles for the child who is about to be born. Jesus, Messiah, and Emmanuel all add depth to the meaning of this birth. What are the other names that speak in worship about the gift of this birth? Lamb of God, Prince of Peace, God from God, Light from Light are some examples. Just as it is confusing for some adults to grasp the various names for Jesus, it may be hard for children to grasp. Try this as a way to help children comprehend the various meanings: their mother may also be someone's wife as a well as a daughter, or sister, or aunt. These names all make up who someone is. Let the children explore the names of Jesus and learn more about this awaited gift of God.

MUSIC FOR WORSHIP

SERVICE MUSIC

A litanic form of the O Antiphons may serve as the entrance music on this day, replacing the entrance hymn and Kyrie. They are pointed for singing to a psalm tone on pages 174–175 of *LBW*. *Praise God in Song* (GIA, 1979) provides a chant setting with a congregational response that may be accompanied by handbells.

GATHERING

| LBW 32 | Fling wide the door |
| WOV 629 | All earth is hopeful |

PSALM 80

DATH 39   Behold and Tend This Vine

Furlong, Sue. "God Of Hosts, Bring Us Back" in PS1.

Haugen, Marty. "Lord, Make Us Turn to You" in PCY, vol. 2.

Jenkins, Stephen. "An Advent Psalm." MSM 80-003. SATB/U, cant, org, cong.

Schaffer, Robert J. "Psalm 80" in *Psalms for the Cantor*, vol. III. WLP 2504.

Witte, Marilyn. PW, Cycle A.

Ylvisaker, John. "Restore Us, O Lord" in *Borning Cry*. NGP.

HYMN OF THE DAY

| WOV 641 | Peace came to earth |
| | SCHNEIDER |

VOCAL RESOURCES

Scott, K. Lee. "Peace Came to Earth." CPH 98-3376. SATB, org, opt cong, opt french hrn.

ALTERNATE HYMN OF THE DAY

| LBW 28 | Savior of the nations, come |
| LBW 34 | Oh, come, oh, come, Emmanuel |

INSTRUMENTAL RESOURCES FOR LBW 34

Albrecht, Timothy. "Veni, Emmanuel" in *Grace Notes VII*. AFP 11-10856. Org.

Organ, Anne Krentz. "Veni, Emmanuel" in *Advent Reflections for Piano and Instrument*. AFP 11-10864. Kybd, fl.

COMMUNION

| LBW 58 | Lo, how a rose is growing |
| WOV 701 | What feast of love |

OTHER SUGGESTIONS

Use choral or instrumental parts of the anthem "What Feast of Love" with the hymn setting in WOV.

Barber, Todd J. "What Feast of Love/ What Child Is This." AFP 11-10674. SATB, pno, fl.

SENDING

| LBW 39 | Joy to the world |
| WOV 638 | Holy Child within the manger |

ADDITIONAL HYMNS AND SONGS

TWC 271	Christ is coming!
UMH 197	Ye who claim the faith of Jesus
W3 365	Hills of the north, rejoice
WOV 634	Sing of Mary, pure and lowly

OTHER SUGGESTIONS

See listings for Mary, Mother of Our Lord (August 15, 1999).

MUSIC FOR THE DAY

CHORAL

Diemer, Emma Lou. "Lift Up Your Heads, O Mighty Gates." PRE 392-00922. SATB, kybd.

Distler, Hugo. "Maria Walks Amid the Thorn." CPH 98-2306. SAB.

Ferguson, John. "He Comes to Us as One Unknown." AFP 11-10742. SATB, org.

Hillert, Richard. "Come, Thou Long-Expected Jesus" in *Church Choir Book II*. CPH 97-56. SAB.

Ierley, Merritt. "Hear, O Thou Shepherd of Israel." CPH 98-216. SATB, kybd.

Schütz, Heinrich. "O Gracious Lord, Our God." CPH 98-155. SS, org.

Sutcliffe, James H. "The Cherry Tree Carol." ECS 4983. SATB.

Willan, Healey, and Carl Schalk. "The Great O Antiphons of Advent." CPH 97-584. SATB.

Young, Jeremy. "Oh, Come, Oh, Come, Emmanuel." AFP 11-10891. 2 pt, kybd, opt cong.

CHILDREN'S CHOIRS

Hopson, Hal. "A Star, A Song." CGA 167. U, kybd.

Roth, John. "Rejoice, Rejoice!" CPH 98-3229 (Logia). U, opt solo, cong. kybd.

KEYBOARD/INSTRUMENTAL

Bach, J. S. "Fugue in g minor," (The Little). Org.

Chauvet, Alexis. *Organ Noels for the Time of Christmas*. CPH 97-6301. Org/kybd.

Clarke, Andrew. "Toccata on 'Veni, Emmanuel'" in *The Oxford Book of Christmas Organ Music*. OXF 01937511240. Org.

Ramsey, Peter A. "Joy to the World!" AFP 11-10719. Inst, kybd, opt vc/bsn.

HANDBELL

Folkening, John. "Come, O Long-Expected Jesus" in *Ten Hymn Accompaniments for Handbells*, set. 1. CPH 97-6022. 3 oct.

Kinyon, Barbara B. "O Come, O Come, Emmanuel." HOP 1565. 2 oct.

Wiltse, Carl. "The Angel Gabriel." Stained Glass Music. 3-4 oct.

PRAISE ENSEMBLE

Chepponis, James. "Magnificat." GIA G-2302. 2 pt, fl, ob, org, cong.

Fry, Steven. "Lift Up Your Heads" in *Integrity's Hosanna! Come and Worship Songbook*. INT.

Hanson, Handt/Murakami, Paul. "Be Near Us, Lord Jesus" in *Spirit Calls, Rejoice!* CCF.

Schramm, Ruth Elaine. "God With Us." ALF GC952. SATB.

MONDAY, DECEMBER 21
WINTER SOLSTICE
ST. THOMAS, APOSTLE

Thomas is perhaps remembered most as "doubting Thomas," the disciple who needed to place his hand in the wounded side of the crucified and risen Lord. Yet Thomas also made one of the strongest confessions of faith in the New Testament: "My Lord and my God."

The observance of Thomas occurs on the winter solstice, the shortest day and longest night of the year. As Thomas needed to see in order to believe, we also long to see the return of the sun and the increase of daylight hours. Thomas is an Advent saint who invites us to name our doubts and fears as we yearn for the coming of the light. As Christmas draws near, it is a day to gather around the four candles of the Advent wreath and sing of the coming light. Consider using "Light one candle to watch for Messiah" (WOV 630).

63

CHRISTMAS

Grace has come to us in Jesus

IMAGES OF THE SEASON

Even where birds of paradise and poinsettias grow wild, it gets dark early this time of year. Even orange groves that nestle colorfully against the foothills by day need smudge pots to chase away the threat of frost at night. At the turn of the year, those who sit on floats or march in parades shiver in their sequins.

Winter in the sunbelt may be more subtle than elsewhere, but it's no less perilous. The danger comes not from dramatic blizzards or subarctic temperatures, but from floods, mudslides, or impenetrable fog. The once-a-decade sprinkling of snow or ice makes headlines and leaves thousands stranded or injured because they don't know how to maneuver in slippery conditions; they have neither the plows nor salt trucks nor special crews that other areas take for granted.

What endangers the body affects the soul. Winter puts both spirit and flesh at risk. Oblique rays of sun are too pale and short-lived for comfort, and the world looks distorted in the sharply slanting light. Skin is raw, and so are nerves. Emotions are brittle as ice. Survival—particularly for the weak and the very young—is anything but assured. Anxiety and depression loom as constant hazards.

And so we huddle together for warmth. We draw together in community to protect one another—especially the most vulnerable—and to strengthen one another in spirit. The whole community is made stronger as we attend to those who are most in need, or allow ourselves to be cared for in our own times of frailty.

We reinforce the bonds of friendship by going out of our way to visit those we otherwise rarely see. We spend time doing nothing but spending time with those we love, enjoying their company for its own sake. We dress up and visit. We feast and sing. In our festivity we proclaim that we are more than creatures frightened by the elements. We insist that life is good.

The human impulse to counter the ravages of winter with spiritual resistance appears to be ancient and deeply rooted. People in frigid climates have long made it a point to come together and make merry, precisely in the words of an eighteenth-century carol, "to drive the cold winter away." (From "All hayle to the dayes," #138 in *The New Oxford Book of Carols*. Hugh Keyte and Andrew Parrott, eds. New York: Oxford University Press, 1992.)

Subtle or harsh, winter begins in late December, on the shortest day of the calendar year. It is—by cosmic definition—as gloomy as it can get. On this date—the winter solstice—a reversal happens. From now on the light will start to grow, even if only by a minute or two each day. Year after year this turning is cause for celebration: night has not prevailed; we've made it through the bleakest point!

What we celebrate at Christmas—the good news, the light in our darkness—is that the Word of God has become *flesh*. Grace has come to us in Jesus of Nazareth, born truly human, flesh and blood—*for us*. We encounter the Word made flesh through our own flesh: in the taste of holiday food, the glow of Christmas tree lights, the sound of caroling. And so secular traditions at home and in public are capable of echoing back the church's joyous strains: stringing lights along the roof . . . touching flaming wick to beeswax candle; carving fruited ham for dinner guests . . . distributing bread and wine among the baptized.

Spiritual renewal occurs through our senses. We come to know the Word of God both through words and through experiences that go powerfully beyond what any of our words can express. "The true meaning of Christmas" is not ethereal, but earthy—embodied—and thoroughly material, if not materialistic. For this reason the pull of nostalgia is not to be disdained. Some of us dream of a white Christmas. Others are homesick for a yuletide walk along the beach, or pastel-flocked trees.

Specific memories and longings are signs of deep connection to the particular relationships and places we cherish. We recall with affection relatives and friends with whom we have shopped at clearance sales, cheered at bowl games, or watched the ball descend at midnight in Times Square. And we meet Jesus Christ not in general, and not only in church, but in the particular people who have touched our lives, in the specific places we have come to live.

Jesus was born, says the author of the book of Hebrews, not to help angels, but the descendants of Sarah and Abraham. We are particular human beings, whose life in the flesh includes sorrow as well as joy. We often confuse celebration with consumerism, or seek pleasure apart from mutual relationship. Many feel acutely the distance between the families they would like, and the actual ones that sometimes betray and disappoint. Many feel their earthly tent wearing away and look for lasting salvation, an end to exile, and a place they can call home.

Good news of great joy: before the foundation of the world God destined us for adoption as children through Jesus Christ. And so Christ is born for us. The Word became flesh and lived—in Greek, "pitched a tent"—among us. Came to dwell in our own house of flesh, becoming like his brothers and sisters in every respect, and changing the family forever.

When a baby is born, there are so many things to do—often, all at once. The infant has to be bathed, and held, and rocked, and changed, and fed. But what's most important—and absolutely essential—is that the caregivers allow themselves to be knocked head over heels with delight over this child in particular; to brim with joy over his or her presence in this particular family, among these particular friends; to approach the child in wonder, awe, and love—and to spend time with the newborn, not "doing" anything beyond taking in the miracle, savoring the goodness, the blessing, of life. With this birth, the home is forever changed.

The story of the birth of Jesus in Bethlehem can remind us to regard ourselves and other children of God with wonder, awe, and love. During these twelve days of Christmas we may find ourselves doing many things: serving at a homeless shelter or singing in a concert. These doings are necessary and good. But other seasons of the year are more suited to action. For these twelve days, we are to spend time not "doing things" so much as taking in the miracle. We delight in those particular people and places God has given us to love. We dwell on the gifts we've been given and enjoy the company around us. We proclaim through our festivity that life is good. We are in the presence of Christ, our brother, knowing our house of flesh to be forever changed, and feeling ourselves to be home at last.

67

ENVIRONMENT AND ART FOR THE SEASON

The environment for the festival of Christmas is in strong contrast to the

period of preparation that preceded this event. Christmas Eve is light,

blazing amid the darkness and despair of the

world. The church environment should reflect this

announcement to the world in creative visual and physical dimension. Planning for a celebration of this importance can be daunting. This celebration must be given renewed attention each year by worship leaders, committees, altar guilds, musicians, and artisans in order to provide a creative, tasteful reflection upon the central drama of the Word revealed to us.

In publicizing events of the Christmas season, design the announcements specifically to serve this season of events. Make clear the reality of Jesus' birth, vital in the life of the parish and its witness to the world. A simple textual listing of the services of the season will not convey the significance of this festive time. Use well-designed graphical art (these days available for use with computers) to tell the story of Christ's birth visually. Look for just one or two good images and use them prominently in newsletters and brochures listing service times and other information about the season. The news of Jesus' birth should not be accompanied by nifty slogans or sweet sentimental gimmicks. The universe and all creation rejoices at the birth of God's son. The environment for this event must be the best that we as God's messengers of this good news can offer.

EXTERIOR ENVIRONMENT

What can be done to work with the architectural style and to embellish this building for this celebration? For many, the use of natural garlands of evergreen or other live greens are useful. Explore combining these greens with slender banners of white and metallic silver or gold fabric. Position these to fall gracefully from porticoes, pediments, and arches. Vertical strands of bells can be affixed to the sides of entrances or to exterior banner standards to mirror this festive occasion with sound as well as sight. Study and refine the decorations to provide the most strikingly tasteful composition, while focusing on the central purpose of the decorations.

Fresh wreaths of pine, holly, ivy, juniper, and bay leaves can be used appropriately to communicate the spirit of celebration. Decorations should enhance the architectural style and scale of the area wherever they are used.

Evening events, especially Christmas Eve, afford an opportunity for a blaze of light upon the church and its decorations. Special flood lighting can be used for this purpose, or if weather and the setting permits use luminaries, ornamental lanterns and other candle stands to define walkways and other spaces. The warmth of candlelight communicates a special sense of hospitality and welcome as one approaches the church.

Carillons, brass, and bell choirs may be positioned to proclaim the joy over Jesus' birth while people are entering.

NARTHEX/ENTRANCE

Just as with the Advent season, the narthex should provide visual clarity about this most special season of the nativity of our Lord. This clarity can be accomplished through the thoughtful use of different media, perhaps changing or expanding with each Sunday or event.

Keep the art timely, discernible, and well illuminated. Depending upon the religious art, candles will

focus subtle attention on the artistic expression. Gauge the amount of decoration carefully, tasteful but not overpowering. Usually this space is especially crowded with people, so all decorations must not impede movement in and out of the church.

An excellent focal point to consider in the narthex and other gathering spaces might be a white seasonal banner that complements the paraments. A banner can be mounted on the wall or placed in a stand, perhaps later to be carried in procession. Banners should have a special place that is secure and well illuminated.

In addition to visual elements, the scent from natural plants and herbs provides a welcome environment for the festival, and can be combined with the decorations in both gathering and worship spaces.

Minimize extraneous nonessential materials throughout the building. Committees should regularly review and establish guidelines for all posters and other materials placed in gathering spaces, corridors, and worship areas. Tired or outdated pieces should be given a new home or discarded.

WORSHIP SPACE

The Christmas Eve environment for worship is in contrast to the more spartan setting used during the Sundays in Advent. This celebration demands special attention to every detail. Brass, silver vessels, and other worship appointments should be polished and sparkling. All vestments must be clean and pressed. New candles should be used.

Practices vary with each congregation, but nothing induces a sense of hospitality, warmth, and wonder as the abundance of candlelight. Beeswax candles in particular offer a subtle fragrance and warmth not offered by the more white stearic candles. While the initial cost of beeswax candles are more expensive, they burn economically when used with followers. The occasion warrants their consideration.

Since many decorations and candles are often used throughout the church at Christmas, always have numerous fire extinguishers ready. Make certain all worship leaders and ushers are familiar with their location and use. Has a regular cycle of maintaining fire extinguishers been followed? More importantly, have safety issues been addressed regarding the use of candles in the worship space? Though many people enjoy pew candles, their use may not be very safe. Consider wall sconces instead (well above people's heads and clothing).

Most important to this festival are the central furnishings and symbols of the church. While decorations, flowers, plants, and greens are important, they are always used in a manner to enhance and embellish the central elements. Altar, pulpit, and font are the central symbols in the worship space. They should not be overwhelmed by other elements or decorations.

White paraments and vestments are used as visual symbols of Jesus' purity and divinity. They should be designed to enhance and complement the liturgical action and space in which they are used. Their symbols should be well designed to reflect the season. Processional style banners of complementing design can also enhance the worship environment. During the services, they should be positioned to embrace the assembly, and not compete visually with the central symbols and places of liturgical action.

The crèche adds a beautiful artistic witness to the incarnation of our Lord. A well-designed and crafted crèche may provide a special lasting image of the season. For many congregations a fine crèche is a unique piece of art to be treasured for generations.

Every season offers distinct environmental opportunity for change and improvement. The Christmas season should use decorative materials that will maintain their shape and freshness for the entire twelve days. Committees and worship leaders need to plan carefully for maintaining the festive character established at Christmas Eve. Dare to introduce new environmental elements as the season progresses. Work with the setting to incorporate meaningful changes in the composition of worship appointments, vessels, different communion breads or wine, candles, and a variety of eucharistic vestments. Be discerning, never allowing wilting plants and decorations to become a visual distraction to the festive environment. Good comprehensive planning and counsel from experienced liturgical designers are two things that may help in the process for improving the environment and art in this and any season.

69

PREACHING WITH THE SEASON

If Advent is to be more than a time of preparation for the celebration of

Christmas, if it is to call up the deepest longings of the human spirit, then

Christmas itself had better be more than a nostalgic celebration of innocence, warmth, and a vague sense of goodwill. There must be more to Christmas than candlelight being passed during the singing of a lullaby, and yet that "more" must in some way include the meanings of candlelight on the longest night of the year and of the impulse to guard and comfort an infant.

During Advent the presence of Christ calls forth in us the sense of longing—for the fulfillment of God's promises, for all of humanity and all of creation to be included in the embrace that has enfolded us, for all of our being to welcome that embrace. During the Christmas season the presence of God's Word calls forth in us the sense of wonder—at the constantly amazing notion of the incarnation, at the "blessed exchange" in which Jesus trades his righteousness for our sin, finitude, and separation, at our inclusion in the mission and the story of the Trinity. What are the central meanings of this festival? How do they illumine this particular facet of Jesus' presence? And how does Christmas fulfill the expectations of its preparatory season?

A clue to the central meaning of Christmas is found in its dual name and nature. Some of the festivals of the church year commemorate an event or person—the

Conversion of St. Paul, for instance, or St. Mary Magdalene. Others center on a doctrine or idea—Trinity or Corpus Christi. Of all the festivals, Christmas is the only one that is by name both an "ideafest" and an "eventfest." It is called both the festival of the nativity of our Lord and the festival of the incarnation. Now, it is not unheard of for an event and a doctrine to be closely connected, such as the ascension and Christ the king. Only here, however, are they linked on a single day.

This juxtaposition provides a clue to the meaning of Christmas. Here are brought together two fundamentally different things—story and reflection, concrete and abstract, "happening" and philosophy, one-time occurrence and habitual mode of communicating. Here they meet and complement each other. The festival of the incarnation keeps the festival of the nativity from being a nice story, irrelevant to our lives or experience. The festival of the nativity keeps the festival of the incarnation from being a bloodless celebration of pantheism, removed from the particular and central person of Jesus.

Because these two themes are juxtaposed, their connection and mutual dependence are inescapable. They are two fundamentally different things brought into a new unity by the person of Jesus. This juxtaposition is a central one for Christianity and one of the reasons why the cross is our central symbol. The cross is not only a reminder of the execution of Jesus, but a summary for his entire ministry. The cross is itself two fundamentally different things—vertical and horizontal lines—juxtaposed in a new reality. At Christmas the cross finds its expression in the festival's central meaning: Jesus is Immanuel, "God with us." Christmas takes great pains to proclaim seriously both the noun and the prepositional phrase in that name/title.

At Christmas, no less than at Christ the King, Jesus is identified with "the least of these" who deserve care, respect, and inclusion. God is with us, and "us" includes such people as unwed mothers and cuckolds, minimum wage shift workers and New Age itinerants—even domestic animals, suitable only for harness and stew pot.

Martin Luther broke through the sentimentality surrounding this story right to its heart and mission (From Roland H. Bainton, *The Martin Luther Christmas Book*. Philadelphia: Fortress Press, 1958):

> There are many of you in this congregation who think to yourselves: "If only I had been there! How quick I would have been to help the Baby! I would have washed his linen. . . ." You say that because you know how great Christ is, but if you had been there at that time you would have done no better than the people of Bethlehem. Childish and silly thoughts are these! Why don't you do it now? You have Christ in your neighbor. You ought to serve him, for what you do to your neighbor in need you do to the Lord Christ himself. (P. 38)

Such an insight would also be valuable to the preacher assigned December 27, even if the lessons for the First Sunday after Christmas are used instead of those for John the Evangelist. The massacre of the innocents, which is the gospel reading for the First Sunday after Christmas, reminds us that in some way all such victims are martyrs, whether or not they die because of their faith. It also reminds us that the *logos* is not without rivals in claiming ultimate allegiance and importance.

70

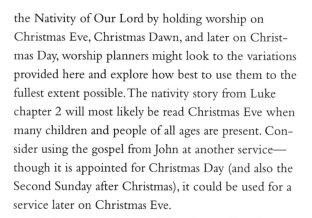

PLANNING AHEAD FOR THE SEASON

While many people may think that the season of Christmas stops with

Christmas Day itself, according to the church's calendar it has only begun.

In the not-so-distant past, congregations often

gathered on Christmas Eve for hanging of the greens and Christmas carol singing (Christmas worship itself was typically not until Christmas Day). With several days between the Fourth Sunday in Advent (December 20) and Christmas Eve this year, a tree decorating party on the afternoon of the last Sunday in Advent, followed by carol singing and a warm punch served in the fellowship hall might be a good tradition to begin (or renew). This gathering could be an adequate response to the oft-heard lament that "we don't sing enough Christmas carols."

Encourage groups and organizations of the congregation to schedule Christmas parties and programs during the twelve days of Christmas (December 25–January 5) so that Advent can retain its own distinct character. While this notion may be unpopular at first, the week between Christmas and New Year's Day is actually a quieter time for many people, with schools on vacation and many workers having extra days off. Even though a number of people may be traveling to visit relatives, for others, it can also be a less hectic time than the days leading up to Christmas. People may enjoy having the opportunity to focus on the more spiritual aspects of the season now.

Congregations with names relating to the twelve days of Christmas—Nativity, Incarnation, St. Stephen (December 26), St. John (December 27), Christ or Immanuel (Name of Jesus, January 1)—may be encouraged to make more of this time, perhaps with a "potluck" supper followed by the Sunday school Christmas program. It is also the time to plan carol singing by groups to homebound members' homes and to nursing homes. Those with calendars booked solid in the days before Christmas may have some free time now to enjoy these worthy pursuits.

While few congregations will take complete advantage of the lectionary's three sets of readings for

the Nativity of Our Lord by holding worship on Christmas Eve, Christmas Dawn, and later on Christmas Day, worship planners might look to the variations provided here and explore how best to use them to the fullest extent possible. The nativity story from Luke chapter 2 will most likely be read Christmas Eve when many children and people of all ages are present. Consider using the gospel from John at another service—though it is appointed for Christmas Day (and also the Second Sunday after Christmas), it could be used for a service later on Christmas Eve.

Perhaps more than anything else, reading the majestic first chapter from the gospel according to John on Christmas Day provides a purpose for worshipers to gather. Even if your congregation has not had the practice of gathering for worship on Christmas Day, consider it as a possibility. While Christmas Day may never achieve the popularity that Christmas Eve has with worshipers, it could meet a variety of needs—those who must work or travel on Christmas Eve, some who prefer not to come out at night, and yet others who may appreciate the relative quiet of Christmas Day worship. Christmas Day also has a full set of carols and anthems that are most appropriate for the morning: "Oh, come, all ye faithful" (LBW 45), "When Christmas morn is dawning" (LBW 59), and "All hail to you, O blessed morn!" (LBW 73). Of the many reasons for coming together to worship on this day, consider the overwhelming fact that God is worthy to be praised!

While many people may welcome the relative quiet in the days following Christmas, some may experience it as a kind of "let down." College students and others who have returned home for the holidays may appreciate opportunities for fellowship and service during this time. Gathering for an evening of informal carol singing at homebound members' homes, followed by refreshments and board games in the church hall or a

71

member's home may be just what is needed during this lull after Christmas. Furthermore, this kind of gathering might be more possible in the last week of December than it could be during the frequently more crowded social calendars prior to Christmas. This opportunity can be especially good for those who are no longer a part of the week-to-week life of the congregation to feel as if they do still have a home within it.

Consider also having post-high school young people take part in the worship leadership on the First Sunday after Christmas (this year also the festival of St. John, Apostle and Evangelist). Some may be able to serve as lectors, musicians, communion assistants, or in a variety of other ways. At the same time, be sensitive to the fact that they may want to have another opportu-

nity to worship with their families. A special fellowship time for young adults following worship on this Sunday could be planned. Arrangements could be as simple as calling out for pizza.

The festival of St. John, Apostle and Evangelist may be observed by many congregations in lieu of the First Sunday after Christmas. The festival is one way to elaborate on the season of Christmas itself, rather than a departure from the twelve days. The first two readings for the festival of St. John continue with the light and darkness images that are so much a part of the Christmas celebration, as well as being a major part of the gospel according to John. Congregations named after St. John might find special ways to observe the festival this year, especially since it happens to fall on a Sunday.

ORDO FOR THE SEASON

For the festival services of the Christmas season, worship leaders might plan not to include a brief order for confession and forgiveness prior to the service, especially if the season of Advent included one each week. Even when a confes-

sional rite does not precede the liturgy, there still can (or should) be opportunity for confessing our corporate misdeeds and failures as a part of the prayers.

Festive services during the Christmas season might include both the Kyrie and the hymn of praise (or perhaps the hymn of praise alone) as part of the gathering rite. Though this portion of the liturgy deserves to be somewhat more extended during this season than at others, be careful about not making it unduly long. How much music is needed for the assembly to gather? A beloved carol as an entrance hymn, a Kyrie, and a hymn of praise are certainly plenty to get everyone in. If your congregation has genuine interest in keeping services so that they not go too long, here is one area to watch.

Most congregations regularly exchange the peace during the Holy Communion liturgy. If your congregation does not do this, consider making it a part of the

Christmas season, since peace is one of the gifts we celebrate at this time of year. Remember that the greeting is a sharing of the *Lord's* peace. Our greetings of peace to one another are ways in which God's love is incarnated.

Eucharistic Prayer B for Christmas from page 66 of *WOV, Leaders Edition* might be used during this season. The more festive liturgies during this season (particularly Christmas Eve) seem to long for yet a more complete eucharistic prayer, either Prayer I or Prayer II in *LBW, Ministers Edition*. The aspects of remembering many of the things God has done throughout history are particularly strong in either of the first two prayers presented in *LBW*, and for that reason are especially fitting for the Christmas festival. The congregational responses indicated in Eucharistic Prayer I and Eucharistic Prayer II of *LBW* also seem to add to the joy of the celebration. They are strong ways in which we acclaim that we are a part of God's story ourselves.

ASSEMBLY SONG FOR THE SEASON

Although our secular world tells us that December 25 (or perhaps January 1) is the end of the Christmas season, the church is again asking us to walk a bit out of step with culture. What fun it can be to show that the church parties for twelve

whole days, long after the wrappings are cleaned up and gifts have been exchanged. A casual remembrance of a historic event may take only one evening to complete, but celebrating the God-made-flesh, present in our time and place in history, takes much longer. It also takes people and energy, both of which can be difficult to locate on December 26. Some congregations are in areas where everyone seems to head to some other home for the holidays. Others are in the hometown to where everyone is heading. Knowing your community is critical for worship planning during the twelve days of Christmas. Developing a Christmas choir for the liturgies within the twelve days may be a way to incorporate the voices of those home for the holidays and/or to provide music when many regular singers are away.

At Christmas, it may be possible to use liturgical music from other parts of the church year, making an aural connection. Some examples:

- The same music that accompanies the Alleluia announcing the gospel on Easter Day could be used at Christmas.
- In some traditions, where the Trisagion (see WOV 603, for an example) is sung during the procession of the cross at the Good Friday liturgy, it is also sung in place of the Kyrie at Christmas, making a connection between the wood of the crib and the wood of the cross.
- To be effective for worshipers, these musical connections would need to be used consistently over a period of years. Although not every worshiper can articulate what is being done, the subconscious effect can be powerful.

For musicians, rarely is there a concern about finding appropriate music for Christmas. More often, the challenge is how to use all the great music available. A few possibilities to incorporate more music are:

- Singing many carols as the prelude (or as part of the prelude), as well as during communion.
- Using appropriate Christmas music throughout the twelve days and even until the Presentation of our Lord on February 2 or the Transfiguration of our Lord.
- Using familiar carols as liturgical music, such as "What child is this?" as the offertory song, or "Good Christian friends" after communion.
- Have a hymn/carol sing during the twelve days. Often a "post-Christmas" depression sets in after December 25 when activity subsides suddenly.

In some places, additional worship opportunities are common throughout Advent, with little happening during the twelve days of Christmas. However, those weeks of Advent are filled with an overabundance of activity while little happens between Christmas and Epiphany. A simple service of evening prayer could work well in providing daily opportunities for worship through the days of Christmas. When trained appropriately, laypersons can lead this service, providing an opportunity for pastors to be worshipers themselves. Many congregations have several members, especially youth, who can play piano. They could be recruited and trained as early as summer to lead the singing for Christmas evening prayer. One worship folder could be prepared, if needed at all, with only readings and hymns changing each day. Such simplicity may be a pleasant and rewarding relief to the clutter that often accompanies this season.

73

MUSIC FOR THE SEASON

VERSE AND OFFERTORY

Boehnke, Paul. *Festive Verse Settings for Christmas, Epiphany and Transfiguration.* MSM-80-100. SATB, opt kybd.

Hillert, Richard. *Verses and Offertory Sentences I: Advent through Christmas.* CPH 97-5501. U.

Wetzler, Robert. *Verses and Offertories: Advent 1–Baptism of Our Lord.* AFP 11-09541. SATB, kybd.

CHORAL MUSIC FOR THE SEASON

Bach, J. S./John Leavitt. "Christmas Joy: Chorales from the Christmas Oratorio." AFP 11-10510. SATB, kybd.

Ellingboe, Bradley. "Jesus, Jesus Rest Your Head." AFP 11-10725. SATB.

Ferguson, John. "Unto Us Is Born God's Son." AFP 11-10449. SATB, org.

Gardiner, John. "Tomorrow Shall Be My Dancing Day." OXF 84.356. SATB, kybd.

Hurd, David. "A Cradle Song." AFP 11-10460. SATB, org.

Koehring, David. "Rejoice and Be Merry." PLY CC-108. SATB, org.

Larson, Lloyd. "Bring You Good News." ALF 16449. SATB.

Lovelace, Austin. "The Angels' Gloria." AFP 11-10580. SAB, kybd.

Praetorius, Michael. "In dulci jubilo." GIA G-4151. SB.

Schalk, Carl. "Before the Marvel of This Night." AFP 11-2005. Fl/ob, hrn, str 11-2004; hb, harp/gtr, str bass 11-5180. SATB, org.

Schalk, Carl. "Where Shepherds Lately Knelt." AFP 11-2456. SATB, org.

Schram, Ruth Elaine. "The First Christmas Gift." WAR 6540300801. SATB, opt hb.

Seivewright, Andrew. "Lullaby of the Madonna." AFP 11-10584. SATB, org.

Shepperd, Mark. "Shepherd Play Your Pipes Tonight." AFP 11-10728. STAB, pno, opt ob.

Somerset Anthem Books for SAB Choirs, vol. IV: Christmastide. ECS 5140.

Spencer, Philip. "I Sing the Birth Was Born Tonight." AFP 11-10583. SATB, kybd, C inst.

CHILDREN'S CHORAL MUSIC FOR THE SEASON

Collins, Dori Erwin. "Hasten Now, O Shepherds." AFP 11-10726. U, desc, pno, fl, gtr, perc.

Ford, Sandra. "Once on a Quiet Night." ABI 081246. U, opt 2 pt, kybd.

Schulz, Johann, and David Cherwien. "Your Little Ones, Dear Lord." CPH 98-3356. U or SA, fl, org.

Young, Philip M. "When Christ, the Son of Mary." AFP 11-10779. U, kybd, opt hb.

INSTRUMENTAL MUSIC FOR THE SEASON

Farlee, Robert Buckley. "Carols for Oboe and Organ." AFP 11-10865. Org, ob/cl.

Held, Wilbur. "Two Traditional Carols." AFP 11-831. Org, fl/vln.

Leavitt, John. "Christmas Suite: Six Carols for Organ." AFP 11-10857.

Lind, Robert. "On December Five and Twenty!" AFP 11-10395.

Lochstampfor, Mark. "'Twas in the Moon of Wintertime." AFP 11-10613. Org.

Osterland, Karl. "I Wonder as I Wander." AFP 11-10859. Org.

Pelz, Walter. "Hymn Settings for Organ and Brass, set 3." AFP 11-10433. Brass 11-10434. Org, brass.

Ramsey, Peter. "Joy to the World: Two Carols for Solo Instrument, Keyboard and Bass Continuo." AFP 11-10719. C/B-flat inst, kybd, vc/bsn.

Wasson, Laura E. "A Christmas Season Tapestry: For Piano." AFP 11-10861. Pno.

Young, Jeremy. "Pianoforte Christmas." AFP 11-10716. Pno.

HANDBELL MUSIC FOR THE SEASON

Helman, Michael. "The Friendly Beasts and We Wish You a Merry Christmas." AFP 11-10807. 3-5 oct.

Helman, Michael. "There's a Star in the East" in *Rise Up, Shepherd.* AFP 11-10721. 2-3 oct.

Larson, Katherine. "Children at the Manger: A Christmas Medley." AFP 11-10623. 3-4 oct.

McChesney, Kevin. "Angel Glory." AFP 11-10515. Hb.

Moklebust, Cathy. "Rise Up, Shepherd, and Follow." CGA CGB184. 2-3 oct, perc.

Tucker, Margaret R. "A German Christmas." CGA CGA595. 3-5 oct hb CGB134; 2-3 oct hb, fl CGB135; str pts CGB136. SATB.

Tucker, Margaret R. "A Scandinavian Christmas." CPH 97-5927. 4-5 oct.

ALTERNATE WORSHIP TEXTS

CONFESSION AND FORGIVENESS

In the name of the Father, and of the ✝ Son, and of the Holy
     Spirit.
Amen

The true light has come into the world
in the Word made flesh.
Let us bring our sin into the light of God,
that we may be healed.

Silence for reflection and self-examination

God of our salvation,
we have failed to respond to your life-giving Spirit
in our relationships with you, with one another,
and with your creation.
Have mercy for the sake of Jesus, your gift to us.
Forgive us by grace,
renew us in love,
and lead us with joy
so that we may bear your peace to all the earth. Amen

Blessed be God
who chose you in Christ!
God forgives all your trespasses;
in Christ you are children of the Most High;
you are marked with the seal of the Holy Spirit,
that you may live to the glory of God.
Amen

GREETING

To us is born this day a Savior, Jesus Christ our Lord.
Alleluia, alleluia, alleluia!
The grace, mercy, and peace of God be with you always.
And also with you.

OFFERTORY PRAYER

Ever-sustaining God,
you bless us with life,
with a world to sustain us,
and with one another.
Receive these gifts we offer
so that through us, all people may know
your steadfast love in Jesus, our Savior. Amen

INVITATION TO COMMUNION

God is with us in Jesus, our Immanuel.
Come to this table where God comes to us.

POST-COMMUNION PRAYER

Gracious God, you gave your only Son
that we may know and love you
with body, heart, and mind.
United in the body of Christ,
may we glorify and praise you in our lives
for all that we have heard and seen
in the wonder of the Word made flesh,
Jesus Christ our Lord.
Amen

BENEDICTION

May God, who in these last days
has spoken to us by a Son, bless you.
May Christ, born of Mary,
enthroned in a manger, bless you.
May the Holy Spirit,
power of the Most High, bless you.
Amen

DISMISSAL

Glory to God in the highest!
Peace to God's people on earth!
Go in peace. Serve the Lord.
Thanks be to God.

75

SEASONAL RITES

BLESSING OF THE NATIVITY SCENE

This blessing may be used after the sermon or after the communion of the people on Christmas Eve.

O Lord our God, with Mary and Joseph, angels and shepherds, and the animals in the stable, we gather around your Son, born for us. Bless us with your holy presence and inspire us to help those who have no place to dwell. Be with us that we might share Christ's love with all the world, for he is our light and salvation. Glory in heaven and peace on earth, now and forever.

Amen

LITURGY FOR CHRISTMAS EVE

Christmas Eve liturgies sometimes include additional elements, such as congregational and choral music and the lighting of candles held by the congregation. Care should be taken that these elements support rather than obscure the primary gathering of the community around word and sacrament. It is most appropriate that the eucharist be celebrated on Christmas Eve, for in this holy mystery, the Word is made flesh for us as we receive the gift of Christ's body and blood. Here are suggestions for incorporating seasonal elements within the basic structure of the liturgy.

GATHERING RITE

An extended period of pre-service music may precede the liturgy and may include congregational carols and hymns, choir anthems, and instrumental pieces.

PROCLAMATION OF THE BIRTH OF CHRIST

The service may begin with the Proclamation of the Birth of Christ, taken from the ancient martyrology. The proclamation should be understood as the announcement of the incarnation within human history rather than a literal counting of years. The lights may be turned down, and, following a period of silence, the proclamation is preferably sung or read; the proclamation may be sung on one note. The congregation may face the reader/cantor at the entrance to the church.

Today, the twenty-fifth day of December,
unknown ages from the time when God created the heavens and
the earth and then formed man
and woman in his own image.

Several thousand years after the flood,
when God made the rainbow shine forth as a sign
of the covenant.

Twenty-one centuries from the time of Abraham and Sarah;
thirteen centuries after Moses led the people of Israel out of Egypt.

Eleven hundred years from the time of Ruth and the Judges;
one thousand years from the anointing of David as king;
in the sixty-fifth week according to the prophecy of Daniel.

In the one hundred and ninety-fourth Olympiad;
the seven hundred and fifty-second year from the foundation
of the city of Rome;

The forty-second year of the reign of Octavian Augustus;
the whole world being at peace,
Jesus Christ, the eternal God and Son of the eternal Father,
desiring to sanctify the world by his most merciful coming,
being conceived by the Holy Spirit,
and nine months having passed since his conception,
was born in Bethlehem of Judea of the Virgin Mary.

Today is the nativity of our Lord Jesus Christ according to the flesh.

Following the proclamation the lights are turned on as the musician(s) introduces the entrance hymn. "Oh, come, all ye faithful" (LBW 45) is an appropriate hymn following the proclamation. The congregation turns to the front as the cross passes them in procession. "Glory to God in the Highest" is the most appropriate hymn of praise for the Christmas season. New settings of Glory to God are found in WOV (WOV 606, 607, 637, and 640). "Angels we have heard on high" (LBW 71) is a hymn which echoes the song of the angels.

76

CANDLELIGHTING: OPTION 1

The liturgy may begin with a service of light as at evening prayer. The congregation may face the entrance to the church and handheld candles may be lit. As the procession passes during the Christmas versicles, all turn to face forward.

CHRISTMAS VERSICLES

These may be sung to the tones given in evening prayer, LBW, p. 142.

The people who walked in darkness have seen a great light.
The light shines in the darkness,
   and the darkness has not overcome it.
Those who dwelt in the land of deep darkness,
   on them has light shined.
We have beheld Christ's glory,
   glory as of the only Son from the Father.
For to us a child is born, to us a Son is given.
In him was life, and the life was the light of all people.

HYMN OF LIGHT

LBW 45   Oh, come, all ye faithful
LBW 49   O savior of our fallen race
LBW 56   The first Noel
LBW 65   Silent night, holy night!

THANKSGIVING FOR LIGHT

Set to music in LBW, p. 144.

The Lord be with you.
And also with you.
Let us give thanks to the Lord our God.
It is right to give him thanks and praise.
Blessed are you, O Lord our God, king of the universe,
   who led your people Israel by a pillar of cloud by day
   and a pillar of fire by night:
   Enlighten our darkness by the light of your Christ;
   may his Word be a lamp to our feet and a light to our path;
   for you are merciful, and you love your whole creation,
   and we, your creatures, glorify you, Father, Son, and Holy Spirit.
Amen
or
Blessed are you, O Lord our God, ruler of the universe.
   In the beginning you created darkness and light
   and in the fullness of time you sent forth your Son,
   the light of the world.
   Enlighten our darkness by the light of your Christ;
   may his word be a lamp to our feet and a light to our path;
   for you are merciful and you love your whole creation,
   and we, your creatures, glorify you,
   Father, Son, and Holy Spirit.
Amen

The service may then continue with the greeting, followed by the hymn of praise and the prayer of the day. Electric lights may be turned on gradually as the hymn of praise is begun (though a rather subdued level of lighting may be desired throughout the service, in order not to overwhelm tree lights and candles). Handheld candles may be extinguished at this time.

CANDLELIGHTING: OPTION 2

Another option for the lighting of handheld candles is to use them at the reading of the gospel. A hymn, such as "The first Noel" (LBW 56) or "Angels, from the realms of glory" (LBW 50), may be sung as hand-held candles are lit. The gospel may be read from the midst of the people. "Silent night, holy night!" (LBW 65) may be sung following the gospel, after which the handheld candles would be extinguished.

CANDLELIGHTING: OPTION 3

A final option for the lighting of handheld candles is at the close of the service. Following the distribution of Holy Communion (or at a service without Holy Communion, following the receipt of the offering and the prayers) handheld candles are lit (instrumental or choral music may accompany the candlelighting).

Reading from John 1:1-14
Fitting if the gospel reading earlier in the service was from Luke 2.
Hymn: "Silent night, holy night!" (LBW 65)
Or other hymn of light, see list in Candlelighting Option 1.

PRAYER

Though written as a post-communion prayer, this prayer also can serve to conclude a service without Holy Communion.

Gracious God, you gave your only Son
   that we may know and love you
   with body, heart, and mind.
   United in the body of Christ,
   may we glorify and praise you in our lives
   for all that we have heard and seen
   in the wonder of the Word made flesh,
   Jesus Christ our Lord.
Amen

BENEDICTION (Sending Hymn)

DISMISSAL

LESSONS AND CAROLS

This service may be used during the Twelve Days of Christmas.

Stand

ENTRANCE HYMN

LBW 45   Oh, come, all ye faithful

WOV 643   Once in royal David's city

DIALOG

The people who walked in darkness have seen a great light.

**The light shines in the darkness, and the darkness has not
overcome it.**

Those who dwelt in the land of deep darkness,

on them light has shined.

**We have beheld Christ's glory, glory as of the only Son from
the Father.**

For to us a child is born, to us a Son is given.

In him was life, and the life was the light of all people.

OPENING PRAYER

The Lord be with you.

And also with you.

Let us pray.

Almighty God, you have filled us with the new light of the Word who
became flesh and lived among us. Let the light of our faith shine in
all we do; through your Son, Jesus Christ our Lord, who lives and
reigns with you and the Holy Spirit, one God, now and forever.

Amen

Sit

First Reading: Isaiah 9:2-7

CAROL

LBW 58   Lo, how a rose is growing

Second Reading: Micah 5:2-5a

CAROL

LBW 41   O little town of Bethlehem

Third Reading: Luke 1:26-35, 38

CAROL

LBW 40   What child is this

WOV 634   Sing of Mary, pure and lowly

Fourth Reading: Luke 2:1-7

CAROL

WOV 642   I wonder as I wander

WOV 644   Away in a manger

Fifth Reading: Luke 2:8-16

CAROL

LBW 44   Infant holy, infant lowly

WOV 636   Before the marvel of this night

Sixth Reading: Luke 2:21-36

CAROL

LBW 184   In his temple now behold him

May also be sung to Regent Square, LBW 50.

Seventh Reading: Matthew 2:1-11

CAROL

LBW 56   The first Noel

WOV 646   We three kings of Orient are

Eighth Reading: Matthew 2:13-18

CAROL

WOV 639   Oh, sleep now, holy baby

or Coventry Carol (*The Hymnal 1982*, 247)

Ninth Reading: John 1:1-14

CAROL

LBW 42   Of the Father's love begotten

LBW 57   Let our gladness have no end

Stand

RESPONSIVE PRAYER

Glory to God in the highest,

and peace to God's people on earth.

Blessed are you, Prince of Peace. You rule the earth with truth and
justice.

Send your gift of peace to all nations of the world.

Blessed are you, Son of Mary. You share our humanity.

Have mercy on the sick, the dying and all who suffer this day.

Blessed are you, Son of God. You dwell among us as the Word
made flesh.

**Reveal yourself to us in Word and Sacrament that we may bear
your light to all the world.**

THE LORD'S PRAYER

BLESSING AND DISMISSAL

Let us bless the Lord.

Thanks be to God.

May you be filled with the wonder of Mary, the obedience of Joseph,
the joy of the angels, the eagerness of the shepherds, the determination of the magi, and the peace of the Christ Child. Almighty God,
Father, ✛ Son, and Holy Spirit bless you now and forever.

Amen

SENDING HYMN

LBW 60   Hark! The herald angels sing

DECEMBER 24, 1998

INTRODUCTION

Three great vigils mark the festivals of the year: Easter, Pentecost, and Christmas. At this vigil celebration, we join with Christians throughout the world to celebrate the great mystery of our faith: God speaks to us in our words so that we might know God's mercy; God comes to us in human flesh—in Christ's body and blood—so that we might share in God's unfailing love.

It is not a baby's birth we celebrate, but the light of redemption. As Paul reminds us, the grace of God has appeared bringing salvation to all. Christ unites himself to our fragile, mortal lives so that we might know he is with us, always offering us life, health, and salvation. With the heavenly host we sing, "Glory to God in the highest heaven."

PRAYER OF THE DAY

Almighty God, you made this holy night shine with the brightness of the true Light. Grant that here on earth we may walk in the light of Jesus' presence and in the last day wake to the brightness of his glory; through your only Son, Jesus Christ our Lord, who lives and reigns with you and the Holy Spirit, one God, now and forever.

READINGS

Isaiah 9:2-7

Originally, this poem was written to celebrate either the birth or the coronation of a new Davidic king. After the fall of Jerusalem, this poem came to be viewed as an expression of the hope that eventually God would raise up a new ruler who would possess the qualities described in the text.

Psalm 96

Let the heavens rejoice and the earth be glad. (Ps. 96:11)

Titus 2:11-14

The brief letter to Titus is concerned with matters regarding church leadership. Here, the letter cites an early confession of faith as an example of sound Christian doctrine.

Luke 2:1-14 [15-20]

Luke tells the story of Jesus' birth with reference to rulers of the world because this birth has significance for the whole earth, conveying a divine offer of peace.

COLOR   White

THE PRAYERS

Beholding the Word made flesh among us, let us offer our prayers for the church, the world, and all those in need.

A BRIEF SILENCE.

For the nations, and for rulers of every land, that they may work to promote peace on earth. Lord, in your mercy,

hear our prayer.

For the church, that it may faithfully announce the good news of great joy that Christ is born in our midst. Lord, in your mercy,

hear our prayer.

For all who are homeless, poor, lonely, or despised in this world, that the humble birth of Christ give them hope. Lord, in your mercy,

hear our prayer.

For those who are hospitalized, homebound, or sick (especially . . .), that God's grace would enfold them with light and healing. Lord, in your mercy,

hear our prayer.

For guests who join us for worship, and for family and friends not present with us, that the joy and gladness of this night stir our hearts to gratitude for the gifts of love and companionship. Lord, in your mercy,

hear our prayer.

For our congregation, that partaking of the Word made flesh among us, we may be signs of his presence in the world. Lord, in your mercy,

hear our prayer.

HERE OTHER INTERCESSIONS MAY BE OFFERED.

We give thanks for all the faithful departed who rejoiced at the Savior's coming. Keep us in union with them, until we join the angelic host in the never-ending song of adoration and praise. Lord, in your mercy,

hear our prayer.

Receive our prayers, gracious God, as we proclaim the wonders of your love to all the earth, through Jesus Christ our Lord.

Amen

IMAGES FOR PREACHING

You needn't be a rocket scientist to notice how the Christmas story affects those who hear it. It can reactivate deep memories and trigger powerful sentiments. But the challenge is to cut through the dense fog laid over this narrative by our culture, the ways we have abstracted and sanitized this birth story into a generic symbol for universal warm-heartedness. So one more time, read Luke's account and listen for its markedly countercultural details. You will discover that little in it seems to fit.

It begins, of course, with the whole absurd premise to which we have become so accustomed—the divine entry into human flesh—as if such a thing were utterly commonplace. But Luke signals a specific place where such an event happens: in occupied Israel, amidst refugee parents, attended by nomadic shepherds. As the story unfolds, angels leave the heavens where they belong, leading shepherds to leave fields where *they* belong and take a sudden interest in urban infants. And three times over, the sign of the manger is given, the resting place for this child where *no* child belongs. In other words, it is a story of the dispossesed, the out-of-place, the *homeless*.

With those who are displaced or rejected or aimless (which includes us all at one time or another), homelessness becomes a doorway into the Christmas story. For the good news tonight is this: God's home is with the homeless. Jesus doesn't shun lives that are adrift, but comes to be with just such people. Our place, our home is wherever Jesus goes: to outcasts and sinners, the abandoned and forgotten. If in those places we find Jesus, our home is there as well, our lives trained into such godliness, to paraphrase Titus. Our mission becomes Christ's: showing hospitality to the least of all, to those who yet long for home.

WORSHIP MATTERS

Christmas themes echo those of Easter. Remember the refrain of the carol, "Christ was born to save!" On this winter night, we do announce the triumph of light over darkness, hope over despair, and life over death.

The tradition of candlelighting on Christmas Eve, enveloping a darkened church with flickering flames, proclaims the message that "Jesus Christ is the light of the world." The ancient church lit candles at its daily evening prayer, adapted from the Jewish practice of lighting candles each evening and on the evening of the sabbath.

Why not link Christmas candlelighting to God's presence in the everyday, by employing parts of the evening prayer service on Christmas Eve? See candle lighting option 1 in the Seasonal Rites section for this season.

LET THE CHILDREN COME

If your congregation has a nativity scene and you have waited through the days of Advent before putting it up, consider a procession during today's worship that brings the figures to the manger. The procession can begin after the sermon, during the hymn of the day. Consider hymns such as "Good Christian friends, rejoice" (LBW 55), "Hark! The herald angels sing" (LBW 60), or "Away in a manger" (WOV 644). Various members of the congregation, led by the children, can hold high the figures during the procession and arrange them in the manger. Consider placing the wise men at various points around the worship space as a sign of their continued journey during the next twelve days.

MUSIC FOR WORSHIP

SERVICE MUSIC

Although a choral or carol replacement for the Gloria in excelsis is a possibility, perhaps this is the night to take the congregation's best known version of this ancient hymn and dress it up—with a fanfare, with descanting instruments or voices, with handbells—so that it is sung with special festivity.

GATHERING

LBW 45	Oh, come, all ye faithful
WOV 643	Once in royal David's city

PSALM 96

Christopherson, Dorothy. "The Lord Is King." AFP 11-10173. U, cong, kybd.

Haas, David, and Marty Haugen. "Psalm 96: Proclaim to All the Nations" in *Gather Comprehensive*. GIA.

Inwood, Paul. "Psalm 96: Today Is Born Our Savior" in STP, vol. 1.

Ollis, Peter. "Today A Saviour Has Been Born" in PS1.

Wetzler, Robert. PW, Cycle A.

HYMN OF THE DAY

LBW 51   From heaven above
               VOM HIMMEL HOCH

VOCAL RESOURCES

Farlee, Robert Buckley. "Choral Fantasy on a Christmas Hymn."
CPH 98-2698. Inst pts 97-5867. SSATB, solo, ob, DB, kybd.

Hill, Jackson. "From Heaven Above." AFP 11-10055. SATB, org.

INSTRUMENTAL RESOURCES

Burkhardt, Michael. "Vom Himmel hoch" in *Easy Hymn Settings for Advent/Christmas*. MSM 10-015. Org.

Folkening, John. "From Heaven Above to Earth I Come" in *Ten Hymn Accompaniments for Handbells*, set 1. CPH 97-6022. 3 oct.

Leavitt, John. "From Heaven Above" in *A Little Nativity Suite*. AFP 11-10351. Org.

Pelz, Walter L. "Vom Himmel hoch" in *Hymn Settings for Organ and Brass*, set 3. AFP 11-10433. Inst 11-1043. Org, brass.

Pepping, Ernst. "Vom Himmel hoch" in *A New Liturgical Year*, ed. John Ferguson. AFP 11-10810. Org.

ALTERNATE HYMN OF THE DAY

LBW 47   Let all together praise our God
WOV 636   Before the marvel of this night

COMMUNION

LBW 41   O little town of Bethlehem
WOV 642   I wonder as I wander
WOV 644   Away in a manger (or LBW 67)

OTHER SUGGESTIONS

DATH 53   Jesus, child of God

SENDING

LBW 65   Silent night, holy night
LBW 60   Hark! The herald angels sing

ADDITIONAL HYMNS AND SONGS

LBW 69   I am so glad each Christmas Eve
WOV 641   Peace came to earth
PsH 192   The people who in darkness walked
LLC 305   Pastores: a Belén/Oh, come to Bethlehem

MUSIC FOR THE DAY

CHORAL

Bach, J. S. "From Heaven Above." in *Christmas Oratorio*, part 2. HM 153. SATB, kybd.

Ebeling, Johann G. "All My Heart This Night Rejoices" in *Be Glad and Sing*. CPH 97-537. SATB, 2 trbl inst, kybd.

Ellingboe, Bradley. "Jesus, Jesus, Rest Your Head." AFP 11-10725. SATB.

Farlee, Robert Buckley. "This Is the Night." AFP 11-10778. SATB, org.

Hassler, Hans Leo. "O Sing unto the Lord." ECS 708. SATB.

Hobby, Robert. " 'Twas in the Moon of Wintertime." CPH 98-3240. U, cong, fl, hb, fc.

Near, Gerald. "O Magnum Mysterium." CAL 6003. U, org.

Proulx, Richard. "It Came upon the Midnight Clear." GIA G4323. SAB, cong, org, tpt.

Prower, Anthony. "Unto Us A Boy Is Born." CPH 98-3129. SATB, org.

Schein, Johann. "From Heaven Above." GIA G-300. SSB, org.

Sedio, Mark. "Therefore Be Merry." AMSI 701. SATB.

Young, Philip M. "When Christ, the Son of Mary." AFP 11-10779. SA, kybd.

CHILDREN'S CHOIRS

Arenson, Carole. "Bring a Torch, Jeannette, Isabella." KJO 6257. U, kybd, opt hb.

Kosche, Kenneth. "Unto Us a Child Is Born." CGA 694. 2 pt, kybd, opt c tpt.

Lindh, Jody W. "Come Let Us Sing." CGA 729. U/2 pt, opt synth, glock, fl.

Manz, Paul. "Antiphonal Carol." MSM 50-1304. U adults and children, kybd.

KEYBOARD/INSTRUMENTAL

Bach, J. S. "Vom Himmel hoch (Variations)" in *Miscellaneous Compositions on the Chorale*. Org.

Gabrieli, Giovanni/Wolff. "Hodie Christus Natus Est." CPH 97-5565. Brass, org.

Osterland, Karl. "A la ru" in *I Wonder as I Wander*. AFP 11-10858. Org.

Reger, Max. "Weihnachten." Op. 145/3. BRE 2270. Org, vln/fl, cl.

Wasson, Laura. "Silent Night" in *A Christmas Season Tapestry for Piano*. AFP 11-10861. Pno/kybd.

HANDBELL

Behnke, John. "Once in Royal David's City." CPH 97-6249. 2-3 oct, org.

Larson, Katherine. "It Came upon the Midnight Clear." AFP 11-10625. 4 oct.

McChesney, Kevin. "Joy to the World." AFP 11-10472. 3-5 oct.

Moklebust, Cathy. "Silent Night." JEF JH S9176FS. Hb pt JH S9176. Cong, 3-5 oct, org.

PRAISE ENSEMBLE

Hanson, Handt, and Paul Murakami. "On Christmas Night" in *Spirit Calls, Rejoice!* CCF.

Kantor, Daniel. "Night of Silence." GIA G-2760. U, inst, kybd.

Kern, Philip. "Rise Up, Shepherd, Behold That Star." ALF 16332. SATB.

Murakami, Paul. "Star of David" in *Spirit Calls, Rejoice!* CCF.

81

DECEMBER 25, 1998

THE NATIVITY OF OUR LORD
CHRISTMAS DAWN (II)

INTRODUCTION

The liturgy proclaims, "To you is born this day a Savior!" The scriptures announce the presence of God among the people of the earth. In Holy Communion we meet the child born of Mary, our crucified and risen Lord. Through Holy Baptism we have become children of the true Light. We go forth to proclaim this news of great joy: God is with us.

PRAYER OF THE DAY

Almighty God, you have made yourself known in your Son, Jesus, redeemer of the world. We pray that his birth as a human child will set us free from the old slavery of our sin; through Jesus Christ our Lord, who lives and reigns with you and the Holy Spirit, one God, now and forever.

READINGS

Isaiah 62:6-12
  Salvation will come to the holy city of Jerusalem.
Psalm 97
  Light has sprung up for the righteous. (Ps. 97:11)
Titus 3:4-7
  Because of Jesus' earthly appearance, we know that we are saved by the grace of God.
Luke 2:[1-7] 8-20
  A song from angels and news announcing Jesus' birth first come to shepherds living in the fields outside Bethlehem.

COLOR   White

THE PRAYERS

Beholding the Word made flesh among us, let us offer our prayers for the church, the world, and all those in need.
  A BRIEF SILENCE.
For the peoples of the world, and for justice and peace in all the earth. Lord, in your mercy,
hear our prayer.
For all the baptized people of God, that their words and deeds proclaim the dawn of salvation. Lord, in your mercy,

hear our prayer.
For those who live with fear, poverty, anxiety, or illness (especially . . .), that the light of this day bring them renewed hope. Lord, in your mercy,
hear our prayer.
For those marginalized in our society, that like the shepherds they may hear the good news of God's great love for all the world. Lord, in your mercy,
hear our prayer.
For our families and those we love, that our hearts be united by the peace of Christ's coming among us. Lord, in your mercy,
hear our prayer.
For ourselves, that in the midst of our Christmas celebration we may ponder, with Mary, all that God has done for us. Lord, in your mercy,
hear our prayer.
HERE OTHER INTERCESSIONS MAY BE OFFERED.
In thanksgiving for all the saints, we glorify and praise God for all that we have seen and heard, until we join them in the splendor of heaven's dawning light. Lord, in your mercy,
hear our prayer.
Receive our prayers, gracious God, as we proclaim the wonders of your love to all the earth, through Jesus Christ our Lord.
Amen

IMAGES FOR PREACHING

To the holiday-weary, hearing Luke's familiar story yet one more time may seem anything but a treat. But the very same words can resonate more deeply when repeated at another time. The tender assurances lovers share when all is dark become yet more solid and sure when heard again at first light. So it is with Christmas dawn. The old narrative of that first holy night is reexamined in the brightness of the new day, and a still more dazzling claim comes into view. Or rather, we hear anew the force of God's counterclaim.

At the start of this familiar tale we meet a claim—of power. Like all those who ever issued such pompous decrees, Augustus was asserting his authority. Here's who is in charge, here's what must be done. Naturally, then, we expect the action to take place on the imperial center stage, the work of noble and mighty Romans. But wait . . . the camera zooms in *where*? On the outposts of Galilee and Judea, far from the seat of power! Ah, this must be a quaint pastoral story, then. Readjusting our expectations, we settle in once more to the predictable flow. Compliant Joseph obeys the decree, traveling home to the city of David. Steeped in the scriptures, we know that claim as well: he's headed for Jerusalem, "the city of David." But wait . . . he's "going up" (as if ascending to the temple) *where*? To the *backwaters* of religious life in Bethlehem!

Just exactly what kind of story steals us away in such unforeseen directions? It is the tale of God's counterclaim. Though familiar centers of power beckon and seduce, God careens off toward the fringes of the world to work salvation there. Isaiah echoed this absurdity. While others might have given the exiles the names they deserved, divine speech calls these rebels Holy, Redeemed, Sought, Unforsaken. God's counterclaim stands against every human assertion and expectation. Indeed, the "great joy for all people" will not descend from heaven like a warrior, but arise from an unassuming city in infant frame. And this is God's great and contrary claim on us.

WORSHIP MATTERS

What is it about Christmas? The songs? The story? Jesus was born of a human family. The good news of the incarnation is God come down to earth. The "ordinariness" of life, even life among the poor and lowly, is exalted. Our families, with many of their Christmas traditions, add to the celebration this time of year.

What traditions are there to honor in our worshiping communities? Young and old alike come to sing familiar carols, and to hear the Christmas story. Can we tell afresh the "good news of great joy for all the people" in a way that utilizes judicious repetition in the phrase of a prayer, or the refrain of a carol? Instead of the image of a pageant or performance, can we proclaim the nativity gospel of Luke as our family's story, where Christ is born for us?

MUSIC FOR WORSHIP
GATHERING
LBW 73	All hail to you, O blessed morn!
LBW 59	When Christmas morn is dawning

PSALM 97
Beckett, Debbie. "This Day New Light Will Shine" in PS1.

The Dameans. "A Light Will Shine/Lord Today" in PCY, vol. 6.

Hopson, Hal H. "Psalm 97" in TP. Cant, cong.

Kreutz, Robert E. "Psalm 97" in *Psalms for the Cantor*, vol. III. WLP 2504.

Wetzler, Robert. PW, Cycle A.

HYMN OF THE DAY
LBW 55	Good Christian friends, rejoice
	IN DULCI JUBILO

VOCAL RESOURCES

Bach, J. S./Pethel. "Good Christian Friends, Rejoice." CPH 3167. SATB.

Hemmerle, Bernhard. "Good Christian Friends, Rejoice" in *For the Crowning of the Year*. AFP 11-10509.

INSTRUMENTAL RESOURCES

Beck, Theodore. "In dulci jubilo." AFP 11-10520. Hb.

Dupré, Marcel. "In dulci jubilo" in *A New Liturgical Year*, ed. John Ferguson. AFP 11-10810. Org.

Leavitt, John. "In dulci jubilo" in *Christmas Suite*. AFP 11-10857. Org.

Wetzler, Robert. "In dulci jubilo" in *Yuletide Carols for Brass and Organ*. AMSI B-7. Org, brass.

ALTERNATE HYMN OF THE DAY
LBW 70	Go tell it on the mountain
WOV 643	Once in royal David's city

COMMUNION
LBW 56	The first Noel
WOV 645	There's a star in the East

SENDING
LBW 70	Go tell it on the mountain
LBW 61	The hills are bare at Bethlehem

ADDITIONAL HYMNS AND SONGS
WOV 642	I wonder as I wander
H82 106	Christians, awake, salute the happy morn
H82 94	While shepherds watched their flocks
DATH 52	For all people Christ was born

83

MUSIC FOR THE DAY

CHORAL

Ferguson, John. "Unto Us Is Born God's Son." AFP 11-10449. SATB, org.

Hillert, Richard. "On This Day Earth Shall Ring." CPH 98-3149. SATB, kybd.

Holst, Gustav. "The Savior of the World Is Born" in *Second Morning Star Choir Book.* CPH 97-470. SATB/2 pt, org.

Proulx, Richard. "A Child Is Born in Bethlehem." GIA G-4156. SAB, hb.

Vivaldi, Antonio/S. Drummond Wolff. "Gloria in excelsis Deo." AFP 11-10582. SATB, org, tpt.

Walter, Johann. "Now Sing We Now Rejoice." CPH 98-204. SATB.

CHILDREN'S CHOIRS

Horman, John. "To Us Emmanuel." HOP A605. U, kybd.

Sleeth, Natalie. "Welcome the Babe." CGA 309. U, kybd, opt perc.

Mitchell, Tom. "Carol of the Children." CGA 473. U, kybd, opt glock.

KEYBOARD/INSTRUMENTAL

Bach, J. S. "In dulci jubilo" in *Miscellaneous Compositions on the Chorale.* Org.

Hassell, Michael. "In dulci jubilo" in *Jazz All Seasons.* AFP 11-10822. Pno/kybd.

HANDBELL

Kinyon, Barbara Baltzer. "Hark! The Herald Angels Sing." HOP 1463. 2 oct.

Larson, Katherine. "When Christmas Morn Is Dawning." AFP 11-10470. 3-5 oct.

Morris, Hart. "Greensleeves." 4-5 oct hb MSM 30-100. Fl/ob, wind ch 30-100A.

Page, Anna Laura. "The First Nowell" in *Hymn Descants for Ringers and Singers*, vol. 1. 3 oct hb ALF 11527. Choral/kybd, 3 oct, kybd, desc 11529.

PRAISE ENSEMBLE

Hanson, Handt, and Paul Murakami. "All Is Christmas" in *Spirit Calls, Rejoice!* CCF.

Hanson, Handt, and Paul Murakami. "Singing Through the Water" in *Spirit Calls, Rejoice!* CCF.

DECEMBER 25, 1998

THE NATIVITY OF OUR LORD
CHRISTMAS DAY (III)

INTRODUCTION

Since the beginning of time, the coming of light has been a sign of life and hope. The sun and the stars transform the darkness into an inhabitable space. On the festival of the Lord's nativity, the church gathers to celebrate the light of God's grace present in Christ. In the holy bath of baptism, he enlightens and claims us as brothers and sisters. In the holy word of scripture, he speaks to us of God's love for each human being. In the holy meal of the eucharist, he gives us the bread of eternal life. From this festive liturgy we go forth to be light-bearers in the ordinary rhythms of daily life.

PRAYER OF THE DAY

Almighty God, you wonderfully created and yet more wonderfully restored the dignity of human nature. In your mercy, let us share the divine life of Jesus Christ who came to share our humanity, and who now lives and reigns with you and the Holy Spirit, one God, now and forever.

READINGS

Isaiah 52:7-10

In chapters 40–55, the prophet announces that the Lord will soon end the exile of God's people in Babylon. In today's reading, the prophet again announces this victory. Note that he is so certain this victory will take place that he announces his message in the past tense, as though it has already happened.

Psalm 98

All the ends of the earth have seen the victory of our God. (Ps. 98:4)

Hebrews 1:1-4 [5-12]

The opening words of this stately epistle present Jesus as the ultimate message of God to us, as the one who perfectly reveals God's glory and being.

John 1:1-14

The prologue to the gospel of John describes Jesus as the creative word of God made flesh, God's true presence among us, the one whose very existence reveals God as "full of grace and truth."

COLOR White

THE PRAYERS

Beholding the Word made flesh among us, let us offer our prayers for the church, the world, and all those in need.
A BRIEF SILENCE.

Strengthen your church to be the messenger that announces peace, and brings good news to all those in despair. Lord, in your mercy,

hear our prayer.

Uphold all who work for justice and equality in our world, and teach us to long for the end of all oppression and violence. Lord, in your mercy,

hear our prayer.

Raise up the lowly and powerless in our world, and let Christ's humble birth shine hope within their hearts. Lord, in your mercy,

hear our prayer.

Surround with your love all who are alone on this day, and shed your light on all whose memories are painful, or whose hopes are dim. Lord, in your mercy,

hear our prayer.

Enfold with your grace all who suffer from depression, grief, or illness (especially . . .), and use us to share with them the joy of Christ's birth among us. Lord, in your mercy,

hear our prayer.

Gladden our hearts through our sharing of the word and eucharist, and let your grace and truth permeate all our days. Lord, in your mercy,

hear our prayer.

HERE OTHER INTERCESSIONS MAY BE OFFERED.

Unite us with all the saints who were bearers of your light, until we join them in the brightness of your glory. Lord, in your mercy,

hear our prayer.

Receive our prayers, gracious God, as we proclaim the wonders of your love to all the earth, through Jesus Christ our Lord.

Amen

IMAGES FOR PREACHING

Reckon the passage of this festival. First the whispers of the eve, then the steady voice at dawn, now the shouts breaking forth to match the majesty of the sun. It's as if the church cannot get enough of the nativity, as if every passing moment must be made to count. But try as we might, nothing about this festival will stand still. The course of the holy infant, now seen in the full light of day, is already speeding on to another destination, part of a larger stream of history. And it is the movement of this *time*, God's and ours, to which Christmas so powerfully alludes.

The opening verses of Hebrews signal this movement: the "long ago" of the ancestors, the "last days" in which we now live. But cutting across all of these time-frames, indeed in contrast to all other creatures and worlds, Christ is marked by "forever." From the beginning ever onward the Son will remain, unchanged and unending. John's gospel opens by singing a similar interplay between the times. In this case, however, the clock is turned back to when history was as yet unborn, back to the eternal Word that was from the beginning. And as gospel melody progresses, note what other moments become part of its flow: real events (the testimony of a prophet), particular reactions (neither knowing nor accepting), concrete benefits (receiving and believing). By their inclusion, these moments receive new dignity. Far from being interruptions to the disinterested trajectory of fate, the specifics of human time are swept into the eternal flow of divine concern.

So much of our days pass as if there were only one sort of time, the kind that condemns us to our yesterdays or paralyzes us about our tomorrows. But God's time, compassionate and complete, interrupts that senseless flow to rearrange its passage and reinvest our moments with lasting value. "The *Word*"—endless divine love for us—"became *flesh*"—embraced that which time decays—"and *lived* among us"—showing the way beyond death's thrall. It is holy time displayed this great festival day, and through the mercy of Christ, it is our time as well.

WORSHIP MATTERS

God speaks to us through the word, and through Jesus, the word made flesh. If the proclamation of the word is central, how can it be a multimedia event?

Do we use a large, substantial book for the proclamation of our scriptures? Do we carry it with honor and joy? Do we allow the word to break into our midst by carrying a book into the middle of the congregation? Do we have a place of honor for the word, an ample lectern or ambo, rather than the minister's seat? Might we on this feast day accent that "the word was God" and "the life was the light of all people" by framing the Bible or lectionary book with candles and/or flowers? How can we creatively make the word visible?

MUSIC FOR WORSHIP

SERVICE MUSIC

LLC 189 (bilingual) combines an easily learned "Gloria" refrain in a *cueca* rhythm with verses that may be sung by a cantor.

GATHERING

| LBW 45 | Oh, come, all ye faithful |
| LBW 73 | All hail to you, O blessed morn! |

PSALM 98

Bell, John. "Sing a New Song to the Lord." GIA G-4380. SATB, cong, org.

Busarow, Donald. "Sing to the Lord a New Song." AFP 11-00698. Inst pts 11-00699. SATB, org, brass, opt cong.

Johnson, Alan. "All The Ends of the Earth" in PS1.

Verdi, Ralph C. "Psalm for Christmas: All the Ends of the Earth." GIA G-2489. SATB, cant, trbl inst, cong, org.

Wetzler, Robert. PW, Cycle A.

GOSPEL SEQUENCE HYMN

| LBW 48 | All praise to you, eternal Lord |
| WOV 788 | Glory to God, glory in the highest |

HYMN OF THE DAY

| LBW 42 | Of the Father's love begotten |
| | DIVINUM MYSTERIUM |

VOCAL RESOURCES

Behnke, John A. "Of the Father's Love Begotten." MSM 60-1000. SATB, cong, hb, org.

Crosier, Katherine. "Of the Father's Love Begotten." GIA G-2837. SATB, cong, hb, opt org.

Gieschen, Thomas. "Of the Father's Love Begotten." CPH 98-2723. SATB, cong, ob, vln, org.

INSTRUMENTAL RESOURCES

Burkhardt, Michael. "Of the Father's Love Begotten" in *Festive Hymn Settings*. MSM-20-171. Org, cong, opt SATB, hb, 2 trbl instr.

Hyslop, Scott. "Of the Father's Love Begotten" in *Six Chorale Fantasias for Solo Instrument and Piano*. AFP 11-10799. Solo inst, kybd.

Leavitt, John. "Of the Father's Love Begotten" in *Hymn Preludes for the Church Year*. AFP 11-10134. Org.

ALTERNATE HYMN OF THE DAY

| LBW 60 | Hark! The herald angels sing |
| WOV 638 | Holy child within the manger |

COMMUNION

| LBW 40 | What child is this |
| LBW 56 | The first Noel |

SENDING

| LBW 57 | Let our gladness have no end |
| WOV 637 | Gloria, gloria, gloria |

ADDITIONAL HYMNS AND SONGS

LBW 43	Rejoice, rejoice this happy morn
CEL 256	Love has come—a light in darkness
H82 84	Love came down at Christmas
NSR 8	When God's time had ripened

MUSIC FOR THE DAY

CHORAL

Bell, John. "Before the World Began." GIA G4381. SATB, cong, ob, opt kybd.

Hyslop, Scott. "Hush You, My Baby." AFP 11-10885. SAB, org, ob.

Praetorius, Michael. "Let All Together Praise Our God." CPH 98-3136. SATB.

Ryan-Wenger, Michael. "In the Beginning Was the Word." AFP 11-10032. SATB, fl, org.

Schalk, Carl. "Let Our Gladness Have No End." CPH 98-3164. SATB, hb.

Scheidt, Samuel. "Sing, Rejoice" (Psallite unigenito). CPH 98-2806. SATB, org.

CHILDREN'S CHOIRS

Burkhardt, Michael, and Rhonda Grobe. "Sing Lullaby and Let Our Gladness Have No End" in *Christmas Songs from Around the World*. MSM 50-1810. U/2 pt, orff.

Grier, Gene, and Douglas Wagner. "Jesus Christ Is Born Today." CGA 692. U, kybd, opt hb.

Maeker, Nancy. "Sing a New Song." CPH 98-3038. 2 pt, orff.

Schalk, Carl. "On Christmas Morning Children Sing." CPH 98-2736.
U, kybd, opt inst.

KEYBOARD/INSTRUMENTAL

Barber, Samuel. "Chorale Prelude on 'Silent Night.'" GSCH. Org.

Dupré, Marcel/ed. Rollin Smith. "Variations on *Adeste Fidelis*."
HWG 11746. Org.

Hassell, Michael. "Go Tell It on the Mountain" in *Jazz December: Piano Arrangements for the Season*. AFP 11-10796. Pno.

HANDBELL

Kinyon, Barbara Baltzer. "Joy to the World." HOP 1393. 2-3 oct.

Krentz, Michael E. "Angels We Have Heard on High." AFP 11-10715.
3 oct.

McChesney, Kevin. "Joy to the World." AFP 11-10472. 3-5 oct.

Moklebust, Cathy. "The Bells of Christmas." CGA CGB146. 2 oct.

PRAISE ENSEMBLE

Hanson, Handt, and Paul Murakami. "Like a Rose in Winter" in *Spirit Calls, Rejoice!* CCF.

Harlan, Benjamin. "African Noel." HAL 3084357. SATB, bass/perc.

Arr. Maddux, Dave. "Joy to the World." AMI. 6B49. SATB, orch.

SATURDAY, DECEMBER 26
ST. STEPHEN, DEACON AND MARTYR

Since the thirteenth century the feasts on the three days after Christmas have been called *comites Christi* ("companions of Christ"). In different ways these three observances further illumine the mystery of the incarnation. Stephen is remembered as the first Christian martyr. In his death he closely imitated the death of Christ, praying for his executioners and commending his soul to the hands of God.

Since Stephen was a deacon who cared for widows and those in need, this day is appropriate for a congregation to remember those who are hungry or homeless. A gift of money, food, or clothing might be delivered to a charitable organization. Amid the sentimental overtones of Christmas, the day of St. Stephen reminds us of one who offered his very life for Christ, and our baptismal call to follow.

87

DECEMBER 27, 1998

ST. JOHN, APOSTLE AND EVANGELIST

INTRODUCTION

The church today remembers John, the fourth evangelist or gospel in our New Testament, and the one many believe to have been "the beloved disciple" in that same gospel. Several people have come to favor his gospel account, no doubt because it is so different from the other three gospels (Matthew, Mark, and Luke—also called the *synoptics*). This gospel is known for its poetic beauty and the many close and personal encounters that people have with Jesus.

As the scriptures are proclaimed today, and as the bread and wine is offered to you, know that Christ is also every bit as close to you as these things are.

PRAYER OF THE DAY

Merciful Lord, let the brightness of your light shine on your Church, so that all of us, instructed by the teachings of John, your apostle and evangelist, may walk in the light of your truth and attain eternal life; through your

Son, Jesus Christ our Lord, who lives and reigns with you and the Holy Spirit, one God, now and forever.

READINGS

Genesis 1:1-5, 26-31
When the world was brought into being through the voice of God, God created humankind in his own image.

Psalm 116:10-17
Precious in your sight, O Lord, is the death of your servants. (Ps. 116:13)

1 John 1:1—2:2
Though no one is without sin, in Jesus Christ we have an advocate who speaks on our behalf.

John 21:20-25
Jesus performed many signs—so great that not all could be recorded in scripture.

COLOR   White

THE PRAYERS

Beholding the Word made flesh among us, let us offer our prayers for the church, the world, and all those in need.

A BRIEF SILENCE.

For the church around the world, that it may faithfully testify to the word of life that we have seen and heard. Lord, in your mercy,

hear our prayer.

For the peoples of the world, that we may be good stewards of creation and the resources of the earth. Lord, in your mercy,

hear our prayer.

For all who live with poverty or discrimination, that we may respond with compassion and generosity throughout the coming year. Lord, in your mercy,

hear our prayer.

For those who are fearful, alone, anxious, or sick (especially . . .), that the light of Christ bring them joy amid their pain. Lord, in your mercy,

hear our prayer.

For ourselves, that the twelve days of Christmas renew our spirits as we prepare to begin a new year. Lord, in your mercy,

hear our prayer.

HERE OTHER INTERCESSIONS MAY BE OFFERED.

For John, apostle and evangelist, and for all who bore witness to the Word made flesh, we give thanks. Make our joy complete until we join all the saints in the light of your endless glory. Lord, in your mercy,

hear our prayer.

Receive our prayers, gracious God, as we proclaim the wonders of your love to all the earth, through Jesus Christ our Lord.

Amen

IMAGES FOR PREACHING

Today provides the chance to see the sanctoral cycle of saints' days intersect the temporal cycle of festivals and seasons that give overall structure to the church calendar. The apostle and evangelist John is commemorated in the middle of three adjacent saints' days that are distinctive in their nearness to Christmas, their antiquity in that calendar location, and their unlikely focus in this season of joy: martyrdom. Stephen (yesterday) represents a martyrdom both voluntary and completed; John (today) recounts a martyrdom voluntary but not completed; and Holy Innocents (tomorrow) recalls a martyrdom completed but not voluntary. Taken together, these three days have been known from earliest times as "Comites Christi," the *companions* of Christ.

Though such companions may seem especially grim during this joyous season, they guide us into a more substantive celebration of the nativity. Today's epistle takes us by the hand and places us in the path of a long testimonial series, making us new recipients of a word already revealed to others long ago. And the substance of that testimony is "that God is light and in him there is no darkness at all." To hear this message from those who suffered for the faith, John and countless others, is a powerful and assuring witness. More comforting still is that this witness is made, as the epistle puts it, "so that you also may have fellowship with us." The companions of Christ's light bid us to be companions with them, heirs of the same promise.

The Jesus we meet this season does not remain an infant forever. His life gestures onward toward the cross, and his companions witness in that same direction. During this time of natal joy, we add our testimony to theirs, declaring to generations yet unborn the light and life won for us. The gospel of John concludes with the sly remark that the "many other things that Jesus did" that were *not* included by the evangelist would, if written, burst earth's very bounds. Many other stories could have been written, indeed were written in the lives of Christ's companions. Our delight on this day, as their fellow companions, is to ask ourselves, "What would mine be?"

WORSHIP MATTERS

With only twelve days to celebrate the glorious mystery that is Christmas, some may ask why we take the time to celebrate festivals of the saints during this season. One of the answers is contained within the celebration of Christmas itself, specifically the mystery that is the incarnation. The good news of Christmas is that God takes on our human nature and endures all that faces a fallen humanity in order to redeem us from sin and death. In the saints we see the work of incarnation continuing, for these are the faithful who, by their example, point us to God, teaching us once more how "God-with-us" transforms life, and empowers for service in the very world God-in-Christ came to redeem. This work of incarnation is especially evident in John the Evangelist, from whose pen the mystery of the incarnation is so eloquently captured: "And the word became flesh and lived among us, full of grace and truth" (John 1:14).

MUSIC FOR WORSHIP

GATHERING

| LBW 57 | Let our gladness have no end |
| WOV 793 | Shout for joy loud and long |

PSALM 116

Daigle, Gary, and Rory Cooney. "Psalm 116: I Will Walk in the Presence of God" in *Gather Comprehensive.* GIA.

Fabing, Bob. "Be Like the Sun" in *Rise Up and Sing.* OCP 9391. U.

Haas, David. PCY, vol. 3.

Hurd, Bob. "Ps. 116: Our Blessing Cup" in STP, vol. 1.

Pavlechko, Thomas. PW, Cycle C.

HYMN OF THE DAY

| LBW 48 | All praise to you, eternal Lord |
| | GELOBET SEIST DU |

INSTRUMENTAL RESOURCES

Bach, J. S. "Gelobet seist du" in *Orgelbüchlein.* Various ed. Org.

Beck, Theodore. "Gelobet seist du" in *Intonations for the Hymn of the Week.* CPH 97-4899. Org.

Busarow, Donald. "Gelobet seist du" in *Five Chorale Preludes for Organ and Two Instruments,* vol. II. CPH 97-5569. Org/kybd, inst.

Manz, Paul. "Hail the Day So Rich in Cheer" in *Improvisations for the Christmas Season,* set. 3. MSM 10-102. Org.

ALTERNATE HYMN OF THE DAY

| LBW 177 | By all your saints in warfare (st. 8) |
| WOV 799 | When long before time |

COMMUNION

| LBW 198 | Let all mortal flesh keep silence |
| WOV 642 | I wonder as I wander |

OTHER SUGGESTIONS

| DATH 55 | There was the Word |

SENDING

| LBW 470 | Praise and thanks and adoration |
| LBW 397 | O Zion, haste |

ADDITIONAL HYMNS AND SONGS

LBW 42	Of the Father's love begotten
LBW 449	They cast their nets
H82 245	Praise God for John, evangelist
UMH 188	Christ is the world's Light

MUSIC FOR THE DAY

CHORAL

Rogers, Sharon E. "Let All on Earth Raise Their Voices." PRE 392-41921. SATB, kybd.

Schubert, Franz. "Sing Praise to God." PRE 392-03028. SATB, pno.

Wesley, Samuel S. "Thou Wilt Keep Him in Perfect Peace." NOV 29 0152 08. SATB, org.

CHILDREN'S CHOIRS

Delmonte, Pauline. "Stars Are for Those Who Lift Their Eyes." CGA 117. U/SA, hp/pno, opt vc.

Kemp, Helen. "God's Great Lights." CPH 98-3072. U/2 pt, kybd.

KEYBOARD/INSTRUMENTAL

Bach, J. S. "Sinfonia" from *Christmas Oratorio* in *The Oxford Book of Christmas Organ Music.* OXF 0193751240. Org.

Brahms, Johannes. "Es ist ein Ros'" in *Orgelwerke.* Henle ed. Org.

Callahan, Charles. "Prelude on Greensleeves for Flute and Organ." MSM 20-162. Org, fl.

Crisafulli, Peter. "Three Carols for Flute and Harpsichord." CPH 97-5559. Kybd, fl.

HANDBELL

Dobrinski, Cynthia. "Lo, How a Rose E'er Blooming." HOP 1655. 3-5 oct, fl.

Gramann, Fred. "Prelude on 'Divinum Mysterium.'" LOR HB332. 3-4 oct.

Morris, Hart. "Go Tell It on the Mountain." 3 oct HOP 1485. 4-5 oct 1533.

PRAISE ENSEMBLE

Delavan, Macon. "You Are My God" in *Integrity's Hosanna! Come and Worship Songbook.* INT.

Ylvisaker, John. "I'll Bless the Lord Forevermore" in *Borning Cry.* NGP.

DECEMBER 27, 1998

FIRST SUNDAY AFTER CHRISTMAS

INTRODUCTION

The gospel reading for this day juxtaposes the birth of Christ with the death of innocent children. Indeed, whenever we sentimentalize the nativity of the Lord, we need to hear this story of the slaughter of the holy innocents. Christian faith does not lead us out of the world of evil rulers, injustice, and death. Rather, the gift of faith strengthens us to contend with any force that threatens the life God has created.

Here is this potent sign: in the holy supper we receive the body and blood of the one who accompanies us in this broken and fragile world.

Today (December 27) is also the festival of John, Apostle and Evangelist.

PRAYER OF THE DAY

Almighty God, you have made yourself known in your Son, Jesus, redeemer of the world. We pray that his birth as a human child will set us free from the old slavery of our sin; through Jesus Christ our Lord, who lives and reigns with you and the Holy Spirit, one God, now and forever.

or

Almighty God, you wonderfully created and yet more wonderfully restored the dignity of human nature. In your mercy, let us share the divine life of Jesus Christ who came to share our humanity, and who now lives and reigns with you and the Holy Spirit, one God, now and forever.

READINGS

Isaiah 63:7-9

These verses sing of thanksgiving and praise because of God's "gracious deeds" and "steadfast love" (v. 7). Both of these terms are translations of the Hebrew word hesed. *It is not a romantic love that grows cold. Rather, this love always treats the other person with unselfish kindness, respect, and loyalty.*

Psalm 148

The splendor of the Lord is over earth and heaven. (Ps. 148:13)

Hebrews 2:10-18

Though Christmas is a joyous season, its meaning cannot be separated from the message of Holy Week. Jesus became like us in order to suffer with us and to destroy the power of death.

Matthew 2:13-23

Matthew describes the terrible slaughter of young Bethlehem boys as a sign of evil present in the world, and to highlight the relationship between the Old Testament and Jesus' life.

COLOR   White

THE PRAYERS

Beholding the Word made flesh among us, let us offer our prayers for the church, the world, and all those in need.

A BRIEF SILENCE.

That as God is faithful to us, may the church recount the steadfast deeds of the Lord in its liturgy and its mission. Lord, in your mercy,

hear our prayer.

That as Herod's rule brought the death of innocent children, may the leaders of nations work for the rights and dignity of children, and the most vulnerable members of society. Lord, in your mercy,

hear our prayer.

That as the holy family sought refuge in Egypt, may we extend hospitality to strangers and to those in exile. Lord, in your mercy,

hear our prayer.

That as Christ was tested by what he suffered, may his compassionate love strengthen all who are sorrowful or sick (especially . . .). Lord, in your mercy,

hear our prayer.

That as Joseph offered his family protection and care, may God bless our families, and strengthen our ties of love. Lord, in your mercy,

hear our prayer.

HERE OTHER INTERCESSIONS MAY BE OFFERED.

That as the birth of Christ was the dawn of salvation, bring us, with John and all your saints, to the light of endless day. Lord, in your mercy,

hear our prayer.
Receive our prayers, gracious God, as we proclaim the wonders of your love to all the earth, through Jesus Christ our Lord.
Amen

IMAGES FOR PREACHING

A discernible rhythm flows through the two Sundays of this little season, even though that rhythm may seem to rush by as quickly as "tick-tock." The first moment of that rhythm resounds through the events immediately after the birth of Jesus, accenting the material and historical reality of that unfolding story. Matthew's gospel provides the dramatic setting with a narrative about three dreams—and a nightmare. Lucky Joseph, that old dreamer, continues to benefit from the kind of angelic clarity that would make our lives so much simpler. Flee! Return! Go there! But these dreams achieve more than the safety of the holy trio. Their final aim is to complete a larger saving story, so that "what had been spoken through the prophets" might thrice be fulfilled.

These dreams, blissful and sweet, receive their counterpoint in the nightmare at Bethlehem. The city that so recently cradled life and hope becomes, through Herod's rage, the horrifying abode of despair and death. We avert our gaze from such senseless carnage. What has the death of these innocents to do with the innocent Jesus we conjure this season? We accept that the holy child's story includes the safety and providence of Joseph's three dreams. But this singular nightmare set in their midst leaves us mute. Surely Jesus has no company with it.

But what if that were so? Where is the hope in that? By contrast, today's reading from Hebrews declares that because Christ shares our flesh and blood, even its horrors, he is the pioneer of our salvation. The one made perfect through suffering became like us "in every respect" in order to make us brothers and sisters. In every respect? Then shocking as it sounds, even the death of the innocents is part of the reality of Christ. Every moment of human history, even the slaughter and brutality that fills the earth to overflowing, is borne in his flesh to the cross. This salvation does not stand at arm's length from worldly sorrow and cruelty. It is instead, as Isaiah knew long ago, God's own presence that saves us, the reality of love that redeems.

WORSHIP MATTERS

Our life's stories are, in large part, defined by all the places we've lived. We live in a mobile society. And in the gospel story of the flight to Egypt, we see Jesus and his family on the move.

Today would be a good day to focus on those who are new to the area, and on all who have come from "somewhere else." Worship etiquette should be welcoming; those in the pews should take notice of visitors and help them find their way. How well do bulletins give instruction? Will people know if they are invited to the communion meal, or to a fellowship gathering?

During the prayer of the church, include petitions for those who travel, those who have come to our land as immigrants, and those who look to find a place of belonging in our communities of faith. We are all on a journey of faith, but it's nice to know we are accompanied by angels and others sent by God to us!

LET THE CHILDREN COME

Note the contrast between the commercial celebration of Christmas and the church's celebration of these same days. Already, the commercial Christmas is into "post-Christmas sales" while the church is only beginning to celebrate Christmas. In what ways can the church help families with children make these twelve days a time to enter the depths of the season? Now would be time to bake cookies or write cards and letters that did not get done because of the pre-Christmas rush. When children on break from school become bored with their gifts, turn them once again to the story that fills these days.

MUSIC FOR WORSHIP

GATHERING

| LBW 50 | Angels from the realms of glory |
| WOV 642 | I wonder as I wander |

PSALM 148

Handel, G. F./Hal H. Hopson. "Praise God, Oh, Bless the Lord." AFP 11-4649. SATB, org.

Ogden, David. "Let All Creation Sing" in PS1.

Powell, Robert J. "Praise the Lord from the Heavens." SEL 422-772. U, kybd.

Rorem, Ned. "Psalm 148" in *Cycle of Holy Songs for Voice and Piano.* PEER 01-073794-212. Solo.

Wetzler, Robert. PW, Cycle A.

91

HYMN OF THE DAY

WOV 639   Oh, sleep now, holy baby
           A LA RU

SUGGESTION FOR WOV 639

Intonation   String or woodwind and kybd
Stanza 1 & 2 Treble solo
Refrain   All with inst

INSTRUMENTAL RESOURCES

Beck, Theodore. "Oh, Sleep, Now, Holy Baby." AFP 11-10521. 2 oct. hb.

Cherwien, David. "A la ru" in *Eight for 88*. AFP 11-10868. Pno, opt. inst.

Osterland, Karl. "A la ru" in *I Wonder As I Wander*. AFP 11-10858. Org.

ALTERNATE HYMN OF THE DAY

LBW 74   A stable lamp is lighted
LBW 47   Let all together praise our God

COMMUNION

LBW 54   It came upon the midnight clear
LBW 72   'Twas in the moon of wintertime

OTHER SUGGESTIONS

LLC 388   Vengo a ti, Jesús amado/Soul, adorn
          yourself with gladness

SENDING

LBW 62   The bells of Christmas
WOV 640   Gloria (Taizé)

ADDITIONAL HYMNS AND SONGS

H82 375   See amid the winter snow
AYG 39   Gentle Joseph heard a warning
DATH 54   Holy Child
LLC 310   María, pobre María/Oh, Mary, gentle
          poor Mary

MUSIC FOR THE DAY

CHORAL

Bach, J. S. "Break Forth, O Beauteous Heavenly Light" in *Church Choir Book*. CPH 97-6320. SATB.

Bass, Claude L. "At Bethlehem." AFP 11-10878. SATB, pno.

Ferguson, John. "Good Christian Friends, Rejoice. MSM 50-4025. SATB, vla.

Praetorius, Michael. "En natus est Emanuel". GIA G-213. SATB.

Proulx, Richard. "From Bethlehem, Fair City." GIA G4155. SATB.

Schroeter, Leonhart. "Let All Together Praise Our God" in *Let All Together Praise*. CPH 97-565. SATB, kybd.

Stevens, Halsey. "Psalm 148: Praise Ye the Lord." MSF EH 2. SATB.

CHILDREN'S CHOIRS

Burke, John T. "Psalm 148" in *Wolfgang Amadeus Mozart for Boys and Girls*. CGA CGC13. U/2 pt, kybd.

Mitchell, Tom. "Sing and Rejoice." CGA 584. 2 pt trbl/mxd.

Sedio, Mark. "The Coventry Carol." SEL 405-234. 2 pt, org.

KEYBOARD/INSTRUMENTAL

Dorian, Mark. "Forest Green" in *Around the World: Six Hymntune Improvisations*. AFP 11-10618. Pno/kybd.

Goemanne, Noël. *Three Fantasies for Organ*. HWG GB00704. Org.

Willcocks, David. "Postlude on 'Mendelssohn'" in *The Oxford Book of Christmas Organ Music*. OXF 0193751240. Org.

HANDBELL

Buckwalter, Karen. "I Wonder as I Wander." SHW HP5323. 3-5 oct.

Dobrinski, Cynthia. "Angel Tidings." HOP 1215. 3-5 oct.

Moklebust, Cathy. "The Hills Are Bare at Bethlehem" in *Rise Up, Shepherd, and Follow*. CGA CGB184. 2-3 oct, perc.

PRAISE ENSEMBLE

Hanson, Handt, and Paul Murakami. "You Alone" in *Spirit Calls, Rejoice!* CCF.

Kauflin, Bob/Tom Fettke. "In the First Light." LIL AN-2623. SATB.

Thomas, André, arr. "Go Where I Send Thee." MFS MF 2044. SATB.

SUNDAY, DECEMBER 27

ST. JOHN, APOSTLE AND EVANGELIST

John is traditionally regarded as the author of the fourth gospel, three epistles that bear his name, and the book of Revelation. During the twelve days of Christmas we read the prologue of John's gospel which speaks of the Word made flesh among us. John is assumed to be the "beloved disciple" to whose care Jesus entrusted his mother at the crucifixion.

According to legend, John's enemies tried to murder him with poisoned wine. His great love, it was said, vanquished the poison's power. Some still observe the medieval custom of blessing and drinking a cup of wine today, making a toast with the words: I drink to you the love of John. Remember John in the prayers today, and with a toast at Sunday dinner. How will your congregation extend the love extolled at Christmas throughout the days of the coming year?

MONDAY, DECEMBER 28
THE HOLY INNOCENTS, MARTYRS

The Innocents were the children of Bethlehem, two years and under, killed by King Herod in his attempt to destroy the infant Jesus. Since they were killed for the sake of Christ, the church honored these Jewish babies as the "buds of the martyrs," killed by the frost of hate as soon as they appeared. This observance so close to Christmas is a bittersweet reminder of the place of suffering and death in the story of our redemption.

It is appropriate today to remember the innocent victims of all ages killed in the slaughters of recent history. It is also a day to hold up the needs of battered children all over the world, and children who live in poverty.

THURSDAY, DECEMBER 31
NEW YEAR'S EVE

FRIDAY, JANUARY 1
THE NAME OF JESUS

This festival marks the naming and circumcision of Jesus eight days after his birth. The observance of the Octave (eighth day) of Christmas goes back to the sixth century, and Lutheran calendars often called it "The Circumcision and the Name of Jesus" until the revision of the calendar in 1973. The festival falls during the twelve days of Christmas and invites continued celebration of Jesus' birth.

Amid New Year's Day events, consider holding a brief service in honor of this liturgical day. Baptized into Christ, we begin the new year in the name of Jesus, our Savior. As an alternate to watching football games, encourage people to make traditional New Year's Day visits to friends or loved ones. The welcoming spirit of baptism encourages us to practice hospitality with others.

SATURDAY, JANUARY 2
JOHANN KONRAD WILHELM LOEHE, PASTOR, 1872

During the nineteenth century Loehe was a parish pastor in the small German village of Neuendettelsau. As a young man Loehe studied in Erlangen, there discovering the Lutheran confessions. He founded a foreign mission society and sent pastors to North America, Australia, and Brazil. He fought for a clear confessional basis for the Bavarian church, and was sometimes in conflict with the ecclesiastical bureaucracy. Loehe taught that Holy Communion was the center of parish life, and that the ministries of evangelism and social ministry flowed from it.

Does your congregation have a mission statement? Is it centered in the gathering of God's people around word and sacrament? How can the Lutheran confessions aid us in defining the heart of our ministry in the late years of this century?

93

JANUARY 3, 1999

SECOND SUNDAY AFTER CHRISTMAS

INTRODUCTION

Today, in the concluding days of the Christmas season, we reflect more deeply on the significance of the Christ who was born at Bethlehem. Our minds may not be able to comprehend just how Jesus existed with God from the beginning of time, as the first chapter from the gospel of John proclaims today. What we do know is this: God comes into our presence today through Jesus Christ. Indeed it happens each Sunday and every other time the church gathers. Through the scriptures as they are read and preached, through the bread and the wine as it is offered to the baptized, God is made flesh among us. The real miracle of Christmas is that God is here now with us—always.

PRAYER OF THE DAY

Almighty God, you have filled us with the new light of the Word who became flesh and lived among us. Let the light of our faith shine in all that we do; through your Son, Jesus Christ our Lord, who lives and reigns with you and the Holy Spirit, one God, now and forever.

READINGS

Jeremiah 31:7-14

The lambs of God's flock frolic joyfully, safe in the careful shepherding of their Lord. God comes to redeem by turning mourning into joy and sorrow into gladness.

or Sirach 24:1-12

Psalm 147:13-21 [Psalm 147:12-20 (NRSV)]

Worship the Lord, O Jerusalem; praise your God, O Zion. (Ps. 147:13)

or The Wisdom of Solomon 10:15-21

We sing, O Lord, to your holy name; we praise with one accord your defending hand. (Wisd. of Sol. 10:20)

Ephesians 1:3-14

God chooses us to be adopted children, holy and without blemish. As children, we have a legacy—redemption and the forgiveness of sin—entrusted to us when we were sealed by the Holy Spirit in baptism.

John 1:[1-9] 10-18

John begins his gospel with this prologue: a hymn to the word

through whom all things were created. This word became flesh and brought grace and truth to the world.

COLOR   White

THE PRAYERS

Beholding the Word made flesh among us, let us offer our prayers for the church, the world, and all those in need.

A BRIEF SILENCE.

That the church may be enlightened with wisdom as it testifies to the grace and truth of Christ. Lord, in your mercy,

hear our prayer.

That the nations may extend care to those living in poverty, and justice to those facing oppression, so all people may know the bounty of God's goodness. Lord, in your mercy,

hear our prayer.

That those who in this glad season live with despair, loneliness, or despondency, may find hope in the light of Christ. Lord, in your mercy,

hear our prayer.

That those who are hospitalized, homebound, or sick (especially . . .) may know the compassion and comfort of God's presence. Lord, in your mercy,

hear our prayer.

That we may value the insights and gifts of children and elderly members of our worshiping communities. Lord, in your mercy,

hear our prayer.

HERE OTHER INTERCESSIONS MAY BE OFFERED.

That with radiant hearts we may give thanks for all the faithful departed, until God gathers us, with them, to the joy of everlasting life. Lord, in your mercy,

hear our prayer.

Receive our prayers, gracious God, as we proclaim the wonders of your love to all the earth, through Jesus Christ our Lord.

Amen

IMAGES FOR PREACHING

The shrewd observer already knows that the opening verses to John's gospel so recently heard on Christmas Day are repeated today as well. Such repetition, however, is part of the historic heartbeat of this season, this Sunday's systole answering last Sunday's diastole. Pulsing through the Church today is the impact of the familiar birth story, a theological reflection on the *cosmic* scope and benefits of the incarnation.

John's great prologue unfolds the course of the eternal Word, leaving nothing untouched. The beginning of creation with its light and life, the testimony of prophets preparing the way, the rebirth of the children of God, all are benefits of Christ, the divine speech. And when the gospel reading reaches its zenith in "the Word became flesh," yet more benefits flow forth: grace and truth and bright glory. But even these dimensions cannot encompass the ultimate aim of the incarnation that breaks the bounds of human comprehension. For through the Son, the very will of the Father is revealed to us. Ponder what that means: the purposes of the one who arranged the planets yet knows when a sparrow falls are, through Christ Jesus, made known to *us*. Nothing hidden, nothing left out, the heart of God revealed for the benefit of our dark hearts.

This same cosmic scope of blessing and grace energizes the opening benediction of Ephesians as well. Yes, we are adopted through Christ, redeemed through his blood, forgiven our trespasses. But greater still is an unimaginable inheritance: to know the mystery of the divine will, the plan for the fullness of time. We, who can barely figure out how to make it through tomorrow without breaking down, are now shown the wisdom and insight that orders the seasons for abundant life. The impact of the birth we acclaim in this little season comes down to but simple, earth-shaking words: death no longer rules, for (to borrow from Jeremiah) we have been redeemed from hands too strong for us. To say anything more would be superfluous.

WORSHIP MATTERS

Our celebration during the twelve days of Christmas emphasizes the lengths to which God will go to love us and to be close to us.

As we focus on the word and the meal in worship, can we also notice one another? Can we smile to one another as we sing hymns, or as someone passes by to receive communion? Can we risk a moment of genuine intimacy in the sharing of Christ's peace?

How can we look at a bulletin, at a hymn book, at a preacher, *and* look to our neighbor in the pew as a way to find the Christ in and around us?

LET THE CHILDREN COME

During the closing hymn children might lead a procession to the manger. The wise men, placed at various spots around the church on Christmas, are still wandering on their way to the Christ child. Since the celebration of the Epiphany is just days away, perhaps the wise men could be brought closer to the manger during this closing procession. Then the children could lead the procession of ministers out of the church. All of this might happen during the singing of "We are marching in the light of God" (WOV 650).

MUSIC FOR WORSHIP

GATHERING

LBW 55	Good Christian friends, rejoice
LBW 50	Angels, from the realms of glory

PSALM 147

Haugen, Marty. PCY, vol. 2.

Hobby, Robert. PW, Cycle A.

PH 255   Now praise the Lord, all living saints

Willcock. *Psalms for the Cantor*, vol. III. WLP 2504.

HYMN OF THE DAY

LBW 57   Let our gladness have no end
           NARODIL SE KRISTUS PÁN

VOCAL RESOURCES

Hess, John. "Let Our Gladness Have No End" CPH 97-6336.
    U, cong, 2 oct hb, org.

Kosche, Kenneth. "Let Our Gladness Have No End" in *Three Carols*.
    CPH 98-3139. SATB, hb.

INSTRUMENTAL RESOURCES

Cherwien, David. "Let Our Gladness Have No End" in *Interpretations*,
    vol. IV. AMSI OR-9. Org.

Leavitt, John. "Let Our Gladness Have No End" in *Hymn Preludes for
    the Church Year.* AFP 11-10134. Org.

Sedio, Mark. *Six Slovak Hymn Improvisations*. MSM 10-833. Org.

ALTERNATE HYMN OF THE DAY

> LBW 64   From east to west
>
> WOV 641   Peace came to earth

COMMUNION

> WOV 642   I wonder as I wander
>
> LBW 56   The first Noel

SENDING

> LBW 39   Joy to the world
>
> WOV 701   What feast of love

ADDITIONAL HYMNS AND SONGS

> PH 556   The world abounds in God's free grace
>
> PsH 218   In the beginning was the Word eternal
>
> UMH 237   Sing we now of Christmas
>
> OBS 48   Beloved, God's chosen

MUSIC FOR THE DAY

CHORAL

> Bell, John. "Before the World Began." GIA G4381. SATB, cong, ob, opt kybd.
>
> Bisbee, B. Wayne. "O Savior of Our Fallen Race." GIA G4122. SATB, hb.
>
> Neswick, Bruce. "The Blessed Son of God." AFP 11-10787. SATB, org.
>
> Roberts, Paul. "The Word Became Flesh." AFP 11-10899. SATB, fl.
>
> Ryan-Wenger, Michael. "In the Beginning Was the Word." AFP 11-10032. SATB, kybd.
>
> "Verbum caro factum est." (15c English carol.) GIA G-4158. SATB.
>
> Willan, Healey. "The Word Was made Flesh" in *We Praise Thee II.* CPH 97-76. SA, org.

CHILDREN'S CHOIRS

> Bach, J. S./Janet Hill. "Alleluia, O Come and Praise the Lord." CGA 174. 2 pt, hpd, org/pno, opt 2 C inst (vln/fl/rec).
>
> Ramseth, Betty Ann. "Sent from God" in *Give Praises with Joy!* BRD 4591-05. U, autohp/kybd.
>
> Wagner, Douglas. "A Round of Praise." CGA 208. U/2 pt, kybd.

KEYBOARD/INSTRUMENTAL

> Ferguson, John. *A Christmas Triptych,* set 2. MSM 10-116. Org.
>
> Lovinfosse, Dennis. "Es ist ein Ros" in *A New Liturgical Year,* ed. John Ferguson. AFP 11-10810. Org.
>
> Wellman, Samuel. "Coventry Carol" in *Keyboard Hymn Favorites.* AFP 11-10820.

HANDBELL MUSIC

> Kinyon, Barbara B. "O Morning Star, How Fair and Bright." HOP 1690. 2-3 oct.
>
> McChesney, Kevin. "Joy to the World." AFP 11-10472. 3-5 oct.
>
> Page, Anna Laura. "Song of the Angels." CGA. CGB176. 2-3 oct.

PRAISE ENSEMBLE

> DeShazo, Lynn and Jamie Harvill. "Heaven and Earth" in *Integrity's Hosanna! Music Songbook 10.* INT.
>
> Hanson, Handt. "Once and For All Time" in *Spirit Calls, Rejoice!* CCF.
>
> Music, Malcolm. "A Christmas Alleluia." SHW. SATB, gtr, bass, drms.
>
> Smith, Michael W., and Wayne Kirkpatrick/Ronn Huff. "All Is Well." WRD 3010538162. SATB, orch.

TUESDAY, JANUARY 5
KAJ MUNK, MARTYR, 1944

Munk, a Danish Lutheran pastor and playwright, was an outspoken critic of the Nazis who occupied Denmark during the Second World War. His plays frequently highlight the eventual victory of the Christian faith despite the church's weak and ineffective witness. Munk was feared by the Nazis because his patriotic sermons and articles helped to strengthen the Danish resistance movement.

Munk's life and death invite us to ponder the power of the gospel in the midst of social and political conflicts. Offer prayers for those who face persecution, and for those who resist and challenge tyranny. This day is another reminder that the joy of Christmas cannot be separated from human suffering, and God's redemptive love made known in the cross and resurrection of Christ.

EPIPHANY

Return home by a different way

IMAGES OF THE SEASON

We take down the ornaments and decorations, pack them up for another year, and haul the Christmas tree outdoors in a shower of brittle pine needles. We might gather out under the stars for the burning of the greens, with dry needles flaming up in an instant, creating their own draft. The fresher ones sizzle and pop as their sap begins to blaze. Indoors, pine needles by the thousands spring up in all directions as we try to sweep the carpeting. Every year it's the same; still, the familiar has the power to surprise us. We vacuum, and move the furniture back to its usual arrangement. The room feels empty—perhaps a little lonely—but also larger. New. We notice things about it we'd forgotten, or had never observed in the first place. Our perspective has shifted.

We return things to where they had been. We return to our daily routine, but the same place, the same sequence, feels different. The house is quiet—a little peaceful and a little sad—the company has gone home. Yet echoing through the quiet are memories of shared stories and laughter, treasure received during the visit. Because of what we have heard and seen, we resume life differently—returning by another road.

The season of Epiphany—revelation—is all about having our perceptions and perspective changed, and seeing things in a whole new way. After an encounter with the holy, ordinary reality seems larger and new. In response, we praise and glorify God.

Epiphany begins with a star pointing the way toward the light of the world, newborn in Bethlehem of Judea. Throughout the season, light shines progressively stronger until we arrive at the mountain of transfiguration, where Christ's glory is revealed in dazzling brilliance.

Light for the nations illumines the night sky, shining on those who were in darkness and the shadow of death, and blazes atop the mountain. Gradually, during the season of Epiphany, we can see further and more distinctly *in* the growing light; we *see* the light; meaning dawns upon us. Our ordinary surroundings appear more expansive; our hearts capable of something new. "What are you looking for?" asks Jesus, of the two disciples who have begun to follow him. We are encouraged to seek and to find.

The season is filled with questions and the journeys they set in motion. "Where is the child who has been born king of the Jews?" ask the star-watchers from the East. "Rabbi, where are you staying?" ask Andrew and his unnamed friend. "Come and see," beckons Jesus. And so we find ourselves in company with foreigners wise enough to know what they don't know, and with the new disciples as they drop their professional fishnets to follow Jesus all around the territory of Galilee.

In the searching and the traveling we discover more and more who Jesus is. Over and over we are met with surprise. This poor Jewish boy is born a threat to tyrants, but not to the genuinely wise who journey for weeks in order to find him. At the River Jordan, Jesus argues with John and insists upon receiving baptism along with all the sinners. With John we name Jesus the Lamb of God for the whole world, and discover his power to inspire and heal. Jesus claims to fulfill the Law and the Prophets—and then converses freely with their living embodiments, Moses and Elijah.

The season is a glorious accumulation of small but significant personal epiphanies—revelations. We come to view others as chosen by God and greatly loved. We can regard ourselves, too, in more gracious light. At times we feel like bruised reeds or dimly burning wicks who have labored in vain and spent our strength for nothing. By worldly standards we may be weak, foolish, and despised. God, knowing this perfectly well replies, "I have called you . . . ; I have given you as a covenant to the people, a light to the nations . . ." (Isa. 42:6). The love of Christ shines in us who share his baptismal life and calling.

These epiphanies open up and widen our perceptions of what is possible. We find abundant room to

98

grow, room to act. And so our vision expresses itself in action. We are to let our light so shine before others that they too may glorify the Father in heaven (Matt. 5:16). We are called to open up eyes that are blind and set free those who are bound (Isa. 24:7). Light shines as we are given the grace to do justice, love kindness, and walk humbly with our God (Micah 6:8).

The will of God is not that we construct dwellings to preserve our visions on the mountaintop, but that we build as needed right where we are. We raise up old and ruined foundations, repair breached city walls, and restore streets that real brothers and sisters can live in. We are to make use of the room we've been given and make room for others, sharing our bread with the hungry and bringing the homeless poor into our house.

But we don't have to start a construction project at the moment while we're caught up in a mountaintop experience. The response God desires to this culminating epiphany is wonder and praise: "It is good for us to be here" (Matt. 17:4).

Transfiguration draws to a close our annual three-season immersion in the mystery of incarnation. In Advent we prepare for Christ's coming in our lives and at the end of time. During the twelve days of Christmas we celebrate his birth and continued presence among us. Epiphany starts with joy, as we respond to what has been revealed. We return to "ordinary time" differently, changed by our experience. We return home, but our new perspective impels us to journey onward to spread the good news and share what we have. Along the road we find that the revelations just keep coming! The one mystery has countless dimensions; as many variations as a snowflake. When we catch a glimpse of how it all comes together, it is dazzling indeed.

During a precious few moments in our lives our strongest response is, "How good it is to be here!" All the more reason to savor them when they do occur, and not diminish them by anticipating their inevitable fading. Joy will illuminate our memory afterward like a lamp shining in a dark place until the day dawns and the morning star rises forever in our hearts.

ENVIRONMENT AND ART FOR THE SEASON

The theme begun Christmas Eve continues. In the Epiphany we recognize how we are the recipients of God's promise and gifts. Epiphany is a feast of light. We recognize that this radiance is not of our own doing, but the love of God shining through the night of darkness. This light cannot be vanquished by our human endeavors and folly. The Epiphany also calls, teaches, and nourishes us to recognize our responsibility as children of light.

The environment for this season changes for several reasons. We begin with the color of white for all banners, paraments, and eucharistic vestments. White celebrates the sign and wonder of the star that called wise men from different nations to Jesus, while also marking Jesus' baptism in the river Jordan. The liturgical colors for the Sundays after the Epiphany change to green, signaling

that through the lectionary readings of this season, Jesus calls us to new growth in being his disciples. Finally, the season concludes with the transfiguration, where the radiance of God's light and glory will re-emerge. Within these few weeks we have an opportunity to provide interesting changes to the environment as well.

What are the basic images of the season that we can visually reinforce? The environment for worship should never be static nor taken for granted. Too frequently, by Epiphany and the Sundays that follow, North Americans want to hibernate as the winter in northern regions continues. The liturgical year, however, calls us to a different commitment of time and energy. Keep people actively informed about the liturgical life of the church, as well as giving witness to the fact that God continues to bring good news to all people.

EXTERIOR ENVIRONMENT

Obviously some of the Christmas decorations need to come down, but a visual presence of this season of light can still remain throughout the season after Epiphany. White, silver, and gold banners may remain, as well as special lighting. To these banners may be added additional colors representing the gentile nations of the world that respond to the brightness of the star (such color may be welcome relief in climates that are either white with snow or a dry brown). The introduction of additional streamers of brilliant fabric colors will add heightened interest for persons passing the church. For those inquiring, it is an opportunity to tell the story of the season and to witness to God's love for all humanity. In addition to the global significance of Epiphany itself, this season's commemoration of Martin Luther King Jr., and the Week of Prayer for Christian Unity give testimony to God's all-inclusive embrace of humanity. Festive streamers and banners may remain until the beginning of Lent.

If the church is blessed with a carillon, it provides another appropriate environmental element that can be used to explore the riches of Epiphany hymnody.

NARTHEX/ENTRANCE

Many decorations remaining from the Christmas season will require replacement. The main task is to continue the festive character of the season. Plants should be kept fresh or replaced with different types, as long as they are harmonious with other decorations.

Many entrance spaces would benefit from the appropriate use of art. Art can take the form of a wood carving, textile, icon, painting, or tile sculpture. In addition to a major work of art that has importance throughout the year, explore more occasional art, perhaps embroidery or prints that reflect the season. Such art should be simple and direct in telling the story. Try for variety that represents different media and styles.

A processional white banner, perhaps with accents of silver or gold, can be used to good advantage in the narthex and then carried into the worship space at the beginning of the service.

WORSHIP SPACE

Since this season reflects the journey of wise men, and of Jesus' journey to the Jordan river to be baptized by John, it is fitting that we use a procession to convey this sense of action and movement. Elements in a procession should include a processional cross and torches that are scaled and well designed for the space. Any banners developed to complement the paraments and vestments should employ appropriate use of color, texture and symbolic content. The lectionary or Bible might be covered in a way that harmonizes with other hangings and vestments.

Beginning with the Second Sunday after the Epiphany, the liturgical color changes to green. Many sets of green paraments have symbols more appropriate for use in summer or for the Sundays after Pentecost. If new paraments are being considered, perhaps it is wise to design a green set that avoids the use of applied symbols that work well for only one time of the year. Alternatively, two different sets of green paraments may be designed—one for use after Epiphany, and one for use after Pentecost.

Candles might be used throughout the season after Epiphany, since it is a celebration of continuing light. With the Epiphany, the use of four torches at the corners of the altar might suggest the spread of Jesus' radiant light to all nations.

Many congregations schedule baptisms on the festival of the Baptism of our Lord. Evaluating the baptismal font and the area surrounding this space is always important, because in this act God's promise of grace and salvation are first revealed to us. The font symbolizes our dying to sin and rising to new life in Christ. Ideally the font should be large enough to convey the theological importance of this sacrament. Since it marks the entrance of a Christian into the church, its location and position in the worship space might actually be located near the entrance. The font should be open, perhaps with flowing water and allowing for access to the water at all times, whether or not a baptism is scheduled. Well-designed embellishment of the baptismal area with carvings, worthy textiles, imaginative tiles and mosaics will enhance and define the area. In addition, a side table is practical to hold a ewer (if needed), shell, baptismal candles, baptismal garment, and oil for anointing. It is customary to place the paschal (Easter) candle here throughout the year, so that it may be a sign of Christ's dying and rising whenever a baptism takes place.

From the Second Sunday after Epiphany to the week before the Transfiguration of Our Lord, green paraments and vestments are used. By this time the decorations of the earlier part of the cycle should be removed from the environment. We still need visual elements that clearly focus upon God's incarnation and the light revealed to us and all people, so it is not a time to remove candles, which are a continuing source of light and life.

The environment in this cycle of the church year may be enriched by using different types of artistic elements that relate to the readings. Items that announce the cosmic significance of Jesus' human birth, as well as Jesus' call to his disciples might be used in various ways. The goal should be to let the light of Christ shine forth with amazing clarity.

PREACHING WITH THE SEASON

Maranatha and Immanuel provide almost automatic themes for the seasons of Advent and Christmas. Epiphany, however, does not seem to have such a self-evident theme. Epiphany seems more a time to recover from Advent and Christmas and to prepare for Lent, with little identity of its own. Indeed, many church calendars omit the season of Epiphany, calling the weeks between the Baptism of Our Lord and the Transfiguration of Our Lord simply "Ordinary Time." Even this designation, of course, would be rife with meaning. If the incarnation involves God's habit of using the everyday for self-revelation, then "ordinary time" is anything but ordinary. It would provide the stage for that return after Christmas to "normal life."

But our calendar does label these weeks as the season after Epiphany, and even a cursory reading of the history, festivals, and lectionary of this time reveals a theme.

The first clue to a theme is the name of the season itself. "Epiphany" has the root meaning of manifesting, showing, shining, or gleaming. "Epiphanes" was a common word in pre–New Testament Greek. It denoted the sudden appearance of a force in battle, and so by extension that of a god as a welcome intervener in human affairs. In the Septuagint, "epiphanes" describes the magnificence that surrounds the appearance of God during theophanies. The word, therefore, denotes a manifestation, an appearance that rescues.

A second place to look is the history of Epiphany. Epiphany started in the East, before Christmas did in

the West, as the feast concentrating on the beginning of Christ's ministry. The church in the East celebrated the birth and baptism of Jesus, and the wedding feast at Cana on the day we now call Epiphany. At some point, East and West exchanged nativity celebrations, so that in most eastern churches the birth narratives moved to December 25, leaving the baptism as the dominant event commemorated on January 6. In the West, for some reason, the Matthean story of the Magi was separated from the nativity celebration on December 25 and assigned to the new feast on January 6, although the three great mysteries (magi, baptism, and Cana) were linked closely together in the celebration.

Epiphany's very history, therefore, indicates that the season completes Christmas by opening up the story of the nativity. To the church in the West, at least, Epiphany not only commemorates the visit of the magi from the East bearing gifts, but is itself a gift sent from the East, an expression of the catholicity and cross-cultural nature of the gospel.

The central theme of the season of Epiphany, then, is this: Jesus acts with evident authority to rescue and relieve. The Word not only heals, strengthens, and makes whole, but by doing so makes its presence obvious to the world. Lent provides us with a time to hear over and over again the message of the cross: the foolishness and weakness of God, which is in fact God's wisdom and strength. Epiphany, on the other hand, proclaims the recognizable glory and strength of God in Christ. The refrain of one of the season's great hymns acclaims Christ as "God in flesh made manifest." It is apparent, even to eyes not yet opened by faith, this Jesus is obviously something special. This manifestation, furthermore, calls forth faith even in gentiles—culture is no barrier to the proclamation of the gospel.

Certainly the readings assigned for Sundays after Epiphany provide support for this general theme. Every year the season is full of the sort of miracles anyone would expect of a Christ. We hear week after week of healing, feeding, exorcism, and authoritative teaching. Often these miracles involve or bring forth faith outside of the people of Israel.

Epiphany must look back to Advent to remember that in this world the kingdom is only breaking in, and that Christ will only become entirely manifest at the end of time. Epiphany must look back to Christmas and forward to Lent to remember that Christ has redefined glory, and that God's greatest epiphany, the truest showing of the divine face, was on the cross.

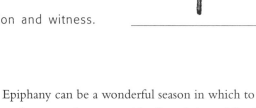

PLANNING AHEAD FOR THE SEASON

Remembering that the Magi came from afar to worship Jesus has often meant that this season has an emphasis on global mission and witness. While midwinter may not be an easy time to get out and tell our story in much of North America,

the congregation may wish to use a variety of opportunities to welcome people into its midst. Public relations and advertising experts know that this season is relatively slower. Why not take advantage of that fact (and the lower advertising rates that may be available during this season) to get the church's message out through a variety of communication channels. Ask people with media expertise in your congregation (or within a cluster of congregations) to help you design something that offers an invitation to people who may not have heard about your congregation in other ways. They also might be able to advise on how a limited advertising budget can be spent most effectively.

People from your area who have been on global mission trips may be happy to speak about their experiences in ways that can delight congregational members of all ages, perhaps in an intergenerational Sunday school program sometime in the Epiphany season. If your congregation has developed global connections through a companion synod program or by helping to sponsor the work of one or more missionaries,

Epiphany can be a wonderful season in which to explore several opportunities for mission while also focusing on the scripture texts used on the Sundays after Epiphany.

January, with its Martin Luther King Jr. Day, and February with its traditional emphasis as Black History month, might encourage congregations to be more intentional about being multicultural. Consider participating in an ecumenical service that has multicultural dimensions during these days, or even sponsoring one of your own. Even if there is little diversity within your own immediate area, it can be an important opportunity to become aware of some of the concerns of the church at large.

Themes in the lectionary encourage us in reaching out to others and may become the central focus for congregational councils and other organizations that reorganize at the beginning of a new calendar year. What is God calling the congregation to be in this community? What long-range goals should be set so that the church continues its growth?

Does your congregation celebrate the festival of the Epiphany in any way? Some congregations have seen this as a time to gather for a festive evening prayer service. Such a service can draw the Christmas season to a close, as well as provide an opportunity for worship apart from Sunday morning. Perhaps an evening prayer service on Epiphany can be an occasion to observe with other congregations, especially with those from other denominations. Even if you would not use it at other times, consider using incense at this service (frankincense is the obvious choice). The service of light in evening prayer is especially fitting on this festival.

The Baptism of Our Lord (January 10) may be observed as a *baptismal festival*—one of the occasions throughout the year when the congregation plans to celebrate the sacrament of baptism. Rather than seeing such a festival as limiting or legalistic, it can be an opportunity for corporate worship to be focused intentionally around baptism. Having scheduled baptismal festivals can lead to better preparation of baptismal candidates, parents, and sponsors. Receptions or congregational fellowship times following baptismal services might also be planned in advance—something that highlights baptism as an entrance into the church. If your congregation offers the option for scheduling baptisms at times other than the preselected baptismal festivals, then congregational members will not view the practice of planned baptismal festivals as inflexible.

When observed, the traditional baptismal festivals serve to highlight one or more aspects of baptism itself: commissioning for ministry in the world (Baptism of Our Lord), incorporation into the death and resurrection of Christ (Easter Vigil), receiving the gifts of the Holy Spirit (Pentecost), and becoming part of a community of faith that extends throughout time and space (All Saints Day/Sunday). A congregation may select these dates as well as additional ones throughout the year in order to plan for baptisms and the extra time they take in the service, rather than having baptisms appear to many people as interruptions in worship.

The Transfiguration of Our Lord may be a time to say farewell to the alleluia. If you have a banner with the word alleluia as a prominent feature on it, consider retiring it after the conclusion of the gospel verse on this Sunday. (Some congregations have gone so far as to bury it in the ground—quite a feat if the ground in your part of the country is still frozen.) If you make a point of saying farewell to the alleluia, the hymn "Alleluia, song of gladness" (WOV 654) is especially fitting. Explaining why the alleluia will disappear during Lent may be useful—for young and old alike. It could serve as an announcement in the bulletin and/or spoken aloud.

103

ORDO FOR THE SEASON

One way to vary the gathering rite from one season or day to another might be never to have all three of the following on a given day: an order for confession and forgiveness, a Kyrie, and a hymn of praise. For the festivals of the Baptism of Our Lord (January 10) and the Transfiguration of Our Lord (February 14), consider using the Kyrie and the hymn of praise, but without an order for confession and forgiveness. For the "green" Sundays after Epiphany, consider using an order of confession and forgiveness, and a hymn of praise, but no Kyrie. Many congregations will likely use an entrance hymn during the gathering rite each week as well. Yet by using an "any two of three" approach, the gathering rite is never unduly extended, even on festival days.

Congregations that like to group baptisms together on scheduled days throughout the year should try to schedule one of those baptismal festivals for the Baptism of our Lord, when the scripture readings focus on baptism and the mission flowing from it. Even if no baptisms actually occur on this day, it can be an opportunity for the entire congregation to join in a renewal of baptism by using, for example, the order for "Affirmation of Baptism" beginning with the address (#12) preceding the creed on page 199 of *LBW*, continuing with the prayers (not necessarily those printed, but that is one option), and concluding with the baptismal covenant on the top of page 201 ("Do you intend to continue in the covenant God made with you in holy baptism . . ."). The entire congregation may join in the response corporately. Additionally, if members of the congregation have made commitments for service both within the congregation and in the community at large for the coming year, the corporate affirmation could be a way to affirm those ministries. Perhaps training and orientation meetings for volunteers would then occur sometime within the following week.

Eucharistic Prayer C for the Epiphany season (*WOV, Leaders Edition,* p. 67) offers another way for the congregation to be mindful of this season's focus upon the light of God in our darkness, and about our role in spreading that light to others. The post-communion canticle throughout the season after Epiphany might be the Song of Simeon ("Lord now you let your servant go in peace . . ."). It also reminds us of Christ's mission to be a light to the nations.

ASSEMBLY SONG FOR THE SEASON

Worship from Epiphany through the Transfiguration of Our Lord opens

important truths about God to us. While the themes of Christmas and

Epiphany center in the incarnation of God—God

becoming human like us and dwelling among us—

the liturgies of Good Friday and the Easter season reflect the divinity of God, an all-powerful and glorious Savior, reigning in heaven for eternity. The Sundays after Epiphany, especially Transfiguration, form a bridge for us between the two natures of Christ. Images of light permeate our Epiphany imaginations, from the star that guides the Magi, to the brilliant light as Jesus was transfigured before his disciples. These images guide us into a deep encounter with both the human and divine Jesus during these weeks.

The radical nature of Jesus' message was that it was for all the world, even for gentiles and unusual visitors from the East. The fact that the visitors who offered lavish gifts to Jesus were from afar, not from the local establishment, is critical in understanding Epiphany and the weeks following. An urgent sense of mission for all people permeates the readings during these weeks.

This season of ministry and mission may provide the opportunity to do more with the sending, the final beat in our liturgical rhythm of gathering, word, meal, and sending. Post-communion songs and closing hymns, appropriate prayers, benedictions, and dismissals that focus on action, inclusion, and mission can assist in provoking God's people to live the liturgy into their homes, workplaces, schools, and wherever they may be during the week.

Epiphany may be an ideal time to introduce music from cultures not normally represented in our particular congregations. As the gaps in our world community become smaller, we have more and more repertoire from the church in all corners of the world. *With One Voice* and many other sources offer a rich variety of songs. Introducing music from unfamiliar styles requires careful preparation. Parish musicians must first do some studying and a lot of listening to begin the discovery of how this music should sound. Then a reality check is

needed. Knowing something about the styles, how can we, with our often limited "western" resources, sing and play this music with integrity? Children are often the best teachers. They have few inhibitions and can learn anything when taught with confidence and enthusiasm.

Two notes of caution, however. Even though children can be the first to learn music from other cultures, this repertoire must never be relegated to them alone. And, music of various cultures ought to become a regular part of a congregation's repertoire, not relegated to "Mission Sunday." These times may be fine for introducing new songs, but only if they lead to fully integrated use.

The popular culture often gets ignored in these conversations, for it is frequently most difficult to grapple with what is in our own backyard. While the church is called to stand somewhat apart from the culture, it cannot ignore it. One senses the great pressure from many people to incorporate popular music styles into Lutheran worship. The reality, however, is that the church will never be able to compete with the secular music business. Our goals and objectives are different. Enabling an encounter with God is not entirely compatible with marketing strategies and consumerism. For this reason, popular music is often dismissed as incompatible with Christian worship. However, it is both unfair and unwise to completely dismiss the possibility of integrating various musics, even popular styles.

For decades, the rise in contemporary Christian music has centered primarily in solo or ensemble (band) music. Some leaders present a feeling of "sing along with us if you can!" That type of focus on performance is hardly full participation by the people of God. Increasingly however, contemporary church musicians are becoming aware of the assembly and what it takes to engage a congregation in song. We need to look carefully and critically for examples from this repertoire that are theologically appropriate, liturgically helpful, and suitable for assembly singing.

MUSIC for the SEASON

VERSE AND OFFERTORY

Boehnke, Paul. *Festive Verse Settings for Christmas, Epiphany and Transfiguration.* MSM 80-100. SATB, opt kybd.

Cherwien, David. *Verses for the Epiphany Season.* MSM 80-200. U, opt hb, org.

Johnson, David N. *Verses and Offertories for Epiphany 2 through Transfiguration.* AFP 11-9544. U, kybd.

Verses and Offertory Sentences, Part II: Epiphany through Transfiguration. CPH 97-5502.

CHORAL MUSIC FOR THE SEASON

Beebe, Hank. "God Shines Forth." CGA 745. U, 2 pt, kybd.

Beethoven, Ludwig van/Richard Proulx. "Give Thanks to God." AFP 11-10648. SAB, kybd.

Bell, John. "Will You Come and Follow Me." GIA G4384. SATB, solo, opt kybd/cong.

Ellingboe, Bradley. "Tandi tanga Jesu." AFP 11-10602. SATB, perc.

Ferguson, John. "He Comes to Us as One Unknown." AFP 11-10742. SATB, org.

Hirten, John Karl. "For Glory Dawns upon You." AFP 11-10650. SB, kybd.

Hopson, Hal H. "New Every Morning." AFP 11-10673. SATB, org, opt cong.

Lassus, Rudolf de/Richard Proulx. "Stars in the Sky Proclaim." AFP 12-400004. SAB.

Leavitt, John. "Come, Follow Me." GIA G-3028. SAB, ob, kybd.

Neswick, Bruce. "Jesus Came from Nazareth." AFP 11-10643. 2 pt, org, solo.

Owens, Sam Batt. "There Is a Balm in Gilead." MSM 50-8832. SATB, solo.

Praetorius, Michael. "Praise Ye the Lord." PRE 312-41067. SATB.

Rotermund, Melvin. "O God of Light." CPH 98-3775. SATB, kybd.

Stainer, John. "How Beautiful Upon the Mountains." NOV 29-0314-08. SATB, org.

Stearns, Peter Pindar. "Your Love, O Lord, Reaches to the Heavens." SEL 410-836. SATB, org.

Willcocks, David. "Rejoice Today with One Accord." OXF A428. SATB, org.

CHILDREN'S CHORAL MUSIC FOR THE SEASON

Cherwien, David. "Ever Since the Savior Came." CPH 98-3351. U, org, opt fl.

Christopherson, Dorothy. "Rise, My Child." CGA 432. U, opt 2 pt, pno, fl.

Christopherson, Dorothy. "The Night of the Star." AFP 11-10890. U, opt desc, pno, fl, perc.

Nelson, Ronald A. "Gather Together!" MSM 50-9450. U or 2 pt trbl, kybd, opt cong, fl, vc.

Ramseth, Betty Ann. "Make Us to Be." CGA 579. U, fl, orff.

Wold, Wayne. "Gloria in Excelsis Deo." MSM 80-101. U, kybd.

INSTRUMENTAL MUSIC FOR THE SEASON

Hassell, Michael. *Jazz Sunday Morning.* AFP 11-10700. Pno.

Kane, Daniel Q. *Selectable Delectables.* AFP 11-10619. Pno.

Leavitt, John. *Hymn Preludes for the Church Year.* AFP 11-10134. Org.

Ramsey, Peter. *Crystal Tide and Falling Stars.* AFP 11-10617. Pno

Sedio, Mark. *Dancing in the Light of God: A Collection for Piano.* AFP 11-10793.

HANDBELL MUSIC FOR THE SEASON

Honoré, Jeffrey. "The Epiphany of Our God." LOR 20/1005. 3-5 oct.

Hopson, Hal H. "Siyahamba." HOP 1869. 3-5 oct, perc, SATB.

Larson, Katherine. "Beautiful Savior." AFP 11-10516. 3-4 oct.

White, Gary C. "An Epiphany Carol." BEC HB59. 3 oct.

Young, Philip M. "In Thee Is Gladness." AFP 11-10624. 4-5 oct.

ALTERNATE WORSHIP TEXTS

CONFESSION AND FORGIVENESS

In the name of the Father, and of the ✢ Son, and of the Holy
    Spirit.
Amen

Confident in the assurance
of forgiveness through Jesus Christ,
let us confess our sin
in the presence of God and of one another.

Silence for reflection and self-examination.

Revealing and healing God,
we confess to you that we choose to walk
in places far from your light.
We neglect opportunities
to do justice, to love kindness,
and to walk humbly with you.
We hide the light that is your gift to us.
Forgive us and guide us in our way,
that we may shine before others
and give you the glory. Amen

Arise, shine, your light has come.
God forgives you all your sins
through the wisdom and power of the cross
and sends the Holy Spirit to rest upon you.
People of God, live no longer in darkness,
but in the light of Christ.
Amen

GREETING

To the church of God in this place,
to those who are called to be saints,
to all those who call on the name
of our Lord Jesus Christ:
Grace and peace be with you all.
And also with you.

OFFERTORY PRAYER

Gracious and loving God,
we bring to your table
these gifts of your creation
and fruits of our labor
for your use in the world.
Receive them for the sake of Christ,
who enlightens our lives
and leads us to the feast
now and forever. Amen

INVITATION TO COMMUNION

Christ is here in bread and wine,
revealing the glorious splendor of God.
Come to the feast of light and life.

POST-COMMUNION PRAYER

O God of love, you have graciously fed us
with the body and blood of your Son.
Let this holy food empower us,
that your dawn may break forth
as we give ourselves to the hungry
and to those who thirst for righteousness;
through Jesus Christ our Lord.
Amen

BENEDICTION

May God, who created the heavens
and spread out the earth,
shine upon you.
May God, whose delight it was
to be revealed to us in Jesus Christ,
uphold and strengthen you.
May God, who guided seekers
by the fire of a star,
bring you to glory.
Amen

DISMISSAL

You are servants of God;
you are light to the nations.
Go in peace. Serve the Lord.
Thanks be to God.

107

SEASONAL RITES

LESSONS AND CAROLS

For Epiphany (January 6) or anytime in the season that follows.

Stand

ENTRANCE HYMN

LBW 55   Good Christian friends, rejoice

LBW 56   The first Noel

DIALOG

The people who walked in darkness have seen a great light.

The light shines in the darkness, and the darkness has not overcome it.

Those who dwelt in the land of deep darkness, on them light has shined.

We have beheld Christ's glory, glory as of the only Son from the Father.

For to us a child is born, to us a Son is given.

In him was life, and the life was the light of all people.

OPENING PRAYER

See Prayer of the Day for Epiphany (LBW, p. 15 or WOV, Leaders Edition, p. 78).

Sit

First Reading: John 1:1-14

CAROL

LBW 42   Of the Father's love begotten

LBW 45   Oh, come, all ye faithful

LBW 57   Let our gladness have no end

Second Reading: John 1:18-25

CAROL

LBW 44   Infant holy, infant lowly

LBW 67   Away in a manger

WOV 644 Away in a manger

Third Reading: Matthew 2:1-12

CAROL

LBW 75   Bright and glorious is the sky

WOV 645 There's a star in the East

WOV 646 We Three kings of Orient are

Fourth Reading: Matthew 2:13-23

CAROL

LBW 177 By All your saints in warfare (st. 9)

WOV 639 Oh, sleep now, holy baby

or Coventry Carol (*The Hymnal 1982*, 247)

Fifth Reading: Luke 2:41-51

CAROL

LBW 417 In a lowly manger born

WOV 634 Sing of Mary, pure and lowly

WOV 643 Once in David's royal city

Sixth Reading: Matthew 3:13-17

CAROL

LBW 85   When Christ's appearing was made known

LBW 88   Oh, love, how deep

WOV 647 When Jesus came to Jordan

Seventh Reading: John 2:1-11

CAROL

LBW 205 Now the silence

WOV 648 Jesus, come! For we invite you

Stand

RESPONSIVE PRAYER

Glory to God in the highest,

and peace to God's people on earth.

Blessed are you, Prince of Peace. You rule the earth with truth and justice.

Send your gift of peace to all nations of the world.

Blessed are you, Son of Mary. You share our humanity.

Have mercy on the sick, the dying, and all who suffer this day.

Blessed are you, Son of God. You dwell among us as the Word made flesh.

Reveal yourself to us in Word and Sacrament that we may bear your light to all the world.

THE LORD'S PRAYER

BLESSING AND DISMISSAL

Let us bless the Lord.

Thanks be to God.

May you be filled with the wonder of Mary, the obedience of Joseph, the joy of the angels, the eagerness of the shepherds, the determination of the magi, and the peace of the Christ Child. Almighty God, Father, ✛ Son, and Holy Spirit bless you now and forever.

Amen

SENDING HYMN

LBW 90   Songs of thankfulness and praise

JANUARY 6, 1999

INTRODUCTION

On this day the church celebrates its catholic nature and mission. In worship we pray that the Holy Spirit would make our lives radiant with the brightness of Christ. From the Lord's table the church goes forth into the world as a witness to Christ's merciful presence. As the stars light up the darkness of night, so the baptized are called to be light in the world.

PRAYER OF THE DAY

Lord God, on this day you revealed your Son to the nations by the leading of a star. Lead us now by faith to know your presence in our lives, and bring us at last to the full vision of your glory, through your Son, Jesus Christ our Lord, who lives and reigns with you and the Holy Spirit, one God, now and forever.

READINGS

Isaiah 60:1-6

The long years of darkness are over. The prophet announces the end of exile in Babylon and looks forward to the restoration of the city of Jerusalem. God's light, reflected in Israel, will draw caravans bearing treasure from all the nations who freely come to praise the Lord.

Psalm 72:1-7, 10-14

All kings shall bow down before him. (Ps. 72:11)

Ephesians 3:1-12

Though it had been hidden for years, Paul now reveals the secret that has shaped his apostolic witness: in Jesus Christ, God's salvation extends beyond the Jews to include all people. The light of Christ shines upon Jew and Gentile alike.

Matthew 2:1-12

The rich symbolism of this story—the Magi, a star in the east, Herod's plots—announces the prophetic hope for an epiphany or revelation that God has entered into our history as one of us.

COLOR   White

THE PRAYERS

Illumined by the light of Christ, let us pray for all nations, and for all in need of his healing presence.

A BRIEF SILENCE.

That the church may joyfully share the gifts of word and sacrament with all who seek to know the mystery of God, we pray:

Send forth your light, O God.

That nations come to your light, and rulers govern with justice and righteousness, we pray:

Send forth your light, O God.

That all who are depressed, lonely, or sick (especially . . .) may see the healing light of God amid their suffering, we pray:

Send forth your light, O God.

That we would share of our wealth with those who live in poverty, we pray:

Send forth your light, O God.

That we welcome those whose cultures and habits differ from our own as Christ welcomes us, we pray:

Send forth your light, O God.

That those on a journey for spiritual fulfillment may be led by the star to the glory of God in a manger, we pray:

Send forth your light, O God.

HERE OTHER INTERCESSIONS MAY BE OFFERED.

That we offer the homage of both worship and service until we join all the saints in the light of God's eternal presence, we pray:

Send forth your light, O God.

In all we ask, O provident God, give us grace to proclaim the coming of your reign in Jesus Christ our Lord.

Amen

IMAGES FOR PREACHING

Like it or not, we are children of the modern age. Reason is our pathway, information our fuel. We demand proof, expect results, want things to make sense. Perhaps this tendency (as well as the usually inconvenient timing of this festival on a weekday) is why Epiphany suffers such neglect in many churches. Who wants to gather to hear that all the evidence in heaven and on earth will never be enough for lasting life? Epiphany is an affront to our cool, calculating discourse. It challenges us instead to rethink what it truly means to be enlightened.

109

To be sure, nature testifies loudly in today's readings. We all know how the star held the magi in its thrall, a light drawing nations to its source. But this peculiar light does less shining than it does rising and moving and stopping, like some beast of burden trudging its well-worn course. Speaking of beasts, even herds of camels (though in Isaiah, not Matthew!) point to God's redemption. So do the minerals and resins offered to the babe by his visitors. Even the abundance of the sea adds its witness, as Isaiah sees it. And the social world offers its own confirmation. Words from gentile outsiders cause not just Herod but the entire holy city to quake with fear.

The irony is that this widespread evidence remains incomplete. The star can only take the magi part of the way. Herod's fright at their words does not tell the whole story. Something more is needed. It takes a special revelation (irony upon irony, through chief priests and scribes!) to say what is truly happening at Bethlehem. Or, as Ephesians remarks, it is the Spirit's work to disclose the mystery hidden for generations. The festival today introduces us modern people, therefore, to an ancient mystery. And the substance of this mystery centers today's epistle reading: "the gentiles have become fellow heirs." What was once only dimly known to reason is now opened before us like treasure. Those who were once far off (and that includes us) are now counted part of God's rich variety. It's a promise stronger than any proof.

WORSHIP MATTERS

What is constant and what is fluid in our worship? Does it take a reliable form, and where is the give and take? We owe our forms of worship to Jewish practices such as the synagogue service, prayers at mealtimes, and sabbath celebrations. Already in the book of Acts, the shape of the liturgy is described as those baptized who "devoted themselves to the apostles' teaching and fellowship, to the breaking of bread and the prayers" (Acts 2:42).

But this shape of worship as word, prayer, and meal has been influenced by both history and culture. Even though we are able to find a normative kind of form for the liturgy, it continues to be adaptable and varied. This process is due to all the influences around us: where we live, the language we speak, and the events of our time. The Epiphany gospel says that "wise men from the East

came to Jerusalem" (Matt. 2:1b). How can we celebrate the gifts of various cultures at Epiphany? What unique gifts can our communities bring to worship?

LET THE CHILDREN COME

Particular attention to the visual environment of the worship space during the weeks after Epiphany is one way to help children identify this season as different from the days of Christmas and the upcoming starkness of Lent. These days are filled with the manifestation of the light of Christ shining out. Consider ways to fill the worship space with light. Suncatchers and mirrored and beveled glass might hang throughout the worship space. Find things that tell the story of the days after Epiphany, things that capture the light, are filled by the light, reflect it, and are changed by it.

MUSIC FOR WORSHIP

GATHERING

LBW 75	Bright and glorious is the sky
WOV 646	We three kings of Orient are

PSALM 72

Della Picca, Angelo A. *Psalms for the Cantor,* vol. III. WLP 2504.

Guimont, Michael. "Psalm 72: Justice Shall Flourish" in RS.

Haugen, Marty. "Every Nation on Earth Will Adore You" in PCY.

Hobby, Robert. PW, Cycle C.

LBW 87   Hail to the Lord's anointed

LBW 530   Jesus shall reign

Smith, Dave. "Let His Glory Fill the Earth" in PS1.

HYMN OF THE DAY

WOV 649   I want to walk as a child of the light
HOUSTON

VOCAL RESOURCES

Lamberton, Dodd. "I Want to Walk as a Child of the Light." MSM 50-8813. SATB, org.

Thomerson, Kathleen. "I Want to Walk as a Child of the Light." GIA G-2786. SATB, kybd.

INSTRUMENTAL RESOURCES

Behnke, John. "I Want to Walk as a Child of the Light" in *Laudate,* vol. 3, ed. J. Kosnik. CPH 97-6591. Org.

Burkhardt, Michael. "I Want to Walk as a Child of the Light" in *Eight Improvisations on 20th Century Hymn Tunes.* MSM 10-707. Org.

Hassell, Michael. "Houston" in *More Folkways.* AFP 11-10866. Kybd, inst.

ALTERNATE HYMN OF THE DAY

| LBW 76 | O Morning Star, how fair and bright! |
| LBW 84 | Brightest and best of the stars |

COMMUNION

| LBW 50 | Angels, from the realms of glory |
| WOV 776 | Be thou my vision |

SENDING

| LBW 518 | Beautiful Savior |
| WOV 651 | Shine, Jesus, shine |

ADDITIONAL HYMNS AND SONGS

LW 79	O Jesus, king of glory
W3 407	What star is this, with beams so bright?
LLC 317	Los magos/The magi who to Bethlehem did go

MUSIC FOR THE DAY

CHORAL

Anon. "Out of the East" in *Later Renaissance Motets.* ed. Matthew N. Lundquist. HM (Musica Sacra Series, I). SATB.

Busarow, Donald. "O Morning Star, How Fair and Bright." CPH 98-281. SAB, cong, trbl inst, org.

Carter, John. "We Have Seen His Star in the East." ECS 4903. SATB, org.

Hirten, John Karl. "For Glory Dawns Upon You." AFP 11-10650. 2 pt mxd, org.

Isele, David Clark. "One Star." ECS 5105. SATB, kybd.

Jennings, Kenneth. "Arise, Shine, for Thy Light Has Come" in *The Augsburg Choirbook.* AFP 11-10817. SATB.

Neswick, Bruce. "Epiphany Carol." AFP 11-10511. U, kybd.

Praetorius, Michael. "O Morning Star, How Fair and Bright." CPH 98-209S. SATB.

Purcell, Henry/Hal H. Hopson. "Arise! Sing Forth!" AFP 11-10253. SAB.

Zgodava, Richard. "Out of the Orient Crystal Skies." AFP 11-2300. SATB, kybd, perc.

CHILDREN'S CHOIRS

Bender, Mark. "Arise, Shine, for Your Light Has Come." CPH 98-2707. 2 pt mxd, org.

Kemp, Helen. "Follow the Star." CGA 484. U, kybd, inst.

Kemp, Helen. "See the Glowing Star." CGA 629. U, kybd, perc.

Neswick, Bruce. "Epiphany Carol." AFP EK11-10511. U, org.

KEYBOARD/INSTRUMENTAL

Buxtehude, Dieterich. "Wie schön leuchtet" in *Orgelwerke.* Org/kybd.

Manz, Paul. "How Lovely Shines the Morning Star." CPH 97-5306. Org, ob.

Vierne, Louis. "Carillon" in *Three Pièces en style libre, livre II.* LED. Org.

HANDBELL

Helman, Michael. "We Three Kings" in *Rise Up, Shepherd: Three for Christmas.* AFP 11-10721. 2-3 oct.

Larson, Katherine. "Celestia" (Bright and Glorious Is the Sky). AFP 11-10622. 3-4 oct.

Moklebust, Cathy. "Meditation on 'Beautiful Savior.'" CGA CGB175. 3-5 oct.

PRAISE ENSEMBLE

Hanson, Handt. "Life In His Hands" in *Spirit Calls, Rejoice!* CCF.

Robinson, Jay, and Steven Urspringer. "Arise, Shine" in *Integrity's Hosanna! Come and Worship Songbook.* INT.

111

JANUARY 10, 1999

THE BAPTISM OF OUR LORD

FIRST SUNDAY AFTER THE EPIPHANY

INTRODUCTION

In the waters of the Jordan, Jesus is baptized by John. The Spirit descends on him and a voice from heaven says, "You are my beloved." Here is the pattern for our entrance into Christ's community and mission: we come to the waters of the font, our Jordan; we are washed by the Word and anointed by the Spirit; we are named God's beloved children. With Christ we are cho-sen to proclaim God's mercy in a suffering world. With Christ we are made public witnesses to God's justice. With Christ we are called to do good and relieve the suffering of the oppressed.

PRAYER OF THE DAY

Father in heaven, at the baptism of Jesus in the River Jordan you proclaimed him your beloved Son and anointed him with the Holy Spirit. Make all who are baptized into Christ faithful in their calling to be your children and inheritors with him of everlasting life; through your Son, Jesus Christ our Lord, who lives and reigns with you and the Holy Spirit, one God, now and forever.

READINGS

Isaiah 42:1-9

The Lord's transformation of something old (something expected) into something new is a major theme of Isaiah 40–55. Today's reading begins with the familiar language of the Lord bringing justice (or "the true way") through a chosen one. What is new is how the Lord brings that about: the servant is not a triumphant warrior, but is one who works quietly and patiently.

Psalm 29

The voice of the Lord is upon the waters. (Ps. 29:3)

Acts 10:34-43

Peter's sermon to the Roman centurion Cornelius tells how the message of God's inclusive salvation came to expression in the ministry of Jesus following John's baptism.

Matthew 3:13-17

Before Jesus begins his ministry, he is baptized by John, touched by the Spirit, and identified publicly as God's child.

COLOR   White

THE PRAYERS

Illumined by the light of Christ, let us pray for all nations, and for all in need of his healing presence.
A BRIEF SILENCE.

For all the baptized, that they may live out their calling within the mission of your beloved Son, we pray:
Send forth your light, O God.

For all who govern and lead, that justice will be brought forth among the nations, we pray:
Send forth your light, O God.

For those weakened by increasing years or illness (especially . . .), that your Spirit anoint them with comfort and hope, we pray:
Send forth your light, O God.

For all who struggle to believe in their self-worth, that the grace of baptism affirm their dignity as children of God, we pray:
Send forth your light, O God.

For our congregation, that we show no partiality, but share God's grace and forgiveness with all people, we pray:
Send forth your light, O God.

HERE OTHER INTERCESSIONS MAY BE OFFERED.

With thanksgiving for the witness of the faithful departed, that we may follow them in faithfulness to our baptismal vows, and in loving service to our sisters and brothers in need, we pray:
Send forth your light, O God.

In all we ask, O provident God, give us grace to proclaim the coming of your reign in Jesus Christ our Lord.
Amen

IMAGES FOR PREACHING

Leaping over three decades in less than a week, we meet a fully grown Jesus who until recently was but an infant. The crowds around him must also have matured a bit. Residents of Jerusalem no longer quake with fear as they did when the magi arrived, but now eagerly go out to the Jordan to confess their sins and be baptized. Surely, then, this water in which they (and later Jesus) will wash provides the centering image for today. But don't be misled. Like good sacramental theology, the natural element is not enough. What grabs us instead are *words* whose energy exceeds even the flowing river.

Jesus steps forward for his turn in the river, and John blurts out like a candidate at the font, "*I* need to be baptized by *you*." The encounter gives Jesus his first chance to speak in Matthew: "It is proper for us in this way to fulfill all righteousness." Those cryptic words are, in some ways, a summary of the entire gospel in which they are contained. Matthew is concerned with showing us a Jesus immersed in the traditions of Israel and humbly obedient to what God requires. But John and Jesus are not the only ones to speak at the riverside. Jesus' ascent from the waters is matched by the descent of the spirit-dove, with an added word for our benefit: "This is my beloved Son." Mark those words well, for the church hears them again at the end of this season of revelation.

Jesus has grown up and learned to speak. As Peter says in Acts, God is "Preaching peace by Jesus Christ." That is, his baptism speaks a reconciling word into our lives. He who has been set apart as the beloved Son

112

now joins the unwashed masses at the Jordan to make them God's beloved children. He who was there when the waters were separated from the waters now enters the water itself, hallowing it for our cleansing. He who until recently had been silent now preaches the strong, creative word—and peace and righteousness come into being.

WORSHIP MATTERS

"(Name), child of God, you have been sealed by the Holy Spirit and marked with the cross of Christ forever." These words, pronounced on the newly baptized while anointing with oil, have their origin in the Greek word for "seal," which is *sphragis*. The concept of seal is related to the way an owner might mark possessions, or a shepherd would mark a sheep. Through anointing at baptism, we become God's own children, a part of Christ's flock.

Oil was a regular part of life in early Christianity. It was used for bathing, cooking, and perfume. It would not seem unusual, then, to use it for initiation into the household of faith.

Other uses of anointing in the ancient church included warding off evil and the promotion of healing. In our own practice, we might consider more frequent use of anointing, by using such rites "Service of the Word for Healing" and "Laying on of Hands and Anointing the Sick" in the *Occasional Services* book. Some churches are using anointing as a part of the process for the catechumenate, to mark incorporation into the way of Christ. How might we promote this gesture as a sign and seal of the Holy Spirit?

LET THE CHILDREN COME

Because of their baptism into Christ, the status of children is equal to adults in the household of faith. Gordon Lathrop points out the paradox of the reversal of status among adults and children in the waters of baptism. The adults are spoken of as infants and called the newborn. Children "baptized as if they were adults, addressed, asked questions, given great promises" (*Holy Things*, Minneapolis: Fortress Press, p. 60). We see this reversal in the rite of Holy Baptism in *LBW*. A mother of a child could be baptized during the same service, and at the end they would be welcomed as "these new sisters." Or, as Peter puts it in today's reading from Acts, "God shows no partiality."

MUSIC FOR WORSHIP

SERVICE MUSIC

If there are baptisms on this day, it may be a good time to introduce the practice of singing a brief acclamation after each baptism. Possibilities: "You have put on Christ" (WOV 694) or "Springs of water, bless the Lord" in *Welcome to Christ: Lutheran Rites for the Catechumenate*.

GATHERING

| LBW 90 | Songs of thankfulness and praise |
| WOV 693 | Baptized in water |

PSALM 29

Batastini, Robert. "Psalm 29: The Lord Will Bless His People" in R.S.

Haas, David. PCY, vol. VIII.

Hobby, Robert. PW, Cycle C.

Marshall, Jane. *Psalms Together, vol. II*. CGA. CGC-21.

Smith, Geoffrey Boulton. "Give Strength to Your People, Lord" in PS1.

Wetzler, Robert. PW, Cycle A.

HYMN OF THE DAY

| WOV 647 | When Jesus came to Jordan |
| | KING'S LYNN |

INSTRUMENTAL RESOURCES

Fruhauf, Ennis. "King's Lynn" in *Ralph Vaughan Williams and the English School*. AFP 11-10826. Org.

Hyslop, Scott. "King's Lynn" in *Six Chorale Fantasias for Solo Instrument and Piano*. AFP 11-10799. Pno, inst.

Johns, Donald. "King's Lynn" in *Eleven Hymn Preludes*, set 2. AFP 11-10559. Kybd.

ALTERNATE HYMN OF THE DAY

| LBW 76 | O Morning Star, how fair and bright! |
| LBW 188 | I bind unto myself today |

COMMUNION

| LBW 486 | Spirit of God, descend upon my heart |
| WOV 697 | Wash, O God, our sons and daughters |

OTHER SUGGESTIONS

| OBS 82 | The journey was chosen |

SENDING

| LBW 189 | We know that Christ is raised |
| WOV 696 | I've just come from the fountain |

113

ADDITIONAL HYMNS AND SONGS

LBW 79	To Jordan came the Christ, our Lord
LBW 83	From God the Father, virgin-born
H82 120	The sinless one to Jordan came
H82 121	Christ, when for us you were baptized
W3 412	When John baptized by Jordan's river
LEV 143	Wade in the water

MUSIC FOR THE DAY

CHORAL

Biery, James. "The Waters of Life." AFP 11-10902. SATB, org.

Hallock, Peter. "The Baptism of Christ." GIA G-2331. SATB.

Lowenberg, Kenneth. "Christ, When for Us You Were Baptized." AMSI 687. SATB, org.

Mathias, William. "Arise, Shine, for Your Light Has Come." OXF A327. SATB, org.

Neswick, Bruce. "Jesus Came from Nazareth." AFP 11-10643. 2 pt mxd, org.

Ore, Charles W. "This Is My Son." CPH 98-3228. SATB, opt cong, tpt, org.

Ridge, M.D. "Wade in the Water." OCP 9785. SATB, cong, cant, kybd, gtr.

Schütz, Heinrich. "The Voice of the Lord Sounds upon the Waters." MER MC40. SATB, kybd.

Thompson, J. Michael. "Come, You Lovers of the Feast." AFP 11-10502. SATB, org.

Uhl, Daniel. "This is My Beloved Son" in *The Augsburg Choirbook*. AFP 11-10817. SATB, org.

CHILDREN'S CHOIRS

Brandon, George. "Carol of the Baptism." MSM 50-2002. SAB/2 pt mxd, org.

Callahan, Charles. "The Baptism of Our Lord." MSM 50-2003. U, opt desc, org.

Kallman, Daniel. "Thy Holy Wings." MFS YS 102. U, desc, kybd, opt inst.

KEYBOARD/INSTRUMENTAL

Hassell, Michael. "I've Just Come from the Fountain" in *Jazz All Seasons*. AFP 11-10822. Pno.

Schaffner, John Hebden. "Variations and Fugue on 'St. Patrick's Breastplate'" in *Organ Music for the Seasons*. AFP 11-10859. Org.

Sedio, Mark. "Thy Holy Wings" in *Dancing in the Light of God*. AFP 11-10793. Pno/kybd.

HANDBELL

Kinyon, Barbara Baltzer. "O Morning Star, How Fair and Bright." HOP 1690. 3 oct, ch.

Moklebust, Cathy. "Thy Holy Wings." CPH 97-6518. 3-4 oct, ch.

Moklebust, Cathy. "We Know That Christ Is Raised" in *Hymn Stanzas for Handbells*. AFP 11-10722. 4-5 oct.

PRAISE ENSEMBLE

Hanson, Handt. "Only for Your Glory" in *Spirit Calls, Rejoice!* CCF.

Haugen, Marty. "Song Over the Waters" in *Gather*. GIA.

Kendrick, Graham/Jack Schrader. "Shine, Jesus, Shine." HOP GC 937. SATB.

WEDNESDAY, JANUARY 13
GEORGE FOX, RENEWER OF SOCIETY, 1691

George Fox is remembered as the founder of the Society of Friends, also known as the Quakers. Fox severed his ties of family and friendship in search of enlightenment. Finding no comfort in the traditional church he became a wandering preacher, teaching the inner light of God as the real source of authority and comfort. His preaching led to the establishment of preaching bands of women and men known as the "Publishers of the Truth."

Since the Quakers are known for the long periods of silence in their meetings, this commemoration provides a congregation to consider how it uses silence in worship. In addition to words and music, are there periods of corporate silence? Consider growing into this practice, allowing silence after the readings, the sermon, during communion, and before the benediction. How are both words and silence part of our spiritual life?

THURSDAY, JANUARY 14
EIVIND JOSEF BERGGRAV, BISHOP OF OSLO, 1959

In 1937, Berggrav was elected bishop of Oslo and primate of Norway. In 1940, he was asked to negotiate with the Nazi regime in order to ascertain its intentions regarding the social and religious life of the Norwegian people. Rejecting any compromise with the occupation forces, he left the negotiations and demanded that the Nazis recognize the rights of the Jews and the autonomy of the church. Deprived of his episcopal title in 1942, he was placed under arrest, only to escape and remain in hiding in Oslo until the end of the war.

During the season of Epiphany the life of Berggrav is another witness to the light of Christ. How does his life encourage us to live our faith in the midst of the issues that face us in the world today?

FRIDAY, JANUARY 15
MARTIN LUTHER KING JR., RENEWER OF SOCIETY,
MARTYR, 1968

Martin Luther King Jr. is remembered as a man who encouraged nonviolent resistance to racism. As the church, we commemorate him as a man of God and Baptist minister whose faith undergirded his yearning for justice. Preaching nonviolence, he demanded that love be returned for hate. He was awarded the Nobel Peace Prize in 1964, and was killed by an assassin on April 4, 1968. His birthday is a holiday in the United States, observed on the third Monday of January.

Congregations may choose to remember King this coming Sunday by naming him in the prayers and by singing "Lift every voice and sing" (LBW 562). Preachers might make a connection between his life and the first reading from Isaiah 49:1-7.

JANUARY 17, 1999
SECOND SUNDAY AFTER THE EPIPHANY

INTRODUCTION

Here is a simple pattern for the church's celebration during Epiphany: Christ is revealed as the servant of all people; Christ is baptized for his mission; Christ proclaims his message in word and deed until he goes up to Jerusalem. Here the season and the readings set forth a pattern for the community of faith: we enter this church, shaped and sustained by Holy Baptism and Holy Communion, with a mission to serve the world. We are called to invite others to come and see the Lord. Come and touch the waters of new life, we say. Come and hear the words of good news. Come and taste the bread of life and the cup of mercy. Let your lives be shaped and sustained by these good things of God's grace.

In addition to the observance of Martin Luther King Jr.'s birthday (USA) tomorrow, it is also the beginning of the Week of Prayer for Christian Unity.

PRAYER OF THE DAY

Lord God, you showed your glory and led many to faith by the works of your Son. As he brought gladness and healing to his people, grant us these same gifts and lead us also to perfect faith in him, Jesus Christ our Lord.

READINGS

Isaiah 49:1-7

Today's reading again picks up the theme of the Lord's transformation of the old into something new. The imagery is familiar: the Lord's appointed one is called before birth and equipped to do the Lord's work. The new thing is that the servant will not only do the Lord's work for the benefit of Israel, but will also work for the benefit of the nations.

Psalm 40:1-12 (Psalm 40:1-11 [NRSV])

I love to do your will, O my God. (Ps. 40:9)

1 Corinthians 1:1-9

Paul's letters to Corinth are addressed to a church beset by many problems. Still, he begins this epistle by emphasizing the faithfulness and grace of God, whose strength will see them through.

John 1:29-42

John the Baptist's witness to Jesus initiates a chain of testimony as his disciples begin to share with others what they have found.

COLOR Green

THE PRAYERS

Illumined by the light of Christ, let us pray for all nations, and for all in need of his healing presence.
A BRIEF SILENCE.

For the mission of Christ's church, that we may invite others to share our worship and witness, we pray:
Send forth your light, O God.

For missionaries around the world, that the gospel may be shared among diverse cultures and peoples, we pray:
Send forth your light, O God.

For the sick and homebound in our community (especially . . .), that our actions may be a sign of your love and compassion, we pray:

Send forth your light, O God.

For all who live with poverty or suffer physical or mental abuse, that they may be rescued from the grip of violence and despair, we pray:

Send forth your light, O God.

For our community of faith, that strengthened with spiritual gifts, we may live as the body of Christ in the world, we pray:

Send forth your light, O God.

HERE OTHER INTERCESSIONS MAY BE OFFERED.

With thanksgiving we remember Martin Luther King Jr. and all who gave their lives in the struggle for racial equality and civil rights. Sustain us with the vision of your light that extends to all nations and peoples. We pray:

Send forth your light, O God.

In all we ask, O provident God, give us grace to proclaim the coming of your reign in Jesus Christ our Lord.

Amen

IMAGES FOR PREACHING

As it was with the last glimmers after Christmas, so also today the church lets the fourth gospel have the final word about Epiphany itself. (In fact, during all three years of the lectionary this second Sunday draws its readings from the first two chapters of John.) Today is something of a hinge between the glory shown to the Gentiles and what that means for our life and mission as church. The way that John forges that connection is through a *sign*—not a miracle as such, but something just as remarkable in its meaning.

We cross paths with John the Baptist once again, though less as a fiery preacher or river liturgist than as a sweeping gesture pointing the way. Twice he makes himself the sign, declaring of Jesus, "Here is the Lamb of God!" Supporting that claim is the sign that John himself has been instructed to await. The spirit, like a dove descending and remaining will be the clear indication of the Son of God. With that mark now confirmed, the Baptist cannot keep silent. And almost immediately he begins to lose followers, not because of some sudden drop in popularity, but because they are moved by the sign John gives. When two of these disciples turn to follow Jesus, he turns to them with his first words in this gospel: "What do you seek?" The question haunts all who would follow. Are we drawn to a sign, or to what it signifies?

The sign on this day is unambiguous: "Here is the Lamb of God." Mark what those words mean. It is more than a remembrance of blood smeared on doorposts in slavery. It is more than a Jewish hope for an end-time champion over evil. Beyond these, Jesus is the kind of lamb who, later in this same gospel, will be sacrificed at the very hour of the Passover celebration for the sins of all. The sign today is significant because it points ahead to the sign of the cross. And as with the first to follow him, Jesus points us onward with a sign of this season: "Come and see."

WORSHIP MATTERS

Augustine called the sacrament of Holy Communion a sort of "visible word." Martin Luther, in his Large Catechism, said "It is appropriately called the food of the soul since it nourishes and strengthens." Psalm 34 exclaims "O taste and see that the Lord is good." In our reception of the meal of our Lord's body and blood, we stand with John the Baptist and Jesus' disciples in discovering Jesus' true greatness. Here is the Lamb of God who takes away the sin of the world! We have found the Messiah! Come and see!

LET THE CHILDREN COME

Some people will argue that liturgical action is too complex for children and that the layers of meaning in worship cannot be comprehended. But, notice how children will watch the same videos over and over or how they will ask to have the same book read to them time and again. Children take delight in seeing or hearing things repeated. By engaging familiar sights and sounds they start to make discoveries and connections. Instead of believing that worship has to be simplified for children, perhaps children will be engaged more by worship done richly and fully.

MUSIC FOR WORSHIP
SERVICE MUSIC

Today's gospel is the source for the litany frequently sung at communion, "Lamb of God." This is a good day for the choir to sing it in one of the classic choral treatments, or to introduce a new congregational setting (see LLC 239 and 240, as well as GS2 48).

GATHERING

| LBW 237 | O God of light |
| WOV 652 | Arise, your light has come! |

PSALM 40

Chepponis, James J. "Here Am I, O Lord." GIA G-3295. SATB, solo, cong, gtr, kybd, opt C inst, hb.

Cooney, Rory. "Psalm 40: Here I Am" in STP, vol. 3.

Forman, Fr. Bruce H. "Hear Me, O God." CGA 578. SATB, cant, cong, kybd, opt gtr.

Nelson, Ronald A. PW, Cycle A.

Ylvisaker, John. "I've Waited Calmly for You," in *Borning Cry*. NGP.

HYMN OF THE DAY

| LBW 87 | Hail to the Lord's anointed |
| | FREUT EUCH, IHR LIEBEN |

VOCAL RESOURCES

Bender, Mark. "Hail to the Lord's Anointed." CPH 98-2888. Inst pts 98-2894. U, SAB, opt desc, cong, org, tpt, opt brass/timp.

Schroeter, Leonhart. "Hail to the Lord's Anointed" in *Parish Choir Book*. CPH 97-757. SATB.

INSTRUMENTAL RESOURCES

Bender, Jan. "Freut euch, ihr Lieben" in *Twenty-three Hymn Introductions,* vol. 5. CPH 97-5788. Org.

Burkhardt, Michael. "Hail to the Lord's Anointed" in *Five Christmas Hymn Improvisations,* set 1. MSM 10-111. Org.

Schramm, Charles, Jr. "Freut euch, ihr Lieben" in *Three Hymn Accompaniments for Brass and Organ,* set 2. CPH 97-5974.

ALTERNATE HYMN OF THE DAY

| LBW 86 | The only Son from heaven |
| WOV 648 | Jesus, come! for we invite you |

COMMUNION

| LBW 205 | Now the silence |
| WOV 768 | He comes to us as one unknown |

OTHER SUGGESTIONS

| DATH 25 | Lamb of God, come take away |

SENDING

| LBW 393 | Rise, shine, you people! |
| WOV 755 | We all are one in mission |

ADDITIONAL HYMNS AND SONGS

LBW 14	Listen! You nations of the world
WOV 752	I, the Lord of sea and sky
LW 78	Jesus has come and brings pleasure eternal
RS 807	You walk along our shoreline

MUSIC FOR THE DAY

CHORAL

Bach, J. S. "The Only Son from Heaven" in *Third Morning Star Choir Book*. CPH 97-497. SATB, ob, vln, vla, cont.

Christiansen, F. Melius. "Lamb of God." AFP 11-013. Also in *The Augsburg Choirbook*. AFP 11-10817. SATB.

Haugen, Marty. "Lamb of God" in *Now the Feast and Celebration*. GIA G-3488. SATB, cong, 2 ww, hb, gtrs, kybd.

Holden-Holloway, Deborah. "Jesus Calls Us O'er the Tumult." SEL 410-304. SAB, rec, perc.

Rotermund, Donald. "The Only Son from Heaven." CPH 98-2820. 2 pt mxd, cong, trbl inst, org.

Saint-Saens, Camille/K. Lee Scott. "Patiently Have I Waited" in *Sing a Song of Joy*. MH AFP 11-8194; ML 11-8195. Solo.

CHILDREN'S CHOIRS

Nagy, Russell. "Follow Me." HSM JH545. 2 pt, kybd.

Spevacek, Linda. "Somebody's Knockin' at Your Door/Rise! Shine! For Your Light Is a-Comin'." TRI 10/1445K. 2 pt, kybd, opt woodblock.

KEYBOARD/INSTRUMENTAL

Cherwien, David. "Rise, Shine You People: Toccata and Fugue for Organ." AFP 11-10523. Org.

Diemer, Emma Lou. "I Love to Tell the Story" in *A New Liturgical Year,* ed. John Ferguson. AFP 11-10810. Org.

Vivaldi, Antonio. "Concerto in G." CPH 97-6516. Org.

HANDBELL

Afdahl, Lee J. "Dear Lord—Lead On." AFP 11-10770. 3 or 5 oct.

Moklebust, Cathy. "Arise, Your Light Has Come" in *Hymn Stanzas for Handbells*. AFP 11-10722. 4-5 oct.

Moklebust, Cathy. "Now the Silence." HOP 1283. 2 oct.

PRAISE ENSEMBLE

Hassell, Michael. "Jesus Loves Me." AFP 11-10790. SATB, sax or B-flat inst.

Ledner, Michael. "You Are My Hiding Place" in *Maranatha! Music's Praise Chorus Book,* 2d ed. MAR.

Spiritual, ed. Earle Ferguson. "Somebody's Calling My Name." WAL WW1062. SATB.

MONDAY, JANUARY 18
THE CONFESSION OF ST. PETER
WEEK OF PRAYER FOR CHRISTIAN UNITY BEGINS

The Week of Prayer for Christian Unity is framed by festivals centered in the two great apostles of the Christian faith—Peter and Paul. Both are jointly commemorated on June 29, but these two days give us an opportunity to focus on two key events from each of their lives. The Confession of St. Peter invites us to declare with him that Jesus is "the Christ, the Son of the living God." This common confession unites us with other Christians.

How often do you get together with congregations in your neighborhood? Consider a joint worship service celebrating the oneness we share in the gospel of Christ. This coming week is the most natural occasion for an ecumenical service. Remember to include petitions for Christian unity in congregational prayers.

TUESDAY, JANUARY 19
HENRY, BISHOP OF UPPSALA,
MISSIONARY TO FINLAND, MARTYR, 1156

Henry became bishop of Uppsala (Sweden) in 1152 and went with the king of Sweden to Finland. After the king returned home, Henry remained in Finland to organize the church. Murdered there in 1156, his burial place became a center of pilgrimage, and he became a popular saint in Sweden and Finland.

Today is an appropriate day to celebrate the Finnish presence in the Lutheran church. Consider singing "Lost in the night," (LBW 394), which uses a Finnish folk tune. During Epiphany we celebrate the light of Christ revealed to the nations. How does Henry inspire us to carry the light to all the world? How can Christian unity be a witness in our missionary efforts?

JANUARY 24, 1999

THIRD SUNDAY AFTER THE EPIPHANY

INTRODUCTION

Today's gospel reading narrates a strange fishing expedition. Jesus utters simple words that change human lives: "Follow me and I will make you fish for people." No glitz, no slick marketing, no extravagant claim; only these words: "Follow me."

Here is the mission that flows from the watery pool of our baptism into Christ. The Christian community goes forth and invites others to see what good things God offers in the waters of rebirth, in the scriptures, in the holy supper, in the community of faith. People can be "caught" in many things. What happens when they are caught in the net of God's mercy?

The Week of Prayer for Christian Unity concludes tomorrow.

PRAYER OF THE DAY

Almighty God, you sent your Son to proclaim your kingdom and to teach with authority. Anoint us with the power of your Spirit, that we, too, may bring good news to the afflicted, bind up the brokenhearted, and proclaim liberty to the captive; through your Son, Jesus Christ our Lord.

READINGS

Isaiah 9:1-4

The people in the northern parts of Israel have experienced "gloom" and "darkness" because of the destruction wrought by Assyrian military forces. To these people, the prophet announces the shining of a great light of salvation. Matthew equates this light with the beginning of Jesus' ministry in Galilee.

Psalm 27:1, 5-13 (Psalm 27:1, 4-9 [NRSV])

The Lord is my light and my salvation. (Ps. 27:1)

1 Corinthians 1:10-18

Three of the most highly respected missionaries in the early church were Paul, Apollos, and Cephas (also known as Simon Peter). Still, as Paul himself attests, respect for any human leader is misplaced if it becomes divisive or obscures devotion to Christ.

Matthew 4:12-23

John the Baptist called everyone to repent, including the ruler Herod, who had him thrown in prison. It was at this point that Jesus began his public ministry, proclaiming the nearness of the reign of God.

COLOR   Green

THE PRAYERS

Illumined by the light of Christ, let us pray for all nations, and for all in need of his healing presence.
A BRIEF SILENCE.

That our unity in Christ may lead the church to oneness at the table of the Lord and in ministry to the world, we pray:
Send forth your light, O God.

That we may follow Christ by proclaiming the good news of the kingdom, and by promoting health and healing in our communities, we pray:
Send forth your light, O God.

That nations torn by conflict and violence may seek reconciliation and peace, we pray:
Send forth your light, O God.

That all who live with grief, anxiety, loneliness, or illness (especially . . .) may find strength in the wisdom of the cross, we pray:
Send forth your light, O God.

That our community of faith may extend hospitality to those of other faiths, and to those different from us, we pray:
Send forth your light, O God.

HERE OTHER INTERCESSIONS MAY BE OFFERED.

We give thanks for all the holy ones who witnessed to the unity of the church, that we may be united with them in the communion of saints. We pray:
Send forth your light, O God.

In all we ask, O provident God, give us grace to proclaim the coming of your reign in Jesus Christ our Lord.
Amen

IMAGES FOR PREACHING

For the first time in this so-called "Year of Matthew" we actually begin to read that gospel in serial order. Last week saw the start of another series of readings from 1 Corinthians, whose opening chapters provide a sec-

ond strand of continuity during the Epiphany season. In both sequences, we meet the quite gritty and imperfect people Christ brings together. Through both the gospel and epistle today, we are bid to hear the call that orders the church and directs its mission.

The first disciples enter the picture a bit differently than we heard in John last week. Here, John the Baptist is already imprisoned, so Jesus goes north to begin preaching. Galilee, a place of diverse cultures and religions, is the object of Jesus' call: Repent! He then approaches two pairs of brothers, all from the same trade, and calls them to vocations with but the slenderest analogy to anything they have ever done before. Yet even so, immediately and wordlessly they leave everything to follow. Matthew sees it as completing Isaiah's prophecy of a call to the gentiles. Ah, for the mission of the church to be this easy: Jesus calls, people follow.

Luckily, this reading from Matthew stands in healthy tension with today's epistle. Paul extends a call to the Corinthians, too, but the call is to stop fighting! Agreement has dissolved, quarrels have erupted, factions have formed. So Paul calls them to task for their behavior, grounding his authority in his own calling to announce Christ crucified, the power of God. And it is just here that Matthew and Paul seem to speak in chorus. To be sure, calls do bring separations. Some folks renounce their home and family; others even renounce their sins! But what unites the church is a call to be "in the same mind and the same purpose" in Christ. The crucified calls the church to repent from all its familiar, sectarian impulses. And then, that same Lord bids us to be about a genuine vocation: calling those who walk in darkness to see a great light.

WORSHIP MATTERS

When we gather on the Lord's Day it is significant. We could be doing anything—perhaps even fishing like the disciples. But when Jesus calls we drop everything (even if only for a brief time). When we gather as latter day disciples, we do so acknowledging Christ's eternal Easter and his risen presence among us.

A cross carried in procession may help draw our focus to Christ, whose words are to be heard and whose meal is to be shared in the worship that follows. Our very coming together on the Lord's Day is both powerful witness and sign of Christ's presence among us.

119

Consider various ways to gather. Perhaps all worshipers gather together and then walk in procession to the place of worship. The congregation might also gather around the baptismal font (particularly if the brief order for confession and forgiveness, or some other form of baptismal remembrance is to be used at the beginning of the service). Gather outside when the weather allows it. Gather in the narthex when space allows it. Gather in silence when the mood calls for it. Dancing or loud sounding praise may begin our gathering. But always we are called from the places where we live and work to follow Jesus.

LET THE CHILDREN COME

Paul has no patience for the divisions among the Corinthians. Though the word *reconciliation* is far from the lips of children, the action and the meaning are a part of their lives. Children squabble and fight with one another. They know the pain of separation and anger with their friends and their family. And they also know what it means to "make up." A simple word such as "sorry" along with a gesture, perhaps a hug, carries the meaning of two people once divided who are now reconciled. In your congregation, what are the ways in which children know the reconciliation and peace of Jesus Christ?

MUSIC FOR WORSHIP

GATHERING

| LBW 252 | You servants of God |
| WOV 651 | Shine, Jesus, shine |

PSALM 27

Kreutz, Robert E. "The Lord Is My Light" in *Psalms and Selected Canticles.* OCP.

Nelson, Ronald A. PW, Cycle A.

Psalms for All Seasons: An ICEL Collection. NPM.

Soper, Scott. "Ps 27: The Goodness of the Lord" in STP, vol. 3.

HYMN OF THE DAY

| LBW 233 | Thy strong word |
| | EBENEZER |

VOCAL RESOURCES

Busarow, Donald. "Thy Strong Word." MSM 60-9000. SAB, cong, 2 tpt, org.

Schalk, Carl. "Thy Strong Word." CPH 97-5167. SATB, tpt, org.

INSTRUMENTAL RESOURCES

Burkhardt, Michael. "Thy Strong Word" in *Seven Hymn Improvisations and Free Accompaniments,* set I. MSM 10-847. Org.

Johns, Donald. "Ebenezer" in *Eleven Hymn Preludes,* set 2. AFP 11-10559. Kybd.

Manz, Paul. "Thy Strong Word" in *Improvisations on Great Hymns of Faith.* MSM-10-839. Org.

McKlveen, Paul. "Come, O Spirit, Dwell Among Us." AGEHR AG45046. 4-5 oct hb, timp.

ALTERNATE HYMN OF THE DAY

| LBW 562 | Lift every voice and sing |
| WOV 784 | You have come down to the lakeshore |

COMMUNION

| LBW 390 | I love to tell the story |
| WOV 761 | Now we offer |

SENDING

| LBW 369 | The Church's one foundation |
| WOV 650 | We are marching in the light of God |

ADDITIONAL HYMNS AND SONGS

WOV 800	Each morning brings us
ASF 29	Christ calls us now, as long ago
RS 811	Will you come and follow me?
RS 805	Those who love and those who labor

MUSIC FOR THE DAY

CHORAL

Haas, David. "Deep Within." GIA G-3338. 2 pt, cant, cong, gtr, acc.

Handel, G. F. "The People That Walked in Darkness" in *Messiah.* HAL 50323760. Bass solo.

Helman, Michael. "Come, Great God of All the Ages." AFP 11-10881. SATB, org, opt cong.

Leavitt, John. "Come, Follow Me." GIA G-3028. SAB, ob.

Marshall, Jane. "He Comes to Us as One Unknown." CFI 6996. SATB, org.

Palmer, Nicolas. "Ubi caritas." OCP 9649. SATB, cant, cong, pno, org, sop inst, vln.

Powell, Robert J. "The Great Creator of the World." AFP 11-10883. SATB, org.

Wesley, Samuel S. "Thou Wilt Keep Him in Perfect Peace" in *Church Anthem Book.* OXF SATTB, org.

Zimmermann, Heinz W. "The Lord Is My Light." CPH 98-217. SATB, kybd.

CHILDREN'S CHOIRS

Hopson, Hal. "We Are Singing for the Lord Is Our Light."
    HOP HH 3949. U/SATB, kybd.

Iona Community. "The Summons" in *Heaven Shall Not Wait.*
    GIA G3646. U/SATB.

Sleeth, Natalie. "The Kingdom of the Lord." AMSI 301. 2 pt, kybd.

KEYBOARD/INSTRUMENTAL

Bridge, Frank. "Adagio in E." NOV 12097. Org.

Kane, Daniel Q. "Lux Benigna" in *More Selectable Delectables.*
    AFP 11-10757. Pno/kybd.

HANDBELL

Afdahl, Lee J. "Dear Lord and Father of Mankind" in *Dear Lord—Lead
    On.* AFP 11-10770. 3 or 5 oct.

Behnke, John A. "I Want to Walk as a Child of the Light."
    CPH 97-6611. 3 or 5 oct.

Honoré, Jeffrey. "Shine, Jesus, Shine." CPH 97-6633. 3-5 oct.

McChesney, Kevin. "We All Are One in Mission." AFP 11-10687.
    3-5 oct.

Moklebust, Cathy. "Arise, Your Light Has Come" in *Hymn Stanzas for
    Handbells.* AFP 11-10722. 4-5 oct.

PRAISE ENSEMBLE

Cymbala, Carol. "His Name Be Glorified." WRD 3010803168.
    SATB, orch.

Moen, Don. "God Will Make a Way" in *Integrity's Hosanna! Come and
    Worship Songbook.* INT.

Ylvisaker, John. "We Are One" in *Borning Cry.* NGP.

MONDAY, JANUARY 25
THE CONVERSION OF ST. PAUL
WEEK OF PRAYER FOR CHRISTIAN UNITY ENDS

The commemoration of Paul's conversion was first celebrated among the Christians of Gaul. It is inspired by
narratives describing this event in the Acts of the Apostles, Galatians, and 1 Corinthians. The risen Christ
appeared to Paul on the road to Damascus and called
him to proclaim the gospel of Christ.

As the Week of Prayer for Christian Unity ends,
use this occasion to reflect on the meaning of baptismal
conversion for our lives of faith. How is baptism more
than a one-time event, but instead a lifelong process?

Does your congregation aid its members in this understanding of faith? In what ways does the church need to
be converted so that its tragic divisions may be healed?
How can your congregation, along with other
churches, more faithfully witness to the light of Christ?

TUESDAY, JANUARY 26
TIMOTHY, TITUS, AND SILAS

Following the festival of the Conversion of St. Paul, we
remember three of his companions. Timothy accompanied Paul on his second missionary journey, and became
the first bishop of Ephesus. Titus joined Paul on the
journey to the apostolic council at Jerusalem, and
became the first bishop of Crete. Silas was a companion
of Paul on his first visit to Macedonia and Corinth.

As you commemorate these three early Christian
leaders, consider the pastors, teachers, and lay leaders
who were influential in your Christian formation. In a
committee meeting or small group allow each person
to name a significant person who was an Epiphany light
for them.

WEDNESDAY, JANUARY 27
LYDIA, DORCAS, AND PHOEBE

Today we remember three women in the early church.
Lydia and her household were baptized by Paul, who
with his companions stayed for a time at her house.
Dorcas was known for her charitable works, and her
skill and generosity in making clothing. Her name was
used in the later Dorcas Societies of church women
devoted to good works. Phoebe was a deaconess or
helper of the church at Cenchreae. Paul praises her as
one who has looked after a great many people.

Today provides an opportunity to give thanks for
women who have served faithfully in the church as pastors, teachers, deaconesses, and lay leaders. How has the
ordination of women as pastors provided the church
with new gifts and resources for ministry and mission?

JANUARY 31, 1999

FOURTH SUNDAY AFTER THE EPIPHANY

INTRODUCTION

What does the Lord ask of us? To do justice, to love kindness, and to walk humbly with God. These are simple words from today's first reading that, nonetheless, remain a challenge for anyone who recognizes the injustice and suffering that mark and mar much of human existence. In the gospel reading, Jesus teaches his disciples a way of seeing those who are blessed in God's sight: the poor, mourners, the meek, those who hunger for righteousness, the merciful, the pure in heart, the peacemakers. These are the people to whom Jesus has constant recourse in his ministry. How does this congregation serve them?

PRAYER OF THE DAY

O God, you know that we cannot withstand the dangers which surround us. Strengthen us in body and spirit so that, with your help, we may be able to overcome the weakness that our sin has brought upon us; through Jesus Christ, your Son our Lord.

READINGS

Micah 6:1-8

With the mountains and the foundations of the earth as the jury, God brings a lawsuit against Israel. Acting first as plaintiff, God charges that though the Lord has provided constant care for the people, they have not responded appropriately. Acting as judge, God indicts Israel for bringing burnt offerings instead of justice and mercy.

Psalm 15

Lord, who may abide upon your holy hill? (Ps. 15:1)

1 Corinthians 1:18-31

In the city of Corinth, many Christians prided themselves on their sophistication and learning. Paul reminds them that God identifies with what is considered foolish, weak, and despised. This message is the wisdom of the cross.

Matthew 5:1-12

Jesus opens the Sermon on the Mount by describing God's care for those who are blessed in the reign of God.

COLOR   Green

THE PRAYERS

Illumined by the light of Christ, let us pray for all nations, and for all in need of his healing presence.

A BRIEF SILENCE.

For the church, that walking humbly with you we may do justice and love kindness, we pray:

Send forth your light, O God.

For those persecuted for their faith, that they find wisdom in the message of Christ crucified, we pray:

Send forth your light, O God.

For the nations of the world, that peacemakers may be a sign of your healing and reconciliation, we pray:

Send forth your light, O God.

For the poor in spirit, and all who suffer due to depression, poverty, or illness (especially . . .), that you may be their strength, we pray:

Send forth your light, O God.

For those who mourn and grieve the loss of loved ones, that you may comfort and console them, we pray:

Send forth your light, O God.

HERE OTHER INTERCESSIONS MAY BE OFFERED.

For all the blessed saints who now see you face-to-face, we give thanks, that we may join them in the everlasting song of praise, we pray:

Send forth your light, O God

In all we ask, O provident God, give us grace to proclaim the coming of your reign in Jesus Christ our Lord.

Amen

IMAGES FOR PREACHING

An "installation" sounds like such an honorable event. Finally you receive the recognition and respect you deserve. It is disquieting, therefore, to learn that this word derives from the Latin verb *installare* (also the basis for a barnyard "stall"), which means "to set in place." So there you have it. Installation is "to be put in your place," like a mechanical cog or a beast of burden. That phrase itself—"to be put in your place"—offends our egalitarian sensibilities. It suggests being powerless before the judgment of another who subjects us to some lower status. So, a warning: be prepared to be offended. The serial readings of Matthew and 1 Corinthians that continue today are deeply concerned with putting us in our place . . . but by way of a great reversal.

The beatitudes, familiar hymnic and homiletic playground, are replete with reversals of fortune. Like Mary's Magnificat in Luke, the "blesseds" with which Jesus begins his great sermon speak of human expectations overturned. All those put in their place by others, all those who pick a place outside the mainstream of greed and domination, will receive a place at the heart of God's own embrace. And note that this change of status is grounded in the worth of another. Those put down "for righteousness sake" and "on my account," those who are like the prophets in bearing the divine word, have their place reestablished through the status granted to Christ.

Paul also bluntly asserts that God alone puts things in their proper place. Wisdom and power, signs and strength shall be brought to shame by the cross. In their stead, God will install at the right hand of glory the weak and lowly and foolish: first the crucified whose ways are humble righteousness, then those who proclaim him and share the same judgment he received. Can you imagine if installations in the church sought neither achievements nor authority, but just simple messengers of the mercy we have through Christ? Everyone clamoring, in Micah's words, "to do justice, and to love kindness, and to walk humbly." What a blessed reversal that would be!

WORSHIP MATTERS

Someone once said that the church, if no one else, will remember the poor. It is important for us to remember this charge to be the church. Our prayers of intercession should reflect this attentiveness to anyone in need. There is no reticence or holding back: "God, remember the sick . . . the dying . . . the lonely . . . the destitute." Our prayer also spurs us to action. As we pray for those in need, so we also serve those in need.

As the offering is presented, enlist all or a few to carry forward donated items for a local food shelf, and lay them at the altar. This action will give a tangible, even visible reminder, that a major part of our gathering each week is for service to one another. Prior to the dismissal, some of these gifts may even be placed in the hands of those who will later distribute them. "Go in peace. Serve the Lord."

LET THE CHILDREN COME

What do children understand in the word "blessing"? They might understand something about the notion of blessing and being blessed from their experience of receiving and giving gifts. The response to receiving a gift is "thank you." The response to receiving a blessing is "amen." Help children to understand the blessing of God as a gift from God for their lives. Help them to see that just as we give gifts to others, we also respond to the gift of God's blessing by blessing others.

MUSIC FOR WORSHIP

GATHERING

| LBW 84 | Brightest and best of the stars |
| WOV 652 | Arise, your light has come! |

PSALM 15

Gelineau, Joseph. "Psalm 15" in R.S.

Haas, David. "They Who Do Justice" in PCY, vol. 3.

Martinson, Joel. "Psalm 15." SEL 421-015. 2 pt mxd, cant, org, ob, opt cong.

Nelson, Ronald A. PW, Cycle A.

Proulx, Richard. "Psalm 15" in TP.

HYMN OF THE DAY

| LBW 425 | O God of mercy, God of light |
| | JUST AS I AM |

INSTRUMENTAL RESOURCES

Cherwien, David. "Just as I Am" in *Interpretations Based on Hymn-tunes.* AMSI OR-1. Org.

Lovelace, Austin C. "Just as I am" in *Hymn Preludes and Free Accompaniments, vol. 4.* AFP 11-9400. Org.

Sadowski, Kevin. "Just as I Am" in *Twenty-One Introductions.* CPH 97-5986. Org.

ALTERNATE HYMN OF THE DAY

| LBW 429 | Where cross the crowded ways of life |
| WOV 764 | Blest are they |

COMMUNION

| LBW 17 | How blest are those who know their need of God |
| WOV 765 | Jesu, Jesu, fill us with your love |

OTHER SUGGESTIONS

| DATH 82 | O loving God |

SENDING

LBW 551   Joyful, joyful we adore thee
WOV 689   Rejoice in God's saints

ADDITIONAL HYMNS AND SONGS

H82 605   What does the Lord require?
REJ 260   Blessed are the poor in spirit
OBS 59   God has called us

MUSIC FOR THE DAY

CHORAL

Ashdown, Franklin D. "Jesus, the Very Thought of You." AFP 11-10886. SATB, org, opt C inst.

Cherwien, David. "God Has Told You." CPH 98-3180. SATB, org.

Davies, H. Walford. "Blessed Are the Pure in Heart" in *New Church Anthem Book.* OXF 0-19-353109-7. SATB, org.

Harris, Jerry Weseley. "The Beatitudes." AFP 11-10591. SATB, kybd.

Kauffmann, Ronald. "The Spirit of the Lord." MSM 50-9071. SATB, opt fl, kybd.

Powell, Robert. "Jesu, the Very Thought of Thee." MSM 50-9070. SATB, org.

Routley, Erik/John Hakes. "What Does the Lord Require?" MFS MF2054. SATB, org.

Toolan, Suzanne. "Beatitudes." GIA G-2132. Cant, cong, acc.

CHILDREN'S CHOIRS

Leavitt, John. "Blessed Are They." CGA 425. U/2 pt, kybd.

Marshall, Jane. "God Speaks: True Goodness." CGA 536. U, kybd.

KEYBOARD/INSTRUMENTAL

Cherwien, David. "Joyful, Joyful We Adore Thee" in *Postludes on Well-known Hymns.* AFP 11-10795. Org.

Cherwien, David. "Rejoice in God's Saints" in *Rejoice in God's Saints.* AFP 11-10713. Org.

Keesecker, Thomas. "Lullaby on *Kuortane*" in *Come Away to the Skies: A Collection for Piano.* AFP 11-10794. Pno/kybd.

HANDBELL

Larson, Katherine. "Be Thou My Vision." AFP 11-10484. 3-4 oct, fl.

Moklebust, Cathy. "Rejoice in God's Saints" in *Hymn Stanzas for Handbells.* AFP 11-10722. 4-5 oct.

Wood, Dale. "Beach Spring" in *American Folk Hymn Suite.* Full score FLA HL5022. Hb pt HL5023. 3 oct, org, hp.

PRAISE ENSEMBLE

Haas, David. "Blest Are They." GIA G-2958. SATB, 2 C inst, kybd, gtr.

Hanson, Handt. "We Love You" in *Spirit Calls, Rejoice!* CCF.

Thompson, John, and Randy Scruggs. "Sanctuary" in *Integrity's Hosanna! Come and Worship Songbook.* INT.

TUESDAY, FEBRUARY 2
THE PRESENTATION OF OUR LORD

Forty days after the birth of Christ we celebrate his presentation in the temple by his parents. Two aged saints, Anna and Simeon, recognize him as the promised messiah. Simeon speaks the words of the beloved Nunc dimittis in which he calls Jesus a "light for the nations."

This day is also called Candlemas, a traditional time to bless candles for the coming year. We are midway between winter and spring, and the custom of the groundhog looking for his shadow symbolizes our hope for the coming light and warmth of spring. Whenever congregational groups gather today let them light candles and read the account of the presentation from Luke. Consider a festive evening prayer service with the church illumined by candlelight. Make sure to sing a setting of the Song of Simeon (such as LBW 339 or 349).

WEDNESDAY, FEBRUARY 3
ANSGAR, ARCHBISHOP OF HAMBURG, MISSIONARY TO DENMARK AND SWEDEN, 865

Ansgar was a missionary who brought the Epiphany light of Christ to the peoples of Scandinavia. A monk of the ninth century, Ansgar was committed to preaching and care for the poor. So deep was his love for the poor that he would wash their feet and serve them at table with food provided by the parish. Ansgar preached in Denmark and then in Sweden where he built the first church. He was named archbishop of Hamburg in 831, and from there he sent missions to the north.

Ansgar is honored by Scandinavian Lutherans today, especially by the Danes. Numerous churches, societies, and educational institutions are named for him. The commemoration of Ansgar allows another opportunity for a parish to reflect on its mission. How do we witness to Christ's light through preaching, education, and social outreach?

FRIDAY, FEBRUARY 5
THE MARTYRS OF JAPAN, 1597

This day commemorates the crucifixion of three Japanese Jesuits, six Franciscans, one Korean, and sixteen Japanese laypersons in the city of Nagasaki in 1597. Fifty years after Francis Xavier brought the Christian faith to Japan, these twenty-six Christians became the first martyrs of the far east. Persecutions extended over the next century in an effort to prohibit the celebration of the eucharist. When Christian missionaries returned to Japan over two hundred years later, they discovered—to their utter surprise—thousands of Christians in the Nagasaki region who gathered to worship in secret.

This commemoration challenges us to consider the cost of discipleship, and to pray for boldness in our witness to Christ. How can the martyrs of Japan inspire the church today to be faithful to its calling to walk in the way of the cross?

FEBRUARY 7, 1999

FIFTH SUNDAY AFTER THE EPIPHANY

INTRODUCTION

Diverse yet complementary actions take place in Holy Baptism: the forgiveness of sins, entrance into a community of disciples, rebirth as children of God, anointing as servants and heralds, union with Christ, receiving the promise of eternal life. The ancient practice of baptism included two rituals inspired by today's gospel reading: salt was placed in the mouth and a burning candle was held next to the newly baptized. Baptism is a moment of enlightenment concerning our truest identity: we are scattered in the world as salt is shaken; we are sent into the world as lights who point to the greater light of God's grace.

PRAYER OF THE DAY

Almighty God, you sent your only Son as the Word of life for our eyes to see and our ears to hear. Help us to believe with joy what the Scriptures proclaim, through Jesus Christ our Lord.

READINGS

Isaiah 58:1-9a [9b-12]

Shortly after the return of Israel from exile in Babylon, the people were troubled by the ineffectiveness of their fasts. God reminds them that outward observance is no substitute for a genuine faith that results in acts of justice and kindness and living in the light of God's presence.

Psalm 112:1-9 [10]

Light shines in the darkness for the upright. (Ps. 112:4)

1 Corinthians 2:1-12 [13-16]

In Corinth, Paul preached the gospel to people enamored with Greek philosophy and wisdom. God's wisdom is proclaimed in the gospel and revealed most clearly in Christ's self-giving.

Matthew 5:13-20

God's blessing, announced in the beatitudes, can be lost unless disciples live in a manner that leads others to praise God.

COLOR   Green

THE PRAYERS

Illumined by the light of Christ, let us pray for all nations, and for all in need of his healing presence.
A BRIEF SILENCE.
For all the baptized people of God, that they may shine forth the light of Christ, and reflect his love in their words and deeds, we pray:
Send forth your light, O God.
For bishops, pastors, and leaders in the church, that they may draw their strength from your wisdom, we pray:
Send forth your light, O God.
For all who serve in the government, that they will lead us all to care for victims of poverty and injustice, we pray:
Send forth your light, O God.

For all who suffer from grief, despair, pain, or illness (especially . . .), that we may minister to them with compassion and love, we pray:

Send forth your light, O God.

For ourselves, that we may be salt and light in our families, congregations, and communities, we pray:

Send forth your light, O God.

HERE OTHER INTERCESSIONS MAY BE OFFERED.

We give thanks for all the faithful departed who have borne witness to the crucified and risen One. Fill us with your wisdom until we behold the dawn of your everlasting glory. We pray:

Send forth your light, O God.

In all we ask, O provident God, give us grace to proclaim the coming of your reign in Jesus Christ our Lord.
Amen

IMAGES FOR PREACHING

Sometimes, the littlest things make the biggest difference. The pebble in the shoe that makes walking unbearable. The untold fear that leaves a life shackled. The steady hand across a wide chasm. The simple word that sets you free. And they are simple words today, these words "salt" and "light." Their very smallness is the real issue. Salt, not used as intended, is worthless. Light, covered and unseen, is wasted. Salt and light exist not for themselves but to be used by others, or they have no purpose at all. But when used as they should, as they can be used, then the whole earth is changed, salted, made bright. Then they make the biggest difference.

Two more simple words, so small that it's easy to miss them: "you" and "I." You are the salt, you are the light. Who is this you? The you of whom Jesus spoke earlier in the beatitudes. You, lowly and rejected ones, you are salt of the earth, you are light of the world. But how can this be? It all rests on that other little word. Jesus said, I have come not to abolish the law, but to fulfill. This law, itself a tiny word, is in reality nothing less than God's order for all creation and human life therein. So here we have a daring claim that in one person, the whole will of God shall meet its fullness, perpetually sustained like a musical passage so beautiful you never want it to end. Through this one person, not even the littlest things of that vast law will ever snare us again. Instead, they will

matter in a new way—as gift once more, as the fruit of faithfulness.

Jesus said, I have come to fulfill; therefore you are salt, you are light. Jesus said, Truly I say to you; therefore you shall have righteousness beyond scribes and Pharisees. Jesus said, I am poured out; therefore the least of you are named greatest in the heavens themselves. Remarkable news: the law and prophets offered to us in a person, the whole will of God poured out in human frame. As biting as salt, as brilliant as light. "The body of Christ, given for you." Such simple words—the simple word that sets you free.

WORSHIP MATTERS

On this Sunday after Epiphany, one preacher handed out sample salt shakers. At one conference, everyone was given flashlights. Jesus says in his Sermon on the Mount that you are salt. You are light. Some congregations use a form of their mission statement as words of dismissal each week, or these words are posted on banners near exterior doors to remind everyone of our calling.

Each week we are filled with the gospel, and we are fed and nourished with food for the journey in God's holy meal. When we are dismissed with "Go in peace. Serve the Lord," we are sent to enlighten others who sit in darkness. If the Spirit of the Lord is upon us, then when we rub shoulders with others from Monday through Saturday, some of that same Spirit will rub off. Spreading the news, sharing the light, doing good. That is our mission from God.

LET THE CHILDREN COME

Each of the Scripture readings today says something about God's power demonstrated or God's grace embodied. Paul speaks of "a demonstration of the Spirit and of power." Jesus' words in the gospel are an invitation to let the light of Christ shine. These words are echoed in the rite of Holy Baptism in *LBW*. "Let your light so shine before others that they may see your good works and glorify your Father in heaven." With the season of Lent approaching, how might children be a part of the congregation's efforts to demonstrate and embody God's grace in outreach to the hungry, the sick, or those who don't know the gospel?

MUSIC FOR WORSHIP
GATHERING

LBW 400	God, whose almighty word
WOV 718	Here in this place

PSALM 112

Proulx, Richard. "A Light Rises in the Darkness." GIA G-3461.

Nelson, Ronald A. PW, Cycle A.

Wright, Helen/Hal H. Hopson. TP.

HYMN OF THE DAY

LBW 393	Rise, shine, you people!
	WOJTKIEWIECZ

VOCAL RESOURCES

Busarow, Donald. "Rise, Shine, You People!" CPH 98-2890. SATB, org, tpt, opt cong.

Wood, Dale. "Rise, Shine!" AFP 11-10737. SATB, org.

INSTRUMENTAL RESOURCES

Cherwien, David. "Rise, Shine, You People! Toccata and Fugue for Organ." AFP 11-10523. Org.

Ferguson, John. "Wojtkiewiecz" in *Hymn Harmonizations for Organ*, book V. LUD O-14. Org.

Linker, Janet, and Jane McFadden. "Rise, Shine, You People!" AFP 11-10628. Hb 11-10629. Org, hb, opt tpt.

ALTERNATE HYMN OF THE DAY

LBW 237	O God of light
WOV 753	You are the seed

COMMUNION

LBW 232	Your Word, O Lord, is gentle dew
WOV 711	You satisfy the hungry heart

OTHER SUGGESTIONS

OBS 59	God has called us

SENDING

LBW 221	Sent forth by God's blessing
WOV 650	We are marching in the light of God

ADDITIONAL HYMNS AND SONGS

G2 468	Bring forth the kingdom
MBW 696	Today we all are called to be disciples
PsH 112	How blest are those who fear the Lord
NCH 309	We are your people
LEV 221	This little light of mine

MUSIC FOR THE DAY
CHORAL

Busarow, Donald. "Forth in Thy Name." MSM 50-9107. SAB, org, treb inst.

Buxtehude, Dietrich. "God Shall Do My Advising." CPH 98-144. U, SATB, org.

Carter, Andrew. "The Light of the World." OXF E161. SATB, org.

Patterson, Joy F. "You Are the Salt of the Earth." MSM 50-9081. SATB, pno.

Routley, Erik. "Light and Salt." GIA G-2300. SATB, org.

Sateren, Leland. "House Him There." AFP 11-10302. SATB.

CHILDREN'S CHOIRS

Handel, G. F./Hal Hopson. "Lord, I Lift My Soul to You." CGA 440. 2 pt mxd, kybd.

Mahnke, Allan. "We Praise You for the Sun." CGA 153. U, opt orff.

Shields, Valerie. "Let Your Light So Brightly Shine." MSM 50-8410. 2 pt, org, opt hb.

KEYBOARD/INSTRUMENTAL

Cotter, Jeanne. "Gather Us In" in *After the Rain*. GIA G-3390. Pno.

Hassell, Michael. "This Little Light of Mine" in *Jazz Sunday Morning*. AFP 11-10700. Pno.

Pachelbel, Johann. "Praeludium in d" in *Selected Organ Works*. KAL 3760. Org.

HANDBELL

Honoré, Jeffrey. "Gather Us In." CPH 97-6556. 3-5 oct.

Matheny, John. "Beach Spring." AGEHR AG35085. 3-5 oct.

Moklebust, Cathy. "Lord of Light" in *Hymn Stanzas for Handbells*. AFP 11-10722. 4-5 oct.

PRAISE ENSEMBLE

Baroni, David/Fitts, Smith, and Cloninger. "Glorious God" in *Integrity's Hosanna! Music Songbook 10*. INT.

Haas, David. "We Are Called." GIA G-3292. 1/2 pt, cong, gtr, kybd.

McLean, Terri. "In Your Heart There Is a Voice" in *Come Celebrate! Jesus*. ABI.

FEBRUARY 14, 1999

THE TRANSFIGURATION OF OUR LORD
LAST SUNDAY AFTER THE EPIPHANY

INTRODUCTION

This festival concludes the Christmas cycle that began in Advent. Today's gospel reading is the inspiration for this feast. On one level it celebrates the manifestation of Jesus as God's beloved child and servant (an echo of the Christmas, Epiphany, and baptism festivals). At the same time, the church's calendar is influenced by the gospel story: after his transfiguration, Jesus announces his impending death in Jerusalem. From the festival of the transfiguration, the church turns this week to Ash Wednesday and its baptismal journey to Christ's death and resurrection celebrated during the Three Days of Maundy Thursday, Good Friday, and the Vigil of Easter/Easter Sunday.

PRAYER OF THE DAY

Almighty God, on the mountain you showed your glory in the transfiguration of your Son. Give us the vision to see beyond the turmoil of our world and to behold the king in all his glory; through your Son, Jesus Christ our Lord, who lives and reigns with you and the Holy Spirit, one God, now and forever.

or

O God, in the transfiguration of your Son you confirmed the mysteries of the faith by the witness of Moses and Elijah, and in the voice from the bright cloud you foreshadowed our adoption as your children. Make us with the king heirs of your glory, and bring us to enjoy its fullness, through Jesus Christ our Lord, who lives and reigns with you and the Holy Spirit, one God, now and forever.

READINGS

Exodus 24:12-18

In the Bible, mountains often serve as places of revelation. Moses' six-day wait on the mountain covered by the cloud is a way of telling the reader that something important is about to be revealed: God's law. Similarly the experience of Jesus, Peter, James, and John on a mountain reveals something important: God's Son.

Psalm 2

You are my son; this day have I begotten you. (Ps. 2:7)

or Psalm 99

Proclaim the greatness of the Lord; worship upon God's holy hill. (Ps. 99:9)

2 Peter 1:16-21

At the transfiguration of Jesus, Peter heard the voice of God speak from heaven. This same voice speaks to us from the holy word.

Matthew 17:1-9

Shortly before he enters Jerusalem, where he will be crucified, Jesus is revealed to his disciples in a mountaintop experience of divine glory called the transfiguration.

COLOR   White

THE PRAYERS

Illumined by the light of Christ, let us pray for all nations, and for all in need of his healing presence.
A BRIEF SILENCE.

That the rulers of nations govern with the vision of a world at peace, we pray:

Send forth your light, O God.

That the church listen faithfully to the word of Christ, and behold the mystery of his presence in the eucharist, we pray:

Send forth your light, O God.

That all who suffer (especially . . .) find comfort in the healing touch of Christ, we pray:

Send forth your light, O God.

That all who live with fear and doubt behold the vision of Christ's glory and live with renewed hope, we pray:

Send forth your light, O God.

That you would transfigure us into the likeness of Christ as we proclaim his grace in our words and deeds, we pray:

Send forth your light, O God.

HERE OTHER INTERCESSIONS MAY BE OFFERED.

In communion with the missionaries Cyril and Methodius and all the saints, we commend our lives to Christ, the bright and morning star. We pray:

Send forth your light, O God.

In all we ask, O provident God, give us grace to proclaim the coming of your reign in Jesus Christ our Lord.

Amen

128

IMAGES FOR PREACHING

How does Jesus appear to you—a friend, a guide, a savior? Have those views ever changed? As the disciples climbed with Jesus, did they sense that all their previous images of him were about to change? In a flash, his brilliant face and dazzling apparel become like the Son of Man, God's great end-time warrior. A cameo visit by Moses and Elijah further confirms his lineage in Israel's covenant. As if that were not enough, the bright cloud completes the apocalyptic scene. And from that cloud, a voice—an echo, really, of the one at Jesus' baptism heard when this season began. To the dimwitted and inattentive it acclaims, "This is my beloved Son . . . listen to him!" But unlike those crowds at the Jordan, the disciples are not unmoved today by this voice. They drop to the ground, overwhelmed by fear at who this Jesus might be.

Instead of the images we carefully construct, Jesus shines today as God's final bringer of justice. But this judgment will appear only through a transformation yet to come. Recall that, at the close of the gospel reading, Jesus silences his disciples until he has been raised from the dead. More appearances are still ahead, it seems: on the cross with the guilty, on the road with the grieving, on the mountain with the faithful. These appearances, too, will echo with the voice of the transfigured Jesus, "Arise, fear not." With words like these, even our visage can shine.

WORSHIP MATTERS

On this day we are invited to bask in the rays of Christ's glory revealed, then called to journey down the mountain to share Christ's power with those in need. One way we live out this calling is in reserving some bread and wine to be shared with homebound folks. We're not just "storing the leftovers," but we are setting apart these eucharistic elements in a way that is respectful of both Christ's glory and those who will be receiving them. It is not simply staking out holy ground. Like Peter on the mountain, we need the reminder to savor and share Christ's glorious presence with others, not to save that glory only for ourselves.

LET THE CHILDREN COME

Today is the day to bury the alleluia. The closing hymn might be one with several alleluias. Children might be invited to process around the worship space during the singing of the hymn. Include all the church's banners with the word alleluia. Have the children wave strips of paper that say alleluia (perhaps made in a Sunday school class). The strips of paper can then be placed in a container that will be buried outside near the entrance of the church. Mark the spot in a way that it can be noticed by the entire congregation on the way in and out of worship during Lent.

MUSIC FOR WORSHIP

SERVICE MUSIC

As the last festival in the Christmas cycle, this day invites special attention to the Gloria in excelsis and the Alleluia before these service elements are set aside during the season of Lent.

GATHERING

LBW 526	Immortal, invisible, God only wise
WOV 651	Shine, Jesus, shine

PSALM 2

Hopson, Hal H. *Psalm Refrains and Tones.* HOP 425.

Wetzler, Robert. PW, Cycle A.

PSALM 99

Hopson, Hal H. *Psalm Refrains and Tones.* HOP 425.

The Psalter: Psalms and Canticles for Singing.

Seltz, Martin. PW, Cycle C.

HYMN OF THE DAY

LBW 76	O Morning Star, how fair and bright
	WIE SCHÖN LEUCHTET

VOCAL RESOURCES

Ore, Charles W. "O Morning Star, How Fair and Bright." CPH 98-3322. SATB, cong, tpt, opt ob, brass, org.

Pelz, Walter L. "O Morning Star, How Fair and Bright." MSM 60-2001. SATB, opt cong, org.

INSTRUMENTAL RESOURCES

Albrecht, Timothy. "O Morning Star, How Fair and Bright" in *Grace Notes VII.* AFP 10856. Org.

Folkening, John. "O Morning Star, How Fair and Bright" in *Ten Hymn Accompaniments for Handbells,* set 1. CPH 97-6022. 3 oct.

Manz, Paul. "Wie schön leuchtet" in *A New Liturgical Year,* ed. John Ferguson. AFP 11-10810. Org.

Sedio, Mark. "Wie schön leuchtet" in *Let Us Talents and Tongues Employ.* AFP 11-10718. Org.

129

ALTERNATE HYMN OF THE DAY

LBW 315	Love divine, all loves excelling
WOV 653	Jesus on the mountain peak

COMMUNION

LBW 518	Beautiful Savior
WOV 728	O Light whose splendor thrills
WOV 701	What feast of love

OTHER SUGGESTIONS

OBS 88	In the desert, on God's mountain

SENDING

LBW 80	Oh, wondrous type! Oh, vision fair
WOV 654	Alleluia, song of gladness

ADDITIONAL HYMNS AND SONGS

CW 97	Down from the mount of glory
NCH 182	We have come at Christ's own bidding
NCH 183	Jesus, take us to the mountain
WGF 71	What glory round us shines!

MUSIC FOR THE DAY

CHORAL

Bouman, Paul. "Christ upon the Mountain Peak." CPH 98-2856. SATB, org.

Farlee, Robert Buckley. "Farewell to Alleluia." AFP 11-10064. SATB, opt cong, org, opt tpt.

Gastoldi, Giovanni. "In You Is Gladness," in *Let All Together Praise.* CPH 97-565S. SATB, kybd.

Hobby, Robert. "Offertory for the Transfiguration of Our Lord." MSM 80-225. SATB, hb, org.

Martinson, Joel. "Transfiguration." PAR PPM 09511. U, org.

Nystedt, Knut. "This Is My Beloved Son." CPH 98-180. SAB, org.

Ore, Charles W. "O God of God, O Light of Light." CPH 98-3297. SATB, cong, brass, org.

Proulx, Richard. "Alleluia, Song of Gladness." GIA G-3984. U, hb, perc.

Schalk, Carl. "Jesus, Take Us to the Mountain." MSM 50-2601. SATB, opt cong, org.

Uhl, Dan. "This Is My Beloved Son" in *The Augsburg Choirbook.* AFP 11-10817. SATB, org.

White, David Ashley. "This Glimpse of Glory." AFP 11-10201. SATB, org, opt tpt.

CHILDREN'S CHOIRS

Ellingboe, Bradley. "Oh, Love, How Deep." KJO Ed 8831. 2 pt mxd, fc, tamb, drm, org.

Johnson, Ralph. "Thee We Adore." KJO Ed 6261. 2 pt mxd, kybd.

Vyhanek, James. "Transform Us." GIA G-4104. SAB, org.

KEYBOARD/INSTRUMENTAL

Benoit, Dom Paul. "The Transfiguration" in *Pieces d' Orgue.* JFB 8774. Org.

Hancock, Gerre. "Schönster Herr Jesu" in *A New Liturgical Year,* ed. John Ferguson. AFP 11-10810. Org.

HANDBELL

Kinyon, Barbara B. "Immortal, Invisible." CGA. CGB172. 3 oct.

McChesney, Kevin. "Immortal, Invisible, God Only Wise." CPH 97-6559. 3-5 oct.

PRAISE ENSEMBLE

Grant, Amy, and Michael W. Smith. "Thy Word" in *Maranatha! Music's Praise Chorus Book.* MAR.

Hayford, Jack. "Majesty." HOP. SATB, kybd.

Tunseth, Scott, and Kathy Tunseth. "Come to the Mountain" in *Celebrate the Seasons of the Church.* LB.

SUNDAY, FEBRUARY 14

CYRIL, MONK, 869, AND METHODIUS, BISHOP, 885; MISSIONARIES TO THE SLAVS

These two brothers are known as the apostles to the southern Slavs. They were sent by the emperor to preach the gospel in Moravia during the ninth century. There they translated the scriptures and the liturgy into Slavonic, the vernacular language. The Czechs, Slovaks, Croats, Serbs, and Bulgars honor Cyril and Methodius as founders of their alphabet, translators of the liturgy, and builders of the foundation of Slavonic literature.

As the Epiphany season concludes these two missionaries are another example of the light of Christ proclaimed to the nations. A congregation could remember them today in the prayers, and the preacher could mention them in the sermon. As the voice from the cloud bid the disciples to listen to Jesus, Cyril and Methodius allowed the Slavic people to hear the gospel in their own language.

FEBRUARY 15

PRESIDENTS' DAY OBSERVED (USA)

LENT

By our own efforts alone we cannot
make a clean break with the past

IMAGES of the SEASON

It's late winter, and cabin fever is raging. If we can't get out of the house where we've been cooped up so long, we know lunacy can't be far. Then, one day, the air is milder and it looks as though we might break free after all. It's warm enough to open a window or door or two, and even go on a walk that isn't an errand. The warm day is a gift. It feels good to be outdoors, and moving again. At the threshold, we notice the contrast between the fresh air outside and the stale atmosphere inside the house. We look closer at the open windows. They're spattered and grimy. The floor shows multiple tracks from winter snow and mud. It's time for spring cleaning.

Lent is the church's season for spring cleaning, and the beginning of our yearly foray into not lunacy but the lunar calendar. The forty days of Lent (not counting the six Sundays) and the fifty days of Easter together make up ninety days—basically a quarter of the year. This cycle wobbles around from one year to the next on our solar-based calendars because it is governed, in part, by the cycle of the moon. To get a feel for the season's origins, we have to travel back in imagination several thousand years.

If we were herders of sheep and goats, we would be acutely aware of how much we depended upon the lives of our animals to sustain our lives. Just about every part of the animal would be a gift for our use: when living, wool and milk; when slaughtered, bone, skin, horn, and meat. Their products would provide us food, clothing, tools, and shelter. By our animals' death, our people could continue to live.

Late winter and early spring would be a time of suspense as we waited for new kids or lambs to be born. Would the births go well and the young survive, safe from predators and disease? Would the flocks we depended on flourish for another generation? We would anticipate new birth, aware of the very real presence of death hovering nearby. At the full moon of high spring, once the young were safely born, we would slaughter an older lamb and smear its blood upon our tentposts. This would protect us and our flocks as we packed our tents and moved from winter grazing areas to summer pastures.

When the God of Abraham, Isaac, and Jacob was revealed, the old practices would take on new meaning, connected to history. Now the lamb would be sacrificed to the God of Israel. The blood of the lamb on the lintels and doorposts of our slave dwellings would avert the angel of death, who would pass over them and instead strike firstborn males among the Egyptians. By the sacrificial death of each household's Passover lamb, our ancestors would live. Passing through the Red Sea waters, they would be freed from slavery and born anew as God's holy people.

We would keep this Passover festival as a way of remembering how God brought us out of Egypt and led us to the land of promise. In Canaan, where we cultivated fields of grain, our neighbors would discard the previous year's sourdough in the spring and start a new batch. New life meant new leavening. We would come to adopt this practice and connect it too with Passover, throwing out food made with yeast or other leavening agents. There would be a clean break between old and new. The commandment to observe a week of consuming unleavened food would be a way of establishing that break and remembering what God had done for us. Forever it would recall the bread of affliction our ancestors ate on the eve of their departure from Egypt, prepared in such haste that it had no time to rise.

Therefore, not even a crumb of the old yeast was to remain in our homes for the Passover celebration. As the holiday approached, in order to make sure that no leaven remained, we would just about turn our homes upside down. Every spring would be a time for thorough and vigorous cleaning—making a fresh start, making all things new.

Early spring for both Jews and Gentiles was a season for preparing to make a fresh start, and purifying oneself and one's surroundings in acknowledgment of complete human dependence upon the divine. The Anglo-Saxon word *lenct,* which survives in our word *lengthen,* names the liturgical season of Lent. The days are lengthening; spring is in the air. For Christians it is a time of spring cleaning as we prepare to celebrate our deliverance out of death into life. We make ready to pass through the waters of baptism or to renew our baptismal promises.

To begin, ashes mark our foreheads in the baptismal sign of the cross. The gritty ashes recall more than mortality: ashes have long been a component of soap, and can sometimes be substituted for soap as a cleansing agent. Paradoxically, the filthy smudge we wear shows our desire to come clean.

We cleanse our hearts the way we clean our homes and garages: by making a more conspicuous mess at first; sometimes becoming overwhelmed at the task; and always proceeding through the grace of God. "Junk drawer" or closet, first we have to get all the stuff out in the open and spread it around to see just what we're dealing with. How did *this* get in here? Why are we keeping *that*? Don't need *those* anymore! Better give them away—and get rid of the dust and cobwebs before replacing anything.

Lent gives us a chance to get our spiritual house in order before participating in the Three Days of our baptismal passage out of slavery into freedom and new life. As we gather, Sunday by Sunday, our scriptures spread out before us the conspicuous mess of our human condition. We recognize ourselves in Adam and Eve, vulnerable to persuasive deceit; in Nicodemus, too apprehensive to approach Jesus by the light of day or risk real commitment; in the panicky and contentious Israelites thirsting in the wilderness; in the blind man whose eyes have to be plastered with mud and spit before he can see; and in the rotting corpse of Lazarus, after four days emitting a stench.

Our scriptures also encourage us with the grace that is ours in Christ as we labor to clean up the messes we've made of things in our relationships with God, others, and ourselves. For our sake, Jesus refuses to be swayed by the seduction of power or the temptation to act helpless (Matt. 4). Aging and barren, Abraham and Sarah nevertheless set out in faith, trusting God's promise of "a land that I will show you" (Gen. 12). And then we see the words we can feed on when we're overwhelmed and know we need more than bread alone: God sent the Son not to condemn, but to save (John 3). "The water that I will give will become . . . a spring of water gushing up to eternal life" (John 4:14). "Go, wash" (John 9:6). "You have seen him, and the one speaking with you is he" (John 9:37).

As discouraged and flawed as we may be, God is with us: in the Spirit, breathing life into our valleys of failure and death; in the Father, who sees in secret and rewards our private struggles; and in Christ, who died for us while we were yet sinners, in whom we have received reconciliation.

Creation and redemption are the work not of our hands, but of the God upon whom we utterly depend. By our own efforts alone we cannot make a clean break with the past. Only the grace of God gives us the discernment and strength to identify the sourdough in our life and get rid of it, so we can make a fresh start with a new batch of leaven. And the result of just about turning our interior house upside down? Not perfection, or even living beautifully; but in the process we may find some things we'd forgotten or lost, including ourselves. We will be prepared to accept the saving power of God as we approach the deep waters. And we will hear addressed to us the words of Jesus: "The Teacher says, 'My time is near; I will keep the Passover at your house with my disciples'" (Matt. 26:18).

ENVIRONMENT AND ART FOR THE SEASON

When entering the church on Ash Wednesday, many worshipers will be

struck by the major change that has taken place since the last celebration.

Gone are the festive hangings and flowers. A stark

but welcoming simplicity greets the congregation.

As somber as it is, Ash Wednesday is not really a time of mourning. Instead it marks the beginning of a period of special discipline. It is also a time for spiritual cleansing and redirection, which should be evident somehow in the liturgical environment.

EXTERIOR ENVIRONMENT

As throughout the year, make good use of exterior signs to identify worship times, announce special services, and to welcome visitors. Consider the use of large purple banners affixed near major entrances to indicate the liturgical season. The placement of large crosses on the church lawn is better left until later in the season—more appropriately for Passion Sunday and Holy Week.

INTERIOR ENVIRONMENT

The narthex should be a place of welcome in any season. In its function as a preparatory space for worship, it should give some indication of the mood or focal points throughout Lent. Artwork in the narthex could depict some of the major gospel stories that will be used during Lent (Cycle A), in particular Jesus' meeting with Nicodemus (John 3), the Samaritan woman (John 4), the healing of the man born blind (John 9), and the raising of Lazarus (John 11). A painting or sculpture relating to any one of these stories could be used throughout the season as a way to draw the attention of worshipers more closely to Jesus' saving activity in the gospels. Use money from memorial gifts and other undesignated funds to commission lasting pieces of religious art from local artists. Works that will be part of a congregation's permanent collection may have the opportunity to tell the gospel story for a generation or more to come.

Arrangements of dried branches, rather than flowers, could be used to decorate gathering and other spaces during this season. For a more restrained version of floral decoration, use natural elements from the surrounding landscape, such as forsythia branches or pussy willows. Whatever is done for decoration, keep things simple throughout the forty days of Lent.

Consider the period of Lent as a time to "cleanse the house." Have paraments, banners, any flags, and other decorations removed for cleaning and to be made ready for Easter. Polish silver and brass worship appointments and communionware. Ceramic communion vessels, or anything with a duller appearance might be considered for this season instead. It is a good time to remove clutter and other extraneous materials from rooms, hallways, and closets. As this is a season for spiritual cleansing, let it also be a time for cleansing the church's house of everything that no longer serves a purpose.

Many churches have the tradition of covering any crosses in the worship space with purple voile. Others use unbleached linen. Still others extend the tradition to cover all crosses and all pictures in the building with the voile or linen.

For Ash Wednesday, paraments and vestments are typically black with little or no symbolism (alternatively they may be purple for the beginning of Lent). Austerity is the key word for Ash Wednesday. Paraments can be coarse, woven pieces in black or dark gray, reminding us of the dust of the ashes. Many use unbleached linen.

Purple is the color for Lent. It represents the penitential nature of the season, as we begin with confession and end with absolution at the Maundy Thursday service. We celebrate the 40 days and all the Sundays in Lent with restraint. In this season it is appropriate to omit symbolism entirely, having simple unadorned fabrics as symbols in themselves.

A generous amount of palms will normally be required for the procession on Passsion (Palm) Sunday. While many congregations may continue to use purple paraments and vestments, scarlet is a color more symbolic of Holy Week, reminding us of the color of blood.

134

PREACHING with the SEASON

Lent is the beginning in the middle of things. The season developed as the church's time to prepare candidates for their plunge into the waters of baptism. At the font, one life would end and another would begin. It was definitely a beginning for them all—for those being baptized and for those preparing them.

But for the church, it always happened in the middle of things. A family history needed to be recounted, stories to be told. Those who were to be adopted into the family needed to learn the family's lore to see where the journey had taken disciples who had preceded them.

The story also had a future. Not everything had come to completion—not yet. The catechumens were central players in this drama yet to unfold. They would carry the story into its next chapter—Jesus had not yet returned; the whole world did not yet know the good news.

In this interim, the church lived between its past and its future. Once again it told the story of salvation. Once again it prepared a new generation of disciples who would advance the good news of God's new day further into the world's life. That it all happened in the springtime was no accident. Yes, the story of Jesus came to its dramatic conclusion and unhinging in the spring. It was Passover. It was a time of liberation. It was a day for new beginnings. The weeks of Lent for us may now take place in the warmth of a Texas spring or the last throes of a New England winter, but always in this hemisphere these weeks are tinged with instability. The atmosphere heaves to throw off the patterns of winter-death, melting the world once again into the tidal flow of summer. Some days creation leans toward its warm future, and other days it slips into its deadly past. Depending on where you happen to find yourself in these weeks, you might face a tornado, a snowstorm, or a nor'easter, and perhaps one of each. But the sun and the tilt of the earth together tip the scales and assure the outcome. There is a comforting inevitability to life.

We celebrate the season best if we view it over the shoulders of those who are about to join the circle.

Once we were on the outside, but we have been brought inside. Can we recall that transformation? For some of us, it began before we were conscious, plunged into new life as infants. But for all of us—newly baptized and venerable ancients who cannot remember a time out of the family—we are always in the process of becoming disciples. Lent is the season for encouraging that process. The preaching of Lent calls catechumen and disciple alike into the journey of faith to take us more deeply into Jesus' new day.

This journey follows only one path. It always goes the way of the cross. No rising can happen without a dying. Grabbing hold of the new day requires a letting go of the worlds around which we so easily build our lives on foundations of self-sufficiency, making our own way, being our own gods. The old Adam and ancient Eve do not die easily or willingly. They need to be crucified. Lent should involve struggle, even as it calls us into discipleship.

We are called to that struggle on Ash Wednesday. We may live in the middle of things but we are easily lulled into a false sense of security thinking we have forever. We do not. The clock is ticking. The ash we will one day become is smeared upon our foreheads here and now and the words are meant to chill us: "Remember that you are dust and to dust you shall return." It is one of the most sobering actions of pastoral care: to mark the ashen cross on the heads of all one's brothers and sisters in Christ. No one escapes mortality: the aged and the infant, the struggling and the comfortable, the best of your friends and the harshest of your critics. Dietrich Bonhoeffer reminded us that when Jesus calls a person to discipleship he bids that person come and die. It is where our baptism leads us. The entire trajectory of Lent, the Three Days and Easter, however, will also help us rediscover that if the way to death goes the way of Jesus' cross, it leads us to new life. Really, these three seasons are one; they need to be analyzed together. It would be good for you to scan the articles for the Three Days and Easter as you think about Lent. How can you know the appropriate place to start unless you have some idea where you are going?

Although the mood of Ash Wednesday is serious and somber, the church does not pass through this season merely to grovel in guilt and inflict misery upon ourselves and each other. The ashen cross is also a symbol of life, a sign of our birthright as sons and daughters of God in Christ. In many places during these weeks, farmers burn their fields. For a while the hills are a deep, ashen black. But when the winter wheat pushes its way through the soot, the green is electric, vibrant with life.

The first readings for the Sundays of this season introduce us to pilgrims from the Hebrew Scriptures, stretching from creation to exile. The gospels present us with characters out of the New Testament. Once we are beyond the First Sunday in Lent, the gospels take us sequentially through the gospel according to John to meet men and women who struggled with issues of darkness and light, death and life, although they were not always aware of it. Together, these two weekly readings create an interesting counterpoint of people living in the middle of things who are in need of new beginnings. In between each Sunday's pair of stories we receive some help from a letter addressed to believers in the early generations of Christian discipleship. These were the folk who had to wrestle early-on with the implications of Jesus' cross and open tomb. It was in their struggles, often set within a context of conflict and persecution, that the church's concepts of the meaning of baptism and discipleship were forged.

Most of the gospels of Lent are extended pericopes that display the evangelists' narrative virtuosity. Worship leaders will want to plan consciously how we might best permit these gospels of Lent to sing to us. Fortunately, the Revised Common Lectionary does not lead us into the temptation of truncating these superbly wrought stories. They are meant to be heard in their entirety and savored. In many ways, they are preparations for the longer narratives in the Three Days. The gospel reader will want to practice reading the stories out loud and could benefit by having the stories read to him or her.

Worship leaders should also reflect on whether our traditional posture of standing during the gospel is

appropriate to these longer narratives. It may be better to invite the congregation to be seated, to settle back and prepare to listen to a good story told well. Finally, the length of the gospels and the austerity of the season might suggest a "leaner, meaner" homiletic style for the season. Sometimes less is more. The preacher may want to consider delivering the homily as an introduction to the lessons for the day, raising the questions of our life and discipleship in such a way that the word itself might be the answer and the challenge to our growth. Other suggestions for approaching these lengthy texts are included in "Preaching with the Season" for the Three Days. It would be good to consider that article as well.

Forty days is not forever, but it is a time in the middle of things. It is a sprint, long enough to move us quickly from here to there, but short enough for us to maintain a maximum effort for a while. If Lent works, we will be different when this time is over. Something will have changed. That change is the root meaning of *repentance*—a new heart and a new mind, a new beginning in the middle of things. And if God offers it and we accept, we will be ready for the plunge into Holy Week that swallows death in life.

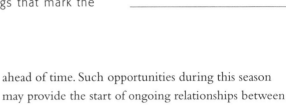

PLANNING AHEAD FOR THE SEASON

Rather than focusing on Lent as a time in which to give up things, think of

it as a time to be more intentional about doing those things that mark the

life of the Christian throughout the year. The Ash

Wednesday liturgy of *LBW* mentions how it is a

time to join in the discipline of the season—repentance, fasting, prayer, and works of love (*LBW, Ministers Edition*, p. 129). If your congregation has the custom of gathering for midweek services throughout the season of Lent, perhaps the various disciplines could give you ideas for weekly sermon topics.

Congregations planning for the baptism of adults at the Easter Vigil (or on Easter Sunday) might enroll such candidates on the First Sunday in Lent and pray for them publicly throughout Lent. Presentations of both the Apostles' Creed and the Lord's Prayer could also occur during this season. Other members of the congregation might join in a reflection on the Apostles' Creed (on or around the Third Sunday in Lent) and the Lord's Prayer (on or around the Fifth Sunday in Lent). Resources for use with candidates for baptism are provided in *Welcome to Christ: Lutheran Rites for the Catechumenate*, pages 18–34. Even when no adult catechumens are present, returning to primary church teachings from the Small Catechism each Lent could be a good basis for midweek Lenten worship.

In addition to many congregations gathering for midweek worship during this season, oftentimes households are provided with additional devotional resources. Resources for daily prayer and Bible reading might be distributed. A simple order for household daily prayer that includes a psalm, a short scripture reading, a hymn, a prayer for the world and for others in need, and the Lord's Prayer, would be one way to introduce a habit that might continue even beyond the season of Lent.

Sunday school classes, small groups, women's circles, and Bible study meetings might covenant to perform works of love during the Lenten season. The social ministry committee (if your congregation has one) might be able to assemble a list of possible projects and community organizations in need of assistance

ahead of time. Such opportunities during this season may provide the start of ongoing relationships between members of the congregation and others experiencing real needs within the community at large.

Congregations that use an extended order for confession on Ash Wednesday (see *LBW, Ministers Edition*, pp. 129–131) might consider delaying any direct announcement of absolution (or statement of forgiveness) until the Maundy Thursday liturgy (see *LBW*, Minister Edition, pp. 137–138). The Ash Wednesday liturgy, at most, provides only an anticipation of forgiveness. Absolutions used throughout Lent might follow a similar pattern, leaving the strong declarative form of absolution ("I declare to you . . .") until Maundy Thursday itself. In that way the season of Lent can be seen as a penitential season or an extended time of spiritual cleansing and renewal. The power of self-examination throughout the forty days of Lent can be brought to a close by providing an opportunity for individual laying on of hands during the absolution on Maundy Thursday (*LBW, Ministers Edition*, p. 138).

Passion (Palm) Sunday provides the opportunity for an elaborate procession or entrance rite at the beginning of the service. The congregation might meet before one of the services on that day in a space other than the space commonly used for worship. Those not wishing to participate in the procession may be seated in the nave prior to the beginning of the service. If possible, find a way for everyone to take part in the procession. If your climate allows, the congregation might actually gather outside, perhaps in a parking lot, a lawn, or even at a location away from the church property. A palm procession can also be quite effective even when it uses an interior route, perhaps going from a parish hall, an educational facility, or even a narthex or hallway into the nave. The processional liturgy is quite brief (*LBW, Ministers Edition*, pp. 134–135), incorporating one of the accounts of Jesus' triumphal entrance into Jerusalem on a donkey. Choirs might sing a jubilant anthem associated with this day (with their loud *hosannas*) at this point of the service. Following a brief blessing of palms and those who will carry them, the procession begins, customarily singing the hymn "All glory, laud, and honor" (LBW 108). Encourage worshipers to wave their palms during the procession.

Though the reading of one of the passion accounts may seem too much for this day, the effect of its use may actually be quite chilling. By the time of the reading of the passion story, the mood of Holy Week shifts dramatically. Can the same crowd that shouted "hosanna" be the same crowd that shouts "crucify him?" (Such has been the basis for many sermons on this day.) With such engaging drama in the procession and the passion reading, a sermon need not be lengthy on this day. It might simply set the stage for the profound moments yet to be experienced in the coming week.

ORDO for the SEASON

The whole season of Lent can be understood to be a suspended time of confession and absolution (see the notes in the "planning for worship" section of this season). Between the extended form for confession on Ash Wednesday (*LBW, Ministers Edition*, pp. 129–131), and the absolution with laying on of hands at Maundy Thursday (*LBW, Ministers Edition*, p. 138), the congregation might gather each week in extended silence and a brief order for confession and forgiveness. To keep the suspension between confession and absolution throughout the season, words that give assurance of God's mercy or pardon could be used, without pronouncing a strong declarative form of absolution ("I therefore declare to you . . .") until Maundy Thursday.

In keeping with the "two of the following three" notion for the gathering rite (introduced in the ordo section of the Epiphany chapter), Lent would be a time to have an order for confession, a Kyrie, but no hymn of praise. A hymn of praise is traditionally not done throughout the Lenten season anyway. The Kyrie in this season might be a hymnic version, such as "Kyrie, God Father" (LBW 168) or "Your Heart, O God, Is Grieved" (LBW 96).

Eucharistic Prayer D for Lent (*WOV, Leaders Edition*, p. 68), helps to convey the sense that the whole period of Lent is a journey towards renewal of baptism. The strong root metaphors referring to Christ as our rock and our water in this prayer give the baptized something to focus on as we travel through the dry desert of Lent. Indeed this prayer could make the longing for the renewal of baptism at the Easter Vigil all that much more intense. Eucharistic Prayer III from *LBW* and *WOV* also contains material that fits nicely into the Lenten season. It echoes words heard on the Second Sunday in Lent (John 3). It also conveys a sense of humility especially appropriate for Lent: "We give thanks to you, Lord God Almighty, not as we ought, but as we are able; and we implore you mercifully to accept our prayers and thanksgiving. . . ."

A brief hymn might replace the post-communion canticle for Lent, especially one that speaks of the continuing Lenten journey such as "O Lord, throughout these forty days" (LBW 99) or "As the sun with longer journey" (WOV 655).

138

ASSEMBLY SONG FOR THE SEASON

In the first reading for Ash Wednesday the prophet Joel advises us to "Return to the Lord, your God, for he is gracious and merciful." Lent is about returning—getting back to basics. The word *Lent* actually means "spring," another reminder that this season is about renewal—about avoiding distractions to see God clearly in our lives. Whether getting ready to enter God's bath yourself, walking with someone who is preparing for baptism, or engaging in a time of renewal and remembrance of our own baptism, Lent is about baptism—about returning to the source of living water that makes us children of God. The images of Lent focus on the effects of baptism: repentance, forgiveness, cleansing, nourishment, enlightenment, healing, and new life.

During this time, the absence of specific sounds may speak more loudly than even the most appropriate musical selection. The church has always customarily excluded "alleluias" in the Lenten fast. The joyful sound of bells or festive stops on an organ may be silenced throughout Lent, adding another layer of aural anticipation for the Vigil of Easter. One musical element that is often nothing more than background sound is the postlude. The surprise of silence may be a conspicuous reminder of the cleansing in which we are now engaged in during Lent. One sentence at the conclusion of the worship folder (such as, "No postludes will be played until the Vigil of Easter") may help to show the intentionality of this omission.

The Bible is the fundamental "textbook" of the Christian life. Lent is a fitting time to focus on the word part of the liturgical rhythm of gathering, word, meal, and sending. In Cycle A of the lectionary, the gospel readings are the "classic" texts used on these Lenten days for centuries: Jesus' temptation in the wilderness, Nicodemus questioning Jesus about being born again, the woman at the well and Jesus' offer of living water, the healing of the blind man, and the raising of Lazarus.

When readings are lengthy, they require conscientious musical selections to accompany them. Participation and response are critical. Therefore, settings of the psalm and gospel acclamation should, if possible, involve the congregation. If a congregation is not used to singing antiphons to the psalm verses, it may be a good time to discover the simple joy of doing so. If antiphons are a part of the regular pattern, omitting them during Lent and singing the psalm text to a simple tone might be appropriate. The congregation can be involved in announcing the gospel reading by flanking the appointed verse (see *WOV, Leaders Edition)* with an appropriate refrain (such as the one at WOV 611b or the refrain to WOV 614). The verse could be sung to a psalm tone by choir or cantor, and would change each week with the congregation refrain remaining the same throughout Lent.

Hymnody has held a place of high regard in Lutheran worship traditions. Martin Luther used hymns as a primary vehicle for involving the congregation in worship. Throughout history, Lutheran authors and composers have been responsible for a wealth of hymns known and loved in many branches of Christianity.

In a world that pushes us toward the new, we often lose sight of the old and faithful. Lent may be an appropriate time to return to the treasury of hymnody from all periods of our history. Opportunities that bring singers of all ages together to share in each other's songs could be of great value. Children's faith can be nurtured by learning some traditional hymnody. Older members need to be reassured about the future of the church by learning newer songs, but not at the expense of those they love deeply. There is room for all. Many people prepare for weekly worship by studying the Sunday readings. Including the hymn of the day in that study, providing it is carefully chosen, could be beneficial for all the faithful.

MUSIC FOR THE SEASON

VERSE AND OFFERTORY

Busarow, Donald. *Verses and Offertories, Part III—Ash Wednesday through Maundy Thursday.* CPH 97-5503. SATB, org.

Cherwien, David. *Verses for the Sundays in Lent.* MSM 80-300. U/2 pt, org.

Farlee, Robert Buckley. *Verses and Offertories for Lent.* AFP 11-10065. U/SATB.

Norris, Kevin. *Verses and Offertories for Lent.* AFP 11-9545. U, kybd.

Schalk, Carl. "Return to the Lord, Your God." MSM 50-3033. SATB, opt kybd.

Schramm, Charles. *Verses for the Lenten Season.* MSM 80-301. SATB, opt org.

CHORAL MUSIC FOR THE SEASON

Bertalot, John. "Amazing Grace." AFP 11-10020. SATB, org.

Chepponis, James. "The Time of Fulfillment: A Lenten Gathering Rite." GIA G-3906. SATB, cant, cong.

DeLong, Richard. "O for a Heart to Praise My God." ECS 4859. SATB.

Erickson, Karle. "Thy Holy Wings." AFP 11-0594. SATB, 2 fl.

Erickson, Richard. "By the Babylonian Rivers." AFP 11-10814. SATB, org.

Fauré, Gabriel. "Cantique de Jean Racine." BBL 801. SATB, kybd/hp.

Keesecker, Thomas. "Jesus, Keep Me Near the Cross." AFP 11-10744. SATB, pno.

Keesecker, Thomas. "Washed Anew." AFP 11-10676. SATB, pno, opt cong, opt 2 oct hb.

Kosche, Kenneth T. "Kyrie, Incline Your Ear." CPH 98-3266. U, cant, hb.

Manz, Paul. "On My Heart Imprint Thine Image." MSM 50-3037. SATB.

Pergolesi/Hopson. "Surely He Has Borne Our Griefs." AFP 11-10587. SATB, kybd.

Proulx, Richard. "Were You There." AFP 11-10571. SATB, S solo.

Sedio, Mark. "By the Babylonian Rivers." SEL 410-850. SATB, vln, vla, or C inst.

Thompson, Randall. "The Best of Rooms." ECS 2672. SATB.

CHILDREN'S CHORAL MUSIC FOR THE SEASON

Jennings, Carolyn. "My Song Is Love Unknown." CGA 559. U, kybd.

Keesecker, Thomas. "Do Not Forget Me." AFP 11-10569. 2 pt trbl, kybd.

Pooler, Marie. "A Song for Lent." AFP 11-10361. U, opt 2 pt, kybd.

Wold, Wayne. "Kyrie Eleison: Lord, Have Mercy." MSM 80-303. U, kybd.

INSTRUMENTAL MUSIC FOR THE SEASON

Biery, James. "Three Gospel Scenes." MSM-10-317. Org.

Cherwien, David. "Toccata on 'In the Cross of Christ I Glory.'" MSM 10-303. Org.

Dupré, Marcel. "Cortége et Litanie." LED. Org.

Ferguson, John. *Thy Holy Wings: Three Swedish Folk Hymn Preludes.* AFP 11-8546. Org.

Hulme, Lance R. "Fantasy on 'Wondrous Love.'" AFP 11-10350. Org.

Leavitt, John. "My Song Is Love Unknown." AFP 11-10828. Org, inst.

Manz, Paul. *Three Lenten Hymns for Oboe and Organ.* MSM 20-361. Org, ob.

Nicholson, Paul. "Wondrous Love." AFP 11-10529. Org, tpt.

Sedio, Mark. *Music for the Paschal Season.* AFP 11-10763. Org.

Uehlein, Christopher. "Pastorale No. 1 and No. 2" in *Blue Cloud Abbey Organ Book.* AFP 11-10394. Org.

Young, Jeremy. "At the Foot of the Cross: Piano for the Lenten Journey." AFP 11-10688. Pno.

HANDBELL MUSIC FOR THE SEASON

McChesney, Kevin. "Pavane." AFP 11-10318. 3 oct.

Nelson, Susan T. "A Plainchant Meditation and Morning Suite." AFP 11-10696. 3 oct.

ALTERNATE WORSHIP TEXTS

CONFESSION AND FORGIVENESS

In the name of the Father, and of the ✝ Son, and of the Holy
    Spirit.
Amen

Before God, who so loved the world as to send a Savior,
let us confess our sin with a contrite heart.

Silence for reflection and self-examination.

Gracious and merciful God,
we confess that we are a broken people
who put ourselves before others.
Too often we have not shared bread with the hungry,
given the homeless a home,
clothed the naked,
and worked for justice among all peoples.
We cry from the depths of our sin, O Lord,
even as we put our trust in your word.
Heal us by your grace, and take from us
all that would separate us from your love. Amen

With the Lord there is mercy and full redemption.
We are refreshed and renewed in the living water of Christ.
Almighty God have mercy on you,
forgive you all your sin,
and bring you to everlasting life.
Amen

GREETING

Come, let us worship and bow down before our Maker.
God is our shepherd, and we are the flock led with care.

The grace of our Lord Jesus Christ, the love of God,
and the communion of the Holy Spirit be with you all.
And also with you.

OFFERTORY PRAYER

God of mercy,
you bless us with gifts that sustain our lives;
you transform us with the priceless gift of grace.
Receive us and these signs of your blessings,
and may our fasting, prayer, and works of love
be an offering of thanksgiving
for all that you have done for us
in Christ, our Lord. Amen

INVITATION TO COMMUNION

Behold the Lamb of God
who takes away the sin of the world.
Happy are those who are called to his supper.
Lord, I am not worthy to receive you,
but only say the word and I shall be healed.

POST-COMMUNION PRAYER

Everlasting God, we have tasted the good food
of your table of grace.
Nourished by the life of your Son,
may we live as children of the light,
sharing your good news;
through Jesus Christ our Lord.
Amen

BENEDICTION

The blessing of God,
who brings you each day to new birth,
who satisfies your thirst with living water,
who breathes life into you by the Holy Spirit,
be among you and remain with you always.
Amen

DISMISSAL

Goodness and mercy shall follow you
all the days of your life.
Go in peace to love and serve the Lord.
Thanks be to God!

141

SEASONAL RITES

MIDWEEK EVENING PRAYER FOR LENT

This flexible order of evening prayer may be celebrated as the midweek service. It is an adaptable form of vespers with readings and music that highlight the Sunday Lenten lectionary themes of God's mercy and forgiveness.

OVERVIEW

Midweek themes from the Sunday readings for Lent, Year A.

Week of 1 Lent
   God commands Adam and Eve not to eat of the forbidden fruit
Week of 2 Lent
   God promises an inheritance to those who share Abraham's faith
Week of 3 Lent
   God pours out living water through Jesus
Week of 4 Lent
   God brings people into the light
Week of 5 Lent
   God breathes life to dry bones

SERVICE OF LIGHT

A lit vesper candle may be processed during the versicles and placed in its stand near the altar.

LENTEN VERSICLES

From LBW, p. 176; these versicles may be sung to the tones given in evening prayer, LBW, p. 142.

Behold, now is the acceptable time;
now is the day of our salvation.
Turn us again, O God of our salvation,
that the light of your face may shine on us.
May your justice shine like the sun;
and may the poor be lifted up.

HYMN OF LIGHT

LBW 248   Dearest Jesus, at your word
WOV 728   O Light whose splendor thrills
WOV 729   Christ, mighty Savior

THANKSGIVING FOR LIGHT

This is set to music in LBW, p. 144.

The Lord be with you.
And also with you.
Let us give thanks to the Lord our God.
It is right to give our thanks and praise.
Blessed are you, O Lord our God, king of the universe,
   who led your people Israel by a pillar of cloud by day
   and a pillar of fire by night:
   Enlighten our darkness by the light of your Christ;
   may his Word be a lamp to our feet and a light to our path;
   for you are merciful, and you love your whole creation,
   and we, your creatures, glorify you, Father, Son, and Holy Spirit.
Amen

PSALMODY

The first psalm may be Psalm 141, as printed in LBW, pp. 145–146, or another setting of this psalm may be used.

An additional psalm may be used for each of the weeks during the Lenten season:

1 Lent   Ps. 1
2 Lent   Ps. 25
3 Lent   Ps. 42
4 Lent   Ps. 27
5 Lent   Ps. 126

HYMN

Possibilities for hymns related to the readings for each of the weeks of Lent follow:

1 Lent
LBW 372   In Adam we have all been one
WOV 733   Our Father, we have wandered

2 Lent
LBW 297   Salvation unto us has come
WOV 699   Blessed assurance

3 Lent
LBW 499   Come, thou fount of every blessing
WOV 696   I've just come from the fountain

4 Lent
LBW 380   O Christ, our light, our radiance true
WOV 649   I want to walk as a child of the light

5 Lent
LBW 488   Breathe on me, breath of God
WOV 799   When long before time

READINGS

Readings for each of the weeks of Lent are given:

1 Lent   Genesis 2:15-17; 3:1-7
2 Lent   Romans 4:1-5, 13-17
3 Lent   John 4:5-42
4 Lent   Ephesians 5:8-14
5 Lent   Ezekiel 37:1-14

A homily or meditation may be given at this time.

Silence is kept by all.

RESPONSE

In many and various ways God spoke to his people of old by the prophets.
But now in these last days he has spoken to us by his Son.

GOSPEL CANTICLE

LBW 180   My soul now magnifies the Lord
or
WOV 730   My soul proclaims your greatness

LITANY

For a musical form of the litany, see LBW, p. 148.

In peace, let us pray to the Lord.
Lord, have mercy.
For the peace from above, let us pray to the Lord.
Lord, have mercy.
For the peace of the whole world, for the well-being of the Church of God, and for the unity of all, let us pray to the Lord.
Lord, have mercy.
For those who are preparing for the Easter sacraments, let us pray to the Lord.
Lord, have mercy.
For the baptized people of God and for their varied ministries within the church, let us pray to the Lord.
Lord, have mercy.
For those who are poor, hungry, homeless, and sick, let us pray to the Lord.
Lord, have mercy.
Help, save, comfort, and defend us, gracious Lord.

Silence is kept by all.

Rejoicing in the fellowship of all the saints, let us commend ourselves, one another, and our whole life to Christ, our Lord.
To you, O Lord.

PRAYER OF THE DAY

From the previous Sunday if a service is held during the week.

THE LORD'S PRAYER

BLESSING

For a musical setting, see LBW, p. 152.
Let us bless the Lord.
Thanks be to God.

The almighty and merciful Lord, the Father, the Son, and the Holy Spirit, bless and preserve us.
Amen

143

FEBRUARY 17, 1999

ASH WEDNESDAY

INTRODUCTION

Christians gather on this day to mark the beginning of Lent's baptismal preparation for Easter. On this day, the people of God receive an ashen cross on the forehead (a gesture rooted in baptism), hear the solemn proclamation to keep a fast in preparation for Easter's feast, and contemplate anew the ongoing meaning of baptismal initiation into the Lord's death and resurrection. While marked with the ashes of human mortality, the church hears God's promise of forgiveness and tastes God's mercy in the bread of life and the cup of salvation. From this solemn liturgy, the church goes forth on its journey to the great baptismal feast of Easter.

PRAYER OF THE DAY

Almighty and ever-living God, you hate nothing you have made and you forgive the sins of all who are penitent. Create in us new and honest hearts, so that, truly repenting of our sins, we may obtain from you, the God of all mercy, full pardon and forgiveness; through your Son, Jesus Christ our Lord, who lives and reigns with you and the Holy Spirit, one God, now and forever.

READINGS

Joel 2:1-2, 12-17

The context of this reading is a liturgy of communal lamentation. The prophet has called the temple-community to mourn a devastating plague of the past and to announce a day of darkness, the day of the Lord. The community is called to repent, to return to God who is gracious and merciful.

or Isaiah 58:1-12

Psalm 51:1-18 (Psalm 51:1-17 [NRSV])

Have mercy on me, O God, according to your lovingkindness. (Ps. 51:1)

2 Corinthians 5:20b—6:10

Out of love for humankind, the sinless one experienced sin and suffering so that the redemptive power of God could penetrate the darkest, most forbidding, and tragic depths of human experience. No aspect of human life is ignored by the presence of God's grace. Because of this, Paul announces that this day is a day of God's grace, an acceptable time to turn toward God's mercy.

Matthew 6:1-6, 16-21

In this passage Matthew sets forth a vision of genuine righteousness illustrated by three basic acts of Jewish devotion: almsgiving, prayer, and fasting. Jesus does not denounce the acts—in the New Testament they are signs of singular devotion to God. Rather, he criticizes those who perform them in order to have a sense of self-satisfaction or to gain public approval. Care for the poor, intense prayer, and fasting with a joyous countenance are signs of loving dedication to God.

COLOR   Black *or* Purple

THE PRAYERS

In these days of Lenten spring, let us pray for the world, the church, and for all people according to their needs.
A BRIEF SILENCE.

For the church and its bishops, pastors, and leaders, that together we may seek reconciliation with you and each other, let us pray to the Lord.

Lord, have mercy.

For all those around the world preparing for baptism at Easter, that they may be brought to newness of life, let us pray to the Lord.

Lord, have mercy.

For those afflicted by poverty, oppression, or discrimination, that we respond with mercy and compassion, let us pray to the Lord.

Lord, have mercy.

For all who seek healing, comfort, and peace, and for all who are sick in mind or body (especially . . .), that you give them endurance in suffering, let us pray to the Lord.

Lord, have mercy.

For this congregation, that our Lenten journey renew our commitment to you, to each other, and to the needs of our community, let us pray to the Lord.

Lord, have mercy.

HERE OTHER INTERCESSIONS MAY BE OFFERED.

For ourselves, that marked with the holy cross we may follow all your saints, who baptized into Jesus' death now share the glory of his resurrection, let us pray to the Lord.

Lord, have mercy.
Hear our prayers, O merciful God, as we eagerly await the day of resurrection and rebirth, through Jesus Christ our Lord.
Amen

IMAGES FOR PREACHING

What is holding you back from life? How has death invaded the middle of things and made you captive? Now is the time—the acceptable time—to do something about it. The ashen cross is placed upon our foreheads once again. Made from the dried palms of our last Passion Sunday celebration, the ashes tie together our endings and beginnings. As in baptism, so in Lent, one life ends and a new life begins. The gospel's DNA twists around full circle spiraling us into the future. In one sense we are where we have been before, but in another sense we are not. Last year's Lent should have changed us. If we seek life now, we must be vulnerable to change and growth.

The ash is a sign of death, the slap in the face to shock us into realizing we do not have forever. Blow the trumpet! Call an emergency meeting! Time is running out. We do not have forever but we do, most likely, have these forty days in which we might act.

What shall we do? Repent, which means to get a new mind/heart. We must fast, which means we let go of those artificial dependencies that hold us back from life. (A fast of the heart, rather than a fast of the belly.) We pray, which means we get into real communication with the God who will save us and raise us from the dead. (Don't hold back!) And we take on acts of charity, committed to life in community with believer and nonbeliever alike. (Isn't that what God had in mind all along? Justice! Compassion!)

The ash is also sign of life, the echo of a baptism that washed over us and anointed us. It is time for us to become what we were meant to be all along. Now!

WORSHIP MATTERS

"*Name*," child of God, you have been sealed by the Holy Spirit and marked with the cross of Christ forever" (Holy Baptism, *LBW*, p. 124). The words are said over all who are baptized by water and the Holy Spirit into the community of God's people. As the words are said, the presiding minister traces the sign of the cross on the forehead of the newly baptized, giving this new member of the body of Christ a permanent share in the priesthood of all believers, and the sign of the cross as a badge of inheritance. Luther reminds us that we return each day to the waters of baptism, to the gifts of forgiveness and new life given in those waters, and to the cross of Christ, the vehicle of our redemption. Luther too urges each of the faithful to trace the sign of the cross upon themselves when saying morning and evening prayers, daily reminders that we have been incorporated into the death and resurrection of Christ. Making the sign of cross is also a customary practice during the assembly's worship. Traditionally, the faithful have made the sign of the cross upon themselves at the invocation, when the words of forgiveness are pronounced, upon receiving the elements of Holy Communion, and at the final blessing.

LET THE CHILDREN COME

Children talk about death to somehow grasp the notion of it. They engage in playacting that imitates death. The rhyme "ashes, ashes, we all fall down," is one example. A key to helping children negotiate the world and mystery of death is having adults who are honest and truthful about it. Avoid euphemisms. Everything dies. At a certain level, children know that. Ash Wednesday is one way to help children speak about death with honesty. They are marked with ashes, a sign of death. These ashes also form a cross, a sign of life that comes from death.

MUSIC FOR WORSHIP

SERVICE MUSIC

Care should be taken on Ash Wednesday that instrumental music be limited, perhaps simply to that which is necessary to sing the service music, hymns, and propers. The austerity of the day points to the "spring house-cleaning" of the heart.

PSALM 51

Bedford, Michael. *Sing Out! A Children's Psalter.* WLP 7191.

Joncas, Michael. "Be Merciful, O Lord." GIA G-3433. SAB/U, gtr, kybd, opt 2 C inst, cong.

Rees, Elizabeth. "O Lord, You Love Sincerity of Heart" in PS2.

Schwarz, May. PW, Cycle A.

Walker, Christopher. "Ps. 51: Give Me a New Heart, O God" in STP, vol. 3.

145

HYMN OF THE DAY

LBW 295   Out of the depths I cry to you
           AUS TIEFER NOT

VOCAL RESOURCES

Ferguson, John. "Psalm 130: Out of the Depths." AFP 11-10749.
    SATB, org.

INSTRUMENTAL RESOURCES

Gore, Richard. "Aus tiefer Not" in *Hymn Settings for Holy Week*.
    AFP 11-10560. Org.

Reger, Max. "Aus tiefer Not" in *30 Short Chorale Preludes, Op. 135a*.
    CFP 3980. Org.

Sadowski, Kevin. "Aus tiefer Not" in *Twenty Hymn Introductions*.
    CPH 97-6026. Org.

ALTERNATE HYMN OF THE DAY

LBW 91   Savior, when in dust to you
WOV 659   O Sun of justice

COMMUNION

LBW 296   Just as I am, without one plea
WOV 734   Softly and tenderly Jesus is calling

OTHER SUGGESTIONS

LLC 442   Crea en mí, oh Dios/Create in me

SENDING

LBW 263   Abide with us, our Savior
WOV 743   Stay with us

ADDITIONAL HYMNS AND SONGS

RS 957   Ashes
NCH 186   Dust and ashes touch our face
NCH 332   As we gather at your table
PsH 255   God, be merciful to me

MUSIC FOR THE DAY

CHORAL

Attwood, Thomas. "Turn Thy Face from My Sins" in *The New Church
    Anthem Book*. OXF 0-19-353109-7. SATB.

Bouman, Paul. "Create in Me a Clean Heart, O God." CPH 98-114.
    SA, org.

Brahms, Johannes. "Create in Me, O God, a Clean Heart."
    GSCH GS 750. SATBB.

Farrant, Richard. "Lord, for Thy Tender Mercy's Sake" in *The New
    Church Anthem Book*. OXF 0-19-353109-7. SATB.

Gerike, Henry. "Create in Me." AFP 11-10746. SAB, org.

Marshall, Jane. "Create in Me, O God, a Clean Heart." CGA 750. U, kybd.

Moore, Bob. "Have Mercy, O Lord: Music for the Imposition of
    Ashes." GIA G-3670. SATB, cant, cong, gtr, acc.

Owens, Sam Batt. "Drop, Drop, Slow Tears." MSM 50-3406. SAB, org,
    opt hb.

Rutter John. "God Be in My Head" in *The New Church Anthem Book*.
    OXF 0-19-353109-7. SATB.

Scott, K. Lee. "Out of the Depths I Cry to Thee." AFP 11-04644. 2 pt
    mxd, kybd.

Wesley, Samuel Sebastian. "Wash Me Thoroughly" in *The New Church
    Anthem Book*. OXF 0-19-353109-7. SATB, org.

CHILDREN'S CHOIRS

Chepponis, James. "Lenten Proclamation." GIA G-2761. 3 equal or
    mxd, hb.

Lovelace, Austin. "God of Beauty." CGA 172. U, kybd.

Marshall, Jane. "Create in Me, O God." CGA 750. U, antiphonal,
    kybd.

KEYBOARD/INSTRUMENTAL

Bach, J. S. "Aus tiefer Not" in *Clavierübung*. Various ed. Org.

Drischner, Max. "Aus tiefer Not" in *Funfundzwanzig Orgelchorale*.
    Schott ed. SCH 6041. Org.

Honoré, Jeffrey. "Ashes" in *Contemporary Preludes for Organ*.
    OCP vol. 15. Org.

Langlais, Jean. "De profundis" in *Neuf Pièces*. BOR. Org.

PRAISE ENSEMBLE

Haas, David. "We Will Drink the Cup" in *Who Calls You by Name,* vol.
    II. GIA G-3622C. SATB.

Ylvisaker, John. "Please Have Mercy on Me" in *Borning Cry*. NGP.

THURSDAY, FEBRUARY 18

MARTIN LUTHER, RENEWER OF THE CHURCH, 1546

Luther taught biblical exegesis at Wittenberg from 1511 until his death on this day in 1546. He posted his *95 Theses* concerning indulgences in 1517. He is honored by the church as a biblical scholar, a translator of the Bible, a reformer of the liturgy, a theologian and educator, and the father of German vernacular literature. His great love of scripture and music, and his profound sense of pastoral care for ordinary people remain prominent aspects of a distinctively Lutheran spirituality.

A Lenten study group might study Luther's Large Catechism. Use the season of Lent to teach the congregation to dip their hands in the baptismal font, make the sign of the cross, and repeat Luther's famous words: *I am baptized!*

146

SATURDAY, FEBRUARY 20
RASMUS JENSEN,
THE FIRST LUTHERAN PASTOR IN NORTH AMERICA, 1620

Jensen was the first Lutheran pastor in North America. He came in 1619 with an expedition sent by King Christian IV of Denmark. The expedition took posses-sion of the Hudson Bay Area, naming it *Nova Dania*. Within a few months of their arrival, most of the members of the expedition died, including Jensen.

Use this occasion to remember the founders of your congregation. Of what synods or districts has it been a part during its history? What has its presence been in the community over the years?

FEBRUARY 21, 1999

FIRST SUNDAY IN LENT

INTRODUCTION

In the early church, those to be baptized at the Easter Vigil were given intense preparation in the preceding weeks. This catechetical process is the origin and purpose of the Lenten season: a time for the church and its baptismal candidates to ponder the meaning of baptism into the death and resurrection of the Lord. The forty days—a scriptural image of testing and renewal—invite us to return to Holy Baptism. On Ash Wednesday we receive the ashen cross of pilgrims (a baptismal gesture) who go forth to the font of new and eternal life.

The weeks of Lent invite us to speak the truth about the keeping of our baptismal promises. The weeks of Lent invite us to hear and taste God's abundant forgiveness in word and sacrament.

PRAYER OF THE DAY

Lord God, you led your ancient people through the wilderness and brought them to the promised land. Guide now the people of your Church, that, following our Savior, we may walk through the wilderness of this world toward the glory of the world to come; through your Son, Jesus Christ our Lord, who lives and reigns with you and the Holy Spirit, one God, now and forever.
or
Lord God, our strength, the battle of good and evil rages within and around us, and our ancient foe tempts us with his deceits and empty promises. Keep us steadfast in your Word and, when we fall, raise us again and restore us through your Son, Jesus Christ our Lord, who lives and reigns with you and the Holy Spirit, one God, now and forever.

147

READINGS

Genesis 2:15-17; 3:1-7
Human beings were formed with great care, to be in relationship with the Creator, creation, and one another. This passage recounts the first in a series of stories that depicts the nature of human sin—wanting to be like God.

Psalm 32
Mercy embraces those who trust in the Lord. (Ps. 32:11)

Romans 5:12-19
Paul describes the effect of Jesus' obedience as analogous to that of Adam's disobedience. Through Christ, God has reversed the consequences of sin and death to offer the free gift of eternal life.

Matthew 4:1-11
Jesus experiences anew the temptations that Israel faced in the wilderness. As the Son of God, he endures the testing of the evil one.

COLOR   Purple

THE PRAYERS

In these days of Lenten spring, let us pray for the world, the church, and for all people according to their needs.
A BRIEF SILENCE.

For all nations torn by war, poverty, or internal strife, that they may know your peace and harmony, let us pray to the Lord.

Lord, have mercy.

For the church, that with Christ we may turn from evil and be obedient to your Word, let us pray to the Lord.

Lord, have mercy.

For all who will be baptized or received into the church at Easter, that you may be their strength, let us pray to the Lord.

Lord, have mercy.

For all those struggling in the wilderness of loneliness, despair, or sickness (especially . . .), that you nourish them with the bread of life, let us pray to the Lord.

Lord, have mercy.

For this community, that we offer you not only the words of worship, but also deeds of justice and compassion, let us pray to the Lord.

Lord, have mercy.

HERE OTHER INTERCESSIONS MAY BE OFFERED.

We give you thanks for all the faithful ones who have journeyed through the wilderness and now dwell in your paradise. Bring us with them to the eternal Easter feast of joy. Let us pray to the Lord.

Lord, have mercy.

Hear our prayers, O merciful God, as we eagerly await the day of resurrection and rebirth, through Jesus Christ our Lord.

Amen

IMAGES FOR PREACHING

What tempts you? We need to be clear from the beginning, for a power will attempt to undo all the good things we resolved Ash Wednesday. It is a crafty, serpentine power. But the real temptation comes from within; that is where we are most vulnerable. What tempts you? T. S. Eliot said it so well in *Murder in the Cathedral*: "The last temptation is the greatest treason: To do the right deed for the wrong reason" (New York: Harcourt, Brace and World, 1963, p. 44). The man and woman want to be like God. Should we not aspire to be like the one who is ultimately good?

Jesus does not. Bread is good, but he chooses the fast. Safety is needed for the journey, but Jesus opts for obedient trust. A world is waiting for its Savior, but Jesus says only God can be God and is the one we must serve.

What tempts you? It's probably not turning stones to bread or hurling yourself from the tallest building in town. The real temptation comes from within. Dietrich Bonhoeffer's masterful *Creation and Fall* suggests that in one important sense the snake did not lie. The great temptation is to want to be like God—to elect ourselves into the position where we will be in control, calling the shots, making the decisions.

The alternative is to enter the wilderness, the place where we could easily lose control. In the wilderness of Lent we meet the new Adam who has gone before us and is waiting for us—the one who invites us to follow him on the way of the cross. It is time to stumble into life.

WORSHIP MATTERS

One of the many images connected with the Lord's Supper is that it is food for the journey of life. That image is most effectively demonstrated when the elements of Holy Communion do indeed bear a resemblance to real bread, the staple of life, and to festive drink (wine), a reminder that each time the faithful gather for the eucharist it is a celebration of the death and resurrection of the Lord Jesus Christ. Many recipes are available for making small loaves of bread, both leavened and unleavened, for use at Holy Communion. The use of a common loaf, as opposed to individual wafers, also provides a powerful symbol of the unity of the body of Christ (as is also the case when a common chalice is used for distributing the wine). While some care must be taken in order not to spill crumbs on the floor when using a loaf of bread, the symbols of unity and sustenance far outweigh this concern.

LET THE CHILDREN COME

As the congregation enters the wilderness of Lent, consider planting some spring flowering bulbs that will be forced into bloom in time for Easter. Amaryllis, tulips, daffodils, crocuses, or lilies might be planted. Some of these bulbs come to flower in five to seven weeks, just the right amount of time for Lent. The bulbs might be planted in clear glass containers so that even the development of the root system can be watched. This way children can mark time through these forty days. At the completion of the forty days, the wilderness of Lent will give way to the full-flower of Easter.

MUSIC FOR WORSHIP

SERVICE MUSIC

Use the litany (*LBW,* p. 168) in place of the confession, gathering hymn, and Kyrie; its themes echo the readings for this day and call to mind the church's "desert journey" during this season. Establish a rhythmic cadence with a slight overlapping of the bids and responses; with choral leadership and a strong cantor, this can be sung a cappella.

GATHERING

| LBW 99 | O Lord, throughout these forty days |
| WOV 657 | The glory of these forty days |

PSALM 32

Cooney, Rory. "Psalm 32" in PCY, vol. 4.

Howard, Julie. *Sing for Joy: Psalm Settings for God's Children.* LTP.

Schwarz, May. PW, Cycle A.

Stewart, Roy James. PCY, vol. 5.

HYMN OF THE DAY

| LBW 230 | Lord, keep us steadfast in your word |
| | ERHALT UNS, HERR |

VOCAL RESOURCES

Busarow, Donald. "Lord, Keep Us Steadfast in Your Word." CPH 98-2602. 2 pt mxd, inst.

Distler, Hugo. "Lord, Keep Us Steadfast." AFP 11-1448. SAB.

INSTRUMENTAL RESOURCES

Behnke, John. "Erhalt uns, Herr" in *Variations for Seven Familiar Hymns.* AFP 11-10702. Org.

Manz, Paul. "Lord, Keep Us Steadfast" in *Improvisations on Reformation Hymns.* MSM 10-803. Org.

Powell, Robert. "Erhalt uns, Herr" in *Sing We to Our God Above.* AFP 11-10230. Org.

Sedio, Mark. "Lord, Keep Us Steadfast" in *Music for the Paschal Season.* AFP 11-10763. Org.

ALTERNATE HYMN OF THE DAY

| LBW 228 | A mighty fortress is our God |
| WOV 660 | I want Jesus to walk with me |

COMMUNION

| LBW 341 | Jesus, still lead on |
| WOV 746 | Day by day |

SENDING

| LBW 343 | Guide me ever, great Redeemer |
| WOV 773 | Send me, Jesus |

ADDITIONAL HYMNS AND SONGS

LBW 454	If God himself be for me
WOV 655	As the sun with longer journey
MBW 337	Christ Jesus knew a wilderness
H82 150	Forty days and forty nights
RS 548	Jesus tempted in the desert
WOV 785	Weary of all trumpeting

MUSIC FOR THE DAY

CHORAL

Bender, Jan. "Begone, Satan." CPH 98-1848. SA/TB, org.

Hassler, Hans L. "A Mighty Fortress Is Our God." CPH 98-198. SATB.

Haugen, Marty. "Tree of Life." GIA G-2944. SATB/U, cong, 1/2 kybd, ww, gtr.

Kitson, C. H. "Jesu, Grant Me This I Pray." OXF 350133-3. SATB, org.

Reagan, Donald J. "Not By Bread Alone." GIA G-2648. SATB, cong, org, gtr.

Schalk, Carl. "In Adam We Have All Been One" in *Second Crown Choir Book.* CPH 97-488. 2 pt mxd, desc, inst, gtr.

Schütz, Heinrich. "Sing Praise to Our Glorious Lord." AFP 12-691170. SATB.

Trinkley, Bruce. "I Want Jesus to Walk with Me." AFP 11-10846. SATB, pno.

CHILDREN'S CHOIRS

Burkhardt, Michael. "O Sinner Man" in *Rise, Children, Gonna Praise the Lord.* MSM 50-9804. U/2 pt.

Christopherson, Dorothy. "There Was a Man." AFP 11-10843. 2 pt, pno, ob.

Powell, Robert. "A Lenten Prayer." CGA 159. U, fl, org.

KEYBOARD/INSTRUMENTAL

Keesecker, Thomas. "Erhalt uns, Herr" in *Come Away to the Skies.* AFP 11-10794. Pno.

Pachelbel, Johann. "Toccata in e" in *Selected Organ Works.* KAL 3760. Org.

HANDBELL

Moklebust, Cathy. "Kyrie." AFP 11-7182. 2 oct.

Nelson, Susan T. "Lenten Prayer." CPH 97-6616. 3 oct, fl.

PRAISE ENSEMBLE

Besig, Don. "Just a Closer Walk." SHW A 7106. SATB, gtr.

Gustafson, Gerrit. "Only by Grace" in *Come and Worship Songbook.* INT.

Ortega, Fernando. "I Will Praise Him, Still" in *Worship Leader Magazine's Song DISCovery,* vol 4.

149

TUESDAY, FEBRUARY 23
POLYCARP, BISHOP OF SMYRNA, MARTYR, 156

Polycarp is an important link between the apostolic age, and the great Christian writers who flourished at the end of the second century. He was burned at the stake for his refusal to renounce the Christian faith. His name means "many fruits," and he has been cherished among Christians as one of the first "saplings" of the church to die for Christ. After the first martyrs mentioned in the New Testament (Stephen, Peter, Paul), Polycarp is considered one of the earliest martyrs for the faith.

During Lent we consider our baptismal call to follow in the way of the cross. How do Polycarp and the other martyrs inspire us to remain steadfast in our calling?

BARTHOLOMAEUS ZIEGENBALG, MISSIONARY TO INDIA, 1719

As a missionary among the Tamil people of India, Ziegenbalg endured imprisonment, illness, and the suspicions of other Christian missionaries. He is believed to be the first Protestant missionary, and he established mission schools, a seminary for native preachers, and built a church called New Jerusalem, which is still in use. Ziegenbalg learned the Tamil language and translated the Small Catechism, the New Testament, parts of the Old Testament, and compiled a grammar.

Ziegenbalg is an example of one who was able to proclaim the gospel in the context of another culture. How can we effectively share the good news within the unique situation of our society today?

WEDNESDAY, FEBRUARY 24
ST. MATTHIAS, APOSTLE

Matthias was chosen to fill the vacancy among the twelve disciples following the death of Judas. Although he is not mentioned elsewhere in the New Testament, the account of his election in Acts 1:15-26 implies that he was a follower of Jesus from the beginning of his ministry. Both Ethiopian and Greek Christians claim him a missionary in their communities.

Since many congregations will be conducting midweek Lenten services today, consider observing the day of St. Matthias. A preacher might consider the ways we set apart someone for service in the church, as well as the ministry of all the baptized. During Lent we return to our baptism, and Matthias can be raised up as a faithful disciple whose call came in a rather unusual way, by the casting of lots. Consider the unique ways God calls us to follow Christ in the way of the cross and resurrection.

THURSDAY, FEBRUARY 25
ELIZABETH FEDDE, DEACONESS, 1921

Fedde was trained as a deaconess, and in 1882 was asked to come to New York to minister to the poor and to Norwegian seamen. Her influence was wide-ranging, and she established the Deaconess House in Brooklyn, and the Deaconess House and Hospital of the Lutheran Free Church in Minneapolis.

The traditional Lenten disciplines are prayer, fasting, and giving alms. Fedde is a Lenten example of selfless service to those in need. How does your congregation reach out to those who are sick, needy, or forgotten? Let this Lenten season be a time of renewed commitment to both prayer and social ministry.

FEBRUARY 28, 1999

SECOND SUNDAY IN LENT

INTRODUCTION

In today's gospel, Jesus directs our attention to the font of Holy Baptism. By water and the word, the Holy Spirit gives us new birth. We are made sons and daughters of God, brothers and sisters of the Lord Jesus, messengers of the Holy Spirit. God makes us God, freely, out of love. From the waters of baptism we rise as a people blessed by God. We are sent forth into the world, not to condemn but to offer mercy.

PRAYER OF THE DAY

Eternal God, it is your glory always to have mercy. Bring back all who have erred and strayed from your ways; lead them again to embrace in faith the truth of your Word and to hold it fast; through Jesus Christ your Son our Lord, who lives and reigns with you and the Holy Spirit, one God, now and forever.

READINGS

Genesis 12:1-4a

Genesis 1–11, often called the "primeval history," provides the background for today's reading. The repeated pattern of human rebellion and God's response ends with the Tower of Babel incident (11:1-9). In today's reading, God begins the relationship with humanity anew, starting with the person of Abram.

Psalm 121

It is the Lord who watches over you. (Ps. 121:5)

Romans 4:1-5, 13-17

Paul has taught that Jews and Gentiles alike are made right with God through faith, and he insists that this has been true since Abraham, the great ancestor of the Jewish people. For this reason, people of "many nations" may share in God's promises to Abraham through faith.

John 3:1-17

The ministry of Jesus drew ambiguous responses from the religious leaders of his day. Some were offended by his challenge to their traditions and rejected him. Others, like Nicodemus, recognized the work of God in him, but needed his teaching to understand how to respond to him and God.

COLOR   Purple

THE PRAYERS

In these days of Lenten spring, let us pray for the world, the church, and for all people according to their needs.
A BRIEF SILENCE.

That the church will faithfully proclaim God's great love for our world, let us pray to the Lord.
Lord, have mercy.

That God's blessing be poured out on all the nations and families of the earth, let us pray to the Lord.
Lord, have mercy.

That our Lenten disciplines turn our hearts toward those most vulnerable in our society, let us pray to the Lord.
Lord, have mercy.

That all those who suffer in mind, body, or spirit (especially . . .) may find help and safety in God's tender care, let us pray to the Lord.
Lord, have mercy.

That those who will be born of water and the Spirit at Easter may grow in grace and faith, let us pray to the Lord.
Lord, have mercy.

HERE OTHER INTERCESSIONS MAY BE OFFERED.

That we may follow all the saints who trusted in Christ lifted on the cross for our salvation, let us pray to the Lord.
Lord, have mercy.

Hear our prayers, O merciful God, as we eagerly await the day of resurrection and rebirth, through Jesus Christ our Lord.
Amen

IMAGES FOR PREACHING

Consider, please, the geography of Lent. The Lenten pilgrimage takes us through a strange land. It is the territory of faith. Things do not happen in this land as they do in other places. In this land, old men are blessed and promised a passel of kids. Land is thrown in so that Abram can start his own nation. There is only one hitch: you have to leave your country and kindred and strike out in a new direction.

151

Nicodemus, too, is called to a new adventure. He is to be born *anothen*. The Greek word is ambiguous—it can mean "again" and it can mean "from above." The biology, however, is crystal clear: You're only born once. "No," says Jesus, "it can happen again"—*anothen*. When the Spirit blows, you cannot predict what might happen.

Starting over—what if you could do it? How might life be different? What would you not do that you did before? What would you do early on that in this life you put off too long?

It is not a hypothetical question; it is reality in the territory of grace. You grasp it by faith, says Paul, but it always comes as the gracious gift in the middle of things. "Another chance," says Jesus. "How can this be?" asks Nicodemus. Jesus replies with a smile and a wink: "Watch me!" And the wind begins to blow.

WORSHIP MATTERS

The hymn, "God is here!" (WOV 719), contains the powerful line: "here the cross has central place. . . ." a reminder that the cross is the chief symbol of our redemption by a gracious and merciful God. Consequently the cross deserves a place of prominence both in church buildings and in the Sunday liturgy.

The use of a processional cross to lead the ministers of the liturgy into the worship space during the gathering rite is a way to signal that it is the crucified and risen one who calls the assembly together and lives in the midst of it. The processional cross may be placed near the altar to serve as a focal point throughout the liturgy, or, if a large cross already hangs in the sanctuary, the processional cross may be placed in a stand to the side. At the end of the liturgy, the cross leads us back into the world, the place where all the baptized bear witness to the crucified one.

LET THE CHILDREN COME

The serpent raised up in the wilderness, described by Jesus in the gospel, finds a counterpart in the church's use of the processional cross. If your congregation does not have one, consider obtaining one and using it regularly. A stationary or permanent cross can get "lost" in the worship space and not noticed. It can become a part of the usual surroundings. If a cross is used in procession, its movement can regularly bring to mind the gift of God in the cross. For children, a processional

cross can be a visual cue to understanding that Jesus' cross leads the way to our salvation.

MUSIC FOR WORSHIP

GATHERING

| LBW 507 | How firm a foundation |
| WOV 693 | Baptized in water |

PSALM 121

Beall, Mary Kay. *Sing Out! A Children's Psalter.* WLP 7191.

Cotter, Jeanne. PCY, vol. 3.

Joncas, Michael. "Guiding Me." GIA G-3438. SATB, cong, gtr, kybd, opt 2 C inst.

LBW 445   Unto the hills

Ogden, David. "I Lift Up My Eyes" in PS3.

Schwarz, May. PW, Cycle A.

HYMN OF THE DAY

| LBW 292 | God loved the world |
| | DIE HELLE SONNE LEUCHT |

INSTRUMENTAL RESOURCES

Bender, Jan. "Die helle Sonne leucht" in *30 Little Chorale Preludes,* Part III. BA BA2429.

Walcha, Helmut. "Die helle Sonne leucht" in *Choralvorspiele für Orgel,* set IV. CFP 8413. Org.

Weber, Stephen. "God Loved the World" in *Four Hymn Preludes.* CPH 97-6089. Org.

ALTERNATE HYMN OF THE DAY

| LBW 194 | All who believe and are baptized |
| WOV 698 | We were baptized in Christ Jesus |

COMMUNION

| LBW 479 | My faith looks up to thee |
| WOV 699 | Blessed assurance |

SENDING

| LBW 102 | On my heart imprint your image |
| WOV 755 | We all are one in mission |

ADDITIONAL HYMNS AND SONGS

WOV 769	Mothering God
NCH 605	As Moses raised the serpent up
DATH 69	Walk across the water
LLC 368	Soplo de Dios/O living Breath of God
LEV 169	Sometimes I feel like a motherless child

MUSIC FOR THE DAY

CHORAL

Berger, Jean. "I to the Hills Lift up Mine Eyes." AFP 11-067. SATB.

Distler, Hugo. "For God So Loved the World." CPH 98-223. SAB.

Goss, John. "God So Loved the World" in *The New Church Anthem Book.* OXF 0-19-353109-7. SATB.

Herbert, Philip A. "Sometimes I Feel Like a Motherless Child." AFP 11-10159. SATB, S solo, fl.

Martinson, Joel. "God So Loved the World." CPH 98-3098. SA, org.

Mendelssohn, Felix. "Lift Thine Eyes." Various ed. SSA.

Schütz, Heinrich. "For God So Loved the World." CHA CLA 671. SATTB.

Scott, K. Lee. "Jesus, Thou Joy of Loving Hearts." CPH 98-3009. SATB, org.

Stainer, John. "God So Loved the World" in *The Crucifixion.* Various ed. SATB.

Tye, Christopher. "To Our Redeemer's Glorious Name" in *Parish Choir Book.* CPH 97-757. SATB.

Yarrington, John. "O Savior of the World." CHA 12-484750. SATB, org.

CHILDREN'S CHOIRS

Barta, Daniel. "Psalm 121." CPH 98-3158. 2 pt equal or mxd, kybd.

Horman, John. "God So Loved the World." CGA 447. U/2 pt, opt fl/vln.

Johnson, Ralph. "As Moses Lifted Up." CGA 550. U, fl, org.

Lovelace, Austin. "Psalm 121." CGA 361. U, fl.

KEYBOARD/INSTRUMENTAL

Albright, William. "Chorale-Partita in an Old Style on 'Wer nur den lieben Gott.'" EV 163-00032. Org.

Ferguson, John. "Cantabile on DUNDEE" in *Three Psalm Preludes.* AFP 11-10823. Org.

Hassell, Michael. "I Need Thee Every Hour" in *Jazz All Seasons: Piano Arrangements.* AFP 11-10822. Pno/kybd.

HANDBELL

Afdahl, Lee J. "If Thou But Suffer God to Guide Thee." AFP 11-10574. 3-4 oct.

Bock, Almon C. "Lenten Meditation." AFP 11-10482. 2/4 oct.

PRAISE ENSEMBLE

Hanson, Handt. "Wind of the Spirit" in *Spirit Calls, Rejoice!* CCF.

Schram, Ruth Elaine. "His Will Was Done." TRI 10/1616T. SATB.

Ylvisaker, John. "The Lord Will Keep Me Safe and Holy" in *Borning Cry.* NGP.

MONDAY, MARCH 1
GEORGE HERBERT, PRIEST, 1633

Herbert, a priest of the Church of England, is remembered for his poetry and other writings. His poems breathe a gentle freshness and grace with a profound love of virtue, and some of his hymns are still sung today. His famous work, *A Priest to the Temple; or the Country Parson,* describes the clergyman as well-read, temperate, given to prayer, and devoted to his flock.

Perhaps Herbert's most popular hymn text is "Come, my way, my truth, my life" (LBW 513). How does this poem shed hope and light on the path of our Lenten journey? How do poets help to express the mystery of our faith, putting into words a truth beyond words?

TUESDAY, MARCH 2
JOHN WESLEY, 1791; CHARLES WESLEY, 1788; RENEWERS OF THE CHURCH

John and Charles were brothers and priests of the Church of England, although their ministry moved them to itinerant preaching, hymn writing, and social outreach on the edges of the established church. Their spiritual discipline or method—frequent communion, fasting, and advocacy of social justice—won them the disparaging title "methodists." Following an experience of religious conversion, John was perhaps the greatest single force in the eighteenth-century revival.

Charles wrote over 600 hymns, twelve of which are in *LBW.* Three are especially appropriate for Lent; consider singing one or more of the following during meetings or other congregational events today: "Christ, whose glory fills the skies" (LBW 265), "Love Divine, all loves excelling" (LBW 315), "Forth in thy name, O Lord, I go" (LBW 505).

153

MARCH 7, 1999

THIRD SUNDAY IN LENT

INTRODUCTION

In the early church, immediate preparation for baptism at Easter was heightened by the proclamation of gospel stories chosen especially for the last Sundays in Lent. In Cycle A, these readings are retained.

Today's gospel is the story of the Samaritan woman asking Jesus for water. It is an image of our great thirst for God's mercy, grace, and forgiveness. It is an image of God's grace freely given to us in scripture, baptism, the holy supper, and the faith of our brothers and sisters. The church invites all who seek God to come to these good things where we encounter the one who gives us life-giving water.

PRAYER OF THE DAY

Eternal Lord, your kingdom has broken into our troubled world through the life, death, and resurrection of your Son. Help us to hear your Word and obey it, so that we become instruments of your redeeming love; through your Son, Jesus Christ our Lord, who lives and reigns with you and the Holy Spirit, one God, now and forever.

or (Year A)

Almighty God, your Son once welcomed an outcast woman because of her faith. Give us faith like hers, that we also may trust only in your love for us and may accept one another as we have been accepted by you; through your Son, Jesus Christ our Lord, who lives and reigns with you and the Holy Spirit, one God, now and forever.

READINGS

Exodus 17:1-7

Today's reading is one of several that tell of experiences during the wilderness wandering. In this case, the people complain because they have a legitimate need and God responds by providing for them. Later in their wanderings, when the people complain because of their wants, God responds with anger.

Psalm 95

Let us shout for joy to the rock of our salvation. (Ps. 95:1)

Romans 5:1-11

Through Jesus' death on the cross, sinners have been put right with God through faith. But being made right with God produces results—ultimately, sure hope for the future produced by God's Spirit.

John 4:5-42

In the culture of Jesus' time, Jews tended to avoid dealings with Samaritans, and men did not converse with women in public. When Jesus crosses these boundaries to speak with a Samaritan woman, he makes himself known as the agent of God who knows all.

COLOR Purple

THE PRAYERS

In these days of Lenten spring, let us pray for the world, the church, and for all people according to their needs.
A BRIEF SILENCE.

Strengthen the church to share the water of life with all who thirst for justice and truth. Let us pray to the Lord.
Lord, have mercy.

Grant peace and reconciliation to all nations and peoples who are estranged from one another. Let us pray to the Lord.
Lord, have mercy.

Refresh with your healing waters all those who are discouraged, fearful, hospitalized, or ill (especially . . .). Let us pray to the Lord.
Lord, have mercy.

Bless with your grace all those to be baptized at Easter, and all who will renew their baptismal vows. Let us pray to the Lord.
Lord, have mercy.

Satisfy the spiritual thirst of all who long for a deeper sense of your presence in their lives. Let us pray to the Lord.
Lord, have mercy.

HERE OTHER INTERCESSIONS MAY BE OFFERED.

Bring us with Perpetua and her companions, Thomas Aquinas, and all martyrs and saints to the river of life in our eternal home. Let us pray to the Lord.

Lord, have mercy.

Hear our prayers, O merciful God, as we eagerly await the day of resurrection and rebirth, through Jesus Christ our Lord.

Amen

IMAGES FOR PREACHING

What are you hiding? Somewhere beneath the surface appearance each of us has a dirty little secret we want no one else to know. We wear our public face and live a grand pretense of illusory respectability.

Thirst comes from within—the hollow place waiting to be filled. When Jesus and the woman begin to talk, it is the semi-friendly, semi-hostile banter of two people from different ethnic worlds. But Jesus sees beneath the surface and starts to look inside the heart of things—sees the hollow places waiting to be filled. The woman discovers in the penetrating gaze of the Jewish prophet the opportunity to be known as she really is, inside and out.

What are you hiding? Would you want to be unmasked? Would you want to be truly known as you really are? It all depends. . . . Paul speaks about a chain reaction that begins with suffering and ends with a hope that does not disappoint. The tragedies of life become the pathway to new life in the strange inside-out world of God's grace. It all depends on whether the one who sees us as we are loves us or judges us. In Jesus, we are loved.

When love looks beneath the surface appearances, it sees not only who we are but what we might become. Our hardened exteriors are melted by grace, and even flinty rock starts gushing water. The places of our encounters with those so different from us become the places of our testing. "They are almost ready to stone me," Moses cries. But God has different ideas about what to do with rocks. The chain reaction begins: suffering, endurance, character, hope, life.

WORSHIP MATTERS

The Sunday assembly is primarily a gathering of the baptized people of God who come to remember their inheritance in God's kingdom, and to be transformed for the work of that kingdom in the world. Placing a large baptismal font filled with water at the entrance to the nave of the church, so that all who enter must pass by, recalls the gathering assembly's baptismal heritage. Worshipers may also be encouraged to dip their hand into the water and make the sign of the cross upon themselves as they enter and leave the worship space as a reminder of baptism. An even more powerful symbol is appropriated if the water flows from a bowl into a larger "pool," or if the water is bubbling, recalling the living waters of baptism. The font may appropriately be surrounded by living green plants (flowering plants at Easter) to further enhance this image.

LET THE CHILDREN COME

Consider the physical characteristics of the baptismal font. The location, the upkeep, the paschal candle, and the candles used in the rite of Holy Baptism all convey a sense of meaning to children. Can children engage in holy play in the waters of the font? Are they encouraged to dip their fingers in it and make the sign of the cross? (If the font is not regularly open and filled with water, you might consider doing so always—whether or not a baptism is planned.) Do the characteristics of the font reflect the importance of baptism in a way that would help children grow in appreciation for their own baptism, and come to know and trust Jesus as the living water?

MUSIC FOR WORSHIP

GATHERING

LBW 301	Come to Calvary's holy mountain
WOV 655	As the sun with longer journey

PSALM 95

Dobry, Wallace. "A Trio of Psalms." MSM 80-706.

Geary, Patrick. "Listen to the Voice of the Lord" in PS2.

Haugen, Marty, and David Haas. "If Today You Hear His Voice" in PCY.

How, Martin. "O Come, Let Us Sing Unto the Lord." MSM 50-73012.
2 pt, org.

Schwarz, May. PW, Cycle A.

HYMN OF THE DAY

WOV 695	O blessed spring
	BERGLUND

VOCAL RESOURCES

Farlee, Robert Buckley. "O Blessed Spring." AFP 11-10544. SATB, ob, org, opt cong.

155

INSTRUMENTAL RESOURCES

Bernthal, John. "O Blessed Spring" in *Lift High the Cross*. AFP 11-10867. Org, C/B-flat.

Cherwien, David. "O Blessed Spring" in *Organ Plus One*. AFP 11-10758.

Farlee, Robert Buckley. "O Blessed Spring" in *Gaudeamus!* AFP 11-10693. Org.

Organ, Anne Krentz. "O Blessed Spring" in *On Eagle's Wings: Reflections for Piano*. AFP 11-10711. Pno.

Sedio, Mark. "O Blessed Spring" in *Let Us Talents and Tongues Employ*. AFP 11-10718. Org.

ALTERNATE HYMN OF THE DAY

| LBW 356 | O Jesus, joy of loving hearts |
| LBW 497 | I heard the voice of Jesus say |

COMMUNION

| LBW 499 | Come, thou Fount of every blessing |
| WOV 772 | The Lord is my song |

OTHER SUGGESTIONS

| GS2 6 | Hamba nathi/Come, walk with us |

SENDING

| LBW 333 | Lord, take my hand and lead me |
| WOV 696 | I've just come from the fountain |

ADDITIONAL HYMNS AND SONGS

WOV 774	Dona nobis pacem
SIC 31	Christ, you give us living water
WAO 40	At Jacob's well, where Jesus sat

MUSIC FOR THE DAY

CHORAL

Busarow, Donald. "I Heard the Voice of Jesus Say." CPH 98-261. SATB, opt cong, fl, org.

Keesecker, Thomas. "Do Not Forget Me." AFP 11-10569. 2 pt trbl, kybd.

Mendelssohn, Felix. "O Come, Every One that Thirsteth" in *Elijah*. Various ed. SATB, org.

Rowan, William. "Woman in the Night." SEL 425-815. SATB, org, opt cong.

Shute, Linda Cable. "What Language Shall I Borrow." AFP11-10844. SATB, org.

Willan, Healey. "God Is a Spirit" in *Twelve Sayings of Jesus*. CPH 97-63. SA, kybd.

CHILDREN'S CHOIRS

Bedford, Michael. "Venite, Exultemus Domino." CGA 631. U/2 pt, kybd, opt C inst.

Hubert, Royce. "Living Rain" in *Two Rainstick Pieces*. CGA 685. U/2 pt, kybd, rainstick.

KEYBOARD/INSTRUMENTAL

Barber, Samuel. "Wondrous Love." GSCH A-1251. Org.

Hassell, Michael. "I've Just Come from the Fountain" in *Jazz All Seasons*. AFP 11-10822. Pno.

HANDBELL

Page, Anna Laura. "Guide Me, O Thou Great Jehovah" in *Hymn Descants for Ringers and Singers,* vol. 4. Hb ALF 16058. Vcs, kybd 16060. 3 oct, kybd, desc.

Moklebust, Cathy. "Guide Me Ever, Great Redeemer" in *Hymn Stanzas for Handbells*. AFP 11-10722. 4-5 oct.

PRAISE ENSEMBLE

Haas, David. "God Is Love" in *Who Calls You by Name*, vol. 1. GIA G-3193C. SATB.

Hanson, Handt, and Paul Murakami. "Water from Heaven" in *Spirit Calls, Rejoice!* CCF.

SUNDAY, MARCH 7
PERPETUA AND HER COMPANIONS, MARTYRS AT CARTHAGE, 202

Perpetua, her servants, and other African catechumens were arrested for their enrollment and participation in the catechumenate. The Roman emperor Severus forbade conversions to Christianity, and Perpetua and her companions were condemned to execution in the arena at Carthage. According to the contemporary account of the martyrdom, Perpetua and Felicity survived the wild beasts and were killed by the sword, having first exchanged the kiss of peace. A preacher might connect their faithfulness with the second reading, where Paul writes of boasting in our sufferings and the hope of sharing the glory of God.

THOMAS AQUINAS, TEACHER, 1274

Thomas Aquinas was a brilliant and creative theologian and philosopher. He was first and foremost a student of the Bible and profoundly concerned with the theological formation of the church's ordained ministers. As a member of the Order of Preachers (Dominicans), he labored to correlate scripture with the cultural questions and philosophical controversies of his day in order to improve preaching.

Several eucharistic hymns have generally been ascribed to Aquinas. Consider using "Thee we adore,

O hidden Savior" (LBW 199) as a communion hymn today. The line "fountain of goodness, Jesus, Lord and God" correlates with the gospel reading describing Jesus as living water.

FRIDAY, MARCH 12
GREGORY THE GREAT, BISHOP OF ROME, 604

Gregory the Great was an important and wealthy figure until he decided to sell his vast property, give the proceeds to the poor, and enter one of the seven monasteries he had founded. He accepted election to the papacy only after great inner struggle, and was a tower of strength to the church in a time of famine, flood, pestilence, invasion, and political struggle. He effected important changes in the liturgy and described his role of pope as "servant of the servants of Christ."

Use Gregory's life to reflect on connections between liturgy and social justice. How does the eucharist form us to be the body of Christ in the world, serving those who are in need? Does our Lenten journey of conversion lead us not only inward, but also outward to struggle against the poverty and injustice in society?

MARCH 14, 1999

FOURTH SUNDAY IN LENT

INTRODUCTION

The gospel for this Sunday is the story of a blind man healed by Christ. It is a profound image of our human condition: we seek after greater clarity and light. It is also a baptismal image of washing and receiving sight, of Christ's desire to enlighten us with the truth of who we are: God's beloved daughters and sons.

PRAYER OF THE DAY

God of all mercy, by your power to heal and to forgive, graciously cleanse us from all sin and make us strong; through your Son, Jesus Christ our Lord, who lives and reigns with you and the Holy Spirit, one God, now and forever.

READINGS

1 Samuel 16:1-13

In chapter 15, Saul's failings have finally caused the Lord to regret having made Saul king over Israel. Now, the Lord directs the prophet Samuel to see to the replacement of Saul, who was made king by popular acclamation of the people. The new king, this time chosen by God, is a simple shepherd boy from Judah.

Psalm 23

You have anointed my head with oil. (Ps. 23:5)

Ephesians 5:8-14

The letter to the Ephesians teaches that through baptism Christians live in God's light. Therefore, we ought to live by doing those things that reflect the light of Christ.

John 9:1-41

Some people in Jesus' day regarded infirmities as signs of divine punishment, and a few even thought Jesus was wrong to help afflicted people. When Jesus is criticized for healing a man born blind, the question arises as to whether such attitudes are not themselves a form of blindness, thereby showing that the heart is far from God.

COLOR   Purple

THE PRAYERS

In these days of Lenten spring, let us pray for the world, the church, and for all people according to their needs.
A BRIEF SILENCE.
For God's holy people, that the light of Christ shine in their words and deeds, let us pray to the Lord.
Lord, have mercy.
For those who govern and lead, that they be anointed with your Spirit of justice and compassion, let us pray to the Lord.
Lord, have mercy.

For those preparing for baptism, that you enlighten them with your grace and mercy, let us pray to the Lord.

Lord, have mercy.

For all who live with poverty, discrimination, anxiety, or illness (especially . . .), that you guide and comfort them, let us pray to the Lord.

Lord, have mercy.

For ourselves, that you open our eyes to your presence in our lives, and to the needs of all of who suffer, let us pray to the Lord.

Lord, have mercy.

HERE OTHER INTERCESSIONS MAY BE OFFERED.

For all the saints who have lived as children of light, we give you thanks. Bring us from darkness to the unending light of Easter. Let us pray to the Lord.

Lord, have mercy.

Hear our prayers, O merciful God, as we eagerly await the day of resurrection and rebirth, through Jesus Christ our Lord.

Amen

IMAGES FOR PREACHING

From blindness to sight; from sight to blindness. What do you see? Do you trust your vision? Do your eyes tell you reality, or are appearances illusions, public lies of convenience for social stability and good order?

He doesn't look like a king, the kid playing with the sheep. But the Lord keeps passing by the attractive candidates, looking for the undiscovered monarch-elect. God has a distinctive, strange shepherding style, giving latitude even for sheep to walk through the valley of the shadow. But they are safe, for they are watched. "The Lord does not see as mortals see."

"Jesus saw a man blind from birth." The seeing starts with Jesus, but before the story is over, the man born blind turns out to have spiritual 20-20. On the other hand, those who have spent their lives with their noses in God's law books have hurt their vision. If you are so totally convinced that you know what you see and see what you know, you might very well end up wrong on both counts.

To be a "child of the light" does not mean we see everything perfectly. Rather, it means that we have been seen by love. "Sleeper, awake! Rise from the dead, and Christ will shine on you." First we are seen; only then can we see. First we must realize that we are dead; only then can we be ready to rise to new life. First we must die and be undone; then we are raised. First we must unknow and then we will know.

"I once was lost but now am found, was blind but now I see."

WORSHIP MATTERS

Scripture reminds us of an ancient tradition of the church as we gather around those who are ill, anoint them with oil, and pray for them, accompanied by the laying on of hands, for "the prayer of faith will save the sick, and the Lord will raise them up" (James 5:14-15). Two forms of a service of healing are provided in *Occasional Services*, one for use at the bedside of a sick person, and the other for use in a communal setting. Both services are marked by prayers for forgiveness and healing, opportunities for proclaiming the word, and anointing the sick with oil accompanied by the laying on of hands. Through word and touch, both services underscore the promise of Jesus, that the coming of God's dominion into the world brings with it wholeness and peace. Pastoral care must be exercised with those for whom instant or permanent healing does not occur following such a service, reminding them that as with all God's gifts, we cannot dictate the time or place in which they are bestowed. We can, however, point to the power and efficacy of all God's promises through regular use of the services for healing.

LET THE CHILDREN COME

We have relied too long on worship that engages adults only by appealing to their intellect and their minds. Unfortunately, "children's sermons" often aim at that same intellectual target; generally they miss the mark. When children see someone adopt a certain posture while blessing or praying, when they see a presiding minister regularly repeat the same actions, and when they associate worship and the smells of candles, wine, and incense, they are developing a sense of church at their own, developmentally appropriate level. Each time children return to something familiar they may also discover something new.

158

MUSIC FOR WORSHIP

GATHERING

LBW 514	O Savior, precious Savior
WOV 745	Awake, O sleeper

PSALM 23

Burkhardt, Michael. "Psalm 23." MSM 50-9051. SATB, opt cong, C inst, org.

Cherwien, David. "Psalm 23: The Lord Is My Shepherd." MSM 80-840. U, cong, org.

Glynn, John. "My Shepherd Is The Lord" in PS2.

Haugen, Marty. "Shepherd Me, O God." GIA G-2950. SATB, cong, kybd, C inst, opt glock/str.

LBW 451   The Lord's my shepherd

LBW 456   The King of love my shepherd is

Ollis, Peter. "The Lord Is My Shepherd" in PS2.

HYMN OF THE DAY

LBW 248	Dearest Jesus, at your word
	LIEBSTER JESU, WIR SIND HIER

INSTRUMENTAL RESOURCES

Burkhardt, Michael. "Dearest Jesus, at Your Word" in *Six General Hymn Improvisations,* set 1. MSM 10-846. Org.

Cherwien, David. "Dearest Jesus, We Are Here" in *Interpretations Based on Hymn Tunes,* book I. AMSI OR-1. Org.

Oliver, Curt. "Variations on 'Liebster Jesu'" in *Built on a Rock: Keyboard Seasons.* AFP 11-10620. Pno/kybd.

ALTERNATE HYMN OF THE DAY

LBW 400	God, whose almighty word
WOV 716	Word of God, come down on earth

COMMUNION

LBW 448	Amazing grace, how sweet the sound
WOV 738	Healer of our every ill

SENDING

LBW 520	Give to our God immortal praise
WOV 737	There is a balm in Gilead

ADDITIONAL HYMNS AND SONGS

LBW 439	What a friend we have in Jesus
WOV 776	Be thou my vision
WGF 54	No eyes so blind as theirs
W3 749	He healed the darkness of my mind

MUSIC FOR THE DAY

CHORAL

Bertalot, John. "Amazing Grace." AFP 11-10020. SATB, org.

Busarow, Donald. "Forth in Thy Name." MSM 50-9107. SAB, org, trbl inst.

Harris, David S. "Come, and Let Us Return unto the Lord." HWG CMR3346. SAB, org.

Kallmann, Daniel. "Walk as Children of Light." MSM 50-9047. SATB, kybd.

Kreutz, Robert. "When We Were Baptized" in *RCIA Suite.* WLP. SAB.

Rutter, John. "Be Thou My Vision." HIN HMC-1035. SATB, org.

Rutter, John. "Open Thou Mine Eyes." HIN HMC-467. SATB.

Willan, Healey. "Now Are Ye Light in the World" in *We Praise Thee,* Part II. CPH 97-7610. U, 2 pt, 3 pt.

Zimmerman, Heinz W. "Psalm 23." AFP 11-638. SATB, DB, org.

CHILDREN'S CHOIRS

Lutz, Deborah. "Loving Jesus, Gentle Lamb." MSM 50-9500. U/2 pt, kybd.

McRae, Shirley. "Psalm 23" from *Let Us Praise God.* AFP 11-7203. U/2 pt, orff.

Ramseth, Betty Ann. "Make Us to Be." CGA 579. U, orff, fl.

KEYBOARD/INSTRUMENTAL

Albrecht, Mark. "Amazing Grace" in *Timeless Hymns of Faith for Piano.* AFP 11-10863. Pno.

Couperin, Francois. "Tierce en Taille" in *Mass for the Convents/Two Masses for Organ.* DOV 0-486-28285-6. Org.

Hassell, Michael. "New Britain" in *Traveling Tunes.* AFP 11-10759. Solo inst, pno.

Kane, Daniel Q. "New Britain" in *More Selectable Delectables.* AFP 11-10757. Pno.

HANDBELL

Gramann, Fred. "Come, Thou Almighty King." CPH 97-6465. 3-6 oct.

Moklebust, Cathy. "Amazing Grace." CGA. Full score CGB200. Hb CGB201. Cong, 3-5 oct, org.

Moklebust, Cathy. "Awake, O Sleeper" from *Hymn Stanzas for Handbells.* AFP 11-10722. 4-5 oct.

Wagner, Douglas E. "Brother James' Air." SMP S-HB25. 3 oct.

PRAISE ENSEMBLE

Haas, David. "I Am the Voice of God" and "Christ Will Be Your Light" in *Who Calls You by Name,* vol. 1. GIA G-3622C. SATB.

Hanson, Handt. "Wake Up" in *Spirit Calls, Rejoice!* CCF.

Underwood, Scott. "You Are God" in *Worship Leader Magazine's Song DISCovery,* vol. 4.

159

WEDNESDAY, MARCH 17
PATRICK, BISHOP, MISSIONARY TO IRELAND, 461

At sixteen, Patrick was captured and taken to Ireland to serve as a herdsman. After his escape, he became a missionary monk, eager to preach the faith to the Irish in their native language. In time he was consecrated bishop, established churches and religious communities, and organized Christian communities he found in the north, bringing Ireland much closer to the Western church. He used the three-leafed shamrock to teach catechumens about the Holy Trinity.

Consider commemorating Patrick at Lenten services today. If there is a community meal, you might serve Irish food and decorate with shamrocks. Use his famous hymn, "I bind unto myself today" (LBW 188) as basis for meditation on Lent's call to return to our baptism.

FRIDAY, MARCH 19
JOSEPH, GUARDIAN OF OUR LORD

Joseph, husband of Mary, was a carpenter who is portrayed in the scriptures as a devout and honest man, showing care for his wife and the child Jesus. The infancy narratives in the book of Matthew portray Joseph as a faithful man who responds to God's leading in visionary dreams. Since Joseph is not mentioned during Jesus' adult life, it is assumed that he died by that time. Joseph is considered the patron saint of the poor, and people in Sicily invite the poor to a festive banquets called "St. Joseph's table."

As you commemorate Joseph, consider the importance of parents, especially fathers, in sharing religious faith with children. How do parents model both devotion to God, as well as just and honorable living?

160

MARCH 21, 1999

FIFTH SUNDAY IN LENT

INTRODUCTION

Today's gospel is the story of Jesus raising Lazarus from the dead. With Martha and Mary we stand at the graves of our beloved dead and hear Jesus say, "I am the resurrection and the life." His words give hope to all who dwell in the shadows of death. But also they are words spoken next to the font of Holy Baptism, where we die to death and rise to life in Christ. In the power and presence of the risen Christ, Christians prepare to renew their baptismal promises and welcome new brothers and sisters at Easter.

PRAYER OF THE DAY

Almighty God, our redeemer, in our weakness we have failed to be your messengers of forgiveness and hope in the world. Renew us by your Holy Spirit, that we may follow your commands and proclaim your reign of love; through your Son, Jesus Christ our Lord, who lives and reigns with you and the Holy Spirit, one God, now and forever.

READINGS

Ezekiel 37:1-14

Ezekiel's earlier vision of the glory of the Lord departing from the temple (Ezek. 10:18ff.) symbolizes Israel's defeat by Babylon and subsequent exile. Now, his vision of the valley of dry bones is a promise that Israel as a nation, though dead in exile, will live again in their land through God's life-giving spirit.

Psalm 130

With the Lord there is mercy and plenteous redemption. (Ps. 130:6-7)

Romans 8:6-11

Paul contrasts two ways of living: The unspiritual life may seek to please God but cannot do so, for it is marked by self-reliance. The spiritual life begins with our justification by God and continues in the power of the Spirit who raised Christ from the dead.

John 11:1-45

The raising of Lazarus is presented as the last and greatest sign in John's gospel. It reveals Jesus as the giver of life. But as John 11:45-53 makes clear, this sign leads to the plan to execute Jesus.

COLOR   Purple

THE PRAYERS

In these days of Lenten spring, let us pray for the world, the church, and for all people according to their needs.

A BRIEF SILENCE.

For the church, that God may breathe new life into its worship and witness, let us pray to the Lord.

Lord, have mercy.

For all those around the world preparing for baptismal death and resurrection at Easter, let us pray to the Lord.

Lord, have mercy.

For the leaders of nations, that they may seek the life and dignity of all people, let us pray to the Lord.

Lord, have mercy.

For those who weep over the loss of loved ones, and all whose lives are marked by despair, addiction, abuse, or illness (especially . . .), that they may be filled with hope, let us pray to the Lord.

Lord, have mercy.

For ourselves, that our Lenten journey would renew our faith in the promise of resurrection and new life, let us pray to the Lord.

Lord, have mercy.

HERE OTHER INTERCESSIONS MAY BE OFFERED.

For all the saints who have been raised by Christ, we give thanks. Keep us steadfast in our faith, until you bring us from death to the eternal life of Easter. Let us pray to the Lord.

Lord, have mercy.

Hear our prayers, O merciful God, as we eagerly await the day of resurrection and rebirth, through Jesus Christ our Lord.

Amen

IMAGES FOR PREACHING

Are you dead? The question sounds ludicrous at first, but through the weeks of Lent the possibility of our death-in-life has loomed ever larger. "Remember that you are dust" were the words that introduced us to this season. "These bones are the whole house of Israel," the Lord says to Ezekiel. The people are physically alive but spiritually dead, cut off from hope and cut off from God.

Paul suggests that "setting the mind on the flesh is death." He does not mean wallowing in carnal lust or enjoying physical beauty and material reality. "The flesh" for Paul is a way of being in the world—a way in which we elect ourselves as our own god and bear the burden of existence on our own shoulders. "What is holding us back from life?" we asked at the beginning of Lent. By now we should be close to the answer: we are. We have elected a life of death because we find it so difficult to trust the God who loves us.

Dead people cannot do much for themselves. The only hope for the dead is a resurrection. The deeper our analysis of our predicament this Lent—the greater our bravery in looking into the mirror and seeing to the heart of matters—the closer we might be to finding the ultimate solution to our death-in-life. "Lazarus is dead." But the one who comes to us in these forty days, who leads the way into the wilderness and teaches the ways of repentance—this one stands beside us as we gaze into the mirror. He says to us as he spoke to Martha, "I am the resurrection and the life."

"See how much he loved him!" You can believe him. If you still have any doubt, the events of the next two weeks should convince you. And when it is time to act, he will do so unequivocally with a loud voice: "Lazarus, come out! Unbind him! Let him go."

The time for living has come.

WORSHIP MATTERS

Increasingly, families are looking to the congregation to provide a place for visitation when a death occurs, not only immediately prior to the funeral liturgy, but also the day before the service. It signals the importance of the ministry of the church, not only in the life of the deceased, but also for all those who gather to grieve and to provide comfort for the family. When the body is brought to the church for visitation, it is appropriate to place the casket in the narthex or gathering space, or in another suitable place where friends and family may gather. This area is also the most appropriate place in which to place floral tributes and other expressions of support. As the time for the funeral liturgy draws closer, the casket is closed and the family follows the casket to the entrance to the nave where all are greeted by the ministers. The liturgy for the Burial of the Dead begins with an opening reading from Romans 6 and the place-

161

ment of the funeral pall. The casket is brought into the
church and placed before the altar, perpendicular to it.
Traditionally the casket is placed so that the deceased
faces the altar, the same position the person occupied in
life each time the community gathered for worship.

LET THE CHILDREN COME

To some people it comes as a surprise that the nature of
groups of children is to form elaborate and complicated
patterns in their play. But it comes naturally as a way to
order the world around them. Leaders and followers are
chosen. Rules are established. What at first glance might
look like aimless play, has a deep structure that transmits
the meaning of the play. A group playing "mom and
kids" will quickly form the rules of the house, and
everyone will take on their roles. The often elaborate
patterns of the liturgy can help children be attuned to
the world of grace around them.

162

MUSIC FOR WORSHIP

GATHERING

LBW 550   From all that dwell below the skies
WOV 777   In the morning when I rise

PSALM 130

Chepponis, James. "Out of the Depths." GIA G-2308. Cong.
Foley, John. PCY, vol. 7.
Haugen, Marty. "With the Lord There Is Mercy" in RS.
LBW 295   Out of the depths I cry to you
Sadowski, Kevin. "Psalm 130." CPH 98-3058. 2 pt mxd, cong, org.
Schwarz, May. PW, Cycle A.
Smith, Alan. "From the Depths I Call To You" in PS2.

HYMN OF THE DAY

LBW 385   What wondrous love is this
           WONDROUS LOVE

VOCAL RESOURCES

Hinkle, Don. "What Wondrous Love" in *Assist Us to Proclaim.*
    AFP 11-10313. SATB.
Johns, Donald. "Wondrous Love." AFP 11-10183. SAB, kybd.

INSTRUMENTAL RESOURCES

Manz, Paul. "Wondrous Love" in *Improvisations for the Lenten Season,*
    set 1. MSM 10-300. Org.
Nicholson, Paul. "Wondrous Love." AFP 11-10529. Org, tpt.

Osterlund, Karl. "Wondrous Love" in *American Hymn Trios.*
    AFP 11-10616. Org.
Page, Anna Laura. "What Wondrous Love Is This" in *Hymn Descants
    for Ringers and Singers,* vol. 2. ALF 11528
Wasson, Laura E. "What Wondrous Love Is This" in *A Piano Tapestry.*
    AFP 11-10821. Pno.

ALTERNATE HYMN OF THE DAY

LBW 325   Lord, thee I love with all my heart
WOV 658   The word of God is source and seed

COMMUNION

LBW 207   We who once were dead
WOV 702   I am the Bread of life

OTHER SUGGESTIONS

GS2 46   Canticle of the Turning

SENDING

LBW 340   Jesus Christ, my sure defense
WOV 780   What a fellowship, what a joy divine

ADDITIONAL HYMNS AND SONGS

WOV 785   Weary of all trumpeting
MBW 338   "Come, Lazarus," the Savior called
NSR 37   When Lazarus lay within the tomb
WAO 44   Martha sent unto the Savior

MUSIC FOR THE DAY

CHORAL

Bach, J. S. "So There Is Now No Condemnation" in *Jesu, Meine
    Freude.* GSCH 14354. SSATB.
Dressler, Gallus. "I Am the Resurrection." CPH 98-2784. SATB.
Ferguson, John. "Lord, In All Love." AFP 11-10788. SATB, org.
Hassler, Hans Leo. "Lord, Let at Last Thine Angels Come."
    CPH 98-2602. SSAATTBB.
Morley, Thomas. "I Am the Resurrection." CPH 98-239. SATB, opt org.
Schalk, Carl. "Lord, It Belongs Not to My Care." AFP 11-1913.
    SATB, org.
Schütz, Heinrich. "I Am the Resurrection and the Life." CFP 6591.
    SATB/SATB.
Thompson, J. Michael. "Taste and See the Lord Is Good." AFP 11-10842.
    SATB, ob, org.
Unruh, Eric W. "Kyrie eleison." AFP 11-10847. SAB, pno.
Willaert, A. "The Raising of Lazarus." RIC 1873. SATB.

CHILDREN'S CHOIRS

Hunt, Robert. "What Wondrous Love Is This." GIA G-2868. 2/3 pt, hb, org.

Ramseth, Betty Ann, and Rudy Ramseth. "Keep in Mind" in *Keep in Mind*. AFP 11-2291. U, gtr.

Williams, Jerome. "Call to Lent." HOP A704. 2 pt mxd.

KEYBOARD/INSTRUMENTAL

Brahms, Johannes. "Fugue in a-flat minor" in *Werke für Orgel*. GHEN. Org.

Lo, Adrian H. "Variations on Wondrous Love for Solo Instrument and Organ." AFP 11-10704.

Nicholson, Paul. "Wondrous Love." AFP 11-10529. Org, tpt.

HANDBELL

Hall, Jeffrey. "I Am the Bread of Life." CPH 97-6659. 3-5 oct.

Moklebust, Cathy. "Come, Holy Spirit." AMSI HB-21. 3-5 oct.

PRAISE ENSEMBLE

Chapman, Steven Curtis. "Listen to Our Hearts" in *Music for Ministry, vol. 2*. EMI.

Haas, David. "Blessing Prayer" in *Who Calls You by Name*, vol. I. GIA G-3193C. SATB.

Larkin, Michael. "I Know the Lord's Laid His Hands on Me." GSCH. A-6697. SATB.

MONDAY, MARCH 22
JONATHAN EDWARDS, TEACHER, MISSIONARY TO THE AMERICAN INDIANS, 1758

Edwards was a Congregational minister of Connecticut who preached and promoted spiritual revival with a special emphasis on original sin. He became well known for his refusal to commune those he believed were not fully "converted" to the faith. After dismissal from his parish, Edwards ministered among the American Indians and then became the president of what would become Princeton University.

Edward's keen intellect and contributions to theology in America and Britain are a reminder of both the mind's contributions and limits in understanding the mystery of God. In light of various spiritual disciplines, reflect on the ways you experience God's presence through intellectual inquiry, meditation, and corporate worship.

WEDNESDAY, MARCH 24
OSCAR ROMERO, BISHOP OF EL SALVADOR, 1980

Romero is remembered for his advocacy on behalf of the poor in El Salvador. After being appointed bishop he preached against the political repression in his country. He and other priests and church workers were considered traitors for their bold stands for justice, especially defending the rights of the poor. After several years of threats to his life, Romero was assassinated while celebrating Mass. During the 1980s thousands of others died in El Salvador.

Romero is remembered as a martyr who gave his life in behalf of the powerless in his country. Our Lenten journey of conversion calls us to be bold in our witness to Christ. Who are the powerless in our society? How can we be their voice in advocating justice and equality for all people created in the image of God?

163

THURSDAY, MARCH 25
THE ANNUNCIATION OF OUR LORD

Exactly nine months before Christmas we celebrate the annunciation in which the angel Gabriel announced to Mary that she would give birth to the Son of God. Ancient scholars believed that March 25 was also the day on which creation began, and the date of Jesus' death on the cross. Thus, from the sixth to eighteenth centuries, March 25 was observed as New Year's Day in much of Christian Europe.

Set within Lent, Mary's openness to the mysterious will of God is an example of faithful discipleship. Observe this important day in the church year by singing "The angel Gabriel" (WOV 632), or a setting of the Magnificat, such as the paraphrase "My soul proclaims your greatness" (WOV 730). Midweek Lenten services on March 24 might celebrate the eve of the Annunciation with a service of Evening Prayer.

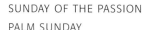

MARCH 28, 1999

SUNDAY OF THE PASSION
PALM SUNDAY

INTRODUCTION

On this day Christians throughout the world begin the great and holy week that culminates in the central celebration of our faith: the Lord's passage from death to new life celebrated in the Three Days. Today's reading of Christ's passion sets forth the central act of God's love for humankind. In the reception of the Lord's body and blood, the church receives this life-giving love. In prayer, hymns, and readings, we hear the great paradox of our faith: Christ is proclaimed the mighty one who reigns from the tree of life.

READINGS FOR PROCESSION WITH PALMS

Matthew 21:1-11

Psalm 118:1-2, 19-29

Blessed is he who comes in the name of the Lord.
(Ps. 118:26)

PRAYER OF THE DAY

Almighty God, you sent your Son, our Savior Jesus Christ, to take our flesh upon him and to suffer death on the cross. Grant that we may share in his obedience to your will and in the glorious victory of his resurrection; through your Son, Jesus Christ our LORD, who lives and reigns with you and the Holy Spirit, one God, now and forever.

READINGS FOR LITURGY OF THE PASSION

Isaiah 50:4-9a

The image of the servant of the Lord is one of the notable motifs in Isaiah 40–55. Today's reading is a self-description of the mission of the servant. This motif became even more important in the early church for understanding the suffering and death of Jesus.

Psalm 31:9-16

Into your hands, O Lord, I commend my spirit. (Ps. 31:5)

Philippians 2:5-11

To illustrate the great self-giving of Christ's passion—the motive for Christian love—Paul quotes an early Christian hymn.

Matthew 26:14—27:66

The story of Jesus' crucifixion in Matthew's gospel emphasizes his rejection by the political and religious institutions of the day. But the events surrounding his death show that he overcame the powers of death. Even the soldiers who crucify him recognize him as "the Son of God."

or Matthew 27:11-54

COLOR   Scarlet *or* Purple

THE PRAYERS

In these days of Lenten spring, let us pray for the world, the church, and for all people according to their needs.
A BRIEF SILENCE.

For the church, that its life and mission may be renewed in the celebration of Jesus' death and resurrection, let us pray to the Lord.

Lord, have mercy.

For all preparing for baptism at Easter, that they may follow Christ in the journey from death to life, let us pray to the Lord.

Lord, have mercy.

For the leaders of nations, that they may strive to serve their people in humility and without self-interest, let us pray to the Lord.

Lord, have mercy.

For those who are sick or dying (especially . . .), that in their suffering they may know that God is with them, let us pray to the Lord.

Lord, have mercy.

For our community of faith, that following the pattern of Jesus we may empty ourselves for the sake of those who are poor, vulnerable, or in need, let us pray to the Lord.

Lord, have mercy.

HERE OTHER INTERCESSIONS MAY BE OFFERED.

We give thanks for all the saints who have walked the way of the cross. Bring us with them to the endless joy and victory of Easter. Let us pray to the Lord.

Lord, have mercy.

Hear our prayers, O merciful God, as we eagerly await

the day of resurrection and rebirth, through Jesus Christ our Lord.
Amen

IMAGES FOR PREACHING

When we come to the Sunday of the Passion, worship planners are faced with a major dilemma: is there really any place for a sermon in this day's liturgy? This question also needs attention in the Three Days, and it would be good for the preacher to look at the discussion under "Preaching with the Season" there.

Holy Week begins as it did in the gospel accounts, with a procession with palms. The processional gospel sets the tone of triumph, which will be undone by the reading of the full passion account. Among North American Lutherans, the image of the palms usurped the entire liturgy for the day, creating "Palm Sunday." The reinstatement of the reading of the passion according to Matthew brings the tension of the day into the liturgy itself. Here is the first opportunity of the faithful to participate in the drama of salvation by entering the narrative and hearing it beginning to end. The goal is not to make our way "station by station" through the story during this week but, rather, to be captivated by the story itself and swept along. Hearing it from beginning to end allows us to do that.

Worship leaders will want to think about how this totality might best be accomplished. The story is powerful by itself, but it is long. If it is read by a solo voice, it might be worthwhile to consider breaking the action of the Passion into scenes separated by stanzas of the alternate hymn of the day:

> Matthew 26:14-56
> O sacred head, now wounded, st. 1
> Matthew 26:57—27:31
> O sacred head, now wounded, st. 2
> Matthew 27:32-54
> O sacred head, now wounded, st. 3
> Matthew 27:55-66
> O sacred head, now wounded, st. 4

The parts may be distributed to various readers or singers. The goal, however, must be clear—to enhance the hearing of the story and encourage the faithful to enter the narrative. "Staging" would be minimal.

We will make our way through the day, from triumph to tragedy, and thus be ready for our undoing in the days of this week: fed at the table, plunged into baptismal waters, made ready for resurrection.

WORSHIP MATTERS

The opportunity to proclaim the passion history, preferably with several readers taking the parts of Christ, the evangelist, and other major characters in the story, is a helpful reminder that careful preparation for proclaiming the word of God in the assembly is always essential. No matter how experienced the readers for the Sunday liturgy are, it is essential to provide opportunities for them to practice reading so that they understand the meaning of the text, can be assured of the pronunciation of difficult words, and have the opportunity to become accustomed to the space in which they will do the reading. Have the readers practice reading aloud so they become accustomed to hearing their voices in the building. Let them become familiar with the ritual editions of the readings so they are not dependent on small sheets of paper on which the lessons are printed. Encourage readers to speak distinctly, slowly, and loudly so that the rest of the members of the assembly can listen to the reading rather than following along on a printed page.

LET THE CHILDREN COME

Well before this morning's worship, teach the children the refrain to "All glory, laud, and honor," (LBW 108). Help them to memorize it so that they can sing it in the procession with palms. Following the presider and other ministers, perhaps the children can lead the procession of the congregation with minimal adult guidance. They will delight in being in charge of the procession. Where might the procession begin? In another part of the building, from one building to another, around the neighborhood?

MUSIC FOR WORSHIP

SERVICE MUSIC

On the Sunday of the Passion, one of the traditional ways in which music has played a significant role in the observance of the day is in the chanting of the Passion narrative. Two simple settings, sung to the classic chant formulas, are available, one in the NRSV translation, the other in the NAB translation:

Kern, Jan. "Chants of the Passion." GIA G-1795. 3 solo vcs. (NAB)

Plater, Ormonde. "The Passion Gospels." CHC 164-8. 3 solo vcs. (NRSV)

A further expanded form of the Matthew Passion for singing is:

Bertalot, John. "Passion of Our Lord According to St. Matthew." AFP 11-10275. Cong 11-10276. SATB, 6 solo vcs, org, cong (in Passiontide hymns). (NRSV)

GATHERING

LBW 108	All glory, laud, and honor
LBW 121	Ride on, ride on in majesty!
WOV 631	Lift up your heads, O gates

PSALM 31

Cooney, Rory. "I Place My Life." GIA G-3613. SATB, cant, cong, gtr, kybd, str qrt, fl.

Farlee, Robert Buckley. PW, Cycle A.

Haas, David. "I Put My Life in Your Hands." GIA G-3949. Cant, cong, SATB, gtr, opt C inst, vc/bsn.

Hopson, Hal H. *Psalm Refrains and Tones.* HOP 425.

Smith, G. Boulton. "Father, Into Your Hands" in PS2.

HYMN OF THE DAY

WOV 661	My song is love unknown
LBW 94	My song is love unknown
	LOVE UNKNOWN or RHOSYMEDRE

VOCAL RESOURCES

Engel, James. "My Song Is Love Unknown" (LOVE UNKNOWN). MSM 60-3000. SATB, C inst, org, cong.

Leavitt, John. "My Song Is Love Unknown" (LOVE UNKNOWN). AFP 11-10113. Choral, org 11-10114. SA/SATB, 2 fl, str qrt, org.

INSTRUMENTAL RESOURCES

Burkhardt, Michael. "Love Unknown" in *Five Lenten Hymn Improvisations.* MSM 10-309. Org.

Kinyon, Barbara. "My Song Is Love Unknown." CGA CGB-127. Hb.

Leavitt, John. "My Song Is Love Unknown." AFP 11-10828. Org, solo inst.

Vaughan Williams, Ralph. "Rhosymedre" in *Three Preludes on Welsh Hymn Tunes.* GAL 1.5087. Org.

ALTERNATE HYMN OF THE DAY

| LBW 116/7 | O sacred head, now wounded |
| WOV 668 | There in God's garden |

COMMUNION

| LBW 111 | Lamb of God, pure and sinless |
| WOV 707 | This is my body |

OTHER SUGGESTIONS

"This is my body" is a good hymn to have the choir, or a soloist, sing first, then repeat with all assembled. A saxophone would be a nice addition playing the tune.

SENDING

| LBW 114 | There is a green hill far away |
| WOV 662 | Restore in us, O God |

ADDITIONAL HYMNS AND SONGS

| LBW 92 | Were you there |
| LBW 105 | A Lamb goes uncomplaining forth |

LITURGY OF THE PALMS

| NSR 29 | Hosanna! The cheering people cry |
| LLC 333 | Mantos y palmas/Filled with excitement |

LITURGY OF THE PASSION

| H82 164 | Alone thou goest forth, O Lord |
| LLC 335 | Jerusalén, ciudad de Dios/Jerusalem, the city of God |

MUSIC FOR THE DAY

CHORAL

Procession with Palms

Brahms, Johannes/Hopson. "Let All the Gates Be Opened Wide." CGA 736. U/2 pt, kybd.

Bunjes, Paul G. "All Glory, Laud, and Honor." CPH 97-451. SATB, cong, tpt. org.

Fleming, L. L. "Ride On, King Jesus." AFP 11-541. SATB, S solo.

Morgan, David C. "A Palm Sunday Antiphon" in *The New Church Anthem Book.* OXF 0-19-353109-7. SATB, org.

Proulx, Richard. "Entrance into Jerusalem and Hymn." OXF 94.248. SATB, cong, org, timp, opt tpt.

Sleeth, Natalie. "Hosanna, Hosanna." CGA 706. U, kybd, opt perc.

Willan, Healey. "Hosanna to the Son of David." CPH 98-101. SATB.

Yarrington, John. "O Thou Eternal Christ, Ride On." AFP 12-477620. 2 pt mxd, org.

Readings/Passion

Anderson, Norma. "The Walk to Calvary." CGA 739. U, kybd.

Bach, J. S. "Crucifixus" in *Mass in B minor.* Various ed. SATB, org.

Cherwien, David. "My Song Is Love Unknown." AFP 11-10708. SAB, org, fl, opt cong.

Ferguson, John. "Ah, Holy Jesus." AFP 11-10572. SATB, org, opt cong.

Ferko, Frank. "Motet for Passion Sunday." ECS 4916. SATB.

Fisher, Bobby. "Gethsemane" in *Play Before God*. GIA G-3380. Gtr, pno, ob, 2 vln, vla, vc.

Hassler/Handel. "O Sacred Head Now Wounded." AFP 11-10680. SATB, 2 fl, org.

Jennings, Carolyn. "My Song Is Love Unknown." CGA-559. U.

Micheelsen, Hans. "A Lamb Goes Uncomplaining Forth" in *Third Morning Star Choir Book*. CPH 97-497. U, org.

Proulx, Richard. "Were You There." AFP 11-10571. SATB, S solo.

Reagan, Donald J. "A Grain of Wheat." GIA G-3105. SATB, kybd.

Schalk, Carl. "My Song Is Love Unknown" (RHOSYMEDRE). CPH 98-223. SB, desc inst, kybd.

Schütz, Heinrich. "St. Matthew Passion." CPH 97-751. SATB, solos, org.

CHILDREN'S CHOIRS

Kemp, Helen. "A Lenten Love Song." CGA 486. U, kybd.

McRae, Shirley. "Come, Let Us Eat" in *Lift Up Your Voices*. CGA 622. U/2 pt, orff.

Pooler, Marie. "Gethsemane." AFP 11-10413. U/2 pt, kybd.

KEYBOARD/INSTRUMENTAL

Decker, Pamela. "Herzlich tut mich verlangen" in *A New Liturgical Year*, ed. John Ferguson. AFP 11-10810. Org.

Dupré, Marcel. "Cortège et Litanie, Op. 19, No. 2." LED 16.850. Org.

Fauré, Gabriel/Basil Ramsey. "Pavane." Org/pno.

HANDBELL

Dobrinski, Cynthia. "Were You There." HOP 1551. 3-5 oct.

Gramann, Fred. "Fantasy on 'King's Weston.'" HOP 1671. 3-6 oct.

Larson, Katherine. "Were You There" AFP 11-10353. 3 oct.

Sherman, Arnold. "Ah, Holy Jesus." HOP 1612. 3-5 oct.

PRAISE ENSEMBLE

Christopher, Tom/Keith Christopher. "Worship His Majesty." WLP 301 0758162. SATB.

Choplin, Pepper. "Jazz Hosanna." FRB BG 2303. SATB.

Hanson, Handt. "For Me" and "Broken in Love" in *Spirit Calls, Rejoice!* CCF.

MONDAY, MARCH 29
MONDAY IN HOLY WEEK
HANS NIELSEN HAUGE, RENEWER OF THE CHURCH, 1824

After a mystical experience Hauge began preaching, first to his own parish, and then throughout Norway.

Itinerant preaching was against the law, and he was frequently arrested. His writings emphasized a person's vocation as service to God, warned against separatism, and urged his followers to remain faithful to the national church. He influenced Norwegians who emigrated to North America by his emphasis on private prayer, devotional reading, Bible study, singing, and preaching.

Observances of Monday in Holy Week might remember Hauge by singing the Norwegian hymn "My heart is longing" (LBW 326) with its devotional response to the death of Christ.

TUESDAY, MARCH 30
TUESDAY IN HOLY WEEK

WEDNESDAY, MARCH 31
WEDNESDAY IN HOLY WEEK
JOHN DONNE, PRIEST, 1631

This seventeenth-century priest of the Church of England is commemorated for his poetry and spiritual writings. Donne was named Dean of St. Paul's Cathedral and became the most celebrated preacher of his day. In his poetry, he mixed sensual passion, intellectual austerity, and fervent devotion.

Since Donne's commemoration falls during Holy Week, consider using his poem "Good Friday, 1613. Riding westward." In it Donne speaks of Jesus' death on the cross: "Who sees God's face, that is self life, must die; What a death were it then to see God die?"

THE THREE DAYS

Christ entered into death
that we might be reborn to eternal life

IMAGES OF THE SEASON

Blood marked the lintel and doorposts of every house among the Israelites

in the land of Egypt. One by one, each household among the captives had

obtained a lamb, killed it, and set it to roast over

a fire. At twilight each household collected the

blood of its sacrificial lamb and used it to stain their entryway overhead and around the edges. Every single dwelling among the slaves was so marked. Once marked, these doorways would never again be places of entry. Beneath these indelibly-stained lintels and between these bloodsoaked doorposts, the slaves would go out, never to come back through again.

Marked for protection and ready for flight, each household divided and ate its unleavened bread and Passover lamb. Loins girded and sandals strapped on, eager to depart the house of slavery, they kept the night of vigil, waiting for the angel of death to pass over. When the moment for freedom arrived, they left their homes for the last time and came together as one people. To escape bondage they had to walk together. On that night, slipping through the bloodmarked doorways and the broken waters of the Red Sea, a new people was born.

It was nothing less than life and death: death to what had gone before; and new life, new birth, brought about by the compassion and power of God. God told Moses: "I have observed the misery of my people. . . . I have heard their cry" (Exod. 3:7). Out of great love, God brought them from slavery to freedom, from despair to joy. But not without cost: the old was to be abandoned forever. There would be no going back. The cost was grave. The triumph would be glorious.

Our Three Days of Maundy Thursday, Good Friday, and the Resurrection of Our Lord are the Paschal (Greek for "Passover") Triduum (Latin for "Three Days"). Together they form our Christian Passover.

The Three Days are about nothing less. We enter as deeply and intensely as possible into the paschal mystery: Jesus gave his life for us, that we might live. God saw our affliction, our human condition of oppression

by evil, and responded to our cries for help. Out of fathomless love God conceived a way of redemption beyond our capacity to envision or comprehend. Christ entered into death that we might be reborn to eternal life. He became our Lamb of God, undergoing the baptism of innocent suffering in order to free us from suffering, and to break the power of death forever.

What we celebrate is the one indivisible mystery: Jesus Christ, crucified and risen for us. What we celebrate each of the Three Days is the mystery as a whole: love and life that prove victorious over the worst excesses of human evil. What we glorify is not suffering, but love that prevails in spite of suffering; love that does not shrink from death; love that is absolutely without conditions. It is not human, but divine.

Christ, our Passover, is sacrificed—and risen indeed. It is the center of our year, the core around which everything else revolves, the source from which all other celebration springs.

These Three Days are sacred time—a time that flows backwards, upside down, inside out. The Three Days are three—but they're not. It is one liturgy that we enter, pause from, and reenter; one mystery of such depth that we need three days even to begin to absorb, articulate, and respond to it. The Three Days are days, but they're not: we reckon them sundown to sundown. We gather at night three nights in a row.

And why are these nights different from all other nights? They are uniquely rich in silence and sound, word and gesture. Uniquely rich—because they're about nothing less than the contending of life with death. And so we see and hear and do things that occur only once a year. We wash feet, strip the chancel, touch the cross. We kindle fire, chant in darkness, praise God for bees. We liberally (and conservatively) retell the best parts of the story of salvation. Sinners are reconciled, catechumens baptized; the whole church is reborn, made new. Stark space and great silence give way to the light of Christ, banks of flowers, ringing alleluias.

But, slow down.

Maundy Thursday takes its name from the old English form of the Latin word *mandatum*, which means "commandment." "A new commandment I give you," Jesus tells his friends on the eve of his betrayal (John 13:34). "Love one another as I have loved you." These are the gospel's *spoken* words on this night; all else takes its cue from them. "As I have loved you"— forgiving you, washing you, acting as your servant; breaking and pouring out my body and blood for you as true food and drink; the sign of the new covenant; sharing my life and self, without reservation; loving you to the end.

We receive forgiveness, allow our feet to be washed, and let ourselves be nourished and cared for. We rest in contemplation of such wondrous love. We watch the emptying of the chancel area and listen to the lament, "My God, my God, why have you forsaken me?" (Ps. 22:1). Love and new life are costly. Ultimately, they cost everything. There is no going back.

Good Friday, the worship area is so bare that the sight startles: bare—empty—silent. We begin and end in silence, as befits the presence of death passing over. We lift our voices on behalf of the empty and silent, the dying and barely living members of the whole human family. We honor the wood of the cross, seeing in it our deepest sorrow and joy combined. We hear Jesus identified as the servant at once exalted and crushed; as a great priest who opens the way to sanctuary through the curtain of his own flesh. In John's crucifixion account Jesus calls himself "I AM"—the name of God revealed to Moses in the burning bush. Throughout the ordeal Jesus acts as a king whose realm is not from this world, whose life is laid down freely.

Saturday night the church or outdoor gathering area is dark. Against the darkness the new fire is kindled, the new paschal candle lit. "Christ our Light" leads the way like the pillar of fire in Exodus, scattering the gloom and radiant with promise. Bathed in the light of Christ, we praise God for the wonders of this night, when heaven is wedded to earth and humankind is reconciled with God. All creation is redeemed; the earth

exults. The church sounds trumpets; angels sing: Christ is risen!

We allow generous time to listen to the stories and songs of God's providence throughout all ages. We begin with the creation of the world and move through covenant, exodus, conquest, and exile. The words of the prophet echo: "Everyone who thirsts, come to the waters!" (Isa. 55:1). And then water is poured and new Christians are made. Old Christians refresh baptismal promises. The table is spread for the simple and glorious feast.

Sunday morning there will be more: more music, more flowers, more people; everywhere, bright eggs and new clothes. It is the first Sunday morning after the first full moon after the spring equinox. This is the day the LORD has made: the first day of the week. For fifty days—a week of weeks—we will be glad and rejoice.

Why do we go through all this—carry wood, splash water, dye eggs, play with fire? Because our paschal celebration is not only about what God wrought for the Israelites in Egypt, or what once happened when Jesus shattered the chains of death and rose triumphant from the grave. It is equally about the resurrections God is accomplishing in and among us here and now. It is the redemption of our own lives and the re-creation of the whole people of God that we celebrate.

One by one, each of us has traced on our forehead the sign of the cross, the mark of the blood that ransoms us from death. One by one we pass through the waters of baptism, where we receive new birth. One by one we are delivered by God—born into a people vastly larger than our immediate family or household. To continue the exodus we have to join people from other dwellings and walk together. Together we walk away from bondage to sin and death; together we learn and remember the story of our redemption; together we taste the feast of victory for our God.

We leave our homes and enter into the liturgy of these Three Days never to come back through our doorways the same. We approach our three-night time of vigil ready to be freed from captivity. We come out on the other shore like Miriam and Moses, singing and dancing our praise of the God who has triumphed gloriously, whose love is everlasting.

171

ENVIRONMENT AND ART FOR THE SEASON

Maundy Thursday marks the first day of the Three Days (or *Triduum*). This

Triduum is the most sacred and important time of year, for it celebrates

the paschal mystery of the death and resurrection

of our Lord. Maundy Thursday, in particular,

observes the commandment to love one another, together with the institution of the last supper.

EXTERIOR ENVIRONMENT

Since these days are important to so many people, especially for persons who may not worship regularly, it is essential that persons responsible for the placement of outdoor signs listing times of services do so carefully. Try drawing attention to just the main days and service times, or refresh the signs each day by removing information from prior days' celebrations that is no longer needed.

Any exterior signs of Lenten observances may be removed by Saturday of Holy Week. If a cross was used as an exterior symbol during Holy Week, consider draping it in white and gold fabrics for the Easter celebration. Church grounds should look as best as they can for this festival (even if it is still too early for spring clean-up in many locales). All of nature joins in the glories of the resurrection. Even the bees which have provided the substance for the paschal candle get into the act (see the Easter proclamation in *LBW, Ministers Edition*, pp. 143–146).

INTERIOR ENVIRONMENT

If the congregation uses scarlet paraments for Holy Week, their use is continued through Maundy Thurday. In lieu of scarlet paraments, white may be considered for Maundy Thursday, but probably different from the white used for the most festive occasions of Easter and Christmas. Even if real bread is not used at other times of the year, its use on Maundy Thursday helps to underscore the meal aspect of Holy Communion on this day.

Another key element of the Maundy Thursday liturgy is footwashing, which focuses on the servanthood of Christ. The footwashing is accomplished with a ceramic bowl and pitcher, a chair and towel for each participant, and a towel and apron for the presiding minister. A practical consideration is to fill the basin with hot water so that by the time it is used it is still warm. The presiding minister removes chasuble and stole during the footwashing.

Yet another highlight of this service is the stripping of the altar, which is symbolic of Jesus' humiliation at the hands of the soldiers on Good Friday. Everything should be removed in an orderly, respectful manner, with vessels, candles, and ornaments removed to the sacristy first, followed by paraments, linens, and other furnishings. Many (if not all) altar guild members may be recruited for duty on this evening in order to empty the worship space of its adornments.

The Three Days continues with Good Friday. The altar is bare, as well as the entire worship space. There are no flowers or paraments. Visually this day is centered on the cross. A rough-hewn cross may be placed before the altar prior to the service, or it may be carried into the space at the appropriate time in the Good Friday liturgy (see *LBW, Ministers Edition*, p. 142). It may be flanked on each side by tall candles that are set on the floor (for a diagram of this see *Manual on the Liturgy*, p. 324). Some provision may be made for kneeling in front of the cross, whether in the form of a special kneeler or loose cushions.

The Vigil of Easter stands at the center of the Three Days, as well as the entire liturgical year itself. The vigil begins the great fifty days of Easter rejoicing, drawing to a close the Lenten period of fasting and special discipline. Paraments, banners, and flowers reappear. The finest white or gold set of paraments that the parish can afford should be used for this festival.

A large fire is typically built in an outside grill or brazier for the first lighting of the paschal candle. The procession begins with the paschal candle (or if incense is used, with a thurifer carrying the burning incense). It is preferable for the entire congregation to be involved in the procession, carrying candles with light that is passed from the paschal candle.

The baptismal font should be filled with water prior to the Easter Vigil. If the font has a cover, it should be removed and made available for all (ideally such availability would be the case throughout the year). Even if no baptisms take place at this service, the font is nonetheless an important focal point for the liturgy.

A new paschal (Easter) candle, which leads the procession into the worship space this evening, is purchased or made especially for this service. (If the paschal candle is made or purchased unadorned, instructions for decorating it are provided in *Manual on the Liturgy*, pp. 326–327). Have the paschal candle stand in place near the altar prior to the service. The base of the stand may be decorated with flowers. Throughout the year the paschal candle proclaims the light of Christ that calls, leads, and guides the faithful on their earthly pilgrimage. (After the Easter season the paschal candle and its

stand is ordinarily placed near the baptismal font.) An evergreen bough may be placed near the baptismal font for use by the presiding minister in sprinkling the congregation during the renewal of baptismal vows.

It almost goes without saying that everything is at its brightest for this evening, as well as for the entirety of the Easter season that follows. A cantor or an assisting minister sings in the Easter proclamation: "This is the night in which all who believe in Christ are rescued from evil and the gloom of sin, are renewed in grace, and are restored to holiness."

The Resurrection of Our Lord continues the festive celebration begun in the Easter Vigil. For many people accustomed to celebrating the Easter Vigil, Easter Day itself seems almost anticlimactic. Yet the worship area and its attendant areas should continue to sparkle on Easter Day, as well as throughout the fifty days. Flowers should be renewed and replaced as necessary. Though Lent may seem long for some people, the season of Easter is even longer. Make it into the "queen of seasons" that it is!

PREACHING with the SEASON

The Three Days are the heart of the matter—the pivot around which the entire liturgical year revolves. It is more than a remembrance of the story of our salvation. It is the drama itself, told again, with the faithful as key actors in the play. The

church knows very well that Jesus died once for all and that his resurrection is an accomplished fact. And yet, even with that theological truth well established, the drama of the Three Days has a profound capacity for bringing the story of salvation into our experience. It is something more than a series of important Bible stories to be retold and remembered again; they are to be lived.

The linchpin for correctly approaching these days is to think of our actions sacramentally. Baptism is the sacrament of initiation, and it is the focus of the church's Easter celebration in the Vigil. Baptism is the action by which we are incorporated into the story of

Jesus: buried with Christ to rise with him. Baptism makes Jesus' story our own: his death is our death so that our death might now be in him. His resurrection is our victory—here and now—over sin, death and Satan, as well as a foretaste of the final victory we will experience at the end of all our stories.

Likewise, this season also revolves around the Holy Eucharist. Jesus structures his words and behaviors at that meal so as to draw us into the action. "For you," Jesus says over the bread. The meal is not meant merely as a symbol of some deeper theological truth. We are to be involved in the action itself. "Here," says Jesus, "take, eat, drink." The good news is to be taken into us and we, too, are drawn into the action at the table. Our guilt and our forgiveness are the subject matter for the meal. "Is it I, Lord? Is it I?" Yes, it is. We cannot hold the action of the eucharist off at arm's length; it is not eucharist that way. No, the meal becomes the meal only when we consume it, take it into ourselves. So, too, these stories of the Triduum are not merely a recounting of a once-upon-a-time. Yes, Christ died once for all. Yes, the sacrifice is complete in itself. But we are drawn into it, dissolved with Christ in baptismal waters, filled with his own flesh and blood in eucharistic bread and wine.

The goal of our celebration is to take up the story and make our way through it again. Our aim, really, is to let the story take possession of us, work its way into our hearts and minds so that from there it may flow through our bloodstream to our hands and feet and mouths. The church has been finding ways of doing this for nearly twenty centuries now, and along the way the faithful have acquired some useful tools to help make it happen. Twentieth-century cyberjunkies imagine they have invented something new in virtual reality. The church has been practicing it and living it for two millennia. And as our recent technologies are discovering, so has the church known for a long, long time, that for virtual reality to be effective it really has to be multimedia; involving, if possible, the whole human sensorium. These days offer us a dazzling array of experiences to hear and see, touch and taste and smell. As Augustine said, sacraments are *visible words*. A good Triduum brings the drama of salvation into the experience of the faithful by making it accessible to our senses.

These days present a major challenge to the preacher. In one sense it is the sheer weight of the entire "great and holy week," which makes the task of proclamation feel so consequential, so difficult as to be almost overwhelming. Since the scope of God's soteriological project is so immense, how can we ever find the words to express it? But the challenge of proclamation in this week is both more simple and, at the same time, more profound. Quite practically, it is not always clear where or when a sermon should happen in the liturgies of Holy Week. The week began with the lengthy reading of the passion according to Matthew, and there is hardly a way (or time) to top that!

Maundy Thursday seems a little more amenable to preaching. It is almost a "regular" eucharist, and so the homily feels at home here. Yet if the order for the

Maundy Thursday liturgy (*LBW, Ministers Edition*, pp. 137–138) is followed, the footwashing may have the effect of preempting the sermon.

Good Friday presents another challenge for the preacher. The Good Friday Liturgy in *LBW* provides for a sermon that "may" occur. And again, we are invited to hear the entire passion from beginning to end, this time from John. Other liturgical traditions are available to congregations for this day. The Tenebrae liturgy can easily be adapted to preaching; sometimes it is combined with meditations on the "Seven Last Words" of Jesus, an artificial conflation of Jesus' saying on the cross from all four gospels. Other liturgies have focused on the stations of the cross with corresponding homiletic reflection.

The Easter Vigil makes it possible to forgo preaching in any traditional sense. The twelve (or seven) lessons could stand on their own, and silence is the mandated response to hearing the word.

So here it is, the Three Days, the center of the church's life, and does the church mean to suggest that the preacher ought to be almost totally silent? Hardly! But what we would like to suggest is that contained within the church's historic liturgical traditions is a deep wisdom and a radical invitation for us to reconsider what the task of proclamation is all about. The idea is both simple and profound: *The church's proclamation of salvation in these liturgies takes place within the liturgical actions themselves.* Our definition of proclamation does not have to be limited to what takes place in a ten (fifteen? twenty? more? stop! please stop!) minute monologue by a pastor standing in a pulpit. The Three Days encourage us to stretch our homiletic imagination in order to see the sermons in long stories well told, bowls of water and dirty feet, broken bread and poured wine, stripped altars, silent darkness, and flint-struck fire.

Perhaps the preacher will do her or his work the best this week not by writing homilies but by paying attention to how stories are read, how furniture is arranged, how movements are made, how feet get washed and candles are lit. Each action is a sermon. Each liturgical antiquity is an invitation for us to expand our homiletic consciousness. But even more, each action becomes a powerful tool for doing the very thing God wants done in baptism and eucharist:

174

to make the gospel real, experienced and lived inside us and between us and through us into the world. Considered from this perspective, the liturgies of the Three Days provide unique opportunities to unfold the drama of our salvation in powerful ways.

The Three Days is really a single liturgy involving the drama of redemption stretching from Thursday evening into the predawn darkness of Easter. The Maundy Thursday eucharist begins with a final confession of sin and receiving of absolution—delayed or anticipated for forty days—giving the faithful an opportunity to repent and amend their lives. The homily is shifted to the beginning of the liturgy, giving the preacher an opportunity to close what began on Ash Wednesday. The rite of footwashing deepens the significance of all Jesus' actions this night and gives Maundy Thursday its name (in Latin, *mandatum*, the new command). Peter's reticence at having his feet washed curiously mirrors that of many moderns: we do not want other people to see our dirty feet! But Peter, and all of us, need to be clear that we need to be washed. Although we want to hold the bad news off and apply it to other people, it has to do with us: our treachery, our unworthiness, our vulnerability to temptation and denial and falling away. We need this night!

The liturgy of Good Friday is the celebration of the triumph of Jesus' cross. The reading of the full passion, this time according to John, is a wonderful way to keep the feast, for in this telling of the tale Jesus, even as he is crucified, is the king lifted high upon his throne, drawing all humanity to himself. Again, a minimalist "staging" of the story might allow the faithful to enter the action more deeply, just as long as the staging does not get in the way of the story itself. Worship planners might also think about the ways in which the cross is visually brought before the people. It can be carried in procession as a "rough hewn cross," or the more ornate and permanent cross in the sanctuary might be unveiled after its forty-day hiding. The service ends quietly. Provision and opportunity might be made for worshipers to kneel before the cross and meditate before they leave in silence.

The Three Days comes to a dramatic climax at the Easter Vigil. Here worship planners will want to give the greatest attention to how symbol and setting might become powerful proclamations of the good news of Jesus' resurrection. A fire struck from flint—sparks of light that can only be seen in the dark—is a dramatic incarnation of the life that comes out of Jesus' death. The spark hits a small clump of dried grass and needs some breath (spirit! *pneuma*! *ruach*!) to make it burst into flame. The paschal candle lifted into the darkness proclaims that the light of Christ conquers sin and death. The growing multiplication of flames mirrors the growing of the body of Christ as more and more saints are taken into the mystery. (It also finally makes clear why it is we give candles to those who are baptized.) The long story stretches out before us from creation through flood and election and prophets' warnings until at last we are brought to the brink of the celebration and the new day dawns above us. Each step along the way we receive the word and take it to heart. Each person's quiet meditations in the silence may speak more eloquently than preached words could possibly achieve, surrounded as we are this night with so much symbol, so many images swirling around our heads: servant bees making wax, the light of the candle reaching to the stars and toward the cosmic Christ risen above all creation, drawing us upward, pulling us into the spiral of the new day and the life to come! Alleluia! Christ is risen indeed! Alleluia!

175

PLANNING AHEAD FOR THE SEASON

Encourage people to worship on each of the Three Days, since the services are intended to be experienced as a whole. In the Maundy Thursday and Good Friday liturgies of *LBW*, no benedictions are given, since each service leads into another one. You might think of these three days as three acts of a grand drama—the total of which proclaims the death and resurrection of Christ. Even visually, each service more or less picks up where the last one left off. The stripped altar at the end of Maundy Thursday becomes the barren set for the Good Friday liturgy. The darkness of Good Friday is where the Service of Light in the Easter Vigil liturgy begins.

If homebound people in your congregation have the expectation of receiving communion during Holy Week (or even on Maundy Thursday or Good Friday itself), try to schedule alternative times in advance (the week before or the week afterwards if necessary). The full energy of worship leaders and all worship participants needs to be devoted to these services that serve as the fulcrum of the entire church year. If everyone is operating at a frenzied pace and being distracted by everything else that needs to be done, the highpoint of the year is lost.

Congregations that have not used the *footwashing* ceremony of the Maundy Thursday liturgy might consider doing so this year. Footwashing is even considered as a sacrament in some traditions. Though the institution of the Lord's Supper is a central part of this day, the washing of feet is also significant in that it visualizes Christ's call to humble service. The footwashing ceremony can have profound meaning on its own, even apart from the scriptures that are proclaimed and the sacrament of Holy Communion that is celebrated on this day. A simple basin, a pitcher filled with water, and a towel are all the elements needed for footwashing. Members of the congregation may come forward to participate in the footwashing spontaneously, though it is usually necessary to ask half a dozen people or more ahead of time to plan on coming forward to participate

in this portion of the service. Two or three chairs placed in the chancel will provide a comfortable place to enable those having their feet washed to sit down. (Note: Footwashing participants should be instructed to dress with footwear that is easily removed.) Footwashing participants should include people of all ages and genders. (It may be especially striking when feet of some of the youngest members of the assembly are washed.) Traditionally only the presiding minister actually washes feet. If others also wash feet, they might begin doing so after the presiding minister has already washed the feet of several participants.

If congregations in the area have participated in a service that sets apart oil used in baptism and the healing ministry of the church, the oil might be brought forward during the offertory procession of the Maundy Thursday liturgy. Oil has traditionally been blessed during Holy Week so that it might be ready for baptisms occurring during the Easter Vigil. Where synods or other regional expressions of the church do not have the practice of blessing oil during Holy Week or shortly before it, congregations of a district/conference/cluster might choose to do this on their own. One resource for use in blessing oil might be the "Dedication of Worship Furnishings," *Occasional Services*, pp. 176–177.

Many different congregational traditions of Good Friday exist. In places where communion has been celebrated on this day, consider encouraging people to commune on Maundy Thursday or during the Easter Day (and Vigil) services, since this is one day in the liturgical year when there ought to be a fast from the sacrament of Holy Communion. *LBW, Ministers Edition* (pp. 139–143) lays out one possibility for worship on this day. Even where congregations have typically used other forms of worship (in particular an adaptation of the *tenebrae* office) elements of *LBW* Good Friday liturgy might still be included, such as a reading of the passion according to St. John, the bidding prayer, and the adoration of the cross. Services geared around "the seven last words" are rather dubious, in that no single gospel account contains all seven "words" attributed to our Lord while on the cross.

The more traditional scripture reading on this day has been from the passion according to St. John. In the course of three years, with the use of the synoptic passion gospels on Passion Sunday and the use of the Johannine passion story each Good Friday, the "seven last words" will in fact be heard, but allowing each of the four gospel accounts to retain their own unique integrity. A dramatic reading of the passion according to St. John (as well as the other passion stories on Passion Sunday) might be assigned to various readers. One can take the part of a narrator, another voice can take all the words spoken by Jesus, while a third voice can take the spoken parts of all the other characters in the drama.

If your congregation has not held an Easter Vigil before, this year may be the year to consider having one. Congregations that have worshiped at Easter Vigil for several years begin to see it as the cornerstone upon which the rest of the liturgical year is built. The great Old Testament readings in the vigil give a summary of salvation history—forming a perfect introduction for baptism. The movement of the service from darkness into light, from subdued hope into profound joy has no other equal throughout the year. You do not have to start big. Just begin.

Schedule your Easter Vigil for Saturday evening just after the sun goes down in your area (a look at the *Farmer's Almanac* or a call to the weather service in your area will inform you of the time). Or schedule your Easter Vigil to start about an hour before sunrise on Easter Day (if your churchyard contains a cemetery, it could be a great place to begin). If you can schedule baptisms for this service, that will ensure you of at least a few people in the congregation for your first vigil. If you can also enlist a number of people as readers, fire builders, acolytes, ushers, communion assistants, singers and instrumentalists, that will also guarantee you a certain minimum number of participants (plus a few family members coming too). Don't be concerned about the numbers just yet. Just do it! Commit yourself to the long range and in a few years this service may eclipse all the other Easter services in popularity. Nothing else conveys the triumph of Easter like the Easter Vigil.

Congregations that hold an Easter Vigil often have a great party following the service. After such a lengthy period of Lenten fasting comes the need to break the fast (a sunrise vigil on Easter Sunday is quite appropriately followed by an Easter break-fast!). Consider having people prepare many types of breads for use at this event (some ethnic traditions have wonderful Easter breads). Easter is the "feast of feasts." Why not let this be the finest party or reception you hold throughout the year?

The lectionary provides scripture readings and a prayer for Easter evening. Where a service at that time of the day is possible, perhaps it might be a festive form of evening prayer. While a congregation might not be willing to return to the church building for yet another service, perhaps holding a service at a nursing home or other institution that did not have a celebration earlier in the day would be possible. The gospel reading from Luke 24 is a marvelous passage when read on this evening. The almost dreamy appearance of Christ to two of the disciples on the evening of the resurrection may match our mood after a big celebration earlier in the day (or the previous night).

ORDO FOR THE SEASON

The Three Days is the only season in which a specific order of worship is proper to each of the days. Having no benediction after the Maundy Thursday and Good Friday liturgies indicates that the time from Maundy Thursday through the Easter Vigil is intended to be experienced as a whole. Members of the congregation might be encouraged to attend services on each of the three days, a strenuous duty to be sure, yet what is celebrated during these three days is absolutely central to the Christian faith.

The *LBW* Maundy Thursday rite begins with a sermon (*LBW, Ministers Edition*, p. 137). The *Commentary on the Lutheran Book of Worship* includes this note: "This unusual arrangement gives the preacher an opportunity to explain the meaning of the day and the actions that are about to take place so that they may flow uninterruptedly and dramatically from this evening through Good Friday and into Easter" (p. 240). Moreover, the footwashing ceremony for this liturgy serves as an enacted sermon, immediately following the gospel. The stripping of the altar, which accompanies the singing or speaking of Psalm 22, concludes the Maundy Thursday liturgy.

The Good Friday liturgy provided in *LBW, Ministers Edition* (pp. 139–143) is a word liturgy, extended by a reading of the entire passion according to St. John, a bidding prayer, and an adoration of the cross.

The Easter Vigil liturgy is the most complex liturgy (typically also the longest) throughout the year. Essentially the parts of this liturgy follow the basic shape of the normal weekly liturgy (see *ordo* section for Advent): a service of light (gathering), a service of readings (word), a service of baptism, a service of communion (meal), and a sending (finally a benediction for the three days). For this one liturgy, it ought to be possible to set clocks and watches aside. The essence of a vigil involves time, waiting, and plenty of silence.

Each portion of the Easter Vigil liturgy is an expanded version of its usual form. The service of light includes an opportunity for a genuine gathering of the congregation outside near a bonfire, and then processing into the darkened nave behind the lit paschal candle. The service of readings offers the possibility for not just one, but several Old Testament readings, each followed by a response, silence, and prayer. The service of baptism is more than the typical baptismal liturgy, in that it calls the entire congregation to remember its baptism (opportunity for the entire congregation to approach the font may be provided). The service of communion might be the only portion of the liturgy that is not elaborated beyond the congregation's usual pattern, though eucharistic prayer II (from *LBW, Ministers Edition*; or *WOV, Leaders Edition*) seems especially appropriate this night. More than the usual post-service reception also seems called for on this night that begins the feast of feasts.

Easter Day continues the festivity begun with the Easter Vigil. Festive arrangements of the hymns and the liturgy might be considered (augmentation by choral descants and additional instruments, for example). An entrance procession with banners and choirs might occur on this day, even if one occurs at no other time. For congregations not yet celebrating Holy Communion each week, this day is certainly a day to offer it at all services. Note that the lectionary for this day provides for a sequence hymn (LBW 137). If used, the hymn might actually follow the reading of the gospel, especially when a gospel procession has been used. Consider also using a eucharistic prayer that befits this day (eucharistic prayer II from *LBW, Ministers Edition*, and *WOV, Leaders Edition*; or seasonal prayer E from *WOV, Leaders Edition*, p. 69).

ASSEMBLY SONG FOR THE SEASON

The liturgical details of Maundy Thursday, Good Friday, and the Vigil of

Easter can appear rather complex. The more complex the rites, the more

direct the music should be to support them.

Allow the choirs and instrumentalists primarily to

be enablers of the people's song, reserving more elaborate choral and instrumental offerings for the fifty days of Easter. Select music worthy of repetition and use it consistently year after year. As these unique liturgies become more familiar, the music can become more varied and involved.

MAUNDY THURSDAY

ENTRANCE

How do the Three Days begin? Flexibility is suggested in *LBW, Ministers Edition*: "The Sermon begins the service. A hymn may precede the Sermon." If a hymn is sung, it needs to set the stage for the entire Maundy Thursday service, if not the entire Three Days.

Consider all the processions and movement that may occur during the three days:

- Entrances on Thursday and Friday
- The entire assembly led by the paschal candle on Saturday
- To receive laying on of hands on Thursday
- To adore the crucified on Friday
- Offertory and communion processions on Thursday and Saturday
- Gospel and sending processions on Saturday

In your architecture, what does the movement and music say? Should they be the same or quite different? Be certain that each procession communicates clearly what you intend.

INDIVIDUAL ABSOLUTION

The movement of worshipers to receive individual forgiveness can be accompanied by silence or something simple and repetitive that does not distract from the powerful gesture of laying on of hands.

FOOTWASHING

A simple, graceful refrain is helpful in experiencing this profound gesture of love and humility. The various possibilities for music might always include a setting of the ancient text, "Ubi caritas et amor, Deus ibi est" (Where charity and love are, there is God). So the people can participate actively or by watching, invite them to sing only the refrains with verses sung by cantor or choir.

STRIPPING OF THE ALTAR

The text of Psalm 22 ("My God, my God, why have you forsaken me?") is spoken or sung as the altar and chancel are stripped bare in preparation for Good Friday. A single voice reciting or intoning the text without accompaniment may be all that is necessary (or possible, if lights are dimmed).

GOOD FRIDAY

ENTRANCE

Profound silence is the best music as the ministers enter at this liturgy. They should treat the silence as music and process in a simple, yet dignified way.

PSALMS, HYMNS, ANTHEMS & OTHER MUSIC

LBW, Ministers Edition suggests specific hymns to be used throughout this liturgy. If at all possible, the organ, piano, and other instruments should be silenced on this day, with only unaccompanied singing. The effect is powerful. Unless all members of the assembly are comfortable with singing in harmony, unison singing is advised, allowing the fullest possible participation. Unless choral selections can be sung unaccompanied with relative ease, they are perhaps best used on Passion Sunday. The choir's role may be to sit in the congregation and lead the singing.

179

ADORATION OF THE CRUCIFIED

Without obscuring the profound simplicity of this portion of the liturgy, these actions can be enhanced with music. "Behold the life-giving cross, on which was hung the salvation of the whole world" and the response "Oh, come let us adore him" could be sung to a psalm tone. Some traditions sing the Trisagion (see WOV 603 for text and one musical setting) during or following the procession; if sung by choir, cantor, or small ensemble, the congregation can focus on the mystery of salvation accomplished on the cross. Especially if the church is dark, it may be awkward to sing a hymn with many words at the end of this liturgy. A simple Taizé refrain or a choral setting may be a more fitting conclusion.

VIGIL OF EASTER

LIGHT

Gathering in silence around a fire may be an excellent prelude to the vigil. If it is an awkward or "chatty" time it may be wise to engage the worshipers in reflective song that does not require printed music as they await the ministers for the start of the vigil.

Allow the visuals of lighting the candle and entering the darkened church to speak for themselves. Keep the musical responses simple. Once in place, the Easter Proclamation is sung by an assisting minister using the light of the paschal candle. The singer needs to know this ancient text backwards and forwards, ideally from memory. With worshipers in a darkened church holding candles, more elaborate settings of the Easter Proclamation can be quite impractical. If sung with confidence and quiet joy, the ancient melody (see settings by Mark Bangert in *Music for the Vigil of Easter*, AFP 3-5330) is perhaps still the best alternative.

READINGS

The Revised Common Lectionary suggests psalms or canticles as responses to each of the Old Testament readings. Since some of these readings are quite lengthy, it is a good idea to involve the congregation in some way. Remember that the church is dark, so simple refrains or familiar hymns are needed. Some solo or choral pieces could be included as long as they serve as a response, not an event in themselves. It can be effective to gradually increase the volume of the accompaniment used during the service of readings, beginning with voice alone, perhaps adding a single drum, then some subtle organ or piano, additional instruments, and finally leading to full-blown organ, brass, bells, and whatever is available, at the hymn of praise.

BAPTISM

The gathering at the font takes place during the singing of the canticle that follows the final reading. No music is necessary during the baptismal (or baptismal renewal) service. However, if the passing through the baptismal waters is the focus of tonight's liturgy, how can we help but sing? Joyful alleluias, with bells and instruments, repeated many times after each baptism can heighten the Easter joy. An evangelical Litany of the Saints can be a dramatic conclusion to the baptismal rite.

EUCHARIST

Immediately before and after the proclamation of the Easter gospel may be splendid times to sing stanzas of an Easter hymn. Music surrounding the offering, great thanksgiving, and sending should be joyful, but remember—there is still Easter morning! Perhaps the big anthems and instrumental music should be reserved for then.

EASTER DAY

It is when most visitors or less-than-regular members will come to Easter worship. Be hospitable and sing some familiar Easter favorites. But also show them that this congregation is moving and growing by including something new and different, perhaps something from another culture with drums and shakers. Today is the day for the choir to offer its grandest Easter anthem, and for the congregation's instrumentalists to join in a joyful concerted prelude or postlude. The liturgy should be fairly straightforward, reminiscent of every other Sunday in the year, but with all the appropriate options included. The complex rites of Thursday, Friday, and Saturday required simple music. The simple rite of Sunday morning calls for more elaborate music.

ALTERNATE WORSHIP TEXTS

MAUNDY THURSDAY

CONFESSION AND FORGIVENESS

Our Lord Jesus knelt to wash the feet of his disciples.
Let us come before God
to confess our need for cleansing.

Silence for reflection and self-examination.

God of love and mercy,
you know the words of our mouths
and the meditations of our hearts;
you know our coming in and our going out.
We confess to you all our sins—
those things done and left undone.
We have not loved one another as you have loved us.
We have not served others as you have served us.
Hear our cry, O Lord.
Accept our repentance.
Cleanse us, restore us, and lead us
that we may love and serve in newness of life
through Jesus Christ our Lord. Amen

In the mercy of almighty God,
Jesus Christ was sent to die for us,
and for his sake, God forgives us all our sins.
As a called and ordained minister of the
church of Christ, and by his authority,
I therefore declare to you the entire forgiveness of all your sins,
in the name of the Father, and of the ✛ Son, and of the Holy
    Spirit.
Amen

OFFERTORY PRAYER

Gracious God,
you gave us the gift of your dear Son,
who humbled himself as a servant before us.
Receive the gifts we offer
as signs of our whole lives
returned to you in humble service to our neighbor,
in the name of Jesus Christ our Lord. Amen

INVITATION TO COMMUNION

The supper is ready; our Lord is host and servant.
Come and share in the bread and cup of salvation.

POST-COMMUNION PRAYER

Lord God, in a wonderful sacrament
you have left us a memorial of your suffering and death.
May this sacrament of your body and blood so work in us
that the way we live will proclaim
the redemption you have brought;
for you live and reign with the Father and the Holy Spirit,
one God, now and forever.
Amen

VIGIL OF EASTER

OFFERTORY PRAYER

God of light and word, water and life,
as we come to your table, receive us and these gifts in thanks-
    giving for the resurrection and the life,
your Son, Jesus Christ our Lord. Amen

INVITATION TO COMMUNION

Christ our Passover has been sacrificed for us.
Therefore let us keep the feast. Alleluia!

POST-COMMUNION PRAYER

We give you thanks, almighty God,
that you have brought us from darkness to light,
from slavery to freedom, from death to rebirth.
Transform our lives with this heavenly food
that we may shine with your love
and take to the world the risen life of your Son,
Jesus Christ our Lord.
Amen

BENEDICTION

Alleluia! Christ is risen.
Christ is risen indeed. Alleluia!
Almighty God, Father, Son, and Holy Spirit
bless you now and forever.
Amen

DISMISSAL

Go in peace. Proclaim the risen Lord. Alleluia, alleluia!
Thanks be to God. Alleluia, alleluia!

181

SEASONAL RITES

GOOD FRIDAY

SERVICE OF LIGHT AND DARKNESS

This service is designed for those parishes that celebrate Tenebrae, yet would like to move toward the revised Good Friday liturgy included in LBW, Ministers Edition (pp. 23–24) as well as in the current Episcopal, Roman Catholic, Methodist and Presbyterian worship books.

Tenebrae (Latin for "darkness") was the name given to the medieval predawn morning prayer celebrated by monks during the last three days in Holy Week. In recent centuries, this monastic liturgy—despite its early morning light imagery—was transferred to Wednesday evening in Holy Week. In the monastic practice, it was a service of prayers and readings from scripture. As the light began to dawn, the candles used for reading were gradually extinguished, so that at the end of the service, the rising sun provided the necessary light for reading and singing. This element has been retained in the contemporary practice but with the curious addition of the removal and return of a single candle, variously interpreted as the presence of the risen Christ.

In the service printed here, these elements have been placed within the reading of the Passion According to St. John, the ancient gospel narrative for the day. With this form, seven or fourteen candles are used, with a larger candle representing Christ. Following each section, one or two candles are extinguished until the eighth reading, at which time the "Christ" candle (not the paschal/Easter candle) is removed without being returned.

It is desirable that the Johannine passion account be read on Good Friday, because the synoptic passion accounts are read in successive years on Palm Sunday/Sunday of the Passion. John's passion account sees Jesus' death as his glorification. Rather than "mourning" the dying or dead Jesus on Good Friday, the cross is acclaimed as the sign of the world's redemption. The procession of the cross and adoration of the crucified Christ become the primary symbolic action of this day. We offer honor and reverence to the one, who lifted up from the earth, draws all people to himself. This service does not end in darkness and sadness, as if the assembly were reenacting the death of Christ. Rather, the liturgy ends with Christ exalted on the cross, an image from the gospel according to John.

For those parishes that have previously used a Tenebrae "service of darkness," there will need to be pastoral preaching and teaching about the place of this liturgy within the Three Days. The procession of the cross has an important connection to the procession of the paschal candle in the Easter Vigil. More importantly, all three days celebrate the mystery of Jesus' dying and rising. We do not wait until Easter Sunday to see what will happen, as if we were participating in a passion play. Already on Good Friday, the church celebrates the Lord's death and resurrection as the central event of our salvation.

GATHERING

The liturgy begins in silence after all have been seated. The ministers process into the worship space in silence.

PRAYER OF THE DAY

READINGS
Isaiah 52:13—53:12

PSALM OR HYMN

THE PASSION ACCORDING TO ST. JOHN
John 18:1-11
First candle(s) may be extinguished.
Hymn: Christ, the life of all the living (LBW 97, st. 1)

John 18:12-27
Second candle(s) may be extinguished.
Hymn: Ah, holy Jesus (LBW 123, st. 2)

John 18:28-40
Third candle(s) may be extinguished.
Hymn: On my heart imprint your image (LBW 102)

John 19:1-7
Fourth candle(s) may be extinguished.
Hymn: O sacred head, now wounded (LBW 117, st. 1)

John 19:8-16a
Fifth candle(s) may be extinguished.
Hymn: Were you there (LBW 92, st. 1)

John 19:16b-22
Sixth candle(s) may be extinguished.
Hymn: O sacred head, now wounded (LBW 117, st. 2)

John 19:23-25a
Seventh candle(s) may be extinguished.
Hymn: O sacred head, now wounded (LBW 117, st. 3)

John 19:25b-30
The large "Christ" candle may be removed.
John 19:31-42
Hymn: Were you there (LBW 93, st. 3)

HOMILY OR MEDITATION

Silence is kept by all.

THE PRAYERS

Bidding Prayer: See LBW, Ministers Edition, *pp. 139–142. For an alternate version, see* Book of Common Worship *(Louisville, KY: Westminster/John Knox Press, 1993), pp. 283–286.*

PROCESSION AND ADORATION OF THE CROSS

A large, rough-hewn cross is carried in and placed in the chancel. The following response is sung or said three times: as the procession begins, halfway to the altar, and as the procession ends at the altar.

Behold, the life-giving cross on which was hung the salvation of the whole world.
Oh, come, let us worship him.

A period of silence is kept. Those who desire may come forward to offer a sign of reverence, such as touching the cross, kneeling briefly, or bowing. Hymns may be sung during this period, or the Solemn Reproaches may be said or sung (see Book of Common Worship, *pp. 288–291).*

HYMNS

LBW 118 Sing, my tongue (may be sung to PICARDY)
LBW 123 Ah, holy Jesus
LBW 124 The royal banners forward go
LBW 482 When I survey the wondrous cross
WOV 668 There in God's garden

We adore you, O Christ, and we bless you.
By your holy cross you have redeemed the world.

The congregation departs in silence. The service continues with the Vigil of Easter.

VIGIL OF EASTER

The following canticle may be sung following the final reading from the Hebrew scriptures as the baptismal party moves to the font.

All creatures, worship God most high!
Sound every voice in earth and sky: Alleluia! Alleluia!
Sing, brother sun, in splendor bright;
sing, sister moon and stars of night:
　　Alleluia, alleluia, alleluia, alleluia, alleluia!

Sing, brother wind; with clouds and rain
you grow the gifts of fruit and grain: Alleluia! Alleluia!
Dear sister water, useful, clear,
make music for your Lord to hear:
　　Alleluia, alleluia, alleluia, alleluia, alleluia!

O fire, our brother, mirthful, strong,
drive far the shadows, join the song: Alleluia! Alleluia!
O earth, our mother, rich in care,
praise God in colors bright and rare:
　　Alleluia, alleluia, alleluia, alleluia, alleluia!

All who for love of God forgive,
all who in pain or sorrow grieve: Alleluia! Alleluia!
Christ bears your burdens and your fears;
in mercy rest, sing through the tears:
　　Alleluia, alleluia, alleluia, alleluia, alleluia!

Come, sister death, your song release
when you enfold our breath in peace: Alleluia! Alleluia!
Since Christ our light has pierced your gloom,
fair is the night that leads us home.
　　Alleluia, alleluia, alleluia, alleluia, alleluia!

O sisters, brothers, take your part,
and worship God with humble heart: Alleluia! Alleluia!
All creatures, bless the Father, Son,
and Holy Spirit, Three in One:
　　Alleluia, alleluia, alleluia, alleluia, alleluia!

Tune: LASST UNS ERFREUEN (LBW 143)

LITANY OF THE SAINTS

See Welcome to Christ: Lutheran Rites for the Catechumenate, *pages 70–71.*

183

APRIL 1, 1999

MAUNDY THURSDAY

INTRODUCTION

On this day the Christian community gathers to share in the holy supper Christ gave the church to reveal his unfailing love for the human family. In the actions of this liturgy, Christ demonstrates this love by speaking his faithful word, washing our feet, and giving us his body and blood. From this gathering we are sent to continue these actions in daily life: to serve those in need, to offer mercy, to feed the hungry.

This first liturgy of the Three Days has no ending; it continues with the worship of Good Friday and concludes with the Resurrection of Our Lord. Together the Three Days proclaim the mystery of our faith: Christ has died. Christ is risen. Christ will come again.

PRAYER OF THE DAY

Holy God, source of all love, on the night of his betrayal, Jesus gave his disciples a new commandment: To love one another as he had loved them. By your Holy Spirit write this commandment in our hearts; through your Son, Jesus Christ our Lord, who lives and reigns with you and the Holy Spirit, one God, now and forever.

or

Lord God, in a wonderful Sacrament you have left us a memorial of your suffering and death. May this Sacrament of your body and blood so work in us that the way we live will proclaim the redemption you have brought; for you live and reign with the Father and the Holy Spirit, one God, now and forever.

READINGS

Exodus 12:1-4 [5-10] 11-14

Israel remembered its deliverance from slavery in Egypt by celebrating the festival of Passover. This festival featured the slaughter, preparation, and consumption of the Passover lamb, whose blood was used to protect God's people from the threat of death. The early church described the Lord's Supper using imagery from the Passover, especially in portraying Jesus as the lamb who delivers God's people from sin and death.

Psalm 116:1, 10-17 (Psalm 116:1-2, 12-19 [NRSV])

I will take the cup of salvation and call on the name of the Lord. (Ps. 116:11)

1 Corinthians 11:23-26

The only story from the life of Jesus that Paul recounts in detail is this report of the Last Supper. His words to the Christians at Corinth are reflected today in the liturgies of churches throughout the world.

John 13:1-17, 31b-35

The story of the Last Supper in John's Gospel recalls a remarkable event not mentioned elsewhere. Jesus performs the duty of a slave, washing the feet of his disciples and urging them to do the same for each other.

COLOR   Scarlet *or* White

THE PRAYERS

Gathered around the table of the Lord and united in love, let us pray for the church, the world, and all those in need.

A BRIEF SILENCE.

That the church may be one at the eucharistic table and in service to the world, let us pray to the Lord.

Lord, have mercy.

That the leaders of nations may seek reconciliation and justice wherever there is conflict and oppression, let us pray to the Lord.

Lord, have mercy.

That those who are unloved, weary, sick, or hospitalized (especially . . .) may find strength in holy communion and in our care for them, let us pray to the Lord.

Lord, have mercy.

That our participation in this holy meal may strengthen us to serve those who are hungry and poor, let us pray to the Lord.

Lord, have mercy.

That those who will be baptized at Easter, and all who gather to celebrate these holy days, may find their life in the mystery of Christ's suffering love, let us pray to the Lord.

Lord, have mercy.

HERE OTHER INTERCESSIONS MAY BE OFFERED.

That you would gather us with the saints of every time and place into your promised reign of love and peace, let us pray to the Lord.

Lord, have mercy.

Hear our prayers, O merciful God, as we eagerly await the day of resurrection and rebirth, through Jesus Christ our Lord.

Amen

IMAGES FOR PREACHING

"Do this." *Do what?* "Break the bread and pass it. Take the cup and share it. Here. It is for you. I am doing this for you."

"Do this." *Do what?* "What you see me doing. Do as I have done to you."

They can understand one command as much as the other—which means almost not at all. How could they? They cannot see the future. Memories of the past swirl around their heads this night—Passover and liberation and years of suffering coming to an end. They would be slaves no more!

How could they understand what he was about to do? How would they understand the suffering and the dying? How could they imagine becoming servants all over again? And most of all, how could they comprehend their own complicity in the crimes that were about to happen? Those are dark truths they (and we) will not fully encounter until tomorrow.

For today, the example is enough. They eat and they drink. They even have their feet washed, although some of them need to be talked into it. They do it, although they cannot fully realize what they do.

And we—do we realize? As we break the bread and take the cup, as we submit to having feet washed? Do we understand? We would like to believe we do. After all, we have spent forty days to get to this moment. But even now, we cannot see the future, and we never fully see the depth of our complicity in the crime about to happen.

Jesus does. He knows. And knowing, he invites us to the table. He takes the bowl and towel into his own hands and kneels before us. "Here. Do this. I am doing it for you."

Over and over we need to be shocked into grace. It *will* happen. Beyond your wildest dreams. Trust him.

WORSHIP MATTERS

The name for this day comes from the Latin word *mandatum*, commandment, a reminder of the new commandment Jesus gives to his disciples the night before his suffering to be servants to one another as he will be the servant of all (John 13:14-15). The liturgy of this day invites us to emulate Jesus' example and to engage in the unfamiliar but powerful practice of washing feet. Once done for the sake of hygiene before the beginning of a meal, this practice allows us the opportunity to demonstrate the servant ministry to which all the faithful are called by virtue of baptism. In some places this ritual is performed by the presiding minister, with twelve representatives of the congregation who represent the twelve apostles. But the purpose of the ritual is not historical reenactment. It is rather an opportunity to recall the one who this night sets out on the path of servanthood, even to the point of death, to bring redemption and grace to God's people. Thus, it is most appropriate for the principle ministers of the liturgy to wash one another's feet, and then to invite all in the congregation who wish to participate to have their feet washed. Ample water to be poured into basins, and plenty of clean towels are necessary in order to demonstrate servant hospitality as the great period of the Three Days begins.

LET THE CHILDREN COME

Is your parish still practicing a kind of "representational" footwashing where only a few persons actively participate in this liturgical action? Make an invitation to the whole worshiping assembly to share in the footwashing. Establish stations, not unlike communion stations, to which people would process and take a seat. A minister would wash the feet of the first person in line. That person would, in turn, wash the feet of the next person in line, and so on, until all have shared in the footwashing. This way parents can wash the feet of children. Siblings, who might usually be rivals, can minister to one another following the example of Jesus to love as he has loved.

185

MUSIC FOR WORSHIP
GATHERING
LBW 104	In the cross of Christ I glory
WOV 666	Great God, your love has called us here

PSALM 116
Brown, Teresa. "The Blessing Cup" in PS2.

Farlee, Robert Buckley. PW, Cycle C.

Glynn, John. "Lord, How Can I Repay" in PS2.

Haugen, Marty. "Ps. 116: Our Blessing Cup" in RS.

Schalk, Carl. "Now I Will Walk at Your Side" in *Sing Out! A Children's Psalter.* WLP 7191.

HYMN OF THE DAY
LBW 126	Where charity and love prevail
	TWENTY-FOURTH

INSTRUMENTAL RESOURCES

Busarow, Donald. "Twenty-fourth" in *All Praise to You, Eternal Lord.* AFP 11-9076. Org.

Hobby, Robert. "Twenty-fourth" in *Three Lenten Hymn Settings.* MSM 10-311. Org.

Long, Larry. "Twenty-fourth" in *By Love We Thus Are Bound.* AFP 11-10519. Org.

ALTERNATE HYMN OF THE DAY
LBW 199	Thee we adore, O hidden Savior
WOV 663	When twilight comes

COMMUNION
LBW 206	Lord, who the night you were betrayed
WOV 710	One bread, one body

OTHER SUGGESTIONS
OBS 92	O grant us, Christ, a deep humility

ADDITIONAL HYMNS AND SONGS
LBW 127	It happened on that fateful night
WOV 709	Eat this bread
AYG 76	With the body that was broken

MUSIC FOR THE DAY
AT THE FOOTWASHING

Aston, Peter. "I Give You a New Commandment." GIA G-4331. 2 pt, org.

Durufle, Maurice. "Ubi Caritas." PRE 312-41253. SATB.

Farlee, Robert Buckley. "Mandatum." AFP 11-10535. SATB.

Leavitt, John. "Ubi Caritas." CLP SV9113. SATB.

WOV 665 Ubi caritas et amor

WOV 765 Jesu, Jesu, fill us with your love

CHORAL

Elgar, Edward. "Ave verum corpus" in *The New Church Anthem Book.* OXF 0-19-353109-7. SATB, org.

Ellingboe, Bradley. "Love Consecrates the Humblest Act." AFP 11-10600. SATB, ob.

Fay, Peter. "O Sacred and Blessed Feast: O Sacrum Convivium." AFP 11-10841. SATB.

Ferguson, John. "Gift of Finest Wheat." GIA G-3089. SATB, org, cong.

Haugen, Marty. "Triduum Hymn: Wondrous Love." GIA G-3544. SATB, cong, gtr, kybd, bass inst.

Kihlken, Henry. "Thee We Adore." MUS M70-22. SATB.

Messiaen, Olivier. "O Sacrum Convivium." DUR 12.742. SATB.

Music, David. "An Upper Room with Evening Lamps Ashine." AFP 11-10068. SATB, kybd, opt cong.

Praetorius, Michael. "O Lord, We Praise Thee." CPH 97-509. SATB, solos, inst/org.

Schack, David. "When You Woke That Thursday Morning." MSM 50-3030. SATB, opt C inst, org.

CHILDREN'S CHOIRS

Kemp, Helen. "A Lenten Love Song." CGA-486. U, kybd.

Livingston Jr., Hugh. "To Thy Table, Lord." LOR 10/1348L. SAB, kybd, opt C inst.

KEYBOARD/INSTRUMENTAL

Biery, James. "Prelude on Ubi caritas" in *Three Plainchants for Organ,* ed. Lynn Trapp. MSM 10-513. Org.

Messiaen, Olivier. "Le Banquet Céleste." LED. Org.

Near, Gerald. "Ubi caritas et amor" in *Saint Augustine's OrganBook.* AUR AE86. Org.

Organ, Anne Krentz. "Partita on 'Adoro te Devote.'" AFP 11-10819. Pno/kybd.

HANDBELL

Helman, Michael. "Gift of Finest Wheat." AFP 11-10872. 3-5 oct, ch.

Nelson, Susan T. "A Plainchant Meditation—Morning Suite." AFP 11-10696. 3 oct.

PRAISE ENSEMBLE

Baloche, Paul, and Claire Cloninger. "As Bread That Is Broken" in *Integrity's Hosanna! Music Songbook,* vol. 10. INT.

Courtney, Craig. "Thy Will Be Done." BEC BP 1263. SATB.

Paris, Twila. "Lamb of God" in *Maranatha! Music's Praise Chorus Book,* 2d. ed. MAR.

186

APRIL 2, 1999

GOOD FRIDAY

INTRODUCTION

On this day the church gathers to hear the proclamation of the Passion, to pray for the life of the world, and to meditate on the life-giving cross. The ancient title for this day—the triumph of the cross—reminds us that the church gathers to offer thanksgiving for the wood of the tree on which hung our salvation.

PRAYER OF THE DAY

Almighty God, we ask you to look with mercy on your family, for whom our Lord Jesus Christ was willing to be betrayed and to be given over to the hands of sinners and to suffer death on the cross; who now lives and reigns with you and the Holy Spirit, one God, forever and ever.

or

Lord Jesus, you carried our sins in your own body on the tree so that we might have life. May we and all who remember this day find new life in you now and in the world to come, where you live and reign with the Father and the Holy Spirit, now and forever.

READINGS

Isaiah 52:13—53:12

Today's reading reinterprets the common idea that suffering is God's punishment for sin: "You get what you deserve." What is new is the idea that the innocent sufferer brings benefits for the community. The suffering and death of the servant serve God's purposes: the redemption of God's people.

Psalm 22

My God, my God, why have you forsaken me? (Ps. 22:1)

Hebrews 10:16-25 *or* Hebrews 4:14-16; 5:7-9

The writer to the Hebrews uses the Hebrew scriptures to understand the meaning of Christ's death on the cross. Like a great priest, Jesus offered his own blood as a sacrifice for our sins so that now we can worship God with confidence and hope.

John 18:1—19:42

On Good Friday, the story of Jesus' passion—from his arrest to his burial—is read in its entirety from the gospel of John.

BIDDING PRAYER

See *LBW, Ministers Edition*, pages 139–142; or *Book of Common Worship*, pages 283–286.

IMAGES FOR PREACHING

What's so good about it? Jesus is dead. Disciples betrayed, denied, and abandoned him. All their hopes were crucified with him—not only the hopes about *him*, but the hope about *themselves* as well, about who they were and what they might become. This is a dark night of disillusionment.

What a strange way for the story to end. With disillusionment! Ah, but there is nothing more deadly than our wish dreams. Remember the beginning of the preparation—the wilderness and the garden? The problem began with a wish dream, with wanting to be like God. "God, save us from our dreams!"

This day, however, is not mired in morose breast-beating and guilt-laden selfrecrimination. It is the *victory* of the cross which is at the center of the celebration. In John's telling of the tale, Jesus goes the way of the cross always in control. The cross is his throne where he holds court. He truly is the king!

But even the victory of the cross does not soften the spasm we experience as we hear the old, familiar story again. Echoes of last night's meal and washing float back: "Here, I am doing this for you." He knew! He knows. Even now. And still he does it: loves us, calls us, dies for us.

Our pilgrimage is really not complete until we are disillusioned, undone. Our wish dreams need to be shattered by the stark reality of this gruesome death. *That* is the victory of the cross. Lots of homiletic talk will not fill the bill this day. John's story, well told, will. Ancient prayers which have a shock value that still disarms us might also do the trick. So will action: the cross carried before us. "Behold, the life-giving cross on which was hung the Savior of the world "And silence. We need to sit and think and take it all in and pray and wait. . . .

187

WORSHIP MATTERS

One of the most ancient traditions of the church is to give those who gather for the liturgy of Good Friday the opportunity to venerate the cross. On this day when we are most directly aware of the great cost of our salvation, it is helpful to place before the assembly a graphic reminder of the lengths to which God has gone to offer salvation to the whole world. A simple form of veneration is included in the liturgy of Good Friday when, as a large wooden cross is brought into the church, the assembly is invited to behold the wood of the cross and then to sing a hymn. Often members of the assembly are encouraged to gather around the cross for prayer at the conclusion of the service. In some places, the assembly is invited to come forward and offer some form of devotion before the cross—kneeling, bowing profoundly, or kissing the cross—while silence is observed. Veneration of the cross takes many forms, but each is designed to impress upon the worshiper that apart from the mystery of the holy cross there is no life for a shattered world.

LET THE CHILDREN COME

Is the Good Friday liturgy a service in which children are welcome? This service is deeply contemplative. There is more silence than usual. The bidding prayers take time. Put together, does this mean that there are fewer children present? Special family services have been tried in some congregations. Might that be out of character with the solemn nature of this day? Good Friday needs to be the way it is. Even though everything is stripped bare, bring children. Make sure worship planners and leaders attend to the details of this day which may interest children: darkness and light, and the substance of a rough-hewn cross. Parents with very small children might know that they could leave at any time without apology.

MUSIC FOR WORSHIP

GATHERING

The liturgy begins in silence on Good Friday.

HYMNS FOR THE PASSION READING

LBW 92	Were you there
LBW 111	Lamb of God, pure and sinless
LBW 115	Jesus, I will ponder now
LBW 116/7	O sacred head, now wounded
WOV 667	Stay here

PSALM 22

Farlee, Robert Buckley. PW, Cycle A.

Haugen, Marty. PCY, vol. 1.

Schiavone, John. "Ps 22: My God, My God, Why Have You Abandoned Me" in STP, vol. 3.

Smith, Alan. "My God, My God" in PS2.

HYMN OF THE DAY

LBW 118	Sing, my tongue
	FORTUNATUS NEW

ALTERNATE HYMN OF THE DAY

LBW 92	Were you there
WOV 668	There in God's garden

ADDITIONAL HYMNS AND SONGS

LBW 482	When I survey the wondrous cross
LW 121	Upon the cross extended
G2 295	Triduum Hymn
UMH 425	O crucified Redeemer

MUSIC FOR THE DAY

CHORAL

Albrecht, Mark. "Lamb of God." AFP 11-10670. SATB, pno.

Bach, J. S. "Crucifixus" in *Mass in B minor*. SATB, org.

Bouman, Paul. "Behold the Lamb of God." CPH 98-108. SA, org.

Copley, Evan. "Surely He Hath Borne Our Griefs." AFP 11-2240. SATB.

Hillert, Richard. "Surely He Hath Borne Our Griefs." CPH 98-159. SATB.

Isaac, Heinrich. "Upon the Cross Extended." GIA G-293. SATB, opt kybd.

Jeep, Johann. "Lamb of God, Pure and Holy" in *Lift up Your Hearts*. CPH 97-621. SATB.

Johnson, David N. "O Dearest Lord, Thy Sacred Head." AFP 11-160. SATB, opt fl, org.

Kihlken, Henry. "We Adore You, Christ Our King." AFP 11-10596. SATB, org.

Mathis, William H. "Ah, Holy Jesus." OXF 3-7800. SATB.

Peloquin, C. Alexander. "My God, My God." GIA G-165. SATB, cant, cong, org.

Pinkham, Daniel. "Near the Cross of Jesus" (STABAT MATER). ECS 4588. SATB, pno.

Proulx, Richard. "Were You There." AFP 11-10571. SATB, sop solo.

Schalk, Carl. "Sing My Tongue" in *Third Crown Choir Book*. CPH 97-596. SAB, org.

Passions

Byrd, William. "The Passion According to St. John." CPH 97-486. SAB, solos.

Kern, Jan. "Chants of the Passion" GIA G-1795. 3 solo vcs.

Victoria, Tomas Luis de'. "The Passion According to St. John." CPH 97-5430. SATB, solos.

CHILDREN'S CHOIRS

Guimont, Michael. "Surely He Bore All My Grief." GIA G-3686. U, vc, kybd/gtr.

How, Martin. "Lenten Litany." BOH OCTB 6080. U/2 pt.

KEYBOARD/INSTRUMENTAL

Brahms, Johannes. "Herzlich tut mich verlangen" in *Orgel Werke*. Henle ed.

Owens, Sam Batt. "They Crucified My Lord" and "Were You There?" in *Three Meditations on Spirituals*. MSM 10-895. Org.

Walcha, Helmut. "Herzliebster Jesu" in *A New Liturgical Year*, ed. John Ferguson. AFP 11-10810.

Young, Jeremy. "Were You There?" (based on *Gymnopedie #3* by Erik Satie) in *At the Foot of the Cross*. AFP 11-10688. Pno.

PRAISE ENSEMBLE

Doane, William H./arr. Lloyd Larson. "Near the Cross." LIN. SATB.

Moen, Don. "All We Like Sheep" in *Integrity's Hosanna! Come and Worship Songbook*. INT.

Smith, Michael W./Robert Sterling. "Agnus Dei." WRD 3010571 16X. SATB.

APRIL 3, 1999

THE RESURRECTION OF OUR LORD
VIGIL OF EASTER

INTRODUCTION

This liturgy's Easter Proclamation announces, "This is the night in which all who believe in Christ are rescued from evil and the gloom of sin, are renewed in grace, and are restored to holiness." It is the very foundation of our Christian faith, and it is what makes this the crowning moment of the church's year. This night the church celebrates the presence of the risen Lord as he brings us to new life in baptism, gives us his body and blood, speaks his word of promise, and comes to us in the Christian community.

PRAYER OF THE DAY

O God, who made this most holy night to shine with the glory of the Lord's resurrection: Stir up in your Church that Spirit of adoption which is given to us in Baptism, that we, being renewed both in body and mind, may worship you in sincerity and truth; through Jesus Christ our Lord, who lives and reigns with you, in the unity of the Holy Spirit, one God, now and forever.

READINGS

Creation: Genesis 1:1—2:4a

Response: Psalm 136:1-9, 23-36

God's mercy endures forever. (Ps. 136:1b)

The Flood: Genesis 7:1-5, 11-18, 8:6-18, 9:8-13

Response: Psalm 46

The Lord of hosts is with us; the God of Jacob is our stronghold. (Ps. 46:4)

The Testing of Abraham: Genesis 22:1-18

Response: Psalm 16

You will show me the path of life. (Ps. 16:11)

Israel's Deliverance at the Red Sea: Exodus 14:10-31; 15:20-21

Response: Exodus 15:1b-13, 17-18

I will sing to the Lord who has triumphed gloriously. (Exod. 15:1)

Salvation Freely Offered to All: Isaiah 55:1-11

Response: Isaiah 12:2-6

With joy you will draw water from the wells of salvation. (Isa. 12:3)

The Wisdom of God: Proverbs 8:1-8, 19-21; 9:4b-6

or Baruch 3:9-15, 32—4:4

Response: Psalm 19

The statutes of the Lord are just and rejoice the heart. (Ps. 19:8)

A New Heart and a New Spirit: Ezekiel 36:24-28

Response: Psalm 42 and Psalm 43

My soul is athirst for the living God. (Ps. 42:2)

The Valley of the Dry Bones: Ezekiel 37:1-14

Response: Psalm 143

Revive me, O Lord, for your name's sake. (Ps. 143:11)

The Gathering of God's People: Zephaniah 3:14-20

    Response: Psalm 98

    Lift up your voice, rejoice and sing. (Ps. 98:5)

The Call of Jonah: Jonah 3:1-10

    Response: Jonah 2:1-3 [4-6] 7-9

    Deliverance belongs to the Lord. (Jonah 2:9)

The Song of Moses: Deuteronomy 31:19-30

    Response: Deuteronomy 32:1-4, 7, 36a, 43a

    The Lord will give his people justice. (Deut. 32:36)

The Fiery Furnace: Daniel 3:1-29

    Response: Song of the Three Young Men 35-65

    Sing praise to the Lord and highly exalt him forever.
    (Song of the Three Young Men 35b)

NEW TESTAMENT READING

Romans 6:3-11

    Christians are baptized into the death of Christ, and are also
    joined to Christ's resurrection.

Response: Psalm 114

    Tremble, O earth, at the presence of the Lord. (Ps. 114:7)

GOSPEL

Matthew 28:1-10

    Christ's resurrection is an earthshaking story. News of it
    spreads with urgency.

COLOR   White *or* Gold

THE PRAYERS

Rejoicing in the resurrection, let us remember in prayer the church, the world, and all those in need.

A BRIEF SILENCE.

Bring your church safely through the waters to the promised land. We pray:

Hear us, risen Lord.

Nourish the newly baptized with your life-giving food and drink. We pray:

Hear us, risen Lord.

Strengthen the leaders of nations to work for the freedom of all who are oppressed. We pray:

Hear us, risen Lord.

Deliver from suffering all who live with poverty, distress, or illness (especially . . .). We pray:

Hear us, risen Lord.

Guide us to care for the earth and its resources. We pray:

Hear us, risen Lord.

Feed us at your table, and use us to declare the glorious triumph of your resurrection. We pray:

Hear us, risen Lord.

HERE OTHER INTERCESSIONS MAY BE OFFERED.

Bring us, with all your saints whose vigil has now ended, to the eternal victory of the Lamb's high feast. We pray:

Hear us, risen Lord.

Receive our prayers and hopes, O God, and fill us with the risen life of Christ our Lord.

Amen

IMAGES FOR PREACHING

The preaching of the Easter Vigil is in the images themselves—atoms of raw experience waiting to ignite and combine as molecules of understanding inside our brains, a biochemistry of new life.

Darkness. Quiet. Gathered outside the worship space. The last time we were in there it was dark and bare. The voice in the night proclaims an illogical contradiction: "May the light of Christ, rising in glory, dispel the darkness of our hearts and minds." Words flung at the darkness. And then, the sound of flint and steel. Sparks flying out of the darkness, a light which could never be seen in the day. The spark hits the tinder, the breath blows and ignites—a flame!

"The light of Christ!" Flames multiplying, light growing. An ancient song passed on and on for centuries and now arriving for us; flames spreading, risen Christ moving, moving into the world, into the future. Waxen wounds bearing the sweetness of incense, a glory hidden in the pain under the mark of the nail. "This is the night!" Here! Now! It is happening again, among us.

The old, old story is once-upon-a-time, but in the telling beside the flaming candle, with the atoms of raw experience so swirling all around us, something happens. Something ignites! This is our story! This is our victory, our new life, just as surely as it is our heads and our bodies which have passed through baptismal waters.

How to make it happen? It already has! But it will happen again. Just do it right. Then, get out of the way. . . .

WORSHIP MATTERS

Just as the reading of scripture requires careful preparation, so also care should be taken to rehearse the actions of the liturgy with those who will lead the celebration.

This carefulness is particularly true for the great Vigil of Easter, a service consisting of four main parts, and including ritual actions that occur only on this night. Everyone with a leadership role for the service should be included, no matter how simple, not only to insure that the service goes smoothly, but so that each person understands the importance of the parts everyone will play. A particularly helpful way to rehearse is to gather the entire group for devotions and for a brief overview of the entire service. Small group rehearsals form the second part of the preparation, with acolytes in one place, readers in another, the baptismal party in a third, ushers in a fourth, and finally the presider and other ministers in a fifth. Finally, all the groups should be brought together to "walk through" the entire service. Simpler, but similar rehearsals, are helpful for the Sunday assembly and for other special services throughout the year.

LET THE CHILDREN COME

One of the most vivid experiences for both children and adults at the Easter Vigil is the service of light. First, the fire gives light to the paschal candle, the light of Christ. Then, the light of Christ is shared with others and given to each person. This action will be repeated at baptisms that night. Before the liturgy, show children how to hold the candles they will receive during the vigil. Show them how to receive the flame from others and how to shield the flame with their hand.

MUSIC FOR WORSHIP
SERVICE MUSIC
AROUND THE GREAT FIRE

Berthier, Jacques. "Within Our Darkest Night" in *Songs and Prayers from Taizé.* GIA.

AROUND THE LIGHT OF CHRIST

Batastini, Robert. "Exsultet (Easter Proclamation)." GIA G-2351.
U chant.

"The Exsultet" in *The Psalter: Psalms and Canticles for Singing.* WJK.

"Rejoice Now, All Heavenly Choirs" in *Music for the Vigil of Easter.* AFP.

AROUND THE READINGS

Reponses to all readings in PW, Cycle C.

First Reading

Hopson, Hal. "O Praise the Lord Who Made All Beauty." CGA 143.
U, kybd.

Smith, Alan. "God's Love is For Ever!" in PS2.

Second Reading

Cherwien, David. "God Is Our Refuge and Strength." MSM 80-800.
U, org.

Third Reading

Inwood, Paul. "Centre of My Life" in PS2.

Fourth Reading

Barker, Michael. "Miriam's Song." CGA 740. U, kybd, opt tamb.

Daw, Carl, Jr. "Metrical Canticles #25 and #26" in *To Sing God's Praise.* HOP 921. Cong, kybd.

Gibbons, John. "Canticle of Moses" in PS2.

Fifth Reading

Lindh, Jody. "Behold, God Is My Salvation." CPH 98-3193. U/2 pt, org.

Rusbridge, Barbara. "Sing A Song To The Lord" in PS1.

WOV 635   Surely it is God who saves me

Sixth Reading

Cox, Joe. "Psalm 19" in *Psalms for the People of God.* SMP 45/1037S.
Cant, choir, cong, kybd.

Ogden, David. "You, Lord, Have the Message of Eternal Life" in PS2.

Seventh Reading

Cox, Joe. "Psalm 43" in *Psalms for the People of God.* SMP 45/1037S.
Cant, choir, cong, kybd.

Howells, Herbert. "Like as the Hart." OXF 42.066. SATB, org.

Hurd, Bob. "As the Deer Longs" in PS2.

LBW 452   As pants the hart for cooling streams

Ninth Reading

Johnson, Alan. "All the Ends of the Earth" in PS1.

Jothen, Michael. "O Sing Ye!" BEC BP1128. U, kybd.

Tenth Reading

WOV 752   I, the Lord of sea and sky

Twelfth Reading

Daw Jr., Carl. "Metrical Canticles 13 and 14" in *To Sing God's Praise.* HOP 921. Cong, kybd.

Proulx, Richard. "Song of the Three Children." GIA G-1863.
U, opt 2 pt, cant, cong, perc, org.

AROUND THE FONT

"A Litany of the Saints" and "Springs of water, bless the Lord" in *Welcome to Christ: Lutheran Rites for the Catechumanate.* AFP 3-142.

Taylor-Howell, Susan. "You Have Put on Christ." CGA 325. U/3 pt, opt orff.

Trapp, Lynn. "Music for the Rite of Sprinkling." MSM 80-901.
SATB, org.

WOV 694   You have put on Christ

PSALM 114

Farlee, Robert Buckley in PW, Cycle C.

Hopson, Hal. *Psalm Refrains and Tones.* HOP 425.

The Psalter—Psalms and Canticles for Singing. WJK.

HYMN OF THE DAY

LBW 210   At the Lamb's high feast we sing
            SONNE DER GERECHTIGKEIT

VOCAL RESOURCES

Cherwien, David. "At the Lamb's High Feast." CPH 98-2864. SATB,
    opt tpt, cong.

Leavitt, John. "At the Lamb's High Feast." GIA G-2980. SATB, cong,
    brass quartet, timp, org.

INSTRUMENTAL RESOURCES

Burkhardt, Michael. "Sonne der Gerechtigheit" in *Five Easter Season
    Hymn Improvisations, set 2.* MSM 10-412. Org.

Ferguson, John. "Partita on 'At the Lamb's High Feast We Sing.'"
    MSM 10-400. Org.

Organ, Anne Krentz. "Partita on 'Sonne der Gerechtigkeit'" in *Reflec-
    tions on Hymn Tunes for Holy Communion.* AFP 11-10621. Pno.

ALTERNATE HYMN OF THE DAY

LBW 189   We know that Christ is raised

WOV 679   Our Paschal Lamb, that sets us free

COMMUNION

LBW 207   We who once were dead

WOV 671   Alleluia, alleluia, give thanks

SENDING

LBW 131   Christ is risen! Alleluia!

WOV 669   Come away to the skies

ADDITIONAL HYMNS AND SONGS

LBW 132   Come, you faithful, raise the strain
H82 187   Through the Red Sea brought at last
NCH 326   Crashing waters at creation
NCH 308   At the font we start our journey
LEV 143   Wade in the water
WOV 670   When Israel was in Egypt's land

MUSIC FOR THE DAY

CHORAL

Bairstow, Edward. "Sing Ye to the Lord." NOV. SATB, org.

Erickson, Richard. "When Long Before Time." AFP 11-10815. SATB,
    pno, opt C inst.

Proulx, Richard. "Our Paschal Lamb That Sets Us Free." CHA 12-106.
    SATB, org.

Sedio, Mark. "O Night More Light Than Day." SEL 405-531. SATB
    div, solo.

Warren, John. "As Many as Have Been Baptized." MUR HNP020.
    SATB.

Willan, Healey. "Christ Our Passover" in *First Motet Book.* CPH 97-484.
    SATB.

KEYBOARD/INSTRUMENTAL

Lovinfosse, Dennis. "Victory" in *A New Liturgical Year,* ed. John
    Ferguson. AFP 11-10810. Org.

Rowan, William. "Trumpet Processional" in *Two Trumpet Tunes.*
    HOP 344. Org.

Webster, Richard. "Paschal Suite for Organ and Trumpet."
    AFP 11-10831. Org, tpt.

HANDBELL

Hopson, Hal H. "This Joyful Eastertide." CPH 97-5922. 3 or 5 oct.

Morris, Hart. "Go Down, Moses." JEF RW8029. 4 oct, perc.

Sherman, Arnold. "The Strife Is O'er." HOP 1847. 3-5 oct.

Young, Philip M. "This Joyful Eastertide." AFP 11-10767. 2-3 oct.

PRAISE ENSEMBLE

deShazo, Lynn. "More Precious than Silver" in *Maranatha! Music's
    Praise Chorus Book,* 2d ed. MAR.

Hanson, Handt. "I Don't Belong to Me" and "Christ Is Risen" in
    Spirit Calls, Rejoice! CCF.

Mullins, Rich. "I See You" in *Come Celebrate Songbook.* ABI.

APRIL 4, 1999

THE RESURRECTION OF OUR LORD
EASTER DAY

INTRODUCTION

Today is the day God began creation, transforming darkness into light. Today is the day Jesus Christ rose from the darkness of the grave to new life. Today is the day when the church celebrates its birth from the waters of baptism and its new life in the holy supper. Though suffering, injustice, and sin continue to mark the world in which we live, the Christian community goes forth from font and table with Christ's mission to heal, liberate, and forgive. In the Fifty Days of Easter rejoicing, the church asks the question: How does our baptism send us forth in joyful service to the world?

PRAYER OF THE DAY

O God, you gave your only Son to suffer death on the cross for our redemption, and by his glorious resurrection you delivered us from the power of death. Make us die every day to sin, so that we may live with him forever in the joy of the resurrection; through Jesus Christ our Lord, who lives and reigns with you and the Holy Spirit, one God, now and forever.

or

Almighty God, through your only Son you overcame death and opened for us the gate of everlasting life. Give us your continual help; put good desires into our minds and bring them to full effect; through Jesus Christ our Lord, who lives and reigns with you and the Holy Spirit, one God, now and forever.

READINGS

Acts 10:34-43

Peter's sermon, delivered at the home of Cornelius, a Roman army officer, is also a summary of the essential message of Christianity: Everyone who believes in Jesus, whose life, death, and resurrection fulfilled the words of the prophets, "receives forgiveness of sins through his name."

or Jeremiah 31:1-6

Psalm 118:1-2, 14-24

On this day the Lord has acted; we will rejoice and be glad in it. (Ps. 118:24)

Colossians 3:1-4

Easter means new life for us as well as for Christ! The Lord has risen to become our life, which is no longer linked to the uncertainties of this world but is securely "hidden" with Christ in God.

or Acts 10:34-43

John 20:1-18

John's gospel describes the confusion and excitement of the first Easter morn: the stone is moved and the tomb is empty; disciples race back and forth, while angels speak to a weeping woman. Finally, Jesus himself appears as the Lord in unity with God.

or Matthew 28:1-10

COLOR   White *or* Gold

THE PRAYERS

Rejoicing in the resurrection, let us remember in prayer the church, the world, and all those in need.
A BRIEF SILENCE.

That the newly baptized and all who renew their baptismal vows may walk in newness of life, we pray:

Hear us, risen Lord.

That the light of Easter guide all who work for justice and peace in our world, we pray:

Hear us, risen Lord.

That the healing power of the resurrection give hope to all who are unloved and forgotten, poor and hungry, hospitalized and sick (especially . . .), we pray:

Hear us, risen Lord.

That you free us from prejudice, so we may show no partiality as we share the good news of the resurrection, we pray:

Hear us, risen Lord.

That you open our eyes to recognize you in this eucharist and in the suffering and joy of daily life, we pray:

Hear us, risen Lord.

HERE OTHER INTERCESSIONS MAY BE OFFERED.

That as we remember all our beloved dead, you would

193

unite our voices with theirs until we join them at the great and promised feast, we pray:

Hear us, risen Lord.

Receive our prayers and hopes, O God, and fill us with the risen life of Christ our Lord.

Amen

IMAGES FOR PREACHING

The Resurrection of Our Lord presents perhaps the most formidable challenge for Christian proclamation. Since this day is the heart of the matter, sooner or later we find ourselves drawn to speak of the totality of the Christian faith. So much is waiting to be said this day, especially when the preacher considers that in the worshiping community are members of the congregation who will not be seen for another year, as well as potential members who have wandered into the community for the first time. How do we help everyone—the curious, the lapsed, the faithful?

Begin with this: Easter is not what you imagine it to be. It is a strange counterpoint of joy, confusion, and fear. Matthew's version of the story says the women left with "fear and great joy." In John, Mary comes to the tomb weeping, and the risen Jesus is easily confused with a gardener. More than tears cloud Mary's vision. Peter works hard in his Pentecost sermon to lay the groundwork, which will slay and raise a mob that days before had screamed for Jesus' crucifixion and gotten it.

Easter is fifty days, not just because the celebration is big, but because we need at least that much time to make sense of this new configuration of reality. The preacher is helped if at least some of the congregation were present for the full experience of the Three Days. Perhaps reminders of those events can allow those who were not present to "see" it for themselves (and maybe resolve to *be there* next year). The preacher, then, should not succumb to the temptation of trying to "say it all" for the sake of those who stumbled through the door. Rather, think of the fifty days as a single feast and today's particular sermon as the first "paragraph" that raises the question and invites others to come back to unpack the mystery. It is not something we can easily view from a distance as bystanders. "We are witnesses," but even more; Paul raises the staggering possibility at the beginning of the second reading—a thought that will take at least fifty days to consider: "If you have been raised with Christ . . . ."

194

WORSHIP MATTERS

One of the joyful challenges facing worship leaders on Easter Day is accommodating the large number of people who gather for worship. Well-rehearsed ritual action, and perhaps an alternative method for distributing Holy Communion, will keep the service within time constraints. Ushers need to be instructed in gracious hospitality while contending with crowds that may necessitate providing extra seating. Are enough greeters present to assist those who may be attending worship for the first time? And finally, how about recruiting and training a few people for directing traffic outside the church in order to facilitate movement in crowded parking lots and at intersections?

LET THE CHILDREN COME

Today begins a fifty-day celebration. Two things need to be done today to help launch the festivities of Easter. It is time to unbury the alleluias first hidden away on the Transfiguration of Our Lord. The children can join in the opening procession waving the strips of paper with the word alleluia. Include alleluia banners as well. And, if the bulbs planted at the beginning of Lent are in full bloom, make sure they are given away to children to take home. After today, how will the children know that the joy of Easter continues for fifty days?

MUSIC FOR WORSHIP

SERVICE MUSIC

All too often the great musical acclamations of the liturgy (the hymn of praise, alleluia at the gospel, Sanctus) seem anticlimactic amidst all the musical hoopla given to Easter hymns on this day. Strive for balance; consider one of the following embellished versions of the *LBW* liturgies:

Cherwien, David. *Alternatives Within.* AFP 11-10611. Org, opt inst.

Ferguson, John. *Festival Setting of the Communion Liturgy* (*LBW*, setting 2). Full score CPH 6127. Choir 98-2994. Org, SATB, opt brass.

Hillert, Richard. *Festival Setting of the Communion Liturgy* (*LBW*, setting 1). Full score CPH 97-5939. Choral desc 97-2755; hb 97-5958. U with desc, org, brass, ob, timp, 3 oct hb.

GATHERING

LBW 142	Hail thee, festival day!
LBW 151	Jesus Christ is risen today
WOV 674	Alleluia! Jesus is risen!

PSALM 118

Farlee, Robert Buckley. PW, Cycle A.

Geary, Patrick. "Rejoice and Be Glad" in PS2.

Hommerding, Alan J. *Sing Out! A Children's Psalter.* WLP 7191.

Hopson, Hal H. "Psalm 118" in *10 Psalms.* HOP HH 3930. SATB, cong, org.

Hurd, Bob. "This is the Day." OCP 9458. SATB, cong, pno, gtr, 2 tpt.

Shields, Valerie. "Psalm for Easter." MSM 80-405. SATB, cong, org, opt tpt, hb, tamb, tri.

GOSPEL SEQUENCE HYMN

LBW 129   Awake, my heart, with gladness
LBW 137   Christians, to the paschal victim
WOV 612   Halle, halle, hallelujah

HYMN OF THE DAY

LBW 135   The Strife is o'er, the battle done
                VICTORY

VOCAL RESOURCES

Gerike, Henry. "Strife Is O'er, the Battle Done." CPH 98-2446. SATB, tpt.

Praetorius, Michael. "The Strife is O'er, the Battle Done." GIA G-279. SAB.

INSTRUMENTAL RESOURCES

Bock, Almon C. "The Strife Is O'er." AFP 11-10486. 2 oct.

Held, Wilbur. "Victory" in *Six Preludes on Easter Hymns.* CPH 97-5330. Org.

Johnson, David N. "Victory" in *Easter Music for Organ and Brass,* vol. 1. AFP 11-9111. Org, brass.

Sherman, Arnold. "The Strife Is O'er." HOP 1847. 3-5 oct.

ALTERNATE HYMN OF THE DAY

LBW 134   Christ Jesus lay in death's strong bands
WOV 678   Christ has arisen, Alleluia

COMMUNION

LBW 352   I know that my Redeemer lives!
WOV 671   Alleluia, alleluia, give thanks

OTHER SUGGESTIONS

OBS 68   In the fair morning

SENDING

LBW 143   Now all the vault of heaven resounds
WOV 675   This joyful Eastertide

ADDITIONAL HYMNS AND SONGS

LBW 148   Now the green blade rises
WOV 677   Alleluia Canon
H82 180   He is risen, he is risen!

MUSIC FOR THE DAY

CHORAL

Bairstow. Edward C. "The Day Draws on the Golden Light" in *The New Church Anthem Book.* OXF 0-19-353109-7. SATB, org.

Burkhardt, Michael. "Christ the Lord Is Ris'n Again." MSM 50-4024. SATB, opt brass qrt, org.

Christiansen, Paul. "Easter Morning." AFP 11-1057. Also in *The Augsburg Choirbook.* 11-10817. SATB.

Ebeling, Johann G. "Awake, My Heart, with Gladness" in *Be Glad and Sing.* CPH 97-537. SATB, 2 trbl inst, kybd.

Ellingboe, Bradley. "Mary at the Tomb." AFP 11-10833. SATB, pno.

Erickson, Richard. "Come Away to the Skies." AFP 11-10816. SATB, fl, fc.

Franck, Melchior. "This Is the Day the Lord Has Made." GIA G-4039. SATB.

Leavitt, John. "Begin the Song of Glory Now." AFP 11-10666. SATB, org, perc.

Owens, Sam Batt. "Christ the Lord Is Risen." SEL 405-518. 2 pt mxd, org.

Parker, Alice, and Robert Shaw. "On Easter Morn." GSCH 995. SATB.

Vaughan Williams, Ralph. "Christ Our Passover." PAR PPM 08702. SATB or U, brass, org.

Wetzler, Robert. "Easter Dawning at the Tomb." AMSI 708. SATB.

Wold, Wayne. "The Whole World Sings Alleluia." CGA 708. U, kybd.

CHILDREN'S CHOIRS

Caceres, Abe. "This Is the Day." AFP 11-10682. U/SAB, kybd.

Hopson, Hal. "On Earth Has Dawned This Day of Days." CGA 709. 2 pt, pno, opt hb.

Horman, John D. "Easter Song." CGA768. 3 pt trbl/mxd, kybd, opt fl, hb.

Kirkland, Terry. "O Bright Easter Day." KIR K-134. U, opt hb, kybd.

Larsen, Libby. "All Shall Be Well." Schirmer 4261. U, opt 2 pt, trbl solo, rec, tri, kybd.

KEYBOARD/INSTRUMENTAL

Argento, Dominick. "Prelude for Easter Dawning." BOH. Org.

Holman, Derek. "Prelude on 'My Dancing Day'" in *The Bristol Collection,* vol. 2. FLA HF 5078. Org.

Webster, Richard. "Paschal Suite for Organ and Trumpet." AFP 11-10831. Org, tpt.

HANDBELL

Moklebust, Cathy. "We Know That Christ Is Raised" in *Hymn Stanzas for Handbells.* AFP 11-10722. 4–5 oct.

Page, Anna Laura. "The Day of Resurrection" in *Hymn Descants for Ringers and Singers,* vol. 2. Hb ALF 11528. Vcs/kybd 11530. 3 oct, kybd, desc.

Tucker, Sondra K. "Christ the Lord Is Risen Today." CPH 97-6623. Hb 97-6638. Cong, 3–5 oct, org, brass.

Wagner, Douglas E. "Easter Hymn" in *Hymn Descants for Handbells,* set 2. BEC HB10. 3 oct.

Young, Philip M. "Good Christian Friends, Rejoice and Sing." AFP 11-10767. 2–3 oct.

PRAISE ENSEMBLE

Harlan, Benjamin. "Worthy Is the Lamb." LIL AN 2597. SATB.

Holm, Dallas. "Rise Again." BEN 25986-0680-7. SATB.

Oliver, Gary. "Celebrate Jesus" in *Come and Worship Songbook.* INT.

Medema, Ken/arr. Robert Sterling. "Come, Sweet Easter Morning." GSCH A-626. SATB, kybd.

Pote, Allen. "On the Third Day." HOP F-1000. SATB, brass, kybd, hb.

Watson, Wayne. "Almighty" in *Come and Worship Songbook.* INT.

APRIL 4, 1999

THE RESURRECTION OF OUR LORD
EASTER EVENING

196

INTRODUCTION

Easter is a feast. And what feasting can be found in scriptures this evening! The news of God's salvation, brought to the world in the death and resurrection of Christ, is worthy of the grandest of celebrations. The gospel from Luke 24 may remind us that the meal we receive in the sacrament of Holy Communion is a share in Christ's death and resurrection. Like the disciples who met with the Lord on the evening of his resurrection, Christ's words and his supper burn in us as well.

PRAYER OF THE DAY

Almighty God, you give us the joy of celebrating our Lord's resurrection. Give us also the joys of life in your service, and bring us at last to the full joy of life eternal; through your Son, Jesus Christ our Lord, who lives and reigns with you and the Holy Spirit, one God, now and forever.

READINGS

Isaiah 25:6-9

God prepares a splendid feast on the holy mountain. All peoples will toast God's salvation.

Psalm 114

Hallelujah. (Ps. 114:1)

1 Corinthians 5:6b-8

Christ clears out the old yeast in all people, making ready for the purity of the new.

Luke 24:13-49

The resurrected Christ makes himself known to two of the disciples in the breaking of bread. Only upon receiving the bread do the disciples make the connection to the words Christ spoke to them earlier on the road.

COLOR White

SUNDAY, APRIL 4

BENEDICT THE AFRICAN, 1589

Born a slave on the island of Sicily, Benedict joined a community of hermits when he was freed. After serving as superior he returned to his former position of cook, and his fame as a confessor brought many visitors to visit the humble and holy cook. Benedict the Moor, as he is called, is the patron saint of blacks in the United States, and is remembered for his patience and understanding when confronted with racial prejudice.

Benedict the African is a witness to the Easter gospel that sets us free from sin, death, and all forms of oppression. In his honor, sing the Tanzanian "Christ has arisen, alleluia" (WOV 678) or the African American spiritual "I'm so glad Jesus lifted me" (WOV 673).

EASTER

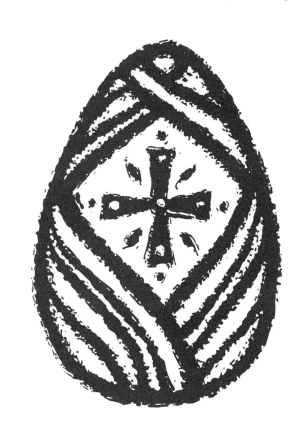

*The meaning of resurrection unfolds
gradually, and keeps expanding*

IMAGES OF THE SEASON

It is a colorful, fertile time. Winter is past; earth awakens. On the high

desert, rains cause the scrubby hillsides to be carpeted for a few weeks

with brilliant purple wildflowers or orange pop-

pies. In other climate zones, bulb flowers paint

the landscape. The scent of lilac travels on the wind. In the city, fresh flowers reappear in sidewalk stands, balcony planters, and window boxes. Hospital and nursing home rooms are brightened by vases of cut flowers from neighborhood gardens. Orchards are places of magic: blossoms pop and unfurl until their trees are so full they can't puff out any more without floating off into the sky as clouds. Then the flowers fade, the trees shrink in volume, and fruit begins to grow and ripen in place of the flowers. But what a vision they had been!

Eastertide is a season of flowering. It is a time of visions and dreams; of waking up (while the earth awakens) to the surprise of resurrection. In early centuries, those newly baptized at the Easter Vigil were given a cup of milk and honey—a symbol of their entry into the land of promise—along with their first taste of Holy Communion. Easter is the church's annual seven-week honeymoon. Like Christmas, it is a season to bask in God's grace, to enjoy the goodness of what God has given. And so we open doors and windows to the temperate air; we create and putter in gardens; we bring nature's gifts of beauty, color, and fragrance into our homes. We marvel at the flowerings of the Spirit as we notice the loveliness flourishing around us. The six weeks of Lent were strenuous and austere. The six months of summer through the end of the liturgical year will provide plenty of opportunity for hard work. For now, we are invited to drink in the wonders of the new life of freedom, sip the milk and honey of the newly reborn in Christ, give play to visions and dreams, and allow the reality of "risen from the dead" to soak in.

The meaning of resurrection unfolds gradually, and keeps expanding. We need time to take it in, and discover what it means for us *this* year, under *these* circumstances. Has it been a relatively quiet year, without dramatic changes? Has there been a recovery from addiction, the

restoration of a broken relationship, healing from an illness? Has there been a death in the family, the loss of a job, the rejection by a loved one? Some years, just surviving is a victory. Our experience affects what we are able to perceive and the meaning we can construct from it. Graduation, confirmation, and marriage are signs of flowering love and maturity. Each transition will bring joy—and unexpected challenges, as well.

It took time for the friends of Jesus to grasp what had taken place at his tomb, although they never grasped it completely. And it took a variety of resurrection appearances—in the morning, at night, beside the tomb, and out along the seashore—to help convince them. In the wisdom of the church the gospel for the Second Sunday of Easter is always the story that begins in a locked room full of frightened people. The doors are bolted against outsiders—and then, suddenly, Jesus is among them, extending peace. He breathes upon them the forgiving, life-giving Spirit, and sends them out in his name. In Cycle A, the Easter season begins *and ends* with this same story—and rightly so: for even we ourselves, who have the first fruits of the Spirit, need repeated encouragement and consolation.

Our Sunday lectionary gospel selection for Easter follows the same structure every year. Easter morning: empty tomb; Second Sunday, Thomas (belief with and without seeing); Third, some other resurrection appearance. The center of the season—week Four—starts with good shepherd; there follow two weeks in Jesus' farewell discourse (and on the 40th day, his Ascension); on the Seventh Sunday, a portion of Jesus' high priestly prayer for the disciples; and on the Day of Pentecost, the gift of the Spirit.

Gradually the risen Lord's physical presence recedes, even as we gain a fuller sense of who he is (the gate for the sheep; the way, the truth, the life) and how he will continue to be among us (through the Advocate, the Spirit of truth). Finally a cloud takes him from our sight, and we spend ten days in prayer waiting to be clothed with power from on high.

Although Jesus has left us, he hasn't left us orphaned. The focus of our liturgical year is about to shift. These ten days give us a chance to prepare for that transition, just as Advent gave us four weeks to prepare for Christ's coming. Since Advent we have immersed ourselves in the mysteries of incarnation and redemption—Christ's identity and ours. During the roughly six months that most Northern Hemisphere residents keep indoors, the focus has largely been inward. We have pondered our baptismal identity: as individuals saved from sin and death, and as a people rescued and formed by God. From the Day of Pentecost until Christ the King—the "outdoors" seasons on our continent—the focus will shift outward: from flowering to bearing fruit. Inspired by the Spirit, we will move out into the world with Christ in mission: spreading the good news of the kingdom, reconciling enemies, healing the sick, and working for justice.

According to the Acts of the Apostles, on the day of Pentecost, Jews from everywhere came on pilgrimage to Jerusalem to thank God for the good gifts of the first fruits of the harvest. The Holy Spirit was poured out upon the believers gathered in the upstairs room, who couldn't wait to proclaim enthusiastically the newest gift from God: sons and daughters shall prophesy; the young shall see visions, and the old shall dream dreams. Acts gives us an exhilarating vision of the young church as it flowers. The baptized—devoted to their life in common, and caring for all in need—did signs and wonders. Daily they spent time in the temple—God's house—and then gathered in their own homes for the breaking of the bread.

They moved from the locked room (where they didn't stay locked up for too long) to the upstairs room—which may have been decorated with bunches of fresh-cut flowers from the surrounding hills; whose walls may have echoed from their stories, songs, and laughter; whose windows may have been open to let in a view of the city by day and the fragrance of warm spring nights. How did they get to this prayerful place of openness to the Spirit?

"In my Father's house are many dwelling places," Jesus had reassured them. "I go to prepare a place for you." Our dream house is already under construction: a place to call home, where we can be free from harm, embraced by love, and inspired to grow. And we ourselves are being built into this spiritual house—*God's* dream house—upon the stone rejected by the builders, the living cornerstone. He is risen indeed! Alleluia, alleluia, alleluia!

199

ENVIRONMENT AND ART FOR THE SEASON

The Easter season is the queen of feasts. It lasts for a "week of weeks." Note that the Sundays within these fifty days are Sundays of Easter, not merely a device for counting the days between Easter Sunday and Pentecost. While spring officially arrived during Lent, its true essence may not appear until sometime during this season. This season is brimming over with festivity. Graduations, Mother's Day, weddings, and the beginning of the summer vacation season on Memorial Day weekend (or Victoria Day in Canada), all lend an air of exuberance during this time of year. But amidst all these more secular pursuits, the church has its story of the resurrection to tell. Let our festivity in this season primarily be in praise of the joy of Easter.

EXTERIOR ENVIRONMENT

Outdoor planting is a sign of the earth's renewal during this season, especially in northern climes. The church can use this natural annual return of another growing season to proclaim new life through the resurrection. In urban areas where parks and lawns may be limited, churches often have at least a small lawn, or just enough open space for window boxes and placing large pots directly on the sidewalk. Take advantage of these spaces to brighten up the neighborhood and to proclaim the joy in new growth. "Now the green blade rises," proclaims the spirited Easter carol. Congregations having larger exterior spaces might consider using them in special ways to proclaim the joy of creation and God's care of the earth.

INTERIOR ENVIRONMENT

In the narthex and other gathering spaces during this season, consider placing containers of spring flowering bulbs. Decorate walls with brightly colored banners or artwork appropriate to this season. Scenes from the various gospels may provide inspiration for seasonal visual artwork used during these weeks: Jesus' appearance to Thomas (John 20), Jesus' appearance on the road to Emmaus (Luke 24), Jesus as the good shepherd (John 10), and the ascension (Luke 24), among others.

The use of banners in the worship space beginning with Easter Day is very appropriate. If alleluia was "buried" prior to Lent, be sure to bring it back now. White paraments, white flowers, and continued use of a lit paschal candle through to Pentecost Day will help to proclaim the special significance of this joyous season.

The paschal cycle comes to a close on the day of Pentecost, with the celebration of the Spirit's sending to the church. Paraments for this occasion are red. Flowers are traditionally red as well, along with members of the congregation being encouraged to dress in red clothing. It is the birthday of the church. All the festivity appropriate to Easter or Christmas is appropriate on this occasion as well.

The final impression on the day of Pentecost is one of explosive expansion. We go beyond the walls of our church. We extend the boundaries of our witness.

PREACHING WITH THE SEASON

The canonical gospels are incredibly conservative in their handling of the resurrection tradition, and this conservatism gives these narratives their ring of authenticity. No canonical gospel describes the act of resurrection itself. Matthew comes closest to a description, recounting the earthquake, the appearance of the angel, and the reaction of the guards. But even in this account, we never see Jesus emerge from the tomb. What the gospels give us, instead, are two distinct traditions concerning Jesus' resurrection. First is the tradition of the empty tomb. Women, and perhaps disciples themselves, come to the tomb and find it empty; an angel interprets its meaning for them. Second, a separate tradition recounts the appearances of the risen Jesus to the disciples. We know these traditions circulated separately because Paul seems to be familiar with the appearances tradition but does not mention the empty tomb. Furthermore, Mark seems to know the empty tomb tradition but never reports an appearance.

Eastertide, however, brings these two traditions together, just as Matthew, Luke, and John do. The fusion of the two traditions, together with the superb narrative skill of the evangelists, creates the unitary celebration of Jesus' resurrection. Although majority scholarly opinion might find it difficult to agree, the gospels' stories, even with their apparent contradictions, feel like they transmit the memory of eyewitnesses to these events. But Eastertide, as the gospels themselves suggest, is far more radical in its assessment of what exactly it is we celebrate in the fifty days.

To understand this more radical celebration, it is important to recognize that the New Testament seems to have four different models of what exactly happened after Jesus rose from the dead. Mark leaves the story dizzyingly open-ended—women running from the tomb in fear, refusing to tell anyone anything; Jesus just "disappears." Luke creates the model that shapes the calendar of Eastertide: the risen Jesus spends forty days with his disciples, then ascends into heaven. Ten days later, the Holy Spirit is given to the disciples and the church is born. Matthew, and to a certain extent also Paul, have yet another model: for them the risen Christ never really departs from his disciples. "And remember, I am with you always, to the end of the age" (Matt. 28.20). Paul also counts the appearance of the risen Lord to him as of equal weight and character with other resurrection appearances (1 Cor. 15:8). And John, finally, has a fourth model—the most radical of them all, with some interesting parallels also to Paul: on Easter evening the risen Jesus stands among the disciples and breathes his Spirit (*ruach, pneuma*) into them. Given biblical anthropology from Genesis 1, this is clearly a new creation. It means that disciples carry within themselves the resurrection life of the risen Christ. We are, to use Paul's phrase, "body of Christ." Or to state it as sharply as we possibly can, Jesus is now alive and well and living in Boulder, Colorado; Poughkeepsie, New York; and Jakarta, Indonesia.

The significance of all this for our paschal celebration and preaching is very profound. These four models of the meaning of Jesus' resurrection each have their own set of implications. Mark's open-ended Easter suggests the story is unfinished and needs to be completed by us. Luke's approach, which has undoubtedly shaped the paschal tradition the most due to its influence on the calendar, sees the "Jesus time" as ended and the "church's time" now here. However, the Matthew/John traditions, with their emphasis on the continuing presence of Christ in his people are, perhaps, the strongest of the four strategies and the scheme that will work the best for the greatest number of persons living in North America in the late 1990s. For us, the Easter stories seem distant, the "sign painted in the faded credulity of earlier ages," to use a phrase from John Updike's "Seven Stanzas at Easter." But Easter is not a spectator sport, something to be viewed at a distance or observed neutrally by an objective witness. No, Matthew and John would urge us to *enter into* the mystery, to let the warm breath of the risen Christ blow into our bodies and raise us with him to new life.

Here it becomes obvious just how important the Three Days are to this entire pivot-point of the Christian faith. We cannot just preach *about* Easter; we must use our words to create a speech-event through which we will experience it with the disciples. And likewise for the disciples themselves, the experience of Jesus' death and resurrection was not simply something that happened *to him*; it also profoundly happened *to them*. When he died, so did they. When he was raised and came among them, not with condemnation but with forgiveness and commissioning, they too were raised to new life. Why, after all, does a death on a cross and a resurrection mean salvation? Where is the magic formula that states that this particular combination of events will fix the world's problems? Christian theology did not come out of a mystic, cosmic recipe book. Rather, it was born out of the experience of women and men who toasted Jesus' death the night before he died (not knowing what they were doing), died with him when they realized they had betrayed/denied/forsaken him, and rose again to his new life when he came among them with forgiveness and a job to do. In the solidarity of that experience they came to believe his own interpretation of this death and resurrection he himself gave to them the night he was betrayed: "Here. Take this. It is for you." The Three Days are the absolutely essential way for the faithful to enter this feast. Their drama and liturgical power provide the necessary experiential ingredients for a proper paschal celebration. And Lent, if it is to do anything, ought to bring the faithful to the Three Days. No one can expect to understand the feast from the inside if they just show up on Sunday morning to smell the flowers and hear the trumpets. They really will find it impossible to be anything more than passive spectators, spiritual gawkers waiting to be entertained.

Once these basic principles are grasped, the rest of the paschal celebration begins to fall into place and make sense. Curiously, from this perspective, the most important day of the season, next to Easter Day itself, is the Second Sunday of Easter. This climax of the fourth gospel states most explicitly the reality of the paschal mystery: *Christ is in you*. Worship leaders will have a choice how they will get to that second Sunday climax,

201

202

since we have an option for the gospel that is to be read on the Resurrection of Our Lord. While choosing Matthew makes sense in order to complete the passion narrative begun a week earlier, John may be the stronger choice since it sets the stage for the Thomas climax a week later. (It also completes the Johannine passion read on Good Friday.) The Third Sunday of Easter has us dip into the appearances tradition, accompanying disciples who speak with the risen Christ on the road to Emmaus. He is hidden from them in their face-to-face conversation but amazingly appears to them in the breaking of the bread, signaling in Luke's own way even his conviction that Christ is now sacramentally present to the church. From the Fourth Sunday of Easter to the close of the fifty days, various pericopes from the Johannine corpus urge us to go back to the words of Jesus once again and hear them in a fresh way, knowing already what the climax of this gospel will be. Yes, he was talking about it all along, even when he was speaking about shepherds, about being the way and truth and life, promising they will not be orphaned, praying for his disciples and claiming "all mine are yours."

The first readings of Eastertide take us into the Book of Acts. The first three weeks give us an opportunity to hear Peter's sermon on the day of Pentecost. It is a gutsy example of politically charged preaching, telling a crowd they are responsible for the death of God's own appointed representative. Viewed naively, the sermon seems profoundly arrogant. But if we realize that its speaker is one who himself had died as a denier and been raised to new life, this sermon becomes a wonderful example of how the early Christian experience is commended to others as a possibility for renewal and new life. The next two Sundays give us glimpses into the life of the early Christian community. They really *are* a community, profoundly reorganizing their communal, social, and economic life in light of the new reality. But they are also a community that continues to share in Jesus' suffering and death as well, as the stoning of Stephen graphically reminds us. The Sixth Sunday of Easter shows us Paul at the Areopagus, suggesting that somehow the risen Christ has already preceded him there and is waiting within a "heathen" culture to greet those who might hear his voice. The remainder of the first readings revolve around the stories of Ascension and Pentecost, helping us to keep those parts of the feast.

Second readings this Eastertide are from the first letter of Peter. Here we see a portrait of a beleaguered church, facing imminent persecution. Is this the new age? Is this what Jesus' victory over death means? Well, yes. The gospel for the Second Sunday of Easter gives us the clue of this victory in a profound but easily overlooked detail: When the risen Jesus comes among the disciples and stands in their midst, the first thing he does is to show them his hands and his side. They still bear the gory marks of his crucifixion! This evidence is incredible. If we were to construct the story we would never frame it this way. The risen Christ is beyond death, and the marks of that suffering should no longer be evident. But no, the risen Jesus carries the wounds of his crucifixion with him into the new age. It is an extremely important dimension of the paschal mystery. Perhaps we come to this feast hoping all our problems will dissolve in the warmth of springtime sun. They will not. To desire such fantasies is to enter again into that world of wish-dreams that was shattered in the Three Days. No, the world of the risen Christ is still a world in which conflicts and headaches and problems clamor to be solved. We may even encounter persecution. But these cannot undo the good news. The good news is that God is using even evil—even the cross—as a tool for new life. We no longer seek to escape our problems. Now we see that the way to life is to pass through them.

Our Lenten pilgrimage has come to its destination. In the Three Days we have been buried with Christ and raised with him. Now it is time to enter the mystery.

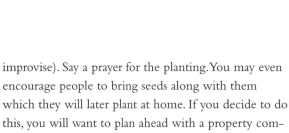

PLANNING AHEAD for the SEASON

Easter is not one day but *fifty* days. How can you keep the festivity going

for a week of weeks? If you have a profusion of flowers for Easter Day but

none in the following weeks, everything else will

be seen as a letdown. Rather than having people

sign up for special flowers that will grace the worship space only on Easter Day, have a list for offering spring flowers on the other Sundays in the Easter season as well. This time of the year has a large number of anniversaries, graduations, and other occasions which people may wish to honor with additional flowers anyway.

If you have a procession on Easter Day consider having a procession for each of the Sundays of Easter. If your congregation has Holy Communion just at designated Sundays of the month and on festivals, consider having communion each week throughout the Easter season, since the whole fifty days are a festival.

If you have celebrated Lent as a season of repentance, Easter is a season for returning to our baptism joyfully. Rather than having a "confession of sin" each Sunday, why not have a brief remembrance of baptism with a prayer of thanksgiving from sin (see the prayer that concludes the *paschal blessing* from morning prayer in *LBW*, p. 141, as an example). Such a remembrance could take place at the baptismal font, with people being invited to come to the font themselves for a baptismal remembrance, or even to be sprinkled with water from the font. An Easter hymn with strong baptismal connections (or a baptismal hymn with strong Easter connections) might follow as the entrance hymn.

Does your congregation pray for the seedtime and planting in any way (particularly appropriate if you observe a harvest festival in the fall)? The three weekdays immediately preceding the Ascension of Our Lord were traditionally a time for remembering the planting (Rogation Days). One way of observing this tradition might be to go outside (weather permitting, of course) at the close of the service on the Sixth Sunday of Easter for a brief time of prayer in the church's lawn or garden (if you don't have such a space, figure out a way to

improvise). Say a prayer for the planting. You may even encourage people to bring seeds along with them which they will later plant at home. If you decide to do this, you will want to plan ahead with a property committee or gardening group. Perhaps it would be a good time to plant a tree or a biblical herb garden.

Is the Ascension of Our Lord ever celebrated in your congregation? One way to celebrate the day may be to combine a Holy Communion service with an evening meal, perhaps even outdoors. It may be an opportunity for more informal worship, but it will still require careful planning. Begin your time together with a hymn and a brief table prayer. Have your meal. While people are still gathered around the tables, continue with the prayer of the day, one or more of the readings (the gospel is key), a sermon (probably brief), intercessions, the peace, the communion (still gathered around tables), and the dismissal. Perhaps you can serve dessert after the dismissal. Keep everything appropriate for persons of all ages. Think about the mechanics of how people will receive the communion elements at tables while seated and how any unconsumed elements will be gathered after distribution.

The Easter season can be a time for each person to reflect on his or her vocation in daily life as a preparation for celebrating an affirmation of vocation at Pentecost. (See resources for affirmations in *Occasional Services*, pp. 147–149; and *Welcome to Christ: Lutheran Rites for the Catechumenate*, pp. 59–61.) Small group experiences, Sunday school sessions, adult forums, and other occasions could all be used as ways to prepare for this (work ahead with appropriate leaders of these ministries). Each person should have the time to reflect on specific opportunities for serving God in daily life. (This reflection is not to be focused on work performed only for the church, but rather on a myriad of work, home, volunteer, and other daily life settings in which God's will can be done.)

203

The day of Pentecost is often celebrated as a baptismal festival in congregations. While a number of congregations may read the Acts passage in half a dozen or more languages on this day, the effect may not be the same as what was actually experienced on the first day of Pentecost, that is, each person hearing the proclamation in *their own language* (for in fact the reading of many languages may simply obscure the one language that everyone is accustomed to hearing at worship).

Congregations that regularly use more than one language at services of worship might consider Pentecost as a time to have bilingual or multilingual worship (if the congregation has members who use sign language, it might be incorporated into the day as well). While it may be rather difficult to provide a simultaneous translation of everything in a service (not to mention taking the time to read everything twice), consider having various parts of the service sung or spoken in some combination of the various languages used while a written translation is provided for worshipers who do not speak the language employed at the moment. In truly multilingual parishes or neighborhoods, the whole range of languages used in that setting might be used in the prayers (while again providing a written translation so that all might understand). Any experiences incorporated into this day should ultimately underscore the unity of the church, rather than having people walk away from services with the feeling of being divided from one another.

ORDO FOR THE SEASON

As the queen of seasons (see the great hymn by John of Damascus, LBW 132, "Come, you faithful, raise the strain"), the whole seven weeks of the Easter season deserves a type of solemnity not accorded to the rest of the year. If at no other time, the gathering rite during this season might include all the options (confession and forgiveness, entrance hymn, Kyrie, and hymn of praise). If an order for confession and forgiveness is desired during this season, one that also emphasizes the joy the baptized people of God have in the resurrection might be used (see the alternate worship texts given here in this season's materials). If the confession is led from the font, the connection to baptism may be further enhanced. Sprinkling the congregation with water from the font immediately following the words of absolution, or during an entrance hymn that follows, may serve to make yet another connection between the forgiveness in baptism and the joy of an Easter people.

If the congregation celebrates designated baptismal festivals, the day of Pentecost is a fitting day for one, since it celebrates the sending of the Spirit, a gift first received in baptism.

Eucharistic Prayer E for the season of Easter (*WOV, Leaders Edition*, p. 69), and Eucharistic Prayer F for the day of Pentecost (*WOV, Leaders Edition*, p. 70) might be used at their respective times, though one of the longer standard eucharistic prayers (especially I and II in *LBW* and *WOV*, also Prayer V in *WOV*) is also appropriate. If the congregation kneels to receive communion throughout the year, you might consider standing throughout the Easter season (a custom expressing joy during this season). A festive Easter hymn might replace the post communion canticle throughout the season (such as LBW 149 or WOV 676, "This joyful Eastertide").

ASSEMBLY SONG FOR THE SEASON

The reading from 1 Peter for the Fifth Sunday in Easter invites us:

"Like newborn infants, long for the pure, spiritual milk, so that by it you

may grow into salvation—if indeed you have

tasted that the Lord is good."

The fifty days of Easter are about having our eyes opened to the mysteries of God—about spiritually growing up. For those who were baptized and first tasted God's love in the eucharist at the Vigil of Easter, these days must be especially meaningful. For many who have been church insiders for several years, it is easy for the Sundays in Easter to deteriorate quickly to little more than the "low Sundays *after* Easter."

The challenge to worship leaders is to keep the fifty days of Easter alive as celebrations of the resurrection. Musicians have a particularly difficult time as evenings grow lighter and rehearsal attendance wanes.

Yet, if Easter is a time to grow spiritually and discover the mysteries of God in our lives, it is an ideal time to challenge musicians and stretch the ears of our worshiping assemblies. Directors need to be open-minded for this continued enthusiasm to occur. Rehearsal days or times may need to be altered. Configurations of choirs may need to change. Perhaps youth and adults can team up together for the fifty days of Easter, leading to a cooperative effort at Pentecost. Working closely with those responsible for education in the congregation, rehearsals could be coordinated with Sunday school classes, freeing up the midweek schedule and enticing new members to join.

In the gospel reading on the Third Sunday of Easter we learn that "Jesus was made known to them in the breaking of the bread." The seven Sundays of Easter, along with the fiftieth day, Pentecost, are ideal times to accent the meal portion of the liturgy. Introducing a new setting of the eucharistic liturgy may not be wise at the Easter Vigil or on Easter Day. However, it could

be appropriate for the weeks following, especially if the setting stretches worshipers musically into a fresh encounter with God.

"Alleluia," that joyful shout of praise the church fasts from during Lent, should return passionately at Easter, especially as it announces the gospel reading each Sunday. As a connection between the spoken word and the sacramental word, the same "alleluia" setting could be sung during communion as well. Choral anthems, solos, antiphons, refrains, and hymns with abundant "alleluias" are easy to find.

Bells of all kinds, especially if included in the musical Lenten fast, can be used imaginatively and frequently throughout the weeks of Easter. Focus their use on the high points in the liturgy, such as the gospel acclamation and the Sanctus. Perhaps several ringers would make the commitment to be present at every liturgy from the Easter Vigil to Pentecost Day to add this special touch and help keep the season alive.

Lent is about preparing for baptism. Easter is about living our baptism. Any music begun during Lent that reflects a congregation's baptismal commitment can be continued and expanded during Easter. The rite of "Affirmation of the Vocation of the Baptized in the World" (see *Welcome to Christ: Lutheran Rites for the Catechumenate*, pp. 59–61) may be used at any time, but is especially appropriate on the fiftieth day of Easter, Pentecost. It is intended not only for those baptized at the Vigil of Easter, but for all the baptized to affirm their Christian identity in whatever corner of the world they live and work. Musicians, sacred and secular, professional and amateur, could affirm their baptism and their calling to communicate the gospel through music at this time.

MUSIC FOR THE SEASON

VERSE AND OFFERTORY

Blersch, Jeffrey. "Alleluia Verses for the Festival of the Liturgical Year."
CPH 98-3230. SATB, org.

Cherwien, David. *Verses for the Sundays of Easter.* MSM 80-400. U, org.

Pelz, Walter L. *Verses and Offertories: Easter—The Holy Trinity.*
AFP 11-9546. SATB, org.

Schalk, Carl. *Verses and Offertory Sentences: Part IV, Easter Day through
Easter 7.* CPH 97-5504.

CHORAL MUSIC FOR THE SEASON

Bach, J. S. "Alleluia! O Praise the Lord Most Holy!" CPH 98-2101.
SATB, org, opt brass.

Berger, Jean. "A Rose Touched by the Sun's Warm Rays."
AFP 11-0953. SATB.

Billings, William. "Arise and Hail the Sacred Day." CPH 98-3272.
SAB, opt kybd.

Billings, William. "I Am the Rose of Sharon." BBL. SATB.

Chepponis, James J. "Eastertime Psalm." GIA G-3907. Cant, cong, opt
SATB, opt tpts, hb.

Dicke, Martin. "Easter Carol." AFP 11-10681. SAB, kybd.

Ferguson, John. "Christ the Lord Is Risen Today." AFP 11-2386.
SATB, snare drm, picc, opt kybd.

Jennings, Kenneth. "With a Voice of Singing." AFP 11-01379. SATB.

Kohrs, Jonathan. "Praise the Spirit in Creation." AFP 11-10542.
SATB, opt cong, fl, org.

Leavitt, John. "Easter." AFP 11-4513. SATB, pno, opt 2 tpt, hrn, 2 tbn,
timp, xyl, glock, cym, tri.

Martinson, Joel. "Awake Arise: An Easter Carol." OXF 94.349. SATB.

Owens, Sam Batt. "Spring Bursts Today." SEL 405-542. 2 pt mxd, org.

Pelz, Walter L. "Peace I Leave With You." AFP 11-1364. SATB.

Proulx, Richard. "Our Paschal Lamb, That Sets Us Free." AFP 12-106.
SATB, org.

Schalk, Carl. "Christ Goes Before." MSM 50-9049. SATB, brass, org.

Scheidt, Samuel. "Arisen Is Our Lord and Christ." CPH 98-3255.
SATB, opt soli, org.

Somerset Anthem Books for SAB choir: vol. II, Easter. ECS 5129.

Telemann/Conlon. "Come Enjoy God's Festive Springtime."
AFP 11-2443. U, cont, vl/C inst.

CHILDREN'S CHORAL MUSIC FOR THE SEASON

Christopherson, Dorothy. "Nature Sings in Celebration."
AFP 11-10547. 2 pt trbl, rec/fl, kybd.

Lau, Robert. "Christ Is Risen! Alleluia!" CGA 674. 2 pt, kybd, opt hb.

Powell, Robert. "With the Lord Arise." CGA 639. 2/3 pt, kybd.

Schalk, Carl. "The Whole Bright World Rejoices Now." CGA 560.
U, org, opt fl/hb.

INSTRUMENTAL MUSIC FOR THE SEASON

Albrecht, Timothy. "The Strife Is O'er" in *Grace Notes III.*
AFP 11-10457. Org.

Martin, Joseph. "Improvisation on Resignation" in *American Tapestry.*
GS HE 5040. Pno.

Martinson, Joel. "Festival Intrada." CPH 97-6193. Org, opt tpt.

Meyer, Lawrence J. "Processional of Joy for Organ or Piano."
AFP 11-10797. Org/pno.

Powell, Robert. "Easter Sonata for Flute and Organ." CPH 97-6472.
Fl, org.

Rendler, Elaine. "Resurrection Fantasia" in *Keyboard Praise,* vol. 2.
OCP 9081. Kybd.

Sedio, Mark. "Music for the Paschal Season." AFP 11-10763. Org.

Webster, Richard. "Paschal Suite for Organ and Trumpet."
AFP 11-10831. Org, tpt.

HANDBELL MUSIC FOR THE SEASON

Behnke, John. "The Head That Once Was Crowned." Full score
CPH 97-6120. Hb 97-6121; SATB 98-2977. Cong, SATB,
2 oct hb, org, brass.

Bock, Almon C. "This Joyful Eastertide and Pastorale." AFP 11-10392.
2 oct.

Hopson, Hal H. "Fantasy on 'Hyfrydol.'" HOP 1048. 2 oct.

Kinyon, Barbara B. "Eastertide Bells." HOP 1342. 2 oct.

McChesney, Kevin. "Cantad al Señor." AFP 11-10690. 2-3 oct, perc.

Moklebust, Cathy. "Crown Him With Many Crowns" in *Hymn Stanzas for Handbells.* AFP 11-10722. 4-5 oct.

Moklebust, Cathy. "Ring to the Lord a New Song." AFP 11-7999. 4 oct.

Page, Anna Laura. "Christ Is Alive!" in *Hymn Descants for Ringers and
Singers,* vol. 2. ALF 11528. Vcs/kybd 11530. 3 oct, org, desc.

Rogers, Sharon E. "Easter Victory." MSM 30-403. 3 oct.

Schalk, Carl/John Behnke. "Thine the Amen, Thine the Praise."
CPH 97-6383. 3-5 oct.

ALTERNATE WORSHIP TEXTS

CONFESSION AND FORGIVENESS

In the name of the Father, and of the ✝ Son, and of the Holy
    Spirit.
Amen

In Christ's dying and rising, we are reborn;
we are no longer dead in our sin.
Let us return to the shepherd and guardian of our souls,
confessing our sin.

Silence for reflection and self-examination.

Almighty God,
we confess before you
our preference for things that pass away,
our silence in the face of injustice,
our reluctance to accept the freedom of forgiveness.
Make us whole again;
renew in us the grace of baptism;
and set our minds on the things that are above.

"All the prophets testify about Jesus
that everyone who believes in him
receives forgiveness of sins through his name."
God, who loves you dearly,
forgives you all your sin,
raises you to new life in Jesus Christ,
and renews you by the power of the Holy Spirit.
Amen

GREETING

Alleluia! Christ is risen.
Christ is risen indeed. Alleluia!

The grace of the risen Lord Jesus Christ, the love of God,
and the communion of the Holy Spirit be with you all.
And also with you.

OFFERTORY PRAYER

Giver of life,
we bring to your table what we have, gifts from you,
the one who makes all things new.
With these signs we bring ourselves,
that we may carry to the world
the victorious life of your Son,
Jesus Christ our Lord. Amen

INVITATION TO COMMUNION

Christ our Passover has been sacrificed for us.
Therefore let us keep the feast. Alleluia!

POST-COMMUNION PRAYER

In this meal, O God, you have strengthened us
by the risen life of your Son.
Send us by your Spirit
to live in peace with one another
and to renew your whole creation;
through Jesus Christ our Lord.
Amen

BENEDICTION

God, who raised Jesus from the dead,
make you stand strong in faith.
Amen. Alleluia!

Jesus Christ, triumphant over the grave,
make you bold to tell the good news.
Amen. Alleluia!

The Spirit of truth abide with you
and guide you into paths of service.
Amen. Alleluia!

DISMISSAL

Go in the power of the Spirit.
Proclaim the risen Lord. Alleluia, alleluia!
Thanks be to God. Alleluia, alleluia!

207

SEASONAL RITES

EASTER HYMN FESTIVAL

PRELUDE

Reading from Exodus 15:1-11
Hymn: Come, you faithful, raise the strain (LBW 132)
    Stanzas: 1-all; 2-women; 3-all; 4-men; 5-all

GREETING

Reading from Leo the Great ("But it is not only the martyrs who
    share in his passion"), from *The Liturgy of the Hours*, as printed
    in *An Easter Sourcebook: The Fifty Days*, Chicago: Liturgy Train-
    ing Publications, 1988, p. 38.
Hymn: I'll Praise My Maker (*The Hymnal 1982*, 429; text and tune
    line may be reproduced from this source)
    Stanzas: 1-all; 2-women, men join at "whose truth forever . . .";
    3-men, women join at "he helps the stranger . . ."; 4-all
or
Hymn: Praise the Almighty (LBW 539)
    Stanzas: 1-all; 2-women; 3-men; 4-all

Reading from the Orthodox Liturgy for Easter Sunday, as printed in
    A Triduum Sourcebook (Chicago: Liturgy Training Publications,
    1983, p. 157).
Hymn: The day of resurrection! (LBW 141)
    Stanzas: 1-all; 2-men; 3-women; 4-all

Reading from Jonah 2:1-10
Hymn: Shout for joy loud and long (WOV 793)
    Stanzas: 1-all; 2-women; 3-men; 4-all

Reading from Balthasar Fischer, "It Is an Unusual Word" from *Signs,
    Words, and Gestures*, as printed in *An Easter Sourcebook*, pp.
    17–18.
Hymn: Good Christian friends, rejoice and sing! (LBW 144)
    Stanzas: 1-all; 2-men; 3-women; 4-all

Reading from Brian Wren, "Lord God, Your Love" as printed in *An
    Easter Sourcebook*, p. 48.
Hymn: My life flows on in endless song (WOV 781)
    Stanzas: 1-all; 2-women; 3-men; 4-all

Reading from Richard Baxter, "Ye Holy Angels Bright", hymn 409 in
    Service Book and Hymnal.
Hymn: The God of Abraham praise (LBW 544)
    Stanzas: 1-all; 3-women; 9-all; 10-men; 11-all

Reading from 1 Corinthians 15:50-57
Hymn: With high delight let us unite (LBW 140)
    Stanzas: 1-all; 2-women; 3-all

OFFERING

Hymn: Christ has arisen, alleluia (WOV 678)
    Stanzas: Refrain-all; 1-all; 2-men; 3-women; 4-all; 5-all

PRAYERS

BLESSING

Hymn: Now all the vault of heaven resounds (LBW 143)
    Stanzas: 1-all; 2-men; 3-women; 4-all

TUESDAY, APRIL 6
ALBRECHT DÜRER, PAINTER, 1528
MICHELANGELO BUONARROTI, ARTIST, 1564

Amid the joy of Easter we commemorate two great artists who revealed, through their work, the glory of God and the wonder of creation. Dürer was a painter and engraver whose work is a close examination of the splendor of creation—the human body, animals, grasses, and flowers. He never renounced the Catholic faith, but was sympathetic with the Reformation. Michelangelo, the most famous late Renaissance artist, earned fame as a painter, sculptor, architect, and poet. His art embodies a new concept of human dignity, projecting the human body on a new scale of grandeur. Michelangelo's contemporaries believed him to be divinely inspired, and he saw in sculpture an allegory of divine creativity and human salvation.

In books of art look at some of the famous works of Dürer and Michelangelo. How do they give witness to the resurrection through the offering of their talents in praise of God? How do all the arts aid us in proclaiming the victory of Easter?

FRIDAY, APRIL 9
DIETRICH BONHOEFFER, TEACHER, 1945

Bonhoeffer was a German theologian who resisted the Nazis, and was linked to a failed attempt to assassinate Hitler. He was arrested in 1943 for his antiwar activities, and was taken to a concentration camp and then to a prison. After conducting a service on April 8, 1945, Bonhoeffer was taken away to be hanged the next day. An English prisoner told of his last words as he was led away: "This is the end, but for me the beginning of life."

Bonhoeffer's courageous life and death is a bold witness to the paschal mystery of Christ's dying and rising. Commemorating him during the Easter season might include reading a passage from his famous work *The Cost of Discipleship*, and singing the hymn "The strife is o'er, the battle won" (LBW 135).

SATURDAY, APRIL 10
MIKAEL AGRICOLA, BISHOP OF TURKU, 1557

Agricola was a Finnish archbishop who carried out a thoroughgoing evangelical reformation in Finland. He worked diligently to translate the prayerbook, the mass, and the New Testament into Finnish, and he devised an orthography which is the basis for modern Finnish spelling. He is remembered as a learned man, moderate and conciliatory, concerned for the well-being of his people.

Remember the Church of Finland in prayers today, and give thanks for the Finnish presence in the former Suomi Synod, one of the Lutheran ethnic groups in this country that merged with others during the past half-century. Sing "Your kingdom come, O Father" (LBW 384), which uses a Finnish folk tune as its melody.

209

APRIL 11, 1999

SECOND SUNDAY OF EASTER

INTRODUCTION

In today's gospel reading, the risen Christ appears to the disciples who have locked themselves into a house. In the midst of their fear he offers his peace so that they might go forth to proclaim God's victory over death. In this Sunday liturgy, Christ offers us his peace anew as we prepare to come to the table where he gives us his body and blood. As we receive bread and cup he says, Do not doubt but believe that I am with you. He sends us forth to be his peacemakers in a community and a world locked in by fear and injustice.

PRAYER OF THE DAY

Almighty God, with joy we celebrate the festival of our Lord's resurrection. Graciously help us to show the power of the resurrection in all that we say and do; through your

Son, Jesus Christ our Lord, who lives and reigns with you and the Holy Spirit, one God, now and forever.

READINGS

Acts 2:14a, 22-32

After the Holy Spirit came to the apostles on Pentecost, Peter preaches the gospel to the gathered crowd. He tells them that Jesus, who obediently went to his death according to God's plan, was raised from the dead by God. Finally, he appeals to scripture, quoting Psalm 16:8-11, to show that Jesus is the Messiah: though crucified, the risen Jesus is now enthroned.

Psalm 16

In your presence there is fullness of joy. (Ps. 16:11)

1 Peter 1:3-9

This epistle was written to encourage Christians who were suffering for their faith. It begins by praising God for the resurrection of Jesus, which produces hope, then and now.

John 20:19-31

One week after Easter, Christ still comes to those who believe in him; he seeks any who may have missed his offer of peace and life through his resurrection.

COLOR   White

THE PRAYERS

Rejoicing in the resurrection, let us remember in prayer the church, the world, and all those in need.

A BRIEF SILENCE.

For the church, born anew to a living hope, that it may joyfully proclaim the resurrection, we pray:

Hear us, risen Lord.

For nations divided by war, oppression, or conflict, that you bless them with peace and reconciliation, we pray:

Hear us, risen Lord.

For all who suffer (especially . . .), that amid their pain they may rejoice in hope, we pray:

Hear us, risen Lord.

For those who face trials, or struggle with doubt and disbelief, that your peace and forgiveness may be made known to them, we pray:

Hear us, risen Lord.

For this assembly, that freed from fear, we may be united at your eucharistic table and in ministry to the world, we pray:

Hear us, risen Lord.

HERE OTHER INTERCESSIONS MAY BE OFFERED.

Let us give thanks for Thomas, and for all the saints who confessed Christ crucified and risen. May we praise you on earth until we receive our eternal inheritance in heaven. We pray:

Hear us, risen Lord.

Receive our prayers and hopes, O God, and fill us with the risen life of Christ our Lord.

Amen

IMAGES FOR PREACHING

The gospel is "John's Pentecost," and brings to a conclusion not only the fourth evangelist's resurrection narrative but really the entirety of this gospel. Jesus appears among the disciples, who are hiding behind locked doors "for fear of the Jews." Of course they are afraid of the mob who demanded their leader's crucifixion, but no doubt they fear one Jew in particular: the one whom they betrayed, denied, and abandoned.

He comes among them with three improbabilities: bearing the wounds of his crucifixion, greeting them with *Shalom*, and commissioning them with his resurrection Spirit/breath. The juxtaposition of these three incongruous elements brings into sharp focus their guilt, his suffering and death, and that divine forgiveness to which they are now to bear witness. They are now capable of forgiving because they know firsthand how forgiveness works. But even more, they will bear in their own bodies the resurrection life of Jesus himself—his Spirit/breath. In this Thomas is absolutely correct and on target: it all has to do with the relationship of his body with Jesus' body ("my finger . . . his side"). Thomas's problem is not doubt but vision. The new Easter epistemology does not arrive at the truth by looking (Mary thought Jesus was the gardener!); knowledge now comes through relationship ("My father and your father," from last Sunday's gospel). Jesus arrives on Easter night to create a relationship more profound than anything they could have imagined: Christ in us!

The rest of the day's images flow out of this: "New birth . . . living hope . . . imperishable inheritance." "This Jesus God raised up, and of that all of us are witnesses."

WORSHIP MATTERS

As the gospel reminds us, the first gift the risen Jesus gives to his disciples is the gift of peace (John 20:19). In bestowing this gift the disciples are assured of Jesus' resurrection, not only because they have seen the risen Lord, but because in bestowing peace and forgiveness, the disciples receive from the crucified but now living one gifts they had received from him during his earthly ministry. The gift of peace, and the forgiveness and oneness with God that accompanies it, continues to be the gift *par excellence* of the reigning Christ. The gift is bestowed in a multitude of ways, not the least of which is when the members of the body of Christ share that gift with one another in the Sunday assembly. By sharing the peace of Christ we are becoming Christ for our neighbor; we embody the grace and peace he bestows upon the church. We share Christ's peace because it is a gift of God who came into the world to transform it, and who invites us by baptism to be a part of that kingdom that comes from the future to meet us.

LET THE CHILDREN COME

How can congregations keep the fifty days of Easter and prevent this season from withering away? Teach the congregation the American Sign Language gestures for a simple Easter greeting. The presider could greet the congregation with the words and gesture, "Alleluia! Christ is risen!" and all could respond in word and gesture, "Christ is risen indeed! Alleluia!" This greeting could mark all the Sundays in Easter. For children, it would help to keep the season alive. Visual movement adds meaning to the words. It could also provide another language in the congregation's vocabulary when Pentecost concludes the season.

MUSIC FOR WORSHIP

GATHERING

| LBW 145 | Thine is the glory |
| WOV 676 | This joyful Eastertide (or LBW 149) |

PSALM 16

Foley, John. PCY, vol. 7.

Haugen, Marty. PCY, vol. 2.

Howard, Julie. *Sing for Joy: Psalm Settings for God's Children.* LTP.

Inwood, Paul. "Centre of My Life" in PS2.

Marshall, Jane. *Psalms Together.* CGA. CGC-18.

Peña, Donna. "Sing Unto the Lord" in *Canten al Señor.* GIA G-3352. Choir, cong, gtr.

Sedio, Mark. PW, Cycle A.

HYMN OF THE DAY

| WOV 675 | We walk by faith and not by sight |
| | DUNLAP'S CREEK |

INSTRUMENTAL RESOURCES

Uhl, Dan. "Dunlap's Creek" in *Easter Suite for Trumpet, Organ and Optional Timpani.* Kybd, tpt, opt perc.

ALTERNATE HYMN OF THE DAY

| LBW 133 | Jesus lives! The victory's won |
| LBW 139 | O sons and daughters of the King |

COMMUNION

| LBW 189 | We know that Christ is raised |
| WOV 774 | Dona nobis pacem |

OTHER SUGGESTIONS

| OBS 50 | Blessing be and glory |
| DATH 65 | Good news, alleluia! |

SENDING

| LBW 147 | Hallelujah! Jesus lives |
| WOV 722 | Hallelujah! We sing your praises |

ADDITIONAL HYMNS AND SONGS

LBW 132	Come, you faithful, raise the strain
WOV 724	Shalom
ISH 21	Show me your hands, your feet, your side
NCH 254	These things did Thomas count as real

MUSIC FOR THE DAY

CHORAL

Bender, Jan. "Peace Be with You." CPH 98-208. SA, org.

Burkhardt, Michael. "O Sons and Daughters of the King." MSM 60-4001. SATB, cong, opt fl, tamb, org.

Haas, David. "Happy Are They Who Believe." GIA G-3500. U, cong, bass inst, gtr, kybd.

Hassler, Hans L. "Quia vidisti me, Thoma" (Because Thou Hast Seen Me, Thomas). CPH 98-174. SATB.

Hogan, David. "O Sons and Daughters of the King." ECS 4885. SAB/ATB, org, tpt.

Lovelace, Austin. "I Saw the Lord Before Me." MSM 50-9022. SATB, org.

Neswick, Bruce. "Peace Be with You." AFP 12-101. SATB, org, ob.

Parker, Alice, and Robert Shaw. "Christ the Lord Hath Risen." HAL 994. TB.

Pelz, Walter L. "Peace I Leave with You." AFP 11-1364. Also in *The Augsburg Choirbook.* 11-10817. SATB.

211

Saylor, Bruce. "Arise, Arise, Lift Up Your Voice." ECS 5096. SATB, org.

CHILDREN'S CHOIRS

Lindy, Jody, and Joe Cox. "Jesus, Son of God Most High." CGA 377. U, opt desc, fl, gtr, opt bass, pno.

Paige, Jon. "There Is a New Song." SHW EA5133. 2 pt trbl, kybd.

KEYBOARD/INSTRUMENTAL

Bach, J. S. "Sinfonia from *Wir danken dir, Gott.*" FEN F530. Org.

Farnam, Lynnwood. "Toccata on 'O Filii et Filiae.'" PRE 113-25819. Org.

Haller, William. "Easter Meditation on a Phrase of Tournemire" in *Back to Life Again.* AFP 11-10319. Org.

Held, Wilbur. "Partita on 'O Sons and Daughters.'" AFP 11-819. Org.

Rutter, John. "Variations on an Easter Theme for Organ Duet." OXF 32-2770.

HANDBELL

Dobrinski, Cynthia. "Good Christians All, Rejoice." HOP 1900. 3-5 oct.

McFadden, Jane. "Hallelujah, Jesus Lives!" AFP 11-10573. 3-5 oct.

PRAISE ENSEMBLE

Gaither, Smith, and Clydesdale/arr. Benson. "Resurrection Song." BEN 25986-067307. SATB.

Kendrick, Graham. "Amazing Love" in *Integrity's Hosanna! Come and Worship Songbook.* INT.

Zschech, Darlene. "Shout to the Lord" in *Integrity's Hosanna! Music Songsheets: Shout to the Lord.* INT.

APRIL 18, 1999

THIRD SUNDAY OF EASTER

212

INTRODUCTION

In this story from Luke's gospel, the risen Christ joins two disciples overcome by the apparent loss of one who was "a prophet mighty in deed and word" (Luke 24:19). Here Luke presents us with two things: our yearning to see the risen Christ, and the Lord's response to that yearning. In word (interpreting the scriptures) and sacrament (breaking the bread) he reveals himself to them and to us. In these two central actions—readings with preaching and thanksgiving with communion—our eyes are opened to see the risen Lord in our midst. Here is the center of our weekly gathering on the Lord's Day.

PRAYER OF THE DAY

O God, by the humiliation of your Son you lifted up this fallen world, rescuing us from the hopelessness of death. Grant your faithful people a share in the joys that are eternal; through your Son, Jesus Christ our Lord, who lives and reigns with you and the Holy Spirit, one God, now and forever.

READINGS

Acts 2:14a, 36-41

Today's reading is the conclusion of Peter's sermon preached following the giving of the Holy Spirit to the apostles on the day of Pentecost. The center of his preaching is the bold declaration that God has made the crucified Jesus both Lord and Christ.

Psalm 116:1-3, 10-17 (Psalm 116:1-4, 12-19 [NRSV])

I will call upon the name of the Lord. (Ps. 116:11)

1 Peter 1:17-23

The First Letter of Peter uses the image of "exile" to describe the experience of new Christians who are no longer at home in the non-Christian world. Their faith in the risen Christ distinguishes them from their ancestors and neighbors and calls them to place their faith and hope in God.

Luke 24:13-35

The colorful story of Jesus' appearance to two disciples on the road to Emmaus answers the question of how Jesus is to be recognized among us. Here, he is revealed through the Scriptures and in the breaking of bread.

COLOR White

THE PRAYERS

Rejoicing in the resurrection, let us remember in prayer the church, the world, and all those in need.

A BRIEF SILENCE.

That bishops, pastors, associates in ministry, diaconal ministers, deaconesses, and all the baptized be filled with genuine love as they set their faith and hope on God, we pray:

Hear us, risen Lord.

That those newly welcomed into the church at Easter may open their hearts to the surprising gifts of your grace, we pray:

Hear us, risen Lord.

That the leaders of nations may rule with justice and truth, we pray:

Hear us, risen Lord.

That in sharing our bread with those who are hungry our eyes may be opened to your presence in our midst, we pray:

Hear us, risen Lord.

That those who suffer with sorrow, loneliness, or sickness (especially . . .) may know the comfort of your abiding love, we pray:

Hear us, risen Lord.

That we may recognize you in the proclamation of the word and the breaking of the bread, we pray:

Hear us, risen Lord.

HERE OTHER INTERCESSIONS MAY BE OFFERED.

Stay with us, O Lord, until we join all the saints at your heavenly feast of unending joy. We pray:

Hear us, risen Lord.

Receive our prayers and hopes, O God, and fill us with the risen life of Christ our Lord.

Amen

IMAGES FOR PREACHING

By this third week in Eastertide we are deep into the appearances tradition of the risen Lord. Just as the canonical gospel accounts of the open tomb are wondrously restrained (see Easter's "Preaching with the Season"), so the appearances traditions are marvelous in their minimalist style so they "rings true." Evidently the risen Lord is hard to see! Disciples on the road to Emmaus never recognize him when they carry on a day-long hike with the risen one. He becomes visible at the very moment when he disappears! It's the breaking of the bread and the memory of an earlier meal that does it.

Peter delivers the grand finale of his Pentecost sermon and his listeners are "cut to the heart." With more than a little panic in their voice they plead, "Brothers, what should we do?" This beginning of new life is not reveling in the sound of trumpets, enjoying the beauty of a lily or the warmth of the returning sun. No, new life begins when we "live in reverent fear during the time of your exile." The challenges and hardships of Lent were not simply an attempt to make ourselves feel miserable so that we will feel so much better when we stop. Rather, the Lenten disciplines were meant to prepare us for life in the new age where, as we heard last week, the risen Lord still bears the marks of crucifixion and where, as we shall hear in weeks to come, those raised with Christ might suffer hardship and persecution. In the midst of such a paradoxical world we break the bread and catch the vision of him out of the corner of our eye and our hearts burn within us.

WORSHIP MATTERS

Four primary actions dominate the Sunday assembly and are always the focus of the assembly's action: gathering, word, meal, and sending. Each is a vital and essential part of the fullness that is the Sunday liturgy, and each benefits from thoughtful reflection on how they are related to the other. In Africa, for example, the gathering rite is an extended portion of the service with singing, drumming, and prayer, calling the people to worship and reflecting what each person brings to the Sunday assembly. At the heart of the proclamation of the word is the reading of the gospel and the homily, testimony to the presence of the risen Christ among the baptized. The focus of the meal is the sharing of the bread and wine as the living Jesus offers the gifts of forgiveness, life, and salvation to the baptized. Finally, the assembly is sent into the world to serve as Christ has served us. It is the place to affirm the vocation of Christians in the world and to help all see that the cross of Christ forms, shapes, and leads our serving. To give prominence to other portions of the liturgy is to obscure the central acts for which the community gathers.

LET THE CHILDREN COME

How do children discern the presence of the risen Christ? Where do they find Jesus today? Worship planners may point to any number of things: pictures, stories, and Christ present in other people. Luke's gospel reminds us that Christ was "known in the breaking of the bread." Will children know Christ's presence in this way? *The Use of the Means of Grace*, a statement on the

213

practice of word and sacrament, offers the reminder that the supper calls for faith; and yet the statement cautions against "narrowing faith to intellectual understanding of Christ's presence and gifts" (38b). How can congregations assist their children of any age to know the presence of Christ in the breaking of the bread?

MUSIC FOR WORSHIP
GATHERING

| LBW 144 | Good Christian friends, rejoice and sing! |
| LBW 210 | At the Lamb's high feast we sing |

PSALM 116

Cooney, Rory, and Gary Daigle. PCY, vol. 4.

Foley, John. PCY, vol. 7.

Glynn, John. "Lord, How Can I Repay" in PS2.

Howard, Julie. *Sing for Joy: Psalm Settings for God's Children.* LTP.

Joncas, Michael. STP, vol. 2.

Sedio, Mark. PW, Cycle A.

HYMN OF THE DAY

| LBW 140 | With high delight let us unite |
| | MIT FREUDEN ZART |

VOCAL RESOURCES

Bobb, Barry. "With High Delight." CPH 98-2670. SAB, cong, org.

Pelz, Walter L. "With High Delight Let Us Unite." CPH 97-5853. Cong, choir.

Yarrington, John. "Mit Freuden zart" in *Ten Hymntune Intradas for Voices and Bells.* AMSI HB-1. SATB, 3 oct.

INSTRUMENTAL RESOURCES

Bender, Jan. "Organ Fantasy and Setting on 'Mit Freuden Zart.'" AFP 12-707380. Org.

Biery, James. "Chorale Chaconne on 'Mit Freuden zart'" in *Three For Easter.* MSM 10-413. Org.

Ferguson, John. "Scherzo on 'Mit Freuden zart'" in *Three Psalm Preludes.* AFP 11-10823. Org.

Keller, Michael R. "Sing Praise to God, Who Reigns Above." HOP 1288. 2 oct.

Pelz, Walter L. "Mit Freuden zart" in *Hymn Settings for Organ and Brass,* set 1. AFP 11-10184.

Sedio, Mark. "Mit Freuden zart" in *Music for the Paschal Season.* AFP 11-10763. Org.

ALTERNATE HYMN OF THE DAY

| LBW 207 | We who once were dead |
| WOV 743 | Stay with us |

COMMUNION

| LBW 214 | Come, let us eat |
| WOV 711 | You satisfy the hungry heart |

OTHER SUGGESTIONS

| OBS 54 | Day of arising |

SENDING

| LBW 219 | Come with us, O blessed Jesus |
| WOV 754 | Let us talents and tongues employ |

ADDITIONAL HYMNS AND SONGS

WOV 769	Mothering God, you gave me birth
PH 505	Be known to us in breaking bread
UMH 309	On the day of resurrection
LLC 362	¿Que venías conversando?/As I walked home to Emmaus

MUSIC FOR THE DAY
CHORAL

Bach, J. S. "Sing Praise to Christ" in *With High Delight.* CPH 97-504. SATB, kybd.

Bertalot, John. "Abide With Me." AFP 11-2570. SATB, org.

Bertalot, John. "Come, Risen Lord." AFP 11-10900. Also in *The Augsburg Choirbook.* 11-10817. SATB, org.

Carter, Andrew. "Love One Another." OXF A422. SATB, org.

Heim, Bret. "Who Is This Who Comes from Nowhere." MSM 50-9050. SATB, org.

Lenel, Ludwig. "With High Delight" in *Second Morning Star Choir Book.* CPH 97-470. U, opt 2 pt, org.

Pelz, Walter L. "Stay With Us." SATB, fl, org CPH 98-2920. SAB, org 98-3073.

Vaughan Williams, Ralph. "O Taste and See" in *First Motet Book.* CPH 97-484. SATB, org.

Ward, M. "In the Breaking of the Bread." WLP 7950. SATB, desc, kybd.

Wesley, Samuel S. "Blessed Be the God and Father." BOH 6335. SATB, org. Also in *The New Church Anthem Book.* OXF 0-19-353109-7.

CHILDREN'S CHOIRS

Bach, J. S./Janet Hill. "Alleluia, O Come and Praise the Lord." CGA 174. 2 pt, hpd, org/pno, opt 2 C inst.

Curtright, Carolee. "Sing, O Sing." CGA 191. U, opt 2 pt, hb, kybd.

Kreutz, Robert. "We Walked Down the Road." CGA-262. U.

KEYBOARD/INSTRUMENTAL

Howells, Herbert. "Saraband for the Morning of Easter" in *Modern Anthology.* HWG 209. Org.

Hyslop, Scott. "Noël Nouvelet" in *Six Chorale Fantasias for Solo Instrument and Piano*. AFP 11-10799. Pno, inst.

Rawsthorne, Noel. "Gelobt sei Gott" in *Easter Glory*. OXF 0862097282. Org.

Young, Jeremy. "The Good Thief (Noël Nouvelet and Llanfair)" in *At the Foot of the Cross*. AFP 11-10688. Pno.

HANDBELL

Frey, Richard. "When in Our Music God Is Glorified" (ENGELBERG). Full score HOP 1370. Hb 1369; Brass 1370B. Cong, 3-5 oct, org, brass.

Helman, Michael. "Processional in C." AFP 11-10768. 3-5 oct.

Moklebust, Cathy. "We Know That Christ Is Raised" in *Hymn Stanzas for Handbells*. AFP 11-10722. 4-5 oct.

PRAISE ENSEMBLE

deShazo, Lynn. "Turn My Heart, Oh Lord" in *Integrity's Hosanna! Come and Worship Songbook*. INT.

Schutte, Daniel/Jack Schrader. "Here I Am, Lord." HOP A687. SAB.

Ylvisaker, John. "On the Road to Emmaus" in *Borning Cry*. NGP.

MONDAY, APRIL 19
OLAVUS PETRI, PRIEST, 1552; LAURENTIUS PETRI, ARCHBISHOP OF UPPSALA, 1573, RENEWERS OF THE CHURCH

These two brothers are commemorated for their introduction of the Lutheran reformation to Sweden. Under the patronage of King Gustavus Vasa (the liberator of Sweden from Danish rule), Olavus was appointed pastor of the city church, and Laurentius became the royal chancellor. From these influential positions, the two brothers worked carefully to establish an intellectual and liturgical foundation for the Lutheran Church of Sweden, including the retention of the historic episcopate.

Remember the Church of Sweden in prayers today, and give thanks for the Swedish presence in the former Augustana synod, one of the Lutheran ethnic synods in this country, which merged with others during the past fifty years. Sing "Thy holy wings" (WOV 741), which uses a Swedish folk tune, and whose text includes baptismal imagery appropriate for the fifty days of Easter.

WEDNESDAY, APRIL 21
ANSELM, ARCHBISHOP OF CANTERBURY, 1109

This eleventh-century Benedictine monk, theologian, and bishop is best known for his theological explanation of the atonement, referred to as the "satisfaction" theory. Anselm is believed to be the greatest theologian between Augustine and Thomas Aquinas, and he understood the pursuit of theology as prayer. He is also counted among the medieval mystics who emphasized the maternal aspects of God. He addressed Christ as our "mother who tasted death in longing to bring forth children to life."

A commemoration of Anselm might include a discussion of ways we use feminine images to speak of the divine. Look at two hymns in *With One Voice* (688 and 769) which are based on texts by two other medieval mystics, Hildegard of Bingen and Julian of Norwich.

215

THURSDAY, APRIL 22
DAY OF THE CREATION (EARTH DAY)

FRIDAY, APRIL 23
TOYOHIKO KAGAWA, RENEWER OF SOCIETY, 1960

Kagawa was from a wealthy Japanese family, and was disinherited by his family when be became a Christian. From his seminary studies he became aware of Christian responsibility in the face of social evils, and he worked on behalf of slum dwellers, labor unions, government relief agencies, and church-sponsored social welfare organizations. He was arrested for his efforts to reconcile Japan and China after the Japanese attack of 1940.

On the Fourth Sunday of Easter (this coming Sunday) we celebrate Christ as the Good Shepherd who lays down his life for his sheep. Kagawa is a model of an Easter shepherd who tenderly cared for the needs of his people. How does his witness inspire us to care for those in need in our community?

APRIL 25, 1999

INTRODUCTION

To some contemporary Christians, the image of Christ as shepherd appears outdated. Yet the continuing popularity of this "Good Shepherd Sunday" and the tender psalm appointed for the liturgy begs the question, Why are moderns attracted to a shepherd? Is it not that we yearn for guidance, protection, and strength in a world filled with much chaos, violence, and fast-paced change? The liturgy this day offers the image of our God as shepherd: the one who guides us—not out of this world, but in and through it with staff and overflowing cup, with word and holy supper.

PRAYER OF THE DAY

God of all power, you called from death our Lord Jesus, the great shepherd of the sheep. Send us as shepherds to rescue the lost, to heal the injured, and to feed one another with knowledge and understanding; through your Son, Jesus Christ our Lord, who lives and reigns with you and the Holy Spirit, one God, now and forever.

or

Almighty God, you show the light of your truth to those in darkness, to lead them into the way of righteousness. Give strength to all who are joined in the family of the Church, so that they will resolutely reject what erodes their faith and firmly follow what faith requires; through your Son, Jesus Christ our Lord, who lives and reigns with you and the Holy Spirit, one God, now and forever.

READINGS

Acts 2:42-47

Today's reading is a description of life in the community following Peter's sermon on the day of Pentecost, when the Spirit was outpoured on God's people. This new community is founded on the teachings of the apostles and sustained in the breaking of the bread.

Psalm 23

The Lord is my shepherd; I shall not be in want. (Ps. 23:1)

1 Peter 2:19-25

The First Letter of Peter addresses the theme of suffering. Jesus, the shepherd and guardian of our souls, models for Christians how one suffers for doing what is right.

John 10:1-10

Jesus uses an image familiar to the people of his day to make a point about spiritual leadership. Good shepherds bring people to life through Jesus, but those who avoid Jesus are dangerous to the flock.

COLOR White

THE PRAYERS

Rejoicing in the resurrection, let us remember in prayer the church, the world, and all those in need.

A BRIEF SILENCE.

For all who gather to hear the voice of the shepherd and feast at his table, that you make them one in ministry to all the world, we pray:

Hear us, risen Lord.

For bishops, pastors, and all who serve as shepherds, that they remain faithful to the apostles' teachings and to the breaking of bread, we pray:

Hear us, risen Lord.

For all who govern and lead, that they may seek justice and the welfare of all people, we pray:

Hear us, risen Lord.

For all who live without adequate food, clothing, or shelter, that your abundance be shared among all people, we pray:

Hear us, risen Lord.

For all who walk through valleys of fear, loneliness, loss, or illness (especially . . .), that you anoint them with your comfort and love, we pray:

Hear us, risen Lord.

For our congregation, that remembering the still waters of our baptism, we may share the loving care of our good shepherd with those in need in our community, we pray:

Hear us, risen Lord.

HERE OTHER INTERCESSIONS MAY BE OFFERED.

For Mark and all the saints who followed Christ the shepherd in life and in death, we give thanks and praise. Make us faithful in our calling all the days of our lives, until we dwell with them in your house forever. We pray:

Hear us, risen Lord.

Receive our prayers and hopes, O God, and fill us with the risen life of Christ our Lord.

Amen

IMAGES FOR PREACHING

If we have already heard the climax of the fourth gospel, we are now ready to listen afresh to some familiar stories and echoes from the earlier portion of the gospel. Jesus as good shepherd plugs into the core of cultural icons by which biblical narrative is publicly identified: Psalm 23, Christmas shepherds in their fields, and images from Sunday school lesson covers that still float into memory. But the heart of the matter, as the Easter climax reveals, is *voice* and *gate*.

His voice is important. It was his voice, you may remember, that pulled Mary into the new age that first Easter Day, jarring her vision so she could recognize she was not looking at a gardener but at her resurrected friend.

Doors are important: the stone that was supposed to keep life and death separated, the locked door in the room meant to keep the risen Lord out and the disciples safe from his justifiable wrath, as well as the anger of the mob. But in Eastertide, doors are either flung open or become strangely irrelevant.

"I am the gate." Some evidence indicates that ancient sheepfolds were C-shaped stone walls and that the shepherd himself would lay in the opening as if to say, "If you want to get to the sheep you will have to get past me." The word of Jesus, especially when he says *Shalom* and commissions us, driven as it is by his resurrection breath, calls us to the new reality. In this new reality we will not necessarily be freed from pain; we might actually suffer injustice. We cannot expect it to be an easy ride—it wasn't for the one who was crucified and raised, either. But in this radically reconfigured world, awe and signs and wonders are the orders of the day. Because we are reconfigured in our relationship to the one who is raised we also find ourselves reconstituted in a new network of relationships. The baptized soon discover that once-important barriers between "mine" and "yours" also begin to melt as we spend time together breaking bread, sharing food, and sharing life with glad and generous hearts.

WORSHIP MATTERS

Most people think of "church" as the building on the corner of First Avenue and Maple Street, the congregation in which they gather each week around the proclamation of the word and the celebration of the sacraments. But the baptized are part of a living, breathing reality that crosses space and time, that in its true universality is the body of Christ wherever and whenever people name the name of Jesus. The church cannot be the church without the local gathering of God's people. But the local assembly is not the whole church, and must always perceive itself to be a part of a greater reality called, gathered, and enlightened by the Spirit of the living Christ. In many traditions, the presence of the bishop helps to signal this reality. As pastor of all the congregations in a synod, the bishop represents the whole people of God, and likewise serves as a symbol of the unity of God's people. For this reason it is appropriate to invite the bishop to visit the congregation and, when present, to preach and preside during the Sunday assembly. As one who serves all God's people in the synod, the bishop provides a link to others in the body of Christ beyond the local community into the whole world.

LET THE CHILDREN COME

Children may not know sheep or shepherds. But they do know about the care shepherds give. They have received comfort, been led, and felt protection. Find stories to share with children on this day that show the care of shepherds. *Psalm 23*, a children's book with illustrations by Tim Ladwig (African American Family Press, 1993) follows an inner-city brother and sister through their day and shows both the constant dangers they face and the safe shelter of their home. The dangers are real but so is the care of the shepherd given by old men in a park, a school crossing guard, and the children's grandmother.

MUSIC FOR WORSHIP

GATHERING

| LBW 352 | I know that my Redeemer lives |
| WOV 791 | Alabaré |

PSALM 23

See listing for the Fourth Sunday in Lent.

HYMN OF THE DAY

| LBW 456 | The King of love my shepherd is |
| | ST. COLUMBA |

VOCAL RESOURCES

Beck, John Ness. "The King of Love My Shepherd Is." BEC BP1247.
SATB, kybd.

Ferguson, John. "Concertato on St. Columba." GIA 4011. SATB, org.

Pelz, Walter L. "The King of Love My Shepherd Is." AFP 11-02002.
SATB, opt cong, kybd, fl.

Pearce, T. "The King of Love My Shepherd Is." MSM 50-9008.
SATB, org.

INSTRUMENTAL RESOURCES

Arnatt, Ronald. "Brother James' Air" in *Hymn Preludes and Free Accompaniments,* vol. 9. AFP 11-9405. Org.

Herald, Terry. "Brother James' Air" in *Hymn Accompaniment for Instrumental Ensembles.* CPH 97-6263. Inst, kybd.

Ore, Charles. "Brother James' Air" in *Eleven Compositions for Organ,* set IV. CPH 97-6013. Org.

Wagner, Douglas E. "Brother James' Air." SMP S-HB25. 3 oct.

ALTERNATE HYMN OF THE DAY

| LBW 451 | The Lord's my shepherd |
| WOV 679 | Our Paschal Lamb, that sets us free |

COMMUNION

| LBW 476 | Have no fear, little flock |
| WOV 731 | Precious Lord, take my hand |

SENDING

| LBW 196 | Praise the Lord, rise up rejoicing |
| WOV 780 | What a fellowship, what a joy divine |

ADDITIONAL HYMNS AND SONGS

LBW 481	Savior, like a shepherd lead us
RS 699	You, Lord, are both Lamb and Shepherd
NSR 96	When Christians shared agape meals

MUSIC FOR THE DAY

CHORAL

Bach, J. S. "Sheep May Safely Graze." GAL 127. SATB, kybd.

Bairstow, Edward C. "The King of Love My Shepherd Is." OXF A 4.
SATB, org.

Bender, Jan. "I Am the Good Shepherd." CPH 98-1992. 2 pt, kybd.

DeLong, Richard. "Loving Shepherd of Thy Sheep." ECS 4795. U, kybd.

Handel, G. F. "He Shall Feed His Flock" in *Messiah.* MSM 50-940.
U, kybd, 2 trbl inst.

Ireland, John. "Greater Love Hath No Man." GAL 1.5030.1. SATB,
B solo, org.

Moore, Donald P. "My Shepherd Will Supply My Need." MSM 50-901.
SATB, org.

Page, Anna Laura. "The Good Shepherd." HIN HMC 1092. 2 pt mxd,
kybd.

Seivewright, Andrew. "Loving Shepherd." GIA G-4467. 2 pt, org.

Smith, Timothy R. "The Lord Is My Shepherd." OCP 10581. SATB,
cong, kybd, gtr, fls.

Tavener, John. "The Lamb." CHE 55570. SATB.

Tomkins, Thomas. "My Shepherd Is the Living Lord."
CPH 98-141A, T. SATB, org.

Zimmermann, Heinz Werner. "Psalm 23." AFP 11-638. Also in *The Augsburg Choirbook* 11-10817. SATB, str bass.

CHILDREN'S CHOIRS

Clausen, René. "I Am Jesus' Little Lamb." MSF YS301. U, opt 2 pt,
kybd.

Lenel, Ludwig. "Loving Shepherd of the Sheep" in *Morning Star Choir Book.* CPH 97-628. 2 pt, kybd.

Roth, John. "David's Song." CPH 98-3184. SA, C inst, kybd.

KEYBOARD/INSTRUMENTAL

Albrecht, Timothy. "Little Flock" in *Grace Notes VII.* AFP 11-10856. Org.

Darke, Harold. "A Meditation on 'Brother James' Air.'" OXF 31.124.
Org.

Kane, Daniel Q. "St. Columba" in *Selectable Delectables.* AFP 11-10619.
Pno.

Wright, Searle. "Prelude on 'Brother James' Air.'" OXF 93.103. Org.

HANDBELL

Kerr, J. Wayne. "A Shepherd's Psalm." CGA. CGB116. 3-5 oct, fl, narr.

Sherman, Arnold. "The Strife Is O'er." HOP 1847. 3-5 oct.

PRAISE ENSEMBLE

Beaker. "Step By Step" in *Come Celebrate!* ABI.

McFerrin, Bobby. "The 23rd Psalm." HAL 0859551. SATB, orch.

Moen, Don. "All We Like Sheep" in *Integrity's Hosanna! Come and Worship Songbook.* INT.

Ray, Robert. "He Never Failed Me Yet." JEN 447080167. SATB,
brass, perc.

MONDAY, APRIL 26
ST. MARK, EVANGELIST (TRANSFERRED)

Mark, though not an apostle, was likely a member of one of the early Christian communities. The gospel attributed to Mark is brief and direct, and is considered by many to be the first gospel. Because of its emphasis on the suffering of Christ it is sometimes called a "passion narrative with a long introduction." The gospel of Mark also challenges the reader to share in Jesus' sufferings. Mark was martyred in Alexandria, and he is the patron saint of Venice where his remains are said to rest. His symbol is the winged lion.

Read Mark's account of the resurrection in chapter 16. The original text of Mark ended at 16:8 with the disciples fleeing in terror and amazement. What additional information do Matthew, Luke, and John include in their accounts of the resurrection?

THURSDAY, APRIL 29
CATHERINE OF SIENA, TEACHER, 1380

Catherine is honored for her service to the church as a political negotiator, a mystic, a reformer, and a minister to the imprisoned and the poor. Though known for her visions of Jesus and for mystical ecstasy, Catherine was also considered a down-to-earth woman. Her most famous writing is *The Dialogue*, a series of conversations between Catherine and the Holy Trinity in which she uses vivid imagery to interpret the life of the Christian, the church, and the ministry. Among Roman Catholics, she is recognized as the first woman to receive the title "Doctor of the Church."

Catherine experienced deep union with Christ and had a significant impact on the public life of her day. Name others who lived a contemplative life while making important contributions to society.

SATURDAY, MAY 1
ST. PHILIP AND ST. JAMES, APOSTLES

Philip was one of the first disciples of Jesus, who after following Jesus invited Nathaniel to "come and see." According to tradition, he preached in Asia Minor and died as a martyr in Phrygia. James, the son of Alphaeus, is called "the less" to distinguish him from another apostle named James, commemorated on July 25. Philip and James are commemorated together because the remains of these two saints were placed in the Church of the Apostles in Rome on this day in 561.

The gospel for this commemoration (John 14:8-14) parallels the gospel for the Fifth Sunday of Easter (John 14:1-14) tomorrow. Preachers might comment on Philip as an Easter saint whose witness calls to invite others to come and see the presence of the risen Christ in word and sacrament.

MAY 2, 1999

FIFTH SUNDAY OF EASTER

INTRODUCTION

The gospel readings for the last Sundays of Easter shift the focus from Christ's presence among the disciples to his care for those who will continue his mission in the world. While the scriptural context is obvious, Christ addresses his contemporary disciples as well. To the community that bears his name he says, You will also do the works that I do. The church keeps Easter's fifty days in order to discern anew its baptismal witness in the world. In our community, at this time, with these gifts, what witness can we offer to the one who is our way, our truth, and our life?

PRAYER OF THE DAY

O God, form the minds of your faithful people into a single will. Make us love what you command and desire what you promise, that, amid all the changes of this world, our hearts may be fixed where true joy is found;

through your Son, Jesus Christ our Lord, who lives and reigns with you and the Holy Spirit, one God, now and forever.

READINGS

Acts 7:55-60

Stephen was one of the seven men chosen by the apostles to serve tables so that the apostles could be free to serve the word (Acts 6:1-6). Stephen does more than distribute food, however. For his preaching of God's word, Stephen becomes the first martyr of the faith.

Psalm 31:1-5, 15-16

Into your hands, O Lord, I commend my spirit. (Ps. 31:5)

1 Peter 2:2-10

The First Letter of Peter has spoken of Christians as people reborn through the resurrection of Christ. Now, those who have experienced this new birth in baptism are encouraged to seek the nourishment of scripture that provides spiritual growth.

John 14:1-14

John's gospel records here some of Jesus' final words to his disciples before his departure. As the one through whom God is known, he promises always to go before them and to continue to act on their behalf.

COLOR   White

THE PRAYERS

Rejoicing in the resurrection, let us remember in prayer the church, the world, and all those in need.

A BRIEF SILENCE.

For bishops, pastors, and leaders in the church, that they may faithfully equip the baptized to fulfill their calling to be the priesthood of all believers, we pray:

Hear us, risen Lord.

For leaders in the world, that they may defend the rights of all people to practice their religious faith, we pray:

Hear us, risen Lord.

For those who live with illness, or whose hearts are troubled (especially . . .), that they find comfort in Christ—the way, the truth, and the life, we pray:

Hear us, risen Lord.

For all who hunger for bread or for truth, that we may share God's bounty with them, we pray:

Hear us, risen Lord.

For this assembly, that nourished by the eucharist, we

may declare the deeds of the one who called us out of darkness into marvelous light, we pray:

Hear us, risen Lord.

HERE OTHER INTERCESSIONS MAY BE OFFERED.

We give thanks for Athanasius, and all the saints who have lived in faith. Bring us with them to the dwelling place prepared for us. We pray:

Hear us, risen Lord.

Receive our prayers and hopes, O God, and fill us with the risen life of Christ our Lord.

Amen

IMAGES FOR PREACHING

The Easter road now starts to turn decisively toward Pentecost. There is a pending departure and we must be prepared for it. Jesus speaks about a destination, a prepared place where he and we can be together. We automatically think of heaven, but is this what he means? How ironic that Thomas asks the question! "How can we know the way?" *I am the way,* says Jesus, but no one at this point (especially Thomas) could begin to anticipate the shocking climax: he will make a home within us!

Stones make a curious encore in these lessons. There are stones and there are stones. Stephen knows the stone as the missile hurled against him. The epistler speaks about a living stone, but the image is hard to grasp since we do not grow houses or castles. Or do we?

Jesus is preparing a place where he and we can be together: it is within our own organic bodies into which he plans to blow his Easter breath. We are his body together: "chosen race, holy nation, God's own people." Stephen discovers even when he is alone before the unbridled fury of the mob he is not alone after all: Jesus is with him. We, too, are called out of darkness into the marvelous light. But we are constituted as a people only when we have tasted mercy. And we can only taste mercy if we can stumble on the stone. Peter did. The disciples did. We do, too. Tasting mercy is the beginning of the light.

But this story is not yet done—not at all! Greater things are still on the horizon, for the risen Christ will multiply his presence and receive a whole new body into which disciples themselves will be constituted—"living stones" after all!

220

WORSHIP MATTERS

Worship is the work of the people of God, of all those who gather to hear Christ's word of forgiveness and to be empowered for service in the world. Similarly, all God's people are invited into leading the Sunday assembly, each with a part to play based upon their calling and their gifts for ministry. *LBW* suggests that an assisting minister be a prominent participant in the liturgy, and it is most appropriate for this person to be a layperson. While in many places the assisting minister does all the portions of the liturgy other than those assigned to the presider, the participation of the whole people of God in the Sunday liturgy is best demonstrated when many more are involved. Laypeople may be invited to read the lessons, write and lead the prayers, bring the gifts of money, bread, and wine to the altar at the offertory, and serve as acolytes, ushers, and greeters. Each role serves a vital part in making the liturgy a true reflection of the community gathered for prayer, and a hospitable place into which newcomers are invited. In all these ways, the risen Lord meets the baptized with grace and mercy, and through them all are invited to give praise and thanks to God.

LET THE CHILDREN COME

By this Sunday all the lilies from Easter Sunday are gone. It is still too early for the celebration of the fifty days to come to an end though. There are a couple more Sundays to go. Invite children and their families to bring spring flowers from their own gardens to worship. Prior to worship, time can be set aside for children to assist the altar guild in preparing the church for the morning's worship. Now that a month of Easter Sundays has passed, it is one way to provide a boost to make it to the end of the Easter season.

MUSIC FOR WORSHIP

GATHERING

| LBW 138 | He is arisen! Glorious Word! |
| WOV 726 | Oh, sing to God above |

PSALM 31

Hopson, Hal H. *Psalm Refrains and Tones.* HOP 425.

Schiavone, John. "Ps 31: Father, I Put My Life in Your Hands" in STP, vol. 1.

Sedio, Mark. PW, Cycle A.

Smith, G. Boulton. "Father, Into Your Hands" in PS2.

HYMN OF THE DAY

| WOV 691 | Sing with all the saints in glory |
| | MISSISSIPPI |

VOCAL RESOURCES

Roberts, William Bradley. "In All These You Welcomed Me." AFP 11-10661. Org, B/C inst.

INSTRUMENTAL RESOURCES

Biery, James. "Sing With All the Saints in Glory" in *Tree of Life.* AFP 11-10701. Org.

Hassell, Michael. "Mississippi" in *More Folkways.* AFP 11-10866. Pno, inst.

Keesecker, Thomas. "On the Mississippi" in *Together Again.* AFP 11-10717. Pno.

ALTERNATE HYMN OF THE DAY

| LBW 143 | Now all the vault of heaven resounds |
| LBW 513 | Come, my way, my truth, my life |

COMMUNION

| LBW 464 | You are the way |
| WOV 671 | Alleluia, alleluia, give thanks |

SENDING

| LBW 557 | Let all things now living |
| WOV 781 | My life flows on in endless song |

ADDITIONAL HYMNS AND SONGS

WOV 704	Father, we thank you
AYG 137	The house of faith has many rooms
BH 383	We are God's people
PsH 533	Church of God, elect and glorious

MUSIC FOR THE DAY

CHORAL

Buszin, Walter, ed. "Jesus Is Our Joy, Our Treasure." CPH 98-107. SATB.

Carter, Andrew. "The Light of the World." OXF E161. SATB, org.

Ferguson, John. "Jesus My Lord and God." AFP 11-2246. U, kybd.

Jennings, Kenneth. "With a Voice of Singing." AFP 11-137. Also in *The Augsburg Choirbook.* 11-10817. SATB.

Luther, Martin. "I Shall Not Die." CPH 98-319. SATB.

Parker, Alice. "The Wells of Salvation." OXF 02.245. SATB, org, hb.

Paynter, John. "The Call." OXF 351125-8. 2 pt, org.

Schütz, Heinrich. "In Thee, O Lord, Do I Put My Trust." PLY SC-117. SATB.

Shaw, Martin. "With a Voice of Singing." GSCH 810. SATB, org.

221

White, David Ashley. "The Call." SEL 418-606. SATB, org.

Wold, Wayne L. "New Beginnings." AFP 11-10849. SATB, org, opt cong.

CHILDREN'S CHOIRS

Handel, G. F./Hal H. Hopson. "Lord, I Lift My Soul to You." CGA-440. 2 pt mxd.

Helman, Michael. "Jesus, We Want to Meet." AFP 11-10734. U, hb, perc, kybd.

Mitchell, Tom. "Celebrate the Good News." CGA 381. 2 pt, opt hb, opt str bass, kybd.

KEYBOARD/INSTRUMENTAL

Guilmant, Alexandre. "Paraphrase (on a Chorus of Judas Maccabaeus)" in *The Organ Music of Alexandre Guilmant,* vol. IV. MCF DM 243. Org.

Harbach, Barbara. "Easter Toccata." VIV 330. Org.

Keesecker, Thomas. "Come Away to the Skies" in *Come Away to the Skies.* AFP 11-10717. Pno/kybd.

HANDBELL

McFadden, Jane. "Hallelujah, Jesus Lives!" AFP 11-10573. 3-5 oct.

Moklebust, Cathy. "Christ Is Made the Sure Foundation" in *Hymn Stanzas for Handbells.* AFP 11-10722. Cong, 4-5 oct, org.

PRAISE ENSEMBLE

Hanson, Handt, and Paul Murakami. "God Without and Within" in *Spirit Calls, Rejoice!* CCF.

Malcolm, Michael Barrett. "He Is the Rock" SHW A 7100. SATB, gtr, bass, perc.

Wilkinson, Steve/David Clydesdale. "Build on the Rock!" WRD 310 0507 169. SATB.

Ylvisaker, John. "No Longer Strangers" in *Borning Cry.* NGP.

SUNDAY, MAY 2
ATHANASIUS, BISHOP OF ALEXANDRIA, 373

Athanasius attended the Council of Nicaea in 325, where as a deacon he defended the divinity of Christ.

From that time on he was a defender of Christian orthodoxy against the heresy of Arianism. He was Bishop of Alexandria for 45 years, and because his enemies accused him of a variety of crimes, he lived in constant danger of death. Athanasius cared for the desert monks and fathers, and his writings introduced the spirituality of the desert monastic community to the West.

Though Athanasius did not write the Athanasian Creed, it was named for him and incorporates his ideas. Since it is one of the three great ecumenical creeds, today would be an appropriate day to recite the Athanasian Creed (*LBW*, p. 54) or portions of it in the liturgy.

TUESDAY, MAY 4
MONICA, MOTHER OF AUGUSTINE, 387

Monica is remembered as the mother of Augustine who prayed fervently for his conversion. Monica was a disciple of Ambrose, and eventually Augustine came under his influence, turning from his wayward life and becoming baptized. In his *Confessions,* Augustine writes tenderly of his mother and her dying wish to be remembered at the altar of the Lord. He speaks of her "truly pious way of life, her zeal in good works, and her faithfulness in worship."

Any parent would do well to ponder these qualities. Why are parents so important in the faith formation of their children? What is the role of parents and sponsors when infants are baptized?

MAY 9, 1999

SIXTH SUNDAY OF EASTER

INTRODUCTION

In today's gospel reading, Jesus speaks clearly of the Spirit he will send to his disciples of every generation. Earlier in John's gospel, Jesus announces that a person comes to birth as a child of God through water and the Spirit. In this reading he calls the Spirit another advocate, the one who will speak to the heart of the baptized who listen in silence for his voice.

In their prayers, hymns, and preaching, Western Christians have tended to place greater emphasis on Christ than the Holy Spirit. In these Sundays, when the role of the Spirit in Christian life is highlighted, it may be appropriate to reflect on our understanding of this seemingly silent yet ever-present person of the Holy Trinity.

PRAYER OF THE DAY

O God, from whom all good things come: Lead us by the inspiration of your Spirit to think those things which are right, and by your goodness help us to do them; through your Son, Jesus Christ our Lord, who lives and reigns with you and the Holy Spirit, one God, now and forever.

READINGS

Acts 17:22-31

In Athens, Paul faces the challenge of proclaiming the gospel to Greeks who know nothing of either Jewish or Christian tradition. He proclaims that the "unknown god" whom they worship is the true Lord of heaven and earth who will judge the world with justice through Jesus, whom God has raised from the dead.

Psalm 66:7-18 (Psalm 66:8-20 [NRSV])

Be joyful in God, all you lands. (Ps. 66:1)

1 Peter 3:13-22

The First Letter of Peter calls Christians, who may be overwhelmed by the challenges of living and working in a non-Christian world, to use their way of life and their words to witness to the power of Easter manifested to them through baptism.

John 14:15-21

John's gospel is concerned for the faith of disciples who no longer have Jesus with them physically. Jesus promises that they will receive the Spirit and that he will continue to reveal himself to those who love him.

COLOR White

THE PRAYERS

Rejoicing in the resurrection, let us remember in prayer the church, the world, and all those in need.

A BRIEF SILENCE.

Send your Spirit to the church, that it may love you by faithfully keeping your commandments. We pray:

Hear us, risen Lord.

Send your Spirit to the nations, that together we might honor the one in whom we live and move and have our being. We pray:

Hear us, risen Lord.

Send your Spirit to all who suffer for their faith, that they may be strengthened by your word and holy supper. We pray:

Hear us, risen Lord.

Send your Spirit to mothers and all who care for children, that your motherly love enfold them. We pray:

Hear us, risen Lord.

Send your Spirit to all who feel orphaned or abandoned, and to all who struggle with poverty, addiction, disease, or illness (especially . . .), that your presence abide with them. We pray:

Hear us, risen Lord.

Send your Spirit to the pastor(s) and leaders of this congregation, that they may grow in love and servanthood. We pray:

Hear us, risen Lord.

HERE OTHER INTERCESSIONS MAY BE OFFERED.

We give you thanks for all the faithful ones who have lived and died abiding in the Spirit of truth. Bring us with them to the great and promised day when we will see you face-to-face. We pray:

Hear us, risen Lord.
Receive our prayers and hopes, O God, and fill us with the risen life of Christ our Lord.
Amen

IMAGES FOR PREACHING

Jesus' assurances to disciples in today's gospel look backward and forward. To Christian worshipers in twentieth-century sanctuaries, these lessons provide an echo of the Easter celebration even as they anticipate the coming feast of Pentecost. And within the fourth evangelist's narrative these sentences of Jesus set the stage for concepts and events that will not be fully understood until the dramatic climax of this gospel at John 20 (which we have heard in the octave of the Resurrection of Our Lord). What Jesus says about receiving the Spirit who will "abide with you and be in you" is not clear until he blows his own Spirit into bewildered disciples on Easter evening.

Therefore, we live in the strange limbo between the accomplished past and the unfolding future. In the difficult present, Christians have sometimes had to deal with persecutions, as the second reading reminds us. In our time, benign neglect is often the worst oppression many Christians have to experience publicly for their faith. However, all of us have opportunity from time to time to "account for the hope that is in you." That hope is Jesus' own resurrection breath, the heartbeat of his new life. As Jesus says, "You will live!"

Sometimes the most difficult circumstances provide the greatest opportunities for witness: suffering for doing good, or standing in front of a crowd of skeptics as Paul does at the Areopagus. How shall we witness? Not by arguing people into believing or moaning about our problems but by passing through baptismal floods and being ready to greet the risen Jesus at those places where we least expect to meet him—even in our suffering, even at the altars of unknown gods. The witness is of him. All you need to do is be willing to open your mouth and utter your amazement: "I wasn't expecting to find you here!"

WORSHIP MATTERS

The rite for Holy Baptism from *LBW* contains two primary focal points for the newly initiated. The first and most important is the washing with water in the name of the Triune God. As Luther reminds us, this central action of baptism communicates most effectively what God accomplishes in this sacrament when large amounts of water are used. In baptism the faithful die with Christ and are raised with him (Romans 6:4), a profound truth that tends to be obscured when the initiate is simply sprinkled with a few drops of water. Traditionally, the second major act of the baptism is anointing with oil and the giving of the sign of the cross to each new member of the body of Christ. Accompanied by a prayer for the gifts of the Holy Spirit, anointing with oil "seals" the act of God in water and the word; it "confirms" what God has accomplished by the use of signs that are reminiscent of the royal priesthood into which the faithful are initiated at baptism. Taken together, both washing and anointing ritually proclaim the fullness of the gifts that are ours by baptism into the death and resurrection of the risen Christ.

LET THE CHILDREN COME

Along with generous use of the water of Holy Baptism, the statement from *The Use of the Means of Grace* reminds us that "other signs proclaim the meaning of Baptism" (Principle 28). These signs include the laying on of hands with prayer, signing of the cross, anointing with oil, clothing with a white garment, and giving a lighted candle. Make sure all of the actions of baptism, beginning with the baptismal washing itself, are done with care and in full view of the children. This multilayered, multisensory reinforcement is the way children learn best, and it is a way that engages them the most.

MUSIC FOR WORSHIP
GATHERING

| LBW 524 | My God, how wonderful thou art |
| WOV 795 | Oh, sing to the Lord/Cantad al Señor |

PSALM 66

Haas, David. PCY, vol. 8.

Jothen, Michael. *Sing Out! A Children's Psalter.* WLP 7191.

Marshall, Jane. *Psalm Together.* CGA. CGC-18. U.

Proulx, Richard. TP. WJK.

Sedio, Mark. PW, Cycle A.

Smith, Alan. "Shout With Joy" in PW2.

Warner, Steven C. "Ps. 66: Cry Out to the Lord" in STP, vol. 2.

HYMN OF THE DAY

    LBW 508   Come down, O Love divine

                 DOWN AMPNEY

VOCAL RESOURCES

    Busarow, Donald. "Come Down, O Love Divine." CPH 98-2335. SAB.

INSTRUMENTAL RESOURCES

    Bender, Jan. "Four Variations for Organ on Down Ampney."
        AFP 11-0807. Org.

    Fruhauf, Ennis. "Changes on Down Ampney" in *Ralph Vaughan*
        Williams and the English School. AFP 11-10826. Org.

    Sedio, Mark. "A Tango for Organ on Down Ampney" in *Music for the*
        Paschal Season. AFP 11-10763. Org.

    Stoldt, Frank. "Pastorale on 'Come Down, O Love Divine.'"
        MSM 20-540. Solo inst, org.

    Wasson, Laura E. "Come Down, O Love Divine" in *A Piano Tapestry.*
        AFP 11-10821. Pno/kybd.

ALTERNATE HYMN OF THE DAY

    LBW 299   Dear Christians, one and all

    WOV 793   Shout for joy loud and long

COMMUNION

    LBW 474   Children of the heavenly Father

    WOV 741   Thy holy wings

SENDING

    LBW 533/4   Now thank we all our God

    LBW 189   We know that Christ is raised

ADDITIONAL HYMNS AND SONGS

    WOV 685   Like the murmur of the dove's song

    PH 285   God, you spin the whirling planets

    NCH 530   God our Author and Creator

    H82 430   Come, O come, our voices raise

MUSIC FOR THE DAY

CHORAL

    Byrd, William. "I Will Not Leave You Comfortless." NOV 29-0123.
        SSATB.

    Hassler, Hans L., and Hugo Distler. "Dear Christians, One and All,
        Rejoice." CPH 98-190. SATB.

    Near, Gerald. "Awake, O Sleeper, Rise from Death." MSM 50-4033.
        SATB, org, opt brass.

    Sjolund, Paul. "Children of the Heavenly Father" in *The Augsburg*
        Choirbook. 11-10817. SATB, org, opt trbl choir.

    Tallis, Thomas. "If Ye Love Me." OXF 42.60. SATB.

    Ward, Michael. "A New Commandment." WLP 7679. SATB, desc,
        cant, fl, kybd.

CHILDREN'S CHOIRS

    Kallman, Daniel. "Thy Holy Wings." MSFYS 102. U, desc, kybd,
        opt inst.

    DeLong, Richard. "All Things Bright and Beautiful." MSM 50-9406.
        U, kybd.

    Vaughan Williams, Ralph. "Unto Him That Loved Us" in *Morning Star*
        Choir Book. CPH 97-628. U, kybd.

KEYBOARD/INSTRUMENTAL

    Cherwien, David. "Suite for Organ on 'When In Our Music.'"
        AFP 11-10765. Org.

    Keesecker, Thomas. "This Is the Feast" in *Piano Impressions for Easter.*
        CPH 97-6695. Pno/kybd.

    Martinson, Joel. "Postlude for a Festival Day." AUR AE 50. Org.

HANDBELL

    Helman, Michael. "Processional in C." AFP 11-10768. 3-5 oct.

    McChesney, Kevin. "All Things Bright and Beautiful." AFP 11-10687.
        3-5 oct.

    McChesney, Kevin. "Cantad al Señor." AFP 11-10690. 2-3 oct, perc.

    Tucker, Margaret. "Northern Lights" (LAC QUI PARLE). AMSI HB-7.
        3-5 oct, fl, perc.

PRAISE ENSEMBLE

    Hanson, Handt. "Be My Home" and "Waterlife" in *Spirit Calls,*
        Rejoice! CCF.

    Klein, Laurie. "I Love You, Lord" in *Maranatha! Music's Praise Chorus*
        Book, 2d ed. MAR.

    Miller, John. "There's a Spirit Here." HIND. SATB.

225

SUNDAY, MAY 9
MOTHER'S DAY

MAY 13, 1999

THE ASCENSION OF OUR LORD

INTRODUCTION

The risen Lord enters the invisible presence of God in order to be present in all times and in all places to the church and to the world. Where shall we find the risen and ascended Lord today? In his word and his bread, in his people and his washing with water and the Spirit, and in all who cry out for mercy.

PRAYER OF THE DAY

Almighty God, your only Son was taken up into heaven and in power intercedes for us. May we also come into your presence and live forever in your glory; through your Son, Jesus Christ our Lord, who lives and reigns with you and the Holy Spirit, one God, now and forever.

READINGS

Acts 1:1-11

Before he is lifted into heaven, Jesus promises that the missionary work of the disciples will spread out from Jerusalem to all the world. His words provide an outline of the book of Acts.

Psalm 47

God has gone up with a shout. (Ps. 47:5)

or Psalm 93

Ever since the world began, your throne has been established. (Ps. 93:3)

Ephesians 1:15-23

After giving thanks for the faith of the Ephesians, Paul prays that they might also see the power of God, who in the ascension has now enthroned Christ as head of the church, his body.

Luke 24:44-53

At the time of his ascension, Jesus leaves the disciples with the promise of the Holy Spirit and an instruction that they should await the Spirit's descent.

COLOR White

THE PRAYERS

Rejoicing in the resurrection, let us remember in prayer the church, the world, and all those in need.

A BRIEF SILENCE.

Enliven the church with your Spirit, that it may powerfully witness to the ends of the earth. We pray:
Come, Holy Spirit.
Guide the leaders of nations, that they may grow in respect and cooperation with one another. We pray:
Come, Holy Spirit.
Raise up those who are poor, discouraged, depressed, sick, or who live without hope (especially . . .), that they may know Christ's abiding presence. We pray:
Come, Holy Spirit.
Deepen our care for the earth, that we may be faithful stewards of its resources, and be mindful of generations still to come. We pray:
Come, Holy Spirit.
Enlighten this congregation with your wisdom, that we may press onward toward the hope to which God has called us. We pray:
Come, Holy Spirit.

HERE OTHER INTERCESSIONS MAY BE OFFERED.

We give thanks for all the saints who now bless God in the heavenly places. Clothe us with power from on high that we may proclaim the crucified and risen one until we join them in glory. We pray:
Come, Holy Spirit.
Receive our prayers and hopes, O God, and fill us with the risen life of Christ our Lord.
Amen

IMAGES FOR PREACHING

Why did he leave, just when the new age was dawning? Would it not have made more sense for him to stay around and direct the new project that had emerged from his open tomb? Although John and Luke have their own particular spins on the way they tell the story they are agreed in this: the risen Jesus needs to leave the scene of his victory in order to make room for the radically new creation that is coming into being. "You will receive power when the Holy Spirit has come upon you," Jesus tells disciples who do not yet grasp what is about to happen. "You are witnesses of these things."

They will be more than passive bystanders, however. This Christ who has been raised from the dead and is now ascended to the right hand, as the second reading reminds us, is the one who now calls the shots in the cosmos. All things are under his feet. We have a friend in high places! But even more: he exercises this executive position for the church, which is his body. Once again we see the incredible linkage between Easter and Pentecost and us!

Why did he leave? Because it was time for us to grow up. But even more, he "left" because he was going to be present in the world a new way: "The church, which is his body, the fullness of him who fills all in all." His ascension, a coronation, is also the beginning of a commissioning of those who will now be his visible presence in the world—which means there is work to be done. It is the work he himself did while he was "with us": proclaiming repentance and forgiveness of sins, loving the unlovable, emptying himself for the sake of others. Just as we celebrated in Lent, the Three Days, and the Resurrection of Our Lord, so we must affirm now: this is our story, our victory, our new life. The preface for Ascension is a real blockbuster and gets close to that exotic doctrine of Orthodoxy known as *theosis*—our "divinization" in Christ, "that he might make us partakers of his divine nature." Alleluia, indeed!

WORSHIP MATTERS

As Jesus takes his earthly leave of the disciples he assures them of his continuing presence and of his forthcoming gift of the Holy Spirit. Farewells are never easy, but they are made more bearable as we recall the gift of baptism that binds us together in Christ's one body, the church. In our increasingly mobile society, people come and go from congregations frequently. Often these members have made a profound impact on the life of the parish through their generous contributions of time and energy, or by their personalities, which bear witness so powerfully to the love of God in Christ.

"Farewell and Godspeed" is a brief rite from *Occasional Services* that allows a congregation a ritual way of saying good-bye to people who have shared a parish's life. Whether it is a student who spent a few brief months, or long-time members who are leaving to retire in another community, this service of prayer and blessing is an appropriate way to recognize the gifts these people have shared within the local community of faith, and to wish them God's richest blessings for the future.

LET THE CHILDREN COME

How can the psalms provide a language of faith for children? One good resource is the translation of the psalms produced by the International Commission on English in the Liturgy (ICEL), *The Psalter* (Chicago: Liturgy Training Publications, 1994). The sentences are short. The language is direct. The imagery is clear and powerful. In Psalm 47, appointed for today, children would hear that God is awesome. Other phrases include, "Shout your joy to God," "God ascends the mountain to cheers and trumpet blast," and "To the king, sing out your praise."

MUSIC FOR WORSHIP

GATHERING

LBW 363   Christ is alive! Let Christians sing
WOV 674   Alleluia! Jesus is risen!

PSALM 47

Brown, Teresa. "God Goes Up" in PS2.

Haugen, Marty. PCY, vol. 1.

Pelz, Walter. PW, Cycle A.

PSALM 93

Hopson, Hal H. *Psalm Refrains and Tones for Singing*. HOP 425.

Hurd, Bob. "The Lord Shall Reign." GIA G-2717. 2 vcs, cong, acc.

HYMN OF THE DAY

LBW 157   A hymn of glory let us sing
               LASST UNS ERFREUEN

VOCAL RESOURCES

Pelz, Walter. "Alleluia, Sing to Jesus." CPH 98-3185. SATB, cong, opt hb, brass, timp, org.

INSTRUMENTAL RESOURCES

Dobrinski, Cynthia. "All Creatures of Our God and King." HOP 1737. Hb.

Mitchell-Wallace, Sue, and John Head. "Ye Watchers and Ye Holy Ones" in *From Humility to Hallelujah*. HOP 299. Tpt, org.

Nelhybel, Vaclav. "All Creatures of Our God and King." HOP 760. Brass, org.

Ore, Charles. "Lasst Uns Erfreuen" in *Hymn Descants for Treble Instruments*. AFP 11-10280. Kybd, trbl inst.

Tryggestad, David. "Lasst Uns Erfreuen" in *Deo Gracias*. AFP 11-10471. Org.

227

ALTERNATE HYMN OF THE DAY

LBW 159	Up through endless ranks of angels	
	(*alternate tune*: PRAISE, MY SOUL, LBW 549)	
WOV 756	Lord, you give the great commission	

COMMUNION

LBW 158	Alleluia! Sing to Jesus
WOV 699	Blessed assurance

SENDING

LBW 170	Crown him with many crowns
WOV 728	O Light whose spendor thrills

ADDITIONAL HYMNS AND SONGS

LBW 156	Look, the sight is glorious
WOV 669	Come away to the skies
H82 218	See the conqueror mounts in triumph
H82 214	Hail the day that sees him rise

MUSIC FOR THE DAY

CHORAL

Erickson, Richard. "Come Away to the Skies." AFP 11-10816. SATB, fl, fc.

Gerike, Henry V. "Up Through Endless Ranks of Angels." CPH 98-270. SAB, cong, tpt, org.

Rose, Michael. "Ye Choirs of New Jerusalem." OXF A412. SATB, org.

Rutter, John. "O Clap Your Hands." OXF A307. SATB, org.

Schütz, Heinrich. "Our God Ascended" in *Three Chorales for Easter and Ascension*. CPH 98-123. SATB.

Titcomb, Everett. "God Is Gone Up." HWG GCMR 2192. SATB.

Vaughan Williams, Ralph. "O Clap Your Hands." ECS 1-5000. SATB, brass, org, perc (orch pts available on rental).

CHILDREN'S CHOIRS

Butler, Donna. "Sing to God." CGA 607. 2 pt trbl, pno, opt hb, opt orff inst.

Cox, Joe. "Poor Little Jesus." CGA 633. U/2 pt, kybd.

KEYBOARD/INSTRUMENTAL

Albrecht, Mark. "On Jordan's Banks I Stand" in *Early American Hymns and Tunes for Flute and Piano*. AFP 11-10830. Pno, fl.

Harbach, Barbara. "Fanfare and Toccata on *Lasst uns erfreuen*." VIV 306. Org.

Vaughan Williams, Ralph. "Bryn Calfaria" in *Three Preludes on Welsh Hymn Tunes*. Galaxy. Org.

HANDBELL

Gramann, Fred. "Fantasy on 'King's Weston.'" HOP 1671. 3-6 oct.

Larson, Katherine. "Beautiful Savior." AFP 11-10516. 3-4 oct.

PRAISE ENSEMBLE

Hanson, Handt, and Paul Murakami. "Spirit Calls, Rejoice!" in *Spirit Calls, Rejoice!* CCF.

Harris, Don, and Gary Sadler. "Lord Most High" in *Integrity's Hosanna! Music Songsheets: He Will Save You*. INT.

Roberts, Leon C. "He Has the Power." GIA G-2476. SATB.

FRIDAY, MAY 14
PACHOMIUS, ABBOT, 348

Pachomius was the founder of cenobitic monasticism, and his rule was later instrumental in formulating the Rule of St. Benedict. He also extended women the opportunity to live in Christian communities in Egypt, establishing the first nunneries in Africa. Give thanks for the African American presence in the church today, and find ways to incorporate African American spirituality in your congregation's worship and musical life.

MAY 16, 1999

INTRODUCTION

"Holy Father, protect them in your name . . . so that they may be one" (John 17:11). With these words, Jesus prays for the unity of his disciples in every age, for their life, and for their mission in the world. Throughout these last days of Easter leading to Pentecost, we could readily pray these words: Holy Father, protect us in your name so that we may be one. In the midst of much economic, ethnic, and cultural diversity, there is ample room for letting what is distinctive about us become divisive. Yet, as Christians, our deepest identity is discovered in baptism, proclaimed in the word, and nourished in the holy supper: we are one people who struggle for the unity that God intends for the entire human family.

PRAYER OF THE DAY

Almighty and eternal God, your Son our Savior is with you in eternal glory. Give us faith to see that, true to his promise, he is among us still, and will be with us to the end of time; who lives and reigns with you and the Holy Spirit, one God, now and forever.

or

God, our creator and redeemer, your Son Jesus prayed that his followers might be one. Make all Christians one with him as he is one with you, so that in peace and concord we may carry to the world the message of your love; through Jesus Christ our Lord, who lives and reigns with you and the Holy Spirit, one God, now and forever.

READINGS

Acts 1:6-14

Today's reading is part of the introduction to the narrative of the outpouring of the Spirit on Pentecost. These verses tell of the risen Lord's conversation with his disciples on the eve of his ascension.

Psalm 68:1-10, 33-36 (Psalm 68:1-10, 32-35 [NRSV])

Sing to God, who rides upon the heavens. (Ps. 68:4)

1 Peter 4:12-14; 5:6-11

Christians should expect to be persecuted, the First Letter of Peter says, whether by violence, ostracism, or simply name-

calling. Firm faith is based on hope in God in defiance of such opposition.

John 17:1-11

John records Jesus' final prayer to his Father before his crucifixion. He prays that his followers, who continue his work in this world, will live in unity.

COLOR White

THE PRAYERS

Rejoicing in the resurrection, let us remember in prayer the church, the world, and all those in need.

A BRIEF SILENCE.

For the church catholic, that it may be one at the Lord's table and in ministry to the world, we pray:

Come, Holy Spirit.

For all who govern, that they may serve with humility and concern for all who face poverty or injustice, we pray:

Come, Holy Spirit.

For those who suffer in body, mind, or spirit (especially . . .), that casting their anxieties on God, they may know God's care for them, we pray:

Come, Holy Spirit.

For farmers and for seasonable weather, that the earth may yield forth food for all its peoples, we pray:

Come, Holy Spirit.

For all who long for justice, peace, or truth, that in their vigil they may be strengthened and upheld, we pray:

Come, Holy Spirit.

For church musicians and all who sing in choirs, that their offering may enrich the corporate praise of our congregation, we pray:

Come, Holy Spirit.

For those who gather around word and table, that we may witness to the unity God desires for the whole human family, we pray:

Come, Holy Spirit.

HERE OTHER INTERCESSIONS MAY BE OFFERED.

For all the faithful departed who share your eternal glory, we offer our thanks, that with them we may glorify you forever, we pray:

Come, Holy Spirit.

Receive our prayers and hopes, O God, and fill us with the risen life of Christ our Lord.

Amen

IMAGES FOR PREACHING

The stage is set. The hour has come. All things are now prepared. What happened once already in the celebration of the fifty days is about to happen again. In fact, it happens over and over. Spirit is coming! Into the void created by Jesus' departure a new body is about to be created.

The cast is chosen. They are named in the first reading—a curious place for the cast of characters, is it not? They watch Jesus ascend and then return to the upper room to wait. Each is named. One is missing; the twelve have become eleven. But they are there. Yes, Judas is gone but those who are left are still a complete cast, women as well as men. They wait. It is the beginning of their vigil.

The image of fire in the second reading is a curious anticipation of Pentecost, but not at all inappropriate. Yes, something strange is about to happen, but do not be surprised. Remember, please, how John the Baptist said *this* baptism would be with fire. Did we think it would be simple? Or painless? It was not for Jesus. Would we expect it to be different for us—we who are his body?

Yes, there may be suffering, but only for a little while. That, too, was how it was for him. The solidarity of the upper room assures us the drama will play itself out to the end. Jesus speaks about it in the gospel: "I am no longer in the world; they are." *There* is the agenda. "They know . . . ."

It is a day of waiting. The preacher would do well to focus on the hollow spots, the vacuums, the places where not everything has come together yet. Sometimes it is only a void. At other times it is filled with the fury of the fire or the roaring of the lion. But either type of place is the place of anticipation, the place for our vigil.

It is coming: tongue of flame, the wind already hurling down the valley and heading straight for us. We are targeted. Just wait!

WORSHIP MATTERS

One of the effects of modern denominationalism is to segregate into separate spheres music, ritual, and traditions that are often equally effective ways of proclaiming the good news. While not every practice, every hymn, each teaching from another tradition is appropriate for use in Lutheran congregations, each of the multitude of traditions that surround us provide a resource to enrich worship. The vast multitude of musical styles available in *LBW*, *WOV*, and a host of other hymnals, is only the most obvious example of vehicles from other traditions that can be used to deepen our faith and broaden our perspective on the God who is active among the whole people of God. While not turning our back on the rich resources of the Lutheran reformation, our Lord's prayer for the unity of all the baptized will be furthered as we draw from the deep well of rich resources contained in the various branches of Christianity.

LET THE CHILDREN COME

Today is the last of the Sundays of Easter. Easter itself is not merely the celebration of a past event, but joy in the ongoing presence of the risen Christ among us. This Sunday does not end that good news. To unfold the continued presence of the resurrected Christ who is with us in all our lives, conclude worship with a procession that includes a return of the alleluia banners and the paper strips buried on Transfiguration and unearthed on Easter Sunday. Have the procession lead everyone out of the church and into the street where Alleluias can be waved at passersby and the entire world.

MUSIC FOR WORSHIP

GATHERING

LBW 369	The Church's one foundation
WOV 719	God is here!

PSALM 68

Marshall, Jane. "Psalm 68" in *Psalms Together II*. CGA. CGC-21. U. Sedio, Mark. PW, Cycle A.

HYMN OF THE DAY

LBW 156	Look, the sight is glorious
	BRYN CALFARIA

VOCAL RESOURCES

Wolff, Drummond. "Look, Oh, Look, the Sight Is Glorious."
CPH 98-2611. SATB.

INSTRUMENTAL RESOURCES

Bisbee, B. Wayne. "Bryn Calfaria" in *From the Serene to the Whimsical.*
AFP 11-10561. Org.

Burkhardt, Michael. "Draw Us to You" in *5 Easter Hymn Improvisations,* set 1. MSM 10-403. Org.

Haller, William. "Bryn Calfaria" in *Back to Life Again.* AFP 11-10319.
Org.

Pelz, Walter L. *Hymn Settings for Organ and Brass,* set 4. AFP 11-10435.
Org, brass.

ALTERNATE HYMN OF THE DAY

| LBW 88 | Oh, love, how deep |
| WOV 756 | Lord, you give the great commission |

COMMUNION

| LBW 198 | Let all mortal flesh keep silence |
| WOV 703 | Draw us in the Spirit's tether |

SENDING

| LBW 260 | On our way rejoicing |
| WOV 742 | Come, we that love the Lord |

ADDITIONAL HYMNS AND SONGS

LBW 173	The head that once was crowned
UMH 312	Hail the day that sees him rise
WOV 685	Like the murmur of the dove's song
WOV 801	Thine the amen, thine the praise

MUSIC FOR THE DAY

CHORAL

Fedak, Arthur. "O Love, How Deep" SEL 425-339. SATB, cong, org,
opt brass, timp.

Hillert, Richard. "Alleluia! Voices Raise!" OXF 94.231. SATB, opt
cong, org, inst.

Keesecker, Thomas. "You Said, Pray Thus." CPH 98-3245. SATB, pno, fl.

Leavitt, John. "Begin the Song of Glory Now." AFP 11-10666. SATB,
org, perc.

Peloquin, Alexander. "A Great Harvest." GIA G-2875. SATB, org.

Pelz, Walter. "O Love, How Deep." CPH 97-567. U, cong, org.

Willan, Healey. "I Will Not Leave You Comfortless" in *We Praise Thee
II.* CPH 97-76. SA, org.

CHILDREN'S CHOIRS

Frahm, Frederick. "Come, Let Us Join Our Cheerful Songs."
CPH 98-3291. SAB, org, opt hb.

Tucker, Margaret. "With Mind and Spirit." CGA 581. U/2 pt, pno,
opt hb.

KEYBOARD/INSTRUMENTAL

Langlais, Jean. "Prelude on Coronation" in *Modern Organ Music,* book 2.
OXF 0193751429. Org.

Porter, Rachel Trelstad. "Day By Day" in *Day by Day.* AFP 11-10772.
Pno/kybd.

Rutter, John. "Toccata in 7" in *A Second Easy Album for Organ.*
OXF 0193751291. Org.

HANDBELL

Moklebust, Cathy. "God Is Here!" in *Hymn Stanzas for Handbells.*
AFP 11-10722. 4-5 oct.

Page, Anna Laura. "How Firm a Foundation." MSM 30-806. 2-3 oct.

Sanders, Patricia. "Day By Day." BEC HB123. 5 oct.

PRAISE ENSEMBLE

Avery, Joann. "With All My Heart" in *Come Celebrate! Praise and Worship.* ABI.

Emerson, Roger. "O Sifuni Mungu" (All Creatures of Our God and
King). HAL 3010467168. SATB.

Hanson, Handt. "God of Glory" in *Spirit Calls, Rejoice!* CCF.

Schram, Ruth Elaine. "Ev'ry Time I Feel the Spirit." WAR 224. SAB,
gtr, bass, drms.

TUESDAY, MAY 18
ERIK, KING OF SWEDEN, MARTYR, 1160

Erik, long considered the patron saint of Sweden, is honored for his crusades to spread the Christian faith in Scandinavia. As king of Sweden, he was a man noted for his goodness, and his concern for those who were poor and sick. On an expedition to Finland he was accompanied by Henry of Uppsala who founded the church in Finland. Erik was murdered by a Danish pagan prince assisted by rebels.

This commemoration could provide a fruitful discussion of the relationship between church and state. Discuss the current changes in the Church of Sweden. Share opinions of the relationship of church and state in this country. What circumstances compromise the relationship between government and religious freedom?

WEDNESDAY, MAY 19
DUNSTAN, ARCHBISHOP OF CANTERBURY, 988

Dunstan is remembered for his role in the revival of monasticism in England. As a monk at Glastonbury he later became abbot, founding new monasteries and developing new rules for their good order. He was made Archbishop of Canterbury, and carried out a reform of church and state. Dunstan corrected abuses by the clergy, encouraged laity in their devotional life, and was committed to concerns of justice. He was also known as a musician, an illuminator, and metalworker.

Consider a retreat to a monastery or abbey in your area. How do places such as these provide renewal for our spiritual lives?

FRIDAY, MAY 21
JOHN ELIOT, MISSIONARY TO THE AMERICAN INDIANS, 1690

As a seventeenth-century missionary among American Indians, Eliot learned their native language and customs. His Algonkian translation of the scriptures was the first complete Bible printed in the colonies. In addition, Eliot trained Native Americans to be missionaries to their own people.

As we pray for a greater sense of respect and justice for Native Americans, use this opportunity to learn of their spirituality and traditions. The response "Helleluyan" (WOV 609) is from the Muscogee (Creek) Indians, and can be used as an acclamation before the reading of the gospel.

MAY 22, 1999

VIGIL OF PENTECOST

232

INTRODUCTION

Pentecost is one of the principal festivals of the liturgical year. Several of the festivals have the tradition of night vigils preceding them. In this night of extended prayer and silence, we anticipate being filled anew with the power of the Spirit, perhaps as the believers were in the second chapter of Acts (an alternate first reading this night). The Spirit gathers the church together. It is the same Spirit that enlightens us by the word, calls us in baptism, and sanctifies us with the bread of life and the cup of salvation. Come, Holy Spirit!

PRAYER OF THE DAY

Almighty and ever-living God, you fulfilled the promise of Easter by sending your Holy Spirit to unite the races and nations on earth and thus to proclaim your glory. Look upon your people gathered in prayer, open to receive the Spirit's flame. May it come to rest in our hearts and heal the divisions of word and tongue, that with one voice and one song we may praise your name in joy and thanksgiving; through your Son, Jesus Christ our Lord, who lives and reigns with you and the Holy Spirit, one God, now and forever.

READINGS

Exodus 19:1-9
God establishes the covenant with Israel at Mt. Sinai.
or Acts 2:1-11
Believers are filled with the Spirit to tell God's deeds.
Psalm 33:12-22
The Lord is our help and our shield. (Ps. 33:20)
or Psalm 130
There is forgiveness with you. (Ps. 130:3)
Romans 8:14-17, 22-27
The Spirit prays for us.
John 7:37-39
Jesus nourishes believers with living water and leads them to the Spirit of God.

COLOR Red

THE PRAYERS

See the prayers for Day of Pentecost, May 23, which follows.

MAY 23, 1999

INTRODUCTION

On this fiftieth day of Easter, the church gathers to celebrate the ongoing life of the Holy Spirit who is its breath, vitality, and inspiration. Through the Holy Spirit, the good news unravels age-old divisions among peoples and nations. In the waters of baptism, the Spirit gives us birth as brothers and sisters of Christ and unites people of different races, tribes, and ethnic groups. In the bread and cup of the holy supper, the Spirit nourishes our unity in worship and witness. Far from celebrating its "birthday" on this day, the church offers thanksgiving to God for the very one who continues to sustain its life in each new generation and makes its prayer possible.

PRAYER OF THE DAY

God, the Father of our Lord Jesus Christ, as you sent upon the disciples the promised gift of the Holy Spirit, look upon your Church and open our hearts to the power of the Spirit. Kindle in us the fire of your love, and strengthen our lives for service in your kingdom; through your Son, Jesus Christ our Lord, who lives and reigns with you in the unity of the Holy Spirit, one God, now and forever.

READINGS

Acts 2:1-21

Pentecost was a Jewish harvest festival that marked the fiftieth day after Passover. After the year 70, this festival came to commemorate the covenant that God made with Israel on Mount Sinai. Still later, Luke associated the outpouring of the Holy Spirit with Pentecost as the fiftieth day after the resurrection. Luke regarded this day as the "birth date" of the church.

or Numbers 11:24-30

Psalm 104:25-35, 37 (Psalm 104:24-34, 35b [NRSV])

Alleluia, or *Send forth your Spirit and renew the face of the earth. (Ps. 104:31)*

1 Corinthians 12:3b-13

In the church at Corinth, some Christians claimed to be more spiritual than others. Paul writes to tell them the Spirit is active in every Christian and in all the varied ministries of the church.

or Acts 2:1-21

John 20:19-23

John's gospel tells us that the experience of Easter comes to fulfillment when Jesus visits his disciples, gives them the Holy Spirit, and sends them out to continue his work of forgiving sins.

or John 7:37-39

COLOR   Red

THE PRAYERS

Rejoicing in the resurrection, let us remember in prayer the church, the world, and all those in need.
A BRIEF SILENCE.

Fill your church with the energy of the holy and life-giving Spirit. We pray:
Come, Holy Spirit.

Breathe your spirit of peace and wisdom on the leaders of nations. We pray:
Come, Holy Spirit.

Reconcile races and nations divided by prejudice, fear, or warfare. We pray:
Come, Holy Spirit.

Comfort with the fire of your love all those who are sick or in pain (especially . . .). We pray:
Come, Holy Spirit.

Inspire us to use our spiritual gifts, and to serve faithfully in the various ministries in the one body of Christ. We pray:
Come, Holy Spirit.

Pour out your Spirit on this congregation, that we may be filled with new insight and noble vision. We pray:
Come, Holy Spirit.

HERE OTHER INTERCESSIONS MAY BE OFFERED.

Unite us with the missionary Ludwig Nommensen and the saints of all times and places until the coming of the great and glorious day of the Lord. We pray:
Come, Holy Spirit.

Receive our prayers and hopes, O God, and fill us with the risen life of Christ our Lord.
Amen

IMAGES FOR PREACHING

They were together: one body but many parts. One Spirit, but many gifts. In one sense it is almost chaotic—a babble of language as if preachers are filled with new wine. It has an element of disorder to it: Eldad and Medad of Exodus—careening out of bounds in unorthodox ways but still somehow managing to get the job done. It causes orderly souls no small amount of consternation.

The gospel poses a choice for us: to review one last time the climax of the fourth gospel, or to dip into an earlier scene where Jesus speaks about the Spirit's coming. The John 7 text is very curious: coming to Jesus because we are thirsty, yet discovering that rivers of living water pour from our own hearts! It makes sense only if his Spirit is within us! The life that pours out of us is his.

The Spirit will be with us in so many ways this day: in Word and words, in bread and wine, and perhaps even in baptismal water. But the Spirit will also be present in unanticipated surprises: the person we always overlooked, his gift we neither saw nor recognized; or the harsh and guttural accents of people who speak languages we do not understand and who come from places we can barely pronounce. Always there will be that part of us that resists the Spirit's coming: "My Lord Moses, stop them." But can you stop the wind? Can you stop the fire when it is driven by the wind? Can you hold back a resurrection? Hardly! So the best we can do is to make sure we are strapped in for the ride. We are taking off!

WORSHIP MATTERS

The festival of Pentecost is a marvelous opportunity to grasp more fully what we confess each week when we say we believe in "one holy catholic and apostolic church." The fact of the matter is that the church exists in a multitude of different settings, with a variety of languages, expressed in differing but dynamic rituals, and bearing witness to the breadth and depth of God's creation and the many gifts of God's kingdom. In many places, the story of Pentecost from the book of Acts is read by several readers, each reading in a different language. The cacophony of sound that results is a powerful testimony to the diversity of the church. But the assembly is also the place that gathers people into one community. A multitude of people bring to the assembly a vast array of experiences, hopes, and burdens. So it is important to speak with a language that seeks as effectively as possible to gather all those experiences into a common expression of God's love and grace. The language of the liturgy should invite into it as many of the people as possible who have gathered, and a language that finally is inaccessible must be altered so that all God's people can join in heaven's song of praise.

LET THE CHILDREN COME

In both the Old and New Testaments, the same word is used for the wind of God's Spirit and the breath that fills our lives. Can the wind of that Spirit fill our worshiping assemblies? At some point in the worship, invite all those gathered to take a deep breath and exhale with all the flair they can muster. You can imagine that the children will delight in this chance to worship with gusto. Have this breath of the Spirit move throughout the congregation: back to front, front to back, side to side. Let the congregation feel the breath of the Spirit move in their lives and among all gathered.

MUSIC FOR WORSHIP
SERVICE MUSIC

On Pentecost, a sequence hymn such as "Come, Holy Ghost, our souls inspire" (LBW 472/3) might be added after or in place of the gospel acclamation. Choir and congregation may alternate, the choir singing stanzas 1, 3, and 5 in the chant version (LBW 472), the congregation singing stanzas 2 and 4 in the chorale version (LBW 473). The Nigerian traditional song "Wa wa wa Emimimo" (WOV 681) is another powerful invocation of the Spirit, which might accompany a Gospel procession.

GOSPEL SEQUENCE HYMN

LBW 472/3   Come, Holy Ghost, our souls inspire
WOV 681   Come, O Holy Spirit, come

GATHERING

LBW 475   Come, gracious Spirit, heavenly dove
WOV 688   O Holy Spirit, root of life

PSALM 104

Bach, J. S./Hill. "Alleluia, O Come and Praise the Lord." CGA-174. 2 pt, kybd, 2 C inst.
DATH 43   When you send forth your Spirit

Kreutz, Robert E. "Lord, Send Out Your Spirit." OCP 9457. SATB, cong, gtr, org, solo inst.

Saliers, Don E. "Psalm 104." OXF 94.234. Cant, cong, SATB, org, hb.

Wright, Andrews. "Send Forth Your Spirit, O Lord" in PS2.

HYMN OF THE DAY

LBW 161   O day full of grace
           DEN SIGNEDE DAG

VOCAL RESOURCES

Christiansen, F. Melius. "O Day Full of Grace." AFP 11-00206. SATTBB.

Schalk, Carl. "O Day Full of Grace." AFP 11-1946. SATB, brass, org, cong.

INSTRUMENTAL RESOURCES

Ferguson, John. "Den Signede Dag" in *Hymn Harmonizations for Organ, Book III.* LUD O10. Org.

Pelz, Walter L. "Den Signede Dag" in *Hymn Settings for Organ and Brass,* set 4. AFP 11-10435. Inst pts 11-10436. Org, brass.

Sedio, Mark. "Den Signede Dag" in *Eight Hymn Introductions.* MSM 10-836. Org.

Wold, Wayne L. "Suite on 'O Day Full of Grace.'" APF 11-10827. Org.

ALTERNATE HYMN OF THE DAY

LBW 163   Come, Holy Ghost, God and Lord
WOV 682   Praise the Spirit in creation

COMMUNION

LBW 508   Come down, O love divine
WOV 684   Spirit, Spirit of gentleness
WOV 683   Loving Spirit

OTHER SUGGESTIONS

OBS 84   We sing the one God

SENDING

LBW 523   Holy Spirit, ever dwelling
WOV 687   Gracious Spirit, heed our pleading

ADDITIONAL HYMNS AND SONGS

WOV 773   Send me, Jesus
NCH 272   On Pentecost they gathered
RS 613   When God the Spirit came
UMH 538   Wind who makes all winds that blow

MUSIC FOR THE DAY

CHORAL

Bach, J. S. "Come, Holy, Quickening Spirit" in *Cantata 22.* CPH 98-283. SAB, kybd.

Burkhardt, Michael. "Come, Holy Ghost, Our Souls Inspire." MSM 50-5551. 2 pt, hb.

Distler, Hugo. "Come, Holy Ghost, Creator Blest." CPH 98-2360. SAB.

Hassell, Michael. "Spirit, Spirit of Gentleness." AFP 11-10850. SATB, pno, sax.

How, Martin. "O Holy Spirit, Lord of Grace." GIA G-4314. SATB, org.

Hurford, Peter. "Litany to the Holy Spirit." OXF E164. SATB, org/pno.

Jeffrey, Richard. "Come to Us, Creative Spirit." AFP 11-10851. SATB, pno, fl, cl, vc.

Leavitt, John. "Come Down, O Love Divine." MSM 50-540. SATB, vln/fl, kybd.

Palmer, Nicholas. "Pentecost Sequence." GIA G-4062. U/2 pt mxd, hb.

Proulx, Richard. "Christ Sends the Spirit." AFP 11-1882. Also in *The Augsburg Choirbook.* 11-10817. SAB, opt cong, org, fl.

Schalk, Carl. "Creator Spirit, Heavenly Dove." CPH 97-5730. SATB, cong, brass qrt, timp, org.

Schein, Johann H. "Come, Holy Ghost, God and Lord" in *Third Morning Star Choir Book.* CPH 97-497. SSB, cont.

Scott, K. Lee. "Gracious Spirit, Dwell with Me." AFP 11-02198. Also in *The Augsburg Choirbook.* 11-10817. 2 pt mxd, org.

Somerset Anthem Books for SAB choirs: vol. III: Holy Spirit. ECS 5139.

Sterndale Bennett, W. "God Is a Spirit" in *The New Church Anthem Book.* OXF 0-19-353109-7.

Willan, Healey. "The Spirit of the Lord" in *Second Motet Book.* CPH 97-5205. SATB.

CHILDREN'S CHOIRS

Cool, Jane. "Pentecost Fire." CGA 502. U, pno.

Patterson, Joy. "Each One Has a Gift." MSM 80-844. U, cant, cong, fl, kybd.

KEYBOARD/INSTRUMENTAL

Goemanne, Noël. *Trilogy on Pentecost.* FLA. Org.

Larsen, Libby. "Veni, Creator Spiritus" in *A New Liturgical Year,* ed. John Ferguson. AFP 11-10810. Org.

HANDBELL

Afdahl, Lee J. "Spirit in the Wind." AFP 11-10698. 3-5 oct.

Moklebust, Cathy. "Come, Holy Spirit." AMSI HB-21. 3-5 oct.

PRAISE ENSEMBLE

DeShazo, Lynn. "Let Your Fire Fall" in *Integrity's Hosanna! Music Songsheets: Holy Fire.*

Hogan, Moses. "I'm Gonna Sing 'til the Spirit Moves in My Heart." HAL 08740284. SATB. INT.

Smith, Michael W., and Deborah D. Smith/Don Marsh. "Great Is the Lord." CEL B-G0528. SATB.

235

SUNDAY, MAY 23
LUDWIG NOMMENSEN, MISSIONARY TO SUMATRA, 1918

The apostle to the Bataks was a man of deep faith, courage, and prophetic vision. In 1861 he left for Sumatra where he worked among the Bataks, a large tribal group then untouched by either Islam or Christianity. The developing church had a thoroughly Batak flavor—a translation of the Bible, acceptance of features of customary law, and the training of Batak Christians as evangelists, pastors, and teachers.

The festival of Pentecost is an opportunity to celebrate the diversity of the church around the world. Setting 6 in *With One Voice* provides an outline of a service that can include liturgical music from all over the world. It is a wonderful way to recognize how the gospel has been proclaimed amid many languages and cultures.

236

MONDAY, MAY 24
NICOLAUS COPERNICUS, 1543;
LEONHARD EULER, 1783, TEACHERS

Scientists like Copernicus and Euler invite us to ponder the mysteries of the universe and the grandeur of God. Copernicus' thirst for knowledge led him to put forth the revolutionary idea that the earth was not the center of the solar system, but that the earth revolved around the sun. Though Copernicus was an intellectual revolutionary, he was also a humble and compassionate man. Euler is regarded as one of the founders of the science of pure mathematics, and made important contributions to mechanics, hydrodynamics, astronomy, optics, and acoustics.

Some people see a conflict between science and religion. How can the church honor the contributions of science to our understandings of the world and universe? What does our Christian faith offer to these understandings?

THURSDAY, MAY 27
JOHN CALVIN, RENEWER OF THE CHURCH, 1564

Calvin, the French reformer and theologian, experienced a conversion in which he embraced the views of the Protestant reformation. He left the Roman Catholic Church, and formulated his theological ideas in the *Institutes of the Christian Religion*. He organized the reform in Geneva with a rigid, theocratic discipline.

As Calvin is considered the father of the Reformed churches, Lutheran congregations might find creative ways to learn more about Presbyterians, and members of the United Church of Christ, and the Reformed Church in America. What do we share in common with the Reformed churches, and how are we reinterpreting matters that previously divided us?

SATURDAY, MAY 29
JIRI TRANOVSKY, HYMNWRITER, 1637

Tranovský is considered the "Luther of the Slavs," and the father of Slovak hymnody. Trained at the University of Wittenberg in the early seventeenth century, Tranovský eventually became a pastor in Slovakia where he issued a translation of the Augsburg Confession, and published his hymn collection *Cithara Sanctorum* (Lyre of the Saints), the foundation of Slovak Lutheran hymnody.

Use this commemoration to pray for the Slovak church, and to give thanks for the gifts of church musicians. Sing one of Tranovský's hymns, such as "Your heart, O God, is grieved" (LBW 96), or "Make songs of joy" (LBW 150).

SUMMER

Losing is finding, following is moving,

and fruitful is the reward

IMAGES of the SEASON

Two words to daunt the bravest heart: "We're moving." Moving is right up there at the top of the stress scale, just below a death in the family. Even if we're looking forward to it, moving automatically involves turmoil, disorientation, and loss.

The cause for the move may bring us satisfaction, pleasure, and anticipation of new opportunities: a promotion, a marriage, or going off to school. It may be that we're finally able to afford a bigger place—or, as the nest empties, a smaller one (with ample closet space). Perhaps we've been itching to rehab an old and charming 100- or 200-year-old house, and it just became available.

Or we may have to move without wanting to, because of circumstances beyond our control: damage from wind, flood, or fire; violence within the home or in the surrounding neighborhood; changes in the landlord's plans, or conversion of rental units to condominiums; the corporation insisting on a transfer. Financial crisis can push us out the door. Illness or advanced age may make it impossible to keep up the property, and necessary to find a residence that will provide adequate care.

Moving is rough because—apart from the pain of trying to get the old place ready for others—we lose our familiar bearings. We don't know where anything *is*. We keep losing track of things, from the ridiculous to the sublime. How do we make a way through the legal and fiscal labyrinth? Where did the markers, scissors, and tape disappear? What box are the dishes packed in? (And if we know which box, do we remember where that *box* is?) Ouch! Where's the light switch? What happened to the phone book? What was that new phone number, again? Where are the schools, businesses, stores in the new neighborhood and environs? Where *are* we? How do we get there from here?

And that's even before asking questions like, can our old friends still reach us? Will we stay in touch? Who will turn out to be trustworthy friends in this new place? What will our new life be like?

Moving is sufficiently draining to body and soul that it's a wonder we do it at all. We don't generally move unless we're forced into it from outside or powerfully impelled from within. We tend to move not for the sake of moving, but in search of a better life for ourselves and those we love. *Life* is what requires movement.

We put up with the chaos and emerge worn out at first, but thankful for what resilience we have been able to tap, thankful to have made it through. If the old home is lost to us, our feelings of anger and grief are mixed with gratitude simply for a place to have landed and the chance to start life over again. If the move happened because we were able to choose more freely, then once we've stopped tripping over boxes and feel we're at least on the way to figuring out where we are, we can feel rewarded by what the new home provides: improved safety and shelter; money or effort saved; enhanced relationship, thanks to its size and location. We endure the move for the rewards at the end.

Our lives follow an overall rhythm of settling in and moving out, getting comfortable and risking the unknown. Sometimes this rhythm feels like a gentle rocking chair; other times we scream as we hold on for the roller-coaster ride. To be fully human, we need both stability and change.

Our life of faith also requires movement. In Christ we are both accepted as we are and called to move beyond it: to stretch, to grow. This call is true for the church as a whole and for every congregation, as well as for every one of us personally. Often, just as it seems we're settled in one spot, we're summoned to pick up and seek new horizons. But God calls us neither merely to dislodge our equilibrium nor merely to enrich our own experiences—though the call may well result in both effects. Rather, God calls us to get moving for the life of the world. Baptism pulls us into the very work of God: the care and redemption of all that God has made. It is for the sake of life—more abundant life for all— that we are called to move.

238

When we have a choice about relocation, many of us move in the summer, when other schedules slacken and the daylight is longest. The liturgical year is the same way. The color of the season after Pentecost is green. It means "go." You may move forward. Winter was a time of frozen stillness. Now the ground and skies are filled with activity. Bees buzz, crickets chirp, fireflies flash. The color green means life, growth, and renewal. The trees are in full leaf; the rows of sweet corn, inching higher; the back yard, a tangle of tomato plants, berries, and flowers. Children and animals romp. Fruit ripens in the trees and on the vines. We have spent six months fasting and feasting, looking inward. Now, as green reappears all around us and twilight comes later and later, we turn our attention outward, to bearing fruit: spreading the good news and helping others to grow.

Liturgical summer starts with the festival of the Holy Trinity. Jesus tells us, "Go therefore and make disciples of all nations." It concludes, at the end of August, with his exhortation, "Take up [your] cross and follow me." *Go . . . follow.* For three months we're on the road, finding unexpected rewards along the way.

We begin in the strong name of the Trinity—The Three in One and One in Three (LBW 188). The trinitarian faith we profess suggests dynamic movement within the life and being of God. The same Holy One has created the human family, is with us always, and sends us forth to teach and baptize. Father, Son, and Holy Spirit are one in creating and restoring life, lifting up the lowly and filling the hungry with good things. It is this very work we are asked to share: "Cure the sick, raise the dead, cleanse those with leprosy, cast out demons" (Matt. 10:8).

As we go with Jesus about all the cities and villages, proclaiming the nearness of God's reign, we travel light and settle in one house at a time. Movement will bring about turmoil, divided households, and even persecution. Sometimes we'll have to shake the dust from our feet. Sometimes as we risk the unfamiliar, we'll falter. Like Peter, we'll be walking toward Jesus on the water; we'll panic and sink. Sometimes our disorientation in

new territory will cause us to shun further vulnerability and thereby misunderstand the mission completely. "God forbid [the cross], Lord! This must never happen to you" (Matt. 16:22). Sometimes in our zeal to bring good news to villages that appear settled, we will forget that our hearers may be coping with upheaval we don't know about.

How good it is, then, that summer is not only a time for laboring in the fields, watching weeds and wheat spring up together, and anguishing over losses to rocky ground, birds, and thorns. Summer is also the season to relax: "Come to me, all you that are weary . . . and I will give you rest" (Matt. 11:28). Mission is not perpetual motion. We have a green light to become re-created by resting and playing outdoors in God's beautiful creation. On quiet evenings in deserted places, sitting on grass-green earth, we share what loaves and fishes we have, knowing them to be blessed. Everyone is filled.

As we catch our breath and our bearings, the Spirit brings to our awareness the rewards for the moves we have made, the risks we have undertaken. With James and John, we discover that the reward for our mission is not the best seats in the house, but something of another order entirely. We will indeed drink the chalice of suffering; we will also be offered cups of blessedly cold water on sweltering summer days. While controversy and rejection are inevitable, even more certain is the gracious welcome we will receive from others who invite us into their homes and lives. Prophets' and disciples' rewards are given and received in hospitality and refreshment, in shared joy at the nearness of the kingdom. Along the road we will witness genuine moments of healing, and watch God's word accomplish its transforming purpose. We will encounter people who truly hear the word and act on it. Just to be with them is a reward.

We move—we risk change—for the sake of life. We dare to take to the road—to take up our cross—because baptism into the death of Christ means being able to walk with him forever in newness of life. Losing is finding, following is moving, and fruitful is the reward.

239

ENVIRONMENT AND ART FOR THE SEASON

Considering the season after Pentecost as three distinct seasons—Summer, Autumn, and November—provides a much broader palette of signs, symbols, and colors to draw upon when designing the environment for worship. Here is an opportunity for worship leaders to expand their artistic thinking beyond a single set of green paraments, which serve the worship setting from the second Sunday after Pentecost to the Sunday before the celebration of Christ the King. Just as lectionary readings of the summer season progress from growth and mission to the autumn of God's work, so might the visual environment suggest the diversity of symbolic image, climate, and light.

EXTERIOR ENVIRONMENT

If your church has a lawn or commons, consider gathering there as a worshiping assembly prior to the start of the service, then processing into the worship space together. This common area can serve as a space to interact with your neighbors, to share in the bounty of your harvest, and show how these gifts, either real or symbolic, can be distributed to the community at large. The space could be decorated with stalks of wheat or other indigenous grains. A processional cross could lead the way into the worship space. Special banners might focus on themes of sowing, growth, and harvest, which relate to several of the gospel stories of this season (particularly those used on the third, seventh, eighth, ninth, and twelfth Sundays after Pentecost this year). Natural materials might be used in conjunction with the more familiar textile appliques.

Create an area on the church grounds for a garden. If this is not possible, ask several members of the congregation to set aside areas at their own homes that could be devoted to a garden supplying the church with fresh flowers. Do not be limited in thinking only of flowers. There are many beautiful vines, greens, and herbs that can stand alone or complement the decoration.

If worship goes outdoors for this season, plan how the available outdoor spaces might be used to maximum benefit for worship. Can certain areas of the church's property be used to frame the worship services? Perhaps there are interesting exterior architectural features of the building, or even sculptures, which would serve as wonderful backdrops, and might otherwise never be enjoyed or used.

Those congregations having outdoor services in the summer, or even those congregations having more informal indoor worship in these months, should still take care that all the elements used in worship are of good quality. Simpler and less expensive communion vessels may be considered, for example, but they still should hold the eucharistic elements with dignity.

INTERIOR ENVIRONMENT

Vestments for this season may need to take into consideration the warmer temperatures, especially in church buildings that are not air conditioned. Green chasubles and stoles might be unlined. Albs used for this season can be made out of loose fitting, lightweight blends (almost shirt fabric) so that liturgical leaders are able to be vested but comfortable. On those very hot days, it may generally be better to eliminate the use of vestments entirely. But be sensible about this. A presiding minister is probably going to be cooler in a loose fitting alb than in a suit coat. Even if street clothes are chosen over other vestments for the warmest of days, a stole may still be worn as a symbol of the pastoral office.

Be creative with the use of containers for floral arrangements and other plants by varying their design, material, and size. Experiment with the location of these containers in the worship space and narthex by setting them on the floor, credence tables, or attached to decorative columns. While it may be easier to have a local florist deliver arrangements, the furnishing of flowers by members of the congregation presents a real opportunity on a weekly basis to impact the worshiping environment in fresh and imaginative ways.

PREACHING WITH THE SEASON

North American summer is a blossoming of abundance as the sun unfurls cities and wildernesses. In the late twilight, children shout across back-yards and balconies, stoops and haylofts, tepee rings and tundra paths, their voices ancient echoes through open windows across the great land. July fireworks spangle swollen waters in rivers and con-crete fountains, rippling reflections of Canadians and Americans celebrating their histories. Seashore to lakeshore, everglades to ice floes, hatching and hoard-ing, feeding and cavorting, every fin, feather, and sting multiplies in a ceaseless riot of getting and begetting. People swarm the out-of-doors: cheering graduates and newlyweds, hawking souvenirs on boardwalks, embrac-ing old and new relatives, and cling-crawling the sides of rocky mountains. Out at sea, summer dawns slide; the deeps of warm waters heave, gestating El Niño.

Not all summer verbs sing green, plenitude, reunion, or rest. Fish flail and flop upon the beaches of bays and lakes, succumbing to new viruses in their watery home. Too early, toxin-damaged eggs break in prairie hawk nests. Children painting church doors in the South Bronx bleed, stung in drug gang crossfire. Acres of crops bend, break, and collapse under the shock of August hailstones. Tempers thin, making cars dominoes of death on holiday weekend highways.

Over the summer of the land's seeding, cultivation, and watering, the church begins with the festival of the Holy Trinity, to be renewed, seeded and watered on Jesus' teaching in order to feed creation's current hunger. Trinity Sunday events dig into our hearts, over-turning them anew, and laying us open to God. All sum-mer, readings rain over the assembly by feeding our faith, while at the same time having us ponder ques-tions. What might it mean to believe that God is with us, come what may? What does it mean to doubt and to follow anyway? What might it require to follow one executed on a cross? How does it sound when one risen from the dead calls you to follow? Why does God trust us to follow Christ as witnesses in our quotidian world?

Holy Trinity Sunday is not a doctrine day, but a day recalling that, by the triune mystery, we live in love, peace, and communion with God. Genesis tells us we are part of God's good, ordered creation. With the Corinthians we are called to put things in order and live in peace, for, like the diminished assembly of doubters and believers at the close of Matthew's gospel, our baptismal calling is to go to all peoples washing and teaching them into the very presence of God the Trin-ity. These readings equip us to move communally through all the Matthean teachings of summer, autumn, and November. With spare liturgies trimmed of festive elements and simplified for ordinary time, the summer assembly follows Jesus on the path to the cross.

In our summer gatherings, with strangers visiting, we rediscover that we too are visitors welcomed in to overhear the teachings at ancient gatherings, and we too—like thousands fed before us—receive bread bro-ken and given for us. Again and again, we watch Jesus making disciples, not with teaching and preaching only, but with attentive caring for the needs of the whole person: meeting sickness with health, overturning death with life, healing exclusion with community, correcting with rebuke, and protecting with retreat.

With the Matthean Jesus, we also follow Paul's explanations of the meaning of being washed into the unconditional love of God in baptism (Rom. 4–13). Summer preaching could easily rest on these readings, exploring our calling to faith like Abraham and Sarah (4:13-25), that plunges us into Christ and into suffering (5:1-8), but frees us from fear of death (6:1b-11) as we offer our whole lives as holy instruments to embody Christ (6:12-23).

241

PLANNING AHEAD FOR THE SEASON

If your congregation is one in which the service schedule is streamlined during the summer (from two services down to one, for example), consider learning something new during this time when you have everyone together. Perhaps you

could learn a new musical setting of the liturgy (and if you have shortened the entrance rite, this will be made even easier). See some of the other alternatives presented in *LBW* or *WOV*. Come fall you may decide to return to more familiar patterns, but in the meantime you will have made friends with something new.

Summer is a time when many congregations decide to have a unison, intergenerational (or "family") choir, while regular choirs take summer breaks. Simplicity is often the key for this to work well. The choir meets for 45 minutes to an hour before the service in order to practice the music for that day (possibly also taking a few moments to look at something for one week hence as well). It can be a choir *du jour*—no one needs to be committed to more than one Sunday at a time. Consider singing unison anthems or even hymns (especially those that are not yet in the congregation's repertoire). A rhythm instrument or two, as well as having people alternate their singing on particular stanzas can dress up an otherwise straightforward piece.

Whatever is done during the summer months should not convey that the church is "on vacation." Keep the interest going. Be realistic (sure, people may be traveling more now), but do not cut away everything so that worship attendance is a self-fulfilling prophecy!

A common practice in Lutheran tradition is to replace a Sunday after Pentecost (also "after Epiphany" or "after Christmas") with a lesser festival when it falls on the same day. This summer the lesser festivals of St.

James the Elder, Apostle (July 25) and Mary, Mother of Our Lord (August 15) occur on Sundays. Worship planners will need to be mindful of this ahead of time, since the congregation (in particular the many worship leaders) will need to know which sets of readings will be used (and consequently which color of paraments and vestments will be used). While the lesser festivals appear to disrupt the flow of the lectionary, some people also see the lesser festivals as a respite from weeks and weeks of "green" or "ordinary" Sundays. The festival of Mary, Mother of Our Lord may be a particularly good opportunity to interrupt the flow of the Sundays after Pentecost since most Protestants have typically underemphasized her importance, even among other saints and biblical figures.

In the United States, Independence Day (July 4) occurs on a Sunday this year. It is often tempting at this time for congregations to abandon the lectionary and the messages associated with it in favor of more patriotic themes. Though Christians live within given countries, the loyalty we have to God should never be confused or replaced with loyalty to flag or country. While the national holiday is rightly remembered in one or more petitions of the prayers—perhaps even the inclusion of a national song among the hymns sung on this day—today's lectionary cautions against triumphalism of any kind. The readings from Zechariah 9:9-12 and Matthew 11:16-19, 25-30 speak about the Lord's gentleness and humility. Any patriotic fervor on this day might be exchanged for an examination of ways in which Christians can be of genuine service to their country and to the world at large.

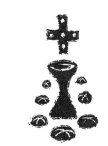

ORDO FOR THE SEASON

If there is a wish to make some of the summertime services shorter, consider shortening those "may be used" portions of the service, rather than "is said" or "is sung" portions, as indicated by the rubrics of the printed orders for Holy Communion

in *LBW* and *WOV*. This long "green" season may be a good time to abbreviate some of the gathering rite. Perhaps all that is needed throughout the summer is an entrance hymn, followed by the apostolic greeting, and the prayer of the day. (Depending on your congregation's custom, a brief order for confession and forgiveness may also precede the liturgy.)

Some things should not be cut, no matter what. Consider keeping all of the readings, along with the psalm. If the word liturgy must be shortened, retain the use of the first reading, either the psalm or the verse, the gospel, and the sermon. Preachers might want to adopt a shorter preaching style during the season (especially if the worship space is uncomfortable during these warmer days). Do not cut out the use of a eucharistic prayer during this season, but consider shorter alternatives, such as the seasonal prayer (*WOV*, p. 71), or the option printed in the order of the Holy Communion (*LBW*, number 33). Note also that neither *LBW* nor *WOV* prescribe the use of a concluding hymn at Holy Communion (though a hymn might replace one of the post-communion canticles).

243

ASSEMBLY SONG FOR THE SEASON

What shall we call this time in the church year? Some church calendars

number these days as "Sundays after Pentecost." That's fairly clear, but it's

not very poetic. Some informally refer to it as the

Pentecost season, but if anything should be

called that, it is the fifty days between Easter and Pentecost. Other denominations have used the word Kingdomtide, emphasizing the many "kingdom of God" stories read during this time. Most well known is the title "Ordinary Time." Without any major festival days during this six months of the calendar, this name refers to the ordinal, the systematic marking of time.

Unfortunately, most people hear the word ordinary and think it says something about the content of the liturgies during this time. Every week, we hear extraordinary stories of God's extravagant love for us, we are challenged to respond to this love. There is nothing ordinary about God's message to us during this time. And neither should our worship and music be "ordinary."

For most people living and working in North American culture, life during the summer months is significantly different from the rest of the year. Even though there is little parallel between the secular school calendars and the church calendar, most congregations operate programmatically in sync with schools. Ironically, we stop many activities just when many people, especially children, have additional time on their hands. Depending on local circumstances, possibilities for continuing involvement may include: intergenerational choirs, instrumental or vocal solos, duets, and other small ensembles. Find a Sunday when your four best singers will be available and schedule a four-part motet. Arrange for your less skilled singers to gather together and sing a simple hymn in unison with some alternate organ or piano accompaniments. See which handbell ringers are available and use them to give pitches and accent the phrases of a simple psalm tone. It is an excellent time to focus on liturgical music, such as singing the psalms and gospel acclamations.

During the summer, if we're not careful, the more relaxed atmosphere can easily turn into carelessness. This "relaxation" is most often evident as the worshipers assemble, often noisily and seemingly nonreverently. These weeks may be an excellent opportunity to focus on the gathering, the first segment of the liturgy. Consider the streamlined gathering rite suggested in "Ordo for the Season," above.

For centuries, worship planners could assume that when worshipers arrived they would sit quietly in their pews waiting for the liturgy to begin, ideally using that silence productively for prayer and meditation. We can no longer assume that an assembly will gather in silence. In some settings, it may be helpful or necessary to engage worshipers in song immediately as they arrive. This time may be an opportunity for singing old favorites or teaching something new. There is a fine line between an engaging participatory gathering and chaos. Once gathered and the time for worship has arrived, worshipers can be greeted and invited to keep a time of silence before proceeding with the liturgy. Just as silence plays a crucial role in the rhythm of any musical piece, so is it critical in the rhythm of the liturgy.

Summer is a common time to take vacations, even for organists. Finding a substitute keyboard player can be a challenge, especially one who understands liturgical worship. Even if the liturgy was completely "out of the book" with every rubric followed exactly, every congregation, with its unique architecture and personnel, has worked out its own way to enact the liturgy. One helpful thing to do for the substitute (and the worshipers) is to prepare liturgical accompaniment books with the music carefully labeled and tabbed. This organization can help in avoiding awkward page turns, and in providing directions regarding such practical matters as cues and timing.

244

MUSIC FOR THE SEASON

VERSE AND OFFERTORY

Cherwien, David. *Verses for the Season of Pentecost,* set 1.
MSM 80-541. U, kybd.

Powell, Robert. *Verses and Offertory Sentences, Part VI* (Pentecost
10–18). CPH 97-5506.

Verses and Offertory Sentences, Part V (Pentecost 2–9). CPH 97-5505.
U/SATB, kybd.

OTHER SUGGESTIONS

During the season after Pentecost, be sure to check the
propers in *WOV, Leaders Edition* for the verse and offertory that corresponds to the RCL proper number.

CHORAL MUSIC FOR THE SEASON

Bertalot, John. "Softly and Tenderly." AFP 11-10212. SAB, org.

DeLong, Richard. "For the Beauty of the Earth." ECS 4797. U, kybd.

Fairbanks, Brian. "You Can Tell the World." PAR PPM09527. SATB.

Hobby, Robert A. "Cantad al Señor." MSM 20-712. Inst pts 20-712A;
choir 50-9063. Cong, 2 tpt, perc, org.

Horman, John. "Small Deeds." CGA-562. U/2 pt, kybd.

Marcus, Mary. "I Come with Joy, a Child of God." HOP A716. SATB,
kybd, opt fl, cong.

Powell, Robert. *Surely the Lord Is in This Place.* AFP 11-10607. Vocal
solos, M.

Proulx, Richard. "Strengthen for Service." AFP 12-400005. SATB.

Roth, John. "Lord, Take My Hand." AFP 11-10379. SATB/U, opt ob,
kybd.

Schalk, Carl. "Our Soul Waits for the Lord." CPH 98-3252. SATB.

Scott, K. Lee. *Rejoice Now My Spirit.* AFP. MH 11-10228. ML 11-10229.
Solo, kybd.

Scott, K. Lee. *Sing a Song of Joy.* AFP. MH 11-8194. ML 11-8195.
Solo, kybd.

Tecson, Andrew. "Sing unto the Lord." CPH 97-6042. Solo, pno.

CHILDREN'S CHORAL MUSIC FOR THE SEASON

Hartland, Betty. "Jubilate." AMSI 695. U/2 pt, kybd.

Lindh, Jody. "Let All the World in Every Corner Sing." CGA 573.
U/2 pt/SATB, hb, kybd.

INSTRUMENTAL MUSIC FOR THE SEASON

Bach, J. S./Jack Schrader. "My Heart Ever Faithful" in *Flute Stylings.*
HOP 154. Fl, pno/synth.

Carlson, J. Bert. "Four Chorale Preludes." AFP 11-10615. Org.

Cotter, Jeanne. "The Love of the Lord" in *After the Rain.*
GIA G-3390. Pno.

Hassell, Michael. "Jazz All Seasons." AFP 11-10822. Pno.

Organ, Anne Krentz. *Reflections on Hymn Tunes for Holy Communion.*
AFP 11-10621. Pno.

Osterlund, Karl. "Holy Manna" in *American Hymn Trios.* AFP 11-10616.
Org.

Wold, Wayne. "Suite on O Day Full of Grace." AFP 11-10827. Org.

HANDBELL MUSIC FOR THE SEASON

Larson, Katherine. "Borning Cry." AFP 11-10517. Hb.

McChesney, Kevin. "Praise God. Praise Him." AFP 11-10630. Hb,
opt perc.

245

ALTERNATE WORSHIP TEXTS

CONFESSION AND FORGIVENESS

In the name of the Father, and of the ✛ Son, and of the Holy
   Spirit.
Amen

Let us confess our failures, fears, and weaknesses to God, asking
   that we be restored to wholeness and peace.

Silence for reflection and self-examination.

God, who cares for all,
we confess that we have not loved you
and have not cared for ourselves,
our neighbors, or the earth you created.
Forgive our lack of care
and our failure to attend to your creation in us and around us.
Take away our fear and our weakness,
and make us strong witnesses in word and action
to your redeeming love. Amen

Our God is merciful, slow to anger, and rich in steadfast love.
I declare to you the entire forgiveness of all your sin
in the name of Jesus, who has restored us to God our maker.
By the power of the Holy Spirit, be renewed to wholeness of life.
Amen

GREETING

The grace of our Lord Jesus Christ, the love of God,
and the communion of the Holy Spirit be with you all.
And also with you.

OFFERTORY PRAYER

Creator God,
the earth and all its fullness belong to you.
We thank you for giving these things into our care,
the growing of grain and grapes,
the money we earn from our work.
We offer these to you as signs of our faith and your love.
Receive them for the sake of Jesus,
who gives us himself in this holy meal. Amen

INVITATION TO COMMUNION

Nothing in all creation can separate us
from the love of God in Christ Jesus our Lord.
Come, delight yourselves in the rich food of God's table.

POST-COMMUNION PRAYER

Merciful God, we give thanks
for the strength we receive at your table.
By your Spirit transform and renew our minds,
that we may do your good, acceptable and perfect will,
in Jesus' name.
Amen

BENEDICTION

Strive first for the righteous reign of God,
and all these things will be given to you as well.
The Lord bless you and keep you.
The Lord's face shine on you with grace and mercy.
The Lord look upon you with favor and give you peace.
Amen

DISMISSAL

Go in peace to love and serve the Lord.
Thanks be to God.

246

SEASONAL RITES

BLESSINGS OF FIELDS AND GARDENS

Let us bless God, the creator of all things. God has given us the earth to cultivate, so that we might receive the bounty of its fruits. Just as the rain falls from heaven and waters the earth, bringing forth vegetation, so God's Word will flourish and will not return empty.

Reading: Genesis 1:1, 11-12, 29-31

PRAYER

Almighty God, we thank you for making the earth fruitful,
so that it might produce what is needed for life:
Bless those who work in the fields;
give us seasonable weather;
and grant that we may all share the fruits of the earth,
rejoicing in your goodness;
through Jesus Christ our Lord.
Amen

HYMN

LBW 409   Praise and thanksgiving
LBW 563   For the fruit of all creation
WOV 760   For the fruit of all creation

BLESSING FOR TRAVELERS

(From *Welcome Home, Year of Luke*, p. 118)
Use this prayer before leaving on a journey

O God,
our beginning and our end,
you kept Abraham and Sarah in safety
throughout the days of their pilgrimage,
you led the children of Israel through the midst of the sea,
and by a star you led the Magi to the infant Jesus.
Protect and guide us now as *we* [*or substitute the names of travelers*] set out to travel.
Make our ways safe and our homecomings joyful,
and bring us at last to our heavenly home,
where you dwell in glory with our Lord Jesus Christ
and the life-giving Holy Spirit,
one God, now and forever.
Amen
© 1997 Augsburg Fortress

247

MAY 30, 1999

INTRODUCTION

Christians have held a festival in honor of the Holy Trinity since the ninth century, when it was celebrated in French monastic communities. In the fourteenth century, the festival was added to the calendar and has been celebrated throughout the world since that time.

Every celebration of baptism and eucharist is a trinitarian celebration, just as every gathering "in the name of the Father, the Son, and the Holy Spirit" is done in union with the Sacred Three.

In the power of the Holy Spirit, the church gathers on Sunday—the day of resurrection—to offer thanksgiving to the Father for Christ's saving life given to us at the table of the word and the table of the eucharist. Listen carefully to the opening greeting, the baptismal "formula," the eucharistic prayer, and the final blessing: we are accompanied in life's journey by a community of persons. We are not alone. Indeed, the church is intended to be a sign in the world of the Holy Trinity's unity-in-diversity.

PRAYER OF THE DAY

Almighty God our Father, dwelling in majesty and mystery, renewing and fulfilling creation by your eternal Spirit, and revealing your glory through our Lord, Jesus Christ: Cleanse us from doubt and fear, and enable us to worship you, with your Son and the Holy Spirit, one God, living and reigning, now and forever.

or

Almighty and ever-living God, you have given us grace, by the confession of the true faith, to acknowledge the glory of the eternal Trinity and, in the power of your divine majesty, to worship the unity. Keep us steadfast in this faith and worship, and bring us at last to see you in your eternal glory, one God, now and forever.

READINGS

Genesis 1:1—2:4a

This creation story reached its current form during or after the crisis of the Babylonian exile of Israel. The writer makes profound declarations of faith concerning the world, human life,

and God. This faith sees the world and humanity under the sovereignty of the God who redeemed Israel: it was Israel's God who was responsible for creation, not Babylon's.

Psalm 8

How exalted is your name in all the world! (Ps. 8:1)

2 Corinthians 13:11-13

Paul concludes his painful letter to the troubled church at Corinth with a final appeal for these Christians to live in peace. His last words form a trinitarian benediction still used in Christian liturgy today.

Matthew 28:16-20

After his resurrection, Jesus summons his remaining disciples and commissions them for mission in the name of the triune God.

COLOR   White

THE PRAYERS

Let us pray for the church, the world, and all who suffer in mind, body, or spirit.

A BRIEF SILENCE.

That the church may live in unity, and thereby give witness to the triune God. Lord, in your mercy,

hear our prayer.

That the nations may live in harmony, according to the will of the God of love and peace. Lord, in your mercy,

hear our prayer.

That all those who are sick or in need (especially . . .) may be strengthened by God's healing power. Lord, in your mercy,

hear our prayer.

That we may see in creation a glimpse of the eternal beauty of God. Lord, in your mercy,

hear our prayer.

That our gathering around word and meal may strengthen us for ministry in the world. Lord, in your mercy,

hear our prayer.

HERE OTHER INTERCESSIONS MAY BE OFFERED.

That we remain steadfast in our faith, and follow in the path of all the blessed saints who have been baptized in

the name of the Holy Trinity, and now dwell in your everlasting glory. Lord, in your mercy,
hear our prayer.
O God, grant us grace to trust your promises, that our lives may bear fruit to the glory of your name, through Jesus Christ our Lord.
Amen

IMAGES FOR PREACHING

Refract the Holy Trinity through the prism of the gift theology of Scripture. Split off three beams from its one ray. Picture God first as the giver. Then as the gift. And finally as the one who helps us open up and use the gift that has been given.

The giver is God in all of God's life-giving manifestations: the creator of heaven and earth, the father of our Lord Jesus Christ, the one who raises Jesus from the dead.

The gift is variously presented in the Scripture: living water, life, salvation, grace, love, communion. Here it is "all authority in heaven and on earth." The gift of all authority is given to Jesus. By whom? The Father, of course. And yet, Jesus is given to us. And so the gift is always ultimately Jesus Christ, the Son, and his cross-won authority to forgive and retain sins and to restore and renew a terminally ill creation. John 3:16 (part of another trinitarian passage) lays it out so clearly. The gift is Jesus.

The gift of Jesus is received by those baptized in the triune name of God. Like a parent giving a gift to a young child, the Holy Spirit is the abiding presence of God (gift and giver) helping us to open up and use the gift that has been given.

It is possible not to receive this gift—to doubt and disbelieve. To not recognize the risen Jesus as God in human flesh is not to receive God in all of God's triune fullness, and thus not to obey what Christ has commanded. Summer is a good time to use the triune name of God and to renew one's bond with the Father's creation, bask in the Son and fling oneself upon the winds of the Spirit.

WORSHIP MATTERS

In what name do we baptize? *The Use of the Means of Grace*, the ELCA's statement on the practice of word and sacrament, sets forth this principle: "Holy Baptism is administered with water in the name of the triune God, Father, Son, and Holy Spirit" (Principle 24). Background material to this principle indicates "the Church seeks to maintain trinitarian orthodoxy while speaking in appropriate modern language and contexts. While a worldwide ecumenical discussion is now underway about such language, we have no other name in which to baptize than the historic and ecumenically received name." Principles 1 and 2 also engage the question of the Trinity. Take time this week in your community to enter into this "worldwide ecumenical discussion" about names of God, language, and formulas for Holy Baptism.

LET THE CHILDREN COME

Children's lives are filled with gestures. There are some basic gestures and meanings that they can immediately identify: a high five, a thumbs-up, and a parent's finger placed over the lips. There are other gestures that children use to express their identity: a hand over the heart during the national anthem, a hand raised for scouts' honor, and all of the actions that accompany the 4-H pledge. The ground is fertile to teach children the sign of the cross. This gesture identifies the life of the church and expresses a child's identity as one who is baptized in the name of the Father, and the Son, and the Holy Spirit.

MUSIC FOR WORSHIP
SERVICE MUSIC

Although a simpler gathering rite is appropriate for the "green" Sundays following Pentecost, this day calls for at least the trinitarian hymn of praise, "Glory to God." A setting of the Te Deum laudamus (see *LBW*, p. 139 or *LLC* 260) also makes a fitting hymn of praise on this day. The Sanctus, with its "thrice-holy" cry of praise, is another element worthy of embellishment on this day.

GATHERING

LBW 393   Rise, shine, you people!
WOV 793   Shout for joy loud and long

PSALM 8

Bell, John. *Psalms of Patience, Protest and Praise.* GIA G-4047.
Cooney, Rory. "How Glorious Is Your Name." GIA G-3412. SATB, gtr, cong, kybd.
DATH 33   Who are we
Geary, Patrick. "Your Name Is Praised" in PS3.
Shute, Linda. PW, Cycle A.

249

HYMN OF THE DAY

LBW 535   Holy God, we praise your name
           GROSSER GOTT

VOCAL RESOURCES

Arnatt, Ronald. "Holy God, We Praise Thy Name." MSM 60-9016.
    SATB, cong, org, opt brass, timp, orch bells.

Busarow, Donald. "Holy God, We Praise Your Name." CPH 98-2530.
    Choir 98-2534; inst pts 98-2531. Choir, brass qrt, timp, org.

Ferguson, John. "Holy God, We Praise Thy Name." GIA G-3167.
    SATB, org, opt brass, cong.

INSTRUMENTAL RESOURCES

Burkhardt, Michael. "Holy God, We Praise Your Name" in *Praise and
    Thanksgiving, Hymn Improvisations,* set IV. MSM 10-754. Org.

Carlson, J. Bert. "Grosser Gott" in *Four Chorale Preludes.* AFP 11-10615.
    Org.

Norris, Kevin. "Toccata on 'Holy God, We Praise Thy Name.'"
    HWG GSTC996. Org.

Peeters, Flor. "Holy God, We Praise Your Name" in *A New Liturgical
    Year,* ed. John Ferguson. AFP 11-10810. Org.

ALTERNATE HYMN OF THE DAY

LBW 400   God, whose almighty word
WOV 799   When long before time

COMMUNION

LBW 165   Holy, holy, holy
WOV 769   Mothering God, you gave me birth

OTHER SUGGESTIONS

OBS 64   In sacred manner

SENDING

LBW 517   Praise to the Father
WOV 796   My Lord of light

ADDITIONAL HYMNS AND SONGS

LBW 188   I bind unto myself today
WOV 794   Many and great, O God, are your works
LW 437   Alleluia! Let praises ring!
NCH 273   Praise with joy the world's Creator
TWC 543   Christ beside me

MUSIC FOR THE DAY

CHORAL

Arnatt, Ronald. "When the Morning Stars Together." ECS 4870.
    SATB, org, opt cong.

Bedford, Michael. "Go Therefore and Make Disciples. CPH 98-3270.
    U, kybd.

Erickson, Richard. "When Long Before Time." AFP 11-10815. SATB,
    fl, org.

Glinka, Mikhail. "Cherubic Hymn." PAR PPM 09501. SATTBB.

Hassell, Michael. "How Exalted Is Your Name." AFP 11-10854.
    SATB, pno.

Hopson, Hal. "Lord, O Lord, Your Name Is Wonderful." CGA 762.
    U, kybd, opt hb.

Hurd, David. "Creating God." GIA G-2891. SATB, org

Leavitt, John. "Festival Sanctus." BEL SV 8821. SATB, pno.

Neswick, Bruce. "Magna et mirabilia." PAR PPM09504. S(S)ATB, org.

Pinkham, Daniel. "In the Beginning of Creation." ECS 2902. SATB,
    tape.

Schalk, Carl. "Go Therefore and Make Disciples of All Nations."
    MSM 50-6200. 2 pt mxd, kybd.

Schütz, Heinrich. "A Song of Praise to the Holy Trinity."
    CPH BA 24. SATB.

Scott, K. Lee. "Trinitarian Blessing." AFP 11-10546. SATB, kybd.

CHILDREN'S CHOIRS

Hopson, Hal. "Do You Know Who Made the Day." CGA 331.
    U, fc/tri, org.

Sleeth, Natalie. "Go Into the World." CGA 209. 2/3 pt trbl/mxd, kybd.

KEYBOARD/INSTRUMENTAL

Bach, J. S. "Allein Gott" settings in *Leipzig Chorales* and *Clavierübung.*
    Various editions. Org.

Cherwien, David. "New Creation: Sketches on the Themes of Bap-
    tism." CPH 97-9089. Org.

Hebden, John Schaffner. "St. Patrick's Breastplate" in *Organ Music for
    the Seasons.* AFP 11-10859. Org.

HANDBELL

Linker, Janet, and Jane McFadden. "Rise, Shine, You People."
    AFP 11-10628. Hb pt 11-10629. Cong, 3-5 oct, org, tpt.

Moklebust, Cathy. "Let All Things Now Living." CGA CGB170.
    3-5 oct.

PRAISE ENSEMBLE

Hanson, Handt. "Go, Make Disciples" in *Spirit Calls, Rejoice!* CCF.

McDonald, Mary. "Holy, True and Faithful God." LOR 010/1456M.
    SATB

Smith, Michael W. "How Majestic Is Your Name" in *Maranatha!
    Music's Praise Chorus Book,* 2d ed. MAR.

MONDAY, MAY 31
THE VISITATION

From the Annunciation (March 25) to Christmas we have the lesser festivals of the Visitation and the Nativity of St. John the Baptist (June 24). Both festivals revolve around the pregnancies of Mary and Elizabeth. The Visitation marks the occasion of Mary visiting her cousin Elizabeth. After Elizabeth calls her "blessed among women," Mary sings the famous song called the Magnificat.

The Visitation celebrates the incarnation of Christ, but it also raises up the hopes and expectations of pregnancy. Even if we have never given birth to a baby, how are we pregnant with the Word, and bearers of Christ to others?

TUESDAY, JUNE 1
JUSTIN, MARTYR AT ROME, C. 165

Born of pagan parents, Justin became a Christian, and taught at Ephesus and Rome. Justin was one of the first Christian thinkers to attempt to reconcile the claims of truth and reason. He and some of his students were denounced as Christians, and upon their refusal to make a pagan sacrifice, were scourged and beheaded. The record of their martyrdom, based on an official court, survives.

Justin's description of early Christian worship is an important document for understanding the beginnings of our liturgy. See page 6 in the front of *WOV* and Justin's description of second-century worship. How is it similar to the pattern of our Holy Communion service today?

THURSDAY, JUNE 3
JOHN XXIII, BISHOP OF ROME, 1963

At age 77, Angelo Roncalli was elected pope. He was expected to be a transitional pope, but he astonished many with his energy and reforming spirit. In 1962 John XXIII convened the Second Vatican Council, the major achievement of his papacy, to "let in the fresh air of the modern world." The reforms of Vatican II brought about changes in Roman Catholic thought and practice, and opened up a spirit of ecumenism among Christians. John was a remarkably humble man, and his death was mourned by the whole world.

Discuss how Lutherans and Roman Catholics have become closer to each other in the past three decades. Has your parish studied the Lutheran–Roman Catholic declaration on justification by faith? Have you shared worship services or bible studies with a neighboring Roman Catholic parish?

SATURDAY, JUNE 5
BONIFACE, ARCHBISHOP OF MAINZ,
MISSIONARY TO GERMANY, MARTYR, 754

An English Benedictine, Boniface was called to missionary work among the Vandals, a warring tribe that lived in Germany. From the outset it was clear that many superstitious and violent practices endured despite the first efforts to plant the gospel. Boniface sent for large numbers of Benedictine monks and nuns who established churches, schools, and seminaries where the faith could be taught and the liturgy celebrated. Much of the Christianization of the Germanic peoples began with Boniface.

Pray for the German people, and recall some of the great German theologians and composers who have shaped our Christian faith.

251

JUNE 6, 1999

INTRODUCTION

The weeks of summer coincide with the beginning of the Pentecost season. Summer brings sunny warmth, growing crops, and the promise of harvest: images of the Holy Spirit's presence and activity in our lives, the church, and the world.

Hosea speaks of God's presence as the dawn, as a gentle shower, as light. In our life together as a community of faith, what needs light, warmth, and watering to grow and flourish? How might we be attentive to others' needs to receive this nourishment through God's words of life and holy supper?

PRAYER OF THE DAY

O God, the strength of those who hope in you: Be present and hear our prayers; and, because in the weakness of our mortal nature we can do nothing good without you, give us the help of your grace, so that in keeping your commandments we may please you in will and deed; through your Son, Jesus Christ our Lord.

READINGS

Hosea 5:15—6:6

Because God's people have trusted in military powers and not God, today's reading begins with the surprising declaration that God will withdraw from Israel and Judah. Perhaps then, the people will recognize their sin and repent. God does not desire pious prayers, but a life of committed action that results in the living out of the covenant.

Psalm 50:7-15

To those who keep in my way will I show the salvation of God. (Ps. 50:24)

Romans 4:13-25

In his letter to the Romans, Paul develops the idea that people are made right with God through faith rather than obedience to the law. To illustrate, he uses here the example of Abraham, whose trust in God's promise is what marks him as righteous.

Matthew 9:9-13, 18-26

Matthew's gospel presents Jesus as a healer of the sick and sinful. Through him, God's mercy overcomes exclusivism, prejudice, disease, and even death.

COLOR   Green

THE PRAYERS

Let us pray for the church, the world, and all who suffer in mind, body, or spirit.

A BRIEF SILENCE.

For bishops, pastors, diaconal ministers, deaconesses, associates in ministry, and all the baptized, that we draw our strength from your mercy and forgiveness. Lord, in your mercy,

hear our prayer.

For the nations of the world, so we may recognize in our sisters and brothers your ancient promise to Abraham and Sarah, that they would be the forebears of many nations. Lord, in your mercy,

hear our prayer.

For all who struggle with guilt, alienation, or despair, that they may know your touch as it brings health and wholeness. Lord, in your mercy,

hear our prayer.

For all who are sick, forgotten, grieving, or dying (especially . . .), that they may know your care and love, and be made well. Lord, in your mercy,

hear our prayer.

For physicians, nurses, therapists, and all who work to promote health, that through their ministries we may know your tender care. Lord, in your mercy,

hear our prayer.

HERE OTHER INTERCESSIONS MAY BE OFFERED.

We give thanks for your faithful people of every time and place. Bring us with them to your heavenly table of mercy and forgiveness. Lord, in your mercy,

hear our prayer.

O God, grant us grace to trust your promises, that our lives may bear fruit to the glory of your name, through Jesus Christ our Lord.

Amen

IMAGES FOR PREACHING

What is different between the Pharisees and the patients Jesus treated is not their need. The Pharisees needed a doctor just as much as the woman with the twelve years of hemorrhaging did. The Pharisees were not self-righteous. They knew they needed medicine that can only come from God. What is different is that the Pharisees wanted to quarantine themselves off from the other sick people. They wanted a private room, while Jesus throws us all into the same ward.

The passage from Hosea confronts us with our need to recognize our illness, even if we are in denial. It builds upon imagery common in medicine, that sometimes God has to open up a wound before God can bind it up and heal it—a procedure many of us have painfully experienced.

God also did a nice piece of work on Abraham and Sarah. God worked in them the miracle of life even though these old, infertile two were terminal. They were "as good as dead" (so much for diagnostic subtleties). Surprise! There is life in these old bones yet. God's specialty is pulled off spectacularly in Jesus Christ. Call it resurrection. The story of Abraham and Sarah begins a pattern consistently logged throughout the Bible's medical journal: We are saved by grace through faith for Christ's sake.

WORSHIP MATTERS

In many parishes the Sunday morning celebration of the Lord's Supper is immediately extended to the sick, homebound, and to those who may need to work. After the worshiping congregation has communed, lay communion ministers come forward to receive bread and wine from the altar. They are blessed and sent on their way as a part of the congregation's dismissal. This is a powerful way for congregations to recognize and include all their members in the Sunday morning assembly. "Distribution of Communion to Those in Special Circumstances" is printed in *Occasional Services*. A dismissal prayer is included among the alternate worship texts appearing in each seasonal section of this book.

LET THE CHILDREN COME

The gospel today is marked with images of touch and healing. A woman reaches out to touch Jesus' cloak. Jesus comes to lay a hand on a girl who has died. For children touch is a sign of reassurance. They know that someone is near enough to touch and to care. For adults, touch is a sign that a child is safe and close by. In worship, children are touched in baptism, in blessings, and in the sharing of the peace. Ensure that touch in worship communicates to children the reassurance of the gospel.

MUSIC FOR WORSHIP

GATHERING

| LBW 543 | Praise to the Lord, the Almighty |
| WOV 782 | All my hope on God is founded |

PSALM 50

Folkening, John. "Six Psalm Settings with Antiphons." MSM 80-700. Choir, cong, kybd.

Hopson, Hal. TP. WJK.

Ogden, David. "Rest Your Love" in PS2.

Shute, Linda. PW, Cycle A.

HYMN OF THE DAY

| LBW 476 | Have no fear, little flock |
| | LITTLE FLOCK |

VOCAL RESOURCES

Pelz, Walter L. "Have No Fear, Little Flock." CPH 97-5692. Org, cong.

INSTRUMENTAL RESOURCES

Albrecht, Timothy. "Little Flock" in *Grace Notes*, vol. VII. AFP 11-10856. Org.

Busarow, Donald. "Little Flock" in *Thirty More Accompaniments to Hymns in Canon*. AFP 11-10163. Org.

Sedio, Mark. "Little Flock" in *Music for the Paschal Season*. AFP 11-10763. Org.

ALTERNATE HYMN OF THE DAY

| LBW 290 | There's a wideness in God's mercy (*alternate tune*: BEACH SPRING, LBW 423) |
| WOV 736 | By gracious powers |

COMMUNION

| LBW 479 | My faith looks up to thee |
| WOV 738 | Healer of our every ill |

OTHER SUGGESTIONS

| GS2 40 | Bread for the Journey |

SENDING

LBW 507	How firm a foundation
WOV 673	I'm so glad Jesus lifted me

ADDITIONAL HYMNS AND SONGS

WOV 737	There is a balm in Gilead
NCH 545	There was Jesus by the water
NCH 461	Let us hope when hope seems hopeless
UMH 340	Come, you sinners, poor and needy

MUSIC FOR THE DAY

CHORAL

Bisbee, B. Wayne. "Teach Me Your Ways, O Lord." AFP 11-10603. 2 pt mxd, kybd.

Marcello, Benedetto. "Oh, Hold Thou Me Up." CPH 98-1046. SS, org.

Parker, Alice. "I Know the Lord." GIA G-4229. SATB, S solo.

Scott, K. Lee. "God Shall the Broken Heart Repair." AFP 11-10530. SATB, kybd.

White, David Ashley. "There's a Wideness in God's Mercy." SEL 420-243. SATB, org.

CHILDREN'S CHOIRS

Jordan, Trilby, and Albert Zabel. "Follow Me" in *The Puzzling Parables.* CGA CGC 31. U/2 pt, kybd.

Page, Sue Ellen. "Sing Alleluia!" CGA 415. U, org, tamb, drm, opt orff.

KEYBOARD/INSTRUMENTAL

Arnatt, Ronald. "Hymn Sonata for Organ #2" (LOBE DEN HERREN, ROYAL OAK, SLANE). ECS 4986. Org.

Linker, Janet. "Variations on 'How Firm a Foundation.'" CPH 97-6586. Org.

HANDBELL

McChesney, Kevin. "My Faith Looks Up to Thee." HOP 1637. 3 oct.

Sherman, Arnold. "Joyful, Joyful, We Adore Thee." HOP 1652. 2-3 oct.

Tucker, Margaret. "Northern Lights." AMSI HB-7. 3-5 oct, fl, perc.

PRAISE ENSEMBLE

Haas, David. "Jesus, Heal Us.". GIA 3248. SATB.

Hanson, Handt, and Paul Murakami. "Jesus, Amazing" in *Spirit Calls, Rejoice!* CCF.

Moen, Don. "Heal Me, Oh Lord" in *Integrity's Hosanna! Music Songbook.* INT.

MONDAY, JUNE 7
SEATTLE, CHIEF OF THE DUWAMISH CONFEDERACY, 1866

Seattle was chief of the Suquamish tribe and became chief of the allied tribes, the Duwamish Confederacy. Unlike many of his day, he rejected war and chose the path of peace. After he became a Roman Catholic, he lived in such a way that he earned the respect of both American Indians and white people. On the centennial of his birth, the city of Seattle—named for him against his wishes—erected a monument over his grave.

Chief Seattle initiated the practice of holding morning and evening prayer in his tribe. When small groups from your congregation gather for meetings and other special events, consider using morning or evening prayer for the devotions.

WEDNESDAY, JUNE 9
COLUMBA, 597; AIDAN, 651; BEDE, 735; CONFESSORS

Today we commemorate three monks from the British Isles who kept alive the light of learning and devotion during the early Middle Ages. Columba was an abbot and missionary who established a community on the island of Iona, and evangelized the mainland and established monasteries on the islands nearby. Aidan, a monk of Iona, was sent to revive missionary work in England. He was admired for both his asceticism and his gentleness. Bede, called "the Venerable," was a biblical scholar and the father of English history. He devoted himself to study, teaching, and writing.

How do we keep alive the light of learning and devotion today? What role do church-related colleges have in this regard? Do our congregations see learning as a lifelong process, rather than one that ends with confirmation?

FRIDAY, JUNE 11
ST. BARNABAS, APOSTLE

In the Eastern church Barnabas is commemorated as one of the seventy commissioned by Jesus, and his observance dates from the fifth century. Barnabas was not actually one of the twelve apostles, but the book of Acts gives him the title of apostle. Barnabas was originally called Joseph, and with Paul he organized the first missionary journey, but he was soon overshadowed by Paul.

At the Council of Jerusalem, Barnabas defended the claims of Gentile Christians in relation to the Mosaic law. Knowing that conflict and disagreement is a given in the church, what kind of wisdom do we seek today in dealing with such situations?

JUNE 13, 1999

INTRODUCTION

In today's gospel reading, Jesus speaks of the church's mission with images drawn from daily life. The harvest is already plentiful, he says, but laborers are needed for work in the fields of daily life.

What are we to do? We are to do what the liturgy invites us to do: let our conversation be shaped by the good news, extend Christ's peace wherever we find ourselves, and share our bread with the hungry.

PRAYER OF THE DAY

God, our maker and redeemer, you have made us a new company of priests to bear witness to the Gospel. Enable us to be faithful to our calling to make known your promises to all the world; through your Son, Jesus Christ our Lord.

READINGS

Exodus 19:2-8a

Upon their arrival at Mount Sinai following the great deliverance at the Reed (Red) Sea, Israel hears the marvelous story of what God has done for them. Because God has delivered them, Israel is called to live in a relationship with God—to live as a priestly people through whom God will work for all.

Psalm 100

We are God's people and the sheep of God's pasture.
(Ps. 100:2)

Romans 5:1-8

For Paul, living in God's grace means experiencing peace with God and hope that does not disappoint. The love of God, evident in Christ's death for the undeserving, has been poured into our hearts and sustains us in our troubles.

Matthew 9:35—10:8 [9-23]

According to Matthew's Gospel, the mission of Jesus' followers is to continue the mission of Jesus himself. Here, he instructs his first disciples as to how they might proclaim the gospel through their words and deeds.

COLOR Green

THE PRAYERS

Let us pray for the church, the world, and all who suffer in mind, body, or spirit.
A BRIEF SILENCE.

For the church around the world, and for missionaries who proclaim the good news. Lord, in your mercy,
hear our prayer.

For all who bear witness to Christ, that they may be strengthened through word and sacrament. Lord, in your mercy,
hear our prayer.

For our nation, that we may work for an end to injustice and hunger in our world. Lord, in your mercy,
hear our prayer.

For the earth God has given us, that we may be good stewards of its resources. Lord, in your mercy,
hear our prayer.

For those who are sick or grieving (especially . . .) and for all who suffer from abuse, addiction, or depression, that they may trust in God's faithfulness. Lord, in your mercy,
hear our prayer.

For our congregation, that we may minister to the needs of our community. Lord, in your mercy,
hear our prayer.

HERE OTHER INTERCESSIONS MAY BE OFFERED.

For servants and witnesses in times past, especially the twelve disciples, we give thanks and praise. May our lives be modeled after their faith and courage. Lord, in your mercy,
hear our prayer.

O God, grant us grace to trust your promises, that our lives may bear fruit to the glory of your name, through Jesus Christ our Lord.
Amen

IMAGES FOR PREACHING

Much of the mission of a disciple is cast in medical terms: cure the sick, raise the dead, cleanse those with leprosy, cast out demons. Certainly the summer sizzles with the symptoms of the sickness of our sin from the physical to the spiritual: deaths due to heat stroke, heart

255

attacks, hot tempers, racial flare-ups, ethnic tensions, demonic spirits, emotional and physiological collapse. Someone once described life as "a sexually transmitted disease with a terminal prognosis." That is the bad news.

The good news is that there is a medicine, at no cost, and in plentiful supply. It is the message of gospel proclamation that while we were still weak, sick sinners, Christ died for us. Christ is the proof of God's own love for us. He is the medicine that gives us hope and endurance through whatever we may suffer now. Love for us is the serum God injects into our veins. Only God doesn't use an IV. God's love pours into our hearts through the Holy Spirit that has been given to us. God uses direct cardiac infusion.

And having been ourselves attended, we are called to tend. Treated patients become P.A.s—physician assistants. Thus we continue that ancient Hebrew tradition of all of God's chosen people participating in the healing arts, or as Moses puts it, being "a priestly and a holy nation." Don't forget that priests had a medical function, too. Having received God's medicine, we are called upon to share it. To do otherwise would be unconscionable.

WORSHIP MATTERS

Having "perfect" Sunday school attendance was a big deal for many children who grew up three or more decades ago. What does honoring "perfect attendance," or even father/son and mother/daughter events do for those households that are products of divorce or other divided loyalties? Are "worship helpers" provided to assist single-parent families—maybe a surrogate grandparent? Do parish activities and announcements assume "traditional" families? Are nontraditional households specifically invited to participate? Is child care provided for siblings when single parents are expected to participate in the Christian education activities of their children?

LET THE CHILDREN COME

Is it time to bring an end to the congregational practice that reserves seating near the back of the church for parents with children? Invite families with children to sit up front near the altar and ambo. This place gives children a chance to see and share in the actions that might otherwise have been blocked from their participation because of an assembly of people. Help congregations adjust to the change of practice by reminding them that

it is one more way for children to participate in worship more fully. It is one more way to let the children come.

MUSIC FOR WORSHIP

GATHERING

| LBW 548 | O worship the King |
| WOV 652 | Arise, your light has come! |

PSALM 100

DATH 41   Come with joy

Howard, Julie. *Sing for Joy: Psalm Settings for God's Children.* LTP.

LBW 245   All people that on earth do dwell

LBW 256   Oh, sing jubilee to the Lord

LBW 531   Before Jehovah's awesome throne

Trapp, Lynn. "Psalm 100." MSM 80-704. Choir, cong, fl, org.

Sweelinck, Jan P. "Psalm 100." ECS 2791. SATB, org.

HYMN OF THE DAY

WOV 756   Lord, you give the great commission
ABBOT'S LEIGH

VOCAL RESOURCES

Taylor/Haugen. "Lord, You Give the Great Commission." GIA G 3200. SATB, cong, opt 2 tpt, 2 tbn, timp, hb.

Wilson, John F. "Lord, You Give the Great Commission." HOP A 618. SATB.

INSTRUMENTAL RESOURCES

Cherwien, David. "Abbot's Leigh" in *Two Hymntune Preludes.* GIA G-4477. Org.

Ferguson, John. "Abbot's Leigh" in *Hymn Preludes and Free Accompaniments,* vol. 17. AFP 11-9413. Org.

Moklebust, Cathy. "Lord, You Give the Great Commission" in *Hymn Stanzas for Handbells.* AFP 11-10722. 4-5 oct.

ALTERNATE HYMN OF THE DAY

| LBW 376 | Your kingdom come! |
| LBW 396 | O God, O Lord of heaven and earth |

COMMUNION

| LBW 403 | Lord, speak to us that we may speak |
| WOV 752 | I, the Lord of sea and sky |

OTHER SUGGESTIONS

OBS 59   God has called us

SENDING

| LBW 390 | I love to tell the story |
| WOV 712 | Listen, God is calling |

ADDITIONAL HYMNS AND SONGS

WOV 722	Hallelujah! We sing your praises
LBW 252	You servants of God
NCH 468	The care the eagle gives her young
NCH 9	We sing to you, O God

MUSIC FOR THE DAY

CHORAL

Bender, Jan. "O God, O Lord of Heaven and Earth." AFP 11-1554. Also in *The Augsburg Choirbook.* 11-10817. SATB, cong, tpt.

Busarow, Donald. "Forth in Thy Name." MSM 50-9107. SAB, org, trbl inst.

Dvorak, Antonin. "I Will Sing New Songs of Gladness" in *Third Morning Star Choir Book.* CPH 97-4972. U, kybd.

Helvey, Howard. "What Wondrous Love Is This." HOP PP 146. SATB, pno.

Mezzogorri, Giovanni N. "Jubilate Deo" (Sing to God). CPH 98-2470. SA/TB, kybd.

CHILDREN'S CHOIRS

Artman, Ruth. "Sing Joy!" CGA 429. U/2 pt, fl, opt perc, pno.

Bedford, Michael. "Jubilate Deo." CGA 647. U, kybd.

Kosche, Kenneth. "Make a Joyful Noise." CGA 620. U/2 pt, kybd, opt C inst.

KEYBOARD/INSTRUMENTAL

Handel, G. F. "Fugue in D" in *Six Little Fugues.* CPH 97-4626. Org/kybd.

Whitlock, Percy. "Toccata" in *Plymouth Suite.* OXF 0193758938. Org.

HANDBELL

Gumma, Victor. "Wondrous Love." 2 oct solo, kybd, opt gtr.

Hopson, Hal H. "Psalm 100." AFP 11-10524. 3 or 5 oct.

Hopson, Hal H. "Variations on 'Kingsfold.'" AFP 11-10703. 3/5 oct.

Moklebust, Cathy. "Arise, Your Light Has Come" in *Hymn Stanzas for Handbells.* AFP 11-10722. 4-5 oct.

PRAISE ENSEMBLE

DeShazo, Lynn. "I Belong To A Mighty God" in *Integrity's Hosanna! Music Songbook 8.* INT.

Klein, Laurie/Jack Schrader. "I Love You, Lord." HOP. GC 936. SATB.

Young, Jeremy. "God, Here Is My Life and My Will." AFP 11-10786. SATB, pno, opt cong.

MONDAY, JUNE 14
BASIL THE GREAT, BISHOP OF CAESAREA, 379; GREGORY OF NAZIANZUS, BISHOP OF CONSTANTINOPLE, C. 389; GREGORY, BISHOP OF NYSSA, C. 385

This day commemorates three Cappadocian fathers from the East. Basil was a defender of orthodoxy, and was known for his eloquence, learning, and great personal holiness. He is considered the father of Eastern communal monasticism. Gregory of Nazianzus, called "the Theologian" in the East, restored the Nicene faith at Constantinople where he was appointed bishop. Gregory of Nyssa, a younger brother to Basil, was also a defender of the Nicene faith, and was a thinker and theologian of great originality and learning.

Since these fathers explored the mystery of the Holy Trinity, discuss some contemporary understandings of trinitarian faith. Do you think these theologies seek to be faithful to orthodoxy?

257

JUNE 20, 1999
FOURTH SUNDAY AFTER PENTECOST
PROPER 7

INTRODUCTION

In today's gospel reading, Jesus gives a brief teaching on the nature of discipleship: do not be afraid, for I am with you; tell others what you hear me say; give your life to the good news and you will discover the riches of life.

This teaching appears simple, yet it is spoken in an anxious and troubled world where it is easier to be fear-ful than courageous and more common to look out for oneself than to care for the neighbor in need.

PRAYER OF THE DAY

O God our defender, storms rage about us and cause us to be afraid. Rescue your people from despair, deliver your sons and daughters from fear, and preserve us all from unbelief; through your Son, Jesus Christ our Lord.

READINGS

Jeremiah 20:7-13

Jeremiah's message of doom earns him only contempt and persecution. Having been beaten, placed in stocks, and then released by Pashur, one of the temple priests, Jeremiah cries out in heart-wrenching lament. Nevertheless, the prophet remains confident of God's care and concludes with resounding praise.

Psalm 69:8-11 [12-17] 18-20
(Psalm 69:7-10 [11-15] 16-18 [NRSV])

Answer me, O Lord, for your love is kind. (Ps. 69:18)

Romans 6:1b-11

In the first part of his letter to the Romans, Paul says that God sent Christ to die for us while we were sinners and so, by grace, accepts us through baptism just as we are. Now, he clarifies that baptism also brings freedom from the slavery of sin and the possibility of beginning a new life.

Matthew 10:24-39

Moved by compassion for the crowds, Jesus has commissioned his twelve disciples to continue his work of preaching and healing. Now he warns them that their ministry will meet with opposition, requiring absolute trust in God and unswerving commitment to their Lord.

COLOR Green

THE PRAYERS

Let us pray for the church, the world, and all who suffer in mind, body, or spirit.

A BRIEF SILENCE.

For the baptized people of God, that they may proclaim the word with courage and power. Lord, in your mercy,

hear our prayer.

For those who suffer persecution for the faith, that they may be given strength and perseverance. Lord, in your mercy,

hear our prayer.

For leaders of the world, that they may work to eliminate war, oppression, and hunger. Lord, in your mercy,

hear our prayer.

For families or churches facing conflict or turmoil, that they may know God's reconciling love and forgiveness. Lord, in your mercy,

hear our prayer.

For fathers and all who model fatherly care, that their love may reveal God's gracious providence. Lord, in your mercy,

hear our prayer.

For those who are sick or in any kind of need (especially . . .), that through Christ's resurrection they may walk in newness of life. Lord, in your mercy,

hear our prayer.

HERE OTHER INTERCESSIONS MAY BE OFFERED.

We give thanks for all your faithful people who, baptized into the death of Christ, now share his eternal glory. Raise us with them to the joy of his endless life. Lord, in your mercy,

hear our prayer.

O God, grant us grace to trust your promises, that our lives may bear fruit to the glory of your name, through Jesus Christ our Lord.

Amen

IMAGES FOR PREACHING

Shhh! Can you keep a secret? The Christians can't. Not when it comes to confessing Christ. Not when it comes to denouncing the violence and destruction of the world. Or proclaiming the peace that God has made through Jesus.

The prophet Jeremiah tried not to speak in the name of the Lord only to discover something like a burning fire shut up in his bones. As much as he resisted, he had to cry out and shout. Jesus commanded many that he healed to say nothing to anyone, but they bubbled up and blabbed. Paul often felt compelled to speak when being quiet would have been safer.

The Christian must speak out because the Christian is "on trial" in every encounter with God and fellow human beings. "Do you promise to tell the truth, the whole truth, and nothing but the truth?" The truth reveals what is hidden and shouts out what many would keep silent—our sinfulness, for one thing, as well as greed, graft, and corruption of self, societies, and systems. God's magnificent pardon and reprieve is in Christ for one another. This God loves us so much that every hair on our head is counted.

The Christian must speak out because our salvation depends upon it. We are emboldened to speak out (in whatever trying situation we are in) as we hear Jesus say in the highest court of them all, "I beg your pardon, Dad. This one belongs to me." And his dad the Judge winks and says, "Dismissed. Next case."

258

WORSHIP MATTERS

Along with constructing larger and more meaningful baptismal fonts, many congregations have also begun to practice immersion baptism. Immersion is getting really wet. Immersion is not necessarily submersion. Immersion does not mean that one's entire body, head and all, must go under the water. Immersion can mean kneeling in the water. It can mean water being poured over the candidate. It can mean movement through a waterspout. Immersion is getting really wet, rather than merely being sprinkled.

Some congregation's worship spaces are well equipped for this abundant use of water in Holy Baptism. The floors around the font are stone or ceramic. There is a floor drain or a shallow pool. Other congregations are asking the question, "How much water should we use for baptisms?" The answer of course will be a local one, guided by the congregation's ability to make the symbol of Holy Baptism as powerful as they are able. (For assistance with renovating the baptismal space in your congregation, call the ELCA's worship unit or Augsburg Fortress's ecclesiastical arts consultants.)

LET THE CHILDREN COME

During the summer months, most congregations have a Sunday schedule that is more relaxed and slower-paced. On one of these Sundays, organize an exploration of the area around the congregation or in a nearby park. Lead the children on a search of the wonders of creation. Flowers and trees are obvious picks. But do not exclude the things children will search out and find as a part of their natural curiosity, such as bugs, eggshells, or even animals that have died. Include a devotional time giving thanks for the gift of life from God.

MUSIC FOR WORSHIP

GATHERING

LBW 554	This is my Father's world
WOV 698	We were baptized in Christ Jesus

PSALM 69

Butler, Eugene. "Save Me, O God" in *The Solo Psalmist*. SMP PP98. Solo, kybd.

Dean, Stephen. "Lord, You Are Good and Forgiving" in PS3.

Haas, David. PCY, vol. 8.

Hopson, Hal H. "You Are My Child." CGA-480. U, opt C inst.

HYMN OF THE DAY

WOV 785	Weary of all trumpeting DISTLER

VOCAL RESOURCES

Distler, Hugo/Richard Proulx. "Weary of All Trumpeting." AFP 11-10897. SAB, org, opt cong, brass.

INSTRUMENTAL RESOURCES

Bender, Jan. "Variations on a Theme by Hugo Distler." AFP 12-706640. Org.

ALTERNATE HYMN OF THE DAY

LBW 366	Lord of our life
LBW 507	How firm a foundation

COMMUNION

LBW 324	O Love that will not let me go
WOV 770	I was there to hear your borning cry

OTHER SUGGESTIONS

LLC 384	Aquí del pan partido tomaré/Here would I feast

SENDING

LBW 487	Let us ever walk with Jesus
WOV 755	We all are one in mission

ADDITIONAL HYMNS AND SONGS

LBW 453	If you but trust in God to guide you
BH 496	Burn in me, fire of God
ISH 77	Servants of the Savior
TWC 720	Christ, whose purpose is to kindle

MUSIC FOR THE DAY

CHORAL

Farlee, Robert Buckley. "O Blessed Spring." AFP 11-10544. SATB, ob, org, opt cong.

Harris, William H. "The Eyes of All Wait Upon Thee." OXF A-142. SATB, org.

Johnson, Roy. "Children of the Heavenly Father." PLY CC-106. 2 pt, kybd.

Mendelssohn-Bartholdy, Felix. "Cast Thy Burden upon the Lord" in *Church Choir Book*. CPH 97-6320. SATB.

Schalk, Carl, "Lord of Feasting and of Hunger." CPH 98-2863. SATB, org.

Sedio, Mark. "Once He Came in Blessing." AFP 11-10452. 2 pt mxd, org, fl.

Warren, John. "As Many as Have Been Baptized." MUR. SATB.

259

CHILDREN'S CHOIRS

Bach, J. S. "God Is Ever Sun and Shield" in *Third Morning Star Choir
    Book.* CPH 97-4972. U, ob/fl, cont.

Coleman, Gerald. "Christ Is with Me." CPH 98-3120. 2 pt mxd,
    C inst, pno.

Wagner, Douglas. "A Round of Praise." CGA 208. U/2 pt, kybd.

KEYBOARD/INSTRUMENTAL

Bruhns, Nicolaus. "Praeludium in g" in *Saemtlich Orgelwerke.* BRE. Org.

Lachenauer, George. "Three Hispanic Carols for Organ."
    GIA G-4494. Org.

Weaver, Georgeann. "Meditation for Cello, Horn or Sax and Key-
    board." AFP 11-10695.

HANDBELL

Afdahl, Lee. J. "Here Would I Feed Upon the Bread of God" in *Two
    Spanish Tunes for Handbells.* AFP 11-10874. 3-5 oct.

McChesney, Kevin. "We All Are One in Mission" in *All Things Bright and
    Beautiful and O Lord, Now Let Your Servant.* AFP 11-10687. 3-5 oct.

McFadden, Jane. "Two Swedish Melodies: Children of the Heavenly
    Father and When He Cometh." AFP 11-10806. 3-4 oct.

PRAISE ENSEMBLE

Christenson, Chris/Fettke. "Song for the Nations." LIL AN-2604.
    SATB.

Hanson, Handt. "Don't Be Anxious" in *Spirit Calls, Rejoice!* CCF.

Smith, Michael W., and Deborah D. Smith/Ed Lojeski. "Great is the
    Lord." HAL 08307231. SATB, SAB, or SSA, gtr, bass, perc.

SUNDAY, JUNE 20
FATHER'S DAY

MONDAY, JUNE 21
ONESIMOS NESIB, TRANSLATOR, EVANGELIST, 1931

Nesib was captured by slave traders and taken from his
Galla homeland in Ethiopia to Eritrea where he was
bought and freed by Swedish missionaries. He became
an evangelist, translated the Bible into Galla, and
returned to preach the gospel in his homeland. His
tombstone includes a verse from Jeremiah 22:29, "O
Land, O Land, hear the word of the Lord . . . ."

Does your congregation support mission work
through synod or churchwide offerings, or do you have
a specific missionary whom you support? How do you
inform your members that their gifts go to support
missions as well as the needs of the local congregation?

THURSDAY, JUNE 24
THE NATIVITY OF ST. JOHN THE BAPTIST

The birth of St. John the Baptist is celebrated exactly six
months before Christmas Eve. John said that he must
decrease as Jesus increases, and from now until Christmas the hours of daylight will become shorter. In many
countries this day is celebrated with customs associated
with the summer solstice. Midsummer is especially popular in northern European countries, which experience
few hours of darkness at this time of year.

The Nativity of St. John the Baptist is a wonderful
day for parishes to have a summertime festival tied to
the unfolding of the liturgical year. Consider a church
picnic, and creatively use John's traditional symbols of
fire and water in decorations and games. It is also a
popular day around the world for bonfires!

FRIDAY, JUNE 25
PRESENTATION OF THE AUGSBURG CONFESSION, 1530;
PHILIPP MELANCHTHON, RENEWER OF THE CHURCH, 1560

On this day the Augsburg Confession, which had been
drafted by Philip Melanchthon and endorsed by
Luther, was read to Emperor Charles of the Holy
Roman Empire. In 1580, when the *Book of Concord* was
drawn up, the unaltered Augsburg Confession was
included as the principal Lutheran confession. In addition to teaching Greek, Melanchthon taught theology
and scripture at Wittenberg. He was a popular teacher,
and with Luther's presence there also, Wittenberg was
one of the leading European universities of the sixteenth century.

What are the gifts of the Augsburg Confession for
our day? Do pastors occasionally refer to it, so that the
laity are familiar with this important document? How is
our heritage of the gospel a gift for the ecumenical
movement today?

JUNE 27, 1999

INTRODUCTION

Without God's loving presence, we are like a parched and waterless land. In the waters of baptism, Christ becomes our life-giving spring, quenching our thirst and pouring God's love into our hearts.

In today's gospel, Christ promises that the disciple who gives a cup of cold water to the little ones serves Christ himself. Our baptism leads us to hear Jesus' words as words concerning our baptismal mission to serve the little ones of this world—with a gesture as simple as offering a cup of cold water.

PRAYER OF THE DAY

O God, you have prepared for those who love you joys beyond understanding. Pour into our hearts such love for you that, loving you above all things, we may obtain your promises, which exceed all that we can desire; through your Son, Jesus Christ our Lord.

READINGS

Jeremiah 28:5-9

The prophets Hananiah and Jeremiah were not at odds simply because of their differing views of upcoming events. Hananiah announces peace and restoration within two years; Jeremiah sees the path to peace as one that requires repentance—recognition of one's sins and reliance on God's forgiveness. Jeremiah knows that when Hananiah's comforting prediction does not come true, all will know that Hananiah has not been sent by God.

Psalm 89:1-4, 15-18

Your love, O Lord, forever will I sing. (Ps. 89:1)

Romans 6:12-23

Paul has told the Roman Christians that in baptism they were not only made right with God through grace, but were also made free from the slavery of sin. Thus, he now claims that those who are accepted by God as sinners may also be used by God for righteousness.

Matthew 10:40-42

When Jesus sends his disciples out as missionaries, he warns them of persecution and hardships they will face. He also promises to reward any who aid his followers and support their ministry.

COLOR Green

THE PRAYERS

Let us pray for the church, the world, and all who suffer in mind, body, or spirit.

A BRIEF SILENCE.

For the church, that it may genuinely welcome all people with hospitality and acceptance. Lord, in your mercy,

hear our prayer.

For the leaders of nations, that they bring a word of peace and reconciliation where there is conflict and violence. Lord, in your mercy,

hear our prayer.

For all who live with addiction, depression, grief, or illness (especially . . .), that they may know your grace and tender care. Lord, in your mercy,

hear our prayer.

For those traveling or on vacation, that they find rest and renewal. Lord, in your mercy,

hear our prayer.

For those who visit the sick, care for the needy, visit the lonely, and work for peace and justice, that they may be strengthened for their tasks. Lord, in your mercy,

hear our prayer.

For our ministries of outreach and evangelism, that we may respond to the spiritual hunger of people in our society. Lord, in your mercy,

hear our prayer.

HERE OTHER INTERCESSIONS MAY BE OFFERED.

We give you thanks for the saints who from age to age have sung of your faithfulness. Welcome us with them into the eternal light of your presence. Lord, in your mercy,

hear our prayer.

O God, grant us grace to trust your promises, that our lives may bear fruit to the glory of your name, through Jesus Christ our Lord.

Amen

261

IMAGES FOR PREACHING

Summer is a time for rewards: a vacation for hard work, a trip to the amusement park for doing well at school, sun and sand for putting up with clouds and cold. Jesus offers a "prophet's reward" to anyone who hospitably welcomes his message and his messengers. And just what is that? What is a "prophet's reward?" The pay is lousy. The clothing allowance meager. The working environment hostile. Jeremiah found it left him lonely, isolated, laughed at. Jesus found it meant a cross with all of its deadly ridicule and rejection.

With a smile as broad as a hen-pecked spouse being right for once, the prophet's reward is "vindication!" Which means being right in the end and having one's faith and hope in the right place. Jeremiah didn't want more money, a better wardrobe, or international acclaim. He wanted to end up on the right side. He wanted to see God come through and have everything God made him say come true. He wanted God to be proven right and God's enemies proven wrong. He wanted vindication. And God could not do it fast enough for him. God stalled over six hundred years and then sent Jesus.

Jesus died guilt-by-association. He offered hospitality to sinners on God's behalf. And he died for it. We are saved grace-by-association. For when we offer hospitality to Christ's message and his messengers, we welcome God into our homes and hearts. The resurrection is Christ's vindication. By it we know that Jesus is "the prophet truly sent." No, it is more than that. Jesus is even better than a prophet. Jesus is nothing less than God in human flesh hospitably associating with us sinners. And through him we have a "reward" and vindication—peace with God that beats all the sun and sand in the world.

WORSHIP MATTERS

In today's gospel Jesus says, "Whoever welcomes you welcomes me." When we welcome a stranger on Sunday morning we simultaneously welcome Christ, and we welcome the stranger to Christ. *Welcome to Christ* is what the ELCA has chosen to call its version of the adult cate-chumenate, an effective and ecumenical way introducing unbaptized adults to Christ. Some theologians are saying that we now live in a post-Christian world. This description recognizes that many adults, now responsible for the faith formation of their own children, had no experience of the church or of the salvation story as children. Today new Christians must be made from adults as well as from children. Read the three volumes of *Welcome to Christ* (see more detail in the bibliography of this book). To find church leaders or congregations near you who are involved in the catecumenate call the ELCA's worship unit or your synod office.

LET THE CHILDREN COME

The late professor of liturgy, Ralph F. Smith, told a story of how children incorporate the symbols and words of liturgy in their own ways. He was sitting in the living room with his older daughter when her younger sister came bounding down the stairs. She wrapped her arms around her older sister, wrestled her to the ground and said, "Confess that you are in bondage to sin and cannot free yourself!" Whatever led to that piece of embodied theology is not known. What is clear is that the images of worship can be trusted to do their work among children, even without endless explanation by adults.

MUSIC FOR WORSHIP

GATHERING

LBW 462	God the omnipotent!
WOV 715	Open your ears, O faithful people

PSALM 89

Fillmore, James. "I Will Sing of the Mercies" in SPW, 52. WRD.

Haas, David. PCY, vol. 8.

Powell, Robert J. "O Praise the Lord, Ye Children." CGA 163. 3 pt canon.

PsH 593   My song forever shall record

Shute, Linda. PW, Cycle A.

Trapp, Lynn. "Four Psalm Settings." MSM 80-701. SATB/U, kybd.

HYMN OF THE DAY

LBW 487	Let us ever walk with Jesus
	LASSET UNS MIT JESU ZIEHEN

VOCAL RESOURCES

Manz, Paul. "Let Us Ever Walk With Jesus." MSM 50-9405. U, org.

INSTRUMENTAL RESOURCES

Burkhardt, Michael. "Lasst Uns mit Jesu Ziehen" in *Seven Hymn Improvisations and Free Accompaniments,* set 2. MSM 10-860. Org.

Busarow, Donald. "Lasset uns mit Jesu ziehen" in *Hymn Preludes and Free Accompaniments,* vol. 8. AFP 11-9404. Org.

Manz, Paul. "Let Us Ever Walk With Jesus" in *Five Hymn Improvisations for Weddings and General Use.* MSM 10-850. Org.

ALTERNATE HYMN OF THE DAY

LBW 429   Where cross the crowded ways of life

WOV 750   Oh, praise the gracious power

COMMUNION

LBW 448   Amazing grace, how sweet the sound

WOV 635   Surely it is God who saves me

OTHER SUGGESTIONS

OBS 72   O grant us, Christ, a deep humility

SENDING

LBW 263   Abide with us, our Savior

WOV 720   In the presence of your people

ADDITIONAL HYMNS AND SONGS

LBW 425   O God of mercy, God of light

WOV 719   God is here!

NCH 29   Let heaven your wonders proclaim

MUSIC FOR THE DAY

CHORAL

Bender, Jan, and S. Drummond Wolff. "Let Us Ever Walk With Jesus" in *Choral Settings for the Hymn of the Day*, IV. CPH 97-5835. SATB.

Farrant, Richard. "Hide Not Thou Thy Face." OXF. SATB, org.

Hobby, Robert. "The Lord Is the Stronghold of My Life." MSM 80-576. SATB, org.

Mendelssohn, Felix. "I Will Sing of Thy Great Mercies" in *Sing a Song of Joy*. MH AFP 11-8194; ML 11-8195.

Schickele, Peter. "Amazing Grace." PRE 362-03402. SATB.

CHILDREN'S CHOIRS

Powell, Robert. "O Praise the Lord, Ye Children." CGA 163. 3 pt, org/pno.

Pavone, Michael. "Psalm 89" in *Seasonal Psalms for Ringing and Singing*. GIA G-3714. U, desc, cong, hb.

Willan, Healey. "I Have Trusted in Thy Mercy" in *We Praise Thee*. CPH 97-7564. U, org.

KEYBOARD/INSTRUMENTAL

Lefébure-Wély, Louis. "Offertoire" in *Favourite Organ Music*, book 1. OXF 0193755270. Org.

Meyer, Lawrence J. "Processional of Joy." AFP 11-10797. Org/pno.

HANDBELL

Moklebust, Cathy. "Amazing Grace." Full score CGA CGB200. 3-5 oct CGB201. Cong, 3-5 oct, org.

Tucker, Sondra. "Meditation on 'Hyfrydol.'" CGA CGB182. 3 oct.

Wagner, Douglas E. "Amazing Grace" in *Five By Five II*. HOP 1476. 3 oct hb qnt.

PRAISE ENSEMBLE

Gordon, Nancy, and Jamie Harvill. "Firm Foundation" in *Integrity's Hosanna! Come and Worship Songbook*. INT.

Hanson, Handt. "Your Constant Love" in *Spirit Calls, Rejoice!* CCF.

Shaw, Kirby. "Children of the Light." HAL 08711241. SATB, inst.

Tunney, Curry. "Let There Be Praise." LOR 08340911. SATB.

MONDAY, JUNE 28
IRENAEUS, BISHOP OF LYONS, C. 202

Irenaeus believed that the way to remain steadfast to the truth was to hold fast to the faith handed down from the apostles. He believed that only Matthew, Mark, Luke, and John were trustworthy gospels. He was strongly influenced by his teacher Polycarp whose teacher had been John the Apostle. Irenaeus was a strong opponent of Gnosticism, dualistic thinking that separated the mind or soul from the body, and he also wrote on the restoration of human nature in Christ.

What does it mean that the church is apostolic? What are ways that the apostolic faith is preserved and passed down through the generations?

TUESDAY, JUNE 29
ST. PETER AND ST. PAUL, APOSTLES

This date commemorating the two great apostles has been observed since at least 258. Peter and Paul were two of the most important leaders in the early church. Both apostles died in the city said to have been founded by the twins Romulus and Remus. Among the early Christians of this city, Peter and Paul were considered the twin founders of the *new* Rome, a city to be transformed by the love of Christ and the blood of the martyrs. An early tradition places their martyrdom at Rome in the same year.

As you observe this festival, reflect on the unique ways that Peter and Paul witnessed to the Christian faith in the first century and how their witness continues for future generations. How do we share the gospel of Christ today? Look at the readings assigned for St. Peter and St. Paul for some insights into these questions.

WEDNESDAY, JUNE 30
JOHAN OLOF WALLIN, ARCHBISHOP OF UPPSALA, HYMNWRITER, 1839

Wallin was consecrated archbishop of Uppsala and primate of the Church of Sweden, and was considered the leading churchman of his day in Sweden, yet his lasting fame rests upon his poetry and his hymns. Of the 500 hymns in the Swedish hymnbook of 1819, 130 were written by Wallin, and approximately 200 were revised or translated by him. For more than a century the Church of Sweden made no change in the 1819 hymnbook.

Name some of the Swedish hymns we continue to sing today, and take a look at the three of Wallin's hymns that are in *LBW*: "All hail to you, O blessed morn!" (LBW 73), "We worship you, O God of might" (432), and "Christians, while on earth abiding" (440).

THURSDAY, JULY 1
CATHERINE WINKWORTH, 1878; JOHN MASON NEALE, 1866; HYMNWRITERS

Neale was an English priest associated with the movement for church renewal at Cambridge, and Winkworth lived most of her life in Manchester, supporting the rights of women among other things. These two hymnwriters translated many hymn texts into English. Catherine Winkworth devoted herself to the translation of German hymns, and John Mason Neale specialized in ancient Latin and Greek hymns. Winkworth has thirty hymns in *LBW*, and Neale has twenty-one. In addition, two texts by Neale are in *WOV*. Use the indexes at the back of both books and research some of their most familiar translations. Sing some of your favorites at congregational events during this week.

JULY 4, 1999

SIXTH SUNDAY AFTER PENTECOST
PROPER 9

INTRODUCTION

Jesus chose to be with people who believed that they were excluded from God's mercy and love: the poor, the sick, the dying, and the deranged. Where many religious people saw only the dark and sinful shadows in these people, Jesus recognized their need for the transforming power of mercy, forgiveness, and healing. To them he said: Come to me and find rest.

Today he comes to us in the waters of healing, in the word of mercy, in the meal of forgiveness. And he asks the church to bring these good gifts—signs of the Spirit's presence—into daily life.

PRAYER OF THE DAY

God of glory and love, peace comes from you alone. Send us as peacemakers and witnesses to your kingdom, and fill our hearts with joy in your promises of salvation; through your Son, Jesus Christ our Lord.

READINGS

Zechariah 9:9-12

The period after the Jews had returned from Babylonian exile was a time of extreme crisis. The return was not the glorious event announced by the prophet (Isaiah 40–55). Serious social, economic, political, and religious problems confronted the people. They then looked to the future when God would intervene on their behalf.

Psalm 145:8-15 (Psalm 145:8-14 [NRSV])

The Lord is gracious and full of compassion. (Ps. 145:8)

Romans 7:15-25a

In his letter to the Romans, Paul argues that we are made right with God through Christ's action rather than through our own works. To illustrate our need for Christ, he offers us a picture of one who tries to do what is right, only to discover good intentions are not enough.

Matthew 11:16-19, 25-30

In Matthew's gospel, John the Baptist and Jesus are described as having very different approaches to ministry, though they both proclaim the same message of God's kingdom. Here,

Jesus chides people who seem to find fault with all preachers as an excuse for ignoring the word of God.

COLOR Green

THE PRAYERS

Let us pray for the church, the world, and all who suffer in mind, body, or spirit.

A BRIEF SILENCE.

That the church faithfully proclaim God's grace and compassion for all people. Lord, in your mercy,

hear our prayer.

That our nation work for peace and justice in all the world. Lord, in your mercy,

hear our prayer.

That we treasure the gift of freedom we enjoy in our country. Lord, in your mercy,

hear our prayer.

That the leaders of government encourage us all to care for those who are poor, hungry, or homeless. Lord, in your mercy,

hear our prayer.

That those who are weary or carrying heavy burdens (especially . . .) will find rest for their souls. Lord, in your mercy,

hear our prayer.

That travelers be kept safe, and vacationers find rest and delight in your creation. Lord, in your mercy,

hear our prayer.

HERE OTHER INTERCESSIONS MAY BE OFFERED.

For all the faithful who have humbly revealed your goodness, we give you thanks. May we celebrate with them the victory of your reign. Lord, in your mercy,

hear our prayer.

O God, grant us grace to trust your promises, that our lives may bear fruit to the glory of your name, through Jesus Christ our Lord.

Amen

IMAGES FOR PREACHING

Summer is when kids congregate in streets and malls to play their games while "wise and intelligent" adults sneer at their antics, oblivious to the fact that much of children's play mimics adult behavior. And so, if the kids look "silly" what does that say about the village that raised them?

Part of his prophetic burden was that young, eligible Jeremiah was forbidden to participate in weddings and funerals—the two most important social/religious events in village culture (Jer. 16:1-9). It was a prophetic sign. The people were under God's judgment. Soon they would be imprisoned. Normal activities would cease. And so, there were no Fourth of Julys, parades, parties, and fireworks for Jeremiah, much to his chagrin.

That Jesus chides the stuffed-shirts in the crowd for not repenting with John (playing funeral) or celebrating with him (playing wedding) shows that the times have changed. With Christ's arrival the people were "to play at" and experience what Zechariah predicted: God's great victory of grace.

If you think America's declaration of independence from Great Britain was big, try this: the victory of Christ. It is at the same time both a wedding and a funeral. It is the marriage of the wounded, but victorious Lamb to his bride the church. It is the death of death. Our "light burden" and great joy is that we get to play at and experience it in worship, witness, and marketplace life. Shoot off the fireworks. Shout. Cheer. Rejoice. Be a kid who plays with Christ. It is foolish and unwise to do otherwise.

WORSHIP MATTERS

In today's gospel, Jesus promises rest to all who are weary and are carrying heavy burdens. How does the liturgy serve these members of our congregations? From week to week worship leaders never know who will arrive with a heavy burden, but we can help assure that any who do arrive seeking rest will find the peace of Christ in our midst. Does your community welcome the hurting, weary, grieving, and burdened? Are space and time provided for personal prayer, small group prayer, mutual conversation and consolation with a pastor or gifted layperson? Does the liturgy assume our daily hurts and invite the community to contribute in some way to the intercessory prayers (even just through silence)? Challenge worship leaders who assume everyone who comes to church should always be happy and upbeat. Does the peace provide opportunity for an embrace in Christian love for the lonely, the grieving, or otherwise burdened? Is Jesus' promise fulfilled by our presence?

265

LET THE CHILDREN COME

Parents know that children can be great traditionalists. Any pattern established around birthdays and holidays, once set in motion, is likely to continue as an annual event. If one detail of decoration or food is overlooked, children may remind their parents that something is not being done the way it is supposed to be. Psychologists say that such patterns are good for children because they provide a sense of stability. This same need for reassurance is what our worship life is about. Rather than thinking that ritual action and life must be tempered in order for it to be meaningful and welcoming to children, what would worship look like if worship planners came to see that just the opposite is the case?

MUSIC FOR WORSHIP

GATHERING

LBW 401	Before you, Lord, we bow
WOV 762	O day of peace

PSALM 145

Folkemer, Stephen. "Psalm 145." GIA G-2337. U, tpt, kybd.

Kemp, Helen. "God Is Always Near." CGA-31. U/2 pt.

Makeever, Ray. PW, Cycle A.

Trapp, Lynn. *Four Psalm Settings.* MSM 80-701. SATB/U, kybd, cong.

HYMN OF THE DAY

LBW 469	Lord of all hopefulness
	SLANE

VOCAL RESOURCES

Pelz, Walter. "Lord of All Hopefulness." CPH 97-5691. U, cong, opt fl, org.

INSTRUMENTAL RESOURCES

Albrecht, Timothy. "Slane" in *Grace Notes V.* AFP 11-10764. Org.

Bender, Jan. "Variations on 'Slane.'" AFP 11-8775. Vln, org.

Burkhardt, Michael. "Slane" in *7 Hymn Improvisations and Free Accompaniments,* set 2. MSM 10-860. Org.

Wagner, Douglas E. "Be Thou My Vision" in *Five By Five.* HOP 1387. 3 oct hb qnt.

Willan, Healy. "Slane—Prelude for Organ." CFP 66034. Org.

Wood, Dale. "Be Thou My Vision" in *Wood Works for Organ.* SMP KK 357. Org.

ALTERNATE HYMN OF THE DAY

LBW 497	I heard the voice of Jesus say (*alternate tune*: KINGSFOLD, LBW 391)
WOV 746	Day by day

COMMUNION

LBW 439	What a friend we have in Jesus
WOV 734	Softly and tenderly Jesus is calling

OTHER SUGGESTIONS

DATH 27	Come unto me

SENDING

LBW 529	Praise God. Praise him
WOV 790	Praise to you, O God of mercy

ADDITIONAL HYMNS AND SONGS

WOV 759	Accept, O Lord, the gifts we bring
ASF 58	We are called to be peacemakers
LW 345	Come unto me, ye weary
NSR 66	Come to me, O weary traveler
DATH 46	God is compassionate

MUSIC FOR THE DAY

CHORAL

Burroughs, Bob. "Come Unto Me." CPH 98-3055. SATB.

Cherubini, Luigi. "Come Unto Me, All Ye Heavy Laden." HTF F6019. SAB, kybd.

Chilcott, Bob. "Just as I Am." OXF E163. SATB, kybd.

Handel, G. F. "Come Unto Him" in *Messiah.* Various ed. Solo.

Howells, Herbert. "O, Pray for the Peace of Jerusalem." OXF 42.064. SATB, org.

Joncas, Michael. "I Heard the Voice of Jesus Say." GIA G-3439. SATB, org, opt inst, cong.

Schubert, Franz. "A Song of Trust" in *Sing a Song of Joy; Vocal Solos for Worship.* MH AFP 11-8194. ML AFP 11-8195.

Schütz, Heinrich. "To Thee We Turn Our Eyes." CPH 98-1885. SATB, opt kybd.

Scott, K. Lee. "God Shall the Broken Heart Repair." AFP 11-10530. SATB, kybd.

Trinkley, Bruce. "I Want Jesus to Walk with Me." AFP 11-10846. SATB, pno.

Willan, Healey. "Come unto Me, All Ye That Labor and Are Heavy Laden" in *Third Morning Star Choir Book.* CPH 97-4972. U, org.

CHILDREN'S CHOIRS

Cherwien, David. "I Heard the Voice of Jesus Say." CGA 643. U, org, opt C inst desc.

KEYBOARD/INSTRUMENTAL

KEYBOARD/INSTRUMENTAL

Franck, César. "Prelude, Fugue and Variation, Op. 18." KAL. Org.

Moore, Bob. "Five Liturgical Meditations." GIA G-4289. Pno, inst.

Wold, Wayne L. "Prelude, Meditation, and Finale on 'Darwall's 148th.'" AFP 11-10809. Org.

HANDBELL

McChesney, Kevin. "Praise God, Praise Him." AFP 11-10630. 2-3 oct, perc.

Sherman, Arnold. "Jesus Shall Reign." 2-3 oct HOP 1708. 4-5 oct 1709.

PRAISE ENSEMBLE

Hanson, Handt, and Steve Swanson. "Rest in My Love" in *Spirit Calls, Rejoice!* CCF.

Joncas, Michael. "Come to Me." GIA G-3432. SATB.

Schrader, Jack. "Just a Closer Walk." HOP GC 990. SAB.

SUNDAY, JULY 4
INDEPENDENCE DAY (USA)

TUESDAY, JULY 6
JAN HUS, MARTYR, 1415

Hus was a Bohemian priest who spoke against abuses in the church of his day. He believed that the Bible and the liturgy should be in the language of the people rather than Latin, and he sought to allow laity to receive both the bread and wine in Holy Communion. As he became more outspoken, Hus was excommunicated from the church and was eventually burned at the stake on this day in 1415. Hus's followers continued as the Czech Brethren and eventually as the Moravian church of today. Use this day to find out more about the Moravian church and its similarities with Lutheranism.

JULY 11, 1999

SEVENTH SUNDAY AFTER PENTECOST
PROPER 10

INTRODUCTION

For the next three Sundays, the gospel readings present the image of the seed. Though it is very small and seemingly insignificant, the seed contains its entire future; with light and nourishment it will grow and prosper. The seed is a vital image of faith in God, baptism, a congregation's life, the word, and the great paradox at the center of Christian faith: God brings flourishing life out of what appears to be little, dormant, even dead. It is a primary image of faith's central mystery: the dying and rising of Christ. There is ground for hope here.

PRAYER OF THE DAY

Almighty God, we thank you for planting in us the seed of your word. By your Holy Spirit help us to receive it with joy, live according to it, and grow in faith and hope and love; through your Son, Jesus Christ our Lord.

READINGS

Isaiah 55:10-13

Preaching to the Babylonian exiles around 540 b.c., the prophet announces the good news that the Lord will bring the exiles home. The effectiveness of God's word is a theme that runs through chapters 40–55. What God says, will happen. Moreover, not only will the people return, the Lord will transform their path through the desert into a paradise.

Psalm 65:[1-8] 9-14 (Psalm 65:[1-8] 9-13 [NRSV])

Your paths overflow with plenty. (Ps. 65:12)

Romans 8:1-11

Paul has explained that, in spite of good intentions, no human being can ever please God by living in complete obedience to the law. Still, we have been reconciled to God through Christ and introduced to the new life of the Spirit.

Matthew 13:1-9, 18-23

In Matthew's gospel, both Jesus and his disciples "sow the seed" of God's word by proclaiming the good news that "the kingdom of heaven is near." Now, in a memorable parable, Jesus explains why this good news produces different results in those who hear.

COLOR Green

THE PRAYERS

Let us pray for the church, the world, and all who suffer in mind, body, or spirit.

A BRIEF SILENCE.

For all the baptized people of God, that your word may be sown in their lives. Lord, in your mercy,

hear our prayer.

For all who preach or teach in the church, that their message will bring forth growth in all who listen and learn. Lord, in your mercy,

hear our prayer.

For peace in the world, and for an end to oppression and injustice. Lord, in your mercy,

hear our prayer.

For all who struggle with guilt, depression, abuse, poverty, or illness (especially . . .) , that they may know the abundance of your love and care. Lord, in your mercy,

hear our prayer.

For farmers and all who till the soil, and for favorable weather, that we may treasure the fruits of the earth. Lord, in your mercy,

hear our prayer.

For all who live with hunger, that we may share the earth's abundance with them. Lord, in your mercy,

hear our prayer.

For this congregation, that nourished at the eucharistic table we may grow and flourish in your grace. Lord, in your mercy,

hear our prayer.

HERE OTHER INTERCESSIONS MAY BE OFFERED.

We give thanks for Benedict, and all the saints who in life have sown the seeds of righteousness, and in death have been gathered to your eternal harvest. Lord, in your mercy,

hear our prayer.

O God, grant us grace to trust your promises, that our lives may bear fruit to the glory of your name, through Jesus Christ our Lord.

Amen

IMAGES FOR PREACHING

The farmlands of America are "poster children" for the parables of Jesus. Despite certain obstacles, there is usually a bountiful harvest. The emphasis in Matthew 13 must not be on the losses but on the success! Even by modern standards, "a hundredfold" is a tremendous yield.

One chore of summer is to tend the garden and yank the weeds competing with the crops. Attention might be given to our receptivity to the greatest seed of all—the mighty word of God. What pathways in our hearts are trampled hard because of other traffic? What precious words get picked off because of flighty thoughts and ravenous temptations? What seeds from God get wasted because we are petrified by worldly concerns and have never taken the time to let our hearts be plowed in readiness for the word to enter in? What initial germinations of God's word get scorched as soon as our life runs into a burning problem?

One joy of summer is to relax in the comfort of what most farmers already know—what happens with seed and soil depends on God and not on us. There is no condemnation for those who are in Christ Jesus. Christ does for us what we cannot do. The word of God shall not return to God empty. Rather, it accomplishes that for which God purposes, and succeeds in the thing for which God sends it. In other words, when you bet on Christ and get to heaven, expect a bumper crop.

WORSHIP MATTERS

Preparing for liturgical change within a congregation is like planting seeds. One or more growing seasons must pass before the fruits are evident and ready to be enjoyed. The church as worshiping community is church at its most basic. Congregations that have resources to do little else, and those that support huge seven-days-a-week operations, both gather for the Sunday assembly. It is a basic definition of who we are. And the liturgy is often seen as a source of stability in a swiftly changing world.

Anything so central to our very being will be closely guarded whenever change is proposed. Ask open questions in forums where people are able to engage in open dialog, while respecting diverse views. Don't assume what the solution will be for your community until there has been serious conversation. Engage the assembly, preach, teach, invite, love, and in time your work together will bear fruit.

LET THE CHILDREN COME

The church calendar marks today as the commemoration of St. Benedict of Nursia, Abbot of Monte Cassino. Benedictine men and women who follow Benedict's rule for monasteries find life in the practice of hospitality. They welcome strangers as if they were welcoming Christ himself. How does your congregation welcome children in worship? Are they seen as interruptions in the order of service? Are they shown ways how they can be welcoming to others?

MUSIC FOR WORSHIP

GATHERING

| LBW 362 | We plow the fields and scatter |
| WOV 713 | Lord, let my heart be good soil |

PSALM 65

Haas, David. PCY, vol. 8.

Makeever, Ray. PW, Cycle A.

PH 200   To bless the earth God sends us

HYMN OF THE DAY

| LBW 234 | Almighty God, your word is cast |
| | ST. FLAVIAN |

INSTRUMENTAL RESOURCES

Johns, Donald. "St. Flavian" in *Eleven Hymn Preludes*. AFP 11-10187. Kybd.

Sadowski, Kevin. "St. Flavian" in *Twenty Hymn Introductions*. CPH 97-6026. Org.

Young, Jeremy. "Forty Days of Grace" in *At the Foot of the Cross: Piano for Lenten Journey*. AFP 11-10688. Pno.

ALTERNATE HYMN OF THE DAY

| LBW 232 | Your Word, O Lord, is gentle dew |
| WOV 658 | The Word of God is source and seed |

COMMUNION

| LBW 235 | Break now the bread of life |
| WOV 705 | As the grains of wheat |

OTHER SUGGESTIONS

Young, Jeremy. "God Has Spoken, Bread Is Broken." AFP 11-10733. SAB, kybd, opt cong.

SENDING

| LBW 221 | Sent forth by God's blessing |
| WOV 760 | For the fruit of all creation (or LBW 563) |

ADDITIONAL HYMNS AND SONGS

LBW 259	Lord, dismiss us with your blessing
WOV 714	The thirsty fields drink in the rain
MBW 780	Seek the Lord, whose willing presence
WGF 64	Song of the sower
LLC 492	Aramos nuestros campos/We plow the fields

MUSIC FOR THE DAY

CHORAL

Englert, Eugene. "Water." OCP 9325. U, cant, cong, kybd, gtr.

Farlee, Robert Buckley. "O My People, Turn to Me" in *Three Biblical Songs*. AFP 11-10604. U, kybd.

Grundahl, Nancy. "For the Beauty of the Earth." AFP 11-10755. SATB, kybd.

Haugen, Marty. "Come to the Feast." GIA G-3543. SATB, gtr, kybd, trbl inst, opt brass/hb.

Lekberg, Sven. "For as the Rain Cometh Down." GSCH 11509. SATB.

Moore, Bob. "The Word Is in Your Heart." GIA G3838. SAB, cong, gtr, kybd, C inst, opt str.

Rutter, John. "For the Beauty of the Earth." HIN HMC550. SATB (2 pt arr also available).

Wetzler, Robert. "Open Now Thy Gates." AMSI 691. 2 pt mxd, org.

Willan, Healey. "The Seed Is the Word of God" in *We Praise Thee II*. CPH 97-7610. U, org.

Zavelli, J. K./Janco. "Sow the Word." GIA G-2928. 3 pt, cant, opt cong, gtr.

CHILDREN'S CHOIRS

Bolt Jr., Conway. "The Kingdom of God." CGA 677. 2 pt, trbl/mxd, kybd.

Christopherson, Dorothy. "Listen to the Rain." CGA 652. U, kybd, rainsticks, perc.

Ziegenhals, Harriet. "Sing, Dance, Clap Your Hands." CGA 625. U, opt desc, kybd.

KEYBOARD/INSTRUMENTAL

Buxtehude, Dieterich. "Fugue in C" in *Orgelwerke*. BRE 6662. Org.

Fields, Tim. "Partita on 'Come, Let Us Eat.'" MSM 10-824. Org.

Hassell, Michael. "All the Way" in *Traveling Tunes*. AFP 11-10759. Pno, inst.

HANDBELL

Anderson, Christine. "The Ash Grove" in *Songs for the Solo Ringer*. HOP 1245. 3 oct hb solo, kybd.

Moklebust, Cathy. "Come, Holy Spirit." AMSI HB-21. 3-5 oct.

Moklebust, Cathy. "God, Who Made the Earth and Heaven" (AR HYD Y NOS) in *Hymn Stanzas for Handbells*. AFP 11-10722. 4-5 oct.

269

PRAISE ENSEMBLE

Founds, Rick. "Lord, I Lift Your Name On High" in *Praise Chorus Book*, 2d ed. MAR.

Haas, David. "Alive in Christ Jesus" in *Who Calls You by Name,* vol II. GIA G 3622C. SATB.

McLean, Terri. "Come and Grow" in *Come Celebrate! Jesus.* ABI.

SUNDAY, JULY 11
BENEDICT OF NURSIA, ABBOT OF MONTE CASSINO, C. 540

Benedict, the founder of western monasticism, was educated at Rome where the licentiousness of society led him to retire to a cave to live as a hermit. A community gradually gathered around him, and Benedict wrote his famous *Rule*, which is a guide to monastic life, dividing the day into periods of prayer, study, work, and rest. He encouraged a generous spirit of hospitality, and even today visitors at Benedictine communities are to be treated as Christ himself.

A small group may choose to read and discuss Joan Chittester's book *Wisdom Distilled from the Daily: Living the Rule of St. Benedict Today* (HarperCollins, 1990). Chittester uses the *Rule of St. Benedict* as a living guide for all people, suggesting that it affirms the spiritual, psychological, and social values of work, leisure, hospitality, community, listening, humility, stability, obedience, service, and care for the earth.

MONDAY, JULY 12
NATHAN SODERBLÖM, ARCHBISHOP OF UPPSALA, 1931

In 1930, this Swedish theologian, ecumenist, and social activist received the Nobel prize for peace. As the primate of the Church of Sweden, Soderblöm worked for ecumenical convergence and greater understanding among the churches. He advocated practical cooperation among Christians on social questions and encouraged the liturgical movement. As archbishop, his work was directed toward intellectuals and working classes alienated from the church.

As you commemorate Soderblöm, sing "The Church's one foundation" (LBW 369) and discuss the ecumenical situation in the church as we face the new millennium. What are some achievements of the past century, and what are some hopes for the future?

THURSDAY, JULY 15
VLADIMIR, FIRST CHRISTIAN RULER OF RUSSIA, 1015; OLGA, CONFESSOR, 969

Olga, princess of Kiev, became a Christian and was one of the first persons in that area to be baptized. Her son continued as a Viking and resisted Christianity, but Olga's grandson, Vladimir, continued the faith of his grandmother. Vladimir's life had been brutal, bloodthirsty, and ruthless, but he took his new religion seriously, and he sent missionaries into remote areas. Over time Vladimir became a humble and devout person. He was known for his kindness toward criminals and his generosity toward the poor. Olga and Vladimir are honored as the first Christian rulers of Russia.

Use this occasion to learn more about the history of the Russian church. Discuss the different ways religion has been practiced in Russia during this century.

SATURDAY, JULY 17
BARTOLOMÉ DE LAS CASAS, MISSIONARY TO THE INDIES, 1566

Las Casas was among the first missionaries in the New World to expose and vigorously oppose the brutal treatment of the indigenous Indian populations by the Spanish explorers. Throughout the Caribbean islands and Central America, he worked energetically to stop the enslavement of the Indians, to halt the brutal treatment of women by the military forces, and to promote laws that humanized the process of colonization. Even after retirement he continued to champion the Indian cause in his writings. Consider these strong words of his: "The Indians are our brothers, and Christ has given his life for them. Why, then, do we persecute them with such inhuman savagery when they do not deserve such treatment?" How does the gospel bid us to work for the human rights of all people?

JULY 18, 1999

EIGHTH SUNDAY AFTER PENTECOST
PROPER 11

INTRODUCTION

The parable in today's gospel reading sets forth what we may experience every day: evil coexists with the good. The conclusion to the parable—the weeds will be burned—seems simple, except for this: the one who speaks gives his life over to death, that God's mercy for all people may be revealed, and that God's power to bring good out of evil may be known. Is it possible that even weeds and thorns will be transformed into beautiful flowers and lush vines?

Here is each Christian's mission: to speak and to act with mercy and justice in a world that knows too well the presence of evil.

PRAYER OF THE DAY

O Lord, pour out upon us the spirit to think and do what is right, that we, who cannot even exist without you, may have the strength to live according to your will; through your Son, Jesus Christ our Lord.

READINGS

Isaiah 44:6-8

Using a dramatic courtroom scene in which God is at once prosecuting attorney, witness, and judge, this prophet of the exile introduces monotheism for the first time: the Lord is not one among many gods; the Lord is the only God.

or The Wisdom of Solomon 12:13, 16-19

Psalm 86:11-17

Teach me your way, O Lord, and I will walk in your truth. (Ps. 86:11)

Romans 8:12-25

Paul encourages us to experience life as more than just mortal existence, which he calls "life in the flesh." Those who are led by God's Spirit discover a hope that sustains them even in their suffering.

Matthew 13:24-30, 36-43

Jesus has just told his disciples the famous parable of the sower, which compares different responses to the word to different kinds of soil in which a seed is planted. Now he tells a second parable about sowing to illustrate the coexistence of good and evil in our world.

COLOR   Green

THE PRAYERS

Let us pray for the church, the world, and all who suffer in mind, body, or spirit.

A BRIEF SILENCE.

That those who lead or govern may do so with justice, compassion, and integrity. Lord, in your mercy,

hear our prayer.

That the church may live as people of hope as we wait for the fullness of redemption. Lord, in your mercy,

hear our prayer.

That we may be faithful stewards of the earth, and protect the environment from pollution, unrestrained development, and toxic waste. Lord, in your mercy,

hear our prayer.

That all who suffer (especially . . .) may know the freedom that comes from trusting in God. Lord, in your mercy,

hear our prayer.

That those who are hungry, neglected, abused, lonely, or afraid will know our love and compassion. Lord, in your mercy,

hear our prayer.

HERE OTHER INTERCESSIONS MAY BE OFFERED.

That gathered with the saints into the harvest of everlasting life, we may shine like the brightness of the sun. Lord, in your mercy,

hear our prayer.

O God, grant us grace to trust your promises, that our lives may bear fruit to the glory of your name, through Jesus Christ our Lord.

Amen

IMAGES FOR PREACHING

While we are pulling out the weeds, let's not be overzealous! Christians do a lot of damage when they try to prune too precisely the vineyard of the Lord. Good gets lost with the bad. It does no good for the surgeon to cut out all the cancer if the procedure kills the patient. The first principal of medicine is "do no harm."

271

Never in scripture are disciples called to reap the crops and judge who is saved and who is not. The harvesting is left to God, the Son of Man, and angels. Disciples are only called to witness. The seed is sown everywhere, to everyone, without regard for ultimate receptivity. Judgment will come soon enough. And so keep your hands off the sickle. Rather, keep your hands in the sack of gospel proclamation. Keep your eyes on the world Christ came to save. And keep casting out the grace.

WORSHIP MATTERS

So many times we want perfect harmony in every aspect of our lives that we seek to root out everything that goes contrary to our wishes. Wise leaders know that conflict is a given within human organizations. In fact a certain amount of it is necessary for growth.

Is it possible that we will not reach perfect harmony in our life together as God's people until the Son of Man comes at the end of the age? This realization doesn't mean that "anything goes." But what differences can we tolerate among ourselves, without demonizing one another or cutting ourselves down?

LET THE CHILDREN COME

Today's gospel provides an opportunity to engage the children in worship for the rest of the weeks of summer. Have them help in starting some plants in a sunny spot within the church, or create a small garden of late season plants outside. During the upcoming weeks, call the progress in growth to the attention of the children. Remind them that this garden is something that they have planted. Make sure that they take responsibility for part of the plants' care. When the plants are watered and nurtured they grow into something alive and green. Cared for, they grow. Neglected they wither and die.

MUSIC FOR WORSHIP

GATHERING

| LBW 407 | Come, you thankful people, come |
| WOV 688 | O Holy Spirit, root of life |

PSALM 86

Handel, G. F./Robert Powell. "Then Will I Jehovah's Praise." CGA 220. U.

Makeever, Ray. PW, Cycle A.

Trapp, Lynn. "Four Psalm Settings." MSM 80-701. U/cant, opt SATB, cong, org.

HYMN OF THE DAY

| LBW 459 | O Holy Spirit, enter in |
| | WIE SCHÖN LEUCHTET |

VOCAL AND INSTRUMENTAL RESOURCES

See the Epiphany of Our Lord.

ALTERNATE HYMN OF THE DAY

| LBW 234 | Almighty God, your Word is cast |
| WOV 760 | For the fruit of all creation (or LBW 563) |

COMMUNION

| LBW 499 | Come thou Fount of every blessing |
| WOV 771 | Great is thy faithfulness |

OTHER SUGGESTIONS

| GS2 14 | Come, the banquet hall is ready |

SENDING

| LBW 540 | Praise the Lord! O heav'ns |
| WOV 795 | Oh, sing to the Lord |

ADDITIONAL HYMNS AND SONGS

LBW 362	We plow the fields and scatter
WOV 714	The thirsty fields drink in the rain
ASF 26	God, whose glory reigns eternal
CHA 695	God of the fertile fields

MUSIC FOR THE DAY

CHORAL

Bairstow, Edward C. "I Will Wash My Hands in Innocency." OXF MA 6. SATB.

Hobby, Robert A. "Open Your Ears, O Faithful People." AFP 11-10752. U, fl, fc, tamb, hb.

Mendelssohn, Felix/Wilbur Held. "Then Shall the Righteous Shine Forth" in *Vocal Solos for Funerals and Memorial Services.* AFP 11-10226. Solo, kybd.

Schalk, Carl F. "Alleluia to Jesus." CPH 98-2350. SATB.

Wesley, Samuel Sebastian. "Lead Me, Lord" in *The New Church Anthem Book.* OXF 0-19-353109-7. SATB, org.

CHILDREN'S CHOIRS

Bisbee, B. Wayne. "Teach Me Your Way, O Lord." AFP 11-10603. 2 pt mxd, kybd.

Shepherd, John. "A Living Faith." CGA 580. U/2 pt, kybd.

KEYBOARD/INSTRUMENTAL

Albrecht, Mark. "Shaker Hymn" and "My God and I" in *Timeless Hymns of Faith for Piano.* AFP 11-10863. Pno.

Busarow, Donald. *Communion Meditations for Flute and Organ.* CPH 97-6690. Org, inst.

Reubke, Julius. "Trio in E-flat" in *Organ Book,* no. 2. OXF. Org.

HANDBELL

Anderson, Christine. "Fount of Blessings." ALF 12394. 3 oct hb solo, kybd.

Dobrinski, Cynthia. "Blessed Assurance." LAK HB90018. 3-5 oct.

Rogers, Sharon E. "Now Thankful People, Come." AFP 11-10804. 2-3 oct.

PRAISE ENSEMBLE

Smith, Henry. "Give Thanks" in *Maranatha! Music's Praise Chorus Book,* 2d ed. MAR.

Smith, Michael W. "Seed to Sow." HAL 40326204. SATB, SAB, 2 pt, inst pts.

Zschech, Darlene. "Shout to the Lord" in *Integrity! Hosanna! Music Songsheets.* INT.

THURSDAY, JULY 22
ST. MARY MAGDALENE

Mary is one of the primary witnesses to the resurrection, and she is sometimes called "the apostle to the apostles." Healed by Jesus, Mary of Magdala became a disciple of the Lord, and walked with him on his journeys. Her intense devotion to Christ was confirmed as she stood at the foot of the cross, his other disciples having abandoned him. In the Eastern church, her faithfulness to Christ at the cross is commemorated with paintings of her holding a bright red egg, a sign of the resurrection.

This commemoration invites a taste of Easter amid summertime. Sing an Easter hymn, share a festive breakfast with eggs and rich breads, and delight in the goodness of creation!

FRIDAY, JULY 23
BIRGITTA OF SWEDEN, 1373

Birgitta was a wealthy woman with a happy marriage and eight children, but she also reached out to the poor, establishing a hospice on her estate. After her husband's death, Birgitta gave all she owned to the poor and entered a monastery. Her life of intense prayer led her to see many of the injustices that flourished in her native Sweden. Birgitta openly criticized the nobility who lived off the oppressive taxes demanded of the poor. She also founded an order that became one of the most important cultural and religious centers of Sweden during the Middle Ages.

Many religious orders today continue to blend a life of prayer with service in Christ's name. Invite members of a religious community to address a group from your congregation about their vocation and the intersection of their particular ministry with their spiritual life.

273

JULY 25, 1999

ST. JAMES THE ELDER, APOSTLE

INTRODUCTION

Today the church celebrates the festival of St. James the Elder, Apostle. He was the only apostle whose martyrdom was recorded in the Bible. James and his brother John were the sons of a prosperous fisherman, Zebedee. Together they left their home in order to answer Christ's call of discipleship.

How does God call us through the words we hear and the meal we receive today? How do we likewise exercise that call in humble service to others?

PRAYER OF THE DAY

O gracious God, we remember before you today your servant and apostle James, first among the Twelve to suffer martyrdom for the name of Jesus Christ. Pour out upon the leaders of your Church that spirit of self-denying service which is the true mark of authority among your people; through Jesus Christ our Lord, who lives and reigns with you and the Holy Spirit, one God, now and forever.

READINGS

1 Kings 19:9-18

After great cataclysmic events, Elijah hears God in the silence.

Psalm 7:1-11 (Psalm 7:1-10 [NRSV])

God is my shield and defense. (Ps. 7:11)

Acts 11:27—12:3a

King Herod orders the death of the apostle James.

Mark 10:35-45

James and John seek the seats of honor in Christ's kingdom. Jesus teaches the disciples that greatness is not measured in terms of honor, but rather in their willingness to be servants of all people.

COLOR Red

THE PRAYERS

Let us pray for the church, the world, and all who suffer in mind, body, or spirit.

A BRIEF SILENCE.

Give to the leaders of nations the wisdom and discernment to govern with justice. Lord, in your mercy,

hear our prayer.

Strengthen your church to proclaim the coming of your reign and to serve those in need. Lord, in your mercy,

hear our prayer.

Grant peace and healing to all who struggle with illness, grief, or anxiety (especially . . .). Lord, in your mercy,

hear our prayer.

Strengthen with your Spirit victims of violence or abuse, and those who suffer for your sake. Lord, in your mercy,

hear our prayer.

Bless this congregation with gratitude for its heritage, and insight and creativity in facing its future. Lord, in your mercy,

hear our prayer.

HERE OTHER INTERCESSIONS MAY BE OFFERED.

We give thanks for St. James and all the saints who treasured your grace in life and in death. Make us faithful servants until we join them at your table in glory. Lord, in your mercy,

hear our prayer.

O God, grant us grace to trust your promises, that our lives may bear fruit to the glory of your name, through Jesus Christ our Lord.

Amen

IMAGES FOR PREACHING

One of the great ironies of Scripture, is that James got exactly what he asked for—honor, prestige, and glory. In the Acts of the Apostles, he has the glory of having his head cut off for Christ. He has the honor of being the only one of the Twelve (outside of Judas) whose death is recorded in the Scriptures. Except for that, we know but little else of him. It is a lesson to us that we should be careful when we seek glory in God's kingdom, for God may very well give us exactly that for which we ask.

James is often chided for his preemptive strike and bold request. But we should not be too hard on him. At least he sensed that something great was happening through Jesus, and he wanted to be in on it. Oh, if only we sought as much! Jesus does not give him a flat "No." Rather in one great sentence he lays out the theme of his administration: "[T]he Son of Man came not to be served but to serve, and to give his life a ransom for many." Jesus sets this pattern for his disciples: "Whoever wishes to become great among you must be your servant, and whoever wishes to be first among you must be slave of all." There is honor, glory, power, and position in God's kingdom. Only they are not things to be grabbed. Rather they are given as God's gifts.

We are called by Christ to the servant's task; to offer up our neck to the sword if necessary, as did James. Or we are called to live to a ripe old age in obedience to Christ as did his brother, John. No matter what we suffer or endure through the cross of Jesus, we get exactly what we asked for—to sit with Christ on his right hand and on the left to share in his eternal glory.

WORSHIP MATTERS

From the early part of the fourth century, when Christian houses of worship were designed after the model of the Roman pantheon, the ministers of the liturgy have traditionally been seated behind the altar, facing the people. Thus able to be seen and heard easily, the presiding and assisting ministers can lead the assembly's proclamation and prayer from their chairs, reserving the ambo for reading and preaching, and the altar for the meal. In this position, the presider normally is seated directly behind the altar, with the assisting minister to the right, and other vested ministers taking a place on either the left or the right.

LET THE CHILDREN COME

See "Let the Children Come" for the Ninth Sunday after Pentecost.

MUSIC FOR WORSHIP

GATHERING

| LBW 500 | Faith of our fathers |
| WOV 689 | Rejoice in God's saints |

PSALM 7

Smith, Jeffrey. "Psalm 103." CPH 98-3025. 2 pt mxd, opt cong, org.

Turner, Ronald. PW, Cycle C.

HYMN OF THE DAY

| LBW 178 | By all your saints in warfare (st. 16) |
| | KING'S LYNN |

INSTRUMENTAL RESOURCES

See January 10, 1999.

ALTERNATE HYMN OF THE DAY

| LBW 176 | For all your saints, O Lord |

COMMUNION

| LBW 230 | Lord, keep us steadfast in your faith |
| WOV 765 | Jesu, Jesu, fill us with your love |

SENDING

| LBW 183 | The Son of God goes forth to war |
| WOV 688 | O Holy Spirit, root of life |

ADDITIONAL HYMNS AND SONGS

ICEL 203	The eternal gifts of Christ the King
H82 276	For thy blest saints, a noble throng
W3 535	God, we praise you! God, we bless you!

MUSIC FOR THE DAY

CHORAL

Bell, John. "For All the Saints Who've Shown Your Love." GIA G-4540. SATB, fl, ob, cello.

Handel, G. F. "Thou Art the King of Glory." PRE 392-41805. SAB, kybd.

Hogan, David. "Lord, Keep Us Steadfast in Your Word. ECS 4902. U, kybd.

Ley, Henry G. "Lo, Round the Throne a Glorious Band" in *The New Church Anthem Book*. OUP 0-19-353109-7. SATB, org.

Pachelbel, Johann. "What God Ordains Is Always Good" in *With High Delight*. CPH 97-5047. U, SATB, cont.

PRAISE ENSEMBLE

Nelson, Ronald A. "Whoever Would Be Great Among You." AFP 11-1638. Also in *The Augsburg Choirbook*. 11-10817. SAB, pno/gtr.

JULY 25, 1999

NINTH SUNDAY AFTER PENTECOST
PROPER 12

INTRODUCTION

The mission of the church and each baptized Christian is to serve the reign of God. But what is the reign of God? In today's gospel reading, Jesus offers images drawn from ordinary life that reveal something of the reign of God. It is like a tree that becomes a safe and sheltering home, like yeast that penetrates and expands, like a treasured pearl, like a net that gains a great catch.

The reign of God is God's steadfast desire to unite the human family, with all its great diversity, in a justice and mercy so great and thoroughly life-giving that people will rejoice at its advent. How are baptism and the eucharist signs of its presence among us?

PRAYER OF THE DAY

O God, your ears are open always to the prayers of your servants. Open our hearts and minds to you, that we may live in harmony with your will and receive the gifts of your Spirit; through your Son, Jesus Christ our Lord.

READINGS

1 Kings 3:5-12

This passage reflects a concern for leadership that is also present in the larger corpus extending from Joshua through 2 Kings. Leadership in the community that lives under the rule of God has its basis in the covenant, and leaders depend upon God's gifts of wisdom and discernment.

Psalm 119:129-136

When your word goes forth, it gives light and understanding. (Ps. 119:130)

Romans 8:26-39

For several chapters in his letter to the Romans, Paul argues that justification by faith produces a life in the Spirit superior to any legal obedience that might be attained through human effort. Now, in the final words of this chapter, his exuberance for this spiritual life leads to a confident hymn in praise of Christ's love.

Matthew 13:31-33, 44-52

Throughout Matthew's gospel, Jesus and his disciples proclaim the good news that "the kingdom of heaven is near!" Here, Jesus offers several brief parables that explore the implications of this announcement for people's lives.

COLOR Green

THE PRAYERS

Let us pray for the church, the world, and all who suffer in mind, body, or spirit.

A BRIEF SILENCE.

Give to the leaders of nations the wisdom and discernment to govern with justice. Lord, in your mercy,

hear our prayer.

Strengthen the church to proclaim the coming of your reign, and to serve those in need. Lord, in your mercy,

hear our prayer.

Grant peace and healing to all who struggle with illness, grief, or anxiety (especially . . .). Lord, in your mercy,

hear our prayer.

Strengthen with your Spirit victims of violence or abuse, and those who suffer for your sake. Lord, in your mercy,

hear our prayer.

Bless this congregation with gratitude for its heritage, and insight and creativity in facing its future. Lord, in your mercy,

hear our prayer.

HERE OTHER INTERCESSIONS MAY BE OFFERED.

We give thanks for James and all the saints who treasured your grace in life and in death. Make us faithful servants until we join them at your table in glory. Lord, in your mercy,

hear our prayer.

O God, grant us grace to trust your promises, that our lives may bear fruit to the glory of your name, through Jesus Christ our Lord.

Amen

IMAGES FOR PREACHING

The wise investor hunts for bargains year around. The prudent shopper is always on the lookout for a sale. What do you watch for? Stocks? Property? Stamps? Coins? Antiques? Sea shells? Low-cost airfares?

The parables of Jesus prod us to seek what is of ultimate importance—the good and gentle rule of God through Jesus Christ. Is it worth all the money in your wallet to buy today what you know for sure will be tomorrow's winning ticket? Of course it is. What we get is God's grace, life, and forgiveness.

God placed this precious treasure on a shelf made by the timbers of a cross. Hidden, yet exposed. Revealed and available. All that it takes is people who know a tremendous bargain when they see one. You have nothing, you say? You have nothing to give in return for Jesus Christ. Bingo! To admit you have nothing is the price.

The choices we make over the summer are a good indication of our priorities. The faithful folk who show up at church on summer Sundays know their weakness and they know Christ's strength. The Spirit of God is what helps us to make the right choice—and to take the plunge—and buy.

WORSHIP MATTERS

A marvel in the body of Christ is its great diversity. We live in a multi-cultural world: geographically, demographically, chronologically, and sociologically. A guiding principle for those who produce this resource is to embrace the diversities present within the body of Christ, believing it more faithful to embrace the diversity of the body than to divide the body based on cultural or stylistic preferences. Some have called this blended worship. We could also call it good theology. Embrace the body of Christ in all its diversity: old and new, local and global, contemporary and traditional, and plan your community's worship "like the master of a household who brings out of his treasure what is new and what is old."

LET THE CHILDREN COME

Children's involvement in the words and actions of worship begins at home. In the service of Holy Baptism, parents and sponsors make promises to teach their chil-

276

dren the Lord's Prayer, the Creed and the Ten Commandments. Parents and sponsors can also teach children the basic gestures of worship: making the sign of the cross on the forehead, and modeling postures of prayer and blessing. All of these can be easily incorporated into family devotions, meals, and prayers at bedtime.

MUSIC FOR WORSHIP

GATHERING

| LBW 463 | God, who stretched the spangled heavens |
| WOV 767 | All things bright and beautiful |

PSALM 119

Haas, David. PCY, vol. 8.

Makeever, Ray. PW, Cycle A.

The Psalter: Psalms and Canticles for Singing. WJK. U, kybd, cong.

HYMN OF THE DAY

| LBW 415 | God of grace and God of glory |
| | CWM RHONDDA |

VOCAL RESOURCES

Arnatt, Ronald. "Cwm Rhondda" in *Hymn Descants and Free Harmonizations.* AFP 11-6710.

Hughes, J./Sam Batt Owens. "God of Grace and God of Glory." GIA G-2953. Inst pts G-2953-INST. SATB, Cong, org, opt brass, timp.

INSTRUMENTAL RESOURCES

Behnke, John. "Cwm Rhondda" in *Variations for Seven Familiar Hymns.* AFP 11-10702.

Manz, Paul. "Cwm Rhondda" in *A New Liturgical Year,* ed. John Ferguson. AFP 11-10810. Org.

Moklebust, Cathy. "God of Grace" in *Hymn Stanzas for Handbells.* 2-3 oct AFP 11-10869. 4-5 oct 11-10722. Hb.

ALTERNATE HYMN OF THE DAY

| LBW 457/8 | Jesus, priceless treasure |
| WOV 753 | You are the seed |

COMMUNION

| LBW 214 | Come, let us eat |
| WOV 706 | Eat this bread, drink this cup |

OTHER SUGGESTIONS

| DATH 25 | Lamb of God, come take away |

SENDING

| LBW 376 | Your kingdom come! |
| WOV 776 | Be thou my vision |

ADDITIONAL HYMNS AND SONGS

WOV 684	Spirit, spirit of gentleness
CHA 491	As grain on scattered hillsides
NCH 540	We plant a grain of mustard seed
RS 775	The kingdom of God is justice and joy

MUSIC FOR THE DAY

CHORAL

Bach, J. S./Randall DeBruyn. "Jesu, Priceless Treasure" in *Classical Choral Series, I.* OCP. SATB, org.

Hobby, Robert. "Immortal, Invisible." MSM 50-9306. U, kybd.

Johnson, Roy. "Children of the Heavenly Father." PLY CC-106. 2 pt, kybd.

Schütz, Heinrich. "Who Shall Separate Us" ed. Larry L. Fleming. AFP 11-10834. SATB, cont.

Scott, K. Lee. "So Art Thou to Me" in *Rejoice Now, My Spirit: Vocal Solos for the Church Year.* MH AFP 11-10228. ML 11-10229.

Wienhorst, Richard. "Lord, to Whom Shall We Go?" in *Two Verse Settings.* CPH 98-2588. SATB, fl.

Young, Jeremy. "Nothing Can Come Between Us." AFP 11-10848. SAB, pno, opt cong.

CHILDREN'S CHOIRS

Beebe, Hank. "A Mustard Seed." KIR K139. 2 pt, kybd.

Hopson, Hal H. "The Treasure and the Pearl." AMSI 462. U/2 pt, kybd.

Hopson, Hal. "Who Shall Separate Us from the Love of Christ?" CGA 286. U, kybd.

KEYBOARD/INSTRUMENTAL

Bender, Jan. "Variations on 'Jesu, meine Freude.'" AFP 11-7110. Vln, org.

Langlais, Jean. "Pasticcio" in *Organ Book.* EV. Org.

Leavitt, John. "Kyrie" in *Simple Gifts.* WAR. Pno.

Perry, Michael/Welch. "Two Regal Settings." MSM 10-946. Org.

HANDBELL

Anderson, Christine. "Children of the Heavenly Father." HOP 1695. 3 oct hb solo, kybd.

McChesney, Kevin. "God of Grace and God of Glory." CPH 97-6584. 3-5 oct.

Wagner, Douglas E. "The Ashgrove." JEF JH-S9072. 2 oct.

PRAISE ENSEMBLE

DeShazo, Lynn. "More Precious Than Silver" in *Maranatha! Music's Praise Chorus Book,* 2d ed. MAR.

Hommerding, Alan J. "Sing Till the Power of the Lord Comes Down." WLP 8602-95. SATB.

Watson, Wayne/Carol Cymbala. "Friend of a Wounded Heart." WRD 3010760167. SATB.

277

SUNDAY, JULY 25
ST. JAMES THE ELDER, APOSTLE

James, son of Zebedee and brother of John, is the only apostle whose martyrdom is recorded in scripture. James is often pictured with a shell, a reminder that he was a fisherman and that he later baptized new Christians. Of the two men named James who became apostles, this James is called the elder, or the greater, because we know more about him. The other James is commemorated with Philip on May 1.

Today would be a wonderful day for baptisms, and to use a shell to scoop water over the head of the persons being baptized.

WEDNESDAY, JULY 28
JOHANN SEBASTIAN BACH, 1750; HEINRICH SCHÜTZ, 1672; GEORGE FREDERICK HANDEL, 1759; MUSICIANS

These musicians used the gift of composition to enrich the worship and devotional lives of Christians in their day and since. Bach is considered one of the greatest composers of all time. In Leipzig he wrote choral cantatas for each Sunday and festival of the church year. Schütz's choral settings of biblical texts show a mastery never surpassed. Handel's music is not church music in the strictest sense, but his oratorios have been cherished proclamations of the scriptures.

Commemorate these three great musicians by playing selections of their great works, or by singing a hymn by each one, such as Bach's arrangement of "Come with us, O blessed Jesus" (LBW 219), "O Spirit of life" (WOV 680), Handel's famous tune used with "Thine is the glory" (LBW 145), and Schütz's tune used with a paraphrase of the Magnificat (LBW 180).

THURSDAY, JULY 29
MARY, MARTHA, AND LAZARUS OF BETHANY

Mary, Martha, and Lazarus of Bethany are remembered for the hospitality and refreshment they offered Jesus in their home. Mary is identified in the fourth gospel as the one who anointed Jesus before his passion. Following the characterization drawn by Luke, Martha represents the active life, and Mary the contemplative. In the gospel of John, Lazarus is raised from the dead by Jesus as a sign of the eternal life offered to all believers. Congregations might commemorate these three by reflecting on the role of hospitality in both home and church.

OLAF, KING OF NORWAY, MARTYR, 1030

Olaf is considered the patron saint of Norway. A year after arriving there he declared himself king of his country, and from then on Christianity was the dominant religion of the realm. In addition, he revised the laws of the nation and enforced them with strict impartiality, alienating some of the aristocracy. After being driven from the country, he died in battle, trying to regain his kingdom. How is Olaf's memory honored in this country?

AUGUST 1, 1999

TENTH SUNDAY AFTER PENTECOST
PROPER 13

INTRODUCTION

In the gospel reading for this day, we hear familiar words about Jesus' meal practice: he took the loaves, blessed them, broke them, and gave them for all to eat. Here the church sees the pattern of the eucharist: the gifts of God's goodness and human labor are presented, the table thanksgiving is spoken, bread is broken and wine is poured, and all are invited to the holy supper.

To this supper the church welcomes all the baptized. The gifts of God are given freely, equally, and without discrimination. "You that have no money," shouts Isaiah, "come and eat." And yet we recognize that this gracious communion takes place in a world where many eat and many go hungry each day. How is this sacred meal a sign of what God intends for life in this world?

PRAYER OF THE DAY

Gracious Father, your blessed Son came down from heaven to be the true bread which gives life to the world. Give us this bread, that he may live in us and we in him, Jesus Christ our Lord.

READINGS

Isaiah 55:1-5

In both ancient Near Eastern history and literature, the building of a temple and the feast held afterward signify the establishment of the kingdom of the temple's builder. Isaiah 54 recounts God's building of a new temple following the exile. Today's reading is the invitation to the feast. Again, the people are invited to be wise and choose what is good rather than what is folly (see also Proverbs 9:5-6).

Psalm 145:8-9, 15-22 (Psalm 145:8-9, 14-21 [NRSV])

You open wide your hand and satisfy the needs of every living creature. (Ps. 145:17)

Romans 9:1-5

In his letter to the Romans, Paul proclaims the good news of Jesus Christ, through whom "nothing can separate us from the love of God." Then, his joy turns to sorrow as he considers those among God's people who have not received the gospel.

Matthew 14:13-21

After John the Baptist is murdered, Jesus desires a time of solitude. Still, his compassion for others will not allow him to dismiss those who still need him but, rather, moves him to perform one of his greatest miracles.

COLOR Green

THE PRAYERS

Let us pray for the church, the world, and all who suffer in mind, body, or spirit.

A BRIEF SILENCE.

For the church, that it may faithfully share all that God has given us with those who are hungry and poor. Lord, in your mercy,

hear our prayer.

For the leaders and legislators of this nation, that they will labor to insure the blessings of food, shelter, clothing, and health care for all who dwell in this land. Lord, in your mercy,

hear our prayer.

For those who grow, harvest, and prepare our food, that we honor their labor and the fruits of the earth. Lord,

in your mercy,

hear our prayer.

For those who struggle with difficult decisions, unemployment, or conflicts in relationships, that you give them courage and strength. Lord, in your mercy,

hear our prayer.

For all who are sick or in special need (especially . . .), that you satisfy their needs with the abundance of your care and compassion. Lord, in your mercy,

hear our prayer.

For ourselves, that you feed us with your word and meal, so we may share of your bounty and goodness. Lord, in your mercy,

hear our prayer.

HERE OTHER INTERCESSIONS MAY BE OFFERED.

Bring us with all your saints to the heavenly table where all people will feast on your never-ending love and grace. Lord, in your mercy,

hear our prayer.

O God, grant us grace to trust your promises, that our lives may bear fruit to the glory of your name, through Jesus Christ our Lord.

Amen

IMAGES FOR PREACHING

"You feed them," Jesus said to his disciples when they thought the hour late. "We have nothing," they replied. How right they were! Preachers of the gospel have nothing of their own to feed God's people; not their own ideas and opinions, political persuasions, personal agendas, or crusades.

We have nothing—except "small fish" words and "mini-pocket-bread" actions which when taken into Christ's hands and blessed by him become a food that is good and a meal that delights—a wine and milk without money and without price. If Jesus can take bread and wine and turn them into sacramental elements (vehicles for forgiveness, life, and salvation), then Jesus can do the same with words. Our sputtering bits of verbiage are transformed into a satiating smorgasbord of grace when they are linked to the mighty word of God.

Here one homiletics professor's play on Luther's Small Catechism is instructive. "How can words do such great things?" he would say mimicking Luther's third question on baptism. And then grandly he would respond, "It is not words indeed that does them, but the word of God which is in and with the words, and faith which trusts such word of God in the words. For without the word of God the words are simple words and not the word. But with the word of God they are the word."

WORSHIP MATTERS

The breaking of the eucharistic bread is both utilitarian and theological. It is from this one loaf that all are fed. It is also in taking and blessing, breaking and giving, that Christ is revealed. Christ is both meal and host. The bread is broken and shared, and broken again. Sometimes the pieces get kind of small, but in the end, everyone is fed. Everyone is included. There is always some bread left over to share.

LET THE CHILDREN COME

How does the parish obtain bread for the celebration of Holy Communion? Maybe on a day such as this, a day filled with eucharistic imagery, recipes for communion bread can be distributed after worship. These can be simple recipes in which children might have an active share in baking. Look in altar guild handbooks or check the internet for such recipes. Make the bread of Holy Communion something that children can "offer with joy and thanksgiving."

MUSIC FOR WORSHIP

GATHERING

| LBW 524 | My God, how wonderful thou art |
| WOV 766 | We come to the hungry feast |

PSALM 145

Haas, David. "I Will Praise Your Name" in *PS2*.

Makeever, Ray. PW, Cycle A.

Sleeth, Natalie. "Everywhere I Go." CGA-171. U/2 pt, opt C inst.

Trapp, Lynn. "Four Psalm Settings." MSM 80-701. U, opt SATB, cong, org.

HYMN OF THE DAY

| LBW 423 | Lord, whose love in humble service |
| | BEACH SPRING |

VOCAL RESOURCES

Bisbee, B. Wayne. "Beach Spring" in *Assist Us to Proclaim,* set 2. AFP 11-10597. SATB, kybd.

Schrader, Jack. "Come, Ye Sinners." HOP HO 1824. SSATB.

INSTRUMENTAL RESOURCES

Anderson, Christine. "Beach Spring." HOP 1707. 3-4 oct hb solo, kybd.

Bisbee, B. Wayne. "Beach Spring" in *From the Serene to the Whimsical.* AFP 11-10561. Org.

Ferguson, John. "Beach Spring" in *Hymn Harmonizations for Organ;* book V. LUD O-14.

Hyslop, Scott. "Beach Spring" in *Six Chorale Fantasias for Solo Instrument and Piano.* AFP 11-10799. Pno, inst.

Sedio, Mark. "Beach Spring" in *Dancing in the Light of God.* AFP 11-10793. Pno.

ALTERNATE HYMN OF THE DAY

| LBW 409 | Praise and thanksgiving |
| WOV 754 | Let us talents and tongues employ |

COMMUNION

| LBW 197 | O living Bread from heaven |
| WOV 702 | I am the Bread of life |

OTHER SUGGESTIONS

| DATH 29 | Just as Jesus told us |

SENDING

| LBW 390 | I love to tell the story |
| WOV 722 | Hallelujah! We sing your praises |

ADDITIONAL HYMNS AND SONGS

LBW 221	Sent forth by God's blessing
WOV 711	You satisfy the hungry heart
NCH 562	Take my gifts and let me love you
NSR 62	Come, satisfy your thirst
LLC 408	Unidos en la fiesta/United at the table

MUSIC FOR THE DAY

CHORAL

Handel, G. F. "Deck Thyself, My Soul, with Gladness." PRE 392-41707. SATB, kybd.

Haugen, Marty. "Come to the Feast." GIA G-3543. SATB, gtr, kybd, trbl inst, opt brass, hb.

Hopson, Hal. "Jesus Fed the Hungry Thousands." HOP JR 221. U, kybd.

Pulkingham, Betty. "Ho! Everyone That Thirsteth." GIA G-1777. SATB, gtr.

Simmons, Morgan. "Bread of Heaven, on Thee We Feed." AFP 12-108. 2 pt mxd, org.

Marcello, Benedetto. "Give Ear Unto Me" in *Second Morning Star Choir Book.* CPH 97-4702. SS, org.

Pethel, Stan. "Bless This Gift." CGA 761. 2 pt mxd, kybd.

Proulx, Richard. "The Eyes of All." CHA 12-109. U, org.

KEYBOARD/INSTRUMENTAL

Langlais, Jean. "Dialogue sur les mixtures" in *Suite Breve.* BOR. Org.

Mathews, Peter. "Pastorale for Clarinet and Organ." MSM 20-966. Org, cl.

Porter, Rachel Trelstad. "Beach Spring" in *Day by Day.* AFP 11-10772. Pno.

HANDBELL

Anderson, Christine. "Fount of Blessings." ALF 12394. 3 oct hb solo, kybd.

Moklebust, Cathy. "Come, Let Us Eat." CGA CGB152. 3-5 oct, perc.

PRAISE ENSEMBLE

Calcotte, Glenn. "My Offering of Praise." DOX DM 147. SATB.

Hanson, Handt, and Paul Murakami. "That We May Be Filled" in *Spirit Calls, Rejoice!* CCF.

Joncas, Michael. "On Eagle's Wings." HOP 16138. SATB.

AUGUST 8, 1999

ELEVENTH SUNDAY AFTER PENTECOST
PROPER 14

INTRODUCTION

"Lord, save me." One of the most ancient prayers of the liturgy is this cry of Peter in today's gospel reading. Lord, save me. How many times in frightening moments have we not shouted or murmured this simple prayer? Faced with a threatening situation or devastating news, we recognize that left to our own devices we will not survive. Such a moment of recognition signals our deep need for God's merciful presence in our lives.

In the liturgy, we hear these words again. Lord, have mercy. Lord, to whom shall we go? Come, Lord Jesus. In our singing and speaking of these words, we ask Christ to strengthen our faith so that we might hear the cry for help in daily life and respond with Christ's own words: Take heart; do not be afraid.

Today is also the commemoration for Dominic, priest (1221), who founded an order of preachers.

PRAYER OF THE DAY

Almighty and everlasting God, you are always more ready to hear than we are to pray, and to give more than we either desire or deserve. Pour upon us the abundance of your mercy, forgiving us those things of which our conscience is afraid, and giving us those good things for which we are not worthy to ask, except through the merit of your Son, Jesus Christ our Lord.

READINGS

1 Kings 19:9-18

On the mountain where God had appeared to Moses with typical signs of God's presence—earthquake, wind, and fire—Elijah is now presented with a dramatic shift in the understanding of where God is to be found. God is not to be found in these signs. Rather, God is among the people, where the will of God is being lived out.

Psalm 85:8-13

I will listen to what the Lord God is saying. (Ps. 85:8)

Romans 10:5-15

Paul is discussing how we may attain the righteousness that leads to salvation. One way, he grants, would be to keep the law, but he has already shown that it is impossible. Then, he proclaims the good news about "righteousness that comes by faith."

Matthew 14:22-33

Matthew's Gospel typically portrays Jesus' disciples as people of "little faith," who fail despite their best intentions. In this story, Matthew shows how Jesus comes to these disciples when they are in trouble and sustains them in their fear and doubt.

COLOR   Green

THE PRAYERS

Let us pray for the church, the world, and all who suffer in mind, body, or spirit.

A BRIEF SILENCE.

For the whole church, that it will listen faithfully to the word of God. Lord, in your mercy,

hear our prayer.

For those who govern in the world, that peace, truth, and righteousness may prevail. Lord, in your mercy,

hear our prayer.

For the earth, that we may be good stewards of its air, water, and other natural resources. Lord, in your mercy,

hear our prayer.

For all who live with illness, doubt, or fear (especially . . .), that they may know the strength of Christ's abiding presence. Lord, in your mercy,

hear our prayer.

For ourselves, that we will honor silence and be attentive to the voice of the Spirit in our busy and noisy world. Lord, in your mercy,

hear our prayer.

HERE OTHER INTERCESSIONS MAY BE OFFERED.

We give thanks for Dominic and all the saints who have confessed the crucified and risen one. Bring us with them to the eternal rest and peace of everlasting life. Lord, in your mercy,

hear our prayer.

O God, grant us grace to trust your promises, that our lives may bear fruit to the glory of your name, through Jesus Christ our Lord.

Amen

IMAGES FOR PREACHING

Peter is often painted as an impulsive fool with shades of yellow cowardliness and green embarrassment to go along with his red temper. But at least he was so overwhelmed, impressed, and emboldened by Jesus that he was willing to take a risk and do something new, different, and unheard of—if not downright dangerous and crazy. He wanted to come to Jesus on the water. Where is our passion to be with Jesus wherever he is? All too often we sit tight in our boats clinging to the gunwales of safety and security; trusting in our little ship of state, the status quo.

But coming to Jesus often means boldly stepping out into a nasty world where winds blow strong and a wavy surface surges and wanes. It means taking some risks and doing something new and different and daring, particularly among the least and lost and little. So

what if we fail? If we are in the neighborhood of Jesus, falling flat on our face will not harm us. Faithlessness— that's what will harm us. When Jesus said, "On this rock I will build my church," he did not mean a church that will never budge. He meant a faith like Peter's that propelled him out with eyes on Jesus.

Peter was doing fine until he took his eyes off Jesus and began to doubt. Beginning to sink, he cried out, "Lord save me!" And the Lord immediately reached out and grabbed him. What Paul says is true: "Everyone who calls on the name of the Lord will be saved." But how can people know that Jesus saves all who ask unless voices out in the stormy recesses of the world are saying and living it? How beautiful are the feet of those who bring good news—even if they are a little wet!

WORSHIP MATTERS

Many congregations plan an outdoor worship service each summer. Some have even scheduled a weekly outdoor liturgy for warm months. These outdoor liturgies call for special attention to issues of hospitality that may not pose problems indoors. Take care to assure that the assembly can hear the leaders and one another. (Open air is not generally conducive to group singing or to hearing worship leaders, unless some type of picnic shelter or natural amphitheater is the setting.)

Don't allow the assembly to be too spread out. Define the worship space creatively with living plants, natural arrangements, or textiles. Arrange the assembly so they are not facing the sun or in direct sunlight. Is the terrain level or smooth? How will physically disabled and/or elderly worshipers be accommodated? Is adequate seating provided? What special attention will the musicians need? Has the assembly been invited to dress for outdoors? Have directions been provided? How will visitors who may be unprepared to be outdoors be welcomed and included (especially if other worshipers are bringing chairs or blankets to use in sitting on a lawn)? Is there a bad weather plan? Who will provide communion vessels and any worship appointments needed? Is there a worthy table for communion? And most importantly, has Christ remained central, in word, in water, in bread and wine in the midst of this crowd? Outdoor worship can be great—but it still needs as much (or even more) careful planning as any other service would receive.

LET THE CHILDREN COME

Congregations continue to explore the implications of *The Use of the Means of Grace.* One question that may linger is the appropriate age at which children begin to commune on a regular basis. Paul's words in 1 Corinthians about the need to discern the body of Christ has been interpreted variously. Perhaps the real question for the worshiping assembly is this: Is the assembly ready to discern the body of Christ in *baptized children* of any age, from the very youngest on up, and welcome them to the Lord's table?

MUSIC FOR WORSHIP

GATHERING

| LBW 507 | How firm a foundation |
| WOV 718 | Here in this place |

PSALM 85

DATH 40   Dancing at the Harvest

Hurd, David. "Show Us Your Kindness." OCP 9874CC. U, SATB, kybd, gtr.

Makeever, Ray. PW, Cycle A.

Smith, Alan. "Let Us See, O Lord, Your Mercy" in PS1.

HYMN OF THE DAY

| LBW 467 | Eternal Father, strong to save |
| | MELITA |

INSTRUMENTAL RESOURCES

Cherwien, David. "Melita" in *Interpretations,* book IX. AMSI SP-106. Org.

Kinyon, Barbara B. "Eternal Father, Strong to Save." HOP 1430. Hb.

Sadowski, Kevin. "Melita" in *21 Hymn Introductions.* CPH 97-5986. Org.

Tryggestad, David. "Melita" in *Deo Gracias.* AFP 11-10471. Org.

ALTERNATE HYMN OF THE DAY

| LBW 366 | Lord of our life |
| WOV 781 | My life flows on in endless song |

COMMUNION

| LBW 334 | Jesus, Savior, pilot me |
| WOV 731 | Precious Lord, take my hand |

SENDING

| LBW 503 | O Jesus, I have promised |
| WOV 780 | What a fellowship, what a joy divine |

ADDITIONAL HYMNS AND SONGS

LBW 417	In a lowly manger born
WOV 768	He comes to us as one unknown
UMH 649	How shall they hear the Word of God?
WAO 39	At evening when the sun was set

MUSIC FOR THE DAY

CHORAL

Barnard, John. "How Can I Keep from Singing." GIA G-4507. SAB, kybd.

Cain, N. "In the Night, Christ Came Walking." GSCH 7967. SATB.

Shepperd, Mark. "I Will Yet Praise Him." AFP 11-10853. SATB, pno.

Strube, Adolf. "Blest Spirit, One with God" in *SAB Chorale Book.* CPH 97-7575. SAB.

Young, Jeremy. "Take a Step." GIA G-3231. SATB, pno.

CHILDREN'S CHOIRS

Davis, Katherine. "Who Was the Man." CGA 110. U.

Mitchell, Tom. "Song of Hope (Canto de Esperanza)." CGA 638. U, kybd, opt desc/inst.

KEYBOARD/INSTRUMENTAL

Couperin, François. "Tierce en Taille" and "Offertoire on the Grand Jeux" in *Two Masses for Organ.* DOV 0486282856. Org.

Uehlein, Christopher. "Pastorales No. 1 and No. 2" in *Blue Cloud Abbey Organ Book.* AFP 11-10394. Org.

HANDBELL

Afdahl, Lee J. "Dear Lord and Father of Mankind" (REPTON) in *Dear Lord—Lead On.* AFP 11-10770. 3-5 oct.

Kinyon, Barbara B. "Immortal, Invisible, God Only Wise." CGA CGB172. 3 oct.

PRAISE ENSEMBLE

Gustafson, Gerrit. "Lord We Pray" in *Integrity's Hosanna! Music Songbook.* INT.

Haas, David. "Come, My Children" in *Who Calls You by Name,* vol. I. GIA G3193C. 2 pt.

Jernigan, Dennis/arr. J. Daniel Smith. "Great Is the Lord Almighty." WRD 301 0810 164. SATB.

283

SUNDAY, AUGUST 8
DOMINIC, PRIEST, 1221

Dominic founded an order of itinerant preachers, known today as the Dominicans. He was a man of study and of prayer, and taught his followers to "bring to others what you contemplate." The Order of Preachers, as it was called, was to use kindness and gentle argument, rather than harsh judgment, when bringing unorthodox Christians back to the fold. Dominic was opposed to the practice of burning heretics at the stake simply because of their unorthodox faith.

Preachers might mention Dominic in their homilies today, especially in relation to the Romans 10:5-15 reading (Proper 14, cycle A), which includes the following quote: "How beautiful are the feet of those who bring good news!" Include a prayer for preachers and all who proclaim the gospel.

TUESDAY, AUGUST 10
LAWRENCE, DEACON, MARTYR, 258

Lawrence lived during the time of persecution under the Roman emperor Valerian. According to legend, when Lawrence learned that he would follow the pope and other deacons to his death as a martyr, he gathered people in need and brought them to a Roman official saying: "Here is the treasure of the Church." Lawrence's martyrdom was one of the first to be observed by the church.

Amid our concerns for the institutional church, reflect on what we consider the treasures of the church today. Are we rooted in the gifts of word and sacrament? Is our response to the needs of the most vulnerable in our society one of obligation, or one that treasures what we can also receive from them?

FRIDAY, AUGUST 13
FLORENCE NIGHTINGALE, 1910; CLARA MAASS, 1901; RENEWERS OF SOCIETY

Florence Nightingale and Clara Maass are examples of women who used their vocation of nursing to forge new paths of service in their day. Among other things, Florence established the first school of nursing in England, and Clara researched and nursed victims of yellow fever. They serve as role models of women who used their gifts and calling to make significant contributions to the times in which they lived.

Give thanks for nurses and other healthcare professionals in your congregation. Do you have a parish nurse on your staff? Some congregations share a parish nurse with a nearby parish. A parish nurse helps keep issues of health and wholeness before the congregation through newsletter articles, classes, and other educational events.

AUGUST 15, 1999
MARY, MOTHER OF OUR LORD

INTRODUCTION

Mary, the mother of Jesus, is traditionally believed to have died on this date. Faithful to the last, Mary has been important to Christian devotion throughout history because in her, the God-bearer, is seen a representation of the church itself. Mary's song (the "Magnificat") is our gospel for the day. It is a powerful statement of justice, still apt for us today as we come with our own neediness to experience God's justice and mercy in word and sacrament. How will we announce this news about God to others who are also in need?

PRAYER OF THE DAY

Almighty God, you chose the virgin Mary to be the mother of your only Son. Grant that we, who have been redeemed by his blood, may share with her in the glory of your eternal kingdom; through your Son, Jesus Christ our Lord, who lives and reigns with you and the Holy Spirit, one God, now and forever.

READINGS

Isaiah 61:7-11

God will cause righteousness and praise to spring up before all nations.

Psalm 45:11-16

I will make your name to be remembered from one generation to another. (Ps. 45:18)

Galatians 4:4-7

Through Christ's birth from a woman, we are no longer slaves, but children of God.

Luke 1:46-55

Upon hearing that she was to become the mother of Jesus, Mary sings a song rejoicing in the Lord.

COLOR   White

THE PRAYERS

Let us pray for the church, the world, and all who suffer in mind, body, or spirit.

A BRIEF SILENCE.

For the church, that like Mary it may magnify the Lord and be a bearer of Christ to the world. Lord, in your mercy,

hear our prayer.

For the nations, that they will share of their wealth with those who are poor and lowly. Lord, in your mercy,

hear our prayer.

For all who face hunger or spiritual emptiness, that you would fill them with the good things of your grace. Lord, in your mercy,

hear our prayer.

For all who suffer or struggle with illness (especially . . .), that you look on them with favor and compassion. Lord, in your mercy,

hear our prayer.

For the children in our community, that we faithfully proclaim to them the promises made to our ancestors in faith. Lord, in your mercy,

hear our prayer.

HERE OTHER INTERCESSIONS MAY BE OFFERED.

We give thanks for Mary, mother of our Lord, and all the saints who proclaimed the greatness of your name, and now share your everlasting joy. Lord, in your mercy,

hear our prayer.

O God, grant us grace to trust your promises, that our lives may bear fruit to the glory of your name, through Jesus Christ our Lord.

Amen

IMAGES FOR PREACHING

Orthodox Christianity honors Mary with the title *theotokos*. The first part of this compound noun is *theos* as in "theology." It is the word for "God." The second part *tokos* is the word for "bearer," as in a pregnant woman "bearing" a child. Mary is theotokos. She is "God-bearer."

And isn't that an awesome thought! A young, common village girl is the mother of God. Without Mary, Jesus would not be Jesus. And Jesus would not be in the position to save us. Prior to his being conceived in Mary, there was no Jesus, only the eternal Son of God. And there was no salvation either from our slavery to sin and death.

We are talking here about logistics—God's placement problem—the problem of getting the right person (Jesus the eternal Son of God) in the right place, at the right time, and in the right fashion. Paul spells it out in Galatians 4. Jesus had to come into our world, our real physical world, in our real historical time, and be under the same real physical law of death and condemnation in order to save us from our real sins. And the only way that it could happen was by being born in a woman's womb. "God sent the Son, born of a woman, born under the law, in order to redeem those who were under the law, so that we might receive adoption as [God's] children."

But let us quickly add that whatever great thing happened in Mary is done by God. Mary magnifies the Lord; she does not magnify herself. God does it all. Mary does nothing, except to let herself be used. Wait a minute! Doesn't that happen to us too? Are we not also *theotokoi*—"God bearers"? Are not we also used by God?

To be sure, none of us can bear Jesus in the womb the way Mary did. None of us can give to him our genetic code or shape his childhood years with our caring or our loving. But we can bear Jesus in some other part of our anatomy—in our mouth, and in our heart, and in our mind, and in our bones, and in our being. We can act like what we are—the adopted children of God—and magnify the Lord by the content of our speech and the patterns of our behavior. Touched by God the Holy Spirit we can allow ourselves to be used by God the Father to bear his Son Jesus in our bodies to the world. Move over Mary. We are *theotokoi*, too! God-bearers.

285

WORSHIP MATTERS

Genuine hospitality in the congregation suggests that care be shown not only to families with young children, but also to those who are expecting a child. Offering prayers for the health of both mother and unborn child is welcome, especially for those for whom pregnancy is a matter of concern. Congregation members can provide support through gifts of food, or the offer to run errands, or to escort the mother-to-be to her doctor appointments. Providing comfortable seating during worship, perhaps in the church's nursery, is also helpful to the expectant mother, and can give her a sense of heightened joy as she awaits the birth of her own child. Throughout the days of a woman's pregnancy words of support and shared expectation make the example of the mother of Jesus more profound.

LET THE CHILDREN COME

See "Let the Children Come" for the Twelfth Sunday after Pentecost.

MUSIC FOR WORSHIP

SERVICE MUSIC

To set apart the lesser festivals that may be celebrated during the season after Pentecost, return the hymn of praise to the liturgy. Today, that hymn of praise might well be a setting of the Magnificat (see *LBW*, p. 147 and Canticle 6; also see listings for the Third Sunday in Advent).

GATHERING

| LBW 224 | Soul, adorn yourself with gladness |
| WOV 632 | The angel Gabriel from heaven came |

PSALM 45

Jennings, Carolyn. PW, Cycle C.

HYMN OF THE DAY

| WOV 634 | Sing of Mary, pure and lowly |
| | RAQUEL |

INSTRUMENTAL RESOURCES

Cherwien, David. "Surely It Is God Who Saves Me" in *Six Organ Preludes*. GIA G-4291. Org.

ALTERNATE HYMN OF THE DAY

| LBW 180 | My soul now magnifies the Lord |

COMMUNION

LBW 42	Of the Father's love begotten
LBW 215	O Lord, we praise you
WOV 730	My soul proclaims your greatness

SENDING

| LBW 533/4 | Now thank we all our God |
| WOV 724 | Shalom |

ADDITIONAL HYMNS AND SONGS

RS 899	I sing a maid of tender years
RS 876	No wind at the window
WGF 70	How can it be, O God most high

OTHER SUGGESTIONS

See listings for Fourth Sunday in Advent.

MUSIC FOR THE DAY

CHORAL

DeLong, Richard. "Of a Rose, a Lovely Rose." ECS 4926. SATB.

Duruflé, Maurice. "Tota pulchra es." PRE 312-416721. SSA.

Holst, Gustav. "Jesu, Thou the Virgin-Born" in *Church Choir Book II*. CPH 97-5610. SATB, org.

Nystedt, Knut. "I Will Greatly Rejoice." HIN HMC-226. SATB.

Schulz-Widmar, Russell. "Mary Said Yes." SEL 405-201. SATB, kybd.

Sedio, Mark. "There Is No Rose of Such Vertu." AFP 11-10784. SATB, org.

Willan, Healey. "The Magnificat" in *We Praise Thee II*. CPH 97-7610. U, SSA, org.

Willcock, Christopher. "Song of the Virgin Mary." OCP 10540. SATB, org, cl.

CHILDREN'S CHOIRS

Bouman, Paul. "Mary's Song of Praise." CPH 98-3194. U, org.

Leitz, Darwin. "The Magnificat." AFP ED12-467281. U, org/gtr, bass.

KEYBOARD/INSTRUMENTAL

Mason, Monte. "The Angel Gabriel." AFP 11-10610.

Organ, Anne Krentz. "The Angel Gabriel" in *Advent Reflections for Piano and Instrument*. AFP 11-10864. Pno, solo inst.

Pachelbel, Johann. "Fugue on the Magnificat" in *Selected Organ Works*. Various ed. Org.

Young, Jeremy. "Mary and the Angel" in *PianoForte Christmas*. AFP 11-10716. Pno.

PRAISE ENSEMBLE

Nystrom, Martin. "As The Deer" in *Maranatha! Music's Praise Chorus Book*, 2d ed. MAR.

Ylvisaker, John. "Magnificat" in *Borning Cry*. NGP.

AUGUST 15, 1999

TWELFTH SUNDAY AFTER PENTECOST
PROPER 15

INTRODUCTION

What parents would not cry out for help to someone who could save their sick or tormented children? Here, in the gospel reading, we see a mother who will not abandon her mission to find relief for her suffering daughter. She is persistent and unflinching in her request for Christ's healing.

In this Canaanite woman, the church finds an image of its mission. The world is filled with people who are tormented, sick, and oppressed. In the prayers, the church asks for God's healing in a world that is troubled and wounded. In the eucharistic meal, the church receives the strength to enter this world and bring comfort, healing, and justice to those in need.

PRAYER OF THE DAY

Almighty and ever-living God, you have given great and precious promises to those who believe. Grant us the perfect faith which overcomes all doubts, through your Son, Jesus Christ our Lord.

READINGS

Isaiah 56:1, 6-8

Whereas the Israelite community, defined by early legal traditions, was expected to live the righteous and obedient life, the prophet makes a new announcement: now righteousness and obedience define who belongs to the Israelite community. In other words, commitment to the Lord makes a person a member of God's people—not race, nationality, or any other category.

Psalm 67

Let all the peoples praise you, O God. (Ps. 67:3)

Romans 11:1-2a, 29-32

As a Jewish Christian, Paul is dismayed that other Jews have not believed in Jesus as their Messiah. In his letter to the Romans, he discusses whether these Jews remain the chosen people of God.

Matthew 15:[10-20] 21-28

Jesus teaches his disciples that true purity is a matter of the heart rather than outward religious observances. Almost immediately, this teaching is tested when a woman considered to be pagan and unclean approaches him for help.

COLOR   Green

THE PRAYERS

Let us pray for the church, the world, and all who suffer in mind, body, or spirit.

A BRIEF SILENCE.

That the church may always be a house of prayer for all people. Lord, in your mercy,

hear our prayer.

That the leaders of nations may seek to keep justice and to practice righteousness. Lord, in your mercy,

hear our prayer.

That Christians and Jews may grow in understanding and respect for one another. Lord, in your mercy,

hear our prayer.

That those who are sick or hospitalized (especially . . .) may know your healing presence. Lord, in your mercy,

hear our prayer.

That we may welcome and accept all who are alienated from the church, or feel unworthy of your love. Lord, in your mercy,

hear our prayer.

HERE OTHER INTERCESSIONS MAY BE OFFERED.

We give thanks for Mary, mother of our Lord, and for all the faithful departed who now keep the endless Sabbath with you, that we may proclaim your praise until we join them at your table of mercy and grace. Lord, in your mercy,

hear our prayer.

O God, grant us grace to trust your promises, that our lives may bear fruit to the glory of your name, through Jesus Christ our Lord.

Amen

IMAGES FOR PREACHING

Jesus tangled with a pit bull when he spoke with the woman from Tyre and Sidon. "It is not fair to take the children's food and throw it to the dogs," he said. "Yes, Lord," she replied, "yet even the dogs eat the crumbs that fall from the master's table."

This kind of toothy tenacity of faith grabs on to the

Savior's hem and doesn't let go. It takes Jesus at his word. It flings into his face his very own words and promises because there is no other way. No other choice. The situation is urgent, and the times are desperate.

This exchange should be of utmost interest to us, since few in the church today are blood relatives of Israel. It fulfills what Isaiah promised—that foreigners also would be gathered and accepted. God is merciful to all. Without denigrating God's promises to the original Israel, foreigners become part of God's new Israel. And look what this woman receives! The answer to her prayers. Instant healing for her tormented daughter. A faith that is declared great. It makes one wonder. If these are "crumbs," then what is the full meal?

WORSHIP MATTERS

Consider for a moment this week what becomes of the bread and wine left over from your celebration of the eucharist. Are the elements immediately distributed to the sick and homebound by lay ministers of communion? Are they consumed by the worship leaders or the assembly after the liturgy? Are they reserved for use by the pastor in ministering to the homebound and hospitalized in the coming week? Are they carried home by those who provided them to be consumed with Sunday dinner? Are they returned to the earth? What seems most appropriate for your community? Discuss this question with your worship committee.

LET THE CHILDREN COME

The church's word and sacrament practices statement indicates that regular communion of children ordinarily occurs "when children can eat and drink, and can respond to the gift of Christ in the Supper." At what age is one able to respond to such a gift? If one were to make a comparison with family gift giving, such giving and receiving begins long before children can articulate any understanding of what it means to receive gifts. In fact, the understanding of receiving comes through the practice that begins at the youngest of ages. Is this any less true for receiving the gift of Christ in the Supper?

MUSIC FOR WORSHIP

GATHERING

LBW 530   Jesus shall reign

WOV 750   Oh, praise the gracious power

PSALM 67

Brown, Teresa. "O God Be Gracious" in PS1.

Folkening, John. "Six Psalm Settings with Antiphons." MSM 80-700. U or SATB, opt kybd.

LBW 335   May God bestow on us his grace

Makeever, Ray. PW, Cycle A.

HYMN OF THE DAY

LBW 359   In Christ there is no east or west
            MCKEE

OTHER SUGGESTIONS

For an inclusive language version of this hymn see *The Presbyterian Hymnal.*

INSTRUMENTAL RESOURCES

Albrecht, Mark. "McKee" in *Early American Hymns and Tunes for Flute and Piano.* AFP 11-10830.

Burkhardt, Michael. "McKee" in *Seven Hymn Improvisations and Free Accompaniments,* set 2. MSM 10-860. Org.

Hassell, Michael. "McKee" in *Jazz Plain and Simple.* AFP 11-10862. Pno.

Powell, Robert. "Postlude on 'McKee'" in *Sent Forth: Short Postludes for the Day.* AFP 11-10612. Org.

Wood, Dale. "McKee" in *Wood Works for Organ,* book 2. SMP KK 400. Org.

ALTERNATE HYMN OF THE DAY

LBW 423   Lord, whose love in humble service

WOV 757   Creating God, your fingers trace

COMMUNION

LBW 360   O Christ, the healer, we have come

WOV 668   There in God's garden

SENDING

LBW 559   Oh, for a thousand tongues to sing

WOV 763   Let justice flow like streams

ADDITIONAL HYMNS AND SONGS

LBW 303   When in the hour of deepest need

WOV 738   Healer of our every ill

MBW 508   To God who gave the scriptures

NCH 179   We yearn, O Christ, for wholeness

MUSIC FOR THE DAY

CHORAL

Bender, Jan. "It Is Not Fair." CPH 98-1847. SA, org.

Bouman, Paul. "God Be Merciful unto Us." CPH 98-2471. SS/SA, org.

Order next year's resources now!

Sundays and Seasons

WORSHIP PLANNING GUIDE, CYCLE B, 2000

Order your copies today and you'll be ready for the next church year! The next edition of *Sundays and Seasons* will continue to supply you with all of the information you need to plan worship, dated specifically for Advent 1999 through Christ the King Sunday in 2000.

3-1204 • 0-8066-3626-2 • $30.00 ea. or buy 3 or more copies for $25.00 ea.

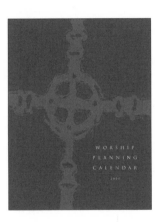

Worship Planning Calendar for the Church

CYCLE B, 2000

Here's the perfect complement to *Sundays and Seasons*. Use this worship planning guide, daily devotional, and appointment calendar as your workbook. Each two-page spread includes propers, hymns, liturgical colors, and general rubrics for the Sunday, principal festivals, lesser festivals, and commemorations that occur during the week.

23-2009 • 0-8066-3814-1 • $20.00

Indexes for Worship Planning

A one-volume reference work of integrated indexes for *Lutheran Book of Worship*, *With One Voice*, and the Revised Common Lectionary. Contains hymns for the church year: a listing of hymns in *LBW/WOV* arranged by the church year, matched with the appointed readings of the RCL. Also contains integrated indexes for *LBW/WOV*: Topical/Liturgical index, Scriptural index, Psalm Paraphrases, Readings & Prayers Index (biblical order), Psalm index (in numerical order) and where used in the lectionary, Tune indexes (alphabetical and metrical), First lines and common titles.

3-400 • 0-8066-2348-9 • $22.50

Church Year Calendar, 2000

This full-color worship planning and devotional resource gives specific dates, Bible readings, hymn of the day, and liturgical color for each Sunday and festival of the church year. Two sides, full-color. 11 x 8.5". 23-2015 • 0-8066-3808-7 • $1.95, 12 for $9.96

Liturgical Wall Calendar, 2000

This full-color calendar features U.S. and Canadian holidays, as well as church festivals. Easy-to-read date blocks note Bible readings from the Revised Common Lectionary for Sundays and festivals, and identify seasonal or festival color. 28 pages. Spiral-bound, hole punched for hanging. 23-2011 • 0-8066-3829-x • $6.95

Shipping and Handling

Note: Prices and availability are subject to change without notice. **Shipping Charges:** Shipping charges are additional on all orders. For orders up through $10.00 add $2.50; $10.01–$20.00 add $4.00; $20.01–$35.00 add $5.50; $35.01 and above add $6.50. Actual shipping charges will be assessed for all orders over 35 lbs. in weight (bulk). Actual shipping charges for expedited shipping service. Additional shipping charges for international shipments. For Canadian orders, actual shipping costs will be charged. This policy is subject to change without notice. Allow 4-6 weeks for all imprinting orders (gold and silver stamping). **Sales Tax:** Add appropriate state/province and local taxes where applicable. Tax exempt organizations must provide tax exempt numbers on all orders. **Return Policy:** All U. S. mail, fax and telephone order returns must be shipped postage prepaid to the Augsburg Fortress Distribution Center, 4001 Gantz Road, Suite E, Grove City, Ohio 43123-1891. Permission is not required for returns. Non-dated, in-print product in saleable condition may be returned for up to 60 days after the invoice date. Defective products, products damaged in shipment, or products shipped in error may be returned at any time and postage will be reimbursed. Special order or clearance items may not be returned. Canadian orders must be returned to the location from which the order was shipped.

Order Form
Worship Planning Resources, Cycle A, 2000

Just complete this order card, affix postage and drop it in the mail. To order by phone: 1-800-328-4648 By fax: 1-800-722-7766 By E-mail: afp_bookstore.topic@ecunet.org

Send to: _____

Address: _____

City: _____ State: _____ Zip: _____

Phone: _____

Bill to: _____

Address _____

City: _____ State: _____ Zip: _____

Method of Payment *(check one)*

☐ Augsburg Fortress Account # _____

☐ Credit Card # _____

Exp. Date: _____

(Must be valid for Sept. 1999. Products ship August 1999)

Signature: _____

(Required on all credit card orders.)

☐ Check *(Place check and order card in an envelope. Send it to address on reverse.)*

Qty.	Title	Price	Total
_____	Sundays & Seasons, Year B, 1999-2000	$30 ea.	_____
	OR $25 ea. for 3 or more		_____
_____	Worship Planning Calendar, 2000	$20.00	_____
_____	Indexes for Worship Planning	$22.50	_____
_____	Church Year Calendar, 2000	$1.95	_____
_____	**OR** 12 for $9.96		_____
_____	Liturgical Wall Calendar, 1999-2000	$6.95	_____

Subtotal _____

Tax Exempt ID# _____

or Tax _____

Shipping and Handling (see left) _____

TOTAL _____

Thank you for your order!

AUGSBURG FORTRESS PUBLISHERS
ATTN POC
PO BOX 59303
MINNEAPOLIS, MN 55459-0303

Hammerschmidt, Andreas. "Let the People Praise Thee, O God."
CPH 98-1826. U, 2 vln, cont.

Parker, Alice. "The Daughter." AFP 11-2279. SATB, vln, vc, org.

Rowan, William. "Woman in the Night." SEL 425-815. SATB, org, opt
cong.

White, David Ashley. "In Christ There Is No East or West."
AFP 11-10598. SATB, kybd.

Willan, Healey. "Let the People Praise Thee, O God" in *We Praise
Thee*. CPH 97-7564. SA, org.

CHILDREN'S CHOIRS

Horman, John. "Psalm 67." CGA 589. U, SATB, cong, kybd.

Lovelace, Austin. "Small Things Count, So Jesus Said." CGA 644.

KEYBOARD/INSTRUMENTAL

Franck, César. "Cantabile" in *Organ Works*. Various ed. Org.

Haydn, F. J. "Sonata for Piano." CFP. Pno.

Kolander, Keith. "Healer of Our Every Ill" in *Laudate!* vol. 4.
CPH 97-6665. Org.

HANDBELL

Mendelssohn, Felix/Anna Laura Page and Christine Anderson. "Cast
Thy Burden upon the Lord." CPH 97-6684. Hb solo, kybd.

PRAISE ENSEMBLE

Hanson, Handt. "Thank You for the Gift" in *Spirit Calls, Rejoice!* CCF.

Leavitt, John. "Call on Him." HAL 08596405. SATB, opt hrn/str.

Hoffman, Elisha. "I Must Tell Jesus." WRD 301 0634 161. SATB.

FRIDAY, AUGUST 20
BERNARD, ABBOT OF CLAIRVAUX, 1153

Bernard was a Cistercian monk and later an abbot of
great spiritual depth. He was a mystical writer who was
deeply devoted to the humanity of Christ and, consequently, to the affective dimensions of medieval spirituality. Bernard also had a great impact on the world beyond
the monastery: secular leaders came to him because of his
peacemaking skills, and he spoke out against excesses of
the clergy and the persecution of Jews.

Does your congregation find ways to nurture a balance in the relationship between contemplation and
action? Do your Bible studies connect with service in
the world? Are your service projects rooted in spiritual
convictions? Does your celebration of the eucharist
nurture your members to serve God in their various
callings?

289

AUGUST 22, 1999
THIRTEENTH SUNDAY AFTER PENTECOST
PROPER 16

INTRODUCTION

At any time and in any place, the Christian may ask
God to forgive sin that separates one from God and
others. At the same time, it is good to remember that
to be a Christian is to be united to a community that
bears the wounds of sin and human folly. The worshiping assembly—as a community—confesses the
truth of its own unloving words, thoughts, and deeds.
And throughout the liturgy, it hears and feels and
tastes the merciful and forgiving love of God: in the
absolution, in the waters of baptism, in receiving the
body and blood of Christ, in the words of forgiveness
spoken by a friend or family member, in the sharing
of the peace.

These acts of confession and forgiveness in the
liturgy are gifts of grace. How, then, might our words
and actions extend this grace in daily life?

PRAYER OF THE DAY

God of all creation, you reach out to call people of all
nations to your kingdom. As you gather disciples from
near and far, count us also among those who boldly
confess your Son Jesus Christ as Lord.

READINGS

Isaiah 51:1-6

*In this text, the writer appeals to a people who seem apathetic,
if not despairing. Isaiah reminds Israel that God's actions in
the past (v. 2) are the basis for hope in the present.*

Psalm 138

O Lord, your love endures forever. (Ps. 138:9)

Romans 12:1-8

Paul offers practical advice to the Roman Christians, suggesting new ways of relating to God, to the world, to the self, and to other believers.

Matthew 16:13-20

At a climactic point in Jesus' ministry, God reveals to Peter that Jesus is "the Messiah, the Son of the living God," and Jesus responds by revealing his vision of the church.

COLOR   Green

THE PRAYERS

Let us pray for the church, the world, and all who suffer in mind, body, or spirit.

A BRIEF SILENCE.

For all who confess Christ as Messiah, that they offer themselves as living sacrifices of spiritual worship. Lord, in your mercy,

hear our prayer.

For all who labor to see justice and peace in the world, that you give them patience and steadfastness in their endeavors. Lord, in your mercy,

hear our prayer.

For our sisters and brothers who suffer in mind, body, or spirit (especially . . .), that you surround them with your enduring love. Lord, in your mercy,

hear our prayer.

For victims of violence, hatred, and prejudice, that your grace transform us to be signs of your reconciliation and freedom. Lord, in your mercy,

hear our prayer.

For our assembly, that we may each use our gifts for the building up of the body of Christ. Lord, in your mercy,

hear our prayer.

HERE OTHER INTERCESSIONS MAY BE OFFERED.

We give thanks for all those who have died confessing Jesus Christ as the Son of the living God. Make us firm in our faith until we join them within the open gates of heaven. Lord, in your mercy,

hear our prayer.

O God, grant us grace to trust your promises, that our lives may bear fruit to the glory of your name, through Jesus Christ our Lord.

Amen

290

IMAGES FOR PREACHING

The first step for accompanying disciples is to confess correctly the true identity of Jesus: "You are the Messiah, the Son of the living God." To solely identify Jesus as a great teacher/healer/prophet (as many do) is to treat him as a fraud and miss his mission. Only a divinely empowered disciple can recognize him as the Christ.

Simon's nickname, Rocky, echoes Isaiah's identification of Abraham and Sarah. Abraham and Sarah are pictured as the stone quarry from which future generations are hewn. Remembering their faithfulness through their long journey and modeling oneself after them equips their descendants (the people of Israel and the disciples of Jesus) for the rugged trip that lies ahead. Or so Isaiah would suggest. Isaiah here is an historical revisionist. Genesis makes it clear that the faithfulness of Abraham and Sarah was itself pretty rocky. It is better to stick with the Psalms. God is the rock. It is the rock-solid, steadfast faithfulness of God that gets them (and us) through.

In any case, following Christ is a trip that requires offering one's body as a living sacrifice and renewing one's mind, not conforming to the world. The payoff is the keys to the gates of heaven. By the grace of God, the cross-won power of Christ becomes the disciple's own. Christ is the cornerstone. And we are chips off the old block. Each one of us has our place and our part.

WORSHIP MATTERS

"Who do people say that the Son of Man is?" In the liturgy we proclaim Jesus as Son of God in the words of the Nicene or Apostles' Creeds. (The other ecumenical creed in *LBW*, the Athanasian Creed, is rarely used in worship, although it is still foundational to the *Book of Concord* and Lutheran identity.) These ecumenical creeds are shared by Christians around the world and are nuanced by the wisdom of the ages. Congregations that distance themselves from these foundational Christian confessions should be very, very careful.

Contemporary "statements of faith" are not the same as these creeds and are not interchangeable with them. Creeds are corporate confessions of faith, which unite us with other Christians beyond our local congregations and denominations. Putting unfamiliar words into the mouth of the assembly and expecting it to proclaim these words as faith can be disrespectful and downright inhospitable. Contemporary statements of faith are usually the work of one person, rarely reviewed by the church at large, and often theologically problematic. Consider ways to make the creed a powerful congregational response in faith to the gospel that has just been heard, and reserve personal statements of faith for the use of witnessing individuals.

LET THE CHILDREN COME

How do children grow to love certain foods? Barbara Kafka, a food writer, reminds us that "It barely needs pointing out that Chinese children eat bean curd and Japanese children eat raw fish; that South American and Bengali children eat very spicy food and French children eat smelly cheese. . . . If our children sit and eat with us, they will have models to follow and will come to consider meal-taking a positive social event" (*Gourmet*, September 1992, p. 80). This modeling of behavior is one way children learn to grow in love for the Lord's Supper. Parents and other adults in the parish set an example of the delight in gathering around the table of the Lord to help children come to love the bread of heaven.

MUSIC FOR WORSHIP
GATHERING

| LBW 500 | Faith of our fathers |
| WOV 692 | For all the faithful women |

PSALM 138

Butler, Eugene. "A Joyous Psalm." CGA-74. U.

Duba, Arlo. "Psalm 138" in TP.

Haas, David. PCY, vol. 3.

Inwood, Paul. "In the Presence of the Angels" in PS3.

Makeever, Ray. PW, Cycle A.

PH 247   I will give thanks with my whole heart

HYMN OF THE DAY

| LBW 365 | Built on a rock |
| | KIRKEN DEN ER ET GAMMELT HUS |

VOCAL RESOURCES

Burkhardt, Michael. "Built on the Rock." MSM 60-9014. Choir 60-9014A; inst pts 60-9014B. SATB, cong, hb, tpt, org.

McFadden, Jane. "Built on a Rock." AFP 11-10714. Cong, 3 oct hb, org, tpt, SATB.

INSTRUMENTAL RESOURCES

Behnke, John. "Kirken den er et gammelt Hus" in *Variations for Seven Familiar Hymns.* AFP 11-10702. Org.

Cherwien, David. "Built on a Rock" in *Interpretations,* book VII. AMSI SP-104. Org.

Manz, Paul. "Built on a Rock" in *Improvisations on Reformation Hymns.* MSM 10-803. Org.

Oliver, Curt. "Variations on 'Built on a Rock'" in *Built on a Rock: Keyboard Seasons.* AFP 11-10620. Pno/kybd.

ALTERNATE HYMN OF THE DAY

| LBW 369 | The Church's one foundation |
| WOV 747 | Christ is made the sure foundation (or LBW 367) |

COMMUNION

| LBW 532 | How Great Thou Art |
| WOV 707 | This is my body |

OTHER SUGGESTIONS

| OBS 51 | Christ, burning Wisdom |

SENDING

| LBW 293/4 | My hope is built on nothing less |
| WOV 704 | Father, we thank you |

ADDITIONAL HYMNS AND SONGS

LBW 345	How sweet the name of Jesus sounds
WOV 781	My life flows on in endless song
REJ 263	Seek ye first the kingdom
LLC 470	Somos uno en Cristo/We are all one in Christ

MUSIC FOR THE DAY
CHORAL

Bertalot, John. "I Stand on the Rock." AFP 11-10852. SAB, org.

Ellingboe, Bradley. "You Are Peter!" MSF MF 2109. SATB.

Fedak, Alfred. "Built on a Rock." SEL 241-503-00. 2 pt mxd, org, kybd, opt bells.

Kirk, Theron. "Seek Ye First the Kingdom of God." CFI CM 8042. 2 pt mxd, pno.

Pote, Allen. "Many Gifts, One Spirit." COR 392-41388. SATB (SSA, SAB also available).

CHILDREN'S CHOIRS

Lindh, Jody. "I Give You Thanks." CGA 561. U, pno, perc, opt bass/synth.

Lord, Suzanne. "Faith That's Sure." CGA 695. U, pno, opt autohp/banjo.

KEYBOARD/INSTRUMENTAL

Hassell, Michael. "How Great Thou Art" in *Jazz All Seasons.*
AFP 11-10822. Pno.

Keesecker, Thomas. "Lac qui Parle" in *Together Again.* AFP 11-10717. Pno.

Mushel, Georgi. "Toccata" in *Modern Organ Music,* book 2.
OXF 0193751429. org.

HANDBELL

Kinyon, Barbara B. "Eternal Father, Strong to Save." HOP 1430. 2-3 oct.

McFadden, Jane. "Built on a Rock." AFP 11-10714. SATB, cong,
3 oct, org, tpt.

PRAISE ENSEMBLE

Greco, Eugene, Gerrit Gustafson and Don Moen. "Mighty Is Our
God" in *Integrity's Hosanna! Come and Worship Songbook.* INT.

Haas, David. "Deep Within" in *Who Calls You by Name,* vol. I.
GIA G-3193C. SATB.

Hine, Stuart/Craig Courtney. "How Great Thou Art." BEC. SATB.

TUESDAY, AUGUST 24
ST. BARTHOLOMEW, APOSTLE

Bartholomew is mentioned as one of Jesus' apostles in
Matthew, Mark, and Luke. The list of apostles in John
does not include him, but rather Nathanael, and they
are often assumed to be the same person. Beyond his
role as a disciple of Jesus, little is known of his life,
though various traditions tell of his missionary work
following Jesus' resurrection. He is symbolically shown
holding a knife, since some believed he was beheaded.

How do we, like Bartholomew, respond to Christ's
invitation to follow? What are the various ways we live
out our baptismal call in daily life? Do you look at this
as your vocation?

SATURDAY, AUGUST 28
AUGUSTINE, BISHOP OF HIPPO, 430

Augustine's conversion to Christianity is described in
Confessions, his autobiographical work, which includes
these famous words: "Our hearts are restless until they
rest in thee." Augustine was baptized by Ambrose at the
Easter Vigil in 387, and became one of the greatest theologians and defenders of the faith. He established a
monastic rule, and more than a millennium later Martin
Luther became a monk of the Augustinian order.

Use Augustine's conversion to pose this question: If
we were baptized as infants, do we ever undergo conversion? Or is baptism a call to lifelong conversion?
Look at the questions in the Affirmation of Baptism
service (*LBW,* p. 198) and discuss our baptismal vocation. Conclude by actually participating in the Affirmation of Baptism liturgy around the font.

MOSES THE BLACK, DESERT MONK, C. 400

A man of great strength and rough character, Moses the
Black was converted to the Christian faith toward the
close of the fourth century. The change in his heart and
life became legendary throughout his native Ethiopia.
Like Augustine, Moses' life was changed because of the
gospel. How do we experience that life-changing
power in our lives of faith?

AUGUST 29, 1999
FOURTEENTH SUNDAY AFTER PENTECOST
PROPER 17

INTRODUCTION

Today's gospel reading reminds us that life in Christ,
rather than simply comforting us or excusing us from
the pain of this world, strengthens us to face what we
fear most: suffering and death. Jesus does not turn from
pain and loss; indeed, he offers strength and hope to his
people.

God's adoption of us in the waters of baptism and
our communion in Christ's body and blood—signs of
healing and community—strengthen us to offer ourselves as servants to a weary and frightened world.

PRAYER OF THE DAY

O God, we thank you for your Son who chose the path
of suffering for the sake of the world. Humble us by his
example, point us to the path of obedience, and give us

strength to follow his commands; through your Son, Jesus Christ our Lord.

READINGS

Jeremiah 15:15-21

The book of Jeremiah contains six personal laments or complaints. Today's reading is the second of these laments. Here the prophet complains that his faithful preaching of the Word of God has brought only angry violence from his hearers. While God responds with a promise of support, note that God does not promise that Jeremiah's task will be easy or painless.

Psalm 26:1-8

Your love is before my eyes; I have walked faithfully with you. (Ps. 26:3)

Romans 12:9-21

Paul writes to the Roman Christians who have experienced rejection and ridicule as a result of their faith. He instructs them on how to live as Christians in an unfriendly world.

Matthew 16:21-28

After Peter confesses that Jesus is "the Messiah, the Son of the living God," Jesus reveals the ultimate purpose of his ministry. These words prove hard to accept even for a disciple whom Jesus has called a "rock."

COLOR Green

THE PRAYERS

Let us pray for the church, the world, and all who suffer in mind, body, or spirit.

A BRIEF SILENCE.

Strengthen your church, that it may follow in the way of the cross, and offer itself for the life of the world. Lord, in your mercy,

hear our prayer.

Uphold all who govern, that a spirit of vengeance may be overcome with compassion and humility. Lord, in your mercy,

hear our prayer.

Draw near to all who are sick or hospitalized (especially . . .), that they may rejoice in hope, be patient in suffering, and persevere in prayer. Lord, in your mercy,

hear our prayer.

Deepen our care for those who are homeless, abused, neglected, or who live with loneliness or despair. Lord, in your mercy,

hear our prayer.

Nourish us at your table to love one another, practice hospitality, and contribute to the needs of others. Lord, in your mercy,

hear our prayer.

HERE OTHER INTERCESSIONS MAY BE OFFERED.

Make us steadfast in our faith, that taking up our cross we may serve you until we join the saints in the glory of eternal life. Lord, in your mercy,

hear our prayer.

O God, grant us grace to trust your promises, that our lives may bear fruit to the glory of your name, through Jesus Christ our Lord.

Amen

IMAGES FOR PREACHING

This week school starts in many places. Matthew 16 marks a new beginning in the disciples' education. Having undergone the lower elementary lessons of "kingdom theology," they were now candidates for the upper elementary lessons of "cross theology." "From that time on, Jesus began to show his disciples that he must go to Jerusalem and undergo great suffering . . . and be killed, and on the third day be raised."

Never was anything said like this before. Never did the Bible say it was the Messiah who had to die and suffer. "God forbid it, Lord! This must never happen to you." Give Peter an "A" in Bible history and for openly admitting he did not care for this new course of study. Give Peter an "F" in divine economics and for failing to catch on to the necessity of it. The path to glory involves a cross both for Jesus and his disciples. Ignore that and even the most vocal, rock-like, well-intentioned disciple can become a stumbling stone.

Here Jesus nails himself to a page from the suffering servant imagery of Isaiah, inspired by the life of Jeremiah—a prophetic cross-bearer if there ever was one— although his call for vengeance must be countered by Christ's call for redeeming grace. The self-denying, cross-determined life style of a Christian is spelled out by the apostle Paul in Romans 12. Genuine love. Mutual affection. Joyous hope. Patient suffering. Prayerful perseverance. Contributions to the needy. Hospitality to strangers. Nonviolent resistance to persecution. And lots and lots of coal heaping by acts of kindness precisely to the people who we detest the most. The bottom line of his lesson book reads: "Do not be overcome by evil, but

293

overcome evil by good." When it comes to discipleship, school is always in session.

WORSHIP MATTERS

"You are a stumbling block to me." Evaluate your worship life and space this week. What stumbling blocks do you observe in the worship life of your congregation. Stumbling blocks can be anything that keep Christ from being at the center of the celebration. They can be anything that keeps the assembly from "seeing Jesus," or from welcoming Christ. Is it the worship folder? Is it the language of the liturgy or the sermon? Is it music or musical leadership? Is it careless presiding or unprepared readers? Is it a bad sound system or sloppy vestments? Is it the worship space itself? Is it bad interior or exterior directional signs? Do these and all other things employed for worship all serve Christ?

A variety of evaluative tools are available, among them are *How Your Congregation Can Become a More Hospitable Community* and *Where We Worship* (both titles available from Augsburg Fortress). Your synod office or the ELCA's worship unit may also be able to recommend others. But seek out the wisdom of your own community first. Ask disabled members, new members, young people, and visitors to identify the stumbling blocks they perceive. Identify the stumbling blocks, then work to remove them.

LET THE CHILDREN COME

In Romans 12, Paul reminds us, "We all have gifts that differ according to the grace given to us." What are some of the gifts that children bring to faith and worship? A sense of wonder and delight. Discovery of their world through their senses. Joy reflected in smiles and easy laughter. Innate generosity and a sharing with others of their wonder, joy, and love. Surely there are more. What are some of the gifts that the rest of the worshiping community can offer as well? Patience, kindness, gentleness might quickly come to mind. Are there others?

MUSIC FOR WORSHIP

GATHERING

LBW 561	For the beauty of the earth
WOV756	Lord, you give the great commission

PSALM 26

Becker, John. PW, Cycle A.

Bender, Mark. "O Lord, I Love the Habitation of Your House." CPH 98-2859. 2 pt.

Gerike, Henry. "Psalm 26." GIA G-2632. U, cong, acc.

HYMN OF THE DAY

LBW 364	Son of God, eternal Savior
	IN BABILONE

VOCAL RESOURCES

Pearce, Thomas R. "Son of God, Eternal Savior." CPH 98-2818. SAB, cong, tpt, org.

Roentgen, Julius. "Son of God, Eternal Savior" in *Choral Settings for the Hymn of the Day,* VII. CPH 97-5865. SATB.

INSTRUMENTAL RESOURCES

Albrecht, Timothy. "In Babilone" in *Grace Notes,* vol VI. AFP 11-10825. Org.

Burkhardt, Michael. "In Babilone" in *Six General Hymn Improvisations,* set 1. MSM 10-846. Org.

Leavitt, John. "In Babilone" in *Hymn Preludes for the Church Year.* AFP 11-10134. Org.

Sedio, Mark. "In Babilone" in *Eight Hymn Introductions.* MSM 10-836. Org.

Wold, Wayne. "Festive Prelude on 'In Babilone.'" AMSI HB-10. 2 oct.

ALTERNATE HYMN OF THE DAY

LBW 398	"Take up your cross," the Savior said (*alternate tune:* ERHALT UNS, HERR LBW 230)
WOV 736	By gracious powers

COMMUNION

LBW 205	Now the silence
LBW 206	Lord, who the night you were betrayed
WOV 743	Stay with us

OTHER SUGGESTIONS

DATH 30	This bread that we break

SENDING

LBW 370	Blest be the tie that binds
WOV 748	Bind us together

ADDITIONAL HYMNS AND SONGS

LBW 455	"Come, follow me," the Savior spake
WOV 670	When Israel was in Egypt's land
BH 285	Take up thy cross and follow me
NCH 170	Your ways are not our own

MUSIC FOR THE DAY

CHORAL

Bock, Fred. "Who Do You Say That I Am?" ECS 4865. SATB, org.

Bouman, Paul. "'Take Up Your Cross,' the Savior Said." SEL 420-617. SATB.

Buxtehude, Dietrich. "In God, My Faithful God" in *Second Morning Star Choir Book.* CPH 97-4702. U, org.

Handel, G. F. "Lord, I Trust Thee" in *The New Church Anthem Book.* OXF 0-19-353109-7. SATB, org.

Hopson, Hal H. "Take Up Your Cross." AFP 11-10570. 2 pt mxd, kybd.

Keesecker, Thomas. "I Am the Living Bread." AFP 11-10684. SATB. kybd, opt cong.

Liebhold. "Commit Your Life to the Lord" in *Second Motet Book.* CPH 97-5205. SATB, opt org.

CHILDREN'S CHOIRS

Cox, Joe. "Lord, Make Me an Instrument of Your Peace." BRN 414978.

Litz, Helen. "Prayer of St. Francis." CGA 242. U/2 pt, kybd/hpd.

Hopson, Hal. "Take Up Your Cross." AFP EK11-10570. 2 pt mxd, org.

KEYBOARD/INSTRUMENTAL

Mendelssohn, Felix. "Praeludium II in G" in *Orgelstücke.* Various ed. Org.

Organ, Anne Krentz. "Partita on 'Adoro te devote'" in *Christ, Mighty Savior: Hymn Reflections for Piano.* AFP 11-10819. Pno.

HANDBELL

Anderson, Christine. "Morning Joy" (BUNESSAN). HOP 1378. 3 oct hb solo, kybd.

McFadden, Jane. "Morning Has Broken." AFP 11-10552. 3-5 oct, kybd/2 hb choirs.

Morris, Hart. "Go Down, Moses." JEF RW8029. 4 oct, perc.

PRAISE ENSEMBLE

Giamanco, Tony. "Sit Down!" AMSI 751. SATB

Hanson, Handt, and Paul Murakami. "Broken Hearts" in *Spirit Calls, Rejoice!* CCF.

Kendrick, Graham. "Turn Our Hearts" in *Integrity's Hosanna! Music Songsheets.* INT.

Ylvisaker, John, and Hal Dragseth. "Stir Up The Love" in *Borning Cry.* NGP.

TUESDAY, AUGUST 31

JOHN BUNYAN, TEACHER, 1688

John Bunyan was one of the most remarkable figures in seventeenth-century literature. His spiritual pilgrimage is revealed in his works, most notably *The Pilgrim's Progress*, which some consider to be the most successful allegory in English literature.

Just as Bunyan believed that God worked through all aspects of his life, it is good for us to be aware of the spiritual movements in our own lives. Consider ways to nurture the gifts of writing among your members. Why not encourage them to keep a journal of their spiritual insights, to prepare a series of devotions based on the church year, or to write an occasional column or brief meditation for your church newsletter.

THURSDAY, SEPTEMBER 2

NIKOLAI FREDERIK SEVERIN GRUNDTVIG, BISHOP, RENEWER OF THE CHURCH, 1872

Grundtvig sought to restore orthodoxy to the Danish church by attacking rationalism and state domination of religion. He challenged the notion that Christianity was a philosophical idea rather than God's revelation made known to us in Christ and in the sacraments.

Grundtvig wrote five volumes of hymns, his most famous being "Built on a rock" (LBW 365). Consider commemorating Grundtvig at a meeting of the worship or education committees, and discuss the ways in which our lives of faith are transformed.

SATURDAY, SEPTEMBER 4

ALBERT SCHWEITZER, MISSIONARY TO AFRICA, 1965

Albert Schweitzer was a theologian, philosopher, musician, and missionary doctor. He believed that the solution to the world's problems was simple: have reverence for life. This conviction led him to warn against the atomic bomb, and to speak out against racial injustice. He not only loved life and all living creatures, he was also committed to ease the suffering of those less fortunate than he.

Schweitzer inspires us to live with a rich spirituality of everyday life in which God is discovered in both the joys of living and the challenges of serving. If your congregation honors the vocations of its members in relation to Labor Day (in a newsletter or in tomorrow's liturgy), Schweitzer could be held up as a model of someone who wisely used his gifts and was creatively involved in many aspects of life in the world.

AUTUMN

The last word belongs to grace

IMAGES OF THE SEASON

Skritch, skritch, skritch . . . tunk! TUNK! We can hear the sounds of home

improvement before you know exactly what the project is, or which yard

it's coming from. Sound seems to carry farther in

the crisp autumn air. Then we get closer, and see

that roof gutters are being swept out. Leaves are being raked into piles for composting or burning. Scraping tools are making chips of summer-blistered paint fly off their walls. Screens are being pried off and storm windows thumped back into place. They're tuckpointing that building and inspecting the chimney caps on this one. The neighbors in the garden over there are digging up the perennial bulbs and separating the segments before burying them back in the soil. Rose bushes have to be trimmed and covered before the first frost. Plowing up the vegetable garden will be next on the agenda, but for the moment we'll leave the pumpkins to swell on their vines. We'd better seal the deck and get that new coat of paint on the house while the air is still warm and dry.

Six months ago it was spring cleaning; now it's the season for home improvement. Our yards and the frameworks of our dwellings become the focus of attention. Many of us make these improvements now because we have to: winter is a few months away, but still approaching. We want to make the repairs while it's still pleasant outside.

Autumn as a season for home improvement stems from the approach of winter. As a season for inward "improvement," it derives both from the American academic context and from the much older Jewish tradition. *Rosh Hashanah*—Jewish New Year—starts somewhere around the fall equinox and initiates ten days of introspection and *teshuvah*—repentance, or return. The Days of Awe are devoted to repairing relationship. Forgiveness is asked of God and of one another. Prayer and almsgiving are part of the work of restoration. On the holiest day of the year, *Yom Kippur* (Day of Cleansing, or Atonement), the slate is cleared between each person and God. As stars appear in the sky, worshipers return to their homes, where many will hammer in the first post

of their new construction for the next holiday. They're starting the new year right by following God's command to build a *sukkah*, or booth.

The Feast of Booths, or Tabernacles *(Sukkot)*, is a joyful eight-day celebration of harvest. It requires the building of some kind of temporary shelter on one's property (in the city, on a balcony or roof). These *sukkot* evoke both poverty and abundance. They serve as reminders of the makeshift shelters the ancient Israelites depended upon during their 40-year wandering in the wilderness. They symbolize everyone's vulnerability to the forces of nature, and especially the lot of the homeless and the poor. *Sukkot* also replicate structures from an age of prosperity. Once the Israelites had settled in the promised land, they built little huts out in their fields to live in during the autumn harvest. Farmers wanted to be close to their crops so they could bring them in quickly. The huts offered a place to sleep at night and protection from the sun during the worst heat of the day.

Present-day *sukkot* are to be places of offering hospitality to others, enjoying the fruits of harvest, and celebrating God's continued providence for the human family in times of both wandering and settlement. As fall gets underway and we work to repair the structures that we hope will last indefinitely, our Jewish neighbors are also constructing symbolic shelters meant *not* to last. What is intentionally impermanent points, by contrast, to what is truly eternal.

The twofold pattern of reparation and rejoicing in harvest takes a little over three weeks in the Jewish calendar. This pattern is reflected—and stretched out—in the periods of Autumn and November within our own liturgical season of Pentecost.

Home repair encompasses the re-forming of our spiritual home, the church. Reformation and daily repentance go hand in hand, as Martin Luther insisted. Our autumn lectionary begins with the discussion of how to repair inevitable broken relationships within churches (Matt. 18:15-20 on September 5); it ends, on Reformation Day, with the celebration of God's amazing power to renew the church as a whole.

As autumn progresses, the tension mounts between grace toward sinners and judgment against the self-righteous. The more radically Jesus proclaims mercy, the higher the conflict escalates. By what authority can he claim that the first will be last, that prostitutes and tax collectors will enter God's reign ahead of priests, elders, and Pharisees? He answers only in riddles.

But the last word belongs to grace. The entire law and the prophets are concentrated in the commandments to love God heart, soul, and mind, and to love one's neighbor as oneself. And we all fall short; even the best-intentioned of repairs eventually falls apart. The human condition is enslavement to sin. We have to be set free by someone besides ourselves. Our liberation comes through one who is beyond us, yet knows our plight from within: Christ Jesus, who, relinquishing equality with God, took the form of a slave, and has therefore been highly exalted above all others.

Together we hear the good news of freedom and then come to the table to eat the bread milled from the grain of the fields and drink the cup of pressed fruit of the vine, the body and blood of Christ. As we receive these harvest gifts, we are incorporated into the new covenant God has made with the house of Israel. We can almost taste the feast of rich food and well-aged wines that will one day be spread for all peoples, when God has freed the human family from contempt, wiped away every tear, and swallowed up death forever. We rejoice in Christ, the son who has made us free indeed, sharing with us his own permanent place in the household of God.

299

ENVIRONMENT AND ART FOR THE SEASON

Throughout much of North America, a rich tapestry of colors is unfolding in the natural world. The liturgical environment might also signal this change through a richer variety of colors and textures. As we experience this seasonal transition, the readings in this liturgical season also prepare us for the future. We are ultimately invited to a rich feast in God's time to come.

EXTERIOR ENVIRONMENT

Though many gardeners in northern climates may have put away their tools for the year, much can still be done outdoors to savor the earth's beauty. Consider fall plantings near entrances that will work well in your climate during autumn. They will help to cheer worshiper's faces, even as the amount of daylight rapidly decreases.

INTERIOR ENVIRONMENT

Though green is still the predominant liturgical color in this season, many eyes might be ready for a difference in the liturgical environment. The autumn months suggest a deeper green than what might have been used throughout the summer (think of forest green, olive green, and even khaki green). Other colors taken from the browns, oranges, golds, and reds of fall foliage might be used to accent green vestments, paraments, and banners. If the summer called for lighter fabrics, the fall suggests heavier, lined materials.

Floral arrangements during this time of year might use dried flowers from local gardens. Deep reds, maroons, and browns suggest the natural landscape in many parts of North America. Shafts of wheat and other dried grains might also be used in imaginative ways. Consider using earthenware containers for floral arrangements and plants that are on display.

Congregations that celebrate Reformation Day will likely use red paraments and vestments for this festival. As well as being used for Pentecost, red is the color used for church dedications and other occasions celebrating the renewal of the church. Some older red paraments were often of a deeper and richer red than what is commonly in use these days. If your congrega-

tion still has an older set of red paraments it does not use, consider whether these might be fashioned into something that could continue to be used, especially on this festival of the Reformation, which recalls our heritage.

PREACHING with the SEASON

Labor Day ushers North Americans out of summer into autumn, returning vacationers home to canning, digging in the garden, and starting Sunday school. Workers return to desks and machines. At this juncture in society's rhythms, the church

turns to the festival of the Holy Cross, a landmark on our movement into darker, shorter days for carrying on the business of study, service, and Sabbath. This stark stump of death is bold against the North American horizon as the land puts its creatures to rest in a blaze of scarlet, orange, brown, and gold dying of the green. All fall we remember that our lives flourish on ancient stock: the great mystery of Michael and all angels, Matthew, Jerome, Francis, Clare, and other saints, and we commemorate their self-giving as blazes of Christ's glory.

Autumn deepens, far north flurries crystallize and descend, nameless figures scour empty boardwalks and chain park gates—homeless mental patients and illegal aliens gathering into the storehouses of their burned out city housing whatever oil drums and wood they can glean from wastelands and roadsides of the civilized. We witness the dying birthing something new as grapes pressed down become wine, crops ingathered become the life of all who eat, and fear becomes joy as students leave home to start school and discover new growth and friends. Like human aging, autumn creeps upon us, ripening, detaching, distilling, and gathering in. Autumn liturgies spread before us God's unquenchable love and undying life upon a harvest home table that knows no end. God calls to the world, "Come."

Coming into God's mercy is an absurd encounter, for Jesus tells Peter to overflow with sheer abundance of

forgiveness (Proper 19). Jesus describes no rule of forgiving, but a way of being that compares God's reign to the unfathomable pity of the slaveowner who liberates the slave's whole household from unredeemable debt. Entering God's dominion impels us into this way of mercy that seeks to redeem life abundantly. Reckoning human need and cost before God, is reckoning an incalculable loss canceled only by God's will to release humanity entirely from our self-made expectation that we can redeem our broken histories. Damages, wounds, and despairs generated over time and embedded in our languages are unanswered by anything less than God's undamaged love for all creation. In God's mercy, which generates all creation, we welcome one another, not to quarrel and compete for survival of the fittest, but to uphold one another in honor and thanks to God. Like trusting Joseph, we do not judge others in the place of God, but weep openly over the brokenness between God's people, providing for all as we are able. Over whom do our assemblies weep and labor now?

Following Jesus means sharing the joy of God's sovereign generosity, not disgruntled second-guessing and grumbling human calculations of justice (Proper 20) nor selfish anger and jealous sulking like Jonah's. As the landowner eschews any hierarchy of worth, so human hierarchies of worth dissolve in one baptism into the Trinity. God spends mercy lavishly, and through Jesus' life spent for all, redeems creation extravagantly. Paul's inquiry to the Philippians is ours, What does it mean, then, to imagine living in such a spirit of generosity and freedom from fear of exclusion? What does it mean to follow Jesus in a manner worthy of this generosity; firm in one spirit; freed to enter into the struggles of faithfulness?

Following Jesus pits believers against other authorities, where the authority of one's actions is revealed in choices enacted (Proper 21). Jesus demonstrates the emptiness of the unenacted words of the two sons who both do the opposite of the spoken responses to their father's calling. Yet the second son allows his mind to be conformed to his father's will and his act is obedience. Those least apparently faithful to God, such as prostitutes and socially despised peoples, experience themselves entering into God's mercy well ahead of those who speak of faith, yet who fail to enact it. Ezekiel's God wills humanity to turn to life and enacts this will in Christ's life for the world; a life shared by baptism, Paul notes, as God works in human beings to fulfill God's desire to save, restore, and create.

Following Jesus calls familiar lives into question. Like a sculptor's chisel against the stone, Jesus' parables strike out all that does not reveal God. Often what falls away is familiar and distracts followers from seeing what remains revealed. The harsh parable of the land owner (Proper 22) reveals God's unfaltering will to plant, establish, and fulfill the dominion of God. Like the vineyard owner consigning to death all that breeds death, and then relentlessly cultivating life, God overturns crucifixion into resurrecting the whole creation, of which the first fruit is Jesus risen. Cheated, betrayed, and dishonored, God never stops willing the cultivation of a fruitful planting. To our bedazzled, unspeakable amazement, God is undefeated. No evil or action arrests God. Isaiah's God does whatever must be accomplished to yield a just and fruitful creation. The truth of God's triumphant life begets faith that can suffer the loss of all things, yet strain forward freely in christic self-giving.

Jesus teaches that God's rule is as indefatigable as the sovereign celebrating the consummation of the future, inviting all peoples to enter into that joy (Proper 23). This invitation cannot be made light of by imagining better preoccupations, for it comes from the sovereign of life and of death. Nor can acceptance be half-hearted, for the sovereign gathers in the homeless, the beggars, and the sojourners in the street—the good and

the bad—and robes them in joy with the invitation to the feast. Those who refuse the garb of gladness are refusing freedom. It is only Isaiah's God who swallows up death forever, restoring all things, and spreading a feast of life before all nations and peoples. Standing firm in this promise, God makes Christ known to us in our eucharist. Believers from ancient Philippi to our hometowns today have no worry about asking God to supply their need. All may rejoice in bringing words of hope to the speechlessness of their times. Rejoicing guards peace, keeping followers unbound in the furnace of daily trials, and clothing us with joy in the doing of the apostolic, holy things: worshiping together as we have been taught around word and sacrament, catechizing inquirers and each other, and helping one another in our callings to serve God.

Land mines litter the way of God's followers, but Jesus springs traps for death, and reveals instead the life of God. Jesus amazes the Pharisees by disarming their trap with the invitation to imagine the things that are God's being returned to God (Proper 24). Who would be disarmed in our day if believers all over the earth ever more seriously imagined together how to return to God what is God's? What might it mean for the earth, and all the species with whom we share the means of life, if we were to imagine that the whole creation bears the title "God's"? Could we all become impartial and deferential? Are we open to amazement and to remembering God's creation before God? Is it possible to remember one another in the work of the gospel, empowered in the full conviction that the living God whom we seek to honor rescues and redeems our labors of faith, love, and hope? Like Cyrus, we are anointed by God, not for kingship over nations, but for faith and for daily stewardship of our baptism as those adopted and named God's beloved offspring. Though we neither intimately grasp nor cleave to God, even so God works in us and saves us because God chooses to do all these things in this way.

Following Jesus for the sake of defeat is to be silenced by his claim: the greatest commandment is two things set side by side: Love God with your entire being, with your whole life, heart, soul, and mind, and love your neighbor as your very self, that is your own heart, soul, and mind (Proper 25). Love yokes God, self, and other. Love is not unbidden emotion, but an enacting of activities of love, which occurs despite mutable feelings, when we attend to honoring God and God's handiwork—ourselves and our neighbors. Faithfulness, even to proclaim the gospel, Paul cautions, is for God's sake, not consumer approval. The gospel of God arouses believers to share their very selves for the sake of God's truth. As Moses first taught the congregations of Israel, to honor the one who is holy is to be loving to the other as to the self. Such love enacts justice, impartiality, building up others, sustaining life, forgiveness, and forbearance.

To follow Jesus is not to be led upwards in a quest of self improvement, for Jesus does not teach a way to be exalted or to be humbled (Proper 26). Yet our imaginations snag on issues of power and stall at Jesus' closing remarks to the crowds and disciples. But Jesus teaches of human unity in God, calling followers to attend to doing and following the teachings of Moses.

Following Jesus is not a solitary exercise, for the way of the truth is utterly communal: remember that you have one teacher, the Messiah, and you are all

students; and you all have one Father, the God of heaven and earth (Proper 28). Jesus abolishes all titles in God's communion, eradicating typical human privileges. People are one: one in need, one in God's mercy, one in being claimed as children of God. Our assemblies best reflect this oneness in one cup, one loaf, and one table welcoming all; one font washing all the dead into the community of the living one. Receiving this word, not as human construct, but as God's active word in us and in the world, means conforming ourselves to this word working in us, as Paul tells the Thessalonians. To believe that God is with us, is not, as the ancient chiefs and rulers of Israel learned, to have all our actions sanctioned by God. Were North American Christian imaginations seized to enact God's word of utter grace and human unity in our conduct, what upheaval might churches and societies experience? Championing our life in God, the Holy Trinity drowns us to death, that in dying we may be born into a new mind, and knit into one risen to harvest all creation into the reign of God.

PLANNING AHEAD FOR THE SEASON

Though it comes toward the end of the calendar year and even closer yet

to the end of the liturgical year, autumn signals the start of many things—

a new school year, new clothes, a new season in

the Supreme Court of the United States, and

even a new television schedule. It is generally a hectic time for most congregations, since it is the start of a new programmatic year. Committees, choirs, Sunday schools, and a whole host of other activities regroup and reenergize. How do these changes affect your worship life?

If your worship schedule returns to a more familiar pattern from the summer, be sure to announce it repeatedly through bulletin announcements, newsletters, newspaper listings, signs on the church lawn, brochures that you hand out, and whatever else can be used to notify people of the changing worship times.

Many congregations will have a rally day for the Sunday school in early September. Often this may be observed at worship through some type of recognition for teachers and other leaders in the education ministry. It may be a time to determine when you might recognize leaders and volunteers in other congregational ministries as well. When are choir members and other worship leaders recognized? What about groundskeepers or those who work with stewardship and finances? Consider appropriate times throughout the year when all other ministries of the congregation might be recognized. The lectionary may also indicate when certain ministries may be recognized.

Congregations often distribute Bibles to children of the congregation at some point in the elementary grades. If your congregation does this, consider having the parents come forward together with their children so that they can actually distribute the Bibles themselves. (Remember what parents and sponsors promised at the baptism of infants or young children?) This event could also be a time to introduce a Bible literacy program for all ages in the congregation—not just for the young readers. Take some time to study some key Bible passages, or even to review the major portions of the Old and New Testaments. Distribute materials that contain suggestions for daily Bible reading.

If your congregation will celebrate a Harvest Festival (or Harvest Home) in the fall, consider whether you will use the regularly appointed readings for that Sunday of the liturgical year, or whether you will use texts appointed for the occasion of a harvest (pp. 185-186 in *LBW, Ministers Edition*). Some congregations take a special collection for a food pantry in their area at a harvest festival (especially useful since many food pantries deplete much of their supplies during the summer months). Work with a social ministry committee, a youth group, or some other organization to determine how a collection of food will be delivered.

Congregations often conduct stewardship campaigns in the fall. It may take some time to plan worship that is faithful to the lectionary and the programmatic needs of the congregation. Why not explore the lectionary texts several months in advance with an eye to the best placement of activities that will serve the total stewardship of the congregation?

Some congregations have a blessing of animals on or near the commemoration of Francis of Assisi, renewer of the church (Oct. 4). An order for this is provided in the seasonal rites for autumn. In many areas of the country this occasion might be a delightful excuse for an outdoor gathering in the fall. Singing Francis's hymn "All creatures of our God and King" (LBW 527) is *de rigueur* for this occasion. Offerings could go to support a program for guide dogs or therapy animals for people who might not be able to afford them.

Reformation Day is celebrated in many places—sometimes even with other congregations. In years past the annual observance of the Reformation was a way in which Lutherans celebrated their own uniquenesses, often to the detriment of other denominational traditions. A more enlightened observance of this festival might examine ways in which we can acknowledge and appreciate all the gifts that several denominations have (including our own). This inclusive attitude could be a helpful way to lead up to the celebration of All Saints Day/Sunday, which is both an older and more universally celebrated festival than Reformation Day.

303

ORDO FOR THE SEASON

If the gathering order was shortened during the summer season, perhaps now is a time to add some of it back (though probably still something less than all of the options). The order for gathering might be: (confession and forgiveness), entrance hymn, apostolic greeting, hymn of praise, and prayer of the day. The Kyrie might be reserved for penitential seasons, and when it is used together with the hymn of praise for festival days and seasons.

The creed, when used, could be the Apostles' Creed, reserving the Nicene Creed for festive days and seasons. A hymn such as WOV 760, "For the fruit of all creation" or LBW 412, "Sing to the Lord of harvest" might replace the offertory hymn during this season, especially if the congregation has a special emphasis of the harvest or of stewardship during these months. Eucharistic Prayer H for Autumn (*WOV*, p. 72) might be used to further enhance the themes and lectionary readings of this season.

ASSEMBLY SONG FOR THE SEASON

The secular calendar calls January 1 the start of the new year. The liturgical calendar tells us that the year starts in Advent. For many North Americans, the year really begins in September when schools resume. Although the church is in the midst of the Sundays after Pentecost, early September is often a "get back to work" time for a congregation. Several of the gospel readings tell stories about laboring in the vineyard—engaging in the serious work of Christ's mission to which all the baptized have been called. And so musicians do just that.

Choirs often resume their regular work at this time. New singers and instrumentalists should be recruited and welcomed intentionally and publicly. Too often, longtime choir members and directors make many assumptions, leaving new members bewildered and frustrated. Take some time with recent recruits (perhaps even preparing a printed resource) to explain the choir's mission and role in worship, as well as practical details, such as vestment care, attendance expectations and fellowship opportunities.

Getting started is often a challenging task. If long-range planning has been done, there is possibly literature from the previous year that can be used with integrity in the early weeks of the choir season, allowing choirs to reenter Sunday worship immediately upon starting rehearsals. Holy Cross Day (September 14) occurs close to the start of the choir season for many congregations. What better way to begin a year of ministry together than to rally around the cross? Perhaps some choral literature from the previous Passion Sunday or Good Friday, recast (different volume, tempo or accompaniment, for example) with a more triumphal character could be an effective way to begin the year. Repeating something learned the previous year can be encouraging for choirs, especially when they are challenged with new literature at the same time.

The "get back to work" attitude of early autumn opens the door to providing education about worship.

It's often a good time to offer classes, articles, and discussion groups about why we worship and how the rhythms of the liturgy intersect with the rhythms of our lives. It is an opportune time for worship planners to take a look at local liturgical practice and music, making certain that what is being done really offers the fullness of the central things and streamlines peripheral words and actions.

In many places, worship attendance increases in the early autumn. Although, we're still in the midst of the Sundays after Pentecost, this increase naturally calls for a more substantial gathering. What was a streamlined gathering could now include the hymn of praise, "Glory to God" between the apostolic greeting and the prayer of the day.

It may also be an excellent time to learn a new hymn or liturgical music. Plan the introduction carefully. Know your community. How much can they handle at once? How do they learn? Holding high expectations together with quality teaching usually results in children learning just about anything. They can, in turn, teach their parents. Brief visits by the director or confident choir members to various parish groups for teaching a new melody in a safe, nonthreatening environment can be well worth the time and effort.

The Lutheran celebration of the Reformation is often observed on the last Sunday in October. This year that would displace the gospel reading (Proper 26), "All who exalt themselves will be humbled, and all who humble themselves will be exalted" proclaimed by many Christians on that day. Perhaps the Reformation would be best celebrated by joining with Christians from all corners of the church in hearing, preaching, and singing about these humbling words.

MUSIC FOR THE SEASON

VERSE AND OFFERTORY

Busarow, Donald. *Verses and Offertories* (Pentecost 21–Christ the King).
AFP 11-09540.

Verses and Offertory Sentences, Part VII (Pentecost 19–Christ the King).
CPH 97-5507.

CHORAL MUSIC FOR THE SEASON

Beethoven, Ludwig van/Richard Proulx. "Give Thanks to God."
AFP 11-10648. SAB, kybd.

Bell, John. "Glory to God in the Highest." GIA G-4296. SATB,
cong, org.

Christopherson, Dorothy, and Tom Colvin. "Jesu, Jesu." CPH 98-3177.
SAB, perc.

Fauré, Gabriel/Marie and Richard Stultz. "Pie Jesu" in *Requiem.*
MSM 50-9906. U, kybd/org/hp.

Hampton, Calvin. "Bread of the World." SEL 410-423. SATB,
B soli, org.

Hassell, Michael. "Jesus Loves Me." AFP 11-10790. SATB, pno, sax.

Hassler, Hans Leo. "We Give Thanks unto Thee." CPH 98-3378. SATB.

Hobby, Robert A. "How Can I Keep from Singing." MSM 20-851.
Cong, brass qnt, org.

MacMillan, Alan. "Three Eucharistic Motets." PAR PPM09530.
SATB (or SA/TB), org.

Marshall, Jane. "Who Hath a Right Like Us to Sing?" ECS 4954.
SATB, org.

Scott, K. Lee. "A Vineyard Grows." MSM 50-9010. Inst pts 50-9010A.
SATB, opt inst, org.

Ylvisaker, John/Daniel Kallman. "The Gift." MSM 50-9103. SAB, org.

CHILDREN'S CHORAL MUSIC FOR THE SEASON

Kreutz, Robert. "God Is Truly Our Good Shepherd." CGA 517. U.

Page, Anna Laura. "Praise Can Be Like Children." KIR 15/1139. 2 pt.

Pethel, Stan. "Come Lift Up Your Voice." COR 392-41826. 2 pt.

Scott, K. Lee. "Best of All Friends." MSM 50-9003. 2 pt, kybd.

INSTRUMENTAL MUSIC FOR THE SEASON

Albrecht, Mark. "Timeless Hymns of Faith for Piano." AFP 11-10863.
Pno.

Arnatt, Ronald. "Hymn Sonata for Organ, No. 2." ECS 4986. Org.

Bedford, Michael. "Come, Holy Spirit, Come" in *Seven Songs for the
Church Year.* CGA-693. U, kybd, opt hb.

Cherwien, David. "Oh, Praise the Gracious Power: Hymn Settings for
Organ." AFP 11-10860. Org.

Diemer, Emma Lou. "Many and Great, O God, Are Thy Things" in
Eight Hymn Preludes for Organ. AFP 11-10349. Org.

Ferguson, John. "Three Psalm Preludes." AFP 11-10823. Org.

Hassell, Michael. "Jazz Plain and Simple." AFP 11-10862. Pno.

Lasky, David. "Variations on 'Morning Song'" in *Eight Hymn Preludes.*
HWG 32-698-703. Org.

Pelz, Walter L. "Aurelia" in *Hymn Settings for Organ and Brass,* set 1.
Full score AFP 11-10184. Inst pts 11-10185.

HANDBELL MUSIC FOR THE SEASON

Anderson, Christine/John Carter. "It Is Well with My Soul."
HOP 1439. Hb duet.

Anderson, Christine/Stephenson. "Beach Spring." HOP 1707. Hb solo.

Hopson, Hal H. "Fantasy on 'Hyfrydol.'" HOP 1048.

Young, Philip. "In Thee Is Gladness." AFP 11-10624. 4-5 oct.

WORSHIP ENSEMBLE FOR THE SEASON

Allen, Dennis. "All Creatures of Our God." GVX 4173-22. 2 pt.

Besig, Don. "Let Us Praise the Lord." Glory Sound A-6893. SATB.

Greer, Bruce. "On the Rock of Christ." INT 08447. SATB. orch.

Haugen, Marty. "Gather Us In." GIA G-2651. 2 pt, 2 ww, gtr.

Larson, Lloyd. "I Will Praise You, O Lord, with All My Heart."
BEC BP1510. SATB.

Medema, Ken. "Sing to the Lord." HAL 08740519. SATB, orch.

Williamson, Dave. "We Know Jesus." INT. SATB, orch.

305

ALTERNATE WORSHIP TEXTS

CONFESSION AND FORGIVENESS

In the name of the Father, and of the ✝ Son, and of the Holy
  Spirit.
Amen

Let us confess our sin in the presence of God and one another,
  praying that God remember us in mercy.

Silence for reflection and self-examination.

God of our days and years,
we confess that we have not used our gifts and time
as you would have us do.
We have turned from the abundance of your grace
and tried to harvest good solely from within ourselves.
We turn to you for forgiveness and mercy,
and pray that you would bring us again
into the fruitful field of your love.

God is merciful and, for the sake of Jesus,
forgives you all your sin.
God grant you joy in all the gifts
God will bring forth from you.
Amen

GREETING

Owe no one anything, except to love one another.
The grace of our Lord Jesus Christ, the love of God, and the com-
  munion of the Holy Spirit be with you all.
And also with you.

OFFERTORY PRAYER

God of wisdom,
in your Son Jesus you teach us to love one another
and to share the gifts of our lives.
Receive these gifts in thanksgiving
for all you have done for us.
Bring forth from us a rich yield
in lives dedicated to your service. Amen

INVITATION TO COMMUNION

Everything is ready;
all who hunger, all who thirst,
come to the banquet.

POST-COMMUNION PRAYER

Lord God, you are the one for whom we have waited.
We rejoice in your salvation.
As you have fed us with the riches of this table,
place us again in your vineyard
to reap the harvest of righteousness;
through Jesus Christ our Lord.
Amen

BENEDICTION

Rejoice in the Lord always; again I will say, Rejoice.
Let your gentleness be known to everyone.
The Lord bless you and keep you.
The Lord's face shine on you with grace and mercy.
The Lord look upon you with favor and give you peace.
Amen

DISMISSAL

Go in peace to love and serve the Lord.
Thanks be to God.

306

SEASONAL RITES

BLESSING OF TEACHERS AND STUDENTS

HYMN
LBW 558   Earth and all stars!

If used on a Sunday morning the following prayer may be used during or following the Prayers.

Let us pray for all who are beginning a new school year,
that both students and teachers will be blessed in their academic
endeavors.

Almighty God,
you give wisdom and knowledge.
Grant teachers the gift of joy and insight,
and students the gift of diligence and openness,
that all may grow in what is good and honest and true.
Support all who teach and all who learn,
that together we may know and follow your ways;
through Jesus Christ our Lord.
Amen

BLESSING OF ANIMALS

This service may be used entirely on its own, perhaps for an observance on or near the commemoration of Francis of Assisi, renewer of the Church, 1226 (October 4). Various elements of this order may also be incorporated into another worship service (though this material is not intended to replace the customary Sunday worship of the congregation). Care should be used in adapting the service to the occasion and to the physical setting in which it is used. For practical reasons this service may be conducted outdoors or in a facility other than a congregation's primary worship space.

The grace of our Lord Jesus Christ, the love of God, and the communion of the Holy Spirit be with you all.
Amen

Let us pray.
O merciful Creator, your hand is open wide to satisfy the needs of
every living creature. Make us always thankful for your loving
providence; and grant that we, remembering the account that
we must one day give, may be faithful stewards of your good
gifts; through your Son, Jesus Christ our Lord.
Amen
or
Almighty God, in giving us dominion over things on earth, you
made us fellow workers in your creation: Give us wisdom and
reverence so to use the resources of nature, that no one may
suffer from our abuse of them, and that generations yet to
come may continue to praise you for your bounty; through
Jesus Christ our Lord.
Amen
Book of Common Prayer, #41, p. 827.

READINGS
Genesis 1:1, 20-28
Genesis 6:17-22
Psalm 8
Psalm 148
Other readings about God's creation and the care of animals may be used. A sermon or an address appropriate to the occasion may also be included.

307

HYMN OR CANTICLE

LBW 18   All you works of the Lord

LBW 409   Praise and thanksgiving

LBW 527   All creatures of our God and King

LBW 554   This is my Father's world

LBW 560   Oh, that I had a thousand voices

WOV 767   All things bright and beautiful

Song of the Three Young Men (PW, Cycle C, Vigil of Easter, Response 12)

The leader may ask all who have brought pets/animals to the celebration to come forward for the following prayer.

The Lord be with you.

And also with you.

Let us pray.

Gracious God, in your love you created us in your image and made us stewards of the animals that live in the skies, the earth, and the sea. Bless us in our care for our pets and animals (names of pets may be added here). Help us recognize your power and wisdom in the variety of creatures that live in our world, and hear our prayer for all that suffer overwork, hunger, and ill-treatment. Protect your creatures and guard them from all evil, now and forever.

Amen

THE LORD'S PRAYER

The Lord almighty order our days and our deeds in his peace.

Amen

SERVICE OF THE WORD FOR HEALING

This service may be celebrated at any time. It may be especially appropriate on or near the festival of St. Luke, Evangelist (Oct. 18).

Stand

HYMN

LBW 360   O Christ, the healer, we have come

WOV 716   Word of God, come down on earth

GREETING AND WELCOME

The grace of our Lord Jesus Christ, the love of God, and the communion of the Holy Spirit be with you all.

And also with you.

We gather to hear the Word of God, pray for those in need, and ask God's blessing on those who seek healing and wholeness through Christ our Lord.

PRAYER OF THE DAY

The proper prayer of the day may be used, or the prayer for St. Luke (October 18), p. 118 in WOV, Leaders Edition, or the following:

Great God our Healer,

by your power, the Lord Jesus healed the sick

and gave hope to the hopeless.

As we gather in his name,

look upon us with mercy and

bless us with your healing Spirit.

Bring us comfort in the midst of pain,

strength to transform our weakness,

and light to illuminate our darkness.

We ask this in the name of Jesus Christ,

our crucified and risen Lord,

who lives and reigns with you and the Holy Spirit,

one God, now and forever.

Amen

Sit

READINGS

These readings, the readings listed for St. Luke, Evangelist (p. 118 in WOV, Leaders Edition), or the readings listed on pp. 96–97 of Occasional Services may be used.

Isaiah 61:1-3a

Psalm 23

The Lord is my shepherd; I shall not be in want

Luke 17:11-19

SERMON

HYMN

LBW 423   Lord, whose love in humble service
WOV 738   Healer of our every ill
WOV 798   Bless the Lord, O my soul

Stand
THE PRAYERS

This litany, or the prayers in Occasional Services *pp. 91–93 may be used.*

God the Father, you desire the health and salvation of all people.
We praise you and thank you, O Lord.
God the Son, you came that we might have life, and might have it more abundantly.
We praise you and thank you, O Lord.
God the Holy Spirit, you make our bodies the temples of your presence.
We praise you and thank you, O Lord.
Holy Trinity, one God, in you we live and move and have our being.
We praise you and thank you, O Lord.

Lord, grant your healing grace to all who are sick, injured, or disabled, that they may be made whole;
hear us, O Lord of life.
Grant to all who are lonely, anxious, or despondent, the awareness of your presence;
hear us, O Lord of life.
Mend broken relationships, and restore those in emotional distress to soundness of mind and serenity of spirit;
hear us, O Lord of life.
Bless physicians, nurses, and all others who minister to the suffering; grant them wisdom and skill, sympathy and patience;
hear us, O Lord of life.
Grant to the dying a peaceful, holy death, and with your grace strengthen those who mourn;
hear us, O Lord of life.
Restore to wholeness whatever is broken in our lives, in this nation, and in the world;
hear us, O Lord of life.
Hear us, O Lord of life:
heal us, and make us whole.

Gracious God, in baptism you anointed us with the oil of salvation, and joined us to the death and resurrection of your Son. Bless all who seek your healing presence in their lives. In their suffering draw them more deeply into the mystery of your love, that following Christ in the way of the cross they may know the power of his resurrection; who lives and reigns forever and ever.
Amen

Sit
LAYING ON OF HANDS AND ANOINTING

Those who wish to receive the laying on of hands (and anointing) come to the altar and, if possible, kneel. The minister lays both hands on each person's head in silence, after which he/she may dip a thumb in the oil and make the sign of the cross on the person's forehead, saying:
(Through this holy anointing) may God's love and mercy uphold you by the grace and power of the Holy Spirit.
Amen

During the anointing, the assembly may sing various hymns and songs, instrumental music may be played, or there may simply be an interval of silence.

Stand
PRAYER

After all have returned to their places, the minister may say:
As you are anointed with this oil,
may God bless you with the healing power of the Holy Spirit.
May God forgive you your sins,
release you from suffering,
and restore you to wholeness and strength.
May God deliver you from all evil,
preserve you in all goodness,
and bring you to everlasting life,
through Jesus Christ our Lord.
Amen

CONCLUDING RITE

THE LORD'S PRAYER

BLESSING AND DISMISSAL

HYMN

LBW 263   Abide with us, our Savior
WOV 721   Go, My children, with my blessing
WOV 737   There is a balm in Gilead

309

SEPTEMBER 5, 1999

INTRODUCTION

Life in community is a precious thing, but it easily breaks down if rumors and idle talk are given free reign. In today's gospel, Jesus prescribes a manner for dealing with conflict in community life, a procedure which is written into most congregations' constitutions. The intent of such a form of church discipline is to restore people to community life.

May all who come to hear and to taste the presence of Christ in word and sacrament today also find communities which seek to understand one another in truth and in love.

PRAYER OF THE DAY

Almighty and eternal God, you know our problems and our weaknesses better than we ourselves. In your love and by your power help us in our confusion and, in spite of our weakness, make us firm in faith; through your Son, Jesus Christ our Lord.

READINGS

Ezekiel 33:7-11

Shortly before the fall of Jerusalem, the Lord commissions Ezekiel to serve as a watchman. The role of watchman is crucial in the hills of Palestine, where early detection of approaching danger can mean the difference between victory or defeat. The prophet's task is also crucial: warn the wicked of the danger of retaining wicked ways.

Psalm 119:33-40

I desire the path of your commandments. (Ps. 119:35)

Romans 13:8-14

Although Paul insists that we are reconciled to God through faith rather than through works of the law, he encourages Christians to practice God's law of love while we wait for the salvation that is to come.

Matthew 18:15-20

Jesus has just said that God's concern for every individual is like that of a shepherd who will leave the entire herd to look for one sheep that is lost. Now, he says, the church should reach out to and welcome members who sin.

COLOR   Green

THE PRAYERS

Remembering the church, the world, and all those in need, let us offer our prayers to God.

A BRIEF SILENCE.

For the church, that through its ministry of reconciliation and forgiveness your gracious love may be revealed. Hear us, O God;

your mercy is great.

For the governing authorities of the nations of the world, that they may rule with justice and honor. Hear us, O God;

your mercy is great.

For those who because of their sins feel separated from you or from your church, and for those who refuse opportunities for reconciliation, that they may come to know the joy and peace of forgiveness. Hear us, O God;

your mercy is great.

For those who are poor, homeless, or outcast; for refugees and for those who face oppression or persecution for their faith; and for those who are sick or in any kind of need (especially . . .), that we extend to them your love. Hear us, O God;

your mercy is great.

For ourselves and this congregation, that honoring your presence among us we be bearers of your reconciliation and love in our daily lives. Hear us, O God;

your mercy is great.

HERE OTHER INTERCESSIONS MAY BE OFFERED.

We give thanks for all the faithful departed who have made known to us your grace and forgiveness. Gather us with them into your reign of justice and peace. Hear us, O God;

your mercy is great.

All these things and whatever else you see that we need, grant us, O God, for your mercy is everlasting, and your faithfulness endures from age to age.

Amen

IMAGES FOR PREACHING

A witness testifies to the truth. Under mosaic law, at least two witnesses had to be in agreement to establish guilt of a capital crime (Num. 35:30; Deut. 17:6; Heb. 10:28). In fact, this principle applied to all judicial procedure (Deut. 19:15). Bearing *false* witness is forbidden in the eighth commandment, and according to the law of Moses, the person who bore false witness suffered the penalty that would have been imposed on the falsely accused (16, 19).

Paul reminded the Romans that all the commandments are summed up in one phrase: "Love your neighbor as yourself" (13:9). Paul referred only generally, however, to most of the commandments, including the eighth, and we must admit we usually do not think much about it. We tend to be more interested in the commandments about murder, adultery, and stealing. When we look at Deuteronomy, though, we see that the witness actually played a huge part in the ordering of the community's life.

The role of the witnesses mentioned in today's gospel reading seems much weightier when we keep in mind the significance of the witness under mosaic law. The witness *must* tell the truth. The two or three witnesses who accompanied an aggrieved party when confronting a member who had sinned could later be called on to testify about what they saw or heard. But this procedure was about more than heading off an argument that merely pits one person's word against another. The witnesses—and the accused—had behind them the power of the whole law.

The eighth commandment and Matthew's instructions are signs of God's continuing care for us, the people of God. They are tools for protecting the powerless, the victim, the innocent. How would our community be changed if we took this commandment as much to heart as we do some of the others?

WORSHIP MATTERS

Today's gospel points us to the practice of confession and forgiveness, mutual conversation, and other opportunities for repentance and renewal in the congregation. Do congregational members know that they can seek out the pastor for *individual* confession and forgiveness, in addition to general orders for forgiveness? Are office hours announced for those needing to speak with a pastor about such matters? Are special services for healing and/or forgiveness held?

Does the congregation, especially among its council, staff, and committee leaders, seek to restore disaffected persons into the life of the congregation? Is Jesus' model from Matthew 18 followed for discipline of members and for approaching one another about difficulties? Or are offending persons oftentimes the last to know about problems? Christian respect demands that we approach one another directly with our concerns, rather than blowing them out of proportion.

LET THE CHILDREN COME

Children come to an understanding of mercy even though the word itself may not be a part of their vocabulary. A scraped knee cleaned, bandaged, and accompanied by a kiss on the forehead offers comfort. A hug when a child is scared provides compassion. A safe place on an adult's lap in the middle of a thunderstorm won't take away the source of the fear, but offers refuge and protection. Find ways to help the children for the mercy of the Lord.

MUSIC FOR WORSHIP
GATHERING

LBW 558	Earth and all stars!
WOV 745	Awake, O sleeper

PSALM 119

Becker, John. PW, Cycle A.

Guimont, Michel. "Ps 119: Happy are They" in RS.

Haas, David. PCY, vol. 8.

Hurd, David. "Teach Me, O Lord." GIA G-2715. SATB, org, cong.

HYMN OF THE DAY

LBW 419	Lord of all nations, grant me grace
	BEATUS VIR

INSTRUMENTAL RESOURCES

Busarow, Donald. "Beatus vir" in *All Praise to You, Eternal God*. AFP 11-9076. Org.

Sedio, Mark. "Lord of All Nations, Grant Me Grace" in *Six Slovak Hymn Improvisations*. MSM 10-833. Org.

ALTERNATE HYMN OF THE DAY

LBW 126	Where charity and love prevail
WOV 739	In all our grief

COMMUNION

LBW210	At the Lamb's high feast we sing
WOV 703	Draw us in the Spirit's tether

SUGGESTION FOR WOV 703

Stanzas 1 and 3, All.

Stanza 2 from the choral octavo, "Draw Us in the Spirit's Tether." BEL GCMR02472. SATB, org.

SENDING

LBW 551   Joyful, joyful we adore thee
WOV 623   Thankful hearts and voices raise

ADDITIONAL HYMNS AND SONGS

WOV 663   When twilight comes
WOV 735   God! When human bonds are broken
UMH 560   Help us accept each other
NSR 153   The Lord is here!

MUSIC FOR THE DAY

CHORAL

Attwood, Thomas. "Teach Me, O Lord." GIA G-3045. SATB, kybd.

Handel, G. F. "Keep Me Faithfully in Thy Paths." GIA G-2355. 2 pt mxd, org.

Harris, Ed. "Gather Together." PRE 392-41543. SAB, kybd.

Hopson, Hal H. "Sing a New Song to the Lord." CGA 204. Hb pt CGA B-204. U, hb.

Schutte, Dan. "Sing a New Song." OCP 9496CC. 3 pt, pno, gtr.

Warner, Richard. "Holy Ghost, with Light Divine." CPH 98-1363. SA, kybd.

Young, Jeremy. "Nothing Can Come Between Us." AFP 11-10848. SAB, kybd, opt cong.

CHILDREN'S CHOIRS

Hopson, Hal. "Love One Another." CGA 741. U/2 pt, kybd.

Marshall, Jane. "God Speaks: The Twin Commandments." CGA 535. U, cong, kybd.

Sleeth, Natalie. "Prayer." CGA 565. U/2 pt, kybd, opt C inst.

KEYBOARD/INSTRUMENTAL

Honoré, Jeffrey. "Sing of the Lord's Goodness" in *Contemporary Postludes,* vol. 14. OCP. Org.

Rorem, Ned. "Pastorale for Organ." SMC. Org.

Sedio, Mark. "Siyahamba" in *Dancing in the Light of God.* AFP 11-10793. Pno.

HANDBELL

Folkening, John. "At the Lamb's High Feast We Sing" in *Ten Hymn Accompaniments for Handbells,* set 2. CPH 97-6035. 3 oct.

McFadden, Jane. "Built on a Rock." AFP 11-10714. SATB, cong, 3 oct, org, tpt.

PRAISE ENSEMBLE

Espinosa/Kilpatrick/Wilson. "Change My Heart/Lord, Be Glorified." HOP. SATB.

Hanson, Handt. "There's A Song" in *Songs of the First Light.* CCF.

Kendrick, Graham. "Where Two Or Three" in *Integrity's Hosanna! Music Songsheets: No More Walls.* INT.

Medema/Schrader. "Lord, Listen to Your Children Praying." HOP GC 850C. SATB.

MONDAY, SEPTEMBER 6

LABOR DAY (USA)
LABOUR DAY (CANADA)

THURSDAY, SEPTEMBER 9

PETER CLAVER, MISSIONARY, 1654

Peter Claver was a Jesuit missionary to the Americas. He served in Cartenga (in what is now Columbia) by teaching and caring for the black slaves. The slaves arrived in ships where they were penned up like cattle in filthy, stinking conditions. Claver met them and attended to their needs, baptizing children that had been born on the voyage. He considered himself a "slave to the slaves," and was committed to speaking more with his hands than with his lips.

Claver's advocacy on behalf of the rights of slaves is a witness to a gospel that is for all people. How are we called to work for the dignity and equality of all God's children? Give examples of contemporary ministries that offer care and compassion to people living in sub-standard living conditions.

SEPTEMBER 12, 1999

INTRODUCTION

In today's gospel reading, Jesus invites us to forgive one another. His invitation, however, is not an optional activity for Christians. It is the heart of the gospel and the distinctive character of Christian life. Out of love for us in our weakness and sin, God forgives us, heals us, and strengthens us to be a forgiving people. The sign of the cross invites us to the ministry of reconciliation in word and sacrament.

On September 14, the church celebrates Holy Cross Day. The cross, marked on our foreheads at baptism and traced over our bodies at the funeral liturgy, assures us of Christ's victory over death and the promise of eternal life.

PRAYER OF THE DAY

O God, you declare your almighty power chiefly in showing mercy and pity. Grant us the fullness of your grace, that, pursuing what you have promised, we may share your heavenly glory; through your Son, Jesus Christ our Lord.

READINGS

Genesis 50:15-21

The story of Joseph is a wisdom story. In it, Joseph plays the role of a wise man. Portrayed in a situation of oppression, he provides an important model of how the wise should act.

Psalm 103:[1-7] 8-13

The Lord is full of compassion and mercy. (Ps. 103:8)

Romans 14:1-12

The Christians in Rome came from a diversity of cultural backgrounds: some Jewish, some Gentile. Here Paul urges them to respect one another's opinions on various religious matters, even though he himself believes that some of the ideas are held by people weak in faith.

Matthew 18:21-35

Jesus has been instructing his disciples about confronting other people who live in ways that are sinful. Now, Peter's question about forgiveness elicits a parable that clarifies this issue. Although the community of faith should challenge sinners to repent, it should also proclaim a forgiveness that reflects the bountiful mercy of God.

COLOR Green

THE PRAYERS

Remembering the church, the world, and all those in need, let us offer our prayers to God.

A BRIEF SILENCE.

For the church, that its divisions be healed, and that a spirit of reconciliation and cooperation grow between separated Christians. Hear us, O God;

your mercy is great.

For our bishops, for our pastor(s), and for all who teach in this congregation, that together they might witness to the richness of your mercy. Hear us, O God;

your mercy is great.

For countries in conflict or threatened by war, for refugees and hostages, and for all those longing for freedom and justice, that your peace may be made known to them. Hear us, O God;

your mercy is great.

For all those burdened by worry, poverty, or sickness (especially . . .), that they may know your compassion and mercy. Hear us, O God;

your mercy is great.

For victims of crime, hate, or injustice, and for those who have been physically or emotionally abused, that they may find healing through forgiveness. Hear us, O God;

your mercy is great.

HERE OTHER INTERCESSIONS MAY BE OFFERED.

We give thanks for all the saints who have revealed to us your abundant mercy and limitless forgiveness. May we follow them by bearing your reconciling word to all the world. Hear us, O God;

your mercy is great.

All these things and whatever else you see that we need, grant us, O God, for your mercy is everlasting, and your faithfulness endures from age to age.

Amen

IMAGES FOR PREACHING

Most of us envision the act of forgiving in this way. The one who has said or done something awful comes to the victim and says, "I'm sorry I did this terrible thing to you. Will you forgive me?" And the injured party, after thinking for a few moments, slowly nods and say, "Yes, I forgive you."

Joseph had that experience with his brothers. Worried that their now powerful brother would use his position to punish them, the brothers told Joseph a lie: "Our father said to tell you that you should forgive us!" Joseph, always a better man than his brothers, wept and assured them, "Do not be afraid, for I will use my power to take care of you and your children." This story is a picture of perfect forgiveness, God's kind of forgiveness.

But what happens when the perpetrator shows no remorse? A number of years ago, theologian Lewis Smedes wrote a wonderful little book, *Forgive and Forget.* Full of sympathy and guidance for those who have been wronged, Smedes also wisely counsels those who have been deeply hurt that they *need* to forgive the one who caused the pain, even if the wrong-doer does not acknowledge the deed.

Perhaps it is just such a situation that was behind Peter's question in Matthew, when he asked, "How often should I forgive?" (Matt. 18:21). After all, why would Peter have even asked the question if another had confessed and promised to straighten up, and Peter had forgiven? But apparently no sinner had come to Peter to say, "I'm sorry." Rather, the person persisted in sin, pushing the exasperated Peter to plead, "How much longer do I have to put up with this? Can't you see, this rascal just won't give up?"

And Jesus, knowing that we need to forgive for our own well-being, not for the well-being of the one we forgive, advised Peter, "You must forgive seventy-seven times. It does not matter what the other person does. You must forgive until you know you have forgiven."

WORSHIP MATTERS

"We offer with joy and thanksgiving what you have first given us. . . ." Each week the liturgy reminds us that we are first and foremost recipients of God's goodness. Having received the grace of God, we then are called to be stewards of God's great bounty. The liturgy calls us to give thanks for our many blessings, while also sending us out into the world to proclaim God's love and care for others.

Our liturgy models an economy of abundance. All are invited to receive, regardless of their ability to pay. Of course this fundamental truth runs counter to the notions of the marketplace. We usually operate by the principle that you get what you earn. Our liturgy proclaims that everything is a gift from God. Do all people in your community know that they are welcome to receive God's gifts through your congregation?

LET THE CHILDREN COME

In many congregations this is the day that starts a new term of Sunday school and educational programs. As children, families, and the parish's teachers rally together for this new start, worship planners may want to set aside time in the service for a blessing of the students and their teachers. As a part of this blessing, consider the possibility of having the children remain seated in the pews but raise their hands in blessing (along with everyone in the congregation) over the teachers who are gathered together near the altar.

MUSIC FOR WORSHIP

GATHERING

| LBW 251 | O day of rest and gladness |
| WOV 750 | Oh, praise the gracious power |

PSALM 103

Becker, John. PW, Cycle A.

DATH 42   Bless the Lord

Folkening, John. "Six Psalm Settings with Antiphons." MSM 80-700.

Haugen, Marty. "Psalm 103: The Lord Is Kind and Merciful" in RS.

LBW 519   My soul, now praise your maker!

LBW 549   Praise, my soul, the King of heaven

HYMN OF THE DAY

| LBW 307 | Forgive our sins as we forgive |
| | DETROIT |

VOCAL RESOURCES

Anders, C./Paul Thomas. "Forgive Our Sins as We Forgive" in *Choral Settings for the Hymn of the Day,* vol. VII. CPH 97-5865. SATB.

Hobby, Robert. "Forgive Our Sins, as We Forgive." CPH 98-2870. SAB, kybd.

314

INSTRUMENTAL RESOURCES

Busarow, Donald. "Detroit" in *Thirty More Accompaniments for Hymns in Canon*. AFP 11-10163. Kybd.

Dorian, Mark. "Detroit" in *Around the World: Six Hymntune Improvisations*. AFP 11-10618. Pno.

Held, Wilbur. "Detroit" in *Seven Settings of American Folk Hymns*. CPH 97-5829.

Hurd, David. "Partita on 'Detroit.'" AFP 11-10225. Org.

ALTERNATE HYMN OF THE DAY

| LBW 126 | Where charity and love prevail (*alternate tune*: ST. PETER) |
| WOV 733 | Our Father, we have wandered |

COMMUNION

| LBW 205 | Now the silence |
| WOV 665 | Ubi caritas et amor |

OTHER SUGGESTIONS

Keesecker, Thomas. "I Am the Living Bread." AFP 11-10684. SATB, kybd, opt cong, opt sop sax/C inst.

SENDING

LBW 527	All creatures of our God and King
LBW 358	Glories of your name are spoken
WOV 721	Go, my children, with my blessing

ADDITIONAL HYMNS AND SONGS

WOV 798	Bless the Lord, O my soul
ASF 1	O God, whom we praise
NCH 457	Jesus, I live to you
LLC 462	Pues si vivimos/When we are living

MUSIC FOR THE DAY

CHORAL

Beaudrot, Charles. "Bless the Lord, My Soul." MSM 50-7025. SATB, org, opt hb.

Giles, Randall. "Ubi caritas et vera." PAR PPM09216. SATB.

Oldroyd, George. "Prayer to Jesus." OXF 43 P 037. SATB.

Parker, Alice. "Pues si vivimos" (While We Are Living). HAL 08596533. SATB, pno.

Rosania, Laurence. "Ubi Caritas." OCP 9661. 3 pt, cong, kybd, gtr, solo inst.

Schalk, Carl. "Where Charity and Love Prevail." CPH 98-2701. 2 pt trbl, ob, org.

Schiavone, John. "Wilt Thou Forgive?" CPH 98-2119. SATB.

CHILDREN'S CHOIRS

Cherubini, Luigi, and Austin Lovelace. "Like As a Father." CGA 156. U and 2 pt mxd, kybd.

Hruby, Delores. "Help Us Accept Each Other." CGA 713. U, kybd, opt fl/gtr.

Larson, Sonia. "Psalm 103." AMSI 636. 2 pt, kybd, opt fl.

KEYBOARD/INSTRUMENTAL

Clerambault, Louis-Nicolas. "Flûtes" in *Suite du Deuxieme Ton*. KAL 3308. Org.

Corl, Matthew H. *Three Sunday School Hymn Settings for Organ*. MSM 10-806. Org.

Young, Jeremy. "How Can I Keep from Singing" in *At the Foot of the Cross: Piano for the Lenten Journey*. AFP 11-10688. Pno.

HANDBELL

Gramann, Fred. "Fantasy on 'King's Weston.'" HOP 1671. 3-6 oct.

Larson, Katherine. "The Ash Grove." AFP 11-10348. 4-5 oct.

Sherman, Arnold. "Jesus Shall Reign." 2-3 oct HOP 1708. 4-5 oct 1709.

Young, Philip M. "In Thee Is Gladness." AFP 11-10624. 4-5 oct.

PRAISE ENSEMBLE

Founds, Rick. "Lord, I Lift Your Name on High." WRD 301 0805 160. SATB.

Hanson, Handt. "I'll Belong To You" in *Spirit Calls, Rejoice!* CCF.

Paris, Twila. "Honor and Praise" in *Worship Leader Magazine's Song DISCovery*, vol. 2.

Red, Buryl. "In Remembrance." BRD 4565-35. SATB.

MONDAY, SEPTEMBER 13

JOHN CHRYSOSTOM, BISHOP OF CONSTANTINOPLE, 407

John Chrysostom was trained in law and theology, and he used his oratorical gifts in preaching, which gave him the title "golden-mouthed" (or "Chrysostom"). He was skilled at the exposition of scripture, able to relate both the author's meaning as well as the practical application, opposing the allegorical interpretation common at the time. He was made patriarch of Constantinople against his wishes, and in that office he reformed the city, court, and clergy.

Share a conversation about the tasks and challenges of preaching today. Ask parishioners to relate particularly memorable sermons, and to discuss the ways that preaching impacts their lives of faith. Pastors may gain insights for their homiletical preparation.

TUESDAY, SEPTEMBER 14
HOLY CROSS DAY

The observance of this day dates from 335 in which a basilica was built by Constantine on the sight believed to be the place of the crucifixion. The cross is one of the primary symbols of Christianity. This festival became very popular, being observed in both the East and West.

Congregations might make mention of Holy Cross Day on Sunday, and sing "Lift High the Cross" as an entrance hymn. Meetings or services during the week might focus on the lessons and themes of the festival. Does the cross have central place in the life of your congregation—in its worship, education, evangelism, and social ministry? Do you teach children (and adults) to make the sign of the cross in remembrance of their baptism into Jesus' death and resurrection?

SATURDAY, SEPTEMBER 18
DAG HAMMARSKJÖLD, PEACEMAKER, 1961

Dag Hammarskjöld was a Swedish diplomat and humanitarian who served as Secretary General of the United Nations. He was killed in a plane crash on this day in 1961 while on his way to negotiate a cease fire between the United Nations and Katanga forces. It was not until after Hammarskjöld's death that the publications of his personal journal, *Markings*, revealed his deep Christian faith. The book revealed that his life was a unique combination of diplomatic service with a personal spirituality.

Through word and sacrament we nurture our congregations to bear witness in their daily lives. Our actions often speak louder than our words. How can we deepen the sense that all of us share a baptismal vocation? Does your congregation find ways to honor the many occupations and various "callings" of its members?

SEPTEMBER 19, 1999

SEVENTEENTH SUNDAY AFTER PENTECOST
PROPER 20

INTRODUCTION

People like to keep score. If our team wins by a point, we rejoice and claim victory. But our relationships begin to dissolve when we count up little mistakes, losing trust and patience.

We learn today that God is not interested in playing counting games. In the reign of God, mercy is freely given to those who come late, as well as to those who have labored for many hours or years. Any claim to partiality, any impulse to keep score, is undercut by the grace of God received in word and sacrament. In the presence of God's mercy, wrote Luther, we are all beggars.

PRAYER OF THE DAY

Lord God, you call us to work in your vineyard and leave no one standing idle. Set us to our tasks in the work of your kingdom, and help us to order our lives by your wisdom; through your Son, Jesus Christ our Lord.

READINGS

Jonah 3:10—4:11

Unlike all other prophetic books, the book of Jonah focuses on the person of the prophet rather than on the prophet's message. The main story begins when Jonah flees God's call to announce destruction of the city of Nineveh, which symbolizes all that is hated by the Israelites. This comic story of a reluctant prophet highlights the very nature of God, the creator of the universe, who "is gracious and merciful . . . and abounding in steadfast love." In the end, every reader must answer the question: should this God not have pity on Nineveh?

Psalm 145:1-8

The Lord is slow to anger and of great kindness. (Ps. 145:8)

Philippians 1:21-30

Paul writes to the Philippians from prison, knowing that he may soon suffer martyrdom for his faith.

Matthew 20:1-16

Jesus tells his disciples a shocking parable about God's gen-

*erosity, which reverses human expectations and offends those
who believe God gives people only what they deserve.*

COLOR   Green

THE PRAYERS

Remembering the church, the world, and all those in
need, let us offer our prayers to God.

A BRIEF SILENCE.

For the church throughout the world, that we may grow
together in your service, and continually invite others to
work with us in your vineyard. Hear us, O God;
your mercy is great.

For church schools and colleges, that you may give wisdom to all who teach and learn. Hear us, O God;
your mercy is great.

For those in charge of world affairs, that they may be
just stewards of the gifts of creation and the labor of
your people. Hear us, O God;
your mercy is great.

For those who are unemployed, and for those who labor
for a living, that all might be able to find work and be
compensated with justice. Hear us, O God;
your mercy is great.

For all who are homebound, hospitalized, or ill (especially . . .), that they may know our compassionate care.
Hear us, O God;
your mercy is great.

For ourselves, that nourished at the Lord's table we may
go forth to serve, not desiring reward, but in thanksgiving for your grace and invitation. Hear us, O God;
your mercy is great.

HERE OTHER INTERCESSIONS MAY BE OFFERED.

For all the holy ones who have died, we give thanks.
Make us faithful stewards of all your gifts until we join
them at the endless feast of joy. Hear us, O God;
your mercy is great.

All these things and whatever else you see that we
need, grant us, O God, for your mercy is everlasting,
and your faithfulness endures from age to age.
Amen

IMAGES FOR PREACHING

Children only four or five years old often imagine what
they are going to be when they grow up. They see
themselves in an exciting or glamorous role—like fire

fighter, movie star, or astronaut. Elders well into their
seventies or eighties recall the years they spent in bank-
ing, nursing, teaching, or carpentry. Whatever age we
are, work is a big part of our identity. It is not surprising, then, that the biblical writers often used images of
work to convey God's truth.

The psalmist extolled God's mighty acts and awesome deeds—the work of God's hands (145:4-6). The
prophet Jonah fled from the work God appointed for
him and sulked when God insisted on showing love for
the wicked Ninevites. Paul wrote to the Philippians that
he did not know whether he preferred living and carrying out "fruitful labor" in Christ's name, or dying and
being with Christ (1:21-22). The gospel writer used a
parable about work and undeserved wages to describe
God's generous love for us.

Former steel company executive William Diehl has
been thinking and writing for years about "ministry in
daily life." Each of us, he explains, is called through baptism to minister in four arenas: family, community,
church, and occupation. (Diehl uses the word *occupation*
rather than *work* because most of us think of "work" as
paid employment.) "Occupation is whatever one primarily does with one's time at any given point in life"
(*Ministry in Daily Life: A Practical Guide for Congregations*,
Bethesda, Md.: The Alban Institute, 1996, p. 13). A
Christian's occupation might be a paid job, the unpaid
job of homemaker and parent, being a student, seeking
a job, or enjoying the many opportunities of retirement.

It makes sense that both four-year-olds and eighty-
year-olds think about work, and that the biblical writers
often refer to work. After all, our work is an important
part about who God created us to be.

WORSHIP MATTERS

"So the last will be first, and the first will be last." How
does your congregation's worship model that God seeks
to break down barriers between status, in groups and
out groups, first and last? Do you have written and
unwritten signs that announce forms of privilege? Perhaps the clothing or the cars that people arrive in to
worship? Does the architecture of your building invite
newcomers to enter, or does it promote a cult of
secrecy?

How are the last first in your community? Do you
have parking spaces reserved for visitors? Do worship

317

leaders commune last as a sign of serving guests first? Do you expect and welcome newcomers publicly? Are children treated with full membership in the community, which their baptism gives them?

LET THE CHILDREN COME

Now that the harvest of gardens and fields is underway, invite members of the congregation to begin to offer fresh produce to local food pantries and soup kitchens. Begin to make plans to develop a congregational garden plot next year that might be used solely for the purpose of feeding the hungry. And look in unexpected places for that plot. Alice Waters, the cookbook author and chef, has had great success developing gardens in the inner city and working with the children of the surrounding neighborhood. With some assistance from adults, the children care for the garden and enjoy eating the harvest.

318

MUSIC FOR WORSHIP

GATHERING

| LBW 389 | Stand up, stand up for Jesus |
| WOV 712 | Listen, God is calling |

PSALM 145

Becker, John. PW, Cycle A.

Haas, David. "I Will Praise Your Name" in PS2.

Haas, David. PCY.

Trapp, Lynn. "Four Psalm Settings." MSM 80-701. Cant/choir, cong, org.

HYMN OF THE DAY

| LBW 405 | Lord of light |
| | ABBOT'S LEIGH |

INSTRUMENTAL RESOURCES

See Proper 6.

ALTERNATE HYMN OF THE DAY

| LBW 297 | Salvation unto us has come |
| WOV 666 | Great God, your love has called us here |

COMMUNION

| LBW 406 | Take my life, that I may be |
| WOV 801 | Thine the amen, thine the praise |

OTHER SUGGESTIONS

| OBS 74 | O sacred River |

SENDING

| LBW 403 | Lord, speak to us, that we may speak |
| WOV 671 | Alleluia, alleluia, give thanks |

ADDITIONAL HYMNS AND SONGS

WOV 734	Softly and tenderly Jesus is calling
H82 541	Come, labor on
NSR 151	May this water keep us aware
TWC 348	We will extol you, ever-blessed Lord

MUSIC FOR THE DAY

CHORAL

Bertalot, John. "I Am the Vine." LOR HRD 287. SATB, org.

Croft, William. "O Give Thanks unto the Lord." CPH 98-1788. SAB, org.

Distler, Hugo. "Salvation unto Us Has Come." CPH 98-1943. SATB.

Hopp, Ray. "Take My Life and Let It Be." SEL 410-331. SATB, org.

Pachelbel, Johann. "On God, and Not on Human Trust." CPH 98-1006. SATB.

Sedio, Mark. "The Thirsty Fields Drink in the Rain." AFP 11-10845. SATB, org.

White, David Ashley. "There's a Wideness in God's Mercy." SEL 420-243. SATB, org.

Wienhorst, Richard. "Let Your Manner of Life." CPH 98-2451. SATB.

CHILDREN'S CHOIRS

Hruby, Dolores. "I Will Bless the Lord at All Times." CGA-452. U, cong, kybd/orff, fc.

KEYBOARD/INSTRUMENTAL

Manz, Paul. "Aria." MSM 10-906. Org.

Mathews, Peter. "Last Song of Summer." MSM 20-960. Vc, org.

Weckmann, Matthias. "Fantasia" in *Freie Orgelwerke*. BRE 8395. Org.

HANDBELL

Folkening, John. "At the Lamb's High Feast We Sing" in *Ten Hymn Accompaniments for Handbells*, set 2. CPH 97-6035. 3 oct.

Larson, Katherine. "Be Thou My Vision." AFP 11-10484. 3-4 oct, fl.

Wagner, Douglas E. "Be Thou My Vision." LOR HB367. 2 oct.

PRAISE ENSEMBLE

Hanson, Handt. "Jesus Be Praised" in *Songs of the First Light*. CCF.

Harris, Ron, and Carol Harris. "In This Very Room." RHP. SATB.

Smith, Michael W., and Deborah D. Smith. "Great Is The Lord" in *Maranatha! Music's Praise Chorus Book*, 2d ed. MAR.

TUESDAY, SEPTEMBER 21
ST. MATTHEW, APOSTLE AND EVANGELIST

Matthew was a tax collector for the Roman government in Capernaum. He is called Levi in the accounts of his call to discipleship, although in the lists of the Twelve he is always called Matthew. Being a tax collector, Matthew was considered a social outcast in his day. Jesus' associations with tax collectors and sinners was considered a scandal to the religious leaders of that time.

This commemoration could lead your worship, social ministry, and evangelism committees to consider whether your congregation is a welcoming place for those considered outcasts in our society. Is your church building and worship bulletin hospitable towards strangers and guests? Do you provide ways to welcome diversity, or does it appear as if the congregation values uniformity?

SATURDAY, SEPTEMBER 25
SERGIUS OF RADONEZH, ABBOT OF HOLY TRINITY, MOSCOW, 1392

Sergius is the most beloved of Russian saints. He renewed monasticism in Russia, and he was known for his peacemaking skills, his kindness to the poor, and his wise, gentle spirit. Sergius turned down being a bishop, preferring the simple life of a monk. He became abbot of Holy Trinity monastery, from which more than 75 monasteries were founded.

The commemoration of Sergius is an opportunity to consider the Russian church. How much do we know of the rich traditions of Russian orthodoxy? What is the role of icons in their worship and spirituality? What do we have in common with Orthodox Christians? Consider these topics in an adult class or forum, or by a visit to an Orthodox liturgy.

319

SEPTEMBER 26, 1999

EIGHTEENTH SUNDAY AFTER PENTECOST
PROPER 21

INTRODUCTION

As we gather today around the table of the word, we become more than a collection of individuals. We have been united to each other in the waters of baptism and welcomed by Christ to his holy supper. While some may be strangers to us, we are invited to recognize the deep communion we share in Christ Jesus. The liturgy does not protect us from others; it teaches us to be a people of hospitality, generous in faith, hope, and love.

PRAYER OF THE DAY

God of love, you know our frailties and failings. Give us your grace to overcome them; keep us from those things that harm us; and guide us in the way of salvation; through your Son, Jesus Christ our Lord.

READINGS

Ezekiel 18:1-4, 25-32

The prophet Ezekiel challenges an old proverb that would see

the exile as punishment for the sins of the exiles' ancestors. Rather, he says, God insists that individuals are responsible for their own sin and their own repentance.

Psalm 25:1-8 (Psalm 25:1-9 [NRSV])

Remember, O Lord, your compassion and love. (Ps. 25:5)

Philippians 2:1-13

Paul quotes from an early Christian hymn to describe the attitude of humble self-sacrifice displayed in Christ Jesus. Although Christians may disagree on many things, he urges them to be of one mind with regard to emulating Christ's self-giving love.

Matthew 21:23-32

Shortly after arriving in Jerusalem, Jesus drives the money-changers out of the temple, heals the sick, and begins teaching there. These activities are challenged by the religious leaders who are supposed to be in charge of the temple.

COLOR   Green

THE PRAYERS

Remembering the church, the world, and all those in need, let us offer our prayers to God.

A BRIEF SILENCE.

For the church, that it may have the mind of Christ, and empty itself for the sake of the world. Hear us, O God; **your mercy is great.**

For civil and political leaders, that they might serve with humility, looking to the interests of others. Hear us, O God; **your mercy is great.**

For those suffering from physical abuse, mental anguish, or broken relationships, that they may know the peace and healing of your presence. Hear us, O God; **your mercy is great.**

For victims of war and violence, and for those living with poverty, anxiety, or illness (especially . . .), that they may know your compassion and love. Hear us, O God; **your mercy is great.**

For our congregation, that we may grow in faith and service, living out our baptismal promises with intentionality and joy. Hear us, O God; **your mercy is great.**

HERE OTHER INTERCESSIONS MAY BE OFFERED.

We give thanks for all the faithful departed who have confessed Jesus as Lord, that we may follow them in the way of righteousness. Hear us, O God; **your mercy is great.**

All these things and whatever else you see that we need, grant us, O God, for your mercy is everlasting, and your faithfulness endures from age to age.
Amen

IMAGES FOR PREACHING

Before gasoline prices began to rise in the early 1970s, families would often take a Sunday afternoon drive in the country. At the beginning of such outings, one geography professor would choose a destination, hand one of his daughters the road map, and say, "OK, now you get us there." If the map reader gave an incorrect instruction and later discovered the family was headed in the wrong direction, it was up to her to get the them back on the right road.

Both Ezekiel and Matthew remind us that God is more concerned about the path a person follows than the path a person points to or talks about but does not follow. We feel judged by texts like these because we believe we have somehow chosen the "right" path. So when we read Ezekiel, we assume we are the righteous—and thus are horrified when the prophet says we are the ones who turn away from righteousness (Ezek. 18:26). When we read Matthew, we first put ourselves in the role of the obedient son, who said, "I go, sir," but did not, and we are aghast when Jesus points out that we are the ones who have not done God's will (Matt. 21:30-31).

The psalmist prayed, "Make me to know your ways, O Lord; teach me your paths" (25:4). Paul described the path the Christian walks as one of compassion, sympathy, harmony, humility, and generosity (Phil. 1:1-3). We learn God's paths from Jesus. Jesus was God but did not presume to be equal with God. Even Jesus humbled himself and took the form of a slave, becoming obedient even to the point of death. It was God who exalted him.

If we depended on our own map-reading abilities, we would always be lost. It is God who puts us on the right path.

WORSHIP MATTERS

"By what authority are you doing these things?" Worship planners might also ask how it is that we do what we do. Do our customs have anything to do with Jesus' commands ("Do this for the remembrance of me." "Go therefore and make disciples of all nations.")? Or do we cherish most those things that are of our own devising and custom?

ELCA congregations that have not yet had opportunity to study *The Use of the Means of Grace* may wish to do so soon. This document is meant both to describe as well as to inform worship practices in our congregations. The principles in that document are shaped by scripture and the Lutheran confessions, as well as having been adopted by the 1997 ELCA Churchwide Assembly. How might this document guide you in determining what is truly central in your congregation's worship life?

LET THE CHILDREN COME

One of the simplest ways for adults to involve children in worship is by acknowledging that they are there. Speak to them, introduce yourself to them, sit with them, and help lead them through the worship service in the book or service folder. In other words, show the same hospitality to children that you might show to visitors in worship. Also be sure to include children in daily prayer and devotion.

MUSIC FOR WORSHIP
GATHERING

LBW 337	Oh, what their joy
LBW 249	God himself is present
WOV 720	In the presence of your people

PSALM 25

Becker, John. PW, Cycle A.

Maeker, Nancy/Don Rotermund. "Sing a New Song" in *Five Psalms/Anthems,* set 2. CPH 97-6041. Speech choir, perc.

Haugen, Marty. "To You, O Lord." GIA G-2653. Cant, cong, opt 2 pt, kybd.

Pelz, Walter. "Show Me Thy Ways." AFP 11-00642. SATB, gtr, ob/fl.

Wellicome, Paul. "Remember Your Mercy, Lord" in PS1.

HYMN OF THE DAY

LBW 179	At the name of Jesus
	KING'S WESTON

VOCAL RESOURCES

Vaughan Williams, Ralph. "At the Name of Jesus." OXF 40-100. SATB.

INSTRUMENTAL RESOURCES

Burkhardt, Michael. "At the Name of Jesus" in *Praise and Thanksgiving, Hymn Improvisations,* set 3. MSM 10-753. Org.

Gramann, Fred. "Fantasy on 'King's Weston.'" HOP 1671. 3-6 oct.

Powell, Robert. "At the Name of Jesus" in *Rejoice Ye Pure in Heart.* AFP 11-10478. Org.

ALTERNATE HYMN OF THE DAY

LBW 230	Lord, keep us steadfast in your Word
WOV 695	O blessed spring

COMMUNION

LBW 492	O Master, let me walk with you
WOV 761	Now we offer

OTHER SUGGESTIONS

Young, Jeremy. "God Has Spoken, Bread Has Broken." AFP 11-10733. SAB, kybd, opt cong.

SENDING

LBW 200	For the bread which you have broken
WOV 723	The Spirit sends us forth to serve

ADDITIONAL HYMNS AND SONGS

LBW 156	Look, the sight is glorious
CEL 568	May the mind of Christ my Savior
H82 358	Christ the victorious
TWC 559	Make room within my heart, O God

MUSIC FOR THE DAY
CHORAL

Bach, J. S. "O Thou Sweetest Source of Gladness." CPH 98-2327. SATB, cont.

Busarow, Donald. "Lord, Keep Us Steadfast in Your Word." CPH 98-2602. 2 pt trbl, fl, org.

Farlee, Robert Buckley. "O Blessed Spring." AFP 11-10544. SATB, ob, opt cong.

Farrant, Richard. "Call to Remembrance, O Lord." HIN HMC-492. SATB.

Frahm, Frederick. "Come, Let Us Join Our Cheerful Songs." CPH 98-3291. SAB, hb, org.

Gallus, J. (Handl)/J. Cozens. "At the Name of Jesus." CPH 98-1051. SATB.

Tye, Christopher (attributed). "Lord, for Thy Tender Mercies Sake" in *Church Anthem Book.* OXF. SATB.

Willan, Healey. "Christ Hath Humbled Himself" in *We Praise Thee.* CPH 97-7564. SA, org.

CHILDREN'S CHOIRS

Handel, G. F./Hal Hopson. "Lord, I Lift My Soul to You." CGA 440. 2 pt mxd, kybd.

Lau, Robert. "Prayer." ALF 4224. SAB, kybd.

Marshall, Jane. "Create in Me, O God." CGA 750. U, kybd.

KEYBOARD/INSTRUMENTAL

Dorian, Mark. "Vesper Hymn" in *Around the World: Six Hymntune Improvisations.* AFP 11-10618. Pno.

Farlee, Robert Buckley. "Rock of Ages" in *Deep Waters: Three Hymns of Faith Arranged for Saxophone or Other Instrument and Organ.* AFP 11-10792. Org, sax/inst.

Johnson, David. "Trumpet Tune in D." AFP 11-805. Org.

HANDBELL

Kinyon, Barbara B. "O Master, Let Me Walk With You." HOP 1573. 2-3 oct.

McChesney, Kevin. "Glorious Things of Thee Are Spoken." LOR HB369. 3-5 oct.

PRAISE ENSEMBLE

Baloche, Paul. "Always" in *Integrity's Hosanna! Music Songsheets.* INT.

Fragar, Russell. "Show Me Your Ways" in *Integrity's Hosanna! Music Songsheets.* INT.

Paris, Twila/Greer. "How Beautiful." WRD BP1440. SATB.

TUESDAY, SEPTEMBER 28
JEHU JONES, THE FIRST AFRICAN AMERICAN LUTHERAN
PASTOR IN NORTH AMERICA, 1852

Jehu Jones was a missionary among urban blacks in the North during the decades before the Civil War. In 1834 he formed St. Paul's Evangelical Lutheran Church in Philadelphia, the first African American Lutheran congregation in the United States. Unable to gain needed financial help from the Ministerium of Pennsylvania, Jones lost the church in 1839, but he remained faithful to missionary work until the end of his life.

Jones is remembered for his faithfulness to the teachings of the Lutheran church, and his missionary calling among African Americans. Is your synod establishing new mission congregations on its territory? Are members of your congregation supporting these endeavors?

WEDNESDAY, SEPTEMBER 29
ST. MICHAEL AND ALL ANGELS

In the book of Revelation, Michael the archangel fights in a cosmic battle against Satan. In the book of Daniel, Michael is portrayed as the heavenly being who leads the faithful dead to God's throne on the day of resurrection.

This day is popular in northern Europe and England, and Michaelmas still marks the beginning of the fall term in some law courts and academic institutions in England.

Angels play an important role in both the Old and New Testaments. Observe St. Michael and All Angels at congregational events today or during the week. Think of biblical stories that include angels, and sing "Ye watchers and ye holy ones" (LBW 175), or a Christmas or Easter hymn that mentions angels.

THURSDAY, SEPTEMBER 30
JEROME, TRANSLATOR, TEACHER, 420

Jerome is known for his translation of the scriptures from Hebrew and Greek into Latin, the common language at that time. The word for his translation, the "Vulgate," comes from the Latin word for the common people. This translation remained the standard Latin version for fifteen centuries.

What translation of the Bible is used in your worship service? The New Revised Standard Version is probably the most common translation used in mainline churches today. Do you give your parishioners help in selecting a translation for themselves? What is the difference between a translation and a paraphrase? Why is there a need for new translations of the scriptures?

OCTOBER 3, 1999
NINETEENTH SUNDAY AFTER PENTECOST
PROPER 22

INTRODUCTION

In today's gospel reading, Jesus tells a parable of the vineyard, an image of Israel, the prophets' mission, and Christ's death. For Christians, the vineyard also speaks of God's love poured out in the blood of Christ, given to us for the forgiveness of sin. Grafted onto Christ the vine at baptism, we are nourished with his blood and drawn to each other by his love.

PRAYER OF THE DAY

Our Lord Jesus, you have endured the doubts and foolish questions of every generation. Forgive us for trying to be judge over you, and grant us the confident faith to acknowledge you as Lord.

READINGS

Isaiah 5:1-7

The prophet sings a sad, parable-like love song about the relationship between God and Israel. Israel is likened to a promising vineyard that now must be destroyed. Despite God's loving care, Israel has brought forth "wild grapes" of injustice and distress where fine grapes of justice and righteousness were expected. Having failed to uphold the covenant, Israel will bear the Lord's judgment.

Psalm 80:7-14 (Psalm 80:7-15 [NRSV])

Look down from heaven, O God; behold and tend this vine. (Ps. 80:14)

Philippians 3:4b-14

Paul has warned the Philippians about Christian leaders who may have impressive credentials but do not witness to the gospel of Christ. Now he offers his own list of credentials, only to reject them all in favor of what he considers truly significant.

Matthew 21:33-46

Jesus tells a parable to the religious leaders who are plotting his death, revealing that their plans will ironically bring about the fulfillment of scripture.

COLOR   Green

THE PRAYERS

Remembering the church, the world, and all those in need, let us offer our prayers to God.

A BRIEF SILENCE.

For the church, that as your vineyard we might be one at the table of the Lord, and produce the fruits of justice, peace, and love. Hear us, O God;

your mercy is great.

For the leaders of our nations, state, and city, that they may be good stewards of the offices entrusted to them. Hear us, O God;

your mercy is great.

For those who live without adequate housing, food, or clothing, that you stir us to share of our abundance with them. Hear us, O God;

your mercy is great.

For those who suffer in mind, body, or spirit (especially . . .), that you give them strength to press on toward what lies ahead. Hear us, O God;

your mercy is great.

For our congregation, that we will reach out to all who are estranged from the church, or who are searching for a spiritual home. Hear us, O God;

your mercy is great.

HERE OTHER INTERCESSIONS MAY BE OFFERED.

We give thanks for all the faithful departed who shared Christ's sufferings and now dwell in the victory of his resurrection. Hear us, O God;

your mercy is great.

All these things and whatever else you see that we need, grant us, O God, for your mercy is everlasting, and your faithfulness endures from age to age.

Amen

IMAGES FOR PREACHING

The psalmist, Isaiah, and Jesus all refer to Israel as a vine or vineyard. We may be so accustomed to this image that we just plunge into the texts, curious to learn what is going to happen—whether the vine will bear rich fruit; grow sickly, wither, and die; or be hacked down and destroyed.

It is interesting to note, however, that throughout history, the vine has been an ambivalent symbol. Grapes are a symbol of "fertility (because of their character as a fruit) and sacrifice (because they give wine—particularly when the wine is the colour of blood)" (J. E. Cirlot, *A Dictionary of Symbols,* 2d ed., New York: Barnes & Noble Books, 1971, p. 121). The vine often carries a similar dual meaning in literature.

This ambivalence is seen, perhaps, in the vines that yield wild grapes (Isa. 4:2, 4), and in the decision made by the owner of the vineyard to lease the vineyard to new tenants (Matt. 21:41). All is not well and good with the vines—nor with Israel and God, or with us and God.

Worshipers might wonder where the gospel hides in the law-laden texts we hear as we approach the end of the season after Pentecost. Where is the good news in the destruction of the vineyard foretold by Isaiah? Is there any grace in Jesus' words: "[The owner of the vineyard] will put those wretches to a miserable death, and lease the vineyard to other tenants who will give him the produce at harvest time" (v. 41)?

The psalmist prays, "Turn again, O God of hosts; . . . have regard for this vine, the stock that your right hand planted" (80:14-15). The good news in this ambivalent symbol is God's desire that the vine be fruitful, God's determination to find faithful tenants. This fruitfulness and faithfulness are indeed ours, through faith in Christ (Phil. 3:9).

323

WORSHIP MATTERS

LBW and *WOV* designate primary worship leaders as "presiding" and "assisting" ministers. Just as a democratic government or institution has public servants who are designated to perform leadership tasks, so the liturgical assembly employs people who will serve its needs. We should note that such leadership is *for* the community, decidedly not against it or in spite of it.

Leadership in the liturgical assembly is precisely so that the assembly may be enabled to do its work (not that leaders usurp or displace the work of the assembly). This joint effort means that many people are needed in order for the liturgical assembly to work well: lectors, musicians, ministers of hospitality, altar guild members, communion ministers, and a whole host of other "voices" (not the least of which is the voice of the assembly itself). The presiding minister functions not unlike someone presiding over any democratic body—calling it together to do its tasks, recognizing other voices, and helping to keep the meeting focused on its reason for being (here keeping the assembly focused on Christ). Such leadership requires strength, humility, and grace; appropriate qualities for any leader, but absolutely essential in the liturgical assembly.

LET THE CHILDREN COME

How do children learn to attend to the silences in worship? Some of it is through modeling offered by the presiding minister, other worship leaders, and other adults in the assembly. The reality is that for children, as for adults, silence can be difficult. Helping them attend to silence is a long-term goal with frustration along the way. Find ways to help children engage in quiet at both home and church. Show how this silence is different from "being quiet," a phrase that has connotations of punishment. Contrast "making noise" with "making silence." Give reasons for the silence of worship: to pray, to listen, to be present with what is happening around them.

MUSIC FOR WORSHIP

GATHERING

LBW 245	All people that on earth do dwell
WOV 747	Christ is made the sure foundation (or LBW 367)

PSALM 80

Becker, John. PW, Cycle A.

DATH 39   Behold and Tend This Vine

Hughes, Howard/Joseph Gelineau. TP.

HYMN OF THE DAY

LBW 378	Amid the world's bleak wilderness	GRANTON

VOCAL RESOURCES

Hillert, Richard. "Amid the World's Bleak Wilderness." AFP 11-1997. SATB, org.

INSTRUMENTAL RESOURCES

Heschke, Richard. "Granton" in *22 Hymn Settings*. CPH 97-6063. Org.

ALTERNATE HYMN OF THE DAY

LBW 421	Lord Christ, when first you came to earth
WOV 668	There in God's garden

COMMUNION

LBW 482	When I survey the wondrous cross
WOV 660	I want Jesus to walk with me

OTHER SUGGESTIONS

Young, Jeremy. "Taste and See." APF 11-10895. U, kybd, opt cong.

SENDING

LBW 383	Rise up, O saints of God!
WOV 733	Our Father, we have wandered

ADDITIONAL HYMNS AND SONGS

LBW 293/4	My hope is built on nothing less
NCH 387	O Christ, the great foundation
NCH 586	Come to tend God's garden
PH 419	How clear is our vocation, Lord
W3 574	A single unmatched stone

MUSIC FOR THE DAY

CHORAL

Ashdown, Franklin D. "Jesus, the Very Thought of You." AFP 11-10886. SATB, org, opt C inst.

Feiten, Dan. "Seed Scattered and Sown." OCP 9920CC. SATB, pno, gtr, fl.

Lang, C. S. "Jesu, the Very Thought of Thee." OXF E95. 2 pt, org.

Neswick, Bruce. "O Taste and See." AFP 11-10592. SATB.

Scott, K. Lee. "A Vineyard Grows." MSM 50-9010. SATB, org. MSM 50-9106. SAB, org.

324

CHILDREN'S CHOIRS

Barnard, Mark. "Sing Alleluia to Our King." UNI 10/1399U. 2 pt,
opt cong, kybd.

Cox, Joe. "Psalm 80:7-14" in *Psalms For the People of God.*
SMP 45/1037S. Cant, choir, cong, kybd.

KEYBOARD/INSTRUMENTAL

Dupré, Marcel. "How Fair and How Pleasant Art Thou" in *Fifteen
Pieces for Organ,* Op. 18. HWG GB 188. Org.

Hassell, Michael. "De Colores" in *Folkways.* AFP 11-10829. Pno, inst.

Porter, Rachel Trelstad. "It Is Well" in *Day By Day: Hymn Arrangements
for Piano.* AFP 11-10772. Pno.

HANDBELL

Dobrinski, Cynthia. "When I Survey the Wondrous Cross."
3 oct HOP 1226; 3-5 oct 1742.

Schalk, Carl/John Behnke. "Thine the Amen, Thine the Praise."
CPH 97-6383. 3-5 oct.

PRAISE ENSEMBLE

Batstone, Bill, and Bob Somma. "I Come To The Cross." in *Worship
Leader Magazine's Song DISCovery,* vol 1.

Dorsey, Thomas A./Jack Schrader. "Precious Lord." HOP GC 968.
SATB.

Hanson, Handt, and Paul Murakami. "May You Run and Not Be
Weary" in *Spirit Calls, Rejoice!* CCF.

MONDAY, OCTOBER 4
FRANCIS OF ASSISI, RENEWER OF THE CHURCH, 1226
THEODORE FLIEDNER, RENEWER OF SOCIETY, 1864

Francis left behind a life of pleasure and riches, and
embraced a way of life marked by simplicity, poverty,
and care for the poor and needy. He associated with
lepers, and acted as a peacemaker between towns at
war. Though Francis embraced a rigid asceticism that
devalued earthly possessions, he had a spirit of gladness
and gratitude for all God's creation. The commemoration of Francis has been a traditional time to bless pets
and animals, as Francis called the animals his brothers
and sisters.

Theodore Fliedner revived the order of deaconesses, and founded a motherhouse in Kaiserswerth,
Germany. His work and his writing encouraged women
to care for the sick, the poor, and the imprisoned.
Inspired by his work Lutherans all over the world commissioned deaconesses to serve in parishes, schools, hospitals, or prisons.

Both Francis and Fliedner call the church to take

its work seriously among the most vulnerable of our
society. What are the ways your parish, synod, or
denomination continue to embody the same concerns
for the poor and needy? Do you remember these agencies and ministries by name in the prayers at your Sunday eucharist?

WEDNESDAY, OCTOBER 6
WILLIAM TYNDALE, TRANSLATOR, MARTYR, 1536

Tyndale is remembered for his English translation of the
Bible. The style of his translation influenced English
versions of the Bible, such as the Authorized Version
and the Revised Standard Version, for four centuries.

The reading of the scriptures is at the heart of the
liturgy of the word. Many congregations value Bible
study as part of their adult education program. Has your
parish considered offering a study of the lessons for the
upcoming Sunday? It could take place during the week,
or during the Sunday morning educational hour. Such
an offering not only deepens the participant's knowledge and experience of scripture, but also prepares
them for the coming Sunday liturgy. Several church
publishers offer studies based on the lectionary, including a new set of educational resources published by
Augsburg Fortress in 1999 that coordinates with the
Revised Common Lectionary.

THURSDAY, OCTOBER 7
HENRY MELCHIOR MULHENBERG,
MISSIONARY TO AMERICA, 1787

Mulhenberg was prominent in setting the course for
Lutheranism in this country. He helped Lutherans make
the transition from the state churches of Europe to the
independent churches of America. Among other things,
he established the first Lutheran synod in America, and
developed an American Lutheran liturgy. His liturgical
principles became the basis for the *Common Service* of
1888 used in many North American service books for a
majority of this century. *LBW* was an attempt to produce
a common service book for Lutherans in North America.

Do you remember some of the Lutheran mergers
during the past forty years? Do you believe our
Lutheran presence and witness is stronger because we
are no longer divided along ethnic lines?

OCTOBER 10, 1999

INTRODUCTION

Three sets of meals cluster around the readings today: the meals of Jesus; the church's celebration of the holy supper; and the wedding feast of heaven. In each meal, the invitation is given to all who hunger for God's love: Come to the banquet.

Come and feast on the bread of heaven; come and drink God's mercy; come and be strengthened for service to the needy. As Augustine once said to his congregation, Become the bread that you hold in your hand. Come to the holy supper and learn what it means to be a Christian.

PRAYER OF THE DAY

Almighty God, source of every blessing, your generous goodness comes to us anew every day. By the work of your Spirit lead us to acknowledge your goodness, give thanks for your benefits, and serve you in willing obedience; through your Son, Jesus Christ our Lord.

READINGS

Isaiah 25:1-9

Today's reading begins with a hymn of thanksgiving and concludes with the promise of the banquet celebrating the day in which the Lord's sovereignty is fully established. This banquet symbolizes not only the establishment of God's reign on earth, it also symbolizes the joy, companionship, and prosperity characteristic of God's reign.

Psalm 23

You spread a table before me, and my cup is running over. (Ps. 23:5)

Philippians 4:1-9

Paul's letter to the Philippians is written from prison at a time when the apostle faced possible martyrdom. Nevertheless, his words reveal concern for the needs of others and convey an attitude of joy, hope, gratitude, and peace.

Matthew 22:1-14

Jesus tells a parable to the religious leaders of his day, indicating that even though God's kingdom is a great feast open to all, its coming will prove disastrous for some.

COLOR Green

THE PRAYERS

Remembering the church, the world, and all those in need, let us offer our prayers to God.

A BRIEF SILENCE.

That the church will invite and welcome all people to your joyful feast of grace. Hear us, O God;
your mercy is great.

That the leaders of nations work to provide all people a just share of the earth's harvest. Hear us, O God;
your mercy is great.

That all who are ill or in any kind of need (especially . . .) may know your peace, which surpasses all understanding. Hear us, O God;
your mercy is great.

That all who mourn may know the consolation of your love and care. Hear us, O God;
your mercy is great.

That through art and music we may be given a vision of your grace and beauty. Hear us, O God;
your mercy is great.

That our participation in the eucharistic feast lead us to share your gifts with all in hunger or need. Hear us, O God;
your mercy is great.

HERE OTHER INTERCESSIONS MAY BE OFFERED.

That we follow the blessed saints in lives of faith and service until we join them at the marriage banquet in heaven. Hear us, O God;
your mercy is great.

All these things and whatever else you see that we need, grant us, O God, for your mercy is everlasting, and your faithfulness endures from age to age.
Amen

IMAGES FOR PREACHING

Three of the four readings for today refer to a banquet or feast, each hosted by God. Where there are banquets, there are guests. In Isaiah and Psalm 23, there is no doubt that the banquet is lavish and joyous, and that the guests

326

are valued. Picture yourself sitting down to a "feast of rich food, a feast of well-aged wines" (Isa. 25:6). Certainly such a fine spread would make you feel important, or at least very fortunate.

The banquet in Matthew's parables is puzzling, however. The guests first invited to the banquet kill the king's servants, and the king in turn destroys them. The guests on the B-list are much better behaved; at least they do not kill the king's servants. But one unfortunate guest is not wearing a proper wedding robe, and the king, making no allowances for the fact that this guest was no doubt surprised to find himself at a wedding banquet, orders the guest thrown into outer darkness. What do we make of this guest's treatment?

In Philippians, Paul tells us a properly attired person of faith wears "whatever is true, . . . honorable, . . . just, . . . pure, . . . pleasing, . . . commendable, . . . excellence and . . . anything worthy of praise" (4:8). And Paul also advises us, "Keep on doing the things that you have learned . . ., and the God of peace will be with you" (v. 9).

WORSHIP MATTERS

Who has been invited to the wedding banquet? Who is welcome to the table? "Customs vary on the age and circumstances for admission to the Lord's Supper. The age for communing children continues to be discussed and reviewed in our congregataions" (*The Use of the Means of Grace*, background 37b). "Admission to the Sacrament is by invitation of the Lord, presented through the Church to those who are baptized," says Principle 37 of the ELCA's *The Use of the Means of Grace*. Invite your worship committee to lead conversations in your congregation about the church's ongoing discussion in the relationship between baptism and communion.

Previous churchwide statements about communion precluded the communing of infants. The current statement enlarges the decision making about the age of communion to the local level. This decision is both a freedom as well as a greater responsibility for congregations.

LET THE CHILDREN COME

What are the hymns that come to mind at various times in your life? What are the hymns and songs that naturally come to mind when you are lonely, afraid, or overjoyed? Perhaps some of them are the great hymns of

faith that have been a part of worshiping assemblies for generations. Can you recall when you learned those hymns and songs? As children learn music in Sunday school and at other times, do not neglect these more traditional songs. Those hymns will surely find a home among future generations and give them words that resonate throughout their lives.

MUSIC FOR WORSHIP

GATHERING

LBW 214	Come, let us eat
WOV 701	What feast of love

PSALM 23

See the Fourth Sunday in Lent.

HYMN OF THE DAY

WOV 789	Now the feast and celebration
	NOW THE FEAST

ALTERNATE HYMN OF THE DAY

LBW 210	At the Lamb's high feast we sing
LBW 203	Now we join in celebration

COMMUNION

LBW 496	Around you, O Lord Jesus
WOV 684	Spirit, Spirit of gentleness

SENDING

LBW 514	O Savior, precious Savior
LBW 552	In thee is gladness
WOV 801	Thine the amen, thine the praise

ADDITIONAL HYMNS AND SONGS

WOV 708	Grains of wheat
ASF 59	The peace of mind that Christ can bring
NCH 332	As we gather at your table
NSR 75	Rejoice in Christ Jesus

MUSIC FOR THE DAY

CHORAL

Barber, Todd. "What Feast of Love/What Child Is This?" AFP 11-10674. SATB, pno, fl.

Hassell, Michael. "This Is the Feast of Victory." AFP 11-10677. SATB, pno, opt cong.

Horn, Richard. "The Peace of God." MSM 50-8904. SATB, org.

327

Kindermann, Johann E. "Dear Christians, Praise God Evermore." CPH 98-1503. U, 2 vln, org.

Pelz, Walter L. "Psalm 23." CPH 98-2676. SATB, fl, org.

Purcell, Henry. "Rejoice in the Lord Always." CPH 97-6344. SATB, solo ATB, org. CPH 97-4472. Str, cont.

Rutter, John. "The Peace of God." OXF E157. SATB, org.

Schack, David. "See What Love." MSM 50-9037. SATB.

Weaver, John. "The Joyful Feast." MSM 50-4011. SATB, org.

Wienhorst, Richard. "We Have Waited for the Lord" in *Three Verse Settings,* set II. CPH 98-2441. SATB, hb/kybd.

Willan, Healey. "Rejoice in the Lord Always" in *We Praise Thee II.* CPH 97-7610. SA, org.

CHILDREN'S CHOIRS

Bedford, Michael. "Now Join We to Praise the Creator." CGA 393. U/2 pt, kybd, opt hb.

Page, Sue Ellen. "The Lord Is Like a Shepherd." HIN HMC-432. U, kybd, opt alto rec/fl.

Pote, Allen. "Praise, Rejoice, and Sing." CGA 392. U/2 pt, opt 2 fl, kybd.

KEYBOARD/INSTRUMENTAL

Organ, Anne Krentz. "Thine" in *Reflections on Hymn Tunes for Holy Communion.* AFP 11-10621. Pno.

Vivaldi, Antonio/S. Drummond Wolff. "Autumn" in *Music from the Four Seasons.* MSM 10-934. Org.

HANDBELL

Folkening, John. "O God, Our Help in Ages Past" in *Ten Hymn Accompaniments for Handbells,* set 3. CPH 97-6058. 3 oct.

Moklebust, Cathy. "Come, Let Us Eat." CGA CGB152. 3-5 oct, perc.

Wagner, Douglas E. "Brother James' Air." SMP S-HB25. 3 oct.

PRAISE ENSEMBLE

Dorsey, Thomas A./Mac Huff. "There'll Be Peace in the Valley for Me." HAL. SATB. 2 tpt, 2 tbn, synth, gtr, DB, perc.

Keaggy, Cheri. "His Banner over Me" in *Worship Leader Magazine's Song DISCovery,* vol 2.

Medema, Ken/Gail Scott. "Bound for Greater Things." GS. SATB.

OCTOBER 11, 1999

DAY OF THANKSGIVING (CANADA)

INTRODUCTION

While North Americans celebrate one day of thanksgiving each year, Christians gather frequently to celebrate a thanksgiving meal at the table of Christ. In the eucharist, the church receives the body and blood of Christ, the food and drink of the promised land. His abundant grace is the reason for our thanksgiving. Indeed, when we gather at the holy supper, there is always enough for everyone. No one is turned away.

At the same time, many people in our rich country go without food, shelter, and clothing. Here, in the eucharist with enough for everyone, we find the source of our service in the world to those who have little or nothing. As Christ has blessed us with the riches of his life, so we are called to give ourselves freely to all in need.

PRAYER OF THE DAY

Almighty God our Father, your generous goodness comes to us new every day. By the work of your Spirit lead us to acknowledge your goodness, give thanks for your benefits, and serve you in willing obedience; through your Son, Jesus Christ our Lord.

READINGS

Deuteronomy 8:7-18

Giving thanks begins with remembering. Even when God's people are well settled in the land, they are to remember the mighty deeds by which God brought them on their pilgrimage to a place of plenty.

Psalm 65

You crown the year with your goodness, and your paths overflow with plenty. (Ps. 65:12)

2 Corinthians 9:6-15

When an earthquake left many people in Jerusalem homeless and destitute, Paul was placed in charge of collecting an offering on their behalf. Here, Paul encourages the Corinthians to express their thanksgiving to God by donating to this collection.

Luke 17:11-19

A Samaritan leper becomes a model for thanksgiving. He does not take for granted the kindness shown to him but takes time to thank Jesus and to glorify God.

COLOR   White

THE PRAYERS

Filled with gratitude for all God's blessings, let us remember our nation, the church, and all those in need.
A BRIEF SILENCE.

Bless our nation with freedom, justice, and equality for all its people. Lord, in your mercy,
hear our prayer.

Nourish the church at the eucharistic table, and let it be a sign of thanksgiving and hope in the world. Lord, in your mercy,
hear our prayer.

Make us generous in sharing the abundance of your blessings with all who are poor, hungry, or in need. Lord, in your mercy,
hear our prayer.

Draw near to all who suffer this day (especially . . .) and fill them with the bounty of your grace and love. Lord, in your mercy,
hear our prayer.

Teach us to treasure your blessings, and open our eyes to your presence in the world. Lord, in your mercy,
hear our prayer.

HERE OTHER INTERCESSIONS MAY BE OFFERED.

Raise us, with all your saints, to the harvest of everlasting life where we will sing the endless song of thanksgiving and joy. Lord, in your mercy,
hear our prayer.

Crown the year with your goodness, O God, that our lives may overflow with thanksgiving, through Jesus Christ our Lord.
Amen

IMAGES FOR PREACHING

The stewardship committee sat around a table in the church's lounge, their brows furrowed. They had just finished reviewing last year's stewardship emphasis, and committee members were feeling dissatisfied. Venita sighed: "Every time we talked about stewardship or planned any educational activities this year, I had the feeling people were just putting up with us, hoping we'd get it over with soon. I wish I could say this con-

gregation was transformed by our work, but if it was, I can't see the change."

Carl nodded in agreement. "I see things the same way, Venita. I wish I could put my finger on what's holding folks back."

How many times is a variation of this conversation repeated in churches each year? Probably dozens. And what *is* the key that will open people's hearts? Perhaps the conviction that God has been unbelievably generous to us.

Humankind is not naturally generous, but it is the very nature of God to be generous, just as it is the nature of God to love and to demand justice. Read the Deuteronomist's list of God's blessings: good land; flowing streams and springs; wheat and barley, vines and fig trees and pomegranates, olive trees and honey; iron and copper (Deut. 8:7-9). Hear the words of Psalm 65, which praises God for awesome deeds of deliverance and the wonders and bounty of creation. Remember the words of Paul: "God is able to provide you with every blessing in abundance" (2 Cor. 9:8a). And take to heart the witness of the leper who was made clean, who threw himself at Jesus' feet and thanked him for healing (Luke 17:16).

"Take care that you do not forget the Lord your God," the Deuteronomist says (Deut. 8:11). Take care that you do not forget: Our God is a generous God!

WORSHIP MATTERS

From the very earliest days of the church, and following the Jewish customs out of which the church grew, the members of the church have offered a prayer of thanksgiving as the bread and wine of Holy Communion are set apart to be for us the body and blood of Christ. Whether simple or elaborate, these prayers recount before God the history of God's saving work on earth. In these prayers the glories of creation are recounted, the fall into sin is recalled, God's gracious activity through Israel and the prophets are announced, and most importantly of all, God's love for the world in the life, death, and resurrection of Jesus is proclaimed. At the heart of the prayers in the eucharist are the words spoken by Jesus on the night before he died, and the prayer for God's Holy Spirit to be active in the midst of the people. This sacrifice of praise and thanksgiving, which for Luther was at the very heart of the Lord's

Supper, sets the stage for our own lives of thanksgiving lived in the world. The prayer calls to mind God's acts among us, and especially the gifts of forgiveness, life, and salvation offered through this meal. By the end of the eucharistic prayer, all creation is summoned to give thanks to God for the mighty deeds of our salvation.

LET THE CHILDREN COME

Help children to learn the basic postures for worship—kneeling, standing, sitting, head bowed, hands folded—in order to "know" what worship means. As you show them the basic postures, ask them how these postures make them feel. When do these same postures happen outside of worship? Listen carefully to the connections they make and offer links between their understandings and the sense of these postures in the context of worship.

MUSIC FOR WORSHIP

GATHERING

LBW 241	We praise you, O God
LBW 412	Sing to the Lord of harvest

PSALM 65

Guimont, Michel. "The Seed That Falls on Good Ground" in RS.

Haas, David. PCY, vol. 8.

Organ, Anne Krentz. PW, Cycle A.

PH 200　To bless the earth, God sends us

Ridge, M.D. "The Seed That Falls on Good Ground." OCP 9460. SAB, cant, cong, desc, kybd, gtr, solo inst.

HYMN OF THE DAY

LBW 533/4　Now thank we all our God
　　　　　　Nun danket alle Gott

VOCAL RESOURCES

Bach, J. S./John B. Haberlen. "Now Thank We All Our God." KJO 5975. Kybd, 2 tpt, timp.

INSTRUMENTAL RESOURCES

Bach, J. S./ed. Michael Burkhardt. "Now Thank We All Our God" in *Music for a Celebration*, set 2. MSM 10-853. Org, opt inst.

Cherwien, David. "Postlude on 'Now Thank We'" in *Postludes on Well Known Hymns*. AFP 11-10795. Org.

Hovland, Egil. "Nun danket alle Gott" in *A New Liturgical Year*. AFP 11-10810. Org.

Karg-Elert, Sigfrid. "Now Thank We All Our God." HWG. Org.

Wagner, Douglas E. "Nun danket" in *Hymn Descants for Handbells*, set 4. BEC HB12. 3 oct.

ALTERNATE HYMN OF THE DAY

LBW 557	Let all things now living
WOV 771	Great is thy faithfulness

COMMUNION

LBW 407	Come, you thankful people, come
LBW 532	How Great Thou Art
WOV 767	All things bright and beautiful

SENDING

LBW 563	For the fruit of all creation (WOV 760)
LBW 527	All creatures of our God and King

ADDITIONAL HYMNS AND SONGS

LBW 409	Praise and thanksgiving
WOV 790	Praise to you, O God of mercy
TWC 373	Praise God for the harvest
DATH 99	Living thanksgiving

MUSIC FOR THE DAY

CHORAL

Anderson, Ronald. "All Good Gifts." AMSI 415. 2 pt, kybd.

Bach, J. S. "Now Thank We All Our God." CPH 98-2102. SATB, 2 tpt, timp, cont.

Bertalot, John. "Let Us with a Gladsome Mind." AFP 11-10754. SAB, org, opt 2 tpt.

Christiansen, F. Melius. "Psalm 50" (Offer unto God) in *The Augsburg Choirbook*. AFP 11-10817. SATB, div.

Ferguson, John. "A Song of Thanksgiving." AFP 11-10505. SATB, org.

Greene, Maurice. "Thou Visitest the Earth." NOV MT 131. SATB, T or B solo, org.

Hobby, Robert. "Offertory for Day of Thanksgiving." MSM 80-600. 2 pt, org.

How, Martin. "Praise, O Praise" in *The New Church Anthem Book*. OXF 0-19-353109-7. 2 pt, org.

Mathias, William. "Praise Is Due to You, O God in Zion." OXF 386. SATB, org.

Pachelbel, Johann. "Now Thank We All Our God." CPH 98-1944. SATB, cont.

Young, Jeremy. "Praise God with the Trumpet" (Psalm 150). AFP 11-10893. 2 pt, kybd, opt brass, cong.

CHILDREN'S CHOIRS

Boyce, William, Jane McFadden, and Janet Linker. "Psalm of Joy." CGA 760. U, opt 2 pt, kybd, opt hb.

Catherwood, David. "Praise The Lord Of Harvest." ALF 11417. U/2 pt, kybd, opt cong.

Dengler, Lee. "Give Thanks and Praise." CGA 727. U/2 pt, kybd, opt perc.

DeLong, Richard. "For the Beauty of the Earth." ECS 4797. U, kybd.

KEYBOARD/INSTRUMENTAL

Callahan, Charles. "Thanksgiving Music for Manuals." MSM 10-601. Org/kybd.

Travis, Al. "Rejoice, Ye Pure in Heart (Toccata)." MSM 10-705. Org.

HANDBELL

Dobrinski, Cynthia. "How Great Thou Art." HOP 1350. 3-5 oct.

McChesney, Kevin. "All Things Bright and Beautiful." AFP 11-10687. 3-5 oct.

McFadden, Jane. "Morning Has Broken." AFP 11-10552. 3-5 oct, kybd/2 hb choirs.

Moklebust, Cathy. "Let All Things Now Living." CGA CGB170. 3-5 oct.

Rogers, Sharon E. "Now Thankful People, Come." AFP 11-10804. 2-3 oct.

PRAISE ENSEMBLE

Hanson, Handt. "Thank You for The Gift" in *Spirit Calls, Rejoice!* CCF.

Sandquist, Ted. "Your Steadfast Love" in *Integrity's Hosanna! Come and Worship Songbook.* INT.

Ylvisaker, John. "O Lord My God" in *Songs for a New Creation.* NGP.

MONDAY, OCTOBER 11
COLUMBUS DAY OBSERVED (USA)

FRIDAY, OCTOBER 15
TERESA OF JESUS (SAME AS THERESA OF AVILA, RENEWER OF THE CHURCH, 1582)

See December 14 for commemoration along with John of the Cross.

331

OCTOBER 17, 1999

TWENTY-FIRST SUNDAY AFTER PENTECOST
PROPER 24

INTRODUCTION

In today's gospel reading, Jesus' words are more than a clever response to a trap set by his opponents. Give the tax that is due to the ruler, he says, but offer to God what is God's: the very life given you by the Creator.

These words of Jesus remind us that no earthly authority can claim the church's ultimate allegiance to God; its life comes from God so that it might serve the world in the labor of love.

PRAYER OF THE DAY

Almighty and everlasting God, in Christ you have revealed your glory among the nations. Preserve the works of your mercy, that your Church throughout the world may persevere with steadfast faith in the confession of your name; through your Son, Jesus Christ our Lord.

READINGS

Isaiah 45:1-7

The prophet announces a radical vision in today's reading.

Late in the period of exile in Babylon, the Persian king Cyrus has taken power in the East and threatens the great Babylonian empire. Seeing this, the prophet announces that God is using Cyrus to accomplish God's purpose of freeing the exiles. Amazingly, God calls Cyrus "his anointed" (a translation of "messiah"), a title earlier reserved solely for Davidic kings.

Psalm 96:1-9 [10-13]

Ascribe to the Lord honor and power. (Ps. 96:7)

1 Thessalonians 1:1-10

Paul's first letter to the Thessalonians is probably the earliest of any of his writings. He opens with a prayer of thanksgiving for the witness these Christians have provided for others to whom he ministers.

Matthew 22:15-22

After Jesus comes to Jerusalem and begins teaching in the temple, the religious leaders try to trap him with trick questions. The first of these questions tries to force him to make an arbitrary choice between devotion to religion or politics.

COLOR Green

THE PRAYERS

Remembering the church, the world, and all those in need, let us offer our prayers to God.

A BRIEF SILENCE.

That bishops, pastors, and other ministers may faithfully proclaim the message of the gospel. Hear us, O God;
your mercy is great.

That all who hold political office may seek the welfare of the most vulnerable members of society. Hear us, O God;
your mercy is great.

That we honor the earth and be faithful stewards of its resources. Hear us, O God;
your mercy is great.

That all who are hospitalized or ill (especially . . .) may be steadfast in hope. Hear us, O God;
your mercy is great.

That you give us faith to use wisely the time, talents, and money entrusted to us. Hear us, O God;
your mercy is great.

HERE OTHER INTERCESSIONS MAY BE OFFERED.

We give thanks for Ignatius and all the saints who revealed your generosity and grace, that we may offer our lives in response to your never-ending love for us. Hear us, O God;
your mercy is great.

All these things and whatever else you see that we need, grant us, O God, for your mercy is everlasting, and your faithfulness endures from age to age.
Amen

IMAGES FOR PREACHING

In the United States, it is not unusual to find the altar in a church flanked by matching flags—the Stars and Stripes on one side, and the so-called Christian flag on the other. Nor is it unusual to read a newspaper account of a court case waged to prevent officials of a small town from erecting a life-size crèche on the courthouse lawn. For some Americans, a "good Christian" is a patriot. Still others believe the Christian's duty is to call civic leaders to the highest moral and ethical standards.

We see in this mix of ideas and behaviors considerable disagreement about the appropriate relationship between church and state. And, indeed, today's readings and the church's history do not provide an entirely uni-form picture of the relationship among God, God's people, and the state.

In the first reading, Isaiah refers to Cyrus as the Lord's "anointed." Cyrus is the only non-Israelite referred to in the Old Testament as "messiah." God affirms, "I call you by your name, . . . though you do not know me" (45:4).

The gospel reading is the most familiar of texts dealing with church-state relations. Jesus does not specifically identify the emperor as God's servant, but he seems at least to promote peaceful coexistence between the emperor and God.

But today is the commemoration of Ignatius, Bishop of Antioch, who was martyred in about 115 during the reign of the emperor Trajan. It would be hard to argue that Trajan was God's chosen servant, or that the emperor and God's people should somehow have peacefully lived together.

God did not confine Cyrus to his own sphere, and the martyrdom of Ignatius warns us that sometimes God, God's people, and the state will be in outright conflict. In those contexts, what do Jesus' words to the Pharisees tell us about how we are to regard the state?

WORSHIP MATTERS

"Render to the emperor . . . ." How shall the church participate in civic observances? Clergy are often called upon to bring an invocation or benediction upon a community gathering. At other times, civic organizations request to bring their celebrations into the church's liturgy. Has your congregation ever wrestled with the various ways that are appropriate for religious and civic functions to be intertwined?

Most people of faith want their government and other public institutions to be responsive to religious and moral teachings. The key matter is *how* they are to be responsive. Witnessing to our faith in the public arena, while at the same time respecting the diverse religious convictions that people have (even *within* the Christian community) is not an easy thing to do. It is a creative tension—no less so for us than it was in Jesus' day.

LET THE CHILDREN COME

The regular Sunday parish schedule often involves compromise and balance between the hours of worship and Sunday school. Rather than seeing the limited hours on

Sunday morning as the stage for competing claims, how can worship and education be linked? If worship and Sunday school must be held at the same time, could Sunday school be thought of as an age-appropriate liturgy of the word? Children could begin worship with their parents, but following the prayer of the day they might be dismissed, with leaders of the children's word liturgy leading the way. The congregation could come together again in the worship space during the offertory procession, in time for Holy Communion.

MUSIC FOR WORSHIP

GATHERING

LBW 437	Not alone for mighty empire
WOV 795	Oh, sing to the Lord/Cantad al Señor

PSALM 96

Becker, John. PW, Cycle A.

Burkhardt, Michael. "Three Psalm Settings." MSM 80-705.

Hassler, Hans Leo/Norman Greyson. "Cantate Domino." BRN ES18. SATB.

Lindh, Jody. "Come, Let Us Sing." CGA-478. U, kybd.

HYMN OF THE DAY

LBW 562	Lift every voice and sing
	LIFT EV'RY VOICE AND SING

VOCAL RESOURCES

Larson, Lloyd. "Lift Every Voice and Sing." GLS A-6772. SATB.

INSTRUMENTAL RESOURCES

Johnson, J. Rosamond. "Lift Every Voice" in *The Hymnal 1982, Accompaniment Edition*, vol. 2. CHC. Kybd.

ALTERNATE HYMN OF THE DAY

LBW 542	Sing praise to God, the highest good
WOV 719	God is here!

COMMUNION

LBW 201	O God of life's great mystery
WOV 699	Blessed assurance

OTHER SUGGESTIONS

Hassell, Michael. "Spirit, Spirit of Gentleness." AFP 11-10850. SATB, sax, pno.

SENDING

LBW 252	You servants of God
WOV 754	Let us talents and tongues employ

ADDITIONAL HYMNS AND SONGS

LBW 465	Evening and morning
LBW 218	We place upon your table, Lord
H82 304	I come with joy to meet my Lord

MUSIC FOR THE DAY

CHORAL

Bender, Jan. "O God, O Lord of Heaven and Earth." AFP 11-10481. Also in *The Augsburg Choirbook*. 11-10817. SATB, org, opt 2 tpt, cong.

Busarow, Donald. "Eternal Ruler of the Ceaseless Round." CPH 98-3078. SATB, opt cong, opt brass, org.

Hillert, Richard. "God, Whose Giving Knows No Ending." AG HSA 105. SATB, cong, ob, opt str, org.

Lovelace, Austin C. "First-Fruits." AG HSA 103. SATB, cong, fl, opt tpt, org.

Schalk, Carl. "Evening and Morning." CPH 98-3314. SATB, org, brass, opt cong.

White, Nicholas. "Take My Life and Let It Be Consecrated." HIN 1336. SATB.

CHILDREN'S CHOIRS

Christopherson, Dorothy. "The Lord Is King." AFP 11-10173. U, opt cong, pno.

Ogasapian, John. "Psalm 96." AFP 11-4607. U, kybd.

Powell, Robert. "From the Rising of the Sun." CGA 463. U, kybd.

KEYBOARD/INSTRUMENTAL

Cotter, Jeanne. "The Love of the Lord" in *After the Rain*. GIA G-3390. Pno.

Harbach, Barbara. "Toccata and Fugue on 'Blessed Assurance.'" VIV 334. Org.

Rheinberger, Josef. "Trio I" (and others in the collection) in *Ten Trios*, Op. 49. KAL 3794. Org.

HANDBELL

Kinyon, Barbara B. "Immortal, Invisible, God Only Wise." CGA CGB172. 3 oct.

Larson, Lloyd. "Holy! Holy! Holy! Lord God Almighty." HOP 1876. Opt tpt 1885. 3-5 oct hb.

McChesney, Kevin. "Immortal, Invisible, God Only Wise." CPH 97-6559. 3-5 oct.

Moklebust, Cathy. "Thee We Adore." CGA CGB166. 2 oct.

PRAISE ENSEMBLE

Brown, Scott Wesley. "This Is the Gospel of Christ" in *Integrity's Hosanna! Music Songbook*. INT.

Gleason, Michael. "Oh Lord Of All" in *Worship Leader Magazine's Song DISCovery*, vol 4.

Saxton, Barbara, and Mark Hayes. "Show Forth My Praise." GVX. SATB.

333

SUNDAY, OCTOBER 17
IGNATIUS OF ANTIOCH, MARTYR, C. 115

Ignatius was bishop of Antioch in Syria where the name *Christian* was first used to describe the followers of Jesus. He is known as a martyr who died for refusing to worship the gods of the state religion. Ignatius believed that in his death he was imitating the passion of Christ. Even as he awaited his own death, his letters encouraged Christians to live in harmony and serve the needy.

This Sunday's gospel includes Jesus' words: "Give to the emperor the things that are the emperor's, and to God the things that are God's." The preacher could use the example of Ignatius as one who remained steadfast in his faith in both life and death.

MONDAY, OCTOBER 18
ST. LUKE, EVANGELIST

Luke was the author of both Luke and Acts, and Paul calls him the "beloved physician." Little else is known of his life. He is commemorated by both the Eastern and Western cultures on this day, and his symbol is the winged ox.

Some congregations use the day of St. Luke to remember and honor those in healing professions. The "Service of the Word for Healing" in *Occasional Services* may be used for the liturgy. When we define healing to include the emotional, spiritual, and physical dimensions of our lives, we all stand in need of God's healing presence. The gestures of laying on of hands and/or anointing with oil give witness to the church's care for the whole person—body and soul.

SATURDAY, OCTOBER 23
JAMES OF JERUSALEM, MARTYR

James became a leader of the early church in Jerusalem. He is identified as a brother of the Lord, though there is disagreement whether Jesus actually had brothers. In Mark Jesus says that "whoever does the will of God is my brother and sister and mother."

How does your congregation define "family"? When trying to understand the will of God for our lives, do we consider the ways we serve Christ as revealed in our sisters and brothers in need? If we are going to talk of family values, then Jesus' words invite us to reach beyond the ties of blood, and beyond the walls of our congregation.

334

OCTOBER 24, 1999
TWENTY-SECOND SUNDAY AFTER PENTECOST
PROPER 25

INTRODUCTION

In the era of "sound bites" and headline news, Jesus' summary of the entire law and the prophets to just two commandments is no doubt quite appealing. But what commandments they are! Love God with all your heart, soul, and mind. And love your neighbor as yourself. These are easy commandments to speak, but they will take more than a lifetime for any of us to be able to put into practice. So we have gathered here this day to deepen our desire and our commitment to love God and to love our fellow human beings. May the words we hear and our communion in the body of Christ strengthen us to do those very things.

PRAYER OF THE DAY

Almighty and everlasting God, increase in us the gifts of faith, hope, and charity; and, that we may obtain what you promise, make us love what you command; through your Son, Jesus Christ our Lord.

READINGS

Leviticus 19:1-2, 15-18

The Lord's people exercise justice and love in their dealings with one another.

Psalm 1

Their delight is in the law of the Lord. (Ps. 1:2)

1 Thessalonians 2:1-8

The apostle Paul demonstrates how he had ministered gently and tenderly among the Thessalonians. He not only shared the gospel, but gave of his very self.

Matthew 22:34-46

Jesus displays his great wisdom among the Pharisees by summing up the entirety of the Old Testament scriptures in just two commandments. He furthermore confounds the Pharisees by demonstrating that the Messiah is far more than simply the son of David.

COLOR Green

THE PRAYERS

Remembering the church, the world, and all those in need, let us offer our prayers to God.

A BRIEF SILENCE.

For the baptized people of God, that your love deepen our love for one another. Hear us, O God;

your mercy is great.

For social service organizations, that their ministries give witness to your unconditional love. Hear us, O God;

your mercy is great.

For our neighbors who live with poverty, injustice, and discrimination, that love motivate our words and deeds on their behalf. Hear us, O God;

your mercy is great.

For the nations and their leaders, that your justice may flourish for all people. Hear us, O God;

your mercy is great.

For those who struggle with addiction, grief, or despair, and for all living with illness (especially . . .), that we extend to them your love and care. Hear us, O God;

your mercy is great.

For this assembly, that our outreach to the community be an extension of your gracious love for the whole human family. Hear us, O God;

your mercy is great.

HERE OTHER INTERCESSIONS MAY BE OFFERED.

For all the saints who loved you in life and death, we give thanks, that we may walk in the way of your two great commandments. Hear us, O God;

your mercy is great.

All these things and whatever else you see that we need, grant us, O God, for your mercy is everlasting, and your faithfulness endures from age to age.

Amen

IMAGES FOR PREACHING

The ordinary Hebrew word for "holy" is *kadosh*. The Greek uses *hagios*. Both mean separated, consecrated, set apart. God announces in the first lesson for today, "You shall be holy, for I the Lord your God am holy" (Lev. 19:2). God is holy because God is infinitely perfect, wide, powerful, just, and good—completely different (and thus separate) from all other beings. Even the angels sing of God's holiness (Isa. 6:3).

God's simple instruction through Moses that the people of Israel are to be holy was both preceded and followed by various commands detailing what holy living is about. How do people who have been separated for a special covenant relationship with God behave? The Holiness Code contained in Leviticus 19–26 laid out everything the people were to do and not do to fulfill their set-apart role.

Jesus knew God called some people to be set apart, and even identified a teaching from the Holiness Code as the second great commandment when he responded to the Pharisees' and Saducees' challenge: "Which commandment in the law is the greatest?" (Matt. 22:36). The person set apart for God—the one who is perfect—is the one who loves the Lord with heart, soul, and mind, and who loves neighbor as self.

Throughout Scripture, God's people are viewed as somehow separate from the rest of humanity and also as under God's special care. The psalmist contrasted the wicked with the righteous—those who delight in the law of the Lord, those who flourish under God's care (1:2, 6). And Paul reminded the Thessalonians that he and his colleagues treated them "like a nurse tenderly caring for her own children" (1 Thess. 2:7).

Because through baptism we are God's chosen ones, people set apart for life in Christ, we live both under the command to be holy and under the promise of God's love.

WORSHIP MATTERS

We live in a communication age. We have an information-based economy. Words, words, words. Everywhere more words coming at us. More words do not necessarily yield greater comprehension though, especially in the liturgy. The liturgy is experiential. It is multisensory. Liturgical speech is the speech of symbol. Liturgical speech is rich in image and poetic in style.

Liturgical speech allows for communication about important, even life-changing events. It is not in the same category as the nightly news or billboards along the highway. Liturgical speech allows for honesty, but within a reasonable order and restraint. Allow the congregation to experience the rhythms and images of the day, to reflect upon them, and to draw some of their own conclusions for life.

Take a cue from Jesus' summary of the commandments to just two. Trust people. Don't explain too much.

LET THE CHILDREN COME

Worship planners can be sure that children would be fascinated by the use of incense because it engages so many of the senses. Children watch the smoke rise. They smell it. The air feels different in a cloud of incense. It might taste like something burning. And, if they are close enough, children can hear the incense crack and burn against the coals. Finally, there is the simple fact that children are attracted to fire. Can a congregation set aside allergies to incense, both emotional and real, to give children the chance to share in this ancient dimension of prayer?

MUSIC FOR WORSHIP

GATHERING

LBW 549	Praise, my soul, the King of heaven
WOV 758	Come to us, creative Spirit

PSALM 1

Cooney, Rory. "Psalm 1: Roots in the Earth." GIA G-3969. U, cong, gtr, kybd.

Haas, David. PCY, vol. 3.

Howard, Julie. *Sing for Joy: Psalm Settings for God's Children.* LTP.

Organ, Anne Krentz. PW, Cycle A.

Schoenbachler, Tim. "Happy are They" in STP, vol. 2.

TWC 342 How blest are they who, fearing God

HYMN OF THE DAY

LBW 513	Come, my way, my truth, my life
	THE CALL

VOCAL RESOURCES

Vaughan Williams, Ralph. "The Call." MSM 50-9912. U, kybd.

INSTRUMENTAL RESOURCES

Heaton, Charles Huddleston. "Come, My Way, My Truth, My Life" in *The Concordia Hymn Prelude Series,* vol. 39. CPH 97-5857. Org.

ALTERNATE HYMN OF THE DAY

LBW 490	Let me be yours forever
WOV 666	Great God, your love has called us

COMMUNION

LBW 199	Thee we adore, O hidden Savior
LBW 325	Lord, thee I love with all my heart
WOV 765	Jesu, Jesu, fill us with your love

OTHER SUGGESTIONS

OBS 48	Beloved, God's chosen

SENDING

LBW 486	Spirit of God, descend upon my heart
WOV 796	My Lord of light

ADDITIONAL HYMNS AND SONGS

BH 580	O God of love, enable me
NCH 383	Come, let us join with faithful souls
NSR 61	By your streams of living waters
DATH 93	Around the Great Commandment

MUSIC FOR THE DAY

CHORAL

Bullard, Alan. "Come, Let Us Join Our Cheerful Songs." GIA G-4312. SAB, org.

Byrd, William. "Lord, Make Me to Know Thy Ways." CPH 98-2935. SATB, opt org.

Goudimel, Claude. "Psalm 1." PRE 312-41098. SATB.

Hogan, David. "O Jesus, King Most Wonderful." ECS 4886. SA/TB, org.

Hopson, Hal. "The Gift of Love." HOP.

Marshall, Jane. "The Twin Commandments." CGA 535. U, kybd.

Schulz-Widmar, Russell. "God Remembers." AFP 11-10882. SATB, kybd.

CHILDREN'S CHOIRS

Hillert, Richard. "Happy Are Those Who Delight." GIA G-4259. U, org, fl, opt str.

Marshall, Jane. "God Speaks: Words of Love." CGA 537. U/2 pt, kybd.

KEYBOARD/INSTRUMENTAL

Bach, J. S. "Jesu, Meine Freude" in *Orgelbüchlein*. CPH 97-5774. Org.

Reger, Max. "Benedictus, Op. 29, Heft II" in *Orgelstücke*. CFP 3008. Org.

HANDBELL

Lorenz, Ellen Jane. "A Procession of Bells." MSM 30-094. 3 oct, snare drm.

Sherman, Arnold. "Joyful, Joyful, We Adore Thee." HOP 1652. 2-3 oct.

Keller, Michael R. "Hymn to Joy." Full score HOP 1458. Hb 1457; brass 1458B; SATB 1687. 3-5 oct, org, brass, SATB.

PRAISE ENSEMBLE

Avery, Joann. "With All My Heart" in *Come Celebrate! Praise and Worship*. ABI.

Espinosa, Eddie. "Change My Heart, Oh God" in *Come and Worship Songbook*. INT.

McHugh, Phil. "Lord of All." WRD 3010680 163. SATB.

TUESDAY, OCTOBER 26
PHILIPP NICOLAI, 1608; JOHANN HEERMANN, 1647; PAUL GERHARDT, 1676; HYMNWRITERS

Lutherans are known for music, especially their robust singing of hymns. One of our unique treasures is the chorale, which refers to both the text and tune of German hymns, especially those of the Reformation era. The Lutheran chorale is known for its unique combination of praise and strong proclamation.

Your congregation might consider having an October hymn festival, and include both classic Lutheran chorales as well as recent hymns in *WOV.* The three hymnwriters commemorated on October 26 could be featured. Nicolai is especially known for both the text and tune of "Wake, awake, for night is flying" (LBW 31) and "O morning star, how fair and bright" (LBW 76). Heerman's most famous hymn text is "Ah, holy Jesus" (LBW 123). Gerhardt has ten hymn texts in *LBW* (see p. 941).

THURSDAY, OCTOBER 28
ST. SIMON AND ST. JUDE, APOSTLES

We know little of either Simon or Jude, two men on the lists of Jesus' apostles. Simon is called a zealot in Luke, and the prayer of the day says "that as they were faithful and zealous in their mission, so may we with ardent devotion make known the love and mercy" of Christ.

We are usually skeptical of people who are overly zealous about their faith. The Sunday assembly around word and meal nourishes us that we might go into the world to serve. It will take a certain Spirit-filled energy to meet the tasks and challenges we encounter there. Maybe we need to be more zealous! Has your congregation council considered the level of commitment and enthusiasm among your members? Do your members look forward to worship as the place where they are strengthened and inspired for service in the world?

OCTOBER 31, 1999
REFORMATION DAY

INTRODUCTION

This day invites the daughters and sons of the Reformation to celebrate the perennial source of reform in the church: the Word of God and the sacraments of forgiveness and new life. Indeed, when the church welcomes a new member in Holy Baptism or gathers around the table of Holy Communion, the Holy Spirit's reforming labor continues among us.

On this day, we acknowledge that our souls are captive to the Word of God, that we share the life of Christ with other Christians through Holy Baptism, and that we are urged by the Holy Spirit to pray for the ongoing renewal of the church in our day.

PRAYER OF THE DAY

Almighty God, gracious Lord, pour out your Holy Spirit upon your faithful people. Keep them steadfast in your Word, protect and comfort them in all temptations, defend them against all their enemies, and bestow on the Church your saving peace; through your Son,

Jesus Christ our Lord, who lives and reigns with you and the Holy Spirit, one God, now and forever.

READINGS

Jeremiah 31:31-34

In contrast to Judah's sin, which Jeremiah describes as "engraved on the tablet of their hearts" (17:1), the prophet envisions a future day when the law will be written "on their hearts" (31:33). To know God in this way is to have a direct and profound connection to God. Forgiveness of sins, which is so complete as to be forgotten, is the motivating force for keeping the law.

Psalm 46

The Lord of hosts is with us; the God of Jacob is our stronghold. (Ps. 46:4)

Romans 3:19-28

Martin Luther and other leaders of the Reformation believed the heart of the gospel was found in these words of Paul written to the Romans. All people have sinned, but God offers forgiveness of sins through Christ Jesus. We are justified, or put right with God, through faith in Jesus.

John 8:31-36

True freedom is not related to ethnic distinctions or social class. Only Jesus can free us from slavery to sin, and he does this through the truth of the gospel.

COLOR Red

THE PRAYERS

Remembering the church, the world, and all those in need, let us offer our prayers to God.

A BRIEF SILENCE.

For the church catholic, that unity may overcome division and estrangement. Hear us, O God;

your mercy is great.

For bishops, pastors, diaconal ministers, associates in ministry, teachers, and all who share the gospel, that your grace be proclaimed courageously. Hear us, O God;

your mercy is great.

For the nations of the world, that amid deceit and sword, we may strive for peace and unity. Hear us, O God;

your mercy is great.

For all who will vote in elections, that you give them wisdom in their deliberations. Hear us, O God;

your mercy is great.

For those living with anxiety, guilt, loneliness, poverty,

or illness (especially . . .), that you be their refuge and strength. Hear us, O God;

your mercy is great.

For children and youth in our congregation, that they may know the truth that sets them free. Hear us, O God;

your mercy is great.

For our family of faith gathered here, and for our friends and loved ones, that where there is misunderstanding or discord, we may receive the grace to forgive and be forgiven. Hear us, O God;

your mercy is great.

HERE OTHER INTERCESSIONS MAY BE OFFERED.

We give you thanks for all who have died in the faith, especially Martin Luther and all who struggled for reform in the church. May their bold witness to the gospel inspire us to walk in grace and to strive for justice. Hear us, O God;

your mercy is great.

All these things and whatever else you see that we need, grant us, O God, for your mercy is everlasting, and your faithfulness endures from age to age.

Amen

IMAGES FOR PREACHING

Each fall when Sam headed north to his "duck spot," the field he and several of his buddies leased from a farmer so they could hunt ducks and geese, he drove past several wild game refuges. The people who selected the land for the refuges obviously knew what they were doing. Sam would moan about the wonderful potholes filled with clean water and lush plants. If he happened to pass a refuge even on the nastiest winter day, he could imagine thousands of birds resting and feeding in the sloughs on their way south for the winter. How he wished that just once he and his friends could hunt in such a wonderful place!

Most of us are not accustomed to thinking of ourselves as people who need a refuge. We learn about such people, refugees, from television or radio news reports or newspaper stories. People who need a refuge live someplace else—Rwanda or Bosnia, someplace with war and not enough to eat and very little water. All of us are indeed refugees, though. We need to find refuge from sin and God's righteous judgment. All of us fall short of God's glory (Rom. 3:23) and need to rely on God's promise to put within us a new heart (Jer. 31:33), so that our relationship with God can be put right.

The hunter who drives by the game refuge sees a fence and "no trespassing" signs. The fence around a refuge is not meant to keep the ducks and geese *in,* as do the fences that confine cattle, hogs, or sheep. The fence around a refuge keeps harm *out,* away from the ones that seek protection. The place that to some eyes looks like a prison is the place, it turns out, that offers perfect freedom.

God is our refuge. In God, we find perfect freedom.

WORSHIP MATTERS

Someone once said that freedom in belief and worship centers around those matters in which you have the opportunity to make a choice. The traditional order of the assembly's worship suggests that the basic structure remains the same: the assembly gathers in the name of Jesus for worship, the word of God is proclaimed, the meal of the new covenant is shared, and the members of the assembly are sent into the world for love and service to all creation. Within that basic structure a great deal of freedom remains: choice of music, who will read the appointed lessons, how best to proclaim the sermon, how extensive the gathering rite will be, the form of the prayers to be said, and so on. In all these ways, the particularity of the community can and should be expressed, even as the community demonstrates its bond with the church throughout the centuries and around the globe in expressing that particularity within the ancient order of the church's worship.

LET THE CHILDREN COME

Children have a natural love for books. They love looking at them over and over again. They are especially fond of books with good pictures, books that are visually interesting. One dimension of the celebration of the Reformation is Martin Luther's love for the word of God, and his love for the Scriptures themselves as the cradle that holds the Christ child. Today, encourage worship leaders to carry the Bible in procession. Hold it high. Treat it with care and love. This visual act indicates to the children and all who are worshiping that this book is most important to the life of the church.

MUSIC FOR WORSHIP

SERVICE MUSIC

The Chorale Service of Holy Communion (*LBW,* p. 120), with its roots in the Lutheran reformation, is an option for this day. Although the athletic tunes may be challenging for many congregations, make an effort to keep in the repertoire at least one or two of these. Other hymn paraphrases from various churches of the Reformation may keep this from becoming a German fest. See *Sundays and Seasons* pages 26–27 for hymn mass.

GATHERING

LBW 228/9	A mighty fortress is our God
WOV 747	Christ is made the sure foundation (or LBW 367)

PSALM 46

Bertalot, John. "God Is Our Hope." CGA-444. 2 pt.

Cherwien, David. "God Is Our Refuge." MSM 80-800. U, cong, org.

Folkening, John. "Six Psalm Settings with Antiphons." MSM 80-700.

Hopson, Hal H. "The Lord of Hosts Is With Us." GIA G-3253. SATB, org, cong, cant.

Wood, Dale. PW, Cycle A.

Ziegenhals, Harriet Isle. *Sing Out! A Children's Psalter.* WLP 7191.

HYMN OF THE DAY

LBW 230	Lord, keep us steadfast in your Word
	ERHALT UNS, HERR

VOCAL RESOURCES

Busarow, Donald. "Lord, Keep Us Steadfast in Your Word." CPH 98-2602. 2 pt mxd, inst.

Buxtehude, Dietrich. "Lord, Keep Us Steadfast in Thy Word." CPH 97-6331. SATB, 2 vln, org.

INSTRUMENTAL RESOURCES

Behnke, John. "Erhalt uns, Herr" in *Variations for Seven Familiar Hymns.* AFP 11-10702. Org.

Manz, Paul. "Lord, Keep Us Steadfast" in *Improvisations on Reformations Hymns.* MSM 10-803. Org.

Powell, Robert. "Erhalt uns, Herr" in *Sing We to Our God Above.* AFP 11-10230. Org.

Sedio, Mark. "Lord, Keep Us Steadfast" in *Music for the Paschal Season.* AFP 11-10763. Org.

ALTERNATE HYMN OF THE DAY

LBW 365	Built on a rock
WOV 712	Listen, God is calling

COMMUNION

LBW 448   Amazing grace
WOV 680   O Spirit of life
WOV 711   You satisfy the hungry heart

OTHER SUGGESTIONS

Keesecker, Thomas. "Remember." AFP 11-10743. SATB, kybd,
2 trbl inst, opt cong.

SENDING

LBW 369   The Church's one foundation
WOV 755   We all are one in mission

ADDITIONAL HYMNS AND SONGS

LBW 355   Through the night of doubt and sorrow
LW 351   By grace I'm saved
MBW 521   Sun of righteousness, arise
OBS 76   Rise, O church, like Christ arisen

MUSIC FOR THE DAY

CHORAL

Bach, J. S. "God Is Ever Sun and Shield" in *Third Morning Star Choir Book*. CPH 97-4972. U, ob or fl, cont.

Bender, Jan. "O God, O Lord of Heaven and Earth." AFP 11-10481. SATB, org, 2 tpt. Also in *The Augsburg Choirbook*. 11-10817.

Bertalot, John. "I Stand on the Rock." AFP 11-10852. SAB, pno.

Fedak, Alfred. "Built on a Rock." SEL 241-503-00. 2 pt mxd, org, kybd, opt hb.

Ferguson, John. "Psalm 46." AFP 11-10748. SATB, org.

Grieg, Edvard/Overby. "God's Son Has Made Me Free." AFP 11-1004. Also in *The Augsburg Choirbook*. 11-10817. SATB, opt kybd.

Lance, Steven Curtis. "If Ye Continue in My Word." CFI CM 8227. SATB.

Mozart, Wolfgang A. "God Is Our Refuge and Strength." CHA CLA 6712. SATB.

Schütz, Heinrich. "Sing Praise to Our Glorious Lord." AFP 12-691170. SATB.

CHILDREN'S CHOIRS

Bertalot, John. "God Is Our Hope." CGA 444. 2 pt, kybd.

Caribbean Tune and Michniewicz. "Halle, Hallelujah." CGA 711. U/2 pt, kybd.

Hogan, David. "Lord, Keep Us Steadfast in Your Word." ECS 4902. U, kybd.

KEYBOARD/INSTRUMENTAL

Albrecht, Timothy. "A Mighty Fortress is Our God" in *Grace Notes* vol. VI. AFP 11-10825. Org.

Bender, Jan. "Ein feste Burg" in *Festival Preludes on Six Chorales, Op. 26*. CPH 97-4608. Org.

Walcha, Helmut. "Ein feste Burg" in *A New Liturgical Year*. AFP 11-10810. Org.

Weckmann, Matthias. "Es ist das Heil" in *Choralbearbeitungen*. BA 62211. Org.

Wellman, Samuel. "A Mighty Fortress" in *Keyboard Hymn Favorites*. AFP 11-10820. Pno.

HANDBELL

Luther/Wagner. "A Mighty Fortress Is Our God." HOP 1256. Director/org score 1257. Hb, org.

Moklebust, Cathy. "A Mighty Fortress Is Our God" in *Hymn Stanzas for Handbells*. AFP 11-10722.

Tucker, Margaret R. "Variations on 'A Mighty Fortress.'" MSM 30-800. 3-4 oct.

PRAISE ENSEMBLE

Choplin, Pepper. "Family of Faith." LOR 10/1657M. SATB.

Grant, Amy, Wes King, and Dennis Allen. "We Believe in God." WRD 301 0769 164. SATB.

Gustafson, Gerrit. "Only By Grace" in *Integrity's Hosanna! Come and Worship Songbook*. INT.

Moen, Don, and Claire Cloninger. "Come to the River of Life" in *Integrity's Hosanna! Music Songbook*, vol. 10. INT.

OCTOBER 31, 1999

TWENTY-THIRD SUNDAY AFTER PENTECOST
PROPER 26

INTRODUCTION

As we come to the final month of a liturgical year, the scripture readings become more urgent, encouraging us to think about things of ultimate importance. Today's readings strongly urge us to obey God's teachings and to act fairly and charitably in our dealings with others. The church, especially, is called into forms of humble service and justice for the sake of the world.

PRAYER OF THE DAY

Stir up, O Lord, the wills of your faithful people to seek more eagerly the help you offer, that, at the last, they may enjoy the fruit of salvation; through our Lord Jesus Christ.

READINGS

Micah 3:5-12

Judgment shall be heaped upon the prophets and the rulers who act unjustly and fail to do what the Lord has commanded.

Psalm 43

Send out your light and truth that they may lead me. (Ps. 43:3)

1 Thessalonians 2:9-13

The apostle Paul shows how his kind fatherly dealings with the Thessalonians aided in their receiving the word of God.

Matthew 23:1-12

Jesus encourages his disciples to obey religious teaching, but not to act like some of their teachers who desire privileged positions or seats of honor.

COLOR   Green

THE PRAYERS

Remembering the church, the world, and all those in need, let us offer our prayers to God.

A BRIEF SILENCE.

For the church catholic, that unity may overcome division and estrangement. Hear us, O God;

your mercy is great.

For bishops, pastors, diaconal ministers, associates in ministry, teachers, and all who share the gospel, that your grace be proclaimed courageously. Hear us, O God;

your mercy is great.

For the nations of the world, that amid deceit and sword, we may strive for peace and unity. Hear us, O God;

your mercy is great.

For all who will vote in elections, that you give them wisdom in their deliberations. Hear us, O God;

your mercy is great.

For those living with anxiety, guilt, loneliness, poverty, or illness (especially . . .), that you be their refuge and strength. Hear us, O God;

your mercy is great.

For children and youth in our congregation, that they may learn the joy of humility and service. Hear us, O God;

your mercy is great.

For our family of faith gathered here, and for our friends and loved ones, that where there is misunderstanding or discord, we may receive the grace to forgive and be forgiven. Hear us, O God;

your mercy is great.

HERE OTHER INTERCESSIONS MAY BE OFFERED.

We give you thanks for Martin Luther and all the saints who were humble servants of the gospel. May their bold witness inspire us to walk in grace and to strive for justice. Hear us, O God;

your mercy is great.

All these things and whatever else you see that we need, grant us, O God, for your mercy is everlasting, and your faithfulness endures from age to age.

Amen

IMAGES FOR PREACHING

For generations, children have climbed to the top of a pile of snow or rocks and begun shouting, "I'm king of the mountain!" Throughout the world, castles, monasteries, and even entire villages are built on hills, from which the residents can see approaching danger and retain the upper hand in battle. When we are in a high place, we feel safe and therefore powerful.

341

How devastated the people of Israel must have felt when Micah warned them that Zion, a city on a hill, would become like a plowed field, a heap of ruins (3:12). Even the temple mount would be stripped. God's dwelling on that holy hill (Ps. 43:3) would be destroyed and the land left bare for decades—long enough so that even in that arid land, trees could grow and cover the hill. The high places would become low-lands, and the people would be left vulnerable.

And how devastated we as individuals might also be in the face of Jesus' warning: "All who exalt them-selves will be humbled" (Matt. 23:12). Most of us seated in a typical Lutheran congregation are people on a hill. Whether we recognize it or not, we are among the exalted in our society—by virtue of the fact that we are financially well-off compared to most of the world's people, or because we are educated, white, or male. And God promises throughout the Bible that the exalted, the powerful, and the mighty will be brought low.

In the presence of God, however, we have already been brought low. Yes, we are the work of God's hands, but we have been created out of the dust of the ground. Yes, we are only a little lower than the angels, but we are a fallen race. And God promises that we brought-low people will be exalted—through the death and resurrection of Jesus Christ.

WORSHIP MATTERS

In today's gospel, Jesus teaches how we should live among one another—as servants. What does it mean for worship leaders to live as servants? Ministers of worship serve the assembly, serve the word, serve the meal, serve the world, and ultimately, serve Christ. To be a servant in the liturgy means to keep Christ at the center. It means to attend to the needs of the weakest in the community. It means to serve in leadership humbly. Jesus' indictment of the scribes and Pharisees is a warn-ing to those of us who stand before the assembly each week. Our place is not to stand in the center and be served, honored, or revered. Our place is to serve the assembly so that they might see Jesus. Carved into the interior of many pulpits are the words from John 12:21: "Sir, we wish to see Jesus." They might serve as a reminder for all leaders of worship.

LET THE CHILDREN COME

One of the easiest ways for worship planners to evaluate how well children can find a part in worship is to con-sider how the words and actions of the various portions of the liturgy can captivate the senses. After all, children make sense of the world around them through the use of all their senses. Any parent who has watched a child eat dirt can testify to this need for sensory experience. Is the worship in your parish as sensory as it can be? Are there tastes, touches, smells, sights, and sounds that can be worship to children?

MUSIC FOR WORSHIP

GATHERING

| LBW 501 | He leadeth me; oh, blessed thought! |
| WOV 718 | Here in this place |

PSALM 43

Hopson, Hal H. *Psalm Refrains and Tones.* HOP 425.

Organ, Anne Krentz. PW, Cycle A.

HYMN OF THE DAY

| LBW 428 | O God of Earth and Altar |
| | KING'S LYNN |

INSTRUMENTAL RESOURCES

Fruhauf, Ennis. "King's Lynn" in *Ralph Vaughan Williams and the English School.* AFP 11-10826. Org.

Hyslop, Scott. "King's Lynn" in *Six Chorale Fantasias for Solo Instrument and Piano.* AFP 11-10799.

Johns, Donald. "King's Lynn" in *Eleven Hymn Preludes,* set 2. AFP 11-10559. Kybd.

Schack, David. "King's Lynn" in *Preludes on Ten Hymntunes.* AFP 11-9363. Org.

ALTERNATE HYMN OF THE DAY

| LBW 539 | Praise the Almighty |
| WOV 750 | Oh, praise the gracious power |

COMMUNION

LBW 508	Come down, O Love divine
LBW 309	Lord Jesus, think on me
WOV 777	In the morning when I rise

SENDING

| LBW 343 | Guide me ever, great Redeemer |
| WOV 776 | Be thou my vision |

ADDITIONAL HYMNS AND SONGS

BH 613	We are travelers on a journey
BH 611	Let your heart be broken
TWC 710	We are called to be God's people
NCH 309	We are your people

MUSIC FOR THE DAY

CHORAL

Bach, J. S. "Lord Jesus Christ, Thou Prince of Peace." CPH 98-1955. SATB/S, vln, cont.

Ellingboe, Bradley. "Love Consecrates the Humblest Act." AFP 11-10600. SATB, ob.

Nelson, Ronald A. "Whoever Would Be Great Among You." AFP 11-1638. SAB, kybd/gtr.

Fleming, Larry L. "Humble Service." AFP 11-2294. SATB.

Harris, William H. "Come Down, O Love Divine" in *The New Church Anthem Book*. OXF 0-19-353109-7.

Wienhorst, Richard. "Lord, Whose Love in Humble Service." MSM 50-9059. SATB, kybd.

CHILDREN'S CHOIRS

Cox, Joe. "Put Your Trust in God" in *Psalms for the People of God*. SMP 45/1037S. Cant, choir, cong, kybd.

Willan, Healey. "Oh, Send Out Thy Light," in *We Praise Thee II*. CPH 97-7610. SA, org.

KEYBOARD/INSTRUMENTAL

Cherwien, David. "Postlude on 'St. Anne'" in *Postludes on Well Known Hymns*. AFP 11-10795. Org.

Read, Gardner. "Meditation on 'Jesu, Meine Freude'" in *Hymns and Carols for Organ*. HWG GB00709. Org.

PRAISE ENSEMBLE

Berrios, Frank, Tom Brooks and Jeff Hamlin. "Why So Downcast?" in *Integrity's Hosanna! Come and Worship Songbook*. INT.

Day, Greg, and Chuck Day/Tom Fettke. "Midnight Cry." LIL AN-1839. SATB, orch.

Liles, Dwight. "We Are an Offering" in *Integrity's Hosanna! Come and Worship Songbook*. INT.

Rambo, Dottie/Camp Kirkland. "We Shall Behold Him." LIL AN 1844. SATB, orch.

SUNDAY, OCTOBER 31
REFORMATION DAY

Reformation Day falls on a Sunday this year. Since in most places Lutherans are the only ones who still observe this festival, why not use it to celebrate the catholicity of the Church, and the oneness we have in Christ? Even Lutheran and Roman Catholic theologians have recently agreed that we are justified by faith, through the good news of the gospel that sets us free from sin and death.

343

NOVEMBER

There is no counting the number of the blessed

IMAGES of the SEASON

As the door to the attic opens, what do we see? Out-of-season decorations, clothes, boxes, and things put away for the time being. Belongings. In the attic, or basement, or closets of our homes go the things we have stored for future reference.

All the same, a trip to the attic or other storage area is a tour backwards in memory and time. The train sets and old toys, the faded photographs and letters, the wedding dress and outgrown uniforms: things that belong to people we care about, things from previous chapters of our own lives. Some are of no practical use. We hold on to them because they connect us to friends or family members now parted from us by distance or death. The belongings help give *us* a sense of belonging—to these particular individuals, in these irreplaceable relationships, through more than a single generation. Some of the things we keep because they hold meaning for us.

Other things we can't bring ourselves to redistribute or throw out; we can't put into words why we have a vague but strong sense that it would be wrong to discard them. And so up into the attic they go, awaiting some future dawning of clarity and insight. The belongings in our storage spaces are signs of our relationships, with all their contradictoriness and intricacy. Jo March knew this instinctively in *Little Women*, where her trip to the garret sparked creative breakthrough.

November is attic, barn, and closet time: the season for gathering in and storing away. It's drab outdoors, so we turn inward. We bring outdoor produce inside: apples, carrots, and potatoes down to the root cellar; fruit preserves, neatly labeled, onto pantry shelves. We stack bales of straw in the barn, pour corn and wheat into secure dry silos.

Agriculturally, November is harvest time, the time of reckoning. What have we reaped from the past growing season? How much is there? How does it add up? Will there be enough to carry us through the cold and dark winter ahead? Harvesting and storage are a matter of sheer physical survival. Once we have collected and assessed our provisions, we can breathe more easily and give thanks for them.

The twofold Jewish autumnal rhythm of reparation and rejoicing in harvest is echoed in part of our liturgical calendar. "Autumn"—September and October—is dedicated to repentance and reformation. "November" is devoted to reckoning and harvest.

At the liturgical year's end, we consider God's harvest. Our scriptures force us to take the measure of our own life: what have we been able to produce, through God's grace, during our spiritual growing season of the year past? How have we grown in Christ? We look honestly at what we will have to take with us into the cold and bleak wintertimes of our life as provisions for the soul. With what spiritual resources will we face loneliness and death?

In many congregations this is the culmination of the stewardship season. What are the gifts of self, time, and possessions we can place in service to God for the life of the world? How much is there to go around; how are we to trade and use it faithfully and wisely? As winter looms, we assess what we can share with the hungry and the homeless—the face of Christ in our midst.

It is a time of reckoning, of measuring, of judgment. The words of the scriptures are harsh: the day of the Lord will be one of wrath and ruin, clouds and thick darkness; the whole earth shall be consumed. It will come like a thief in the night, with sudden destruction for those who are complacent. The choice is stark: entering into the joy of the master or being thrown into the outer darkness; eternal punishment or eternal life. It is a time of sifting, winnowing, and sorting. When death comes, will it find us among the sheep or among the goats? Where will the combination of a lifetime of choices have led? Which side are we on? The contrasts are deliberately shocking. Their goal is that we wake up and die right.

The passages about judgment pull us back to baptismal reality: in baptism we have died, and our old life is hidden with Christ in God. Baptism, that ending which is our beginning, washes us with grace and clothes us in the garments of salvation. We need something besides the prospect of damnation to lead us into genuine, loving new life.

And so we are presented with several visions of blessedness in which we can imagine ourselves. A great multitude from every nation—from all tribes and peoples and languages—wears those baptismal garments. In contrast to the adding up and reckoning that go with the season, there is no counting the number of the blessed: mercy is beyond our ability to compute.

Moreover, there are as many ways to be one of God's saints as there are people—each one irreplaceable, unique. We are reminded of the plural—sometimes contradictory—ways of expressing sanctity within the whole people of God. Blessed are the meek who accept what is, and also those who hunger and thirst for what could be. Blessed are the merciful who know compromise—and those for whom compromise is impossible. Blessed are the peacemakers—and those who get in trouble for the sake of the kingdom.

When the Son of Man comes in glory, he will invite the faithful who have given of themselves in a variety of ways into his inheritance: offering food and drink, providing shelter and understanding, sharing the gifts of time and attention, comfort and respect. The gifts are different, their combinations intricate. Somehow there is a way for us to serve, with our particular set of experiences and talents. Here is where we belong, sharing our harvest.

Liturgical November starts with the festival of All Saints, when we remember in gratitude not only the saints recognized formally by the church, but also the dead who have loved us and touched our lives in so many different ways. We give thanks for the harvest of memory, for the legacy of belongings handed on to us. And we ask that one day our life, our memory, might be a blessing. May our children and our children's children find good things from us when they in their turn open the attic door.

We end the church year with the festival of Christ the King and the prayer that we may know the hope to which God has called us, the riches of God's glorious inheritance among the saints. As the year of Matthew draws to a close, we trust that immersion in his gospel has helped us toward becoming—in that uniquely Matthean image—scribes trained for the kingdom of heaven. For every such scribe is like a householder who knows what's up: who knows what's up above in the attic, and what's up above and beyond the attic. Every such scribe is like a householder who brings out of the household treasure—the attic, the storage place—what is new and what is old. Both memory and hope. A harvest for thanksgiving.

ENVIRONMENT AND ART FOR THE SEASON

Thanksgiving features large into this month of the year. Our thanksgiving is not just in the form of a secular holiday though. In this time of year we give thanks for the harvest, to be sure, but we also give thanks for the community of saints and for God's ultimate salvation in the world to come. During this festive time of year, the liturgical environment should give some indication of its rich bounty.

EXTERIOR ENVIRONMENT

Many parts of the North American landscape are a dull brown by this time of year, if not already covered in a blanket of white snow. Some use of color on the outside of buildings, especially near major entrances, may help to alleviate the monotony. Wreaths and other hangings made from natural elements may offer warmth and invitation to otherwise stark exteriors.

INTERIOR ENVIRONMENT

As the church prepares to remember the witness of God's saints who have lived and died over the course of time, why not prepare to honor some of your own localized "saints" with a display of photographs and other artifacts from your congregation's past? Hang some of the larger photographs in the narthex and in other gathering spaces throughout the entire month. If you have a memorial book, put it on display. Use lighting to enhance these and any other special displays.

The throne of God plays prominently into the readings during this month. On All Saints Day, a great multitude from every nation gathers around God's throne and the lamb (Rev. 7). The festival of Christ the King presents us with the Son of Man coming in his glory and sitting on his throne (Matt. 25). On these days the altar might be dressed in some of the brighter white, or even gold paraments, that the congregation owns. A laudian frontal, which completely surrounds the altar, may suggest the great multitude gathering from all corners of the earth.

Congregations that celebrate Thanksgiving Day or hold some observance of the harvest often attempt to decorate their worship spaces in fall motifs. This theme can easily be overdone. Large cornucopia and displays of fall produce can overwhelm a chancel, even to the point of obscuring the major centers of liturgical activity (pulpit/ambo, altar, font, and chairs for worship leaders). Try working with the space you have so that any seasonal art and decoration tastefully supplements the fixed elements, and does not become a traffic flow problem or fire hazard.

Perhaps the narthex or other gathering spaces might serve as "collecting areas" for food and other items that will be donated to the hungry this season. Bread and wine for the eucharistic table may be set out there as well prior to services. Then during the offertory procession, the monetary offering, as well as symbolic gifts of the earth's bounty, can be brought forward along with the bread and wine.

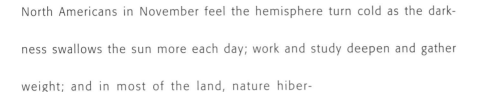

PREACHING WITH THE SEASON

North Americans in November feel the hemisphere turn cold as the darkness swallows the sun more each day; work and study deepen and gather weight; and in most of the land, nature hibernates, withdrawing abundance with darkening,

withering, shedding, scattering, stripping, burrowing, and freezing. Fields are stubble, herds are ice-bearded, and frost lamps are set out in southern orange groves. Cardboard lean-tos of the homeless mushroom on city streets and under trestles. Sunless northern ice fields borrow light from the spectacular aurora borealis.

Precisely as the earth stiffens and chills, iced, gray, and brown, November heralds that the baptized are to be awake and actively enacting our remembering of Christ as the goal, not simply of the year, but of all time. November Sundays gather Christians around God's word and Christ's cup to remember all the saints of every time and place who have died in the faith; to remember, to watch, and to wait in hope and love; to remember who is sovereign of all that is and ever shall be. Such remembering is deeply imaginative and profoundly collaborative. It is not merely a remembering of a past, but an active recollection of the future, and thus a participation in Christ's remembering a world beloved of God.

Christ's remembering requires entering into a mind unique among the minds with which we supply ourselves. The mind of Christ—proposed in the great images of our November texts—imagines saints as refugees, undistinguished by denomination, race, or creed, gathered at the table in the household of God; imagines the living and the dead meeting as they are all caught up to be with God forever; imagines a God whose passion can consume the whole earth; and imagines God as a thief, stealing creation back to paradise, personally gathering in and making equal the whole flock of God's people. These visions of the fullness of time in the mind of Christ are proclaimed amongst peoples whose minds are largely shaped by a learned predisposition to believe in western proposals of reality, whether Canadian or American. But Christ's proclama-

tion of justice, peace, and the fulfillment of creation's purpose is not of the proposals of the West, nor of any culturally constructed power. Flowering through the texts and out of the cup of blessing in November assemblies, God's justice is a gift freely announced to all nations ingathered, indeed all creation; not the construct of one nation. God's saints are all who are robed in Christ's blood; the vision names no denomination, race, or creed.

Drawing the liturgical year to a close, the Sundays of November asks us to gather the harvest of the seeds that were sown from Advent to Pentecost by remembering deeply to whom we belong, and by whom the cry of all the earth is heard. Christian memory frees us to imagine enduring suffering, experiencing joy, and being patient in the face of adversity. Remembering with Christ frees our prayer for the world. At the same time, it frees us to be with the one who first and last remembers and hears us.

All Saints Day calls to mind all the faithful in history, pulling us into the vortex of unity with all those who have gone under the waters of death to be delivered into the life of God. Revelation's voices cry out at the Lamb's table, echoing the witness of the one whose body and blood we share, calling us into light, out of our self-absorption and small-mindedness (Propers for All Saints). All Saints displays our freedom, always, for thanksgiving.

On the festival of Christ the King, the assembly stands by the sea of glass, at the throne of God from whence flows the river of life, having journeyed here on a raft of lessons and memories through ordinary time. The year drops anchor at the throne of Christ who is, who was, and who is yet to come. Contemplating the suffering sovereign enthroned on a bare cross, ruling all in all, we hear Jesus' account of the Son of Man in glory. The image of Christ the king who rules over all nations gathered before the throne of God gives us a personalized snapshot of terror. Jesus seems to say that God's eternal peace is prepared for those who do good works. Jesus seems to promise eternal punishment to those who have not been faithful to the least of the sick, the hungry, the thirsty, the unwelcome, the naked, or imprisoned. Our typical preoccupation with ourselves and our lives makes us hear of the glory of the Son of Man in judgment as merely a description of who will and who will not live forever with God. Isolated in our natural self-absorption, this image becomes individualized or parochialized and hides Jesus' truth. The one telling of the judgment of God is the one who becomes stranger to his followers through their betrayal and abandonment; is taken prisoner of both the temple and Rome; is stripped naked and sickened by the wounds of whip, thorns, and crucifixion; thirsts in his dying moments; and appears separated from humanity and from heaven hanging on the shameful cross. Yet this very one calls out for God to forgive all those who do not embrace him in his miserable dying.

God alone bursts the crucified from his three-day prison, eternally heals the wounds of death, clothes the nakedness of Jesus with the resurrection, and spreads a table by the sea of Galilee. God welcomes the crucified as no stranger to heaven, and returns Jesus risen to humanity as firstborn sibling of a new creation. Christ alone sits at the right hand of God, the advocate of mercy. For others to sit at the right hand of this God can mean only that Christ carries others in the presence, clothed in the love of Jesus, welcomed by adoption into God's household, and nursed at the breast of reconciliation. Through, in, and with Christ, in the unity of God, the family of God is created and gathered.

The one who remembers us before God promises to welcome one of the least of these is to welcome me . . . here I am to be served, to be honored, to be welcomed. I am the hungry, the thirsty, the stranger, the naked, the sick, the imprisoned. Christ's sovereignty is about remembering the need and the possibility of all the gathered nations. The divide between lived wretchedness and lived holiness rests on recognizing God in those suffering.

PLANNING AHEAD FOR THE SEASON

November is a time for remembrance. Throughout much of North America

we think back to the past growing season and warmer weather with a kind

of wistfulness. November calls to mind those

who have served their country with the twin

observances of Veterans Day (U.S.A.) and Remembrance Day (Canada). All Saints Day/Sunday is the church's way of remembering where we have come from, but also where we are headed.

Frequently congregations include the names of those who have died from among their own membership in the year just past. This acknowledgment can be enlarged to include a remembrance of other saints and witnesses also known to members of the congregation who have died within the past year. People may be

encouraged to list names of those they wish to have remembered in a book to be used in intercessory prayers either on All Saints Sunday or throughout the month of November. A blank book can be placed in the narthex before worship for people to write the names of others who have died and whom they wish to have remembered in prayer. If the congregation is large (and the list of names could thus be large as well), a prayer petition simply referring to "the names that are written in this book" could be said as one of the ministers lifts the book of remembrance. Some congregations use this form of listing prayer concerns in a book throughout the year (an assisting minister carries the book during the entrance procession, or an usher takes it forward sometime before the prayers).

If All Saints Day has us thinking primarily of the past, the lectionary readings toward the conclusion of each liturgical year have us looking toward the future. The focus in these days are on the day of the Lord and of God serving as judge. The texts may seem especially relevant this year in that the year 2000 is just weeks away. While most people may be planning more elaborate parties than usual for this coming New Year's Eve, others may be looking at the change of the year with a sense of fear or dread. These weeks may be a real

opportunity to minister to genuine feelings that people have, without sensationalizing any fears.

In one way, the movement from the year 1999 to the year 2000 will be like the passing of any year—it will happen with or without our efforts. But how can the passing into this new millennium be an opportunity for us to proclaim the coming of God's certain judgment and also God's certain grace? Lutheran tradition, steeped as it is in law and gospel, may have a unique contribution to make these days. We can acknowledge our failures and weaknesses, but at the same time we can also announce God's sure forgiveness and genuine hope. The year 2000 will be a year of salvation, too!

ORDO FOR THE SEASON

Framed as it is by the festivals of All Saints Day and Christ the King, the entire month of November has the feel of a festival season. Perhaps the entrance rite will be elaborated to include entrance hymn, Kyrie, and hymn of praise. The

use of an order for confession and forgiveness seems appropriate during this season, especially since the lectionary causes us to be mindful of God's judgment and fulfillment of time. In lieu of a preparatory order for confession and forgiveness, special attention might be given to placing petitions beseeching God's mercy in the prayers.

If baptismal festivals are observed in the congregation, All Saints Sunday is a special day to observe one, since we enter God's communion of saints through our baptism into Christ.

Eucharistic prayer I (that's the *letter* "I", not the roman numeral "I") for November (*WOV, Leaders Edition*, p. 73) might be used throughout the season, since it speaks particularly of God's coming reign of peace and justice.

ASSEMBLY SONG FOR THE SEASON

The festivals of All Saints and Christ the King, along with the Sunday

between them, form a liturgical bridge from one year into the next. Escha-

tological themes are present in November and

Advent. A remembrance and celebration of All

Saints can still occupy a treasured place on the first Sunday in November using the appointed Sunday reading for this year, the wise and foolish virgins, rather than using specific All Saints readings. It is not a choice between liturgical and secular themes during this time that is crucial. Rather, it is creatively discovering the intersection between the themes of God's harvest at the end of time with our nation's accent on the late autumn earthly harvest.

Festive worship for All Saints, Christ the King, and even the Sunday in between, can provide much needed relief from the lengthy period of Sundays after Pentecost. Here is a brief opportunity for a glimmer of

remembrance and anticipation of the resurrection festival. Some musical extravagance with Easter themes can appropriately interrupt our autumn pilgrimage leading to the frantic days and quiet worship of Advent. Yet these glorious days have a certain soberness about them as we remember loved ones who have gone before, and as we look to the end of time with uncertain eagerness and hesitation. These few Sundays can easily be overlooked in the fury of preparation for Christmas. Just as we mourn the death of Christ and simultaneously revel in the mystery of salvation on Good Friday, so too the paradoxical themes of these days deserve conscientious attention. Carefully selected music can be a key ingredient in communicating the power and beauty of these brief but poignant weeks in the church's year.

MUSIC FOR THE SEASON

VERSE AND OFFERTORY

Hobby, Robert. "Verse for All Saints Day." MSM 80-810. 2 pt mxd.

Hobby, Robert. "Offertory for All Saints Day." MSM 80-811. 2 pt mxd.

OTHER SUGGESTIONS

See also the Autumn listings.

CHORAL MUSIC FOR THE SEASON

Billingham, Richard. "Deep River." AFP 11-10783. SATB, pno.

Copland, Aaron. "At the River." BOH B5513. SATB, kybd.

Kellner, Mark. "Christ Is Alive." HOP GC 971. SATB.

Parker, Alice. "Come, We that Love the Lord." GIA G-4245. SATB, S.

Pfautsch, Lloyd. "Christ Is the King." HOP LP 3710. Hb LP 3710HB.
SATB, hb.

Ross, Joel A. "Give Me Jesus." CFI CM8490. SSATB, kybd.

Schalk, Carl. "I Saw a New Heaven and a New Earth."
AFP 11-10803. SATB.

Schalk, Carl. "Thine the Amen, Thine the Praise." AFP 11-02173. SATB.

Schütz, Heinrich. "Blessed Are the Faithful!" Gsch 10114. SSATTB.

Trinkley, Bruce. "Weary Traveler." AFP 11-10514. SATB, trbl solo, pno.

White, Nicholas. "Steal Away." AFP 11-10506. SATB.

Wood, Charles. "Summer Ended." WAL WW1036. SATB, org.

INSTRUMENTAL MUSIC FOR THE SEASON

Farlee, Robert Buckley. "Deep Waters" in *Three Hymns of Faith
Arranged for Saxophone or Other Instrument and Organ.*
AFP 11-10693. Org, sax/inst.

Ferguson, John. "Shall We Gather At the River." AFP 11-10824. Org.

Gabrielson, Stephen. "My God, How Wonderful Thou Art" in *We Are
Your Own Forever.* AFP 11-10473. Org.

Hyslop, Scott. *Six Chorale Fantasias for Solo Instrument and Piano.*
AFP 11-10799. Pno, inst.

Langlais, Jean. "Chant de Paix" in *Neuf Pieces.* BOR. Org.

Organ, Anne Krentz. "Christ, Mighty Savior" in *Reflections on Four
Hymntunes.* AFP 11-10819. Pno.

Wellman, Samuel. *Keyboard Hymn Favorites.* AFP 11-10820. Pno.

HANDBELL MUSIC FOR THE SEASON

Larson, Katherine. "The Ash Grove." AFP 11-10348. Hb.

McFadden, Jane. "Rejoice, Rejoice, Believers." AFP 11-10632. Hb.

Sherman, Arnold. "Jesus Shall Reign." AG 1708. Hb.

Wagner, Douglas. "Crown Him with Many Crowns." HOP 1268. Hb.

Young, Philip M. "Shall We Gather at the River." AFP 11-10633. Hb.

ALTERNATE WORSHIP TEXTS

CONFESSION AND FORGIVENESS

In the name of the Father, and of the ✝ Son, and of the Holy
   Spirit.
Amen

Let us confess our sin before God
and in the presence of one another, trusting in God's mercy.

Silence for reflection and self-examination.

God of grace,
we confess our impatience,
our failure to pray,
our inhospitable actions,
our unwillingness to recognize Christ
in the least of our brothers and sisters.
Forgive us for wanting to restrict your love
to match our own understanding.
In your mercy, renew us
in ways of harmony and peace. Amen

God loves you and, for Jesus' sake,
forgives you all your sin.
As your life is renewed by the Holy Spirit,
may you rejoice in hope, be patient in suffering,
persevere in prayer, and live in harmony with one another.
Amen

GREETING

From God our maker,
from Christ our sovereign,
from the holy Comforter,
grace and peace be with all the saints.
And also with you.

OFFERTORY PRAYER

Loving God,
we give you only what is yours, whatever our gift may be.
All that we have is yours alone, a trust given into our care.
May we receive your bounty as true stewards,
and return to you the first fruits of the harvest of our lives.
Amen

INVITATION TO COMMUNION

Holy things for the holy people.
One is holy, one is Lord, Jesus Christ.

POST-COMMUNION PRAYER

We give you thanks, loving God,
for this meal, a gift from your goodness.
Now let us go in peace to serve our neighbor;
and at the end, with our own eyes,
let us see our Savior, forever and ever.
Amen

BENEDICTION

May the God of abundance fill you with grace.
May the God of wisdom rule in your thoughts, words, and deeds.
May the God of consolation walk beside you and give you peace.
Amen

DISMISSAL

Surrounded by a great cloud of witnesses,
go in peace to love and serve the Lord.
Thanks be to God.

354

MONDAY, NOVEMBER 1
ALL SAINTS DAY

The custom of commemorating all of the martyrs of the church on a single day goes back at least to the third century. Our All Saints Day celebration commemorates not only all the martyrs but all the people of God, living and dead, who form the mystical body of Christ, as the prayer of the day makes clear.

Today many congregations remember their members who have died during the past year. Consider reading these names during the prayers or during the eucharistic prayer, when we join with the church on earth and the hosts of heaven around the table of the Lord. If you use Eucharistic Prayer I (*WOV, Leaders Edition*, p. 73), add the following before the second paragraph from the end: "We remember before you all our departed friends and relatives, especially those who have died during the past year (the names are then read)."

TUESDAY, NOVEMBER 2
ELECTION DAY (USA)

WEDNESDAY, NOVEMBER 3
MARTIN DE PORRES, 1639

Abandoned by his wealthy Spanish father, Martin and his sister lived in poverty with their black mother in Peru. As a young man Martin gained knowledge as a druggist and "physician," and the sick and needy came to him because of his great kindness. As a Dominican he served the infirm in the monastery, and he also brought sick and homeless persons from the wider community into vacant rooms there.

The Latin American churches recognize Martin's important work on behalf of the disenfranchised, and he is seen as the patron of interracial justice. He stands as a model for us as we continue to work for justice and equality in our country.

355

NOVEMBER 7, 1999

ALL SAINTS SUNDAY

INTRODUCTION

As November heralds the dying of the landscape in many northern regions, the readings and liturgy call us to remember those who have died in Christ. As the liturgical year draws to a close, we hear warnings about the end of time, stories of crisis and judgment, and parables of loss and death. The Christian community speaks honestly about human frailty and mortality.

At the same time, we confess our faith in the risen Lord, in the communion of saints, the resurrection of the body, and life everlasting. While we may face dying or death with fear, the liturgy calls us to hear the Lord's promise that he is with us in life and in death.

Christ has claimed us in Holy Baptism. He nourishes us in the Holy Communion of his body and blood. He leads us to the new Jerusalem. There we shall join all the saints in praise of God, who has turned our graves into the doorway to eternal life.

Today is also the commemoration of John Christian Frederick Heyer, missionary to India, 1873.

PRAYER OF THE DAY

Almighty God, whose people are knit together in one holy Church, the body of Christ our Lord: Grant us grace to follow your blessed saints in lives of faith and commitment, and to know the inexpressible joys you have prepared for those who love you; through your Son, Jesus Christ our Lord, who lives and reigns with you and the Holy Spirit, one God, now and forever.

READINGS

Revelation 7:9-17

The book of Revelation is written to seven churches in western Asia Minor during a time of great oppression (in A.D. 95 or 96). Today's reading provides a response to the question asked in 6:17: "Who is able to stand?" The writer responds to the faithful with the assurance of God's protection and a vision of eventual victory.

Psalm 34:1-10, 22

Fear the Lord, you saints of the Lord. (Ps. 34:9)

1 John 3:1-3

John encourages us to hope in God's love and trust the promise that we shall see God's face.

Matthew 5:1-12

In the beatitudes, Jesus provides a unique description of those who are blessed with God's favor. His teaching is surprising and shocking to those who seek wealth, fame, and control over others.

COLOR   White

THE PRAYERS

Surrounded by a great cloud of witnesses, let us offer our prayers before God's throne of grace.

A BRIEF SILENCE.

For the holy church of God throughout the world, that it may faithfully proclaim the blessedness of new life in Christ, we pray:

Your kingdom come.

For the leaders of nations, that they may work tirelessly as peacemakers and ambassadors of goodwill among all people, we pray:

Your kingdom come.

For those who are meek and pure in heart, for those beset by persecution for righteousness' sake, and those weighed down by trial and distress, that the example of the saints may give them endurance and courage, we pray:

Your kingdom come.

For those who live with poverty or who are poor in spirit, and for all who are homebound, hospitalized, or sick (especially . . .), that you fill them with hope, we pray:

Your kingdom come.

For those who mourn the loss of loved ones, that they would find comfort in the promise of eternal life, we pray:

Your kingdom come.

HERE OTHER INTERCESSIONS MAY BE OFFERED.

We give thanks for the missionary John Christian Frederick Heyer, and all the saints who now rest from their labors and dwell in your eternal light. May their mem-

ory stir our imagination, and deepen our hope of sharing with you the endless feast of victory. We pray:

Your kingdom come.

Rejoicing in the fellowship of all the saints, let us commend ourselves, one another, and our whole life to Jesus Christ our Lord.

Amen

IMAGES FOR PREACHING

Companies pay hundreds of thousands of dollars for thirty seconds of television commercial time to persuade us to buy breakfast cereal, soft drinks, beer, and fast food. And we do not necessarily eat because our stomachs let us know we *need* to; we eat because a star athlete or cartoon character tells us we *want* to. Still, millions of people all over the world, most of them children, go to bed hungry each night and know the wrenching physical pain of an empty stomach.

Augustine, in a well-known confession, described another kind of hunger, a yearning for God: Our hearts are restless until they find their rest in God. And the biblical writers regularly used the images of being hungry and being well fed to describe our relationship with God. The psalmist observed, "Young lions suffer want and hunger, but those who seek the Lord lack no good thing" (34:10). In Revelation, John shared a vision of the redeemed before the throne of God: "They will hunger no more, and thirst no more" (7:16). And Jesus' Sermon on the Mount includes perhaps the most familiar teaching about spiritual hunger: "Blessed are those who hunger and thirst for righteousness, for they will be filled" (Matt. 5:6).

How is our hunger for God made manifest in our lives? Do we covet possessions—a bigger house, a newer car, nicer clothes? Are we willing to do whatever it takes to get that job promotion—and a generous paycheck, more vacation, and an office with a door? Do we try to fill the emptiness in our heart with food, sex, or alcohol?

When we find ourselves aching for *something,* but we do not know what we are looking for, we would do well to consider: Is my hunger for God?

WORSHIP MATTERS

To be holy is to be set apart by God for a specific task, itself designed to demonstrate some aspect of God's grace active in the world. That holiness is always at God's initiative, who bestows the gifts needed to fulfill this calling by the Holy Spirit. So the church, the members of the body of Christ, are holy by being set apart through the waters of baptism to be God's people. We are holy because God has called us into the service of the kingdom, in order to point to the grace, peace, and love God intended from the foundation of the world. So also is it true that some things are holy precisely because they are set apart by God to become vehicles of divine grace. As we show care and concern for the holy people who surround us, so we do well to show the same kind of care for these simple things of the earth that communicate so great a gift.

LET THE CHILDREN COME

On this day, congregations often take time in worship to acknowledge those who have died. Rather than limiting an understanding of "saint" to those who have died in the Lord, expand the acknowledgment to include all those who have been baptized since last All Saints Day. Perhaps the acknowledgment of those who have died can include the date of their birth, the date of their baptism, and the date of death. The acknowledgment of the baptized can include their date of birth and baptism. A candle can be lighted for both the dead and the baptized. It is one way to show the sainthood all children share in as a gift of their baptism.

MUSIC FOR WORSHIP

SERVICE MUSIC

Toll a single handbell after the reading of each of the names of those who have died during the past year.

GATHERING

| LBW 553 | Rejoice, O pilgrim throng! |
| WOV 690 | Shall we gather at the river |

PSALM 34

DATH 34   I will bless you, O God

Hobby, Robert. "I Will Bless the Lord." MSM 80-707. U, cong, org.

Kreutz, Robert. "Jesu dulcis" (The Taste of Goodness). GIA G-2304. SATB, cong.

Organ, Anne Krentz. PW, Cycle A.

Walker, Christopher. "Taste and See" in PS3.

WOV 706   Eat this bread, drink this cup

HYMN OF THE DAY

| LBW 174 | For all the saints |
| | SINE NOMINE |

VOCAL RESOURCES

Hinkle, Don. "For All the Saints" in *Assist Us to Proclaim.* AFP 11-10313. SATB.

Ley, Henry G. "For All the Saints." OXF 27.761. SATB, opt cong, org.

Mueller, Jonathan R. "For All the Saints." MSM 60-8100. Choir 60-8100A; inst pts 60-8100B. SATB, org, brass qnt, timp, cong.

INSTRUMENTAL RESOURCES

Cherwien, David. "Postlude on 'For All the Saints'" in *Postludes on Well Known Hymns.* AFP 11-10795. Org.

Fruhauf, Ennis. "Sine Nomine" in *Ralph Vaughan Williams and the English School.* AFP 11-10826. Org.

Held, Wilbur. "Sine Nomine" in *Organ Music for Funerals and Memorial Services,* book I. AFP 11-07625. Org.

Page, Anna Laura. "For All the Saints" in *Hymn Descants for Ringers and Singers,* vol. 3. ALF 16057. Vcs/kybd 16059. 3 oct, kybd, desc.

Pelz, Walter L. "Sine Nomine" in *Hymn Settings for Organ and Brass,* set 2. AFP 11-10272.

ALTERNATE HYMN OF THE DAY

| LBW 314 | Who is this host arrayed in white |
| WOV 691 | Sing with all the saints in glory |

COMMUNION

| LBW 331 | Jerusalem, my happy home |
| WOV 764 | Blest are they |

OTHER SUGGESTIONS

Wetzler, Robert. "Take of the Wonder." AFP 11-10647. SATB, opt fl, gtr, cong.

SENDING

| LBW 351 | Oh, happy day when we shall stand |
| WOV 742 | Come, we that love the Lord |

ADDITIONAL HYMNS AND SONGS

WOV 689	Rejoice in God's saints
NCH 380	O saints, in splendour sing
NSR 102	Onward, you saints, in joyous celebration
WGF 38	Clouds of witnesses surround us
DATH 102	Death Be Never Last

357

MUSIC FOR THE DAY

CHORAL

Bell, John. "In Zion." GIA G-4541. SATB, solo.

Christiansen, Paul. "For All the Saints." SHM 8041. SATB div, opt brass, org.

Harris, Jerry W. "The Beatitudes." AFP 11-10591. SATB, kybd.

Hassler, Hans L. "Lord, Let at Last Thine Angels Come." CPH 98-1026. SATB/SATB.

Ley, Henry G. "Lo, Round the Throne a Glorious Band" in *Church Anthem Book*. OXF. SATB, org.

Neswick, Bruce. "O Taste and See." AFP 11-10592. SATB, kybd.

Nicholson, Paul. "Jerusalem." AFP 11-10501. SATB, org, tpt, opt cong.

Schalk, Carl. "I Saw a New Heaven and a New Earth." AFP 11-10803. SATB.

Svedlund, Karl Erik. "There'll Be Something in Heaven." AFP 12-113. SATB.

Thompson, J. Michael. "Taste and See the Lord Is Good." AFP 11-10842. SATB, ob, org.

Tye, Christopher. "How Glorious Zion's Courts Appear" in *Four Motets*. GIA G-4647. SATB.

Vaughan Williams, Ralph. "O Taste and See." OXF 43-909. SATB, S solo.

CHILDREN'S CHOIRS

Exner, Max. "Saints of God." AFP EK11-2356. U, kybd.

Herman, David. "I Sing a Song of the Saints of God." CGA 446. 2 pt.

Leavitt, John. "Blessed Are They." CGA 425. U/2 pt, kybd.

Telemann, G. P., and Susan Cherwien. "I Want to Praise the Lord All of My Life." CPH 98-3350. 2/3 pt, kybd, opt orff inst and C inst.

KEYBOARD/INSTRUMENTAL

Cotter, Jeanne. "Blest Are They" in *After the Rain*. GIA G-3390. Pno.

Ferguson, John. "Shall We Gather at the River." AFP 11-10824. Org, cong.

Harbach, Barbara. "Fantasy and Fugue on 'Swing Low, Sweet Chariot.'" VIV 338. Org.

Hassell, Michael. "Swing Low, Sweet Chariot" in *Jazz December*. AFP 11-10796. Pno.

Peeters, Flor. "Elegy." LEM. Org.

Vierne, Louis. "Requiem Aeternam" in *Pièces de Fantaisie*. LEM. Org.

Willan, Healey. "Elegy" in *Modern Anthology*. HWG 209. Org.

HANDBELL

Afdahl, Lee J. "Rejoice in God's Saints." AFP 11-10808. 3-5 oct, opt perc.

Honoré, Jeffrey. "Jesus in the Morning and Somebody's Knockin' at Your Door." AFP 11-10626. 2 oct.

Moklebust, Cathy. "Behold a Host." CPH 97-6377. 3-4 oct.

Nelson, Susan T. "Elegy." AFP 11-10554. 2 oct, opt inst/solo ringer, pno.

Young, Philip. "Shall We Gather at the River." AFP 11-10633. 3-5 oct.

PRAISE ENSEMBLE

Brown, Scott Wesley. "All Around Your Throne" in *Integrity's Hosanna! Music Songbook*, vol.10. INT.

DeShazo, Lynn, and Jamie Harvill Heaven. "And Earth" in *Integrity's Hosanna! Music Songbook*, vol.10. INT.

Hogan, Moses. "I Want Jesus to Walk with Me." HAL 08740785. SATB.

Joncas, Michael/Mark Hayes. "On Eagle's Wings." ALF 16104. SATB, orch.

NOVEMBER 7, 1999

TWENTY-FOURTH SUNDAY AFTER PENTECOST
PROPER 27

INTRODUCTION

Why does the bridegroom come so late to the wedding celebration? Why, asked the early Christians, does Christ seemingly delay his promised return? And we, who live in an unjust and violent world may ask, Where is the Lord when we need him?

We do not know the hour of his final advent. But we do know that Christ has claimed us in Holy Baptism as his servants in this world. We have the witness of the word and sacrament to enlighten our path in life. We are strengthened in Holy Communion as heralds of the coming reign of God's justice and peace. Between his first advent and his final coming, the church is called to serve the Lord Jesus in faith, hope, and love.

PRAYER OF THE DAY

Lord, when the day of wrath comes we have no hope except in your grace. Make us so to watch for the last days that the consummation of our hope may be the joy of the marriage feast of your Son, Jesus Christ our Lord.

READINGS

Amos 5:18-24

In this speech, Amos takes up one of the central themes of Israel's faith and turns it against his Israelite audience. The Day of the Lord was understood to be a day of disaster and judgment for the Lord's enemies, but one of salvation and deliverance for the Lord's people. Now, Amos declares, because the people have turned away from God and failed to pursue justice and righteousness, Israel will be numbered among the Lord's enemies.

or The Wisdom of Solomon 6:12-16

Psalm 70

You are my helper and my deliverer; O Lord, do not tarry. (Ps. 70:6)

or The Wisdom of Solomon 6:17-20

The beginning of wisdom is the most sincere desire for instruction. (Wisd. of Sol. 6:17)

1 Thessalonians 4:13-18

The Thessalonian Christians were eagerly awaiting the return of Christ and became distressed when loved ones died before this occurred. Paul's words about the second coming offer hope to all who grieve.

Matthew 25:1-13

In this chapter, Jesus tells three parables about the second coming. The first of these emphasizes the need for readiness at all times.

COLOR   Green

THE PRAYERS

Surrounded by a great cloud of witnesses, let us offer our prayers before God's throne of grace.

A BRIEF SILENCE.

For the church, that through its proclamation and witness it may be a lamp of hope for all who live with darkness and despair, we pray:

Your kingdom come.

For political leaders, that they may be watchful and responsible, and so give the light of peace to a world threatened by war and violence, we pray:

Your kingdom come.

For those oppressed and treated unfairly, that your justice

may roll down like waters, and your righteousness like an everflowing stream, we pray:

Your kingdom come.

For those without food, shelter, and clothing; for those without dignity and self-esteem; and for those whose spirits are broken by addiction, abuse, or depression, that your light may give them hope, we pray:

Your kingdom come.

For those living with illness, or who find it difficult to face the future (especially . . .), that they would find encouragement in the Lord's promise to come again, we pray:

Your kingdom come.

For ourselves, that we may seek to be wise, living with our eyes open, watchful and alert to the signs of your grace in the world and in our lives, we pray:

Your kingdom come.

HERE OTHER INTERCESSIONS MAY BE OFFERED.

We give you thanks for the missionary John Christian Frederick Heyer, and all the saints who have joyfully celebrated this banquet and now partake of the eternal marriage feast. May their memory enliven our faith and deepen our hope. We pray:

Your kingdom come.

Rejoicing in the fellowship of all the saints, let us commend ourselves, one another, and our whole life to Jesus Christ our Lord.

Amen

IMAGES FOR PREACHING

Surprises can be wonderful. Walking into a room full of friends unexpectedly gathered to celebrate a birthday or anniversary can be a delightful reminder that these people care about us. But not all surprises are welcome. Sometimes surprises are about loss and we feel sad, as we do when someone dies suddenly. Sometimes surprises are frightening. For example, the day of the Lord, Amos said, is as if someone "went into the house and rested a hand against the wall and was bitten by a snake" (5:19). Sometimes we are surprised because we are not prepared. Jesus illustrated such surprise in the parable of the wise and foolish maidens.

And sometimes surprises are indeed wonderful. Paul reassured the Thessalonians about one surprise— the coming of the Lord. Paul did not want them to feel sad that some members of their community had died before the Lord's return. He did not want them to feel afraid about what was coming. And he wanted them to be prepared to meet the Lord and be with him forever.

The coming of God's reign will be a surprise, but we need not feel sad or afraid. Rather, we can live in a state of constant readiness, even eagerness, to meet our Lord.

WORSHIP MATTERS

Weddings, funerals, and baptisms are the church's liturgies but congregations also feel great pressure on these occasions to bend to families and individuals who would make these individual rites of passage. Policies and outlines that clearly explain the expectations of the congregation for such events are helpful.

The wedding banquet is a powerful biblical symbol for the fulfillment of all God's promises. Use what we know of God's relationship with us to teach about Christian marriage. Also use what we understand about Christian marriage to teach about how it is that the Lord would be with the church. Encourage all members of the community to attend wedding liturgies. Prepare the congregation for the coming day with published banns, petitioning the prayers of the people for the wedding couple. Encourage the congregation to assist the wedding couple with their plans and preparations, for ultimately the couple will need the help of the whole community to support their relationship through all that the years will bring.

LET THE CHILDREN COME

Do the bread and wine of Holy Communion convey the actual forms of bread and wine? One of the pioneers of the liturgical movement in the United States, Godfrey Diekmann, is often attributed with saying that it takes less of a step of faith for people to believe that the bread of the eucharist is really the body of Christ than it does for people to believe that the little wafers we are accustomed to using are really bread. Surely this struggle of belief is true for children as well.

MUSIC FOR WORSHIP

GATHERING

| LBW 383 | Rise up, O saints of God! |
| WOV 669 | Come away to the skies |

PSALM 70

Hallock, Peter. "Psalm 70" in TP.

Hopson, Hal H. *Psalm Refrains and Tones*. HOP 425.

Organ, Anne Krentz. PW, Cycle A.

HYMN OF THE DAY

| LBW 31 | Wake, awake, for night is flying |
| | WACHET AUF |

VOCAL AND INSTRUMENTAL RESOURCES

See the First Sunday in Advent.

ALTERNATE HYMN OF THE DAY

| LBW 25 | Rejoice, rejoice, believers |
| WOV 799 | When long before time |

COMMUNION

| LBW 346 | When peace, like a river |
| WOV 699 | Blessed assurance |

OTHER SUGGESTIONS

Before or after singing "Blessed Assurance," play piano setting "Assurance" by Michael Hassell in *Jazz Sunday Morning*. AFP 11-10700.

SENDING

| LBW 529 | Praise God. Praise Him |
| WOV 780 | What a fellowship, what a joy divine |

ADDITIONAL HYMNS AND SONGS

LBW 526	Immortal, invisible, God only wise
WOV 627	My Lord, what a morning
MBW 709	Come, let us join our friends above
NCH 369	Keep your lamps trimmed and burning

MUSIC FOR THE DAY

CHORAL

Bach, J. S./Hal H. Hopson. "The Lord Will Soon Appear." AFP 11-10888. SATB, kybd.

Bender, Jan. "Lord, Lord, Open to Us." CPH 98-1833. U, org.

Bouman, Paul. "Rejoice, Rejoice, Believers." MSM 50-0004. SATB, org.

Goss, John. "If We Believe That Jesus Died." BBL 219-7. SATB, org.

Handel, George F. "Deck Thyself, My Soul, with Gladness." PRE 392-41707. SATB, kybd.

Parry, C. H. H. "O Day of Peace." GIA G-2689. SATB, org, opt brass, timp.

Posegate, Marie. "The Lord Will Come." RME. SATB.

Proulx, Richard. "Immortal, Invisible." SEL 425-842. SATB, org, tpt, opt cong.

Purcell, Henry. "Thou Knowest, Lord, the Secrets of Our Hearts." OXF 44.236. SA, kybd.

Thomas, Andre. "Keep Your Lamps!" HIN HMC-577. SATB, conga drm.

CHILDREN'S CHOIRS

Hobby, Robert. "Immortal, Invisible." MSM 50-9306. U, kybd.

Honore, Jeffrey. "Rejoice, Rejoice, Believers." CGA 746. 2 pt mxd, kybd, opt rec/tamb.

Praetorius/D. Wagner. "We Will Praise You." CGA 350. 2/3 pt, kybd.

KEYBOARD/INSTRUMENTAL

Albrecht, Timothy. "St. Denio" in *Grace Notes V*. AFP 11-10764. Org.

Mozart, W. A. "Fantasy in d" in *Complete Piano Works*. DOV. Pno.

HANDBELL

Larson, Katherine. "A Scottish Melody: Come, O Thou Traveler Unknown." AFP 11-10771. 3-5 oct, opt inst.

McChesney, Kevin. "When We Are Living." AFP 11-10631. 3-5 oct, opt chimes.

PRAISE ENSEMBLE

Haas, David. "My Lord Will Come Again." GIA G-3654. SATB.

Hanson, Handt. "Life in His Hands" in *Spirit Calls, Rejoice!* CCF.

Harvill, Jamie, and Nancy Gordon. "Because We Believe" in *Worship Leader Magazine's Song DISCovery*, vol. 4.

SUNDAY, NOVEMBER 7

JOHN CHRISTIAN FREDERICK HEYER, MISSIONARY TO INDIA, 1873

Heyer did mission work in India, but he also served as an evangelist and teacher in the United States. He valued Christian education, and helped establish Sunday schools in Lutheran parishes.

When our congregations consider their mission, they usually look both inward and outward. How do we teach, preach, and care for our own members? How do we reach out to the needs of our communities, especially to those in need, or on the fringes of society? How do we share the good news with people who have not heard the gospel, or who live with the everyday realities of poverty or injustice? Does your congregation include all these elements in its overall ministry? Could the commemoration of Heyer invite you to review your mission statement?

THURSDAY, NOVEMBER 11

MARTIN, BISHOP OF TOURS, 397

Martin became a hermit, and was known for his care for the poor. In time he was elected bishop of Tours in France. Martin is also remembered as a saint for peace, since earlier in his life he had been a soldier who left the army because he was unable to reconcile killing someone in battle with his Christian faith.

This day, sometimes called "Martinmas," was chosen to commemorate the end of the First World War. Veterans Day now honors Americans who fought in wars during this century. How can congregations follow in Martin's steps and work tirelessly for peace in the world? We pray for peace in our liturgies, but are there other ways we can practice peacemaking in our families, congregations, and nation?

SØREN AABYE KIERKEGAARD, TEACHER, 1855

Kierkegaard is not only the founder of modern existentialism, he also was a theologian whose writings reveal his Lutheran heritage and his commitment to a faith that is experienced rather than merely intellectualized. He invites our congregations to consider whether doubters and questioners would feel comfortable in our communities of faith. Do we provide opportunities for persons who struggle honestly with issues of faith? Do pastors make themselves available to those who are questioning what they believe? Is not this dimension of pastoral care important within the life of the congregation?

VETERANS DAY (USA)

REMEMBRANCE DAY (CANADA)

NOVEMBER 14, 1999

INTRODUCTION

In a world marked by much suspicion and back-biting, those who offer encouragement, trust, and hope are like an oasis of green-growing life. In a world wounded by rugged individualism, cutthroat competition, and much greed, the Holy Spirit blesses each Christian with the ability to use one's gifts for the greater and common good, to build up the body of Christ, and to serve those who suffer injustice.

The gospel reading for this day encourages us to use our God-given talents wisely while we still have time to do so. We do not know the hour of the Lord's final advent among us. But we do know that we have been formed into a body of servants who live according to the light of faith, nourished by word and sacrament, eager to share the riches of God's love with all in need.

PRAYER OF THE DAY

Lord God, so rule and govern our hearts and minds by your Holy Spirit that, always keeping in mind the end of all things and the day of judgment, we may be stirred up to holiness of life here and may live with you forever in the world to come, through your Son, Jesus Christ our Lord.

or

Almighty and ever-living God, before the earth was formed and even after it ceases to be, you are God. Break into our short span of life and let us see the signs of your final will and purpose, through your Son, Jesus Christ our Lord.

READINGS

Zephaniah 1:7, 12-18

Like last week's reading, today's lesson revolves around the concept of the Day of the Lord, the day of destruction of the Lord's enemies and of salvation for the Lord's faithful. This little-known prophet declares to the people of Jerusalem that sin without repentance will lead to destruction.

Psalm 90:1-8 [9-11] 12

So teach us to number our days, that we may apply our hearts to wisdom. (Ps. 90:12)

1 Thessalonians 5:1-11

Paul encourages the Thessalonian Christians to look forward to the return of Christ as a day of salvation.

Matthew 25:14-30

In the second of three parables concerning the second coming, Jesus indicates that merely maintaining things as they are is not sufficient. As Christians await his return, we are to use wisely the gifts of God.

COLOR   Green

THE PRAYERS

Surrounded by a great cloud of witnesses, let us offer our prayers before God's throne of grace.

A BRIEF SILENCE.

That the church faithfully proclaim the day of the Lord, inviting us to live each day with integrity and wisdom, we pray:

Your kingdom come.

That those who know abundant blessing may share of their wealth with those in need, we pray:

Your kingdom come.

That nations beset by ruin, destruction, or distress may know the justice and peace of the Lord's reign, we pray:

Your kingdom come.

That all who are troubled, fearful, or ill (especially . . .) may find refuge and hope in God, we pray:

Your kingdom come.

That we may be faithful stewards of the resources of the earth, the talents, and the treasure we have each been given, we pray:

Your kingdom come.

HERE OTHER INTERCESSIONS MAY BE OFFERED.

That we follow all the saints in light until the great and promised day of the Lord, we pray:

Your kingdom come.

Rejoicing in the fellowship of all the saints, let us commend ourselves, one another, and our whole life to Jesus Christ our Lord.

Amen

362

IMAGES FOR PREACHING

It is no coincidence that the word *talent,* which in Jesus' parable is an amount of money equal to about fifteen years' wages of a laborer, is the word we use to refer to a person's abilities or gifts. The English *talent* is actually derived from the Greek *talanton,* meaning the pan of a scale used to weigh goods, including precious metal, as well as the monetary value of the metal itself. Whether we are talking about the talents loaned to the three slaves in the parable, or about an individual's talents, we are dealing with something of great worth.

The lessons for these last days of the church year, which focus on the end times, are often overshadowed by congregations' emphases on the annual budget process and "stewardship Sunday." Here, though, are texts that suit both agendas.

The first reading and the psalm work together to paint a picture of life as brief and sorrowful. We are people of the dust (Ps. 90:3), and so we pray, "Teach us to count our days that we may gain a wise heart" (v. 12). Zephaniah points to the day of the Lord as a time of intense distress and devastation.

Jesus and Paul, however, teach us how to prepare for that day: We make good use of our talents. Modern Bible scholars believe the parable of the talents is an allegory, and the core image is of a slave who buried the talent, that is, who failed to pursue a life of righteousness. We ready ourselves for the return of the master by being alert and sober (1 Thess. 5:6), by putting on the "breastplate of faith and love, and for a helmet the hope of salvation" (v. 8). In this way, we pursue righteousness, using our talents to encourage and build up one another (v. 11).

WORSHIP MATTERS

Have you ever offered an adult education class on preparation for death? Has your worship committee ever talked about parish funeral practice? Has a workshop on wills or estate planning ever been conducted?

Parishoners are often interested to talk together and with their pastor about funerals. Most have never considered the shape of a Christian funeral, why we do what we do, and how they are different from what a funeral director might suggest. People are very curious about celebrating Holy Communion at a funeral. They may also not be aware that conducting a funeral from the church is even possible (and even preferred).

Use these days of November between All Saints and Christ the King, when the scripture readings turn to the end time, to invite the congregation into discussion and reflection about dying and living. How church leaders talk about death and the disposition of our life's assets can help all of us to face the end times with less fear.

LET THE CHILDREN COME

Take time after the worship service to lead the children on an exploration of the church's candles. Let them enjoy the smell of the beeswax, the touch of the soft wax, and the warmth of the flame. The smell, feel, and look may not have any theological content in and of itself. But just as smells associated with a wide range of events can trigger our imagination and memory, the smells of the church can do the same.

MUSIC FOR WORSHIP

GATHERING

LBW 312   Once he came in blessing
WOV 745   Awake, O sleeper

PSALM 90

Farrell, Bernadette. "Restless Is the Heart" in STP, vol. 2.

Folkening, John. "Six Psalm Settings with Antiphon." MSM 80-700.

Gelineau, Joseph. "In Every Age" in RS.

LBW 320   O God, our help in ages past

Organ, Anne Krentz. PW, Cycle A.

HYMN OF THE DAY

WOV 778   O Christ the same
            LONDONDERRY AIR

INSTRUMENTAL RESOURCES

Hassell, Michael. "Londonderry Air" in *Folkways.* AFP 11-10829. Pno, inst.

Kane, Daniel Q. "Londonderry Air" in *More Selectable Delectables.* AFP 11-10757. Pno.

McFadden, Jane. "O Christ the Same." AFP 11-10769. 2-3 oct, C/B-flat inst.

ALTERNATE HYMN OF THE DAY

LBW 405   Lord of light
LBW 408   God whose giving knows no ending

363

COMMUNION

LBW 389	Stand up, stand up for Jesus
WOV 649	I want to walk as a child of the light
WOV 712	Listen, God is calling

OTHER SUGGESTIONS

| OBS 75 | Rich in promise |

SENDING

| LBW 495 | Lead on, O king eternal |
| WOV 754 | Let us talents and tongues employ |

ADDITIONAL HYMNS AND SONGS

WOV 744	Soon and very soon
UMH 730	O day of God, draw near
CHA 703	When all is ended, time and troubles past
PH 211	Lord, you have been our dwelling place
WGF 60	How small our span of life, O God

MUSIC FOR THE DAY

CHORAL

Attwood, Thomas. "Turn Thee Again, O Lord" in *Church Anthem Book*. OXF. SATB.

Isaac, Heinrich. "O World, I Must Be Parting." GSCH 8425. SATB.

Manz, Paul. "E'en So, Lord Jesus, Quickly Come." CPH 98-1054. SATB.

Moore, Undine Smith. "I Will Trust in the Lord." AFP 11-2505. SATB, div.

Sedio, Mark. "Once He Came in Blessing." AFP 11-10452. 2 pt mxd, org, fl.

Stout, Alan. "The Great Day of the Lord." CFP 6883. SATB, org.

Vaughan Williams, Ralph. "Lord, Thou Hast Been Our Refuge." GSCH 9720. SATB/SATB div, org/orch.

CHILDREN'S CHOIRS

Hruby, Dolores. "Go Now to Love and Serve the Lord." CGA 354. U, fl, kybd.

Ramseth, Betty Ann. "Make Us to Be." CGA 579. U, fl, orff, woodblock, fc, autohp.

KEYBOARD/INSTRUMENTAL

Manz, Paul. "Reprise" (Reflection on E'en so, Lord Jesus, Quickly Come). MSM 10-950. Org.

Pachelbel, Johann. "Ciacona in f" in *Selected Organ Works*. KAL 3760. Org.

HANDBELL

McKlveen, Paul A. "O God, Our Help in Ages Past." Full score JEF JH-S9157FS; 3-5 oct hb JH-S9157; brass JH-S9157B.

PRAISE ENSEMBLE

Hanson, Handt. "Holy, You Are Holy" in *Songs of the First Light*. CCF.

Tunney, Curry/arr. Greer. "All Creation Sing His Praise." BMG AG-1002. SATB.

Wyrtzen, Don. "Flow, O Mighty Holy River." INT 01197. SATB, orch.

WEDNESDAY, NOVEMBER 17
ELIZABETH OF THURINGIA, PRINCESS OF HUNGARY, 1231

Elizabeth is remembered for her care for the sick, the elderly, and the poor. She founded two hospitals, and many hospitals have been named after her. The commemoration of Elizabeth might be a time for congregations to sponsor forums or classes related to issues of health care. What is the church's role in ensuring that the poor and elderly receive adequate health care? How might we as a community of faith promote wholistic health and preventative medicine? Perhaps your congregation could gather a panel to discuss such issues and include a physician, nurse, social worker, nursing home administrator, and family members.

NOVEMBER 21, 1999

CHRIST THE KING
LAST SUNDAY AFTER PENTECOST
PROPER 29

INTRODUCTION

The Lord Jesus was not wealthy or famous. He did not promise his followers that they would possess riches, power, or prestige. He was named a king only in his death. He reigned from the cross, leaving his disciples the treasure of his body and blood.

Today we gather at the table of Christ, our merciful and loving ruler. We wear the crown of baptism and trace his royal sign—the holy cross—over our brows and bodies. We leave here strengthened to serve those who are hungry, thirsty, strangers, naked, sick, and imprisoned. We look for the day when all earth's people will see him coming with the scepter of peace and the crown of justice.

PRAYER OF THE DAY

Almighty and everlasting God, whose will it is to restore all things to your beloved Son, whom you anointed priest forever and king of all creation: Grant that all the people of the earth, now divided by the power of sin, may be united under the glorious and gentle rule of your Son, our Lord Jesus Christ, who lives and reigns with you and the Holy Spirit, one God, now and forever.

READINGS

Ezekiel 34:11-16, 20-24

The term "shepherd," which was another image for "king" in the ancient Near East, was suggestive of the care, concern, and protection that a shepherd/king was to show on behalf of his flock of citizens. When Israel's kings prove to be bad shepherds, Ezekiel declares from exile in Babylon that the Lord will assume the role of shepherd.

Psalm 95:1-7a

We are the people of God's pasture and the sheep of God's hand. (Ps. 95:7)

Ephesians 1:15-23

On Christ the King Sunday, we read this prayer of thanksgiving for the Ephesian Christians, a prayer that exalts Christ as head of the church and Lord of the universe.

Matthew 25:31-46

Jesus tells three stories about the second coming in this chapter. The final story—today's gospel—contains a surprise: when he does return, people will discover he has come to them before, in ways they did not recognize.

COLOR   White

THE PRAYERS

Surrounded by a great cloud of witnesses, let us offer our prayers before God's throne of grace.
A BRIEF SILENCE.
That the church minister faithfully to all considered least in our society, we pray:
Your kingdom come.
That bishops and pastors serve as faithful shepherds among their people, we pray:
Your kingdom come.
That the leaders of government work to provide for the needs of those who are hungry, naked, homeless, or in prison, we pray:
Your kingdom come.
That through us your care may be extended to all who are sick or in pain (especially . . .), we pray:
Your kingdom come.
That your reign of justice be made known to our community through our ministries of love and compassion, we pray:
Your kingdom come.
HERE OTHER INTERCESSIONS MAY BE OFFERED.
That you bring us with all the saints to the promised day of judgment and mercy, we pray:
Your kingdom come.
Rejoicing in the fellowship of all the saints, let us commend ourselves, one another, and our whole life to Jesus Christ our Lord.
Amen

IMAGES FOR PREACHING

Christ, who was raised from the dead and given great power by God, is seated at the right hand of God

365

(Eph. 1:19-20). It is from this seat, a throne, Jesus says in Matthew 25:31ff, that the Son of Man will judge all nations and separate righteous and unrighteous people, as a shepherd separates sheep from goats.

What does it mean to us that the risen Christ is seated on a throne? Many of us are more comfortable with an image of Jesus as a patient shepherd, a kind man who holds children on his lap, an inspiring teacher, a gentle friend who carries us when we are weary. What do we make of Christ, the king, who rules in majesty from his throne at the right hand of God?

First, we need to keep in mind that Christ is king *because* Christ is God. No one who is not God could be king of creation and ruler of heaven. Yes, Jesus Christ is fully divine and fully human, but Christ as king is about Christ as God. Second, Christ is king because he was present at creation and is our maker (Ps. 95:5-6; John 1:1-3). Third, as king, Christ is judge of all humankind (see the readings from Ezekiel and Matthew). And finally, because Christ is king, he is worthy of our praise (Ps. 95:1-3). Let us kneel before the throne!

WORSHIP MATTERS

This week, think about how the worship life of your congregation is linked to its social ministries. "You gave me food . . . something to drink . . . welcome . . . clothing . . . took care of me . . . visited me." It is for these activities that the liturgy seeks to prepare us and shapes us. The sending from worship is all about mission. The world stands in need of food and drink, care and clothing. Our meal together is a hungry feast in honor of the poor. God's word calls us to action. Our worship is so we can regroup for another week of service. The king we celebrate this day is a servant king who reigns from the cross, and who calls us to be about his kingdom in the world.

How does the liturgy empower your congregation's service? God bless your work and prayer this day and through another year of grace.

LET THE CHILDREN COME

The leadership of the presiding and assisting ministers can help ritual from becoming idle repetition and continue to appeal to children. Children are drawn to actions and events that they see someone carrying out with care and energy. Worship leadership that is focused and not sloppy, and actions that are done well and show that someone cares about what is being done, have a better chance to appeal to children than they would if they were done without any notion of their meaning.

MUSIC FOR WORSHIP

SERVICE MUSIC

The Kyrie and "This is the feast of victory" are strong acclamations of the sovereign Christ; this may be one of the days when both are used.

GATHERING

LBW 530	Jesus shall reign
LBW 518	Beautiful Savior
WOV 744	Soon and very soon

PSALM 95

DATH 5   Oh, come, let us worship

Dobry, Wallace. "A Trio of Psalms." MSM 80-706.

Geary, Patrick. "Listen to the Voice of the Lord" in PS2.

Joncas, Michael. "Come, Let Us Sing." GIA G-3473. SATB, cong, kybd.

NSR 52   To God with gladness sing

Organ, Anne Krentz. PW, Cycle A.

HYMN OF THE DAY

LBW 363	Christ is alive! Let Christians sing
	TRURO

VOCAL RESOURCES

Busarow, Donald. "Truro" in *All Praise to You, Eternal God.* AFP 11-9076. Org.

INSTRUMENTAL RESOURCES

Burkhardt, Michael. "Truro" in *4 Hymn Improvisations for Holy Week.* MSM 10-318. Org.

Hopson, Hal H. "Christ Is Alive!" in *A Creative Approach to Hymn Ringing.* HOP 1638. 3-5 oct.

Page, Anna Laura. "Christ Is Alive!" in *Hymn Descants for Ringers and Singers,* vol. 2. ALF 11528. Vcs/kybd 11530. 3 oct, kybd, desc.

Pelz, Walter L. "Truro" in *Hymn Settings for Organ and Brass,* set 1. AFP 11-10184.

ALTERNATE HYMN OF THE DAY

LBW 173	The head that once was crowned
WOV 801	Thine the amen, thine the praise

COMMUNION

LBW 423	Lord, whose love in humble service
LBW 456	The King of love my shepherd is
WOV 740	Jesus, remember me

OTHER SUGGESTIONS

Before or after singing "The King of Love My Shepherd Is" play the organ and solo instrument setting by David Cherwien in *Organ Plus One*, AFP 11-10758.

SENDING

| LBW 171 | Rejoice, the Lord is King! |
| WOV 787 | Glory to God, we give you thanks |

ADDITIONAL HYMNS AND SONGS

WOV 729	Christ, mighty Savior
G2 551	God of day and God of darkness
NCH 302	Eternal Christ, you rule
DATH 61	Strange King

MUSIC FOR THE DAY

CHORAL

Beadell, Robert. "I Am the Alpha and the Omega." CPH 98-3083. SATB, org.

Bender, Jan. "Come, O Blessed of My Father." CPH 98-1834. 2 pt, kybd.

Copland, Aaron. "Sing Ye Praises to Our King." BOH 6021. SATB.

Desprez, Josquin. "God, the Lord, Now Reigneth." CPH 98-3213. SATB.

Hopson, Hal. "Love One Another." CGA 741. U/2 pt, kybd.

Marchionda, J./M. Rachelski. "I Was Hungry." WLD 7996. SATB, fl, kybd.

Micheelsen, Hans F. "Jesus Has Come and Brings Pleasure." CPH 98-2783. SATB/SAB, org.

Proulx, Richard/Rosser. "Look for Me in Lowly Ones." GIA G-2145. Inst pts G-2145-INST. SATB, org, brass, cong, timp.

Schalk, Carl. "Lo, He Comes with Clouds Descending" in *Second Crown Choir Book*. CPH 97-4882. 2 pt mxd, trbl inst, kybd.

Tye, Christopher. "O Jesus, King Most Wonderful." GIA A-3113. SATB.

Weber, Paul D. "I Will Sing the Story of Your Love." AFP 11-10839. SATB/U, org, opt cong.

CHILDREN'S CHOIRS

Carter, Sydney. "I Come Like a Beggar." ECS W150. U, pno.

Helman, Michael. "Christ Is King." TRI 10/1727K. 2 pt, kybd.

Powell, Robert. "With the Lord Arise." CGA 639. 2/3 pt, kybd.

KEYBOARD/INSTRUMENTAL

Bach, J. S. "Jesu, Joy of Man's Desiring." HWG. Org.

Benoit, Dom Paul. "Christ the King" in *Pieces d'Orgue*. JFB 8774. Org.

Organ, Anne Krentz. "Christ, Mighty Savior" in *Christ, Mighty Savior: Reflections on Four Hymntunes*. AFP 11-10819. Pno.

HANDBELL

Behnke, John. "The Head that Once was Crowned." CPH 97-6120. Hb 97-6121; choir 98-2977. Cong, SATB, 2 oct, org, brass

McFadden, Jane. "Blessing and Honor." AFP 11-10573. 3-5 oct.

Schalk, Carl/John Behnke. "Thine the Amen, Thine the Praise." CPH 97-6383. 3-5 oct.

PRAISE ENSEMBLE

Evans, Darrell. "My God Reigns" in *Integrity's Hosanna! Music Songsheets*. INT.

Hayford, Jack and Tom Fettke/arr. Keith Christopher. "Worship His Majesty." WRD 301 0758 162. SATB.

Paris, Twila. "We Will Glorify" in *Maranatha! Music's Praise Chorus Book*, 2d ed. MAR.

Thomas, Andre. "The Kingdom." HIN. SATB.

TUESDAY, NOVEMBER 23

CLEMENT, BISHOP OF ROME, C. 100

Clement was a bishop of Rome during the first century. Little is known of his life, but he is remembered for his letters, one of which challenges the divisions in the Corinthian community. He offered pastoral counsel by urging a spirit of peace and kindness.

It is not surprising that the church of our day continues to face disagreement, division, and occasionally mean-spiritedness. Clement reminds us that a pastoral love for people must be present amid our differing views of authority, scripture, or social ministry. Can we be united in the central affirmations of our faith, and still embrace diversity in other matters? How does your congregation deal with disagreement or conflict?

MIGUEL AGUSTIN PRO, 1927

Miguel Pro grew up among oppression in Mexico where revolutionaries accused the church of siding with the rich. After studying for the priesthood in Belgium, he returned to Mexico to work on behalf of the poor and homeless. Living amid constant danger, eventually Miguel and his two brothers were shot, falsely accused of throwing a bomb at the car of a government official.

With Thanksgiving two days away, a commemoration of Miguel invites reflection on the widening gap between the rich and the poor. How do those who live with abundance share with those living in poverty?

NOVEMBER 25, 1999

DAY OF THANKSGIVING (USA)

See Day of Thanksgiving (Canada), pages 328–331.

THURSDAY, NOVEMBER 25

ISAAC WATTS, HYMNWRITER, 1748

Watts is one of the most well-known writers of English hymn texts, and was important in establishing hymn singing in the English church. Many of his hymns are based on psalms, and they reflect a strong and serene faith.

LBW includes thirteen of his texts. Several are especially appropriate for Thanksgiving services: "From all that dwell below the skies" (LBW 550), "Before Jehovah's awesome throne" (LBW 531) or "Come, let us join our cheerful songs" (LBW 254).